Ecocide

Djalma Alvarez Brochado Neto

Ecocide

Massive Damage to the Environment and the International Criminal System

Springer

Djalma Alvarez Brochado Neto
Law School
Unichristus
Fortaleza, Ceará, Brazil

ISBN 978-3-032-07756-1 ISBN 978-3-032-07757-8 (eBook)
https://doi.org/10.1007/978-3-032-07757-8

The original submitted manuscript has been translated into English. The translation was done using artificial intelligence. A subsequent revision was performed by the author(s) to further refine the work and to ensure that the translation is appropriate concerning content and scientific correctness. It may, however, read stylistically different from a conventional translation.

This Springer imprint is published by the registered company Springer Nature Switzerland AG.
The registered company address is: Gewerbestrasse 11, 6330 Cham, Switzerland

Foreword

Ecocide: Massive Environmental Damage and the International Criminal System

I am honored by the invitation to present such a significant work. Reflecting on and understanding ecocide as a legal phenomenon is to recognize the urgent need to protect the natural world and its essential role in the survival of humankind. In terms of importance, this work goes beyond the boundaries of International Criminal Law.

I participated in the thesis defense of Professor Dr. Djalma Brochado Neto, whose research was submitted for his doctorate through a joint program between the Federal University of Ceará (Brazil) and the University of Pisa (Italy), under the supervision of Professors Gustavo Cabral and Leonardo Pasquali. Djalma's command of the subject and the confidence with which he presented his findings were remarkable, earning enthusiastic praise from the committee and strong encouragement to publish the thesis as soon as possible.

Equally impressive was the breadth and quality of the sources used to produce a study that is both rich and up-to-date, while also contributing meaningfully to a topic that is both urgent and fundamental to legal scholarship. The author's use of premier research institutions—including the Cujas Library in Paris, UN libraries in Geneva and New York, the International Criminal Court, and the International Court of Justice in The Hague, as well as academic libraries—demonstrates the depth of his effort and its reward, especially for us readers.

Humanity has long faced major environmental disasters. Massive damage caused by oil exploitation, chemical spills in oceans, rampant pollution, rising global temperatures, dam failures, and the ongoing loss of biodiversity all raise alarms about the future of life on Earth.

As with the best legal scholarship, each chapter of this work offers a precise historical overview, allowing readers to trace the development of the subject. In Chap. 2, the author examines large-scale environmental damage through some of the most paradigmatic events, such as the use of Agent Orange in Vietnam by U.S. military forces and pollution disasters caused by oil companies.

Chapter 3 explores climate litigation and international law, drawing on historical context and key hard cases such as Urgenda and Shell in the Netherlands. The evolution of the concept of ecocide is addressed in Chap. 4, with particular attention to its comparison with genocide and war crimes. Chapters 5 and 6 analyze how domestic legislation and legal reform projects in various countries have responded to, and shaped, the concept.

The author's definition of ecocide deserves full citation, as it encapsulates its legal relevance:

> Causing, by any means, massive damage to the environment in a way that prevents short-term recovery (resilience), directly or indirectly affecting human populations, either through harmful physical alteration of ecosystems or the extinction of species within a given natural area, with repercussions for one or more States, regardless of administrative authorization for the conduct, knowing or having reason to know the consequences of one's actions for the natural environment.

In Chaps. 7 and 8, Djalma reaches the apex of the work, critically discussing the strengths and weaknesses of ecocide's normative framework, contributing to its serious consideration by legal scholars, institutions, and the international community. Among the issues addressed are the possibility of including ecocide within the jurisdiction of the International Criminal Court, its relevance as *jus cogens*, the challenges of defining it within criminal law dogmatics, the obstacles posed by international sovereignty, and the potential for immediate implementation of ecocide as a means of environmental protection.

It is unacceptable to continue tolerating impunity for serious environmental crimes. Regulatory frameworks have proven increasingly insufficient to provide effective responses, especially considering that such crimes often transcend national borders and operate as interconnected chains of consequences—such as in global warming, where local actions can have worldwide impacts.

In sum, this work successfully outlines the criminal repercussions of massive environmental crimes through concrete cases. It also traces the evolution of the concept to demonstrate the plausibility of individual criminal liability. Most notably, it highlights the key challenges related to legal classification, jurisdictional structure, and the mental element (*mens rea*).

Ideally, ecocide should be addressed by the international community before irreversible damage occurs—if it hasn't already—reversing the historical pattern seen with crimes against humanity and genocide, which were only prosecuted in international courts after the most atrocious acts had already taken place.

Today, much is debated—especially through the principle of complementarity—about the role of the International Criminal Court in raising awareness and preventing the gravest crimes against humanity. Perhaps, with the recognition of ecocide and its inclusion within the Court's jurisdiction, we can significantly enhance environmental protection with immediate practical effects on domestic legislation. The author aptly states:

> Establishing ecocide as a crime under the ICC symbolizes the affirmation of the intrinsic connection between human values and the environment—an inseparable bond in a society that seeks justice and security.

Ultimately, addressing environmental crimes with this level of depth and dedication shows how the legal field can help ensure a dignified life for human beings—or at least prevent the annihilation of the world as we know it. We need more works like this, which tackle major questions about the planet's future with seriousness, critical thinking, and responsibility. I congratulate Professor Dr. Djalma Brochado Neto for his courage in revealing, exposing, and elevating the standard of discussion on massive environmental damage—an issue of utmost importance to humanity.

Master's Program in Forensic Psychology
UTP
Curitiba, Paraná, Brazil

Rodrigo Faucz Pereira e Silva

Foreword

The publication of the English language version of *Ecocide: Massive Environmental Damage and the International Criminal System*, just a few years after the original book in Portuguese, is a remarkable event for the studies in International Environmental Law and Criminal Law. Unfortunately, the issue addressed here is tragically current, considering the increasing amount of massive environmental damages in recent years. The sense among specialists is that the existing legal mechanisms within domestic legal systems and even on the international level may not be sufficient to address actions of such gravity.

As mere human conventions, state boundaries are unable to contain the effects of serious problems like those described in this book. It becomes urgent to consider them from the transnational perspective that should guide reflections on the environment, especially considering the high destructive capacity of certain events.

Djalma Brochado's proposal goes precisely in this direction. In this work, which is the result of a doctoral thesis in Law carried out in a cotutelle program between the Federal University of Ceará (Brazil) and the University of Pisa (Italy), as well as a research period at the University of Paris (France), the author proposes elements that characterize a legal category that, despite its concrete realization, still lacks a clear definition that needs to characterize criminal offenses.

The numerous cases presented throughout the following pages, coupled with a detailed description of the legislative debates that have occurred in many countries, not only prove the timeliness of the subject but also the need to consider ecocide as a matter of International Law, with strong and necessary domestic repercussions. Brochado carefully explores the numerous challenges this option faces, offering, in the end, a work that is essential for deepening debates on ecocide.

Therefore, this is a must-read book for anyone interested in the debate on ecocide. I am convinced of the relevance of this work not only for the academic environment in which it was born but also for the national and international public debate, considering the urgency of implementing concrete measures to effectively combat ecocide in all countries, including Brazil, and the international level. Within this version in English, the book certainly will reach a broader audience and will influence the international debate on ecocide.

Law School, Federal University of Ceará
Fortaleza, Brazil
January 2025

Gustavo César Machado Cabral

Preface

Ecocide: Why Now?

The term "ecocide" has existed for over 50 years, evolving from a theoretical offence against the environment in a war situation[1] to reality as a crime typified in penal codes. Concurrently, international criminal law itself has developed in doctrine and practice, reaching its peak with the operation of the International Criminal Court,[2] a permanent court dedicated to prosecuting the most serious crimes.

The need to define the most important crimes on the international level, through *The Code* (Code of Crimes Against Peace and Security of Humanity), and the topic of ecocide have been together in some circumstances, in recent decades. However, the understanding of the environment as a legal good deserving of international criminal protection, to this day, is not fully developed. In part, this resistance is related to what was understood—customarily—as *jus cogens*, traditionally linked to human rights[3] and situations of armed conflict (internal or external).

Thus, based on the study presented in this book, the question that arises is: in the current context—given the growing understanding of the impact of human activity

[1] Inspired by the United States' herbicide attacks in Vietnam, studied in Chap. 2.

[2] "Despite being based on a classic international law instrument, an international treaty, whose ratification or adherence is a sovereign and voluntary decision of the States, it is evident that the Rome Statute, creator of the International Criminal Court, is one of those multilateral agreements that, like the United Nations Charter or the main human rights and international humanitarian law treaties, aspires to universality. For this, a campaign for universal ratification is permanently made (by some States, the European Union and NGOs), which is also echoed in resolutions annually adopted by the Assembly of States Party to the ICC (ASP), the political body where all State Parties sit, as well as observer States, and which meets at least once a year, being responsible for the management and also legislative body of the ICC" (Teles, 2014).

[3] "It should be highlighted that the conception of human rights to be considered is the one in force at the time of interpretation, and not at the time of the treaty's elaboration – in this case, the Rome Statute". (Ambos, 2008, p. 113). "Such conception becomes relevant as Human Rights are in frank evolution, and cannot be restricted to the conceptions still existing in the last century. Recall that the Statute is dated July 1998" (Reiss, 2017). 2017, p. 115).

on the environment,[4] the development of the concept of ecocide and the evolution of international criminal law—Is there both theoretical and practical feasibility for including a crime of massive environmental destruction, in times of peace, within the limited list of crimes set out in the Rome Statute?

To affirmatively answer the demand, it is necessary to identify: the existence of an acceptable concept of ecocide and a trend of universalisation of the prohibition of massive environmental destruction among the States; the environment as a universal legal good; compatibility between ecocide and the ICC, in addition to the advantages of this addition; and whether the current moment is appropriate.

The lack of precision regarding what constitutes ecocide was used as an argument to exclude it from the *Draft*[5] of international crimes, between the 1970s and 1990s, at the *International Law Commission*. Indeed, the vagueness of the concept, originally designed by Galston, stands in contrasts to the principle of legal certainty and specificity required of criminal norms. Nevertheless, the general contours of the crime are identifiable: the large-scale destruction of the environment, to such an extent that its short-term recovery (resilience) becomes impossible, directly or indirectly impacting human populations—whether through harmful physical alterations of biomes or the extinction of species[6] within a given natural area.

---

[4] The UN discusses both the impacts of man on nature and how to promote harmony between them, especially since 2011, with the convening of an interactive dialogue on "Harmony with Nature", through Resolution 65/164, of the General Assembly, developed until 2017: "As can be read in the analysis of the 'Interaction of human beings with the Earth', contained in United Nations Resolution A/67/317 of 17 August 2012, among the various known aspects of humanity's devastating influence on planet Earth, with risks for the future of humanity, climate change stands out. As a result of it, large amounts of soil are suffering from erosion; rich pastures are desertifying; the ancient ice formations are melting and species are being pushed to extinction. Fertiliser substrates wash fields and flow down rivers, creating stretches of water where nothing grows, except algae. Atmospheric carbon dioxide may be at its highest level in 15 million years" (MORAES, 2018, p. 692).

[5] "The draft Code of Crimes against the Peace and Security of Mankind is intended to strike at the worst crimes, those which affect the foundations of human society. While it is clear that under normal conditions of peaceful coexistence even phenomena of massive pollution or other degradation of the environment can easily be fitted into the available network of cooperation in criminal matters, this would not be the case any more if damaging the environment formed part of a general strategy on the part of a Government or a private group to exert terrorist pressure on the world community. It is precisely in such situations of a general breakdown of law and order and a sense of responsibility towards humankind that the draft Code is called into operation. The draft Code is certainly not necessary for states of normalcy, which should be taken care of pursuant to routine patterns that have long since stood the test of time. However, exceptional situations do require exceptional responses. To maintain that such situations should be tackled only after they have arisen would be short-sighted" (ILC, 1996, p. 22).

[6] The extinction of species is a phenomenon that has occurred since the origin of life on the planet, at varying rates and reasons. Nowadays, "the overexploitation of living organisms (including wildlife trade), the introduction of alien species, air, soil and water pollution, and climate change are direct consequences of such activities and a huge source of pressure on wild species". (…) "scientists now agree that the rate of extinction is far greater than the rate of speciation, which is also negatively influenced by human activities such as transport, which causes distant populations in the process of speciation to reunite, neutralizing the process. If you spend more than you earn, it is

These boundaries guided the development of the first criminal definitions of ecocide, which emerged during the Vietnam War and later spread to countries that arose from the dissolution of the former Soviet Union and, more recently, countries of the American and European continent. In addition, legislative bodies in various countries propose bills addressing the subject. A common feature—particularly in the most recent laws and proposals—is a more detailed and precise definition of the crime,[7] defined as the maximum infraction, in the environmental field.

At the international level, the proposal of the *Ecocide Law Foundation*, now officially a Bill to Amend the Rome Statute,[8] seeks to design ecocide as a viable crime within the ICC, leveraging the Court's existing technical infrastructure. The conceptual framework remains intact, as is the understanding of the infraction, as the most serious possible against the environment during peacetime.

Defining the upper threshold of damage is relatively straightforward, as it can be envisioned as a global catastrophe resulting from deliberate human action. However, the challenge lies in determining its lower threshold—identifying the minimum level of conduct necessary to constitute ecocide. In this regard, the laws/bill proposals that carry explanatory norms are increasingly common, in order to carry out the subsumption—fitting the concrete case to the norm in abstract—correctly. With the parameters outlined in this work, transnationality (immediate) of the damage is not a mandatory requirement, particularly given the existence of countries with continental dimensions.[9] Thus, it is the damage in nature that is relevant (and the direct and indirect impacts on the human being), when it overflows the own limit of resilience of the natural environment. In the realm of criminal law, a degree of flexibility in legal specificity is warranted, akin to crimes of genocide and crimes against humanity. This allows for a broader conceptualization of ecocide, sending a clear message to humanity that severe environmental harm is unacceptable under any circumstances.

The proliferation of criminal definitions and proposals on ecocide reflects a significant evolution in the conceptualisation of the crime,[10] as well as the

---

only a matter of time that you go bankrupt. That is exactly what human activity is causing on the Planet in the Anthropocene: the irreversible bankruptcy of Life, at least at a human timescale". (Rodríguez-Rodríguez, 2024, p. 16).

[7] For example, in Brazilian Bills, explanatory norms are proposed, detailing the meaning and scope of each term, in order to seek respect for legality and the simplicity of the future norm.

[8] As studied in Chap. 6.

[9] As an example brought in this book (Chap. 2), the disasters of Brumadinho, Mariana and Bhopal did not transcend the borders of Brazil and India, given the size of the countries. If a similar environmental damage occurred in Europe, it would directly affect various States, and indirectly the entire continent.

[10] The awareness of ecocide was very strong from the beginning of the 19th century: "whether it is deforestation, climate change or mass extinction, the different aspects of ecocide are widely perceived as moral failures, violations of divine or natural laws that should lead to the death penalty by civilisation. Secondly, the discourse on ecocide is not limited to a small circle of 'whistleblowers' or visionaries crying alone in the desert. It can be found in books or articles widely distributed to an educated general public" (Bounoua, 2020, p. 32).

universalisation—in progress—of the prohibition of this conduct.[11] In addition to various States individually taking action (through their parliaments) to address ecocide, the most relevant international organisations are also increasingly engaging with the issue. The European Union has officially advocated for the construction of ecocide as an international crime;[12] the Security Council links the environment to international security and peace; as well as the UN recognises access to a clean and healthy environment as a universal human right,[13] in addition to the *International Law Commission.*[14]

These developments, in addition to evidencing a universalisation[15] of the prohibition of ecocide—given that all humanity lives in an interconnected and interdependent environment—reinforce the understanding of the environment as a universal legal good, when framed from an anthropocentric perspective. That is, regardless of the approach, the fundamental objective is the reinforcement of protection, without allowing one interest to overshadow another.[16]

---

[11] When a certain concept or mode of responsibility exists in a large number of national jurisdictions, the concept is considered 'widely accepted' (Yanev et al., 2019).

[12] European Parliament 2021. Strasbourg, Feb. 2022.

[13] United Nations 2022.

[14] It is not enough to assert that there is a clearly identifiable need "to proscribe attacks on the environment by making them acts punishable under criminal law. Additionally, it has to be asked whether environmental crimes cannot be adequately dealt with by domestic jurisdictions or in accordance with the methods and procedures of international cooperation in criminal matters as provided for in a dense multilateral network of international treaties. These traditional methods and procedures have many advantages. First of all, they do already exist. No additional monies are required to establish new institutions or devise new mechanisms. Secondly, application of the provisions of national criminal codes may sometimes be more effective than treating an offence as a crime against the peace and security of mankind, given the fact that common rules of criminal law lack the political element which is inherent in the draft Code. Lastly, it might be argued that massive pollution of the environment invariably constitutes a consequence of armed conflict, not requiring any new treatment in view of the existence of article 55 of Additional Protocol I to the Geneva Conventions of 1949 and the Convention on the Prohibition of Military or any Other Hostile Use of Environmental Modification Techniques (ENMOD Convention). And yet, many situations can be conceived which cannot be dealt with in a satisfying manner within the framework of the existing substantive and procedural rules" (ILC, 1996, p. 22).

[15] The Portuguese Constitution, for example, "deals with the environmental issue, both from an objective point of view, as a fundamental task of the State (article 9, paragraphs d) and e)), and from a subjective point of view, by establishing a fundamental right to the environment and quality of life (article 66)" (Silva, 2015, p. 263).

[16] LORA 2021.

Although the adoption of a Declaration of the Rights of Nature[17] remains unrealized,[18] raising the environment as a universal legal good already provides a basis to consider ecocide as *jus cogens*, that is, a peremptory norm of international law that prohibits the infliction of massive environmental damage under any circumstances. Within this limited spectrum of prohibition, ecocide finds its place among the most serious conduct offenses peace and international security; therefore, today, it is capable of composing the list of crimes of the Rome Statute, dedicated to the most egregious acts affecting the planet.

There are no technical obstacles—material restriction (thematic), for example—to the inclusion of ecocide into the ICC; once the procedures are overcome,[19] any conduct can, in theory, be incorporated into the Treaty as a new crime (as evidenced by the efforts of insular State Parties in the pro-ecocide campaign at the ICC, with an official proposal in 2024). As the only permanent court with aspirations of universal jurisdiction,[20] capable of prosecuting and judging the most serious crimes that shake peace and international security, the International Criminal Court, with more than half of the world's countries as a member, is the most suitable Court to investigate ecocide.[21]

[17] "In April 2017, during the Interactive Dialogues, at the commemorative session of International Mother Earth Day, Fernando Hunancuni Mamani, speaking as Minister of Foreign Affairs of Bolivia, highlights the challenge for the 193 States of the United Nations to reach a consensus on the Universal Declaration of the Rights of Mother Earth, through mechanisms that allow, in an inclusive way, to contribute to the fulfilment of a comprehensive vision of the objectives of sustainable development. It recalls that its country has been building an economic model in harmony with Mother Earth" (Moraes, 2018, p. 710).

[18] The main objective of the Mother Earth Rights movement is "encourage creative diversity rather than to impose uniformity', and to 'open spaces within which different and unconventional approaches can spring up, perhaps to flourish, perhaps to run their course and die'. In this sense, the Rights of Mother Earth is an invitation to think and act in a non-anthropocentric world" (Sólon, 2018, p. 128).

[19] Article 121, Rome Statute.

[20] As demonstrated in Chap. 8.

[21] Unsuccessfully addressed for many years, within the scope of the work of the ILC, the international criminalisation of serious attacks on the environment remains an imperative need, under the assumption of impunity for environmental crime: "This trend converges towards the possibility of extending outright the material competence of the International Criminal Court to serious environmental offences. These views are shared between the possibility envisaging the addition of a definition element to crimes against humanity or that consisting of defining an autonomous crime in addition to the four crimes constituting the ratione materiae of the ICC which would include all serious environmental offences committed in peacetime. Thus, the apprehension of acts of serious environmental damage by the law of the ICC will depend on a restructuring of the Rome Statute which will take into account the rules of the Vienna Convention on the Law of Treaties and the provisions of the Rome Statute on revision and amendments. In essence, it will be necessary to review the provisions relating to crimes, the quality of those responsible for these acts, the operation of the Court thinking about experts on the prosecution of these kinds of crime. The other aspects of restructuring concern not only the definition of the elements of the crime, but also the regime of reparation and the penalties of the ICC for environmental crimes. This adaptation will take into account restorative justice, transitional justice, the penalties intended for legal entities. It goes without saying that the hypothesis envisaging this restructuring of the ICC in favour of the

The criminalisation of the conduct at the international level would serve as a declaration that the environmental disasters, both past and future—which have so far lacked a specific legal designation—are unacceptable, finally gaining an official *nomen iuris,*[22] 'ecocide', and conferring a dimension to massive environmental damage similar to genocide and crimes against humanity. The immediate practical effect would be the criminalisation—therefore, standardization—of the conduct across all State Parties, resulting in a significant symbolic weight, whether through actual sanctions or the mere implication of criminal liability, particularly for individuals and corporations[23] seeking to avoid association with an international crime.

The convergence of the maturation of the international criminal system and the conceptualisation of ecocide provides the appropriate tools for drafting a proposal and incorporating the crime into the ICC's jurisdiction. The timing is propitious, even considering the constant technological increase of human capacity for large-scale environmental destruction[24] (as seen in Alberta, Canada), the far-reaching

prosecution of these acts is worth its weight in gold so much, despite vehement criticisms about the politicisation of the Court, it remains the only institution which, by its experience, its record and its history, can effectively face the terrifying resurgence of environmental crime" (Banungana, 2017, p. 242).

[22] To promote the use of the name and awareness around ecocides, understood as "causing serious damage or destroying the environment, so as to significantly and durably alter the global commons or ecosystem services upon which certain human groups rely" (Paul, 2017), different activist digital platforms, such as eradicatingecocide.com have contributed to the construction of new forms of victimhood to enhance cultural and social recognition of the condition of being a victim. Thus, ecocide can be defined as an attempt to label as criminal the human activities that destroy the well-being of ecosystems and species" (Varona, 2020, p. 669).

[23] From an economic point of view, it can be said that "the rule of prohibiting ecocide" safeguards the economic benefits of countries "and seeks to ensure the security of the order and economy of the societies, since ecocide, collapses local, national, regional, and international economy. So, if we closely investigate ecocide based on any economic approach (even pure growth pattern) and in the light of any economic theory (even pure liberal), it has to be condemned and prevented, due to the fact that ecocide is completely economic loss. Because in the event of repetition and continuity of ecocides, no economy would remain. With the loss of the natural resources factor, the other two factors which are capital and human resources will destroy, and production and supply and demand and finally, markets would collapse. Therefore, making a common global policy against ecocide so as to face this phenomenon, especially with intensifying the global crisis of climate change is an undeniable necessity" (Mehra et al., 2019, p. 15).

[24] The damage that humanity inflicts on the environment, "as well as the animal and plant kingdoms, appears as the subversion of the natural order of things. Many are those for whom such subversion should entail, as punishment, the decline, even the collapse of civilisation, the material, political, social and cultural ruin of humanity. But this punishment would not be of human origin: as societies have not defined crimes against nature in their law, it is not up to human justice to punish the guilty" (Bounoua, 2020, p. 3).

effects of certain damages (such as deforestation,[25] desertification, and similar phenomena) to climate changes[26] and the substantial loss of biodiversity.[27]

Even though ecocide does not directly criminalise[28] conduct against global climate change,[29] it indirectly offers mechanisms to combat some of the causes, such as wildfires. Therefore, the argument of climate protection[30] is not entirely incompatible with the crime, serving as a foundation to underpin the new national and international classification.[31]

This is the purpose[32] of the Rome Statute: to announce the conducts deemed unacceptable by humanity, as such acts are fundamentally incompatible with the

---

[25] "Acceleration is recognisably a fundamental trait of our time and this includes the global rate of deforestation over the last 200 years. Deforestation is caused by the combination of seven factors, all accelerating: timber extraction, advancement of agricultural frontiers, fires, mining, hydroelectric plants, urbanisation and the roads opened in the forest as a result of these factors (...). Since the 1980s, global deforestation seems to have reached its peak, as recent estimates suggest that a quarter of the global forest loss over the last ten millennia was destroyed in the last 30 years" (Marques, 2018, pp. 86–88).

[26] Some of the effects of climate change are: "rise in average temperature, changing patterns of precipitations, rise in a sea level, increase and extreme weather events, including heat waves, droughts, cyclones/hurricanes, floods and wildfires. Effects of climate change: habitat change, flooding of coastal areas (deltas, low-lying islands and river basins), negative health effects, food and freshwater shortages, loss of and threats to livelihood, increased migration (mega-cities in developing nations), increase social conflict. (…) Climate change clearly has a range of negative effects, with the extent and severity of these effects virtually certain to increase in coming decades. Further, certain of these effects, such as the loss of livelihood, have clear implications for crime. Nevertheless, criminologists have largely ignored climate change as a source of crime, with exception of a few 'green' or environmental criminologists. (…). As a critical and environmental criminologists point out, certain legal acts cause far more harm than many state-defined crimes, with these legal acts harming people, nonhuman animals, and the natural environment more generally" (Agnew, 2020).

[27] ILC 2019.

[28] There are statistics on the relationship between climate changes and the occurrence of crimes, the former influencing the criminal dynamics of certain regions (Ranson, 2020).

[29] White and Kramer (2015).

[30] It is important to highlight the significance of other fields of law for the formation of a complete legal framework in the fight against climate changes, undoubtedly one of the most serious problems of humanity currently. In this aspect, a crime like ecocide would join climate litigations, of civil, tax, consumerist order, etc., building a network of legal protection more coherent with reality.

[31] "For criminologists concerned with global warming and the environmental harms flowing from it, there is currently no established body of international or domestic law that offers a legal framework to bring these harms within the boundaries of criminology. (…). Indeed, unless criminologists escape the juridical trap that mandates they only study that with states, through their law-making systems, tell them is a crime, the social injuries caused by the most powerful actors in the contemporary world, transnational corporations and national states, will remain forever outside their reach" (Kramer, 2020, p. 87).

[32] It is necessary to reiterate how the Statute "claims in its essence a preeminent role, primarily because of its symbolic function as a tool for global agreement. From this nature derives the imperative for dialogue as a rule that must guide international criminal law in all its expressions" (Di Landro, 2018, p. 118).

existence of peace and security. In this context, the absence of ecocide as an international crime represents a paradox—one that can be resolved through an amendment to the list of crimes under the jurisdiction of the International Criminal Court.[33] Finally, there are now available technical devices to consider the environment as a legal good worthy of protection from an international crime, when it comes to massive destruction. The political will for this, despite being volatile and permeated with crises,[34] seems, despite everything, also to emerge, driven by the climate urgency increasingly felt worldwide.

This book seeks, in a clear and objective manner, to reveal whether—and how—the technical foundation of the crime allows ecocide to transition from discourse to reality as an international crime within ICC. The task undertaken here is still incipient in doctrine, largely due to the relatively recent advancement of the crime in national legislations, as well as the inherent conservatism of international law, especially in the criminal field. Nevertheless, it is evident that the barriers are gradually being overcome, at different levels. This work aims to unify and systematize these foundations, constructing the arguments that ultimately affirm the technical feasibility of ecocide as a crime in the international criminal system.[35]

Fortaleza, Brazil Djalma Alvarez Brochado Neto

References

Agnew, R. (2020). Dire forecast: a theoretical model of the impact of climate change on crime. In R. White, (Ed.) *Environmental crime*. (Vol. II, pp. 17–38). Cheltenham: Elgar.

Banungana, C. T. (2017). La Judiciarisation des Atteintes Environnementales: La Cour Pénale Internationale à la Rescousse. *Quebec International Law Review* 205–243.

Bounoua, S. (2020). Penser l'écocide au XIXe siècle: crimes contre la nature, châtiment divin et vengeance de la Terre. Criminocorpus. Revue d'Histoire de la justice, des crimes et des peines. Available via https://journals.openedition.org/criminocorpus/8041. Accessed March 8, 2025.

Bounoua, S. (2020). Thinking ecocide in the 19th century: crimes against nature, divine punishment and revenge of the Earth. Criminocorpus. *Journal of the History of Justice, Crimes and*

[33] "When life is endangered because of abuses of governments and their acolytes, human rights must be more efficient to give a minimum protection to these populations which are going to disappear in the near future because of destruction of their natural environment. In this regard environmental protection is not only a political or scientific issue but must be also regarded as an issue of justice. Legal courts must remain concerned when fundamental rights are in danger. For that purpose the position of the courts have evolved in response to changing social conditions, and account has been taken of the increasing importance of environmental protection" (Gilbert, 2003, p. 97).

[34] Among the most recent, mention the war between Ukraine and Russia (involving the European Union and NATO), and the trade battle between China and the United States.

[35] "The recognition of the need to criminalize actions of destruction of nature in large proportions demonstrates the advance of the vision in relation to nature as a living being, integrated with the human being, after all, a component element of the cosmologies of the thousands of indigenous cultures existing in the world." (Moribe et al., 2023, p. 40).

Punishments. Available via https://journals.openedition.org/criminocorpus/8041. Accessed March 8, 2025.

Di Landro, A. (2018). La responsabilità per l'attività autorizzata nei settori dell'ambiente e del territorio: Strumenti penali ed extrapenali di tutela. G Giappichelli Editore.

European Parliament. (2022). Human rights and democracy in the world—annual report 2021. Strasbourg, Feb 2022.

Gilbert, J. (2003). Environmental Degradation as a Threat to Life: A Question of Justice. *Trinity College Law Review 6*:81–97.

ILC. (1996). Document on crimes against the environment, prepared by Mr. Christian Tomuschat, member of the Commission. ILC(XLVIII)/DC/CRD.3.

ILC. (2019). Provisional summary record of the 3460th meeting. A/CN.4/SR.3460, Geneva.

Kramer, R. C. (2020). Carbon in the atmosphere and power in America: climate change as state-corporate crime. In R. White (Ed.), *Environmental crime*. (Vol. II, pp. 84–101). Elgar, Cheltenham.

Lora, L. A. (2021). The legal regulation of crimes against the environment in international law: challenges for the definition of ecocide as an international crime. *Anuario Iberoamericano de Derecho Internacional Penal 9*.

Marques, L. (2018). *Capitalismo e colapso ambiental*. (pp. 86–88). São Paulo: Unicamp Publisher.

Mehra, N., Gholipour, G., & Babakhani, E. (2019). Ecocide: a Crime against Sustainable Development. *Ankara Üniversitesi SBF Journal 15*. Available via https://hal.parisnanterre.fr/hal-03156805/document. Accessed March 8, 2025.

Moraes, G. de O. (2018). Os diálogos das Nações Unidas 'harmonia com a natureza' e a proposta de declaração internacional dos direitos da mãe Terra. *Nomos 38*(2):687–712. Available via https://repositorio.ufc.br/bitstream/riufc/43864/1/2018_art_gomoraes.pdf. Accessed March 10, 2025.

Moribe, C. M., Pereira, F. de L. B., França, N. P. C. De. (2023). Ecocide: A new challenge for the international criminal law and for humanity. *Journal of International Criminal Law 4*(1):28–40.

Ranson, M. (2020). Crime, weather and climate change. In: White, Rob (Ed.), *Environmental crime*. (Vol. II, pp. 39–67). Cheltenham: Elgar.

Reiss, M. W. (2017). O Tribunal Penal Internacional no Contexto da Mundialização do Direito: Análise do Estatuto de Roma com base no Direito Penal de inspiração anglo-saxã, no Direito Penal de inspiração romano-germânica e no Direito Penal brasileiro. Doctoral Thesis, Pontifical Catholic University of Rio de Janeiro. Available via https://www.maxwell.vrac.puc-rio.br/36273/36273.PDF. Accessed March 10, 2025.

Rodríguez-Rodríguez, D. (2024). The great family of life. In *The great family of life: Rethinking the place of Homo sapiens in the Biosphere*. Springer Nature Switzerland.

Silva, V. P. da. (2015). My right to green—the right to the environment as a fundamental right. In A. P. B. Homem, & C. Brandão (Eds.), *From natural law to human rights*. (pp. 263–284) Coimbra: Almedina.

Sólon, P. (2018). The rights of mother earth. The climate crisis. South African and global democratic eco-socialist alternatives. (pp. 107–130). Available via https://library.oapen.org/bitstream/handle/20.500.12657/29462/9781776143306.pdf?sequence=1#page=119. Accessed March 8, 2025.

Teles, P. G. (2014). O Tribunal Penal Internacional e a evolução da ideia do combate à impunidade: uma avaliação 15 anos após a Conferência de Roma. *JANUS.NET, e-journal of International Relations 5*(2):2–14.

United Nations. (2022). UN General Assembly declares access to clean and healthy environment a universal human right. *Climate and Environment*. 28 Jul 2022. Available via https://news.un.org/en/story/2022/07/1123482. Accessed March 10, 2025.

Varona, G. (2020). Restorative pathways after mass environmental victimization: Walking in the landscapes of past ecocides. *Onati Socio-Legal Series 10*(3):664–685. Available via https://www.opo.iisj.net/index.php/osls/article/download/1077/1255. Accessed March 10, 2025.

White, R., & Kramer, R. C. (2015). Critical criminology and the struggle against climate change ecocide. *Critical Criminology 23*(4):383–399. Available via https://link.springer.com/content/pdf/10.1007/s10612-015-9292-5.pdf. Accessed March 10, 2025.
Yanev, L. D. et al. (Eds.) (2019). *Modes of liability in international criminal law*. Cambridge University Press.

Acknowledgements

Writing a book with an international scope is no simple task. While writing itself is often a solitary activity, the development and construction of ideas—and the organization of life around them to make everything possible—is the work of many people and institutions. This book followed this script: a lot of individual energy, but also a lot of support from remarkable individuals, without whom it would not be possible to be addressing you now. I will be brief, so as not to risk naming many and accidentally omitting someone. The list is long, and I offer my deepest thanks (as I have done personally on many occasions).

This work would not exist without the unwavering defences of my doctoral supervisors, Dr. Gustavo Cabral (Federal University of Ceará, Brazil) and Dr. Leonardo Pasquali (Università di Pisa, Italy). Their deep knowledge of academic and institutional pathways added strength to the thesis, which would later become this book. My Brazilian supervisor, Dr. Gustavo, has been the intellectual guide behind the path I continue to walk today. In their names, I thank these two exceptional institutions, which opened their doors to high-quality research. I also thank the staffs of the Université de Paris (France), Mercer University (USA), Fordham University (USA), UCLA (USA), The Hague Academy of International Law (Netherlands), International Criminal Court Library (Netherlands), United Nations (USA and Switzerland), Université de Strasbourg (France), and other digital platforms that enabled me to collect the essential materials for this research.

I would also like to thank the publisher Springer Nature, represented by Karolina Araújo Martino, a consummate professional who believed in my work from the beginning—even when it was first published in Brazil in 2023. Now, in 2025, she has championed its international release through this major publisher—something I could never have imagined, not even in my wildest dreams. I also thank my friend Rodrigo Faucz, one of the most accomplished criminal lawyers in Brazil, who believed in the manuscript, encouraged me to publish it, and referred me to one of the leading publishers in the country. Thank you from the bottom of my heart.

My deepest gratitude goes to my family—the most essential part of this journey—who believed in me during both the best and the most difficult moments. Grandparents, aunts, cousins, Xerina: without her, I would never have made it here.

The pride of the family, however modest my work may be, is what drives me forward. My mother, Karen Brochado, and my siblings Carolina and Leandro have always supported my dreams, travels, and long absences—understanding that there was a purpose, even if it seemed impossible: to learn about the world and how it works. My admiration for them is eternal.

To my wife, Sarah Lima, and my daughter, Nicole—you are not only my foundation as a family, but my foundation in every sense. Sarah, an international scholar of the highest caliber, undertook the task of reading every part of this book, offering insights and comments that were vital for refining its ideas. I will never be able to fully repay her support and care over these years. Every member of this family can count on me for whatever they need, always.

Finally, I wish to thank two people who are no longer on this Earth, but who remain present in my life at every moment: my grandfather Djalma Brochado and my father Marcus Brochado—sensitive, honest artists who passed on many beautiful things that I continue to discover a little more each day. Art, I've come to understand, is not only in oil paintings or ceramic sculptures; it lives, above all, in the way we face and live through this complex world. I am forever grateful for their trust and teaching.

It is astonishing how the desire to learn, travel, read, and write can carry someone from the northeastern region of Brazil, from the state of Ceará, from a city called Fortaleza—so far. I am deeply grateful to everyone who has crossed my path in a positive way. Fortunately, there are many. This book represents a small slice of my life, but one filled with meaning. My ambition for it is no greater than the pride and joy I feel in contributing, even in a modest way, to such an important global discussion.

The dream of a better and more equitable world will endure as long as people and institutions like those remembered here continue to exist. Sometimes, the first and most essential step toward real change is simply to believe.

Contents

Chapter 1
Introduction

On 8 August 2019, the Brazilian Federal Public Prosecutor's Office sent a letter (660/2019-PRM/IAB/GAB1) to IBAMA[1] in Santarém, in the state of Pará,[2] inquiring whether the environmental authority was aware of, and had a contingency plan for, a planned demonstration by farmers who intended to use fire to clear forest areas for pasture, as reported by a local newspaper.[3] The Institute responded that, without support from the Military Police of Pará, it could not inspect.[4]

Two days later, Brazilian public and private monitoring agencies recorded a staggering 1923% increase in fire outbreaks in the state, compared to the same period (August 10 and 11) in the previous year.[5] Soon after, it was reported in the press[6]

---

[1] Brazilian Institute of the Environment and Renewable Natural Resources, https://www.gov.br/ibama/pt-br.

[2] Brazilian state entirely within the Legal Amazon (https://www.ibge.gov.br/geociencias/cartas-e-mapas/mapas-regionais/15819-amazonia-legal.html?=&t=o-que-e).

[3] Link: https://www.extraclasse.org.br/ambiente/2019/09/dia-do-fogo-terrorismo-contra-a-floresta-amazonica/. Accessed on: 10 Mar 2025.

[4] In the Official Letter of 12 August 2019, the General Coordinator of Environmental Inspection responded: "In response to the official letter no. 660/2019-PEM/IAB/GAB1, I inform that on 8 August 2019, after the receipt of the document, the Coordination of Inspection Operations and the Intelligence Nucleus of the Superintendency of Pará were alerted to the manifestation. Due to the various attacks suffered and the absence of support from the Military Police of Pará, the inspection actions in the state are impaired because they involve risks related to the security of the field teams. I point out that letters have already been sent requesting support from the National Security Force, however until now there has been no response. Finally, I note that on this date an additional vehicle was sent to strengthen the Prevfogo brigade in the municipality of Itaituba". (OFFICIAL LETTER N° 274/2019/GEREX-SANTARÉM-PA/SUPES-PA, proc. 02048.001402/2019-29).

[5] Links: https://www1.folha.uol.com.br/ambiente/2020/08/dia-do-fogo-em-2019-gerou-poucas-multas-ambientais.shtml, accessed on: 10 Mar 2025; https://www.greenpeace.org/brasil/florestas/dia-do-fogo-completa-um-ano-com-legado-de-impunidade/, accessed on: 10 Mar 2025.

[6] https://www.bbc.com/portuguese/brasil-49453037, accessed on 10 Mar 2025; https://g1.globo.com/pa/santarem-regiao/noticia/2019/10/23/dia-do-fogo-foi-combinado-em-grupos-de-mensa-

D. A. Brochado Neto, *Ecocide*, https://doi.org/10.1007/978-3-032-07757-8_1

that the atypical growth was due to what became known as "Fire Day", when farmers, coordinating actions via *WhatsApp*, deliberately set fire (a mixture of diesel and petrol) at multiple points of the Amazon Rainforest (the National Institute for Space Research—INPE—detected 1457 heat sources in the state). The goal: to create pasture for future annexation and regularization of the burned area.[7]

Over 5 years later, no individuals have been indicted or prosecuted in the Federal Court, despite the Federal Public Prosecutor's investigation and identification of several farms, perpetrators, and instigators. Afterwards, prosecuting authority itself requested the dismissal of the Inquiry due to the "inability to establish culpability."[8] In contrast, in 2020 alone, the Pantanal had 6 months of record-breaking wildfires; by May 2021, deforestation in the Legal Amazon had reached the highest for the month ever recorded. In August 2024, the Amazonas state saw an increase of 89% in fire hotspots, increases with similar surges across other Brazilian states-including Pará (105%), Mato Grosso (457%), and Mato Grosso do Sul (1845%), all compared to August 2023.[9]

These repeated instances of human-caused environmental destruction in Brazil reflect a global crisis.[10] According to a joint UNEP and INTERPOL report, environmental crimes surged by 26% between 2014 and 2016, with the most prevalent being wildlife poaching and trafficking, illegal waste dumping,[11] and forest related crimes.[12] Environmental crime is already the third most profitable criminal industry

---

gens-revela-policia-federal.ghtml, accessed on 10 Mar 2025; https://reporterbrasil.org.br/2019/10/investigacoes-apontam-fazendeiros-e-empresarios-de-novo-progresso-como-organizadores-do-dia-do-fogo/, accessed on 10 Mar 2025.

[7] This fact caused international commotion, even leading to discussions about international intervention in the Amazon (Toledo, 2019).

[8] https://www.mpf.mp.br/pa/sala-de-imprensa/documentos/2021/manifestacao_mpf_pede_arquivamento_inquerito_incendio_alter_do_chao_pa_set_2019.pdf/at_download/file, Accessed on: 7 Dec. 2024.

[9] INPE: Fire Programme. August 2024. Link: https://dataserver-coids.inpe.br/queimadas/queimadas/Infoqueima/2024/2024_08_infoqueima.pdf. Accessed on: 10 Mar 2025.

[10] Among the civil society groups that catalogue environmental damage situations, the website Environmental Justice Atlas (https://ejatlas.org/) is an interactive platform that documents situations of conflict involving the environment worldwide.

[11] Illegal disposal is further exacerbated by organised environmental crime involving hazardous waste, making it difficult to measure the dire consequences of this behaviour (Bugarski, 2015).

[12] The document points to another significant criminal activity, involving air pollution and companies: "According to the International Energy Agency, industrial activities account for almost a third of the global energy consumption and 36 per cent of carbon dioxide emissions. In this context, a market-based carbon pricing system ('cap-and-trade') aimed to decrease carbon emissions was developed. Under this emissions trading scheme, companies can emit carbon set to a certain limit (cap). If they exceed it, they can offset their surplus emissions by purchasing carbon credits from another company. Alternatively, spare carbon credits can be sold to those requiring more (trade). As a new market, emissions trading schemes present gaps in their regulatory framework. These constitute opportunities for unscrupulous companies to circumvent the system in place: To obtain carbon credits: some companies overstate their estimates or engage in corrupt practices in order to claim or receive more carbon credits; To sell carbon credits: certain companies have been involved in the sale of fake or already used carbon credits. Others also manipulate carbon prices, allowing

on the planet,[13] growing three times more than the global gross domestic product in the last decade.[14]

The increasing magnitude of these environmental disasters and their impacts have also been evident in recent years: oil exploration in the tar sands of Alberta (Canada),[15] oil spills at sea,[16] massive oil pollution in the Amazon rainforest (Ecuador),[17] melting permafrost in the Arctic region,[18] global temperature rise,[19] drastic reduction in biodiversity,[20] tailings dam failures,[21] environmental damage resulting from Russia's invasion of Ukraine,[22] among others.

Common to all these cases, regardless of the country (in addition to, at some point, being identified as "ecocide"),[23] is the difficulty in judicially determining administrative, civil, and especially criminal responsibilities. Even more notable is the complete absence of criminal regulation at the international level—this is the focus I intend to address in this research.

For the purposes of this book, ecocide is considered to be causing, by any means, massive environmental damage that renders short-term recovery (resilience) unfeasible, affecting directly or indirectly human populations, either through the harmful physical alteration of ecosystems or extinction of species within a given natural space,[24] with repercussions for one or more States, regardless of whether the

---

them to make significant profits. Overall, the new nature of carbon markets has generated loopholes which are fully exploited by disreputable firms at different stages of the supply chain". (INTERPOL-UN 2016, p. 19).

[13] Link: https://www.interpol.int/News-and-Events/News/2020/INTERPOL-marks-a-decade-of-tackling-serious-organized-environmental-crime. Accessed on: 9 Mar. 2025.

[14] "In the EU, annual revenues from the illegal traffic of non-hazardous waste reach the level of 1.3–10.3 billion euros, from the traffic of hazardous waste - 1.5-1.8 billion euros, and the volume of illegal trade in rare species of flora and fauna, threatened with extinction, is 20 billion euros per year, constituting the second illegal market in the world, after that of drugs". (Bucur, 2023, p. 14).

[15] Lynch (2016).

[16] One of the most famous cases is the Deepwater Horizon oil rig, owned by the British company BP, which collapsed in 2010 after an explosion, leaking 780 million liters of oil into the Gulf of Mexico (Cruden et al., 2016).

[17] Crasson (2017).

[18] Brisman (2013).

[19] Fisher et al. (2017).

[20] Ash, Kyle (2007).

[21] The Brazilian cases of Mariana (2015) and Brumadinho (2019) are one of the largest environmental disasters in Brazil (Thome et al., 2019).

[22] Duunova et al. (2024).

[23] For example, Tregaskis, Shiona. Ten worst 'ecocides'. The Guardian, London, 4 May 2010. Available at: https://www.theguardian.com/environment/gallery/2010/may/04/top-10-ecocides. Accessed on: 10 Mar. 2025, and Oliveira, Regiane. "The mining disasters in Brazil can be judged as crimes against humanity". El País. São Paulo, 26 Feb. 2019. Available at: https://brasil.elpais.com/brasil/2019/02/22/politica/1550859857_043414.html. Accessed on: 10 Mar. 2025.

[24] For instance, predatory hunting resulted in the deliberate and conscious extinction, in 1821, of the great auk, a large bird, incapable of flying, similar to penguins, that inhabited North America

conduct was administratively authorized, provided that the perpetrator knew or should have known the consequences of their actions for the natural environment.[25]

In fact, most of the aforementioned disasters (and their effects) are transboundary (regional impact) or of concern to the global community. Supporting this reasoning, international legal attention to the environment has been growing over the past 50 years, marked by High-Level meetings such as the United Nations Conference on the Environment, and others focused on specific themes (a process known as the "sectorisation" of IEL, or International Environmental Law),[26] such as the United Nations Conference on Climate Change and the United Nations Convention to Combat Desertification.

In criminal matters, however, there remains a largely overlooked gap in the international environmental field. This work will delve into this gap, specifically addressing the crime of ecocide, both as a legal reality (already codified or proposed in domestic laws in certain countries) and as a project under discussion at international level.

Regarding the time frame of this investigation, international criminal law[27] materialized in practice with the establishment of the first ad hoc international courts in 1945.[28] However, it achieved global reach with the creation of the International Criminal Court in 2002,[29] defining the first genuinely international crimes.

The connection between international criminal law and the environment was first established only in the 1970s, when the term "ecocide"[30] emerged. To this day, it remains the only agenda that intersects both areas in international legal discussions.

---

and Europe. Docile, it was easily killed and transformed into food, bait, feathers, etc., serving as cheap sustenance to vessels (Kolbert, 2015, pp. 65–67).

[25] The construction of a definition of ecocide, even preliminary, serves to select past cases that would fit into the crime (Chap. 2), as well as to compare ecocide projects and laws worldwide (Chaps. 5 and 6).

[26] Antunes (2020, p. 269).

[27] Here, terminologically, I refer to international criminal law to deal with crimes at the international level, recognised at this level (and their procedures), i.e., the crimes listed in the Rome Statute; international criminal law refers to the internal criminal law of countries, whose crimes in some way have repercussions beyond borders (Misutra, 2018).

[28] "The massive and unprecedented crimes committed during the Second World War led states to recognise essential values whose serious violation was likely to threaten the very foundations of the international legal order, namely: international peace and security, first, and human dignity, then" (Bellivier et al., 2018, p. 9).

[29] Link: https://www.icc-cpi.int/resource-library/documents/rs-eng.pdf

[30] The development of the debate on ecocide as an international crime, from the 70 s to the present day, takes place in Chap. 3, when the arguments used at the time to support it and, later, to exclude it from the final draft of The Code, the draft Code of crimes against peace and security of humanity, prepared by the International Law Commission (ILC), an agency linked to the UN. This document was the legal basis/inspiration for the Rome Statute.

The objective here is to contribute to resolving the open questions that hinder the effective recognition of ecocide as an international crime. This will be achieved through an analysis of the legal treatment—particularly in the criminal sphere—given by States to major environmental disasters, the existing crimes and ecocide proposals worldwide, documents related to the International Criminal Courts (such as the Statutes of the ad hoc criminal courts and, especially, of the ICC), and the doctrinal proposals developed so far.

Although this approach incorporates elements of domestic law (when discussing cases and criminal liability), it is predominantly international, focusing on existing mechanisms and institutions[31] of international criminal law and related fields.

Specifically, the objectives are also: (1) to identify the criminal repercussions of massive environmental damage on paradigmatic cases, in order to reveal the existing mechanisms to assist in procedural instruction, cases outcomes, and the legal approach to climate change, with focus on accountability and criminal sanctions; (2) to trace the evolution of the notion of ecocide as a crime at both the international and national plans (in jurisdictions where legislation or proposals on the subject exist), to unveil the obstacles preventing its codification at the international level; and (3) to develop arguments for overcoming the main barriers to the recognition of ecocide at the international level, based on the existing legal tools on competence, jurisdiction, the mental element, and the environment as *jus cogens*.

Initially, it is important to note that there is no precise or universally accepted definition of environment.[32] However, for the purposes of this book, the concept introduced at the United Nations Conference on the Environment, in 1972, is sufficient: the environment is understood as a set of components (physical, chemical, biological, and social) capable of causing direct or indirect effects, in a short- or long-term, on living beings and human activities.[33] The concept of environmental crime is more restricted, referring to acts explicitly defined as crimes by law, including both the proscribed conduct and the corresponding sanction.[34]

In criminal law, damage is understood as a harmful alteration of a legally protected good. Thus, even if one considers that the environment should be safeguarded per se, rather than solely due to harm inflicted upon individuals, the meaning of

[31] As an example of the mechanisms considered in this work, mention is made in the ICC (Rome Statute) of the attraction of complementary competence (art. 1), denunciation by the Security Council (art. 13, b) and the regime of international cooperation (art. 86 and following).

[32] For example, for José Afonso da Silva, the environment is the interaction of the set of natural, artificial and cultural elements that promote the balanced development of life for all living beings (SILVA, 2000, p. 20). For a discussion on the 'types' of environment, see: Geraldino, 2014.

[33] United Nations, 1972.

[34] Even so, in international law, there is no consensus: "'Environmental crime' does not have a commonly accepted legal definition. The United Nations Environment Programme (UNEP) and Interpol use the term 'environmental crime' to refer to all illegal activities harmful to the environment that benefit individuals, groups or companies, by harming, trading or stealing natural resources, and which include serious crimes and transnational organised crime" (Bellivier et al., 2018, p. 199).

"damage" remains unchanged.[35] The issue, however, lies in determining the intensity of the damage—this variable is what establishes its legal relevance, distinguishing an insignificant act (such as the theft of a candy from a supermarket) from a war crime (such as an attack on the environment as a military target).[36]

International criminal law is a field of study that gained practical application only after the World Wars. Previously, the prevailing understanding of sovereignty as an absolute characteristic of states prevented the cognition of a punitive authority beyond national borders. The ad hoc military tribunals of Nuremberg (1945 to 1946) and Tokyo (1946 to 1948) marked the beginning of this paradigm shift, assuming, since then, the possibility of criminal sanction at the international level.[37]

From that point onward, sovereignty[38] could no longer serve as an impenetrable shield against violations of legal interests deemed essential for harmonious coexistence among States. In this context, attending to the principle of minimal intervention of criminal law, the legal interests subject to external procedural scrutiny were all linked to war. This confirmed the existence of common values—non-negotiable and intolerant of violations—at least in the war context, a principle that remains in effect to this day.[39]

---

[35] Benjamin argues that "one of the main consequences of the assertion that the environment must be protected per se operates in the field of civil liability, where the notion of "environmental damage" (damage to the environment itself) begins to be dissociated from the idea of harm (personal or economic) to the individual". Even so, he continues: "Damage to nature, almost always, turns against the human being himself, haunting him and, often, harming him in an inevitable way" (Benjamin, 2011, pp. 95–96).

[36] The difficulty in measuring the extent of the damage—which compromises the very application of criminal law –, is a problem even in the ICC: "If environmental damage does not meet such standards, it will not give rise to a war crime and the individual that caused it will not be subject to criminal responsibility. However, there is one further complication: there is no agreed upon definition-not even in the ICC's Elements of Crime-of the terms 'widespread', 'long-term,' or 'severe'" (2018. p. 219).

[37] "The first mention of the personal responsibility of military personnel in times of war comes from the Lieber Code Published in 1863, during the Civil War, by the government of the United States. (...) The idea of a sanction for violations of an emerging law of war therefore stems from the desire to regulate armed conflicts and limit atrocities. A draft of individual criminal responsibility - the obligation for an individual to answer for the offences he has committed and resulting in a sanction - is then put in place by the Geneva Conventions of 1906 and 1927, as well as a state's civil liability - the obligation to repair by compensation a damage caused - by the IV Hague Convention of 1907". (Nollez-Goldbach, 2018, p. 15).

[38] On sovereignty and the environment: "The effects of climate change on the material existence of the territory (for example under the effect of submersion) and on the presence of its population generate consequences on the state's ability to manage activities on its territory and to exercise its sovereign rights. This also calls into question its essential functions such as ensuring the security of its nationals on its national territory. However, international law imposes a requirement of governmental effectiveness, therefore a capacity to actually exercise state functions, as a legal condition for the existence of the state. Can we really consider that a state is sovereign when it is not able to face climate risks, especially events of great intensity such as cyclones, or phenomena such as the rise in sea level with the risks of induced submersion?". (Michelot, 2018, p. 2).

[39] Finally, with the typification of conduct crimes in the Rome Statute (1998, with validity in the international order on 1 July 2002).

This logic prevailed in the following ad hoc tribunals, which were established to prosecute and adjudicate crimes committed in the context of war or armed conflict: The International Criminal Tribunal for the former Yugoslavia[40] (1993–2017) and the International Criminal Tribunal for Rwanda[41] (1994–2015),[42] as well as the internationalized courts in Kosovo, Bosnia Herzegovina, East Timor, and Cambodia, and the hybrid courts[43] of Sierra Leone and, more recently, of Lebanon.[44]

The consolidation of the United Nations (UN, 1945), successor to the ill-fated League of Nations (1919[45]–1946), plays an important role in the construction of internationally recognized and accepted values.[46] This fact is evident when analysing the issues addressed by the Security Council and the General Assembly. Over the last 60 years, in order to ensure the maintenance of global peace and security, the UN has significantly expanded the range of obligations of States, which, in case of non-compliance, may even face military intervention—even in contexts that initially appear to be purely internal affairs.[47]

Meanwhile, environmental issues were gradually gaining international attention. The first global-scale regulations[48] aimed at environmental protection emerged from

[40] Resolution 827 of the UN Security Council. See: https://www.icty.org/.

[41] Resolution 955 of the UN Security Council. See: https://unictr.irmct.org/.

[42] "It should be remembered that the creation of these two ad hoc Tribunals, by decision of the Security Council, in light of Chap. 7 of the United Nations Charter, came not only to meet public pressures in the face of atrocities committed in the former Yugoslavia and Rwanda, but also to contribute to preserving the belief in an international legal order in which those responsible for serious violations of human rights and International Humanitarian Law are judged and sanctioned, thus preventing future crimes". (Trindade, 2010. p. 39).

[43] The distinction of nomenclature is necessary here. "The courts created through national legislation and which are part of the national judiciary are the internationalised courts, (...), since international participation was inserted into the existing judicial system, even if in an isolated chamber", while "hybrid courts are those that come closest to the model of a purely international court (...), they operate independently of the affected State and the international body that created them. Their creation is made by international agreement or by resolution of the Security Council and it is the fact that they are also constituted by elements of national origin (...)". (Annoni et al., 2015).

[44] The latter, differing from the others, investigates crimes of terrorism. Annoni et al. (2015).

[45] League of Nations, conceived in Versailles, on 28 April 2019.

[46] Alain Pellet comments that "It would certainly be excessive to claim that the United Nations has ensured the rule of law in international relations but, concretely, international law has, during the 50 years of life of the new system, played a role much greater than that assigned to it by the letter of the Charter, some provisions of which have had an unexpected fortune". (Pellet, 1995, p. 402).

[47] For example, considering the duty to protect of States as intrinsic to the exercise of sovereignty, the Security Council has already determined humanitarian intervention (Resolution 1542, of 2004, in Haiti) and military (Resolution 1973, of 2011, in Libya), in situations that, in principle, relate to internal affairs.

[48] For some authors, the first international judicial environmental dispute took place in 1941, in the case Trail Smelter, disputed between the United States and Canada, presented by the former to the International Joint Commission, based on the Boundary Waters Treaty, of 1909 (Parrish, 2005, p. 363–430). As for Treaties, one of the first drafted was the London Convention on the Preservation of Fauna and Flora in their Natural State, of 1900 (Convention for the Preservation of Wild Animals, Birds, and Fish in Africa), which, for not reaching the minimum number of signatures,

the International Conference for the Human Environment in Stockholm in 1972. By then, it was already clear that human activity had the potential to cause irreparable damage to nature indiscriminately[49] affecting the community. The main concern was to securing recognition by States of the finiteness of natural resources, urging the international community to cooperate on matters related to "protection and improvement of the environment".[50]

The next significant step in establishing more concrete goals for environmental protection came with the United Nations Conference on the Environment and Development held in Rio de Janeiro, in 1992, known as the Earth Summit (or Eco-92). In addition to reaffirming the commitments determined in Sweden, the meeting sought to define a new global agenda, introducing key concepts in conventions and multilateral treaties[51]—most notably the precautionary principle, which was a central element of the Rio Declaration.[52]

The precautionary principle was elevated to the status of an international principle-rule,[53] requiring the adoption of all possible measures to prevent environmental damage.[54] Together with the principle of prevention,[55] it aims to protect the

was replaced by another Convention, in 1933. (https://www.ecolex.org/details/treaty/convention-relative-to-the-preservation-of-fauna-and-flora-in-their-natural-state-tre-000069/). Before the Stockholm Conference, the African Convention on the Conservation of Nature and Natural Resources (Algiers Convention), replacing the London Convention, of colonial nature (Erinosho, 2013). It is important to mention two other documents, in the period between World Wars, dealing with indiscriminate whaling: the Geneva Convention for the Regulation of Whaling, of 1931, and the Agreement for the Regulation of Whaling, of 1937. Both, despite being little effective, constituted the legal basis for the signing, in 1946, of the International Convention for the Regulation of Whaling, already under the mantle of the UN (Fitzmaurice, 2017).

[49] From the Declaration of the UN Conference, June 1972, point 6: "We have come to a point in history where we must shape our actions around the world with particular attention to the consequences that can to the environment. Out of ignorance or indifference, we can cause immense and irreparable damage to the earth's environment on which our life and well-being depend".

[50] Principle 24 of the Conference Declaration: "All countries, large and small, should deal with international issues related to the protection and improvement of the environment in a spirit of cooperation and on an equal footing. It is essential to cooperate to control, prevent, reduce and effectively eliminate the harmful effects that activities carried out in any sphere, may have on the environment, through multilateral or bilateral agreements, or by other appropriate means, respecting the sovereignty and interests of all states".

[51] Guimarães et al. (2012), p. 21.

[52] Principle 15: In order to protect the environment, the principle of precaution should be widely observed by States, according to their capabilities. When there is a threat of serious or irreversible damage, the absence of absolute scientific certainty will not be used as a reason to postpone economically viable measures to prevent environmental degradation

[53] Brochado et al. (2018).

[54] "The basis of such a requirement will once again be human solidarity, both with the present generation and with future generations. Thus, solidarity begins to play the role of a limiting instrument, establishing a link between generations, and even provoking a form of social control". (Marques, 2012, p. 46).

[55] For Denise Hammerschmidt, "the principle of prevention is a rational conduct in the face of a harm that science can objectify and measure, which moves within the certainties of science.

environment by avoiding harm before it occurs. However, if damage does take place, there is no sanction for whoever causes it, whether the harm was caused intentionally or negligently.

Ten years later (2002), the World Summit on Sustainable Development,[56] known as Rio + 10, took place in Johannesburg, South Africa. This summit marked progress in recognizing sustainable development as a key element in UN activities, calling on various stakeholders to take actions to ensure the implementation of the Millennium Declaration[57] and Agenda 21.

It is worth mentioning that this Conference took place exactly 1 year after the terrorist attacks in the United States, carried out by Osama bin Laden's Al-Qaeda. These events underscored the importance of environmental concerns, even amid the newly initiated "War on Terror".[58]

At the United Nations Conference on Sustainable Development (2012), known as Rio + 20,[59] which was again in Rio de Janeiro, the agreements made 10 years earlier were reiterated: the Final Declaration, known as "The Future We Want", reaffirms the commitments made in previous Conventions, with the goal of strengthening international cooperation, focused on sustainable development.[60]

Regarding anthropogenic climate change,[61] following the adoption of the United Nations Framework Convention on Climate Change (UNFCCC) in 1992, the first significantly impactful milestone occurred in 2005, with the entry into force of the Kyoto Protocol.[62] This treaty established binding targets, particularly for major

---

Precaution, on the other hand, faces the other nature of uncertainty: the uncertainty of scientific knowledge itself", and concludes: "The principle of prevention refers to concrete danger and the principle of precaution refers to abstract danger". (Hammerschmidt, 2002, p. 111).

[56] Link: https://sustainabledevelopment.un.org/milesstones/wssd.

[57] Link: https://www.oas.org/dil/port/2000%20Declara%C3%A7%C3%A3o%20do%20Milenio.pdf.

[58] According to Stanford, the so-called 'War on Terror', that is, on terrorism (faceless, without a flag), promotes a constant state of war, more susceptible to human rights violations (Stanford, 2015).

[59] Link: https://sustainabledevelopment.un.org/rio20.

[60] According to Guimarães and Fontoura, "Rio + 20 was not centred, nor was it designed, with the aim of culminating negotiations on fundamental aspects for the future of the planet's environment, focusing only on discussions, almost academic, around 'green economy in the context of sustainable development and the eradication of poverty' and on 'the institutional framework for sustainable development'. With the world immersed in the deepest economic crisis since the Great Depression of 1929, it was really difficult to convince world leaders to travel to Rio in June to simply discuss these themes, but without having to make decisions, moreover, not identified at any time for their ratification and implementation, except in the vague political declaration 'The Future We Want'." (Guimarães et al., 2012, p. 26).

[61] On the importance of international negotiations about climate change, see OTT, 2001.

[62] Agreement affirmed at COP-3, in Japan, in December of 1997. Available at: https://treaties.un.org/Pages/ViewDetails.aspx?src=TREATY&mtdsg_no=XXVII-7-a&chapter=27&clang=_en. Accessed on: 10 Mar. 2025.

greenhouse gases emitters, in an effort to slow down global warming,[63] identified there as the major threat to humanity's future.

The greenhouse effect and its consequences—such as rising sea levels, droughts, desertification, loss of biodiversity, epidemics—directly impact human populations, leading to social degradation and a decline in individual quality of life. The risks associated with such disasters, including forced migrations, were the subject of the World Conference on Disaster Risk Reduction in Kobe, Hyogo, (Japan), in 2005.[64]

The most recent and important initiative to curb the rise in global temperatures was the signing of the Paris Agreement at COP-21 in December 2015, which aims to limit global warming to 2° C by the end of the century,[65] through decarbonization (control of greenhouse gas emissions) of economies. At the last summit meeting, COP-29, a new financial target was set to assist countries in protecting their populations and economies from climate disasters while ensuring the equitable distribution of the benefits of clean energy.[66]

On the international stage, then, protection mechanisms have become more sophisticated[67]—and some, legally binding—focusing on the prevention and reduction of environmental risks. There are, in fact, frameworks for environmental governance on the global level, linked to national legislation, which seek to regulate environmental issues both within and beyond state borders on a supranational scale.[68]

---

[63] The human impact is noticeable in the present and future, as Kotzé highlights: "(...) the result of anthropogenic impacts has taken on spatial-temporal- causal dynamics where, for example, present automobile emissions in a city cause not only respiratory diseases in that city but also contribute to greenhouse gas concentrations that fuel global climate change, which, in turn, could affect unborn future generations across the globe for years to come". (Kotzé, 2014).

[64] "Disaster loss is on the rise with grave consequences for the survival, dignity and livelihood of individuals, particularly the poor, and hard-won development gains. Disaster risk is Compared to pre-industrial average levels. However, the ideal, according to the Agreement itself, is to limit the temperature increase to 1.5 °C (Article 2, 'a'). The number is agreed upon among scientists, according to the Intergovernmental Panel on Climate Change (IPCC, see: https://www.ipcc.ch/).

[65] Compared to pre-industrial average levels. The ideal, however, according to the Agreement itself, is to limit the temperature increase to 1.5 °C (Article 2, 'a'). This number is agreed upon by scientists, according to the Intergovernmental Panel on Climate Change (IPCC, see: https://www.ipcc.ch/).

[66] Link: https://unfccc.int/news/cop29-un-climate-conference-agrees-to-triple-finance-to-developing-countries-protecting-lives-and. Accessed on: 7 Dec. 2024.

[67] Important principles were established, such as the prohibition of environmental regression: "(...) the principle of non-regression is, in addition to a principle, the expression of a duty of non-regression that is imposed on the Administration. A positive formula, like a 'principle of progression', was not chosen by us because it is too vague and because it applies, in fact, to every norm as an instrument, functioning in the service of the ends of society". (Prieur, 2010, p. 14).

[68] "Global environmental governance has recently emerged as a collective descriptive term and normative construct that encapsulates the countless (and growing) political, legal and institutional arrangements at the international, regional, sub-regional, national and sub-national levels that seek to respond to environmental problems. Generally speaking, all of these arrangements aim to influence human behaviour vis-à-vis the environment. They consist of complex political and diplomatic processes; a plethora of legal arrangements such as international multilateral environmental agreement (MEA) regimes; regional, sub-regional, national and sub-national laws; state actors, various

However, the escalation of massive environmental damage in recent years reveals not only the possible inefficiency but certainly the insufficiency of preventive measures.[69] Criminal intervention[70] in environmental matters, as ultima ratio, emerges as a possible tool,[71] and is increasingly discussed in legal doctrine,[72] national parliaments,[73] and international forums.[74] This is precisely the investigative hypothesis of this work.

Within the international repressive system, environmental damage was historically been considered a crime only in context of war. When analysing the Vietnam War (1955–1975), where nature was, for the first time, systematically targeted for

---

public- and private-sector organisations and other non-state actors; numerous private- and public-sector arrangements and networks; and a host of monitoring, research, information sharing, enforcement and dispute resolution mechanisms". (Kotzé, 2012).

[69] An example of failure in crime prevention was the international fight against so-called "blood diamonds". The Kimberley Process (KP) certification was created, which would guarantee the origin of the precious stone, supposedly ensuring control in mineral exploration and respect for human rights. However, the solution found, apparently, institutionalises and masks the practice of crimes, now under a supposed seal of authenticity (Alt, 2015).

[70] The international human rights protection systems (global and regional) lead to the criminal responsibility of individuals at the international level: "(...) it would be worthless to have guaranteed the right of access to international human rights bodies (whether within the UN or regional organisations) if there was not also the obligatory counterpart in the criminal sphere, beyond the obligations already existing in the civil sphere" (Mazzuoli, 2019, p. 1408).

[71] Environmental crime affects societies as a whole, having consequences in various areas, such as health and economic, directly affecting the security of countries. International law proves powerless in the face of successive violations of the environment, requiring a focus on international criminal law, in order to promote greater legislative integration between States (Martin-Chenut et al., 2015 p. 543–544).

[72] As an example, in free research on the Hein Online site (private database service specialising in legal materials), the number of articles with the term "ecocide" in the title published between 2015 and 2020 is over 60% higher than the period between 1971 and 2014 (27 articles were found, 17 of them published in the first indicated period). Google Scholar records approximately 13,000 documents with the term 'ecocide' between 1970 and 2019, while only between 2019 and 2024 almost 14,000 documents are found.

[73] Some of the main countries today discussing ecocide as a crime are France, Belgium and Brazil. In the United Kingdom, in 2011, the Supreme Court held a mock trial on ecocide (https://www.dw.com/en/uk-supreme-court-explores-ecocide-in-mock-trial/a-15425719). Today, the country has a Bill, presented in 2023.

[74] The International Law Commission (ILC), in 2019, discussing species extinction, ecocide and jus cogens on the international level, stated: "(...) some 500 biodiversity experts had gathered to discuss the Global Assessment Report on Biodiversity and Ecosystem Services produced by the Intergovernmental Science-Policy Platform on Biodiversity and Ecosystem Services. The report concluded that some one million species were facing extinction and that many could disappear completely within a decade if nothing was done. Unlike genocide, however, "ecocide" was not a jus cogens norm. While protection of the environment and natural resources might not have been recognized as a peremptory norm in the past, it was a potential candidate for inclusion on a future list of jus cogens norms. The manner in which the Commission elaborated an illustrative list should not hinder the potential inclusion of such norms. The list adopted by the Commission must not be fixed in the year 2019, but must remain open-ended" (ILC, 2019, p. 7).

military destruction, Richard Falk used the term ecocide,[75] originally coined by Arthur Galston from the word "genocide," to refer to American attacks involving herbicides, particularly Agent Orange. In this sense, the protection of the environment, for criminal purposes, was linked to crimes against peace and humanity.[76]

During the negotiations for the drafting of *The Code*, the technical basis of the Rome Statute, the inclusion of ecocide as an international crime in times of peace (the fifth crime of global relevance)[77] was initially considered, but in the preliminary draft, in 1998, it was excluded[78] any mention of this offence, restricting the issue solely to war crimes.[79] Even so, the provision remains vague and difficult to apply in practical case.[80]

---

[75] "Therefore, it is important to understand the extent to which environmental warfare is linked to the overall tactics of high-technology counter-insurgency warfare, and extends the indiscriminateness of warfare carried on against people to the land itself. Just as counter-insurgency warfare tends toward genocide with respect to the people, so it tends toward ecocide with respect to the environment". (Falk, 1973, p 1–2).

[76] "Crimes against the peace and security of mankind might therefore be characterized as acts which seriously jeopardized the most vital interests of mankind, violated the fundamental principles of jus cogens and threatened individual nations, ethnic groups, civilization and the right to life. Perhaps the Special Rapporteur could also consider the relationship between the provisions of the draft code and those of article 19 of part 1 of the draft articles on State responsibility. He would also not object if the list of international crimes included "ecocide", as a reflection of the need to safeguard and preserve the environment, as well as the first use of nuclear weapons, colonialism, apartheid, economic aggression and mercenarism" (Yearbook of The International Law Commission, 1987, V. 1.Available at: http://legal.un.org/ilc/publications/yearbooks/english/ilc_1987_v1.pdf , accessed on: 13 Mar. 2025).

[77] Cabanes (2018, pp. 265–278).

[78] This point is detailed in Chap. 3. The idea is, when describing chronologically the discussion about ecocide in the Code by the ILC, showing that the technical—and political—issues pointed out at the time, today find new lights, which allows a reanalysis about the possibility of changing the Rome Statute (art. 121 of the Statute) to include the crime of ecocide.

[79] Decree 4388, of September 25, 2002, promulgating the Rome Statute. Article 8, 8(2)(b) (iv) states: "For the purposes of this Statute, 'war crimes' are understood as: iv) Intentionally launching an attack, knowing that it will cause incidental loss of human lives or injuries to the civilian population, damage to civilian property or extensive, long-lasting and severe damage to the environment that are clearly excessive in relation to the concrete and direct overall military advantage anticipated".

[80] "À première vue, les défenseurs de l'environnement devraient donc être ravis de voir des règles sur les dommages causés à l'environnement en temps de guerre—qui ne faisaient auparavant même pas partie du régime des infractions graves—élevées au rang de crimes de guerre à la Cour pénale internationale. Cependant, notre analyse des éléments de l'article 8, paragraphe 2, alinéa b-iv) du Statut de la CPI et de leur application à des exemples classiques de dommages intentionnels à l'environnement en temps de guerre a montré que le champ d'application de cette règle est extrêmement limité. En effet, au vu des critères élevés fixés pour les dommages causés, de la difficulté que pose l'exigence de connaissance, et de la notion de « proportionnalité/nécessité » élargie et donc facile à invoquer, on peut se demander, comme Heller et Lawrence, s'il sera possible de condamner qui que ce soit pour dommages à l'environnement en temps de guerre en vertu de cette disposition de la CPI". (Wyatt, 2010).

Despite this setback, there has been a growing number of studies in recent years on the feasibility of punishing serious environmental offences through international criminal law. Environmental disasters[81] with international consequences/repercussions, amplified by successive and increasingly accurate scientific reports on climate change[82] have broadened the debate beyond academia, reaching civil society, such as the campaigns *Eradicating Ecocide* (which resulted in a document presented at the United Nations in 2010[83]), *Friends of the Earth International,*[84] *Stop Ecocide Foundation*[85] (which focused, in 2021, on the technical definition of the crime, by a panel of experts), in addition to robust independent research, such as proposals for international conventions on ecocrimes and ecocide.[86]

At the end of 2016, the Office of the Prosecutor of the International Criminal Court released a policy document on case selection and prioritization.[87] The document established that if one of the crimes (already under the jurisdiction of the ICC) is committed through environmental destruction, or if this causes significant suffering to the victims, the investigation and prosecution of these offenses will take precedence over others.[88]

More recently, on 19 May 2021,[89] the European Parliament, in addressing climate change and human rights, expressly encouraged the EU and its Member-States to support, within the framework of the International Criminal Court (ICC), new negotiations to recognise "ecocide" as an international crime, under the Rome Statute, "in order to combat the impunity of perpetrators of environmental crimes at a global level".[90]

---

[81] For the purposes of this work, the term "disaster", associated with the "environment", does not necessarily imply the inevitability or the natural causes of the event, but rather relates to the magnitude of the environmental damage, whatever the cause.

[82] As an example, the successive Bulletins of the World Meteorological Organization (WMO), a specialized agency of the UN, which, year after year, report record increases of CO^2 in the atmosphere, heating the planet, leading the UN Secretary-General, commenting on the latest report (WMO. Bulletin: The journal of the World Meteorological Organization, v. 70, n. 1, 2021), to state: "the world is on the brink of the 'abyss' of climate change, as the increase in temperature continues" (Link: https://news.un.org/en/story/2021/04/1090072. Accessed on: 10 Mar. 2025).

[83] Eradicating Ecocide. Relevant international crime history. Available at: http://eradicatingecocide.com/the-law/history/#_ftn8. Accessed on: 15 Mar. 2025.

[84] Link: http://www.foei.org/.

[85] Link: https://www.stopecocide.earth/.

[86] NEYRET (2015).

[87] International Criminal Court (2016, p. 14).

[88] Misutra (2018. p. 219).

[89] Previously, in January 2021, the European Parliament adopted Resolution 2020/2208(INI), calling for the recognition and promotion of ecocide as an international crime under the Rome Statute of the International Criminal Court (European Union, 2021a, 2021b).

[90] European Union (2021a, 2021b) (2).

In November 2023, the European Council formally adopted a new directive on environmental crimes, including provisions to criminalize cases "comparable to ecocide".[91]

Previously, at the national level, some countries, such as Russia,[92] had already included the crime of ecocide in domestic legislation,[93] but with different criteria and applicability. However, the lack of a clear and consistent definition of "ecocide" has remained one of the biggest obstacles to its recognition as a criminal offense. Two recent legislative proposals illustrate this difficulty: Bill 2.787/2019, in Brazil,[94] and Bill 2353/2019,[95] in France. Among the most common criticisms are the weak distinction between the proposed crime and other environmental offences already codified in law. Additionally, determining the threshold of damage required to characterize ecocide has proven problematic in legislative projects from[96] and Mexico.[97]

Even so, ecocide has been embraced by non-governmental organizations (NGOs), as well as civil and political movements that advocate for the introduction of this crime on the international stage. The term has gained popularity in

---

[91] European Union (2024).

[92] Despite being defined as a crime for over 2 decades in the Criminal Code of the Russian Federation (art. 358), there is no record of any conviction for ecocide to date (Link: https:// strelka-mag.yc.strelka.com/ru/article/pochemu-vse-govoryat-pro-ekocid . Accessed on: 12 Mar. 2025).

[93] These are Russia (1996, with amendment in 2012), Vietnam (1999), Armenia (2003), Belarus (1999), Moldova (2002), Ukraine (2001), Georgia (1999), Kazakhstan (1997), Kyrgyzstan (1997) Tajikistan (1998). (Cabanes, 2018, p. 276).

[94] After this Bill, two others have already been proposed, all in progress in the Brazilian Congress: PL 2933/23 and PL 2875/2024.

[95] The French Bill, inspired by the Citizens' Convention for Climate (created in 2019, composed of French citizens, to formulate proposals on the theme of environment and ecological transition. See: https://www.conventioncitoyennepourleclimat.fr/), is controversial for downgrading ecocide from a crime to a mere offence (Bill amended to 3875/2021), in discrepancy with the popular desire revealed in the Convention.

[96] The Bolivian Bill 137/2020-2021, called "Bill against ecocide and protection of Mother Earth", does not specify what is "serious and significant damage", inaccuracy that directly affects the applicability of the penal norm. Thus, art. 365 is provided: "Whoever causes serious and significant damage to Mother Earth, putting at risk the continuity of her life cycles, structure and functioning will be punished with the penalty of deprivation of liberty from (15) fifteen to (30) thirty years without prejudice to the civil and/or environmental liability that may result from the damage caused".

[97] The Federal Bill, presented by Senator Samuel Alejandro Garcia Sepúlveda in 2020, is also imprecise in explaining what is "serious, massive and extensive damage", compromising the future practical application of the crime. Thus, art. 416 bis in the Federal Penal Code is provided: "Commits the crime of ecocide who by himself or by interposed person derived from the activities he carries out, causes a serious, massive and extensive damage, in surface and temporality, to the natural resources, flora, fauna, water quality, soil, subsoil or the environment, whose result is the affectation of a certain ecosystem" (Available at: sil.gobernacion.gob.mx/Archivos/Documentos/2020/03/asun_4025989_20200324_1584567385.pdf. Accessed on 12. Mar. 2025). Note that another Bill was presented in 2023, to include art. 417 bis in the Mexican Federal Penal Code bringing the crime of ecocide in the terms proposed in the International Criminal Court.

newspapers and magazines[98]—not as a formally defined criminal offense but rather as a public policy issue highlighting serious crime against the environment.[99] There have been numerous calls for the inclusion of ecocide among the crimes under the jurisdiction of the International Criminal Court, the only permanent criminal court[100] on the planet.[101]

In 2020, Vanuatu and Maldives, two island nations highly vulnerable to rising sea levels, officially advocated[102]—at the Assembly of the Parties of the ICC—for the inclusion of ecocide in the Rome Statute, receiving support throughout the year from Belgium, France,[103] and others. In March 2021, a group of researchers, coordinated by Philippe Sands and Dior Fall Sow,[104] gathered hundreds of suggestions on the crime of ecocide, presenting in June of the same year a theoretical definition designed to meet the technical requirements of an international criminal offense, in order to make it viable as a norm.

---

[98] Even during the Covid-19 pandemic, environmental issues and the possibility of criminalising ecocide remained prominent topics in various international news outlets e. Some headlines: Lawyers Are Working to Put 'Ecocide' on Par with War Crimes. Could an International Law Hold Major Polluters to Account? (Time, 19.2.2021); To stop climate disaster, make ecocide an international crime. It's the only way (The Guardian, 24.2.2021); Ecocidio: a new crime against peace to save the planet (Huffingtonpost, 27.3.2021); Is it time for "ecocide" to become an international crime? (The Economist, 28.2.2021); Ecocidio', a new crime to protect the planet from humanity (El País Spain, 21.3.2021); Ecocide: Should killing nature be a crime? (BBC, 6.11.2020).

[99] Brochado et al. (2018).

[100] In 2014, in reaction to the action of the ICC in investigations in African continent countries (see item 7.2), the African Union (AU) adopted the Protocol on Amendments to the Protocol on the Statute of the African Court of Justice and Human Rights (Malabo Protocol), which extends the jurisdiction of the yet to be established African Court of Justice and Human Rights (ACJHR) to international law crimes and transnational crimes. However, there is no mention of environmental crimes in this extended list (Amnesty International, 2016, p. 11. "On this occasion, African leaders were building a penal structure with competences identical to those of the ICC, however with the guarantee that it would not be the target of the action of this jurisdictional body, that is, they created an immunity for themselves" (Leite & Cabral, 2018).

[101] There are also suggestions for the creation of a new Court, exclusive for the environment, which would judge crimes, among other demands. In the permanent context of economic crisis—and now, pandemic—it is highly unlikely the construction of an international treaty specific for this, considering the necessary cost (Neyret, 2017).

[102] The speech of the ambassador of the Republic of Vanuatu in the European Union took place at the 18th Session of the Assembly of States Parties to the Rome Statute, in The Hague, in December 2019 (Link: https://asp.icc-cpi.int/iccdocs/asp_docs/ASP18/GD.VAN.2.12.pdf).

[103] It was expected that France would seek more support within the Union from 2022, presiding over the European Union (Le Parlement Européen demande à la Cour Pénale Internationale de reconnaître le crime d'écocide. Novethic, 29 Jan. 2021. Available at: https://www.novethic.fr/actualite/environnement/pollution/isr-rse/le-parlement-europeen-demande-a-la-cour-penale-internationale-de-reconnaitre-le-crime-d-ecocide-149459.html. Accessed on: 410Mar. 2025).

[104] See: www.ecocidelaw.com, composed by researchers from the projects Stop Ecocide Earth, chaired by Jojo Mehta, and Promise Institute for Human Rights from UCLA School of Law. Definition of ecocide elaborated by the panel: https://static1.squarespace.com/static/5ca2608ab914493c64ef1f6d/t/60d7479cf8e7e5461534dd07/1624721314430/SE+Foundation+Commentary+and+core+text+revised+%281%29.pdf, accessed on: 13 Mar. 2025.

Finally, on 9 September 2024, Vanuatu, Fiji, and Samoa officially proposed an Amendment to the Rome Statute before the Assembly of the Parties, seeking to include ecocide as the fifth crime under the jurisdiction of the Court, using the definition developed by the panel of experts.[105]

Now more clearly, the ICC emerges as a previously considered but now tangible alternative for prosecuting and adjudicating acts of massive destruction of the environment in peacetime.[106] Beyond being physically operational, with 125 signatory states,[107] the Court has accumulated trial experience,[108] allowing for adjustments and refinements to its legal mechanisms after two decades of operation.[109] However, despite growing consensus on the Court's potential jurisdiction over this new crime, significant technical challenges remain—with its "limited" competence over the Member-States.

The ICC exists by virtue of an "international treaty",[110] binding only the States that ratify it. However, the Rome Statute contains a provision allowing the UN Security Council to refer any situation where crimes may have occurred, thus expanding the original jurisdiction of the Court. This mechanism theoretically establishes a form of universal jurisdiction.[111] However, among the five permanent

[105] ICC (2024).

[106] It is, at least, incongruent that, for the Rome Statute, destroying the environment in a context of war (when almost everything is allowed) is a crime, while doing the same, in peacetime, is not (Brochado et al., 2020).

[107] The last country to become a member was Ukraine, on 25 October 2024.

[108] There is an important criticism of the Court's action, treated as 'Eurocentric' for focusing, in most of the cases admitted to the Court, on people from the African continent, leading certain countries, such as Kenya, Uganda and Namibia, to consider withdrawal (art. 127) from the Rome Statute (Pasquali, 2019, p. 5).

[109] The Court is complementary to criminal jurisdictions international (art. 1 of the Rome Statute). That is, the Court is not in conflict with the States Parties, "(...) that complementarity must not function as a principle that separates national from international jurisdiction or puts them in conflict with each other, but as a principle that in fact requires interaction between them while keeping the Court in an 'avant-garde position'. The idea of international criminal justice is not to build a supranational system that excludes national courts, but to provide an example and to contribute to the progressive rapprochement—thus harmonisation—of national criminal justice systems. Such an objective is obviously difficult to attain given the considerable differences between national systems, including on such major issues as the death penalty and torture and inhumane or degrading treatment. And yet, harmonisation has been occurring as States Parties have transposed the ICC Statute, which contains definitions of crimes and conditions of responsibility, into their legislation. In the long term, harmonisation will hopefully be strengthened under the influence of international human rights instruments and through the principle of complementarity". (Delmas-Marty, 2006 p. 7).

[110] There are authors who consider the term "international treaty" redundant, as 'treaty' is necessarily negotiated/ratified between sovereign states, hence the international character is inherent to all agreements.

[111] Despite that, as seen in the case of Libya, it does not transform the non-signatory state into a State Party, that is, it does not have obligations to the Court, such as, for example, cooperation.

members of the Security Council,[112] only France and the United Kingdom are States Parties to the Statute, raising concerns that the power of veto could, in practice, block this universalization.

However, it would not be the first time that the Security Council would be stalled by the lack of agreement among the permanent members. The General Assembly, the UN's main deliberative body, has previously stepped in to compensate for such inaction often due to Cold War-era deadlocks—on matters concerning the Council. In a 1961 advisory opinion, the International Court of Justice (ICJ)[113] recognized the possibility of Assembly intervention, including in matters of international security. By broadening the view of the circumstances that affect peace to include environmental issues, it is reasonable to anticipate increased interaction and cooperation between the organisms.

Defining what "ecocide" means and its scope within criminal law[114] —and its respective penalty[115] is essential—but far from the only challenge in establishing it as an international crime.

Assuming the task of defining it, with clear boundaries of its scope, it is necessary to point out, among other aspects, to whom the rule is intended. This is essential for this type of crime, whose conduct is primarily carried out by legal entities. Far more devastating than individuals, it is large corporations that are commonly attributed significant damage to the environment.

The jurisdiction of the ICC is, however, restricted to natural persons. Despite there being a Bill, from the year 2015, presented to the Secretary-General of the

---

[112] The United States and Russia did sign the Statute, on 17 September and 31 December 2000, respectively, but later expressed their non-adherence to the Court. China, on the other hand, did not even sign the document (United Nations, 2021).

[113] Amorim (2015, p. 57).

[114] That is, respecting the principle of legality, with clear description of the conduct, parameterisation of what would be 'massive damage' and, finally, the penalty.

[115] The functions traditionally attributed to penalties are preventive, retributive and rehabilitative. Prevention, in the sense of example to discourage similar conduct; retributive, in the form of traditional punishment to the agent who commits the illicit; and rehabilitative, when the State reinstates the offender as part of society. However, for national criminal law these concepts are generic, enclosing various problems in the specialised doctrine, which judge them disconnected from practice. Also, "to understand that International Criminal Law is the basis of international punishment or that it is linked to the application of the penalty as a justifying instrument from a nebulous plethora of empirically unprovable theories is to fall into a problem long indicated and criticised by the critical analysis of the functions of the penalty. (...) As Zaffaroni identified, this is about justifying the irrational search for revenge that pacifies only the spectator of the process and, even so, in a tense, anguished and temporary way". (Dissenha, 2013, p. 312).

United Nations[116] for the punishment of transnational corporations (TNCs),[117] there is no mechanism in international law that attracts their criminal liability for environmental damage.[118]

In Brazil, for example, criminal liability of legal entities for environmental crime is permitted,[119] regardless of whether a natural person is prosecuted.[120] At the international level, a possible the way forward may involve revisiting the very concept of legal personality,[121] or, alternatively, maintaining the prosecution of individuals by analysing their actions within a defined chain of command.

This approach also mitigates a second problem in the prosecution of environmental crime: establishing the causal link between conduct and resulting harm. It is generally easier to attribute responsibility to a company for specific environmental damage than to identify a particular individual within that company, whose actions are often embedded within complex hierarchical decision-making procedures.

Nonetheless, when it comes to environmental damage, this task can be extremely difficult, if not impossible.[122] For instance, linking the collapse of the Brumadinho

---

[116] "The Treaty should include a reference to Ecocide caused by the direct or systemic violations by TNCs. Ecocide is the extensive damage to, destruction of or loss of ecosystem(s) of a given territory to such an extent that peaceful enjoyment by the inhabitants of that territory has been or will be severely diminished, or when systemic death and extermination of species occur. The inclusion of Ecocide in international law aims to prohibit mass damage and destruction of the Earth and creates a legal duty of care for all inhabitants—including all living beings—that have been or are at risk of being significantly harmed due to Ecocide. The duty of care applies to prevent, prohibit and preempt both human-caused Ecocide and natural catastrophes United Nations (2015).

[117] Indeed, TNCs (from English, transnational companies), accumulate economic and political power unparalleled in human history: "The non-governmental organisation Global Justice Now conducts a ranking that compares the business figures of major companies with the budgetary income of countries. According to this list, if the American supermarket chain Walmart were a state, it would occupy the tenth place, behind the USA, China, Germany, Japan, France, United Kingdom, Italy, Brazil and Canada. In total, 69 of the 100 main economic entities are companies. The 25 corporations that earn the most surpass the GDP of numerous countries". See: https://brasil.elpais.com/brasil/2017/11/03/economia/1509714366_037336.html, and https://www.globaljustice.org.uk/news/69-richest-100-entities-planet-are-corporations-not-governments-figures-show/. Accessed on: 20 Mar. 2025.

[118] Shell Nigeria was recently (January 2021) condemned, in the Netherlands, to repair Nigerian farmers and fishermen for damages resulting from oil spills, in the cities of Oruma and Goi (Link: https://www.istoedinheiro.com.br/shell-e-condenada-a-indenizar-agricultores-nigerianos-por-vazamentos-de-petroleo/. Accessed on: 20 Mar. 2025). The resolution of the case, of a civil nature, is considered paradigmatic, in a context of successive environmental violations and human rights in Nigeria, involving the oil company (Lambooy & Rancourt, 2008).

[119] Brazilian Federal Constitution, art. 225, §3°, and art. 3°, of Law 9.605/98 (Environmental Crimes Law).

[120] RE 548181/PR, rel. Min. Rosa Weber, 6.8.2013 (Link: http://portal.stf.jus.br/processos/downloadPeca.asp?id=273427698&ext=.pdf. Accessed on: 24 Mar. 2025).

[121] Chaumette (2009).

[122] There are doubts about "the degree of causation between the activity allegedly causing the damage, and the damage itself, it might be extremely difficult, if not impossible, to establish causation between the relevant human activity and the damage provoked with a sufficient degree of certainty, so as to impose criminal responsibility" (Misutra, 2018, p. 224).

dam (environmental destruction, deaths, etc.) to the company responsible is less complex than identifying the individual (natural or legal person) responsible for the melting of the polar ice caps or global warming. In addition to the constructing the causal link, one must also assess the psychological element—the intention behind the criminal action.

The perpetrator, by carrying out certain act conscious and voluntary, must either intend—or at the very least foresee—the harmful outcome.[123] Across legal traditions, are civil law and common law[124] (or often hybrid models, including elements of Muslim law),[125] the principle of *nullum crimen, nulla poena sine praevia lege poenali* prevails: there can be no crime nor punishment without prior legal definition. In all cases, intent (*mens rea*, in common law terminology), must be present and proven.[126] In short, it is necessary to establish the will to commit the conduct described as a crime.

In environmental cases, this technical requirement presents considerable challenge. Most environmental disasters are not, a priori, caused with direct intentionality. They commonly occur due to accidents stemming from negligence, incompetence, or recklessness—or, at most, from the agent's awareness of the potential harm and acceptance of the risk (i.e., *dolus eventualis* or indirect intent).

Beyond the procedural challenges of demonstrating harm and intent, another persistent issue—applicable not only to environmental crimes—is the evidentiary burden in international criminal proceedings. At the ICC, the book Rules of

---

[123] This is what is commanded by art. 30, "psychological elements", of the Rome Statute: "1. Unless otherwise provided, no person may be criminally liable and punished for a crime within the jurisdiction of the Court, unless he acts with the will to commit it and knowledge of its material elements. 2. For the purposes of this article, it is understood that one acts intentionally who: a) Regarding a conduct, proposes to adopt it; b) Regarding a effect of the crime, proposes to cause it or is aware that it will take place in a normal order of events. 3. Under the terms of the present article, "knowledge" is understood as the awareness that a circumstance exists or that an effect will take place, in a normal order of events. The expressions "to have knowledge" and "with knowledge" should be understood accordingly".

[124] Even in traditionally common law countries, crimes have been almost entirely codified, that is, they are no longer directly determined by customs or courts. It should be noted, however, that the Courts are not mere enforcers of the law. In practice, the interpretation of the provision can change it, if not create new definitions: "Judicial crime creation is still explicitly permitted in several states. And even in those jurisdictions that have abrogated criminal common law, we can find criminal prosecutions that can only be explained in terms of judicial crime creation. What is more, legislatures appear to have implicitly embraced common law crimes. Legislatures routinely fail to define statutory terms, and they rely on qualitative standards that necessarily require decisions about the scope of criminal law to be made on a case-by-case basis.53 That is to say, legislatures write statutes that delegate their lawmaking authority; the scope of those statutes can only be determined as a matter of criminal common law". (Hessick, 2019).

[125] Barrozo (2021).

[126] For example, the prosecution of the International Criminal Court for the former Yugoslavia appealed, in 2012, to a project to extract the genocidal intent of General Ratko Mladić from the identification, analysis, categorisation and contextualisation of evidence in speeches, discourses and media announcements. (Dojčinović, 2020, p. 179).

Procedure and Evidence[127] outline, in Sects. 4.1 and 5.3, the mechanisms for collecting and organizing evidence. Allied with the international cooperation rules of Chap. 11, these are the tools for the evidentiary framework in the Court.[128]

In response to these challenges, this book is structured in seven chapters. Its objective is not only to present the state of the art regarding the subject but also to identify and promote technical solutions and legal adaptations to make the international criminalization of ecocide viable.

To that end, the first chapters critically examine emblematic cases of massive environmental destruction and their respective legal responses—including the emerging phenomenon of climate litigation. The discussion then turns to the development of the concept of ecocide, from its earliest theoretical formulations in the 1970s to existing ecocide statutes and recent legislative proposals, highlighting the obstacles to criminalization. With this foundation, the book seeks to deepen the debate[129] on overcoming such challenges in light of the evolution of international criminal law and assess the feasibility of ecocide as an international crime.

By following this roadmap, the aim is, by illuminating issues today restrictive to the understanding and application of the crime of ecocide,[130] to offer both practical

[127] See: https://www.icc-cpi.int/iccdocs/pids/legal-texts/rulesprocedureevidenceeng.pdf.

[128] In practice, there is extreme dependence on two events: international cooperation and witness testimony. The former requires the benevolence of the local country of the crime, which does not always occur, as an example, the non-compliance by Libya, of the arrest warrant for Muammar Gaddafi, issued by the Court in 2011. The arrest, until his death, in the same year, never occurred. The country also refused to hand over his son, Saif al-Islam Gaddafi, in 2012. (Sekularac & Gumuchian, 2012). It should be noted that here there is a controversy about the obligation of Libya, since it is not a signatory to the Rome Statute, activated due to a call from the Security Council: "It was only when certain states parties refused to cooperate with the Court in the arrest of Sudan's then sitting (now former) Head of State, Omar Al Bashir, that the Court started to reflect further upon the issue. For the first time, it asserted that the Statute is 'a multilateral treaty which acts as an international criminal code for the parties to it' and so 'cannot impose obligations on third states without their consent'". (Dias, 2019). About the witnesses, as Faucz warns, "despite being the most used means of proof, the memory of witnesses is subject to numerous influences during and after the crime, making narratives not necessarily reflect the experienced reality and can generate unfair convictions. In fact, the information from the eyewitnesses directs the police investigation from the beginning, since recognitions and other diligences are carried out from this". (Silva, 2019, p. 4). These were, for example, the main problems identified in the performance of the Chambres Africaines Extraordinaires (CAE), a Court created to judge international crimes that occurred in Chad, between 1982 and 1990 (Téliko, 2020).

[129] Debates are today fostered by various international actors such as the European Union, and within civil society, through organisations that, with the support of academics, former judges and lawyers from International Criminal Courts, seek to propose the new crime, especially in the ICC (Link: https://www.stopecocide.earth/expert-drafting-panel. Accessed on: 7 Dec. 2024).

[130] The call for the swift adoption of ecocide as an international crime is, as Valérie Cabanes explicitly states, aware that this "speed" is measured in years, considering the traditional speed of changes - when there are any - in international law: "for the ICC to adopt the ecocide definition and amend the Rome Statute it would take a few steps. One of the International Criminal Court's 123-member countries (which do not include the U.S., China or India) would have to submit a definition to the United Nations secretary-general. The proposal must then be voted on by a majority of members of the ICC at the annual assembly in December in order to be considered. Between the

and theoretical tools that can enable the establishment of an international legal mechanism. Such a mechanism—through incorporation into the Rome Statute—would serve to nationalize the criminal prosecution and sanctioning of the most harmful conduct inflicted upon the planet.

The intention, therefore, is to demonstrate that the crime of ecocide can follow a trajectory similar to that of genocide and crimes against humanity: from theoretical—once regarded as unlikely to materialize—to internationally ratified treaties enforced by a permanent international court. In the cases of genocide and crimes against humanity, it took the atrocities of a world war and a holocaust to galvanize international action. In recent decades, the impact of human activity on nature is no longer speculative—it is real, measurable, transboundary, and transgenerational. It has also, to a certain extent, captured the attention of international legal framework. This book, within the parameters it sets forth, aspires to contribute to the next step: providing the legal and conceptual foundations necessary for the recognition of ecocide as a crime under international criminal law, thereby reinforcing domestic legal frameworks and strengthening environmental protection on a global scale.

References

Alt, V. (2015, 19 fevereiro). The fallacy of Blood Diamond certification. Politike, Carta Capital.

Amnesty International. (2016). Malabo protocol: Legal and institutional implications of the merged and expanded African Court. https://www.amnesty.org/en/documents/afr01/3063/2016/en/.

Amorim, J. A. A. (2015). *The UN and the environment* (p. 57). Atlas Publisher.

Annoni, D., Mendonça, C. D., & de Araujo. (2015). Mixed courts: An analysis of the concept. *Nomos, 35*(1) http://www.periodicos.ufc.br/nomos/article/view/1520/1551

Antunes, P. d. B. (2020). International environmental law particularities. *Veredas do Direito, 17*(1), 263–294.

Ash, K. (2007). Why "Managing" biodiversity will fail: An alternative approach to sustainable exploitation for international law. *Animal Law Review, 13*, 209–250.

Barrozo, P. (2021). Law in time: Legal theory and legal history. *Yale Journal of Law & the Humanities, 31*(2), 316–361. https://doi.org/10.29327/529171.1-12

Bellivier, F., Eudes, M., & Fouchard, I. (2018). Law of international crimes. Thémis.

Benjamin, A. H. (2011). Nature in Brazilian law: Thing, subject or none of that. *Nomos, 31*(1), 79–96.

Brisman, A. (2013). Not a bedtime story: Climate change, neoliberalism and the future of the Arctic. *Michigan State International Law Review, 1*(1).

Brochado, N., Djalma, A., & Mont'Alverne, T. C. F. (2018). Ecocide: Proposal for a policy criminalising international environmental crimes or a crime itself? *Brazilian Journal of Public Policies, 8*(1), 209–226. https://www.publicacoes.uniceub.br/RBPP/article/view/5203

Brochado, N., Djalma, A., & Mont'Alverne, T. C. F. (2020). Massive damage to the environment: Crime in war, but not in peacetime? Intergovernmental organisations and the next step in global environmental governance. *Scienza e Pace, XI*(2), 37–55.

formal proposal of an ecocide crime by a member country and ratification, however, an amendment process could take years. Once the final text for an amendment is discussed and agreed upon, two-thirds of member countries must vote in favour. When the vote is ratified in General Assembly of the ICC states parties, it must be enforced in countries a year later". (Cabanes, 2023, p. 582).

Bucur, M.-C. (2023). Ecocide and environmental policies. *Public Administration & Regional Studies, 1*(13–23), 14.

Bugarski, T. (2015). Challenges of organized environmental crime. *Zbornik radova Pravnog fakulteta, Novi Sad, 49*(3), 1097–1107. https://doi.org/10.5937/zrpfns49-9883. Accessed on: 10 Mar. 2025.

Cabanes, V. (2018). Holding states and companies accountable for climate change: From planetary boundaries to the crime of ecocide. In C. Cournil & L. Varison (Eds.), *Climate trials: Between national and international* (pp. 31–46). Pedone.

Cabanes, V. (2023). Ecocide. In *Handbook of the Anthropocene: Humans between heritage and future* (pp. 579–583). Springer.

Chaumette, A.-L. V. (2009). *The subjects of international criminal law: Towards a new definition of international legal personality?* Pedone.

Crasson, A. (2017). The case of Chevron in Ecuador: The need for an international crime against the environment? *Amsterdam Law Forum, 9*(3), 29.

Cruden, J. C., O'rourke, S., & Himmelhoch, S. D. (2016). The Deepwater horizon oil spill litigation: Proof of concept for the manual for complex litigation and the 2015 amendments to the Federal Rules of civil procedure. *Michigan Journal of Environmental & Administrative Law. [s. l.], 6*(1), 65–150.

De Dias, T., & Souza. (2019). The nature of the Rome statute and the place of international law before the international criminal court. *Journal of International Criminal Justice, 17*(3), 507–535. https://doi.org/10.1093/jicj/mqz034

Delmas-Marty, M. (2006). Interactions between national and international criminal law in the preliminary phase of trial at the ICC. *Journal of International Criminal Justice, 4*(1), 2–11. https://doi.org/10.1093/jicj/mqi087

Dissenha, R. C. (2013). *For a universal criminal policy: A critique of International Criminal Courts* [PhD Thesis, University of São Paulo].

Dojčinović, P. (2020). In the mind of the crime: Proving the *mens rea* of genocidal intent in the words of Ratko Mladić and other members of the joint criminal enterprise. In P. Dojčinović (Ed.), *Propaganda and international criminal law: From cognition to criminality* (p. 179). Routledge.

Duunova, T., et al. (2024). International humanitarian law and ecocide: The war in Ukraine as a case study. *European Journal of Environmental Sciences, 14*(1), 14–23.

Erinosho, B. T. (2013). The revised African convention on the conservation of nature and natural resources: Prospects for a comprehensive treaty for the management of Africa's natural resources. *African Journal of International and Comparative Law, 21*(3), 378–397.

European Union. (2021a, 21 janeiro). Resolution 2020/2208 of the European Parliament: Human rights and democracy in the world and the European Union's policy on the matter.

European Union. (2021b, 19 maio). Resolution P9_TA(2021)0245 of the European Parliament: Regarding the effects of climate change on human rights and the role of environmental defenders in this matter.

European Union. (2024, 13 março). *Directive PE-CONS 82/23: On the protection of the environment through criminal law and replacing directives 2008/99/EC and 2009/123/EC.*

Falk, R. (1973). Environment warfare and ecocide: Facts, appraisal and proposals. *Belgian Review of International Law, 11.*

Fisher, E., Scotford, E., & Barritt, E. (2017). The legally disruptive nature of climate change. *Modern Law Review, 80*(2), 173–201.

Fitzmaurice, M. (2017). International convention for the regulation of whaling. *United Nations Audiovisual Library of International Law*, 1–7.

Geraldino, C. F. G. (2014). A definition of environment. *GEOUSP—Space and Time, 18*(2), 403–415.

Guimarães, R. P., Fontoura, Y. S., & dos Reis da. (2012). Rio+20 or Rio-20?: Chronicle of a foretold failure. *Environment & Society—USP, 15*(3), 19–39.

Hammerschmidt, D. (2002). Risk in contemporary society and the principle of precaution in environmental law. *Sequência: Legal and Political Studies*, 97–122. https://periodicos.ufsc.br/index.php/sequencia/article/view/15317

Hessick, C. B. (2019). The myth of common law crimes. *Virginia Law Review, 105*(5), 965–1024.

International Criminal Court. (2016). Office of the Prosecutor Policy Paper on case selection and prioritization. https://www.icc-cpi.int/itemsDocuments/20160915_OTP-Policy_Case-Selection_Eng.pdf.

International Criminal Court Assembly of States Parties. (2024). *Report of the working group on amendments* (ICC-ASP/23/26). Proposal submitted by Vanuatu to amend the Rome Statute. Annex II, Article 8ter Ecocide. https://asp.icc-cpi.int/sites/default/files/asp_docs/ICC-ASP-23-26-ENG.pdf.

International Law Commission. (2019). Provisional summary record of the *3460th meeting* (A/CN.4/SR.3460).

Kolbert, E. (2015). The sixth extinction: An unnatural history. Intrínseca.

Kotzé, L. J. (2012). Arguing global environmental constitutionalism. *Transnational Environmental Law, 1*(1), 199–233.

Kotzé, L. J. (2014). Rethinking global environmental law and governance in the Anthropocene. *Journal of Energy & Natural Resources Law, 32*(2), 121–156. https://doi.org/10.1080/02646811.2014.11435355

Lambooy, T., & Rancourt, M.-E. (2008). Shell in Nigeria: From human rights abuse to corporate social responsibility. *Human Rights & International Legal Discourse, 2*(2), 229–276.

Leite, R., & Cabral, R. L. (2018). The Hissène Habré case and the possibilities of innovation in the matter of regional criminal courts. *Legal Space: Journal of Law, 19*(2), 593–614. https://dialnet.unirioja.es/descarga/articulo/7277474.pdf

Lynch, M. J. (2016). A proposal for the political economy of green criminology: Capitalism and the case of the Alberta Tar Sands. *Canadian Journal of Criminology and Criminal Justice. [s. l.], 58*(2), 137–160.

Marques, C. (2012). Environment, solidarity and future generations. *Nomos, 32*(2) http://www.periodicos.ufc.br/nomos/article/view/350/332

Martin-Chenut, K., Neyret, L., & Perruso, C. (2015). Towards the internationalisation of criminal protection of the environment: From ecocrimes to ecocide. *International Law Review, 12*(2).

Mazzuoli, V. O. (2019). Course of public international law. Forense.

Michelot, A. (2018). International climate protection and state sovereignty. *VertigO, 18*(1). https://doi.org/10.4000/vertigo.19685

Misutra, A. (2018). Is there space for environmental crimes under international criminal law? The impact of the office of the prosecutor policy paper on case selection and prioritization on the current legal framework. *Columbia Journal of Environmental Law, 43*(1), 181–226.

Neyret, L. (Ed.). (2015). *From ecocrimes to ecocide: Criminal law to the rescue of the environment*. Bruylant.

Neyret, L. (2017). From ecocrimes to ecocide: Protecting the environment through criminal law (C-EENRG Reports). University of Cambridge.

Nollez-Goldbach, R. (2018). *The international criminal court*. Presses Universitaires de France.

Ott, H. E. (2001). Climate change: An important foreign policy issue. *International Affairs, 77*(2), 277–296. https://academic.oup.com/ia/article-abstract/77/2/277/2434674

Parrish, A. L. (2005). Trail Smelter Deja Vu: Extraterritoriality, international environmental law, and the search for solutions to Canadian-U.S. Transboundary water pollution disputes. *Boston University Law Review, 85*(2).

Pasquali, L. (2019). The limits set by African countries to the institutionalisation of cooperation between states in the judicial repression of international crimes. *Federalismi.it, 9*, 2–51.

Pellet, A. (1995). The formation of international law within the framework of the United Nations. *European Journal of International Law, 6*(3), 401–425. https://doi.org/10.1093/oxfordjournals.ejil.a035928

Prieur, M. (2010). The principle of prohibition of environmental regression. In R. Rollemberg (Ed.), *Principle of prohibition of environmental regression* (pp. 63–86). Federal Senate.
Sekularac, I., & Gumuchian, M.-L. (2012, 5 abril). ICC rejects Libya's request over Gaddafi son surrender. Reuters. https://www.reuters.com/article/us-libya-icc/icc-rejects-libyas-request-over-gaddafi-son-surrender-idUSBRE8331BJ20120405.
Silva, J. A. d. (2000). *Environmental constitutional law* (3rd ed.). Malheiros.
Silva, R. F. P. (2019). *Witness testimony from research on memory conformity in the criminal field* [PhD Thesis, Federal University of Minas Gerais].
Stanford, B. (2015). The 'War on Terror': Perpetual emergency. *Edinburgh Student Law Review, 2*(4).
Téliko, S. (2020). The extraordinary African chambers and the repression of international crimes in Africa. L'Harmattan-Sénégal.
Thome, R., Ribeiro, L. G., & Goncalves. (2019). The decommissioning of tailings dams and the mine closure plan as risk mitigation instruments in mining. *Veredas do Direito, 16*(2), 63–86.
Trindade, A. A. C. (2010). Contemporary international courts and the pursuit of the ideal of international justice. *Revista da Faculdade de Direito UFMG, 57*, 37–68.
United Nations. (1972). *Report of the United Nations conference on the human Environment* (Stockholm, 5–16 June).
United Nations. (2015). *Written statement submitted by friends of the earth international* (A/HRC/WG.16/1/NGO/13). Human Rights Council. https://www.ohchr.org/Documents/HRBodies/HRCouncil/WGTransCorp/Session1/A.HRC.WG.16.1.NGO.13.pdf
Wyatt, J. (2010). Le développement du droit international au carrefour du droit de l'environnement, du droit humanitaire et du droit pénal: Les dommages causés à l'environnement en période de conflit armé international. *Revue Internationale de la Croix-Rouge, 92*, 301–360.

Chapter 2
Massive Environmental Damage in the World

The recognition of the environment as a legal interest[1] worthy of protection by States—whether directly[2] or indirectly[3]—has led to its engagement across multiple areas of law, including environmental, agrarian, civil, labour, administrative, tax, and international law. As a *last resort*, criminal law intervenes to protect the environment only when all other legal mechanisms prove insufficient to achieve the desired protection.

It is important to note that concern for environmental protection typically arises first at the national level before extending to the international sphere.[4] In this context,

[1] "There are dogmatic and material arguments that support the definition of the right to a healthy environment or, in the wording of Brazilian constitutional law, ecologically balanced both as human rights, in their international perspective, as well as fundamental rights in their internal dimension" (SAMPAIO, José Adércio Leite; COSTA, Beatriz Souza (2015) The complicated interrelationships between the internal and international systems of protection of the right to a healthy environment. International Law Review, Brasília, v. 12, n. 2, p. 785–803, p. 787).

[2] As in some Andean countries, where elements of the environment itself (rivers, mountains, for example) are holders of rights, and can appear as parties in legal proceedings, without, necessarily, there being a direct interest of a natural person. "The 'ecocentric' approach aims to overcome the anthropocentric perception of the ownership of rights, questioning the priority given to human needs, to the detriment of other forms of life and of nature itself" (FONSECA, Fúlvio Eduardo (2007) The convergence between environmental protection and the protection of the human person in the scope of international law. Brazilian Journal of International Politics, v. 50, p. 121–138, p 129).

[3] This is the case in most countries, where legal protection of the environment occurs in an anthropocentric context, when a good or right of a person—natural or legal—is affected through environmental damage. This worldview supports all the governance structures of contemporary industrial society, economy, education, religion and law, and has fostered the belief that the natural world is just a collection of objects for human use (MALONEY, Michelle (2016) Building an Alternative Jurisprudence for the Earth: The International Rights of Nature Tribunal. Vermont Law Review, vol. 41, no. 1, p. 129–142, p. 132).

[4] ANTUNES, Paulo de Bessa (2020) International Environmental Law: particularities. Paths of Law: Environmental Law and Sustainable Development, v. 17, n. 37, p. 263–294, p. 265.

D. A. Brochado Neto, *Ecocide*, https://doi.org/10.1007/978-3-032-07757-8_2

environmental issues are addressed by both private and public law[5]; with the latter forming the primary focus of this work.

Among the various branches of public law is international environmental law[6] (IEL), which is concerned with the international norms specifically directed at environmental matters.[7] However, the fragmentation of IEL—and of environmental protection law more broadly—has often produced the opposite effect of what is intended: the proliferation of predominantly symbolic documents rather than enforceable legal instruments.[8]

Moreover, despite the plurality of legal provisions addressing environmental issues, there remains a striking normative deficit in the field of international environmental crime.[9] Even acknowledging the anthropocentric nature of criminal law,

---

[5] The difference between private and public international law lies fundamentally in the object of study: "in public international law, the concern is with the law that regulates the relations between States or between States and other international actors", while "private law is focused on relations between individuals, such as contracts between companies or resolution of conflicts without the presence of the State" (VARELLA, Marcelo Dias (2017) Public international law. 6th ed. São Paulo: Saraiva, p. 21/22).

[6] "International environmental law is one of the responses given by the international community to the deterioration of environmental resources on a planetary scale. It is a legal response, originated in the common understanding of the subjects of International Law in the sense that only a uniform and articulated action among the various international actors is capable of solving problems that go beyond the border of a single state" (ANTUNES, Paulo de Bessa (2020) International Environmental Law: particularities. Paths of Law: Environmental Law and Sustainable Development, v. 17, n. 37, p. 263–294, p 265).

[7] "International environmental law (or international environmental law) refers to the part of international law relevant to issues arising from ecology, environmental protection and sustainability, which have stimulated and catalysed the development of legal knowledge in this domain." (FONSECA, Fúlvio Eduardo (2007) The convergence between environmental protection and the protection of the human person in the scope of international law. Brazilian Journal of International Politics, v. 50, p. 121–138, p 122).

[8] Numerous international treaties impose, for example, criminal responsibility for damage to certain species of animals. Although such treaties recognise the need to protect non-human life, "*they adhere to the reductionist problem of environmental law. Reductionism entails the development of environmental laws that aim to protect constituent parts of ecosystems resulting in compartmentalisation and fragmentation of environmental law*" (MWANZA, Rosemary (2018) Enhancing Accountability for Environmental Damage under International Law: Ecocide as a Legal Fulfilment of Ecological Integrity. Melbourne Journal of International Law, vol. 19, no. 2, pp. 586–613, p. 607).

[9] In the anthropocentric view of criminal law, man (natural person) is the greatest victim—and, in most countries, the only one—of crimes, as a subject of rights. In a biocentric (or ecocentric) view, nature itself is a subject of rights, can be a victim of crimes, holder of legal actions and, therefore, deserving per se of state protection. "*Rights of nature tap into a place that anthropomorphism and its pragmatism, for all their importance, cannot touch: a powerful link to the human heart. They provide a baseline not easy for humans to manipulate, backed by this undeniable bond. Their contribution to the world at large could be yet greater, not limited to changing outcomes in particular cases, nor to empowering local communities, nor to creating new protected areas and restoring old ones before they too disappear, nor even to finding a place in corporate sustainability codes, gross domestic product, and other instruments of the prevailing economic order. Through each of these means and more, in framing a new way to perceive the world, an old way really, a world we will*

it is notable that no comprehensive legal framework exists to address massive environmental destruction. This Chapter aims to present cases of major international relevance where environmental harm—considered as instances of ecocide—occurred, and to analyse their respective legal repercussions.

First, it should be considered whether environmental crime is a matter of international or national law. Indeed, as the very structure of international law presupposes, there is no hierarchy between domestic and external law.[10] Thus, the interest of international law, in the criminal field, will always also involve national law, given the complementarity and subsidiarity relationship between jurisdictions.

In the case of massive environmental damage, considering the importance of the legal interest to be protected for the regular exercise of all human rights, the scale of the harm will determine whether there is international legal attention to the case. Often, the consequences of environmental disasters are transnational,[11] raising doubts about the boundary between national and international law (i.e. when regional and/or global interests are implicated).

In these situations, it is important to verify whether the conduct that caused the damage is classified as a crime under domestic law, even where there are extraterritorial elements. In such cases, prosecution would normally fall within the competence of the national judiciary, potentially in parallel with the laws of another affected country, if applicable.[12]

There are also cases of environmental disasters occurring exclusively within a single territory, but which nonetheless have international relevance (such as fires[13] in natural parks or forests, extinction of species important for biomedicine, or events

---

continue to dominate but may come to acknowledge -as entitled to life, liberty, and a pursuit of happiness all its own". (HOUCK, Oliver A. (2017) Noah's Second Voyage: The Rights of Nature as Law. Tulane Environmental Law Journal, vol. 31, no. 1, pp. 1–50, p. 50).

[10] "*It has almost become a commonplace to state that the organisation of international law does not follow a hierarchical model. It is sometimes said to be "anarchic", in that it would not be based on a relationship of authority, with a superior power that would regulate subjects to whom it would impose "its law". (…). It is also with reference to this horizontal conception of the "society of States" that it is sometimes considered that international law would first be the sum of the self-limitations of States, the product of its commitments, and not a set of laws dictated by a superior entity*" (SANTULLI, Carlo (2013) Introduction to international law: formation, execution, application. Paris: Editions Pedone).

[11] As, for example, the drying up of the Aral Sea, largely due to the irrigation programmes of the former Soviet Union (WHEELER, William (2021) Environment and Post-Soviet Transformation in Kazakhstan's Aral Sea Region: Sea Changes. London: UCL Press).

[12] It is possible that the materially transnational crime may also be the subject of an international convention, which considers them legally as transnational crimes. In these cases, there is no interference from international judges in the proceedings, with common criminal law prevailing in the States (BELLIVIER, Florence; EUDES, Marina; FOUCHARD, Isabelle (2018) Law of international crimes. Paris: Themis Droit, p. 5).

[13] In recent years, 'natural' and intentional large-scale fires have been identified in Australia, Brazil and, more recently, the United States (for more information on the relationship between ecocide and fires, especially the Australian one, in 2020, see: WALTERS, Reece (2023) Ecocide, climate criminals and the politics of bushfires. The British Journal of Criminology, v. 63, n. 2, pp. 283–303.

influencing climate changes). These scenarios cannot be discarded as potential ecocide at the international level merely because the immediate damage is restricted to one State; some countries have continental dimensions (e.g. Brazil and Canada are slightly smaller than the entirely of Europe, including western Russia),[14] and certain cases of massive environmental damage would undoubtedly cross borders if they occurred in a geographically smaller region like Europe.

On the other hand, supranational crimes are a response to offences of such magnitude and gravity that they threaten the foundations of the international order[15]—today primarily addressed by the only permanent criminal court in existence, the ICC. Here lies a notable gap: the Rome Statute does not currently provide for a specific criminal offense addressing massive environmental destruction in times of peace, despite the global scale of harm that demands international concern.[16]

Criminal law remains exclusively a domain of public law, even at the international level. Thus, the predominant regulatory tools of modern international law—such as technical standards, ratings, benchmarks, rankings, codes of conduct, and digital protocols[17]—are not appropriate instruments for defining crimes, establishing due process, or imposing sanctions.

Given this restrictive framework, analysing legal cases of ecocide at the international level would, in theory, be impossible when adhering to the strict definition of "crime"—that is, a legally prohibited conduct linked to a corresponding sanction.[18] However, based on definitions of ecocide found in existing national laws, legislative

---

[14] Brazil ranks fifth in territorial extension, with 8,515,767,049 km^2, while Europe has 10,180,000 km^2; Canada, in second place, has 9,970,610 km^2 (ALBUQUERQUE, Dominic (2022) The 10 largest countries in the world. SoCientífica Blog, 17 Aug. 2022. Available at: https://socientifica.com.br/os-10-maiores-paises-do-mundo/. Accessed on: 18 Mar. 2025).

[15] BELLIVIER, Florence; EUDES, Marina; FOUCHARD, Isabelle (2018) Law of international crimes. Paris: Themis Droit, p. 9.

[16] Environmental disasters of global interest, such as the nuclear accidents in Chernobyl and Fukushima, the production and improper disposal of nuclear waste in Tibet by China, are not covered by any international criminal standard. To deal with the Chinese case, for example, it is necessary to understand it as genocide of Tibetans to consider it an international crime (HEISCHMIDT, Christina M. (2010) China's dumping ground: Genocide through nuclear ecocide in Tibet. Penn State Environmental Law Review, v. 18, n. 2, p. 213–233).

[17] VAN WAEYENBERGE, Arnaud (2017) Global Law: A suitable theory to think about environmental law? International Law Review, v. 14, n. 3, p. 15.

[18] It is important to note that the principle of legality in international law can be less restrictive than in national law: "The evolution of jurisprudence shows an internationalisation of the principle of criminal legality which, from a transversal principle to internal criminal rights, would be on the verge of becoming a general principle of international law—PIL and HRL –, by taking a distance from internal conceptions. Indeed, the fundamental structural differences between international legal order and internal legal orders oppose a mechanical transposition in the international order of the strict conception of the principle of legality. Moreover, and above all, the specific nature of certain international crimes commands not to apply to the letter the principle of legality under penalty of contradicting its spirit "(BELLIVIER, Florence; EUDES, Marina; FOUCHARD, Isabelle (2018) Law of international crimes. Paris: Themis Droit, p. 5).

proposals, and ICC amendments initiatives, doctrine and civil society[19] have begun classifying certain instances of massive environmental destruction as ecocide, thereby enabling legal analysis, if not always in the criminal field, then at least in the compensatory domain.

Even so, it is not possible to definitively establish when the first act of massive and systematic environmental destruction by human hands occurred. Nevertheless, certain cases and situations can be identified based on specific parameters. First, the reprehensibility of the act—environmental harm—should be considered, at least morally if not legally, according to the standards of the time. Second, the potential for litigation, whether nationally or internationally, should be assessed. Third, the destructive potential of the event should be measured, taking into account the technological capacity to alter the environment.

Following this outline, the first international movements attentive to human capacity for environmental destruction[20] took place at the 1970s. The American attacks during the Vietnam War (1955–1975), particularly the use of Agent Orange, were harshly criticized at the United Nations Conference on the Human Environment, held in Stockholm, where the term "ecocide" was mentioned for the first time at a Summit meeting. From that point forward, there was exponential growth in international instruments aimed at protecting the environment. Some countries began to include ecocide in their legislation, and the UN itself considered its inclusion in the Draft Code of Crimes Against the Peace and Security of Mankind. Paradoxically, however, the incidence of cases involving massive environmental destruction has also grown since then.

From a situation of war (the environment as a military target in Indochina) to disasters such as the dam collapses in Brumadinho and Mariana (Brazil), massive environmental damage predominantly occurs outside the context of armed conflict.[21] This fact is significant because, as previously noted, while the Rome Statute

---

[19] In doctrine, the term ecocide is mentioned since the use of Agent Orange in Vietnam; as for civil society, the term, for example, became popular in the media, as seen in The Guardian (The Guardian, London, 4 May. 2010. Available at: https://www.theguardian.com/environment/gallery/2010/may/04/top-10-ecocides. Accessed on: 11 Apr. 2025), and, more recently, referring to large-scale environmental destruction in Ukraine (AHMED, Kaamil; GAYLE, Damien; MOUSA, Aseel (2024) 'Ecocide in Gaza': does scale of environmental destruction amount to a war crime? The Guardian, 29 Mar. 2024. Available at: https://www.theguardian.com/environment/2024/mar/29/gaza-israel-palestinian-war-ecocide-environmental-destruction-pollution-rome-statute-war-crimes-aoe. Accessed on: 7 Dec. 2024).

[20] Point 6, of the UN Conference Declaration, June 1972, due to the International Conference for the Human Environment in Stockholm.

[21] The War between Russia and Ukraine, a continuous and prolonged conflict of, at least, 2014, but with significant deterioration of relations from 2021, is considered by many researchers as an example of ecocide, given the destruction of natural resources, pollution of water, air and soil, in addition to the risk of nuclear catastrophe: "*Ukraine has entered the fight for accountability for ecocide based on international norms and instruments. The filing of lawsuits against Russia in international judicial bodies, particularly the International Court of Justice, demonstrates Ukraine's seriousness in holding the aggressor state accountable for damaging the environment during the invasion. Although the concept of ecocide does not yet have a universal definition in*

provides for a specific crime concerning attacks against the environment during wartime,[22] there is no equivalent provision to criminalize such destruction in times of peace.[23]

Thus, although the term "ecocide" was originally coined from a warlike conduct, its meaning today encompasses a variety of other situations.

The extraction and use of oil have been responsible—particularly since the Industrial Revolution—for exponential technological development worldwide, but also for some of the greatest environmental disasters caused by human activity.[24] From the pollution inherent to the activity itself to failures in processing and transport, the frequency of incidents has grown in direct proportion to global demand for the *commodity*. Among the most serious cases[25] are the exploitation of the Niger Delta (Nigeria), the extraction of oil from the bituminous sand of Alberta (Canada) and the practice of *fracking* (United States).

Accidents such as the chemical pollution in Bhopal (1984), India, and the collapses of the Mariana (2015) and Brumadinho (2019) dams in Brazil reveal that large-scale environmental destruction can also occur due to negligence of natural persons, corporate entities, and even the State itself, when ineffective in enforcing its own environmental protection laws.

By the end of this section, it will become clear that, despite the recurrence and variety of cases of massive environmental destruction caused by humans across the planet, legal responses have been almost always non-existent or insufficient, either in punishing the perpetrators or compensating for the damage caused. Such

international law, there are initiatives and proposals to establish the international legal status of ecocide as a separate crime". (DUIUNOVA, Tetiana et al. (2024) International humanitarian law and ecocide: the war in Ukraine as a case study. European Journal of Environmental Sciences, v. 14, n. 1, p. 14–23, p. 21).

[22] Art. 8, 8(2)(b) (iv), of the Rome Statute.

[23] BROCHADO NETO, Djalma Alvarez; MONT'ALVERNE, Tarin Cristino Frota (2020) Massive environmental damage: a crime in war, but not in peacetime? Intergovernmental organisations and the next step in global environmental governance. Scienza e Pace, v. XI, n. 2, p. 37–55. Available at: https://scienzaepace.unipi.it/index.php/it/call-for-papers/item/download/430_e5761931728ba84456238f2abebf5ac7.html. Accessed on: 10 Mar. 2025.

[24] Regarding oil, there are several possible forms of environmental pollution, such as "*oil spills, oil well blowouts, effluent emission (gas flaring), equipment failure, abandoned oil facilities, artisanal refining (oil bunkering), and improper industrial waste disposal*" (BROWN, Cleverline T.; OKOGBULE, Nlerum S. (2020) Redressing harmful environmental practices in the Nigerian petroleum industry through the criminal justice approach. Journal of Sustainable Development Law and Policy, v. 11, n. 1, p. 18–55, p. 32).

[25] It is worth highlighting the crude oil spill that occurred in September 2019, in Brazil. More than 3000 kilometres of beaches were surprised by the material from the sea, from the Amazon coast to Rio de Janeiro, becoming the most extensive and damaging oil environmental disaster in the country's history. In this case, there was an absence/failure of measures from the Federal Government (headed by Jair Bolsonaro) to deal with the environmental emergency (SOARES, Marcelo de Oliveira et al. (2020) Oil spill in South Atlantic [Brazil]: environmental and governmental disaster. Marine Policy, v. 115, p. 1).

shortcomings are rooted in the precariousness of environmental legislation and the technical and procedural difficulties inherent to the complexity of these cases.

These problems are even more pronounced in cases of international environmental harm—situations where the impacts extend to two or more countries. In the criminal field, there is currently neither a treaty nor a court specifically mandated to address massive environmental damage.[26] The following sections will examine emblematic cases and the corresponding judicial repercussions.

2.1 The First "Ecocide": Indochina

The term *ecocide* was coined by Arthur W. Galston (Pereira, 2020, pp. 179–224), a physiologist and plant biologist, in the late 1960s in response to the American military attacks in the Indochina region. Before delving into the subject, however, it is important to provide brief contextual background.

Following the onset of the Cold War (1945), the countries of Western Europe struggled with the colonial legacies left in Southeast Asia after World War II. The United States perceived fight against communism—embodied by the Soviet Union—led it to intervene in the Korean War (1950) and the Vietnam War (1956), two conflicts that, though distinct, were seen by the Americans as part of the broader struggle against communist expansion (Wiest, 2003, p. 13).

At the time, the 1925 Geneva Protocol[27] prohibited the use of asphyxiants or poisonous gases, as well as bacteriological methods, in warfare. Although the United States was among the Protocol's drafters, it did not ratify it initially. Concurrently, scientific research of herbicides for agricultural use produced the first "plant killers," designed to target specific weeds, any plants useless or harmful to human needs: 2,4-D (2,4-Dichlorophenoxyacetic acid) and 2.4.5-T (2,4,5-Trichlorophenoxyacetic acid) (Zierler, 2011, p. 1).

A mixture of these two compounds, known as Agent Orange (50:50 mix),[28] was used extensively by the U.S. military in Vietnam between 1961 and 1971. Operation "Ranch Hand" aimed to eliminate Viet Cong's strategic advantage[29] by defoliating dense forests, which facilitated ambushes against foreign forces, and by destroying

[26] There is no international environmental crime in peacetime. The crime set out in art. 8, 8(2)(b)(iv), of the Rome Statute, whose objective is to punish attacks on the environment in a war context, is discussed in Chap. 7.

[27] 1925 Geneva Protocol. Available at: https://unoda-web.s3-accelerate.amazonaws.com/wp-content/uploads/assets/WMD/Bio/pdf/Status_Protocol.pdf, accessed on: 20 Mai. 2025.

[28] Other less known mixtures are still widely used in agriculture, such as Agent Blue, based on arsenic, for rice plantations, and Agent White, specially constructed with 2,4-D (ZIERLER, David (2011) The invention of ecocide: Agent Orange, Vietnam, and the scientists who changed the way we think about the environment. Athens: University of Georgia Press, p. 5).

[29] Members of the so-called National Front for the Liberation of Vietnam, belonging to the communist north of the country.

subsistence crops. Between 1966 and 1969 alone, 15 to 20 million gallons of the herbicide were dumped by planes, defoliating more than 20,000 square kilometers[30] of vegetation,[31] including forests and mangroves.

Beyond the visible scale of environmental destruction, Agent Orange caused widespread human suffering: cancers, diabetes and congenital malformations in descendants among both Vietnamese[32] and Americans veterans exposed to the chemical.[33]

The magnitude of this environmental and human disaster captured the attention of scientists and environmentalists alike. It was, however, the scientific community that made the greatest impact on U.S. military herbicide policy. In 1970, the Conference "War Crimes and American Conscience" was held, conceived by American researchers. Arthur W. Galston presented his findings after 4 years of studying the ecological and human effects of herbicides warfare in Vietnam, concluding that the actions in Indochina constituted "ecocide" —drawing a parallel to the crime of genocide.[34]

---

[30] An area equivalent to the State of Israel.

[31] "As part of the broader counterinsurgency mission, Kennedy sought innovative means to neutralize the NLF's ambush tactics. The president's strategy was simple: deny guerrillas their only tactical advantage with chemicals, not infantry" (ZIERLER, David (2011) The invention of ecocide: Agent Orange, Vietnam, and the scientists who changed the way we think about the environment. Athens: University of Georgia Press, p. 2).

[32] "The aim was to reveal enemy combatants hidden by the otherwise dense vegetation, but among the unwanted side-effects were a series of ecologically damaging events, including a loss of minerals from the ecosystem due to increased nutrient dumping, soil erosion and gulleying, replacement of valuable species like teak by useless and noxious weeds like scrub bamboo, and the destruction of some crops by deliberate or accidental drifting of the aerial spray. In addition, it was later discovered that Agent Orange contained potentially toxic levels of dioxins, amongst the most harmful materials ever synthesized. Vietnam veterans, whose service led to them being sprayed, received many millions of dollars in compensation from the manufacturers of Agent Orange after a lengthy court battle87, but no recompense has yet been offered to Vietnamese mothers who may have given birth to teratogenic babies or suffered from other toxic effects" (GALSTON, Arthur W. (2001) Plant biology: retrospect and prospect. Current Science, p. 143–152, p. 150/151).

[33] Studies on the correlation between Agent Orange and the various diseases related to it continue to this day, with the extent of the herbicide's impact on those directly or indirectly affected remaining unclear. Even so, at the time, it was understood that the United States, with this conduct, was committing war crimes: "*But the question that truly vexed most dissenters in the Vietnam war was not if but how the war was illegal. That is, to challenge the entire basis of the American intervention in Vietnam required a certain intellectual detachment from the war as it was being waged day to day*" (ZIERLER, David (2011) The invention of ecocide: Agent Orange, Vietnam, and the scientists who changed the way we think about the environment. Athens: University of Georgia Press, p. 6).

[34] During the panel "Technology and American power", Galston noted that humanity condemns the destruction of a people or culture, calling this crime against humanity genocide; therefore, the complete and permanent destruction of the environment, where people can live, has similarity with that crime, being designated as 'ecocide'. (ZIERLER, David (2011) The invention of ecocide: Agent Orange, Vietnam, and the scientists who changed the way we think about the environment. Athens: University of Georgia Press, p. 19).

Galston's motivation in criticizing the U.S. use of herbicides differed from that of environmentalists, whom he also criticized.[35] His concern transcended the immediate environmental devastation and human exposure to toxic chemicals; he was driven by fears of future ecological dystopias and health epidemics resulting from increasingly sophisticated chemical warfare.

This "biological approach" was crucial to differentiating Galston and his colleagues from the general anti-war movement, allowing them to participate in high-level diplomatic discussions. Their goal was to ensure a global prohibition on the use of herbicides as instruments of war. Their campaign extended beyond U.S. borders, attracting international condemnation from both adversaries and allies.

The group's expertise in international law was enhanced by the participation of Professor Richard Falk,[36] whose work remained focused on combating ecocide caused by Agent Orange rather than addressing the political motives behind the Vietnam War.[37] Falk's thinking aligned with Galston's, centering on safeguarding humanity's future by advancing a deeper understanding of the relationship between humans and the environment,[38] particularly in the context of armed conflict.

---

[35] Galston emphasized more the "cide" than the "eco", in lobbying to ban the use of herbicides in wars. He believed the environmental movement to be dilettante, "passionate", stirring up a social upheaval for "Coca-Cola bottle clean-ups" on the beaches, advocating the prioritization of the natural over the non-natural, devoid of a pro-human technical analysis. Therefore, for the biologist, if the campaign against the conduct in Vietnam was motivated by the preservation of an ecological-indigenous Eden, the operation could not be called "ecocide" (ZIERLER, David (2011) The invention of ecocide: Agent Orange, Vietnam, and the scientists who changed the way we think about the environment. Athens: University of Georgia Press, p. 18).

[36] In his most important article for the time of War, in 1973, Falk argued the need for the United States to respect the Geneva Protocol: "*It seems clear that an overwhelming majority of governments regards 1) the Geneva Protocol as binding on non-parties, and 2) as extending its prohibition to cover military herbicides. The protocol is binding because it enjoys the status of customary international law, a status that the United States has not seriously challenged. Indeed, the U.S. Government has argued its adherence to the terms of the Protocol, contending only that its prohibition does not extend to military herbicides (or riot control gases)*". (FALK, Richard (1973) Environmental warfare and ecocide. Facts, appraisal and proposal. Bulletin of Peace Proposals, v. 4, n° 1, p. 80–96, p. 90).

[37] For Falk, Agent Orange was the Auschwitz of environmental values, and, just as the Convention on Genocide formalized the repulsion to this crime, an Ecocide Convention was needed to condemn methods of war with herbicides (ZIERLER, David (2011) The invention of ecocide: Agent Orange, Vietnam, and the scientists who changed the way we think about the environment. Athens: University of Georgia Press, p. 25).

[38] "*With respect to action, I think there is an emerging consensus that somewhere between three and ten decades hence, a world order solution will prove necessary to meet the environmental challenge. This solution will necessitate, among other things, two principal adjustments. First, the economic basis of collective existence will have to be rearranged to achieve a relationship of environmental equilibrium. Secondly, we will have to bring about a substantial equalisation in life standards, or more modestly, the attainment of sufficient equity to eliminate extreme poverty. The only areas in which there is significant room for doubt concern the amount of time available for these profound adjustments, whether the earth's carrying capacity requires levelling down or allows for levelling up to achieve substantial equalisation, and the extent to which these two processes of adjustment (one on the level of economic behaviour, the other on the level of social*

The campaign reached official forums when, at the International Conference for the Human Environment in Stockholm,[39] in 1972, the Swedish Prime Minister,[40] Olof Palme,[41] used the term *ecocide*[42] to describe the environmental disaster occurring in Indochina and cross-border pollution (Ahmed, 2018, pp. 139–147).

Internal and international pressure[43] ed. the United States to ratify the Geneva Protocol, in 1975, 50 years was first proposed.[44] Thus, the scientists succeeded in

---

behaviour) can occur within the framework of the present world order system, a system comprised mainly of competing sovereign states which are highly diverse in ideology, culture, capability, and level of development" (FALK, Richard A. (1975) The Global Environment and International Law: Challenge and Response. Kansas Law Review, v. 23, p. 390).

[39] The Conference marked the beginning of the operation of the United Nations Environment Programme (UNEP), aimed at protecting the environment and promoting sustainable development. Link: www.mma.gov.br/estruturas/agenda21/_arquivos/estocolmo.doc

[40] Olof said: "*The immense destruction brought about by indiscriminate bombing, by large-scale use of bulldozers and herbicides is an outrage sometimes described as ecocide, which require[s] international attention*". At the same Conference, the Prime Minister of India, Indira Gandhi, also denounced the war and the dangers to the environment (GREENE, Anastacia (2018) The campaign to make ecocide an international crime: quixotic quest or moral imperative? Fordham Environmental Law Review, v. 30, p. 10).

[41] The Prime Minister's speech was given against the wishes of the Americans, who conditioned their participation in the event to no mention by the participants of the Vietnam War and the use of Agent Orange. In fact, criticism of the conduct of the war by the United States was constant only in the two parallel forums, especially in the so-called *Woodstockolm*, which concentrated serious discussions among researchers, marches and rock concerts (ZIERLER, David (2011) The invention of ecocide: Agent Orange, Vietnam, and the scientists who changed the way we think about the environment. Athens: University of Georgia Press, p. 165).

[42] The construction of the term ecocide "*was born from science. The plant biologist and chair of the Department of Botany at Yale University Arthur Galston first publicly used the term ecocide in 1970 after researching herbicides*" (LAY, Bronwyn et al. (2015) Timely and Necessary: Ecocide Law as Urgent and Emerging. The Journal Jurisprudence, v. 28, p. 433).

[43] The reaction of international institutions to the "environmental war" was discreet, although there were some attempts to hold the United States accountable for the conduct of the conflict. With the UN Security Council locked due to the Cold War, it was up to the UN General Assembly to be the place for the advancement of legal and political debates: "*In 1966 a debate started within the UNGA, with Hungary accusing the US of violating international law and the Geneva Protocol by using herbicides in Vietnam. The UNGA passed Resolution 2162 (XXI), calling for a 'strict observance by all States of the principles and objectives of the Protocol' and condemning 'all actions contrary to those objectives'. Although the resolution did not address the scope of the Geneva Protocol with regard to specific weapons and used general language, it marked the first time that the US had to defend its military strategies in Vietnam before the international community. In 1969 the UNGA went further and adopted Resolution 2603 to clarify the scope of the Geneva Protocol*" (CUSATO, Eliana (2018) From Ecocide to Voluntary Remediation Projects: Legal Responses to Environmental Warfare in Vietnam and the Spectre of Colonialism. Melbourne Journal of International Law, vol. 19, no. 2, p. 494–520, p. 502).

[44] There was intense internal political debate about the interpretation of the Protocol, to determine whether the prohibition on the use of chemical weapons reached the use of herbicides, since the former targets humans, while the latter targets the environment. In fact, the American fear was that, by ratifying the treaty, which they always argued to comply with, they would automatically assume its violation, incurring international sanctions and reprimands. In the end, the vague language of

their campaign against the use of herbicides in warfare, with no comparable situation to Vietnam having occurred since then.[45]

The legal repercussions, however, did not directly address environmental concerns. Among the claims brought—all seeking reparations for damage—against herbicide-producing companies, the primary focus was on the aftermath of Agent Orange on former combatants, civilians, and descendants. Three major cases stand out: two in the United States and one in France.

In 1977, American veteran soldiers, suffering from various health problems, approached the *Veteran Administration* (VA) to report the consequences of exposure to Agent Orange. Many complaints came from ground troops in Vietnam, who believed they had been sprayed with, or had consumed water contaminated by, the herbicide—a fact consistently denied by the United States Department of Defense (Hansen, 1981, pp. 29–36).

The largest class action lawsuit for product liability at the time was filed in January of 1979 in the Federal District Court of New York, on behalf of the veterans and their families, against chemical companies that manufactured Agent Orange.[46] The plaintiffs sought the creation of a trust fund, administered by the Court, to reimburse the government for compensation and medical care provided to military personnel and their children affected by dioxin.[47]

The plaintiffs alleged that the chemical companies knew of Agent Orange's extreme danger but failed to warn either the Department of Defense or the soldiers who might be exposed.[48] The defendants denied liability, arguing that the herbicides

the Protocol encouraged the signature, with the caveat of using the method of war in case of defence against attacks using the same tactic (ZIERLER, David (2011) The invention of ecocide: Agent Orange, Vietnam, and the scientists who changed the way we think about the environment. Athens: University of Georgia Press, p. 157).

[45] Also, "environmental damage became explicitly prohibited in international armed conflict in 1977, as it became included in Additional Protocol I to the 1949 Geneva Conventions (Articles 35[3] and 55 of 'Protocol Additional to the Geneva Conventions of 12 August 1949, and Relating to the Protection of Victims of International Armed Conflicts [Protocol I]. This was almost entirely in response to the methods and means of warfare employed by the US Army in the Vietnam War" (SMITH, Tara (2012) Creating a framework for the prosecution of environmental crimes in international criminal law. Companion to International Criminal Law: Critical Perspectives. Farnham: Ashgate Publishers, p. 9).

[46] The five chemical companies indicated as defendants are Dow Chemical Company, Monsanto Company, Thompson Hayward Chemical Company, Hercules, Inc. and Diamond Shamrock Corporation.

[47] In re Agent Orange Prod. Liab. Litig., 373 F.Supp.2d 7, 19 (E.D.N.Y.2005), Available at: https://caselaw.findlaw.com/us-2nd-circuit/1177960.html, accessed on: 20 Apr. 2025.

[48] The American Department of Defense enjoys, in front of other federal agencies, several exemptions from compliance with environmental regulations, especially when representing a "threat to national security". The most recent and broad request in this sense occurred after the terrorist attacks of September 11, 2001, when the Pentagon requested several general exemptions to federal environmental laws, in order to avoid potential restrictions on military training and combat operations. In return, the DoD has significant initiatives in favour of the environment, such as the unequivocal recognition of climate change as a threat to national security, in the last 30 years; the commitment to reducing dependence on fossil fuels and the transition to renewable energy sources;

sold to the military pose no threat to human health, and further contending that any harm caused resulted from the improper use of the product, which otherwise would have been safe (Hansen, 1981, pp. 29–36).

The case, consolidated by the Judicial Panel on Multidistrict Litigation in the New York Court (for all similar federal actions), reached the stage of procedural discussions and debate over the Government's possible inclusion as a defendant (liability was excluded in November 1980). It ultimately ended with a global settlement shortly before trial, in May 1984.[49] The companies, while denying liability, agreed to establish a settlement fund (Abboud, 2017). Dow and Monsanto's lawyers described their acceptance of the settlement, without admission of guilt, as an act of goodwill (Zierler, 2011, p. 13).

The resulting Agent Orange Settlement Fund distributed $180 million[50] among registered VA claimants until the depletion of funds in September 1997.[51]

The next two cases did not meet with the same "success". In the first, the Vietnamese Association for Victims of Agent Orange,[52] along with individual Vietnamese plaintiffs, filed a lawsuit in the United States (Federal District Court of New York), seeking compensation from the chemical manufacturers under grounds similar to those asserted by American veterans.[53] The plaintiffs alleged (with an amendment to their initial filing in September 2004) that the U.S. military's use of Agent Orange violated international, U.S., and Vietnamese law, and that the companies either aided and abetted these violations or committed independent violations by supplying the herbicides.[54]

---

and land management programs at its facilities (Cranston, Curtis (2019). The US military's environmental protection efforts: Unexpected eco-friendly solutions to land management problems. Boston College Law Review, 60, 1023–1072, p. 1029).

[49] Agent Orange I Settlement Op., 818 F.2d at 152–55.

[50] Many Vietnam War veterans reported dissatisfaction with the settlement, which amounted to $3800 (three thousand and eight hundred) dollars per person. They claimed that, in addition to the paltry amount, there were unanswered questions about the responsibility of chemical product manufacturers. No claim has been successful, with all new actions on the subject being denied in American justice (ABBOUD, Alexis (2017) In re Agent Orange Product Liability Litigation (1979–1984). Embryo Project Encyclopedia).

[51] U.S. Department Of Veterans Affairs, Agent Orange Settlement Fund. Available at: https://www.benefits.va.gov/compensation/claims-postservice-agent_orange-settlement-settlementFund.asp, accessed on: 20 Apr. 2025.

[52] Vietnamese Association for Victims of Agent Orange (VAVA).

[53] The authors alleged as a consequence of exposure to Agent Orange, among others, miscarriages, birth defects, breast cancer, ovarian tumours, lung cancer, Hodgkin's disease and prostate tumours (U.S. Court Of Appeals For The Second Circuit, *Vietnam Association for Victims of Agent Orange/Dioxin v. Dow Chemical Co.*, 05-1953-cv, 2008, p. 14. Available at: https://www.asser.nl/upload/documents/DomCLIC/Docs/NLP/US/AgentOrange_AppealsJudgement_22-2-2008.pdf, accessed on: 20 Apr. 2025).

[54] U.S. Court Of Appeals For The Second Circuit, *Vietnam Association for Victims of Agent Orange/Dioxin v. Dow Chemical Co.*, 05-1953-cv, 2008, p. 15. Available at: https://www.asser.nl/upload/documents/DomCLIC/Docs/NLP/US/AgentOrange_AppealsJudgement_22-2-2008.pdf, accessed on: 20 Apr. 2025.

On 25 March 2005, the District Court dismissed the case. Regarding claims under the Alien Tort Statute,[55] the Court concluded that the plaintiffs failed to establish a cause of action, finding that neither the military's use of Agent Orange nor the companies' agreement to supply it violated any well-defined and universally accepted international norm (such as those under the Geneva Protocol or the Conventions protecting war victims)[56] prohibiting the use of herbicides in armed conflict. After an appeal to the Second Circuit Court of Appeals, the case was ultimately denied by the U.S. Supreme Court (Zierler, 2011, p. 13).

The third case was brought in Évry (Île de France) by Tran To Nga, a 79-year-old Franco-Vietnamese woman, against 14 American chemical companies, in 2014. Tran To Nga claimed that these companies were responsible for the ecocide in her native country and for her serious health problems, which included type 2 diabetes, alpha thalassemia, numerous bodily nodules and calcifications, immune system damage, and the death of her first daughter due to a severe congenital heart defect. The Plaintiff alleged that the companies had prior knowledge of Agent Orange's toxicity and failed to inform U.S. authorities or take corrective action.[57] The crux of the matter, once again, is the human cost of the herbicidal method of warfare.

The companies' defense's arguments, raised previously in U.S. courts, included claims of jurisdictional immunity (based on Articles 32, 122, and 771 of the French Code of Civil Procedure and Article 1382 of the French Civil Code). They also referred to the decisions of American courts, particularly the New York Court's ruling that exempted herbicide producers from liability under international law.[58]

---

[55] 28 U.S.C. § 1350: The district courts shall have original jurisdiction of any civil action by an alien for a tort only, committed in violation of the law of nations or a treaty of the United States.

[56] The nuclear issue was whether the use of Agent Orange violated international law and was actionable under the ATS. Judge Weinstein rejected the claim, arguing that the 1907 Hague Regulations, which prohibit the use of poison and poisoned weapons, did not apply because "poison" did not have a defined concept; there are different interpretations of the term and, in any case, the prohibition was not generally considered to apply to the use of lethal gas weapons used against people in World War I, much less to herbicides targeted at plants. As for the 1925 Geneva Protocol, which prohibits the use of asphyxiating, poisonous and other gases, the United States only ratified it in 1975 (after the end of the Vietnam War and the fumigation), and any customary norm evidenced by this treaty would have only covered the types of gases used in World War I, such as mustard gas, intended to have an immediate incapacitating effect on people, as opposed to herbicides, designed to remove the leaves from plants, with potential unintentional effects on people (ROBERTS, Anthea (2005) The Agent Orange Case: Vietnam Ass'n for Victims of Agent Orange/ Dioxin v. Dow Chemical Co. American Society of International Law, v. 99, p. 387. Available at: http://www.jstor.org/stable/25660031. Accessed on: 20 Apr. 2025).

[57] Judicial Court Of Évry, 10th of May, 2021, n ° 14/04980. Available at: https://www.doctrine.fr/d/TJ/Evry/2021/U0C32CC99EED863A0B1B8#decision-table-of-contents-4, accessed on: 20 Apr. 2025.

[58] Judicial Court Of Évry, 10th of May, 2021, n ° 14/04980. Available at: https://www.doctrine.fr/d/TJ/Evry/2021/U0C32CC99EED863A0B1B8#decision-table-of-contents-4, accessed on: 20 Apr. 2025.

On 10 May 2021, the Court dismissed the action. While citing Article 6.1 of the Convention for the Protection of Human Rights and Fundamental Freedoms[59] to recognize the admissibility of the case, the Court emphasized that the article does not establish an absolute right of access to a court. Specifically, the Court invoked the principle of sovereign immunity under customary international law, expressed in the maxim *par in parem non habet imperium*, as codified in Article 5 of the United Nations Convention on Jurisdictional Immunities of States and Their Property (adopted in 2004 and ratified by France in 2011).[60] The Court concluded that the companies, by acting on behalf of the State, were entitled to sovereign immunity.[61]

As demonstrated, the American actions in Vietnam had significant human and environmental harm. The term "ecocide", coined in response to the massive environmental destruction, initially bore a different meaning than it holds today: it referred exclusively to the attack on the natural environment through the use of herbicides in the context of war. The primary concern at that time was with humanity and its future habitability on a planet that was contaminated by advanced chemical weapons.[62] The understanding prevailing at the time emphasized the intentionality

[59] Article 6-1: Everyone has the right to have their case examined, fairly and publicly, within a reasonable time by an independent and impartial court, established by law, which will decide, either on the determination of their civil rights and obligations, or on the basis of any criminal charge against them. The trial must be public, but access to the courtroom may be prohibited to the press or the public during the whole or part of the process, when in the interest of morality, public order or national security in a democratic society, when the interests of minors or the protection of the private life of the parties in the process require it, or, to the extent deemed strictly necessary by the court, when, under special circumstances, publicity could be harmful to the interests of justice. Link: https://www.echr.coe.int/documents/d/echr/convention_ENG, accessed on: 2nd Jan. 2025.

[60] Judicial Court Of Évry, 10th of May, 2021, n ° 14/04980. Available at: https://www.doctrine.fr/d/TJ/Evry/2021/U0C32CC99EED863A0B1B8#decision-table-of-contents-6, accessed on: 2nd Fev. 2025.

[61] The benefit of this immunity in civil proceedings aims at the legitimate objective of observing international law in order to promote courtesy and good relations between States, guaranteed by respect for the sovereignty of another State. Once the link between the conduct pointed out by the Plaintiff and the action of a sovereign State is established, the French civil jurisdiction is ruled out (Judicial Court Of Évry, 10th of May, 2021, n ° 14/04980. Available at: https://www.doctrine.fr/d/TJ/Evry/2021/U0C32CC99EED863A0B1B8#decision-table-of-contents-6, accessed on: 2nd Fev. 2025).

[62] Today, the concern also lies with the organised crime of pesticides: "*As the world value of the legitimate pesticides industry is approximately amounting to USD 60 billion (FAO, 2012), there are a variety of market and strategic incentives for organized criminal groups and networks to produce and distribute illicit goods, including pesticides. Profit margins are high—with none of the traditional costs or liabilities associated with developing, producing and marketing a brand-name product. Estimates of the worldwide market for illicit pesticides range from USD 6–10 billion annually (based on a 10–15% of market estimate) and the European market accounts for approximately USD 1.1 billion*" (UNICRI (2016) Illicit pesticides, organized crime and supply chain integrity. Torino: United Nations. Available at: http://www.unicri.it/illicit-pesticides-organized-crime-and-supply-chain-integrity. Accessed on: 3rd Fev. 2025).

of the action as a condition for qualifying the conduct as ecocide, drawing parallels to the crime of genocide.

The victories of Galston and Falk, crowned by the U.S. ratification of the 1925 Geneva Protocol,[63] did not yield significant judicial outcomes regarding the harmful consequences of Agent Orange[64] dispersal nor was it the objective of the researchers. Nevertheless, their work laid the foundation for what is now understood as ecocide: a broader concept focused on the environment,[65] while still acknowledging its wartime origins and the involvement of private corporations.

Subsequent sections will examine major environmental disasters linked to oil extraction– also regarded as instances of ecocide.

2.2 Environmental Disasters and Black Gold

The economic importance of oil and the transnational scale of the corporations that operate in this sector are key factors that hinder legal accountability for environmental disasters.[66] In recent years, however, efforts have emerged—at both national

---

[63] For a study on the Geneva Protocol of 1925 and ecocide, see: JOHNSTONE, L. Craig (1971) Ecocide and the Geneva Protocol. Foreign Affairs, v. 49, n. 4, p. 711–720.

[64] The American and Vietnamese initiatives to address the legacy of the war cannot be considered as damage repair. "*Even if one wanted to claim that the American government's intention to 'make good' could be implied 'facta concludentia', the ways these programmes are implemented, and who their beneficiaries are, raise further questions. The issue of whether individuals have rights under the laws of armed conflict, including the right to reparation in case of violation, is highly debated in the literature. Historically, war reparations were settled through inter-state agreements, which included the payment of a lump sum and waiver of individual claims. As such, the beneficiary of the international obligation to provide reparation remained the injured state. Yet, in the last couple of decades, a different perspective has emerged. In a few cases, individual victims were granted the right to bring claims and ultimately awarded compensation for violations of the laws of armed conflict.* (…). *The funding of environmental clean-up projects in Vietnam presents some similarity with the practice of* ex gratia *payments, often associated with episodes of transboundary environmental damage or incidents involving the shutting-down of civilian or military airplanes*". (CUSATO, Eliana (2018) From Ecocide to Voluntary Remediation Projects: Legal Responses to Environmental Warfare in Vietnam and the Spectre of Colonialism. Melbourne Journal of International Law, vol. 19, no. 2, p. 494–520, p. 511).

[65] It was from the studies carried out in the 1970s that ideas emerged to include ecocide as an international crime: "*During the 1970s, the idea of expanding the 1948 Convention on Genocide led to an inquiry by the UN as to how the Convention could be improved. This included the possibility of criminalising ecocide alongside genocide. The International Law Commission (ILC) considered the inclusion of an environmental crime within the Draft Code of Crimes against Peace and Security of Mankind (hereafter 'the Code'), which later became the Rome Statute—the founding document of the ICC*" (MALHOTRA, Saloni (2017) The International Crime That Could Have Been but Never Was: An English School Perspective on the Ecocide Law. Amsterdam Law Forum, vol. 9, no. 3, p. 49–70, p. 52).

[66] "*Since SPDC is a Nigerian joint venture company, Nigeria would be the logical place to commence proceedings. In principal, victims cannot file a claim against the local company before a court in another country. Secondly, successfully asserting a claim against Shell, the ultimate par-*

and international levels —aimed at securing at least financial reparations for the damages inflicted on people and nature. As will be shown, the duty to provide redressal is increasingly grounded in the recognized relationship between human rights treaties and business enterprises.

In underdeveloped countries—particularly those that are former European colonies— the difficulty of holding perpetrators accountable is even greater. Nigeria, for example, which gained independence from the United Kingdom only on October 1, 1960 (Lambooy et al., 2008, p. 229), has oil as its primary export commodity and hosts the continent's most significant petroleum industry.

In 1958, even before independence, Shell—an Anglo-Dutch company—began oil extraction in the country's southeastern region, specifically in the Niger River Delta, through its subsidiary, Shell Petroleum Development Company of Nigeria (SPDC). Over the following 60 years, repeated oil spills turned the Delta—a 70,000 square-kilometer expanse of swamp and mangrove—into one of the most polluted regions in the world.

The absence of effective management, emergency response strategies, and preventive policies[67] led to the neglect of pipeline maintenance. As a result, frequent leaks and blowouts released large quantities of crude oil into the environment.[68] In addition to devastating ecosystems, the contamination of land, water, and air caused serious health issues among the local Ogoni population.[69]

---

ent company of SPDC—which consisted of a dual-company structure, registered both in The Netherlands and in the UK—is not an easy undertaking. The parent company would basically assert that it is only the (indirect) shareholder of SPDC and has no influence upon the wrongdoings of the local SPDC management. Parent-companies establish local legal entities for protection against commercial risks and other liabilities incurred by their subsidiary ventures". (LAMBOOY, Tineke; RANCOURT, Marie-Eve (2008) Shell in Nigeria: From human rights abuse to corporate social responsibility. Hum. Rts. & Int'l Legal Discourse, v. 2, p. 229, p. 241/242).

[67] SOARES, Marcelo de Oliveira et al. (2020) Oil spill in South Atlantic [Brazil]: environmental and governmental disaster. Marine Policy, v. 115, p. 3.

[68] Many oil spills were deliberately ignored by the company, allowing the pollution to worsen. (MORIMOTO, Tetsuya (2005) Growing Industrialization and our Damaged Planet-The Extraterritorial Application of Developed Countries' Domestic Environmental Laws to Transnational Corporations Abroad. Utrecht L. Rev., v. 1, p. 134, p. 140).

[69] In addition to health problems, pollution also led to various public protests against oil extraction in the Niger Delta. In 1993, after protests against environmental devastation, SPDC suspended its operations in Ogoniland (one of the richest oil regions). The following year, nine protesters, accused of inciting the death of Ogoni leaders favourable to the government (whose leniency towards SPDC was criticised), were convicted and executed after trial. (MORIMOTO, Tetsuya (2005) Growing Industrialization and our Damaged Planet-The Extraterritorial Application of Developed Countries' Domestic Environmental Laws to Transnational Corporations Abroad. Utrecht L. Rev., v. 1, p. 134, p. 140). After the executions, "*the ethnic minorities have raised their voices, insisting to be included in the economic development of their region and to be heard in their struggle for social and ecological justice*", drawing international attention to the human rights of Indigenous Peoples to self-determination (LAMBOOY, Tineke; RANCOURT, Marie-Eve (2008) Shell in Nigeria: From human rights abuse to corporate social responsibility. Hum. Rts. & Int'l Legal Discourse, v. 2, p. 229, p. 240).

Notably, Nigeria has several laws regulating oil activities and environmental protection.[70] However, as often occurs in politics, most of these laws were enacted only in response to disasters—and even then, they have proven insufficient to resolve the country's environmental crisis. Sanctions are typically limited to negligible fines, and there are no records of imprisonment for violations.[71]

For example, Nigeria's legal framework includes no crimes specifically targeting oil-related pollution, except when classified as sabotage.[72] In such cases, the law defines various acts as sabotage,[73] punishable by up to 21 years in prison, with exclusive jurisdiction conferred on the Federal High Court.

Some cases[74] in Nigerian courts have seen partial success. In *Shell v. Ijaw Aborigines of Bayelsa State* (2006), the Nigerian subsidiary was ordered to pay 1.5 billion U.S. dollars, in compensation for damages to communities in Bayelsa State

[70] Among these laws and regulations, include "*Oil Pipelines Act, Mineral Oils (Safety) Regulations (1963), Oil in Navigable Waters Act, Petroleum Act, Associated Gas Re-injection Act, the National Environmental Standards and Regulations Enforcement Agency (NESREA) Act, the National Oil Spill Detection Response Agency (NOSDRA) Act, the National Policy on Environment 1989, Environmental Impact Assessment (EIA) Act and the Department of Petroleum Resources (DPR)-initiated Environmental Guidelines and Standard for the Petroleum Industry in Nigeria (EGASPIN), 2002*". (BROWN, Cleverline T.; OKOGBULE, Nlerum S. (2020) Redressing harmful environmental practices in the Nigerian petroleum industry through the criminal justice approach. Journal of Sustainable Development Law and Policy, v. 11, n. 1, p. 18–55, p. 26)

[71] There is a notable discrepancy in the sanctions applied especially when corporations are the defendants, existing, at most, outdated monetary penalties. Indeed, the Nigerian legal framework seems to cover the basics in terms of environmental damage, but the lack of application, coupled with the precariousness of supervision and control, reflects the various incidents of environmental pollution recorded by the *Oil Spill Monitor*, which contains data collected from various oil companies. (BROWN, Cleverline T.; OKOGBULE, Nlerum S. (2020) Redressing harmful environmental practices in the Nigerian petroleum industry through the criminal justice approach. Journal of Sustainable Development Law and Policy, v. 11, n. 1, p. 18–55, p. 28–30). Furthermore, "*the same corruption and weak governance are said to affect the ability of the government to deliver its obligations to protect the environment against the negative impacts of the oil industry*" (LAMBOOY, Tineke; RANCOURT, Marie-Eve (2008) Shell in Nigeria: From human rights abuse to corporate social responsibility. Hum. Rts. & Int'l Legal Discourse, v. 2, p. 229, p. 235).

[72] Petroleum Production and Distribution (Anti-Sabotage) Act—CAP. P12 L.F.N. 2004, Link: https://laws.lawnigeria.com/2018/04/24/lfn-petroleum-production-and-distribution-anti-sabotage-act/, accessed on: 10 Fev. 2025.

[73] "The Act refers to the offence of sabotage as any wilful act done with the intent to obstruct or prevent the production or distribution, procurement of petroleum products for distribution in any part of Nigeria or any wilful act done in respect of any vehicle or any public highway with intent to obstruct or prevent its use for the distribution of petroleum products, thereby causing any interruption in the production or distribution of petroleum products in any part of Nigeria" (BROWN, Cleverline T.; OKOGBULE, Nlerum S. (2020) Redressing harmful environmental practices in the Nigerian petroleum industry through the criminal justice approach. Journal of Sustainable Development Law and Policy, v. 11, n. 1, p. 18–55, p. 49).

[74] For other cases involving oil companies in Nigeria, see: BROWN, Cleverline T.; OKOGBULE, Nlerum S. (2020) Redressing harmful environmental practices in the Nigerian petroleum industry through the criminal justice approach. Journal of Sustainable Development Law and Policy, v. 11, n. 1, p. 18–55, p. 37–42.

for the degradation of their waterways and the destruction of crops and fisheries. However, the amount was never paid, as the case became entangled in appeals and corruption allegations (Lambooy et al., 2008, p. 229, 252).

In another case, the *Ejama-Ebubu* people filed a suit in 1991 against SPDC for oil spills resulting from pipeline ruptures in the 1970s. After the company was ordered to pay 17 billion naira in 2010, the Nigerian Supreme Court dismissed the final appeals in 2020. In August 2021, Shell Nigeria agreed to pay 45.7 billion naira (approximately US$ 110.9 million) "for full and final satisfaction" of the case.[75]

The legal alternative for many affected by pollution was to pursue claims in foreign courts (Brown et al., 2020, pp. 18–55), reaching the parent companies of the oil firms involved.[76]

Two legal actions merit particular attention, as they reflect a shift in the understanding of parent company liability for environmental harm: one in the Netherlands (Hague Court of Appeal) and the other in the United Kingdom (Supreme Court).

In the first case, four Nigerian farmers[77] filed a civil lawsuit for damages in 2008 before Dutch courts against Royal Dutch Shell—the parent company of Shell Petroleum Development Company of Nigeria (SPDC)—for oil spills that devastated three villages in the Niger Delta (Oruma, Goi, and Ikot Ada Udo). The plaintiffs claimed that Shell had violated its duty of care by responding inadequately to the spills and failing to implement a leak detection system that could have helped to identify incidents more rapidly.

The company initially argued that it bore no responsibility for the actions—or failings— of its Nigerian subsidiary, on the merits, it claimed that the leaks were caused by sabotage and, therefore, it could not be held liable. Moreover, the company asserted that it had acted to contain and clean up the oil, restoring the affected areas.

On 29 January 2021, the Hague Court of Appeal held SPDC liable for the consequences of the first two oil spills in Nigeria[78] (excluding Ikot Ada Udo, where

[75] Links: https://www.worldoil.com/news/2021/8/11/shell-to-pay-110mm-for-full-and-final-satisfaction-of-nigeria-oil-spill-suit, accessed on: 11 Fev. 2025

[76] It is not simple to seek reparation for damages from the parent company based in another jurisdiction. Civil litigations in the United States and the United Kingdom have fostered the doctrine of *forum non conveniens*, protecting the parent companies from actions against the subsidiaries spread in developing countries: "*A parent company will typically bring up this defence stating that the complaint or the facts on which the case is based have a closer link with another jurisdiction and that it would be more appropriate to litigate the case there. In other European Union (EU) countries, Article 2 of the Brussels Convention on Jurisdiction and the Enforcement of Judgments in Civil and Commercial Matters precludes the application of this doctrine where the defendant is based in the EU*" (LAMBOOY, Tineke; RANCOURT, Marie-Eve (2008) Shell in Nigeria: From human rights abuse to corporate social responsibility. Hum. Rts. & Int'l Legal Discourse, v. 2, p. 229, p. 244).

[77] Shell Nigeria was notified, on 26 June 2005, of a leak from an underground pipeline near the village of Oruma, leaving the soil visibly bubbling with oil.

[78] Procedurally, an important point reached was about the burden of proof, when the Dutch court recognised the Nigerian legislation to impose on the defendant company the burden of proof about the allegation of pipeline sabotage, which must be demonstrated beyond any reasonable doubt

sabotage was confirmed, although the Court ordered transparency regarding the status of environmental remediation). The ruling also extended to Royal Dutch Shell, recognizing its duty of care under customary law, even in relation to plaintiffs residing in a third country. The Court ordered the installation of an adequate leak detection system, while compensation and environmental restoration—yet to be quantified—were attributed to SPDC.

In the second case, nearly 40,000 residents of the Ogale community in the Niger Delta brought a lawsuit in the United Kingdom against Royal Dutch Shell in October 2015, holding its subsidiary SPDC responsible for numerous oil spills from pipelines and infrastructure operating near their communities. The plaintiffs alleged widespread environmental contamination, including serious pollution of water and soil, without proper cleanup or repair. As a result, the affected communities were unable to use natural water sources for drinking, fishing, agriculture, washing, or recreation.[79]

In January 2017, the English High Court initially dismissed the case on jurisdictional grounds, concluding that Royal Dutch Shell owed no duty of care to its Nigerian subsidiary and was therefore not a proper party to the proceedings. In 2018, the Court of Appeal upheld the ruling but authorized an appeal to the UK Supreme Court.[80]

Finally, in February 2021, the UK Supreme Court recognized the possibility of adjudicating claims against Shell's parent company based on the degree of control and effective management it exercised (duty of care), in relation to the alleged environmental and human rights violations committed by the Nigerian subsidiary.

Although the case remains in the procedural phase, it is notable for recognizing the potential liability of a multinational corporation for environmental damage caused by its subsidiaries in third countries.

(link: https://www.foei.org/news/justice-shell-compensate-nigerian-farmers-oil-spill, accessed on 8 Apr. 2025).

[79] Supreme Court of the United Kingdom, *appeal from*: [2018] EWCA Civ 191, 12 Feb. 2021.

[80] The evidence consisted of "*witness testimony and supporting documentary evidence adduced by both parties, including 26 witness statements and expert reports adduced by the appellants, and 17 witness statements and expert reports adduced by the respondents*". (Supreme Court of the United Kingdom, *appeal from*: [2018] EWCA Civ 191, 12 Feb. 2021).

Environmental disasters linked to oil exploitation are not limited to poorer countries.[81] Oil extraction from tar sands[82] in Canada is considered one of the most environmentally destructive activities in the world.

Canada holds the world's largest deposit of tar sands, located in Alberta, along the Athabasca River. The extraction process is categorized as "unconventional" due to its departure from traditional drilling methods (Cruden et al., 2016, p. 65, 141). In this case, oil is located near the surface and is mixed with other substances, requiring five barrels of water for every barrel of oil, along with significant chemical input.[83] Extraction involves clearing vast stretches of tundra, leaving the exposed soil crisscrossed by toxic waste ponds, pipelines, and acid rains.[84]

Oil extraction began in 1969 and has since accelerated, driven by high global demand and commodity prices. While the industry has contributed significantly to regional economic development,[85] it is widely regarded as the most severe ongoing ecocide, causing not only environmental degradation but also severe health effects

---

[81] In the United States, for example, the use of the technique of *fracking* to extract shale gas was the subject of discussion in the 2020 American elections. The procedure, which involves 'fracturing' the soil through the injection of a large amount of water, added to various chemicals (many of them toxic), with the aim of extracting the gas, promotes pollution of groundwater (badly built cement ducts), of the air (release of methane), being prohibited in various American states, but, at the same time, is the economic basis of others. President Joe Biden, with a speech combating climate changes, encounters resistance when trying to ban *fracking*. (Link: https://edition.cnn.com/2021/01/27/business/fracking-ban-biden-federal-leasing/index.html, accessed on: 7 Dec. 2024). Still in the United States, in April 2010, the oil platform *Deepwater Horizon* exploded, killing 11 people, injuring another 17, leaking nearly 800 million litres of oil into the Gulf of Mexico, for 87 days. The company responsible for the largest accident of this nature in the country, British Petroleum—BP, is facing over 300 lawsuits in the United States, in addition to continuing today the clean-up work. Civil lawsuits and class actions (under the command of various laws, from maritime laws to defective products laws) have accumulated in different courts, until they were all united in the Multidistrict Litigation Judicial Panel. (CRUDEN, John C.; O'ROURKE, Steve; HIMMELHOCH, Sarah D. (2016) The Deepwater Horizon oil spill litigation: proof of concept for the manual for complex litigation and the 2015 amendments to the federal rules of civil procedure. Michigan Journal Environmental & Administrative Law, v. 6, p. 65, p. 98.)

[82] Known as *oil sands* or *tar sands*, they are deposits of bitumen, a semi-solid form of crude oil that impregnates the rocks, composed of sand and clay.

[83] RAOUL, Emmanuel (2010a, 2010b) Under the bituminous sands of Canada. Le monde Diplomatique, São Paulo, 1st of April 2010. Available at: http://diplomatique.org.br/sob-as-areias-betuminosas-do-canada/. Accessed on: 10 Mar. 2025.

[84] LEAHY, Stephen (2019) This is the world's most destructive oil operation—and it's growing. National Geographic, Alberta, 11 Apr. 2019. Available at: https://www.nationalgeographic.com/environment/article/alberta-canadas-tar-sands-is-growing-but-indigenous-people-fight-back. Accessed on: 17 Jan. 2025.

[85] The relationship between companies and the State is also influenced by the economic contribution from oil: "*a related concern is the overall nature of how the state regulates corporate behaviour that causes ecological disorganization. In the case of the oil sands, lax enforcement allows for an increase in production. For example, a review of nearly 9262 environment incidents associated with oil sands production in Alberta between 1996 and 2012 suggests that enforcement is lax and that only 0.9% of all reported incidents are subject to enforcement*" (LYNCH, Michael J.; STRETESKY, Paul B.; LONG, Michael A. (2016) A proposal for the political economy of green

among local Indigenous populations, including leukaemia, lymphoma, and colon cancer (Crook & Short, 2014, pp. 298–319).

The oil industry's activities (by both corporations and the State) have frequently been challenged in court. In one such case, the Fort McKay First Nation (FMFN)—a community surrounded by three open-pit oil fields—filed a lawsuit against the province of Alberta[86] over its authorization of another field (managed by Prosper Petroleum) in the last remaining undeveloped area, known as Moose Lake. The project, they argued, would prevent the exercise of traditional practices, such as hunting and fishing, in violation of *First Nation's Treaty 8*.[87]

In 2018, Alberta's Energy Regulator (AER) approved the project, finding it in the public interest and asserting that there was no evidence that oil extraction would impair treaty rights. However, on appeal in 2019, the FMFN prevailed. The Court held that any project potentially infringing on Indigenous rights—and therefore touching on constitutional obligations—could not be considered in the public interest,[88] as it would compromise the *honour of the Crown*.[89] As a result, the regulatory agency was ordered to re-evaluate the project's public interest status in light of Indigenous treaty rights.

In another case, also based on *Treaty 8*, the Blueberry River First Nations challenged the Supreme Court of British Columbia's authorization of industrial development within their territory, alleging cumulative harm to their constitutional rights to hunt, trap, fish, and maintain their traditional way of life.[90]

In a landmark July 2021 ruling, the Court found that while no single project caused catastrophic harm, the cumulative impact of multiple industrial activities over time had violated the basic rights of the First Nations. The Court banned the issuance of new permits for projects that failed to account for cumulative impacts,

criminology: Capitalism and the case of the Alberta Tar Sands. Canadian Journal of Criminology and Criminal Justice, v. 58, n. 2, p. 137–160, p. 151).

[86] Alberta Court of Appeal, Fort McKay First Nation v Prosper Petroleum Ltd., 2020 ABCA 163. Link: https://www.canlii.org/en/ab/abca/doc/2020/2020abca163/2020abca163.html?autocompleteStr=2020%20ABCA%20163&autocompletePos=1, accessed on: 17 Fev. 2025.

[87] The *Treaty 8* was signed on 21 June 1899 by the Crown and the First Nations of the Lesser Slave Lake area, granting the indigenous peoples involved administrative autonomy and rights to maintain their ways of life (Link: https://www.thecanadianencyclopedia.ca/en/article/treaty-8, accessed on: 17 Fev. 2025).

[88] Alberta Court of Appeal, Fort McKay First Nation v Prosper Petroleum Ltd., 2020 ABCA 163, item 68–70. Link: https://www.canlii.org/en/ab/abca/doc/2020/2020abca163/2020abca163.html?autocompleteStr=2020%20ABCA%20163&autocompletePos=1, accessed on: 17 Jan. 2025.

[89] On what is understood by *honour of the Crown*: DICKSON, Jamie D. (2019) The honour and dishonour of the Crown: Making sense of aboriginal law in Canada. Purich Publishing, p. 12.

[90] British Columbia Supreme Court, *Yahey* v. *British Columbia*, Link: https://www.canlii.org/en/bc/bcsc/doc/2021/2021bcsc1287/2021bcsc1287.html?resultIndex=1#_Toc75942631, accessed on: 17 Jan. 2025.

but suspended the order for 6 months to allow the parties to negotiate changes to the relevant regulatory framework.[91]

The most recent project connected to tar sands oil involves a proposed pipeline system linking Alberta's reserves to the Pacific Ocean, with the aim of expanding Canadian oil exports to Asia. The most controversial of these projects, the Trans Mountain Pipeline, would cross the British Columbia mountain range. After legal challenges by Indigenous groups—Squamish Nation, Tsleil-Waututh Nation, and Coldwater Indian Band (collectively known as the First Nations) —and environmental activists, the Supreme Court of Canada, in July 2020, upheld the Federal Court of Appeal's decision authorizing the project to proceed.[92]

It is worth recalling that Canada was the defendant in the first decision of an international Court or Tribunal on transboundary pollution, when it was sued by the United States (Parrish, 2005, p. 363, 364) in 1941. The *Trail Smelter Arbitration*[93] involved a Canadian smelter that emitted sulphur dioxide, which damaged the crops of American farmers.[94]

As can be seen, Canada maintains a contradictory approach,[95] it promotes climate action —receiving even Supreme Court support for the Paris Agreement[96]— and, on the other, it continues to expand oil operations in the tar sands. Despite this dichotomy, legal challenges tend to address environmental destruction only tangentially or indirectly, usually by alleging non-compliance with required administrative procedures or violations of Indigenous rights—the most frequent claims arising from oil exploitation in Canada. The mere existence of environmental laws per se,

[91] British Columbia Supreme Court, *Yahey* v. *British Columbia*, 2021, item 1891. Available at: https://www.canlii.org/en/bc/bcsc/doc/2021/2021bcsc1287/2021bcsc1287.html?resultIndex=1#_Toc75942631, accessed on: 17 Jan. 2025.

[92] Supreme Court of Canada, *Case* 39111, Coldwater Indian Band, et al. v. Attorney General of Canada, et al., Link: https://www.scc-csc.ca/case-dossier/info/dock-regi-eng.aspx?cas=39111, accessed on: 17 Jan.2025.

[93] United Nations. Trail smelter case (United States, Canada): 16 April 1938 and March 1941. Reports of International Arbitral Awards, v. III, p. 1905–1982, 2006. Link: https://legal.un.org/riaa/cases/vol_III/1905-1982.pdf. Accessed on: 30 Jun. 2025.

[94] The arbitral decision "established for the first time the principle, later consolidated by custom, that 'no state has the right to use or allow the use of its territory in such a way as to cause damage to others'". (TOVO, Carlo (2011) International Criminal Court of the Environment: roots, perspectives, alternatives. Group of the Progressive Alliance of Socialists & Democrats in the European Parliament, p. 4).

[95] Canada has some credibility on the subject of climate change, "as early as 2007, Alberta's provincial government instituted a carbon tax on large industrial emitters, which has raised U.S. $350 million (C $463 million) for energy research. At the Paris climate summit in 2015, Canada pushed for the ambitious 2.7 degrees Fahrenheit (1.5 degrees Celsius) global warming target. A national carbon tax went into effect April 1, 2019" (Link: https://www.nationalgeographic.com/environment/article/alberta-canadas-tar-sands-is-growing-but-indigenous-people-fight-back, accessed on: 8 Apr. 2025).

[96] Supreme Court of Canada. Reference re Greenhouse Gas Pollution Pricing Act. Available at: https://www.scc-csc.ca/case-dossier/cb/2021/38663-38781-39116-eng.aspx. Accessed on: 8 Apr. 2025.

it is clear, does not inhibit the occurrence of massive environmental destruction, when oversight is weak and when the State itself is complicit of—or even actively encouraging—such activities.

2.3 The Relationship Between "Accidents" and Criminal Laws

The largest chemical disaster in history occurred in December 1984, in the city of Bhopal, India (Martins, 2021). A pesticide plant operated by *Union Carbide India Limited* (UCIL), the Indian subsidiary of the American *Union Carbide Corporation*, released 40 tons of lethal gases (including methyl isocyanate), instantly killing more than 2000 people,[97] currently leaving almost 600,000 individuals with sequelae, extending into the third generation of victims,[98] in addition to severe soil and groundwater contamination.[99]

The accident was the result of a combination of operational failures, negligence, design flaws, cost-cutting measures, and a lack of both training and emergency containment systems (Morimoto, 2005, p. 134, 138). Two years before the disaster, company safety experts had—in a confidential memo— warned of a "potential release of toxic materials". That information was ignored by Warren Anderson, president of the American parent company, who continued downsizing the staff and deactivating essential safety systems (Sarangi, 2002, pp. 47–52).

Although the environmental damage was local in scope, it nonetheless prompted international legal scrutiny due to the potential liability of a U.S.-based corporation.

[97] After the passage of most of the toxic cloud, life in the region had been exterminated. In the words of a witness: "*everyone was dead. After a few hours [...] second day, 4th December. We saw, at the time, the plants had no leaves; and the fruits had busted. And no plants had leaves. And then we continued and we saw on the left-side and right-side, everywhere, dead animals, dead bodies, people around dead bodies. Everywhere: dead bodies, cats, dogs, people, cattle… everywhere. I was disturbed. And no one was there to take them*". (MARTINS, Bruno Sena (2021) Revisiting the Bhopal Disaster. In: SANTOS, Boaventura De Sousa; MARTINS, Bruno Sena. The Pluriverse of Human Rights: The Diversity of Struggles for Dignity, Routledge).

[98] "The first acute effects of the toxic gases on the body were vomiting and burning sensations in the eyes, nose and throat, and many of the deaths were attributed to respiratory failure. In some cases, the toxic gas caused such severe internal secretions that their lungs became obstructed; in others, the airways closed leading to suffocation. Many of those who survived the first day were diagnosed with respiratory problems. Later studies with the survivors also pointed out neurological symptoms, such as headaches, balance disorders, depression, fatigue and irritability, as well as damage to the musculoskeletal, reproductive and immune systems" (Available at: https://greenpeace.org.br/bhopal/docs/Bhopal_desastre_continua.pdf, accessed on: 8 Apr.2025).

[99] After the accident, the company abandoned the factory, "*today, over 20,000 people in the surrounding area rely on drinking water contaminated with chemicals that have seeped into the ground water from the plant, causing cancer and other disease*" (SARANGI, Satinath (2002) Crimes of Bhopal and the global campaign for justice. Social Justice, v. 29, n. 3 (89), p. 47–52, p. 47)

Shortly after the accident, over 140 lawsuits[100] were filed in various federal courts in the United States, the first in 1984 by the victims themselves, known as *Dawani* et al. *v. Union Carbide* (Moltó, 2016, p. 9). The cases were consolidated in February 1985 before the U.S. Judicial Panel on Multidistrict Litigation in the Southern District Court of New York (Morimoto, 2005, p. 134, 139).

Once again, the U.S. judiciary declined jurisdiction in 1986, invoking the doctrine of *forum non conveniens* on the grounds that Indian courts were better suited to adjudicate the matter and that the relevant private and public interests were all located in India.[101]

Meanwhile, the Government of India passed the *Bhopal Gas Leak Act* (1985),[102] assuming exclusive representation of the victims. After the failed attempt to litigate in U.S. courts, the Indian government filed a criminal case before the District Court of Bhopal, charging *Union Carbide Corporation*, *Union Carbide Corporation Eastern,* and *Union Carbide India Ltd*, along with eight company executives—including Warren Anderson[103]—with various offenses against the person, including causing death by negligence.[104]

[100] In addition to the greed of American lawyers (who collected, a week after the accident, the signatures of victims of the event in Bhopal), Indian jurists themselves advised claiming the rights to compensation directly in the United States. "*Indeed, lawyers in both Delhi and Bhopal were aware that since the eighteenth century when the British had begun to establish common law in India, the codification of procedural, criminal and business law had been adapted to the colonizers' standards and rules, but that tort law, which should deal with civil offences committed by physical or juridical persons, had, surprisingly, not been codified. So, after assessing the limited legislative development, the jurisprudence and the lawyers' almost complete inexperience in this kind of law, it was decided that any civil action in India was doomed to failure, as its legal system was considered "underdeveloped, weak or dying*" (MOLTÓ, Jose Elias Esteve (2016) The close interdependence between transnational corporations criminality and human rights and environmental international law violations: Bhopal case lessons. Electronic Journal of International Studies, n. 32, p. 8).

[101] The decision also justified the verdict, unfavourable to all the plaintiffs, that judging the case in the United States would be an act of "imperialism" in relation to India, "*when it was precisely neocolonialism that availed itself of the impunity of transnational corporations and the humiliation of the Indian victims who showed their lack of protection in their own courts in an exercise that Nkrumah considered 'power without responsibility and exploitation without redress'*" (MOLTÓ, Jose Elias Esteve (2016) The close interdependence between transnational corporations criminality and human rights and environmental international law violations: Bhopal case lessons. Electronic Journal of International Studies, n. 32, p. 9).

[102] The Bhopal Gas Leak Disaster (Processing of Claims) Act, 1985.

[103] The president of the *Union Carbide Corporation* was arrested the day after the catastrophe, accused of homicide, but was released, on bail.

[104] Charges based on Section 304A 336,337 and S.338 r/w, section 35 of the Indian Penal Code, 1860 (Case n° 8460/1996, Link: https://www.countercurrents.org/UCIL.pdf, accessed on: 18 Jun. 2025).

In February 1989, the Supreme Court of India approved a settlement between the Indian government and the *Union Carbide* and its Indian subsidiary, setting the compensation at 470,000 dollars[105]—amounting to less than $10,000 per victim.

Another civil action was filed in 1999 in the United States (*Bano v Union Carbide*), alleging violations of human rights, environmental law, and international criminal law. Regarding compensation, in 2006, the U.S. court held that the 1989 Indian Supreme Court settlement barred any subsequent civil action. As to environmental remediation, the Court ruled that it could not supervise the cleanup of groundwater and aquifers located within the sovereign territory of another State, and therefore dismissed the claims.[106]

As for the criminal proceedings, in 2010, the Indian courts confirmed the conviction of the company, Warren Anderson, and other executives, sentencing them to 2 years in prison and fine. As Anderson failed to appear for trial, an international arrest warrant was issued and extradition requests were submitted to the United States, which were ultimately denied in 2004.[107]

Union Carbide was acquired in 2001 by another American company, Dow Chemical, which has since refused to accept responsibility for the environmental damage resulting from the accident.[108] Thus, the Bhopal case is widely regarded as a judicial failure—both nationally and internationally—for having failed to achieve justice in either civil or criminal courts, despite the severe human and environmental harm identified even 40 years after the event.

Among the broader consequences of the disaster, the Supreme Court of India has sought to facilitate public interest litigation by reinterpreting constitutional

---

[105] The decision was heavily criticised at the time, first for not admitting, in the process, active voice of the victims, excluded by the Bhopal Gas Leak Disaster Law; second, about the value: "*curiously enough, this figure is the same as that initially offered by the company to the victims, and is a far cry from the 3.3 billion dollars originally claimed by the Indian government. Moreover, the compensation would be covered almost in its entirety by the insurance companies, according to an analysis by Muchlinsky, economist and professor at the London School of Economics. In short, the judicial settlement 'was clearly a victory for Union Carbide', whose shares rocketed in the New York stock exchange*" (MOLTÓ, Jose Elias Esteve (2016) The close interdependence between transnational corporations criminality and human rights and environmental international law violations: Bhopal case lessons. Electronic Journal of International Studies, n. 32, p. 18).

[106] MOLTÓ, Jose Elias Esteve (2016) The close interdependence between transnational corporations criminality and human rights and environmental international law violations: Bhopal case lessons. Electronic Journal of International Studies, n. 32, p. 23.

[107] The arrest warrant remained open until the director's death in 2014. (MOLTÓ, Jose Elias Esteve (2016) The close interdependence between transnational corporations criminality and human rights and environmental international law violations: Bhopal case lessons. Electronic Journal of International Studies, n. 32, p. 20).

[108] In addition to arguing its procedural illegitimacy, the company makes its position clear on its own website: "*Did The Dow Chemical Company (TDCC) inherit any liability for Bhopal when it purchased the shares of Union Carbide (UCC) in 2001? No. While UCC's stock is owned by TDCC, UCC remains a separate company as a TDCC subsidiary. Under well-established principles of corporate law, both in India and the United States, TDCC did not assume UCC's liabilities as part of the 2001 transaction*"(Link: https://corporate.dow.com/en-us/about/legal/issues/bhopal/tragedy.html, accessed on: 18 Jun. 2025).

provisions to equate environmental issues with human rights—particularly Article 21, which guarantees the fundamental right to life and liberty[109]—in order to strengthen the Court's authority over governmental agencies.[110]

Two more recent disasters in Brazil also caused massive environmental damage, loss of life, and prompted judicial and legislative responses: the collapses of tailings dams[111] in the municipalities of Mariana and Brumadinho, both in the state of Minas Gerais.

On November 5, 2015, a waste dam in Mariana, part of an iron ore mining complex operated by Samarco (a binational company jointly owned by Brazil's Vale S.A. and the Anglo-Australian firm BHP Billiton), burst, releasing between 40 and 60 million cubic meters of toxic sludge. The material flowed into the Doce River,[112] covering the 663 kilometres of the river, until it reached the Atlantic Ocean off the coast of Espírito Santo.[113]

The environmental impact was visible from space.[114] The sludge rendered the Doce River 6000 times more turbid than legally permitted levels, silted its bed, and

---

[109] Globally, the coalition between human rights and the environment is increasingly pressing, the latter being a prerequisite for the enjoyment of the former (SZIEBIG, Orsolya Johanna (2024) The Crime of Ecocide through Human Rights Approach: The "Universal" Right to a Healthy Environment as a Driving Force Calling for Ecocide Legislation. Acta Humana: Hungarian Centre for Human Rights Publications, v. 12, n. 2, p. 75–89).

[110] "*In India, promoted by the Bhopal chemical plant disaster, the Indian Supreme Court has made particular use of new environmental provisions of the Indian Constitution in facilitating public interest litigation against state governments. Its decisions have included the explicit adoption of a right to life approach in cases concerning pollution and environmental harm*" (HAN, Xiuli (2011) ATCA as an avenue of overseas environmental protection and its implication to China's overseas investors. Frontiers of Law in China, v. 6, n. 2, p. 219–240, p. 233).

[111] There are 19,388 dams in Brazil, of which 5285 are subject to the National Dam Safety Policy (PNSB). Of these, 8% are mining waste containment dams. In the 2019 report from the National Water Agency, 12 accidents and 58 incidents with dams were reported, figures much higher than in previous years (Federal Government Of Brazil (2019) National Water and Sanitation Agency. Annual Dam Safety Report. Brasília).

[112] Ironically, the Doce River gave its name to the company that polluted it, Vale do Rio Doce, until the name was changed to Vale S.A. after the purchase of the Canadian mining company Inco. (CUCOLO, Eduardo (2016). Vale buys Canadian company and becomes 2nd largest in the world. G1, São Paulo, 27 Dec. 2016. Available at: http://g1.globo.com/Noticias/Economia_Negocios/0,,AA1322545-9356,00.html. Accessed on: 19 Jun. 2025).

[113] The waste reached the municipality of Bento Rodrigues, and, in 12 s, destroyed 80% of the 257 buildings, killing 19 people. It also hit a Permanent Preservation Area (APP), ruining 1469 hectares of natural vegetation. (DIAS, Carlos Alberto et al. (2018) Impacts of the Mariana dam break on the water quality of the Doce River. Revista Espinhaço. Available at: http://www.revistaespinhaco.com/index.php/revista/article/view/141/146. Accessed on: 19 Jun. 2025).

[114] Images show before and after of area of dams in Mariana. G1, São Paulo, 12 Nov. 2015. Available at: http://g1.globo.com/minas-gerais/noticia/2015/11/imagens-mostram-antes-e-depois-de-area-das-barragens-em-mariana.html. Accessed on: 19 Jun. 2025.

depleted its oxygen, causing mass mortality among its ichthyofauna—many of which were endemic or threatened with extinction.[115]

In the civil arena, several Terms of Commitment[116] and settlement agreements were signed with the defendant companies.[117] However, these were widely considered insufficient, as they failed to involve many of the affected parties, resulting in additional reparatory lawsuits.[118] More than half a decade after the disaster, no group of affected individuals has been fully compensated (the amount of compensation remains undetermined), the village of Bento Rodrigues has not been rebuilt, and the environment remains unrecovered.[119] Only in October 2024 did Brazilian Federal Government, through the Attorney General's Office (AGU), sign a comprehensive judicial settlement with the defendant companies for the full and final reparation of damages caused by the collapse of the Fundão dam. The agreement includes the removal of nine million cubic meters of waste from reservoirs and a staggered payment of R$ 100 billion (Brazilian reais), to be used for victim compensation and environmental restoration of the affected areas.[120]

---

[115] DRUMMOND, Gláucia Moreira; SUBIRÁ, Rosana Junqueira; MARTINS, Cássio Soares (2021) Red Book of the aquatic biota of the Rio Doce threatened with extinction post Fundão dam rupture: Mariana, Minas Gerais: crustaceans, ephemeroptera, odonata and fish. 1. ed. Belo Horizonte: Biodiversitas Foundation. Available at: https://biodiversitas.org.br/wp-content/uploads/2021/08/Livro_Vermelho_Biodiversitas_Renova_Rio-Doce.pdf. Accessed on: 19 Jun. 2025.

[116] The first ones were established in November 2015. The first, Preliminary Socio-environmental Commitment Term, was signed in the State of Espírito Santo, between the Federal Public Prosecutor's Office/Espírito Santo, Labour (MPT), the State of Espírito Santo (MPES) and Samarco Mining S.A., urgently, in order to safeguard the rights of the people involved, protect evidence and present immediate measures to mitigate the socio-environmental impact. The second, Preliminary Commitment Term, signed by Samarco Mining S.A., at the initiative of the Federal Public Prosecutor's Office/Minas Gerais and the Public Prosecutor's Office of Minas Gerais, established a security deposit of one billion reais to safeguard the means to repair the damage caused by the disaster in the State (AZEVEDO, E. M. de; FARIA JÚNIOR, A. C. de (2021) The Samarco case disaster-crime: the five-year balance of corporate environmental criminal responsibility. Journal of the Federal University of Minas Gerais, Belo Horizonte, v. 27, n. 2, p. 616–645).

[117] Link: http://www.mpf.mp.br/grandes-casos/caso-samarco/atuacao-do-mpf/atuacao-na-1a-instancia/acordos, accessed on: 22 Jun. 2025.

[118] Among the existing agreement execution actions, the Public Prosecutor's Office of Mariana advocated for the segmentation of the liquidation and execution of the sentence, prioritising the compensation of the direct victims of the disaster (proc. n° 0400.15.004335-6, 2nd Court of the District of Mariana/MG. Link: https://www.conjur.com.br/dl/mariana-mp.pdf. Accessed on: 22 Jun. 2025).

[119] Link: http://www.mpf.mp.br/mg/sala-de-imprensa/noticias-mg/caso-samarco-cinco-anos-de-uma-tragedia-sem-fim. Accessed on: 18 Jun. 2025.

[120] Judicial agreement for full and definitive reparation related to the rupture of the Fundão dam. Available at: https://www.samarco.com/wp-content/uploads/2024/10/Repactuacao-TTAC-Mariana.pdf. Accessed on: 8 Dec. 2024.

In addition to civil proceedings, the Federal Public Prosecutor's Office (MPF)[121] filed the principal public criminal action[122] in October 2016 indicting 21 individuals and four legal entities (Samarco Mineração S.A., Vale S.A., BHP Billiton Brasil LTDA, and VOGBR Recursos Hídricos) for violations of environmental[123] and criminal law.[124] It is worth noting that the most serious environmental offense, under Article 69-A of Law No. 9.605/1998, carries a penalty of 3 to 6 years of imprisonment, plus a fine.[125]

In 2019, The Federal Regional Court of the 1st Region (TRF-1) granted a habeas corpus[126] petition filed by one of the defendants, ruling that the charges of 19 counts of homicide (with eventual intent) and three cases of grievous bodily harm could not proceed. The ruling was extended to all individual defendants in the case. The Court held that the deaths and injuries, as described in the indictment, were consequences of the crime of flooding (a public danger offense) and thus did not allow for the characterization of homicide, since the victims were indeterminate and not individually targeted.[127]

---

[121] The action n° 0023863-07.2016.4.01.3800, in progress at the 12th Federal Court of Belo Horizonte/MG, is against the Union, the states of Minas Gerais and Espírito Santo, in addition to the companies Samarco Mining S.A, Vale S/A and BHP Billiton Brasil Ltda. The value of the case is estimated at 155 billion reais (Link: http://www.mpf.mp.br/mg/sala-de-imprensa/docs/acp-samarco. Accessed on: 19 Jun. 2025).

[122] Before the indictment, in November 2015, the Federal Public Prosecutor's Office and the Public Prosecutor's Office of Minas Gerais signed a Preliminary Commitment Term with the company Samarco, setting a socio-environmental security deposit of 1 billion reais, in order to guarantee the funding of minimum preventive emergency, mitigating, repairing or compensatory measures.

[123] From the Environmental Crimes Law (Law 9.605/98), the indictment (no. 0002725-15.2016.4.01.3822, in progress at the Federal Court of the District of Ponte Nova/MG) pointed out the crimes of qualified pollution, against fauna, flora, urban planning and cultural heritage, against environmental administration. The Public Ministry also pointed out the crime of preparing and presenting a false or misleading stability declaration and of omission of information in the Annual Mining Report (BRAZIL. Federal Public Ministry. Samarco Indictment. Belo Horizonte: MPF/MG, 2016b. Available at: http://www.mpf.mp.br/mg/sala-de-imprensa/docs/denuncia-samarco. Accessed: 8 Apr. 2025).

[124] The indictment includes the crimes of qualified homicide with eventual intent, flooding, collapse and serious bodily injuries. (BRAZIL. Federal Public Ministry. Samarco Indictment. Belo Horizonte: MPF/MG, 2016b. Available at: http://www.mpf.mp.br/mg/sala-de-imprensa/docs/denuncia-samarco. Accessed: 8 Apr. 2025).

[125] Law 9.605/98: Art. 69-A. To prepare or present, in licensing, forest concession or any other administrative procedure, a study, report or environmental report that is totally or partially false or misleading, including by omission: Penalty—imprisonment, from 3 (three) to 6 (six) years, and fine.

[126] HC 1033377-47.2018.4.01.0000, TRF-1, 4th Chamber, Federal Judge Olindo Menezes, judged on 23 April 2019. Available at: https://politica.estadao.com.br/blogs/fausto-macedo/wp-content/uploads/sites/41/2019/04/Aco%CC%81rda%CC%83o-HC-MARIANA.pdf. Accessed: 24 Jun. 2025.

[127] The Federal Court also points out in the ruling that "The indictment did not describe the volitional element of the homicide, essential to the configuration of the intent, eventual or direct, which would be more imposed as it describes only a common danger crime. As one mistake attracts another, it described the material causality of the deaths (consequence of the flooding by the mud

Of the 21 individuals originally charged, eight remained accused of specific offenses under Articles 254 (flooding), 256 (collapse) —both in their qualified forms—and Article 258 of the Brazilian Penal Code, along with 12 additional environmental crimes under Law No. 9.605/1998.[128] However, the proceedings moved slowly, raising concerns within the MPF over the potential statute of limitations.[129]

Ultimately, in November 2024, the Federal Court in Ponte Nova (MG) acquitted all defendants—both corporate entities and individuals—in the criminal case regarding the Mariana dam collapse. The Court found no causal link between the individual conduct of the defendants and the resulting harm and determined that there was no intent or negligence in the planning and reporting necessary for the dam's operation and regulatory approval.[130] The justice system, therefore, failed to establish criminal liability.

A second disaster struck Brazil just over 3 years later. On 25 January 2019, Dam I at the Córrego do Feijão Mine in Brumadinho (MG) collapsed, releasing 13 million cubic meters of mining waste. Although the volume was smaller than in the Mariana case, the denser physical properties of the waste led to the deaths of 270 people, including employees of Vale S.A. and the German company Tüv Süd.[131]

This event—considered the largest occupational accident in Brazil's history[132]—confronted public authorities (state and federal prosecutors, public defenders, and

of waste) without describing at what point the intention of the patient or another defendant to kill or cause bodily injury would reside". (HC 1033377-47.2018.4.01.0000, TRF-1, 4th Chamber, Federal Judge Olindo Menezes, judged on 23 April 2019).

[128] Criminal Action no. 0002725-15.2016.4.01.3822, in progress at the Federal Court of the District of Ponte Nova/MG.

[129] MPF, ID 440164918, proc. no. 0002725-15.2016.4.01.3822: "Having more than 4 years passed since the receipt of the indictment referring to the largest socio-environmental crime in the country, on 16.11.2016, and it not having been possible, to date, to overcome the instructional stage of the criminal procedure, the MPF identifies a real and concrete risk that some crimes charged in the indictment are on the verge of being hit by the institute of prescription, according to the rules brought by item V, of art. 109, of the Penal Code. Despite this D. Court having ordered the resumption of the procedural instruction at the beginning of 2020, with the designation of hearings for the testimonies of the defence, the advent of the COVID-19 pandemic meant that only 2 (two), of the 141 (one hundred and forty-one) witnesses listed (according to the Court's count), were heard in the year that ended".

[130] The accusatory body claimed that the "Declaration of Stability pertaining to the Fundão dam" report was false (misleading), a document issued shortly before the disaster, a necessary periodical for the dam's regularisation. The Federal Court of Minas Gerais understood that "the document should be understood as a 'snapshot' indicative of the dam's situation (stable or not) at the time it was drawn up, it being certain that numerous circumstances arising subsequently can substantially alter the safety conditions, especially given the dynamism and complexity of such a type of construction" (BRASIL. Federal Court. Acquittal sentence. Proc. no. 0002725-15.2016.4.01.3822, Federal Court of Ponte Nova/MG, 14 Nov. 2024. Available at: https://www.conjur.com.br/wp-content/uploads/2024/11/sentenca-absolvicao-Samarco-Mariana.pdf. Accessed on: 8 Dec. 2024).

[131] Indictment Public Prosecutor's Office of the State of Minas Gerais, proc. no. 0003237-65.2019.8.13.0090, in progress at the 2nd Court of the District of Brumadinho/MG.

[132] In the technical sense of Convention no. 174 of the International Labour Organisation (SILVA, Mariano Andrade da et al. Overlap of risks and impacts in the Vale disaster in Brumadinho. Sci. Cult., São Paulo, v. 72, n. 2, p. 21–28, Apr. 2020).

victims' associations), the companies involved, and the judiciary with unprecedented legal challenges. Like Mariana, it exposed significant legal gaps in managing cases involving multiple actors, large-scale environmental harm, and an indefinite number of victims. Despite the experience—both successful and flawed—gained from the 2015 disaster, procedural errors were repeated.

In the civil domain, numerous precautionary actions,[133] class actions,[134] and public civil lawsuits were filed seeking compensation for both environmental damage—natural and artificial—as well as loss of life.[135]

In July 2019, the 6th Public Treasury Court of Belo Horizonte/MG ruled jointly on two environmental actions—one precautionary and one public civil action—ordering Vale S.A. to fully repair all damages resulting from the collapse of the Córrego do Feijão iron ore tailings dam in Brumadinho maintaining the freeze of R$ 11 billion in assets, the court noted at the time that further investigation was still required to determine the full extent of human and environmental damages.

A new global agreement was signed in February 2021[136] for full compensation, amounting to nearly R$ 38 billion reais. The settlement also provided for the termination of legal proceedings related to the socio-environmental damages caused by the rupture, as well as those concerning socio-economic compensation for *lato* sensu collective and indivisible homogeneous individual damages.

In the criminal field, the Public Prosecutor adopted a strategy similar to that used in the Mariana case. In January 2020, the State Prosecutor's Office of Minas Gerais filed charges against 18 defendants, including two legal entities (Vale S.A. and Tüv Süd Bureau of Projects and Consultancy Ltd). The natural persons were charged with the crimes (270) of qualified homicide (committed by means resulting in common danger and in a manner that hindered or prevented the victims' defense, pursuant to Article 121, § 2°, items III and IV, of the Brazilian Penal Code), in addition to

[133] One of the first precautionary measures reached an agreement, still in 2019, guaranteeing the payment of 1 minimum wage to each resident of the city of Brumadinho, for a period of 1 year, as maintenance income (proc. no. 5010709-36.2019.8.13.0024, in progress at the 6th Public Treasury Court of Belo Horizonte/MG).

[134] Among the popular actions, the Superior Court of Justice (STJ) established jurisdiction in the Federal Court of Minas Gerais, in detriment of another action in progress in Campinas (SP), of the process that requests, among others, the blocking of Vale's financial assets of 4 billion reais (Popular action no. 1001868-13.2019.4.01.3800, 17th Federal Court of the Judicial Section of the State of Minas Gerais. At the STJ, Conflict of Jurisdiction no. 164362, Rel. Min. Herman Benjamin, judgement 22/05/2019).

[135] Among the labour demands, in the main one, in progress at the 5th Labour Court of Betim/MG, the court of first instance condemned, in June 2021, Vale to the payment of R$ 1 million reais as moral damage for each worker killed in the disaster. Vale appealed. (Proc. no. 0010165–84.2021.5.03.0027, in Progress at the Regional Labour Court of the 3rd Region).

[136] The agreement was sealed at the Judicial Centre for Conflict Resolution and Citizenship of the Second Degree, of the Court of Justice of Minas Gerais, in continuation of the joint decision of July 2019 (Link: https://www.mg.gov.br/sites/default/files/geral/ata_acordo_vale_04-02-2021_1.pdf, accessed on: 10 Apr. 2025).

environmental crimes against fauna,[137] flora,[138] and the crime of pollution.[139] The legal entities were charged with environmental crimes.

At first glance, two critical issues stand out in the indictment: the inclusion of homicide charges and the jurisdictional competence to hear the case.

Regarding the first point, the formulation of homicide charges repeated the same error found in the complaint from the Mariana case, which was later rejected by the TRF-1 in April 2019. The absence of a thorough examination of the mental element—*mens rea*—even under the theory of *dolus eventualis* (indirect intent)—undermines the initial complaint. It imputes the same supposed *animus necandi* to all defendants in relation to all victims, without establishing a minimal causal nexus. If the homicide charges were excluded, the case would no longer fall within the jurisdiction of the Jury Court, which would inevitably delay the proceedings.

The second issue proved decisive for the dismissal of the complaint. The Superior Court of Justice (STJ), ruling on an appeal in habeas corpus (HC)[140] filed by one of the defendants, held that the 2nd State Court in Minas Gerais lacked jurisdiction, as the case clearly involved a direct and specific interest of a federal regulatory agency and the Union, and entailed environmental damage to archaeological sites—thus falling under federal jurisdiction.[141]

As a result of the habeas corpus ruling, all proceedings before the 2nd Brumadinho Court were declared null, and the case was remanded to the Federal Public Prosecutor's Office for the filing of a new complaint. Once again, the statute of limitations—particularly for the environmental offenses charged against the corporations—looms large.

The temporal—and physical—proximity between the two Brazilian disasters is revealing, as are the legal outcomes observed thus far. Both events, Mariana and Brumadinho, occurred in similar contexts and involved the same corporate actors. Together, they illustrate institutional fragility in handling complex, large-scale cases: persistent procedural and strategic errors, poor judicial coordination,

---

[137] Art. 38, art. 38-A, art. 40 and art. 48, these combined with art. 53, clause I, of Law no. 9.605/1998.

[138] Art. 54, § 2°, clause III, of Law no. 9.605/1998.

[139] Art. 13, § 2°, items "a", "b" and "c", combined with art. 18, clause I, *in fine*, and with art. 29, all of the Penal Code and combined with art. 2 of Law no. 9.605/1998.

[140] RHC 151.405—MG (2021/0228782-1), Rel. Min. Olindo Menezes (Judge Appointed from TRF-1), judged on 19 Oct. 2021.

[141] The search for accountability for the deaths of 270 people and environmental damage is based on the practice of an act whose origin is the provision of false documents, leading the National Mining Agency (ANM) to the wrong conclusion about safety standards for tailings dams in Brumadinho. Although the indictment does not include the crimes of document and ideological falsity (since the prosecutors understood they were absorbed by the crime of homicide), the link with federal interests is clear (Summary 122 of the STJ), to the point of being evaluated even in the strict parameters of a HC (Judgement RHC 151.405—MG, Rel. Min. Olindo Menezes [Judge Appointed from TRF-1], judged on 19 Oct. 2021 Available at: https://processo.stj.jus.br/processo/revista/documento/mediado/?componente=ATC&sequencial=136206970&num_registro=202102287821&data=20211112&tipo=5&formato=PDF, accessed on 10 Apr. 2025).

leniency towards defendant companies, and inadequate compliance practices (Fernandes, 2020, pp. 231–246).

The weakness of the legal framework for addressing massive environmental destruction is also evident. While Brazil's Environmental Crimes Law is relatively comprehensive and reflects the will of the constitutional legislator,[142] by encompassing a wide range of conduct, its penalties are negligible in the face of large-scale disasters. This facilitates the expiration of the statute of limitations, especially in complex cases requiring extensive time for investigation, multiple parties, expert reports, and voluminous documentation.

Moreover, there is currently no crime under Brazilian law that fully encompasses the level of destruction observed, highlighting a normative gap. The Mariana and Brumadinho disasters spurred the introduction of Bill No. 2787/2019, now under consideration in the National Congress. The proposed bill creates two new criminal offenses: causing dam collapse and ecocide. In theory, therefore, under the principle of specialty, incidents such as those in Minas Gerais would not currently be classified as ecocide in Brazil, but rather as dam-related crimes.

When environmental destruction is linked to climate change, a new and innovative approach is emerging both nationally and internationally: climate litigation. This strategy seeks to hold companies accountable for contributing to global warming, particularly those involved in the production and emission of greenhouse gases.

This is the subject of the next chapter.

References

Abboud, A. (2017). In re agent Orange product liability litigation (1979–1984). Embryo project encyclopedia.

Ahmed, N. (2018). Proof of ecocide: Towards a forensic practice for the proposed international crime against the environment. *Archaeological and Environmental Forensic Science, 1*(2), 139–147.

Ahmed, K., Gayle, D., & Mousa, A. (2024). 'Ecocide in Gaza': Does scale of environmental destruction amount to a war crime? The Guardian, 29 Mar. 2024. Available at: https://www.theguardian.com/environment/2024/mar/29/gaza-israel-palestinian-war-ecocide-environmental-destruction-pollution-rome-statute-war-crimes-aoe. Accessed on December 7, 2024.

Albuquerque, D. (2022). The 10 largest countries in the world. SoCientífica Blog, 17 Aug. 2022. Available at: https://socientifica.com.br/os-10-maiores-paises-do-mundo/. Accessed on March 18, 2025.

Antunes, P. d. B. (2020). International environmental law: Particularities. *Paths of Law: Environmental Law and Sustainable Development, 17*(37), 263–294.

Azevedo, E. M. d., & Faria Júnior, A. C. d. (2021). The Samarco case disaster-crime: The five-year balance of corporate environmental criminal responsibility. *Journal of the Federal University of Minas Gerais, Belo Horizonte, 27*(2), 616–645.

[142] In addition to determining that the ecologically balanced environment is a common good of the people, the Federal Constitution assigns to the Public Power and the community various duties, according to art. 255. In addition, it allows for the criminal punishment of the legal entity, according to § 3° of the same article.

Bellivier, F., Eudes, M., & Fouchard, I. (2018). *Law of international crimes*. Themis Droit.
Brochado Neto, D. A., & Mont'alverne, T. C. F. (2020). Massive environmental damage: a crime in war, but not in peacetime? Intergovernmental organisations and the next step in global environmental governance. *Scienza e Pace, XI*(2), 37–55. Available at: https://scienzaepace.unipi.it/index.php/it/call-for-papers/item/download/430_e5761931728ba84456238f2abebf5ac7.html. Accessed on March 10, 2025
Brown, C. T., & Okogbule, N. S. (2020). Redressing harmful environmental practices in the Nigerian petroleum industry through the criminal justice approach. *Journal of Sustainable Development Law and Policy, 11*(1), 18–55.
Cranston, C. (2019). The US military's environmental protection efforts: Unexpected eco-friendly solutions to land management problems. *Boston College Law Review, 60*, 1023–1072.
Crook, M., & Short, D. (2014). Marx, Lemkin and the genocide—ecocide nexus. *The International Journal of Human Rights, 18*(3), 298–319.
Cucolo, E. (2016). Vale buys Canadian company and becomes 2nd largest in the world. G1, São Paulo, 27 Dec. 2016. Available at: http://g1.globo.com/Noticias/Economia_Negocios/0,,AA1322545-9356,00.html. Accessed on June 19, 2025.
Cusato, E. (2018). From ecocide to voluntary remediation projects: Legal responses to environmental warfare in Vietnam and the spectre of colonialism. *Melbourne Journal of International Law, 19*(2), 494–520.
Dias, C. A. et al. (2018). Impacts of the Mariana dam break on the water quality of the Doce River. Revista Espinhaço. Available at: http://www.revistaespinhaco.com/index.php/revista/article/view/141/146. Accessed on June 19, 2025.
Dickson, J. D. (2019). *The honour and dishonour of the crown: Making sense of aboriginal law in Canada*. Purich Publishing.
Drummond, G. M., Subirá, R. J., & Martins, C. S. (2021). Red book of the aquatic biota of the Rio Doce threatened with extinction post Fundão dam rupture: Mariana, Minas Gerais: Crustaceans, ephemeroptera, odonata and fish. (1st ed.). Belo Horizonte: Biodiversitas Foundation. Available at: https://biodiversitas.org.br/wp-content/uploads/2021/08/Livro_Vermelho_Biodiversitas_Renova_Rio-Doce.pdf. Accessed on June 19, 2025.
Duiunova, T., et al. (2024). International humanitarian law and ecocide: The war in Ukraine as a case study. *European Journal of Environmental Sciences, 14*(1), 14–23.
Falk, R. (1973). Environmental warfare and ecocide. Facts, appraisal and proposal. *Bulletin of Peace Proposals, 4*(1), 80–96.
Falk, R. A. (1975). The global environment and international law: Challenge and response. *Kansas Law Review*, 23.
Federal Government of Brazil. (2019). National water and sanitation agency. Annual Dam Safety Report. Brasília.
Fernandes, G. L. (2020). *Mariana and Brumadinho: Why didn't compliance practices prevent those tragedies? Compliance and sustainability: Brazilian and Portuguese perspectives* (pp. 231–246). Legal Institute.
Fonseca, F. E. (2007). The convergence between environmental protection and the protection of the human person in the scope of international law. *Brazilian Journal of International Politics, 50*, 121–138.
Galston, A. W. (2001). Plant biology: Retrospect and prospect. *Current Science*, 143–152.
Greene, A. (2018). The campaign to make ecocide an international crime: Quixotic quest or moral imperative? *Fordham Environmental Law Review, 30*, 1.
Han, X. (2011). ATCA as an avenue of overseas environmental protection and its implication to China's overseas investors. *Frontiers of Law in China, 6*(2), 219–240.
Hansen, J. C. (1981). The Vietnam veteran vs. agent Orange: The war that lingers. *The Government Accountability Office Review, 16*, 29–36.
Heischmidt, C. M. (2010). China's dumping ground: Genocide through nuclear ecocide in Tibet. *Penn State Environmental Law Review, 18*(2), 213–233.

Houck, O. A. (2017). Noah's second voyage: The rights of nature as law. *Tulane Environmental Law Journal, 31*(1), 1–50.

Johnstone, L. C. (1971). Ecocide and the Geneva protocol. *Foreign Affairs, 49*(4), 711–720.

Lambooy, T., & Rancourt, M.-E. (2008). Shell in Nigeria: From human rights abuse to corporate social responsibility. *Human Rights & International Legal Discourse, 2*, 229.

Lay, B., et al. (2015). Timely and necessary: Ecocide law as urgent and emerging. *The Journal Jurisprudence, 28*, 433.

Leahy, S. (2019). This is the world's most destructive oil operation—and it's growing. National Geographic, Alberta, 11 Apr. 2019. Available at: https://www.nationalgeographic.com/environment/article/alberta-canadas-tar-sands-is-growing-but-indigenous-people-fight-back. Accessed on January 17, 2025.

Lynch, M. J., Stretesky, P. B., & Long, M. A. (2016). A proposal for the political economy of green criminology: Capitalism and the case of the Alberta Tar Sands. *Canadian Journal of Criminology and Criminal Justice, 58*(2), 137–160.

Malhotra, S. (2017). The international crime that could have been but never was: An English school perspective on the ecocide law. *Amsterdam Law Forum, 9*(3), 49–70.

Maloney, M. (2016). Building an alternative jurisprudence for the earth: The international rights of nature tribunal. *Vermont Law Review, 41*(1), 129–142.

Martins, B. S. (2021). Revisiting the Bhopal disaster. In B. D. S. Santos & B. S. Martins (Eds.), *The Pluriverse of human rights: The diversity of struggles for dignity*. Routledge.

Moltó, J. E. E. (2016). The close interdependence between transnational corporations criminality and human rights and environmental international law violations: Bhopal case lessons. *Electronic Journal of International Studies, 32*.

Morimoto, T. (2005). Growing industrialization and our damaged planet-the extraterritorial application of developed countries' domestic environmental Laws to transnational corporations abroad. *Utrecht L. Rev., 1*, 134.

Mwanza, R. (2018). Enhancing accountability for environmental damage under international law: Ecocide as a legal fulfilment of ecological integrity. *Melbourne Journal of International Law, 19*(2), 586–613.

Parrish, A. L. (2005). Trail smelter déjà vu: Extraterritoriality, international environmental law, and the search for solutions to Canadian-US transboundary water pollution disputes. *Boston University Law Review, 85*, 363.

Pereira, R. (2020). *After the ICC Office of the Prosecutor's 2016 policy paper on case selection and prioritisation: Towards an international crime of ecocide? Criminal law forum* (Vol. 31, pp. 179–224). Springer.

Raoul, E. (2010a). Under the bituminous sands of Canada. Le monde Diplomatique, São Paulo, 1st of April 2010. Available at: http://diplomatique.org.br/sob-as-areias-betuminosas-do-canada/. Accessed on March 10, 2025.

Raoul, E. (2010b) Under the bituminous sands of Canada. Le monde Diplomatique, São Paulo, 1st of April 2010. Available at: http://diplomatique.org.br/sob-as-areias-betuminosas-do-canada/. Accessed on February 20, 2018.

Roberts, A. (2005). The agent orange case: Vietnam Ass'n for Victims of Agent Orange/Dioxin v. Dow Chemical Co. American Society of International Law. (Vol. 99, p. 387). Available at: http://www.jstor.org/stable/25660031. Accessed on January 2, 2022.

Sampaio, J. A. L., & Costa, B. S. (2015). The complicated interrelationships between the internal and international systems of protection of the right to a healthy environment. *International Law Review, Brasília, 12*(2), 785–803.

Santulli, C. (2013). *Introduction to international law: Formation, execution, application*. Editions Pedone.

Sarangi, S. (2002). Crimes of Bhopal and the global campaign for justice. *Social Justice, 29*(3), 47–52.

Silva, M. A. d., et al. (2020). Overlap of risks and impacts in the Vale disaster in Brumadinho. *Scientific Culture São Paulo, 72*(2), 21–28. Available at: http://cienciaecultura.bvs.br/scielo.php?script=sci_arttext&pid=S0009-67252020000200008&lng=en&nrm=iso. Accessed on November 20, 2021

Smith, T. (2012). Creating a framework for the prosecution of environmental crimes in international criminal law. In *Companion to international criminal law: Critical perspectives*. Ashgate Publishers.

Soares, M. d. O., et al. (2020). Oil spill in South Atlantic [Brazil]: Environmental and governmental disaster. *Marine Policy, v*, 115.

Sziebig, O. J. (2024). The crime of ecocide through human rights approach: The "Universal" right to a healthy environment as a driving force calling for ecocide legislation. *Acta Humana: Hungarian Centre for Human Rights Publications, 12*(2), 75–89.

Tovo, C. (2011). International criminal court of the environment: Roots, perspectives, alternatives. Group of the Progressive Alliance of Socialists & Democrats in the European Parliament.

UNICRI. (2016). Illicit pesticides, organized crime and supply chain integrity. Torino: United Nations. Available at: http://www.unicri.it/illicit-pesticides-organized-crime-and-supply-chain-integrity. Accessed on February 3, 2025.

Van Waeyenberge, A. (2017). Global law: A suitable theory to think about environmental law? *International Law Review, 14*(3).

Varella, M. D. (2017). *Public international law* (6th ed.). Saraiva.

Walters, R. (2023). Ecocide, climate criminals and the politics of bushfires. *The British Journal of Criminology, 63*(2), 283–303.

Wheeler, W. (2021). *Environment and post-soviet transformation in Kazakhstan's Aral Sea region: Sea changes*. UCL Press.

Wiest, A. (2003). *The Vietnam war 1956–1975*. Osprey Publishing.

Zierler, D. (2011). *The invention of ecocide: Agent Orange, Vietnam, and the scientists who changed the way we think about the environment*. University of Georgia Press.

Cruden, J. C., O'rourke, S., & Himmelhoch, S. D. (2016). The Deepwater Horizon oil spill litigation: proof of concept for the manual for complex litigation and the 2015 amendments to the federal rules of civil procedure. *Michigan Journal Environmental & Administrative Law, 6*, 65. 141.

Chapter 3
Climate Litigation and International Law

Of the current environmental issues, the topic of anthropogenic climate change[1] is the main problem highlighted in all international forums. Since the beginning of the industrial revolution, in the eighteenth century, man has been consuming natural resources in geometric progression, generating, as a primary product, greenhouse gases (GHG: carbon dioxide, CO2, accounting for two-third of the gases in the atmosphere, and methane, CH4) resulting from the burning of fossil fuels.

The link between the average increase in global temperature and human activity is, with each international scientific report (especially the IPCC,[2] under the United Nations), more clear. The warming of the planet disrupts natural climate systems, triggering countless disturbances to the environment: heat extremes in most inhabited regions, occurrence of heavy rain in some places, likelihood of drought and rainfall deficits in other regions; global average rise in sea level; impacts on biodiversity and ecosystems, including loss and extinction of species; acidification and decreases in oxygen levels in the oceans; health problems, livelihoods, food security, water supply, human security, and economic growth, among others.[3]

In this regard, it is estimated that human activities have caused around 1 °C of global warming above pre-industrial levels (with a likely range of 0.8 °C—1.2 °C).

[1] At the centre of climate justice is the research and understanding of inequalities associated with global warming: "*In seeking to apprehend all dimensions of vulnerability to climate change, particularly social vulnerability, the concept of climate justice contributes to developing our responsibility to face the climate emergency*" (Michelot, A. (2019). Climate justice: Facing the responsibility of climate change? International Journal of Bioethics and Science Ethics, 30(2), 17–39).

[2] "*It is unequivocal that human influence has warmed the atmosphere, ocean and land. Widespread and rapid changes in the atmosphere, ocean, cryosphere and biosphere have occurred*" (IPCC, Summary for Policymakers, 2021, p. 5).

[3] Intergovernmental Panel on Climate Change (IPCC). (2018). *Global warming of 1.5 °C. Special Report of the Intergovernmental Panel on Climate Change*. https://www.ipcc.ch/pdf/special-reports/sr15/sr15_spm_final.pdf, accessed on: 20 Jun. 2025.

D. A. Brochado Neto, *Ecocide*, https://doi.org/10.1007/978-3-032-07757-8_3

Global warming is projected to reach 1.5 °C between 2030 and 2052, the temperature stipulated by scientists as the limit to extreme climate change.[4] The latest Report was released in March 2023,[5] the same year in which there were 25 records among the 35 vital planetary signs (even higher in 2024), including extreme temperatures on the continents and the ocean surface, reduction of Arctic and Antarctic ice periods, among others (Ripple et al., 2024, pp. 812–824).

The most recent international agreement aimed at keeping the planet's average temperature within acceptable limits was designed in France, in December 2015, coming into force in November 2016: the Paris Agreement.[6] This document is the most used,[7] as a legal basis (almost) binding,[8] in the recent movement of climate litigation,[9] which seeks to question the actions of polluting countries and companies

---

[4] There is a calculated tolerance of 2 °C for the increase in average global temperature by the end of the twenty-first century, even so, considered risky, for practical effects. (Intergovernmental Panel on Climate Change (IPCC). (2018). Global warming of 1.5 °C. Special Report of the Intergovernmental Panel on Climate Change. https://www.ipcc.ch/pdf/special-reports/sr15/sr15_spm_final.pdf, p. 7).

[5] It was stated in the Report that global warming is caused by the unsustainable and unequal use of energy and land, in addition to the burning of fossil fuels; thus, climate impacts will be more extreme and comprehensive than predicted (Intergovernmental Panel on Climate Change (IPCC). (2023). Climate Change 2023: Synthesis Report. Summary for Policymakers. https://www.ipcc.ch/report/ar6/syr/downloads/report/IPCC_AR6_SYR_SPM.pdf, accessed on: 12 Dec. 2024.

[6] The Paris Agreement came into force 30 days after the ratification of at least 55 countries responsible for a minimum of 55% of global greenhouse gas emissions. Previously, the Kyoto Protocol, signed at COP-3 in Japan in 2005, sought to set objectives adapted to the capacity of each major polluter, among them the promotion of sustainable forms of agriculture, research and promotion of renewable energy sources and progressive reduction of tax incentives to the sector emitting polluting gases (Agreement affirmed at COP-3 in Japan in December 1997. Available at: https://treaties.un.org/Pages/ViewDetails.aspx?src=TREATY&mtdsg_no=XXVII-7-a&chapter=27&clang=_en. Accessed on: 20 Jun. 2025, pp. 34–35.).

[7] Other foundations/arguments of international law are sought in the United Nations Conference on the Human Environment Declaration (1972), which establishes principles and behaviours aimed at environmental protection; in the Montreal Protocol on Substances that Deplete the Ozone Layer (1987); in the Convention on Biological Diversity (1992), which points out (art. 6) general measures for conservation and sustainable use of natural resources; in the Rio Declaration on Environment and Development (1992), which provides that states have the responsibility to ensure that activities under their jurisdiction or control do not cause damage to the environment of other states or areas beyond the limits of national jurisdiction; in the very United Nations Framework Convention on Climate Change (UNFCCC, 1992); in the United Nations Declaration on the Rights of Indigenous Peoples (2007), which guarantees (art. 29) the right to conservation and protection of the environment and the productive capacity of their lands, territories and resources; in addition to the Kyoto Protocol.

[8] Through the mechanisms of Nationally Determined Contribution (NDC) and the Carbon Market.

[9] A process is considered as 'climate litigation' when used as a legal tool capable of triggering the Judiciary and extrajudicial bodies to assess, supervise, implement and enforce rights and obligations related to climate change, its causes and consequences (Hautereau-Boutonnet, Mathilde. (2018). Les procès climatiques par la « doctrine du procès climatique ». In Christel Cournil & Leandro Varison (Orgs.), Les procès climatiques: Entre le national et l'international (pp. 31–46). Paris: Pedone).

through the judiciary, at the national and international levels, approaching civil liability.

National and subnational governments articulate commitments to mitigate and adapt to climate change, especially after the ratification of international agreements,[10] through legislation, regulations, and public policies. In this way, States and their agencies become vulnerable to administrative and judicial legal challenges, which contest the commitments made and their practical application. This effect also falls on companies[11] and other institutions that do not meet their own climate change objectives.[12]

Despite there not being a consolidated doctrine of climate litigation and a still nascent transnational communication, it is possible to outline four groups of general objectives— simultaneous or not—of this type of process: reduction of greenhouse gas emissions (mitigation); reduction of vulnerability to the effects of climate change (adaptation); repair of damages suffered (losses and damages); and management of climate risks.[13]

The "climate law" is often related, in the processes, to the violation of constitutional and international rights to life, health, food, water, freedom, and family life,[14]

---

[10] "*The decentralized framework of the Paris Agreement, with its bottom-up system of NDCs supplemented by international transparency and review mechanisms, invites—and perhaps even requires—activism by domestic political constituencies to hold governments to account for achieving the objectives set out in national commitments and ratcheting these up over time*" (Peel, Jacqueline, & Osofsky, Hari M. (2020). Climate change litigation. Annual Review of Law and Social Science, 16, 21–38, p. 34).

[11] *Corporate liability and responsibility.*

[12] United Nations Environment Programme (UNEP). (2021). Global Climate Litigation Report: 2020 Status Review. https://wedocs.unep.org/bitstream/handle/20.500.11822/34818/GCLR.pdf?sequence=1&isAllowed=y, accessed on: 10 Jun. 2025.

[13] In mitigation climate litigation, plaintiffs demand from the Public Power the implementation of measures aimed at reducing GHG emissions, in order to ensure the effectiveness of reduction targets or carbon markets assumed, supervising actions to combat deforestation, measures in urban planning and environmental licensing processes. In adaptation litigation, accountability is given by risk assessment and obligation of actions necessary to combat adverse impacts. In loss and damage litigation, the aim is to hold governmental entities and major emitters accountable for damages caused due to extreme climatic events and significant changes in livelihood (e.g., melting of glaciers and their impacts on traditional peoples). Finally, risk litigation involves the consideration of climate risks in environmental licensing processes, environmental impact studies and the preparation of sectoral plans related to climate issues (such as energy and mobility). It seeks the provision of information about risks and assessment of mitigation measures, up to financial and socio-environmental support (Conectas Human Rights. (2019). Climate litigation in practice: strategies for climate litigation in Brazil.

[14] United Nations Environment Programme (UNEP). (2021). Global Climate Litigation Report: 2020 Status Review. https://wedocs.unep.org/bitstream/handle/20.500.11822/34818/GCLR.pdf?sequence=1&isAllowed=yUNITED NATIONS ENVIRONMENT PROGRAMME. Global Climate Litigation Report: 2020 Status Review. 2021, p. 19, available at: https://wedocs.unep.org/bitstream/handle/20.500.11822/34818/GCLR.pdf?sequence=1&isAllowed=y, accessed on: 10 Jun. 2025.

that is, correlating to human rights[15] (including the right to participation and environmental information).[16] However, a set of cases are identified that question climate change through the rights of nature, in the sense that these are intrinsically related to those.[17]

Despite the legal and technical framework on the causes, consequences, and projections of the impacts of climate change and the variety of types of lawsuits, a common set of difficulties permeates all cases. The most frequent questions are about the appropriate party to demand action (legitimacy); the source of rights or obligations related to the climate and the damages suffered; and the competence (forum) to judge the cause. This implies that, in most cases, climate actions are hindered by formal, legal, and practical (preliminary) issues, before delving into the merits.[18]

Climate litigation also encounters another significant obstacle: the separation of powers,[19] which limits the action of the Judiciary within the authority granted to it

[15] In this regard, the Universal Declaration of Human Rights (1948) is the international document that underpins the legal and institutional discussions, increasingly linked to climate standards, as in the case of the Cancún Agreements, adopted at COP-16 of the Framework Convention on Climate Change (2010); in the context of corporate accountability, the Guiding Principles on Business and Human Rights, approved by the UN Human Rights Council (2011); and the International Covenant on Economic, Social and Cultural Rights (1966).

[16] On this topic, the Escazú Agreement (Regional Agreement on Access to Information, Public Participation and Access to Justice in Environmental Matters in Latin America and the Caribbean, Link: https://repositorio.cepal.org/bitstream/handle/11362/43611/S1800493_pt.pdf) was signed by Brazil in 2018, with the aim of supporting the application of Principle 10 of the Declaration on Environment and Development in Latin America and the Caribbean, which establishes the rights of access to information, public participation and justice in environmental matters. The National Environmental Policy provides for the principle of participation, especially in art. 2, item X, when it states that through environmental education the citizen would effectively participate in decisions involving the environment; In Brazil, Law No. 10,650/2003 establishes public access to data and information existing in the bodies and entities of SISNAMA (Conectas Human Rights. (2019). *Climate litigation in practice: strategies for climate litigation in Brazil.*, p. 42–43).

[17] United Nations Environment Programme (UNEP). (2021). Global Climate Litigation Report: 2020 Status Review. https://wedocs.unep.org/bitstream/handle/20.500.11822/34818/GCLR.pdf?sequence=1&isAllowed=yUNITED NATIONS ENVIRONMENT PROGRAMME. Global Climate Litigation Report: 2020 Status Review. 2021, p. 19, available at: https://wedocs.unep.org/bitstream/handle/20.500.11822/34818/GCLR.pdf?sequence=1&isAllowed=y, accessed on: 10 Jun. 2025, p. 17.

[18] The doctrines of justiciability are theoretically agnostic as to the merits of the action, that is, neither the importance of the cause nor the strength of the evidence presented by the plaintiff are relevant if the claim cannot technically be heard. (United Nations Environment Programme (UNEP). (2021). Global Climate Litigation Report: 2020 Status Review. https://wedocs.unep.org/bitstream/handle/20.500.11822/34818/GCLR.pdf?sequence=1&isAllowed=yUNITED NATIONS ENVIRONMENT PROGRAMME. Global Climate Litigation Report: 2020 Status Review. 2021, p. 19, available at: https://wedocs.unep.org/bitstream/handle/20.500.11822/34818/GCLR.pdf?sequence=1&isAllowed=y, accessed on: 10 Jun. 2025, p. 37).

[19] Among the arguments that underpin the judiciary's distancing from merit decisions about the establishment of public policies, it is pointed out that "the Courts hardly represent the different segments of society, as they are usually composed of a select and highly educated group of judges

by a constitution or other laws. This is relevant when discussing in the processes the pertinence/scope of a public policy for the environment, the action/omission of the Executive in the face of climate change, or the fragility of an existing legal framework. This factor can, even if preliminary issues are overcome, result in the futility of the action, due to the legal impossibility of the request.

Lastly, among the difficulties inherent to this type of process is the construction of the causal link between the conduct and the damage. Attributing a defendant's GHG emissions to climate change in general (source attribution) and linking them to specific impacts of global warming (impact attribution)[20] is the most important task in many climate cases, especially those seeking to compel national governments to take action or hold companies accountable for their contribution to the problem.[21]

(...), judicial procedures do not constitute the most appropriate forum for debate among the different sectors of society, as such procedures have defined deadlines, usually incompatible with the time needed for maturation and deliberation on contradictory and complex interests (...), they also hinder citizen participation, as they involve the need for participants to have legal knowledge, apart from issues of active legitimacy, judicial costs (...), judges they are not technically prepared to predict the consequences of these decisions, nor do they have the necessary legitimacy to make decisions of this nature in relation to global warming" (Lameira, Vinicius. (2017). Climate Change: litigation strategies and the role of the judiciary in combating the causes and effects of global warming in the Brazilian context. Journal of the Public Prosecutor's Office of Rio de Janeiro, 64, 197, p. 82–83.

[20] The attribution of impact is a challenge for the parties, requiring the demonstration that a certain extreme weather event was caused by anthropic climate change. In the case *In re Upstream Addicks & Barker (Texas) Flood-Control Reservoirs v. USA* (Fed. Cl. 2021), the plaintiffs sued the Government after intense rains during Hurricane Harvey flooded reservoirs controlled by the United States and caused flooding on the plaintiffs' properties. Both parties cited climate change to support their arguments: the plaintiffs pointed to the amount of unusual but predictable rain, in light of climate change. The government, in turn, argued that, precisely because of this fact, climate change, extreme rains could not have been predicted. Both parties, therefore, question whether and to what extent a certain weather event can be caused or aggravated by climate change. The court decided that the flooding was predictable and that the plaintiffs were entitled to compensation (Link: https://ecf.cofc.uscourts.gov/cgi-bin/show_public_doc?2017cv9001-354-0, accessed on: 25 Jun. 2025).

[21] In the case *Juliana v. United States* (947 F.3d 1159, 9th Cir. 2020), for example, the plaintiffs submitted more than 1000 pages of expert reports, detailing the fundamental science of climate change, its observed and projected impacts, as well as the ways in which the US government and the fossil fuel industry contributed to the problem. In response, the defendants submitted hundreds of pages of their own expert reports, challenging the reliability, robustness, and validity of the plaintiffs' claims. The attribution of sources has been a major challenge in several cases, and the courts have reached varied results (United Nations Environment Programme (UNEP). (2021). Global Climate Litigation Report: 2020 Status Review. https://wedocs.unep.org/bitstream/handle/20.500.11822/34818/GCLR.pdf?sequence=1&isAllowed=yUNITED NATIONS ENVIRONMENT PROGRAMME. Global Climate Litigation Report: 2020 Status Review. 2021, p. 19, available at: https://wedocs.unep.org/bitstream/handle/20.500.11822/34818/GCLR.pdf?sequence=1&isAllowed=y, accessed on: 10 Jun. 2025, p. 44).

Despite the practical difficulties,[22] climate litigation is evolving globally and becoming increasingly recurrent,[23] especially in the last decade, with international courts more willing to overcome preliminary restrictions to, at least, analyse the merits.

An example is the case *Duarte Agostinho and others v. Portugal and 32 others*, filed in September 2020, at the European Court of Human Rights (ECHR), when six Portuguese youths[24] held 33 countries accountable for contributing to the climate crisis, with global emissions within and outside their territorial limits, without making the necessary effort to reduce them.[25] The aim is to overcome the understanding that States, due to their direct and continuous contact with the vital forces of their countries, are, in principle, better positioned than an international judge (from the ECHR, for example) to deal with issues related to the implementation/interpretation of an Agreement (such as Paris).[26] For this, it is argued that climate change is the

[22] There are broader discussions, seeking to answer the question: what constitutes "justice" in the context of climate change? "*A striking feature of the philosophical literature on climate change ethics and justice over recent years is the broad level of agreement amongst philosophers that wealthy countries bear the greatest ethical duties in terms of mitigation and adaptation. This is not to deny that significant disagreement continues in terms of specific cases, such as appropriate use of technology in climate mitigation. As noted above, there is no single universally accepted ethical justice framing in relation to climate change. Nevertheless, some influential framings such as that based on human dignity (...), and those resting on core human rights (...), arguably rest on values that are universally accepted. The more significant barriers seem to be linked to the bridge between ethical or justice principles and action* "(Van Dijk, Nicky., Linehan, Jan., & Lawrence, Peter. (2018). Introduction to the special issue: Imagining a different future, overcoming barriers to climate justice. University of Tasmania Law Review, 37(2), 1–24, p. 14).

[23] The growth in the number of lawsuits is notable since the Paris Agreement. It was estimated that there were at least 660 actions with this object in the United States, 80 in Europe (especially Anglo-Saxon), 80 in Australia, and another 230 in the world (Hautereau-Boutonnet, Mathilde. (2018). Les procès climatiques par la « doctrine du procès climatique ». In Christel Cournil & Leandro Varison (Orgs.), Les procès climatiques: Entre le national et l'international (pp. 31–46). Paris: Pedone. p. 34). In 2020, there were already over 1550 cases, with 1200 only in the United States (United Nations Environment Programme (UNEP). (2021). Global Climate Litigation Report: 2020 Status Review. https://wedocs.unep.org/bitstream/handle/20.500.11822/34818/GCLR.pdf?sequence=1&isAllowed=yUNITED NATIONS ENVIRONMENT PROGRAMME. Global Climate Litigation Report: 2020 Status Review. 2021, p. 19, available at: https://wedocs.unep.org/bitstream/handle/20.500.11822/34818/GCLR.pdf?sequence=1&isAllowed=y, accessed on: 10 Jun. 2025, p. 9).

[24] Link: https://youth4climatejustice.org/.

[25] The argument is that States should be held accountable for emissions arising from: 1) fossil fuels they export, 2) production of goods they import and 3) activities abroad of multinationals under their jurisdiction (Form and Petition submitted to the European Court of Human Rights, available at: https://youth4climatejustice.org/wp-content/uploads/2020/12/Application-form-annex.pdf, accessed on: 20 Jun. 2025).

[26] The aim is to overcome the understanding that States, due to their direct and continuous contact with the vital forces of their countries, are, in principle, better positioned than an international judge (from the ECHR, for example) to deal with issues related to the implementation/interpretation of an Agreement (Liston, Gerry. (2020). Enhancing the efficacy of climate change litigation:

greatest threat to human rights on the planet, in violation of the main legal provisions of international humanitarian law.[27]

In the latest report[28] developed by the United Nations Environment Programme (UNEP), in partnership with the Sabin Center for Climate Change Law at Columbia University, in 2023, it was concluded that climate policies are far short of what is necessary to keep global temperatures within the terms of the Paris Agreement, encouraging the search for judicial solutions. The total number of cases more than doubled since the first report, in 2017, from 884 to 2180, in 2022.

Moving forward, two cases that represented significant victories against states and companies are analysed, guiding subsequent studies and proceedings.[29] Afterwards, climate litigation is contrasted with criminal law, highlighting the difficulties of compatibility between the topics.

3.1 The Urgenda Case

The *Urgenda v. Netherlands* case is the first climate litigation of significant success on the global stage. In 2013, the Urgenda Foundation[30] and another 886 natural persons[31] filed a lawsuit against the Dutch state, in the District Court of The Hague,

---

how to resolve the 'fair share question' in the context of international human rights law. Cambridge International Law Journal, 9(2), 241–263).

[27] Form and Petition submitted to the European Court of Human Rights, available at: https://youth4climatejustice.org/wp-content/uploads/2020/12/Application-form-annex.pdf, accessed on: 20 Jun. 2025, p. 21.

[28] United Nations Environment Programme. (2023). Global Climate Litigation Report: 2023 Status Review (p. 11). https://wedocs.unep.org/bitstream/handle/20.500.11822/43008/global_climate_litigation_report_2023.pdf?sequence=1&isAllowed=y. Accessed on: 12 Dec. 2024.

[29] In addition to the cases studied here, between States and companies as defendants, other important ones are cited: *Massachusetts v. EPA* (2007), *Affaire Klimaatzaak* (2015), *Leghari v. Federation of Pakistan* (2015), *Ridhima Pandey v. Union of India and others* (2017), *Youth v. Colombia* (2018), *The elders for climate protection v. the Swiss Confederation* (2018), *The People's Climate Case v. European Union* (2019), *Our case to all and others v. the French State* (2019), *Cases Greta Thunberg, Teitiota and Torres* (2019–2020), *Earthlife Africa Johannesburg v. Ministry of Environmental Affairs and others* (2017), *Greenpeace Nordic Ass'n and Nature and Youth v. Ministry of Petroleum and Energy* (2018–2020), *Indigenous Environmental Network v. US Department of State* (2018–2019), *Native Village Of Kivalina v. Exxon Mobil Corp.* (2012), *City of New York v. BP, Chevron, Conocophillips, Exxonmobil, and Royal Dutch Shell* (2018), *Greenpeace Southeast Asia and others v. Carbon Majors* (2015–2020), *Our case to all and others v. Total* (2020), *Climate activists v. Credit Suisse and the public prosecutor* (2020), Allegation of Non-compliance with Fundamental Precept—ADPF 708/DF (2020).

[30] The Dutch Urgenda Foundation aims for a rapid transition to a sustainable society, focusing on the circular economy and exclusive use of renewable energies. Link: https://www.urgenda.nl/en/home-en/.

[31] The legitimacy of the 886 people was questioned by the Dutch state. The Court of First Instance found that the Urgenda Foundation had legitimacy in its own name, under a Dutch law that specifically allowed for collective actions brought by interest groups. The Court initially rejected the

demanding that the country fulfils its part in reducing greenhouse gas emissions (particularly CO2), between 25% and 40% compared to 1990, by the end of 2020, as its greenhouse gas emission mitigation policy was not satisfactory.

The plaintiffs based their claims on the duty of care of the Dutch state, grounded in arts. 2 and 8 of the European Convention on Human Rights,[32] art. 21 of the Dutch Constitution[33] and the general duty of care, art. 6:162, of the Dutch Civil Code.[34] Urgenda also argued that, due to the Dutch contribution to climate policy, the state wrongly exposes the international community to the risk of dangerous climate change, resulting in serious and irreversible damage to human health and the environment.[35]

The Netherlands contested, stating that it had committed to reducing GHG emissions, also based on European agreements, through appropriate climate policies, achieved by the discretionary power of the Government. Therefore, the state could not be forced by law to pursue another "climate policy", at the plaintiff's discretion.[36]

The District Court, on 26 June 2015, partially upheld Urgenda's claim. The Court considered that Urgenda could not rely on the European Convention on Human Rights, as the Foundation itself was not a direct or indirect victim of a violation of arts. 2 and 8 (under the terms of art. 34 of the Convention). It also could not directly invoke the Constitution, as art. 21 imposes a duty of care on the state in relation to the habitability of the country and the protection and improvement of the environment, but does not provide certainty about the way in which this duty of care

argument that the 886 individual applicants had legitimacy, however, due to the practical aspect, since their claims could not result in a different decision from the Urgenda case, they were accepted as part of the case, represented by the Foundation. The District Court's decision was upheld in the Court of Appeals and was not contested when the parties reached the Dutch Supreme Court (United Nations Environment Programme (UNEP). (2021). Global Climate Litigation Report: 2020 Status Review. https://wedocs.unep.org/bitstream/handle/20.500.11822/34818/GCLR.pdf?sequence=1&isAllowed=yUNITED NATIONS ENVIRONMENT PROGRAMME. Global Climate Litigation Report: 2020 Status Review. 2021, p. 19, available at: https://wedocs.unep.org/bitstream/handle/20.500.11822/34818/GCLR.pdf?sequence=1&isAllowed=y, accessed on: 10 Jun. 2025, p. 39).

[32] Right to life and right to respect for private and family life (Link: https://www.echr.coe.int/documents/convention_por.pdf)

[33] *Article 21: It shall be the concern of the authorities to keep the country habitable and to protect and improve the environment.* (Constitution of the Kingdom of the Netherlands).

[34] Dutch Civil Code, "*Article 6:162 Definition of a 'tortious act': A tortious act is regarded [as] a violation of someone else's right (entitlement) and an act or omission in violation of a duty imposed by law or of what according to unwritten law has to be regarded as proper social conduct, always as far as there was no justification for this behaviour*".

[35] District Court of The Hague, 4.1, 24/06/2015, ECLI:NL:RBDHA:2015:7196, Link: https://elaw.org/system/files/urgenda_0.pdf, accessed on: 25 Jun. 2025.

[36] District Court of The Hague, 4.2, 24/06/2015, ECLI:NL:RBDHA:2015:7196, Link: https://elaw.org/system/files/urgenda_0.pdf, accessed on: 25 Jun. 2025.

should be exercised, so that the task to be performed is covered by the government's own discretionary powers.[37]

The Court, however, accepted that the state violated its duty of care under the Dutch civil code, which requires parties to take precautionary measures to mitigate a risk situation. Even so, it considered the United Nations and European Union climate agreements, along with the principles of international law and climate science, to define the scope of the state's duty of care in relation to climate change, as reflected in national legislation.[38]

Other important points were raised in the decision. The Court declared that the implementation of adaptation measures, per se, will not satisfy the duty of care and should consider measures to mitigate GHG emissions.[39] It also rejected the state's argument that the unilateral reduction of emissions by the Netherlands meant a decrease in global emissions of less than 0.1%, therefore "irrelevant". It was established that any anthropogenic emission of greenhouse gases, no matter how small, contributes to an increase in CO2 levels in the atmosphere and, therefore, to climate change. Therefore, the state cannot exempt itself from the duty of care, and a sufficient causal relationship can be presumed between Dutch gas emissions, global climate change, and the effects, present and future, on the Dutch living climate.[40]

Finally, the Court condemned the Dutch state to limit the total volume of annual greenhouse gas emissions by at least 25% by the end of 2020 compared to the level of the year 1990.[41]

The Dutch state appealed to the Hague Court of Appeal, against the definition given by the District Court to the duty of care and the consequent conviction. In October 2018, the appeal was denied, confirming in full the first instance decision.[42]

At long last, after a new appeal, the case reached the Supreme Court of the Netherlands. The final decision was issued on 20 December 2019, with the denial of the Dutch objection.[43] In the decision, the Court highlighted that the risk of anthropogenic climate change is of a global nature, with GHG emissions not only from

[37] District Court of The Hague, 4.36 to 4.45, 24/06/2015, ECLI:NL:RBDHA:2015:7196, Link: https://elaw.org/system/files/urgenda_0.pdf, accessed on: 25 Jun. 2025.

[38] District Court of The Hague, 4.52, 24/06/2015, ECLI:NL:RBDHA:2015:7196, Link: https://elaw.org/system/files/urgenda_0.pdf, accessed on: 25 Jun. 2025.

[39] District Court of The Hague, 4.73–4.75, 24/06/2015, ECLI:NL:RBDHA:2015:7196, Link: https://elaw.org/system/files/urgenda_0.pdf, accessed on: 25 Jun. 2025.

[40] District Court of The Hague, 4.79–4.90, 24/06/2015, ECLI:NL:RBDHA:2015:7196, Link: https://elaw.org/system/files/urgenda_0.pdf, accessed on: 25 Jun. 2025.

[41] District Court of The Hague, 5.1, 24/06/2015, ECLI:NL:RBDHA:2015:7196, Link: https://elaw.org/system/files/urgenda_0.pdf, accessed on: 25 Jun. 2025.

[42] Court of Appeal of The Hague, 09/10/2018, ECLI:NL:GHDHA:2018:2610, Link: https://www.urgenda.nl/wp-content/uploads/ECLI_NL_GHDHA_2018_2610.pdf, accessed on: 25 Jun. 2025.

[43] "*The Supreme Court concludes that the State's appeal in cassation must be rejected. That means that the order which the District Court issued to the State and which was confirmed by the Court of Appeal, directing the State to reduce greenhouse gases by the end of 2020 by at least 25% compared to 1990, will stand as a final order*" (Supreme Court of the Netherlands, *Opinion of the Supreme Court*, 20/12/2019, ECLI:NL:HR:2019:2007, Link: https://www.urgenda.nl/wp-content/

Dutch territory, but from all over the world, with consequences experienced also across the planet. The Netherlands, as part of the United Nations Framework Convention on Climate Change (UNFCCC), committed to maintaining the concentration of greenhouse gases in the atmosphere at a safe level. The UNFCCC is based on the premise that all member countries must take measures, according to their responsibilities and specific options. Each country is, therefore, responsible for its share. This means that a country cannot escape from its share of responsibility under the argument that, compared to the rest of the world, its own emissions are relatively limited in scope and that a reduction would have negligible impact on a global scale. The State is, therefore, obliged to reduce GHG emissions from its territory in proportion to its share of responsibility.[44]

Within this state duty, the Supreme Court sought to define what it means to "do its part", considering the obligations assumed internationally. For this, it reinforced the scientific understanding, widely supported and accepted in the world, embodied, especially, in the IPCC reports.[45] The Dutch state, in turn, was unable to demonstrate that the proposal to accelerate the reduction of emissions after 2020 would be viable and sufficiently effective to meet the targets for 2030 and 2050 and, thus, keep the targets of 2 °C and 1.5 °C average global temperature within reach.[46] Hence, the correctness of the lower courts in determining the reduction of emissions by at least 25% by the end of 2020, leaving it up to the State to choose the measures necessary to comply with the conviction.[47]

Following this decision, the number of articles, papers, and processes on climate litigation multiplied,[48] with a growing diversity of interdisciplinary

---

uploads/ENG-Dutch-Supreme-Court-Urgenda-v-Netherlands-20-12-2019.pdf, accessed on: 25 Jun. 2025).

[44] Supreme Court of the Netherlands, 20/12/2019, *Global problem and national responsibility,* ECLI:NL:HR:2019:2007, Link: https://www.urgenda.nl/wp-content/uploads/ENG-Dutch-Supreme-Court-Urgenda-v-Netherlands-20-12-2019.pdf, accessed on: 25 Jun. 2025.

[45] "*At the annual climate conferences held in the context of the UNFCCC since 2007, virtually every country has regularly pointed out the necessity of acting in accordance with the scenario of the IPCC and achieving a 25–40% reduction of greenhouse gas emissions in 2020. The scientifically supported necessity of reducing emissions by 30% in 2020 compared to 1990 has been expressed on multiple occasions by and in the EU*" (Supreme Court of the Netherlands, 20/12/2019, *What, specifically, does the State's obligation to do 'its part' entail?,* ECLI:NL:HR:2019:2007, Link: https://www.urgenda.nl/wp-content/uploads/ENG-Dutch-Supreme-Court-Urgenda-v-Netherlands-20-12-2019.pdf, accessed on: 25 Jun. 2025).

[46] Supreme Court of the Netherlands, 20/12/2019, *The policy of the State,* ECLI:NL:HR:2019:2007, Link: https://www.urgenda.nl/wp-content/uploads/ENG-Dutch-Supreme-Court-Urgenda-v-Netherlands-20-12-2019.pdf, accessed on: 25 Jun. 2025.

[47] Thus, the Dutch Supreme Court avoids the discussion about disrespect for the separation of powers (Supreme Court of the Netherlands, 20/12/2019, *The courts and the political domain*, ECLI:NL:HR:2019:2007, Link: https://www.urgenda.nl/wp-content/uploads/ENG-Dutch-Supreme-Court-Urgenda-v-Netherlands-20-12-2019.pdf, accessed on: 25 Jun. 2025).

[48] "*The court's decision immediately made headlines around the world. It's worth stating upfront: it surprised the legal community, who were torn between tension and admiration10. But it also sparked emulation and enthusiasm in many countries. Legal actions increased significantly follow-*

perspectives—extending beyond the legal studies niche to the broader social sciences, involving an ever-increasing range of actors in litigation (moving away from previous models of actions, exclusively individual or through non-governmental organizations against governments) (Peel & Osofsky, 2020, pp. 21–38).

It also became clear that one of the greatest difficulties, within the litigation, concerns the individualization of the State's responsibility in relation to human rights, but also in a broader context, characterized by the need for a global response, on a planetary scale, in terms of the decision of the Supreme Court of the Netherlands, when stating that it is incumbent on Dutch public authorities to do "their part".[49] The "drop in the ocean" argument was, therefore, rejected.[50]

The Urgenda case was the first where a Court demanded a State to reduce GHG emissions, contrary to the majority of jurisdictions and legal traditions, whose difficulties in proving causality prevented the progress of civil liability litigation from the beginning, not even entering the merits (Lin, 2015, pp. 65–81).

It should be noted that the decision in Urgenda was significantly based on the understanding of the obligations internationally assumed by the Dutch state, in relation to climate change. This means that the argument of the action would not serve, at least in this part, countries that do not have international agreements on climate, among them, some of the largest polluters. Also, even if the approach adopted by the Dutch courts is replicated globally, it is not guaranteed that global warming global will be maintained at the 2 °C target, as this decision is based on (Liston, 2020, pp. 241–263).

Next, another case relevant to climate litigation will be analysed, this time featuring a transnational company as the defendant.

---

ing the June 2015 ruling, becoming more diverse. Urgenda created a ripple effect." (Misonne, Delphine. (2020). Netherlands v. Urgenda (2019). In C. Cournil (Ed.), The major climate cases, Confluence of rights (p. 209). International, Comparative and European Rights).

[49] Responsibility derived, firstly, from the principle of common responsibility, considering the differentiated and asymmetrical characteristics of climate governance, where the environmental project has always been intertwined with the demands for development made by countries; secondly, concurrent with the affirmation, by the States, of the role they committed to assume, in the so-called "Annex I" of the UNFCCC. Also remember the reference to "Principle 21", known as the "*no-harm principle*", from the Stockholm Declaration on the Environment (1972), elevated to the category of general principles of international law, stating that States have the sovereign right to exploit their own resources, according to their own environmental and development policies, and have the duty to ensure that activities carried out within their jurisdiction or under their control do not cause harm to the environment in other States or in areas without any national jurisdiction (Misonne, Delphine. (2020). Netherlands v. Urgenda (2019). In C. Cournil (Ed.), The major climate cases, Confluence of rights (p. 209). International, Comparative and European Rights, p. 217).

[50] "*The court in that case ruled that, in such cases of 'cumulative causation', individual parties will be held liable for their share in causing the harm and will pay a corresponding share of the damages awarded*" (Lin, Jolene. (2015). The first successful climate negligence case: A comment on Urgenda foundation v. the state of The Netherlands (Ministry of Infrastructure and the Environment). *Climate Law*, *5*(1), 65–81, p. 79).

3.2 Shell and CO2 Emissions in the Netherlands

Relying on the precedent set by the Urgenda decision, a case that exemplifies another approach to climate litigation was proposed by the environmental group *Milieudefensie* (*Friends of the Earth Netherlands*) and others[51] against the oil company *Royal Dutch Shell*. While the first exemplifies a conflict against states for lack of adequate and effective measures in the face of climate change, the second represents a dispute against private actors,[52] especially those who work with fossil fuels.[53]

Actions against private individuals are not uncommon. Before the case *Earth Netherlands (Milieudefensie) v. Royal Dutch Shell*, there was, especially in the United States, a significant number of actions linking climate change (GHG emissions) and companies.[54] However, two barriers are relevant to the success of this type of proceedings: difficulty of cognizance of the action and construction of the causation link (Canali, 2018, pp. 68–83).

In the first, the very merit of the cause ceases to be analysed, due to the low justiciability of climate issues, often associated with political decisions (raising the argument against judicial action of violation of the separation of powers), in addition to the questionable interest of private plaintiffs (almost universally recognized as the existence of an injury [*injury-in-fact*], traceable line between the injury and

---

[51] Included among the co-plaintiffs are other NGOs (*ActionAid NL, Both ENDS, Fossielvrij NL, Greenpeace NL, Young Friends of the Earth NL, Waddenvereniging*) and more than 17,379 citizens. The NGO *ActionAid NL* and the individual claimants had their claims rejected, as their operations were not aimed at Dutch citizens, their interests were already served by the collective action and they did not present independent interests (Climate Case Chart. (2019). Milieudefensie et al. v. Royal Dutch Shell plc...).

[52] The idea of suing companies for the damage caused by climate change, initially extreme, is gaining more and more ground in the courts, especially after numerous studies linking the influence of human activities to global warming. When it comes to companies, "*a small number of them have contributed significantly to past GHG emissions. Moreover, companies were aware of the scientific data on climate change. Instead of taking alternative measures to fossil fuels, some have funded studies to contest the existence of climate change*" (Canali, Laura. (2018). Climate litigation against companies: assessment and prospects. In Cournil, C., & Varison, L. (Eds.), *Climate trials between the national and the international* (pp. 68–83). Paris: A. Pedone Editions, p. 68–69).

[53] Among the research that portrays the role of multinationals in destabilising the climate, the *Carbon Majors* report is cited, pointing out that between the years of 1751 and 2010, 63.04% of GHG emissions on the planet are the responsibility of the 90 largest companies that handle fossil fuels, such as oil, natural gas, coal (Heede, Richard. (2014). Carbon Majors. Accounting for carbon and methane emissions. Methods & Results Report. Climate Mitigation Services. https://climateaccountability.org/pdf/MRR%209.1%20Apr14R.pdf. Accessed 25 Jun. 2025).

[54] Another report that associates greenhouse gas emissions with "carbon giant" companies was made in 2017, pointing out that, despite the IPCC, in 1988, pointing to the relationship between global warming and human activity, the fossil fuel industry expanded prodigiously, doubling the contribution of GHGs in the atmosphere in just 28 years, compared to the entire period prior to 1988, since the beginning of the industrial revolution (Griffin, Paul. (2017). *The carbon majors database: CDP carbon majors report 2017*. London: Carbon Disclosure Project (CDP) UK. http://www.truevaluemetrics.org/DBpdfs/Carbon/CDP/CDP-Carbon-Majors-Report-2017.pdf, accessed on: 12 jun. 2025).

the conduct [*causation*] and possibility of the damage being repaired by a judicial decision [*redressability*]).[55]

The second barrier is inherent to the complexity of the climate change topic. Once the initial procedural premises are overcome, it is rare to see secure links (evidence) constructed in the processes between the behaviour considered harmful and the damages incurred, necessary for holding a person accountable. Among the factors that complicate the burden of proof, one way to mention the spatial distance between the cause and the damage,[56] the multiple causes of global warming, and the distribution of responsibility.[57]

The case *Earth Netherlands (Milieudefensie) v.Royal Dutch Shell*[58] overcame these technical barriers, at least at first instance. The oil company received, in April 2019, a court summons from the District Court of The Hague, accusing it of its contribution to climate change and violating its duty of care under the Dutch law and human rights obligations.

The legal basis was similar to that proposed by Urgenda: seeking a reduction in CO2 emissions by 45% by 2030, on the part of the defendant, compared to 2010 levels, and to 0 by 2050, the plaintiffs to pointed alignment with the Paris Climate Agreement, violation of the duty of care, of Art. 6:162, of the Dutch Civil Code, and arts. 2 and 8 of the European Convention on Human Rights. Other important elements, pointed out by the authors, are the defendant's endorsement of the guiding principles of the United Nations on Business and Human Rights, the UN Global Compact, and the OECD guidelines for multinational companies, in addition to the

---

[55] As examples, the cases *Baker v. Carr* (369 U.S Sup. Ct. 186), *Connecticut v. American Electric Power* (406 F. Supp. 2d 265, 267), *Saul Luciano Lliuya v. RWE* (2 O 285/1520), *Massachusetts v. EPA* (49 U.S 497, 518, 2017), *Native Village of Kivalina and City of Kivalina v. Exxon Mobil Corporation* et al. (663 F. Supp. 2d 863, 883, 2009) (Canali, Laura. (2018). Climate litigation against companies: assessment and prospects. In Cournil, C., & Varison, L. (Eds.), *Climate trials between the national and the international* (pp. 68–83). Paris: A. Pedone Editions, p. 69–72).

[56] "*Unlike pollution cases, GHGs do not directly and locally affect humans and ecosystems. They start as individual emissions, before dispersing into the atmosphere. Their multiplication and accumulation warm the surface of the globe to finally trigger a long series of damages. The link between a localised source of emissions and a locally identified damage is then difficult to demonstrate*" (Canali, Laura. (2018). Climate litigation against companies: assessment and prospects. In Cournil, C., & Varison, L. (Eds.), *Climate trials between the national and the international* (pp. 68–83). Paris: A. Pedone Editions, p. 73).

[57] The indivisibility of the causal link continues to be the main reason for the impossibility of quantifying the role of the different antecedents of climate damage. The difficulty of prosecuting all the co-authors responsible for climate change, so that each one answer for its well-defined share in global warming, ends up making the repair of damages unfeasible (Canali, Laura. (2018). Climate litigation against companies: assessment and prospects. In Cournil, C., & Varison, L. (Eds.), *Climate trials between the national and the international* (pp. 68–83). Paris: A. Pedone Editions, p. 75).

[58] *Earth Netherlands (Milieudefensie) v.Royal Dutch Shell*, ECLI:NL:RBDHA:2021:5339.

preparation of misleading statements, even with Shell's long knowledge of climate change.[59]

Shell contested the process in November 2019, arguing that it does not have control over the use of its products (Scope 3),[60] and that GHG emissions derived from the burning of oil extracted by the company should not be considered as its carbon footprint. Its actual emissions would therefore be, insignificant. Nevertheless, it claimed to be taking the necessary measures to achieve the objectives of the Paris Agreement (Duthoit, 2020, p. 538).[61]

The first instance decision[62] was made on 26 May 2021. For the first time, a company was legally held responsible for climate change. Shell (both directly and through the companies and legal entities included in its annual consolidated accounts and with which it forms a group) was ordered to limit, or cause to be limited, the aggregate annual volume of all CO_2 emissions into the atmosphere (Scope 1, 2, and 3) by at least 45% net by the end of 2030, compared to 2019 levels.[63]

The Court declared that the obligation to reduce emissions arises from the standard of care applied to the company's policies, especially in relation to GHG emissions and their consequences; to human rights and to international and local legal obligations relating to climate protection.[64]

Shell appealed to the Hague Court of Appeal on 20 July 2022,[65] in November 2024, after the Court reversed the decision.[66] Despite reaffirming the company's legal duty of care to contain climate change, in accordance with the country's civil liability law, the Court annulled the judgement, removing the imposition of a specific target for emission reduction. It concluded that there is not enough scientific

---

[59] The Hague District Court, *Earth Netherlands (Milieudefensie) v.Royal Dutch Shell*, ECLI:NL:RBDHA:2021:5339, 26 May 2021, p. 22.

[60] CO_2 emissions generated by a business activity are divided into three levels, according to GHG (Greenhouse Gas Protocol, Link: https://ghgprotocol.org/): Scope 1, consisting of emissions released as a direct result of the company's operations; Scope 2, indirect emissions, arising from the electricity purchased for the company's own use; and Scope 3, covering all other indirect emissions not included in Scope 2, resulting from the activities of the organisation, but occurring from GHG sources owned or controlled by third parties, such as other organisations or consumers, including emissions from the use of crude oil and gas purchased from others.

[61] Duthoit, Louis. (2020). Milieudefensie et al. v. Shell (2019). In C. Cournil (Ed.), The great climate affairs, Confluence of rights. International, Comparative and European Rights, p. 538).

[62] The parties presented their evidence in the months of September and October 2020, followed by 4 days of hearings in December of the same year. The hearing documents can be accessed here: https://en.milieudefensie.nl/news/overview-of-legal-documents-climatecase-against-shell

[63] The Hague District Court, *Earth Netherlands (Milieudefensie) v.Royal Dutch Shell*, ECLI:NL:RBDHA:2021:5339, 26 May 2021, p. 44.

[64] The Hague District Court, *Earth Netherlands (Milieudefensie) v.Royal Dutch Shell*, ECLI:NL:RBDHA:2021:5339, 26 May 2021, p. 26.

[65] Link: https://climatecasechart.com/non-us-case/milieudefensie-et-al-v-royal-dutch-shell-plc/, accessed on: 12 Dec. 2024.

[66] Hague Court Of Appeal, 12/11/2024, ECLI:NL:GHDHA:2024:2100, Available at: https://climatecasechart.com/wp-content/uploads/non-us-case-documents/2024/20241112_8918_judgment.pdf. Accessed on: 12 Dec. 2024.

consensus on a specific reduction percentage or path that an individual company like Shell should adhere to in practice (especially for Scope 3). The case can still be taken to the Dutch Supreme Court.

Even with the turnaround in the Hague Court of Appeal, the case proved to be an important precedent in climate litigation, having the potential for global propagation of legal effects. Based on human rights standards[67] and international instruments on climate change, the decision—if corroborated by the Dutch Supreme Court, as in the Urgenda case—can serve as a basis for other ongoing actions and new proceedings. Undeniable, however, is the impact—of a dimension yet to be measured—of the second instance decision in the country, reflecting the difficulty of this type of legal action.

Nevertheless, the same restrictions described for the Urgenda case apply to this litigation or others against companies: the reasoning used in the Dutch cases cannot be automatically replicated in all countries, as the legal instruments are different; furthermore, there are no guarantees that the limitations imposed judicially will be sufficient to contain global warming.

The context of climate litigation presented was, primarily, of civil scope, more specifically of civil liability. However, even considering the gravity of the "climate change" theme, the action of the most restrictive arm of the law—the criminal law—is still timid in these cases. In the next topic, we seek to work on the theme, questioning the fight against anthropogenic global warming through the crime of ecocide.

3.3 Is There Room for Criminal Law in Climate Litigation?

There is no law or penal code on the planet that criminalizes the emission, per se, of greenhouse gases, the main driver of climate change. Therefore, obeying the principle of legality, there is no way to criminally prosecute someone directly for causing global warming. Fitting criminal law into climate litigation, therefore, is only feasible indirectly.

Even so, forms of climate litigation are being developed, especially in the United States, involving simultaneous civil and criminal demands, in the latter, under the command not of the victims or representatives, but of the State itself, through the

[67] This aspect is what finds the most resonance with international jurisdictions, since it constitutes a viable path to the connection between environmental law and human rights: "From the analysis that the environment, as a common use good, is responsible for all economic-social-cultural development of humanity, we can affirm that it is present in all dimensions of Human Rights. In this perspective, the maintenance of an ecologically balanced environment, essential for the quality of life, so that present and future generations can enjoy the economic and social benefits that its preservation brings to the life of each individual and to society as a whole is fundamental" (DO CARMO, Thaís Maria Leonel; CAMARGO, João Henrique Fagundes Prestes. The environmental dimension of human rights and the adoption of climate litigation to reduce vulnerability to climate change. Chile: Revista Inclusiones, Vol: 8 num Special. p. 38–55, 2021).

Public Prosecutor's Office (Canali, 2018, pp. 68–83). The aim of the criminal investigations is to discover how some large companies integrated their knowledge about climate change into their governance, accounting and organizational planning, to identify possible crimes, such as fraud, document falsification, disinformation campaigns, aimed at deceiving the public and investors about the scientific reality of climate change.[68]

The criminal liability of the legal person (such as oil companies), is, in itself, controversial, in national legislations. The mechanism for distributing responsibilities of natural and fictitious entities is diverse (Mongillo, 2018, p. 449), fluctuating between accumulation, alternativity, and impossibility of punishment. The exclusive sanction of the legal entity is, however, an exception, as occurs, for example, in Brazil and the United Kingdom.[69]

In the international criminal sphere, taking into account the only permanent Court, the International Criminal Court, climate litigation against companies proves more problematic to become a reality. The first restriction is inscribed in arts. 22 and 23 of the Rome Statute,[70] which make a direct reference to the principle of legality. There is no provision in the Treaty for any crime or penalty related to climate change. Second, legal entities are not prosecuted in the Court, according to art. 25 of the same document.[71]

It is important to remember another traditional principle of criminal law, also present in the Rome Statute: the principle of non-retroactivity.[72] This restriction to

[68] This type of action is not intended to hold companies accountable for repairing climate damage, but to condemn the negligent, or fraudulent, behaviour of some defendants. "One of the ongoing actions is led by the New York State prosecutor and is based on the law relating to securities fraud (Martin Act). The investigation aims to determine whether ExoonMobil has hidden studies showing the harmful role of fossil fuels for climate change and to what extent the company has funded climate-sceptic research. In parallel, several federal state prosecutors have launched the same lawsuits". (Canali, Laura. (2018). Climate litigation against companies: assessment and prospects. In Cournil, C., & Varison, L. (Eds.), *Climate trials between the national and the international* (pp. 68–83). Paris: A. Pedone Editions, p. 83).

[69] There is still debate about the need for criminal punishment of the legal entity: "The arguments about the criminal-political necessity of penalties directed against collective entities are essentially divided into two groups: 1) the gravity - in terms of entity, spread and territorial extension - of the criminal output of companies; 2) the genetic context of risk-crime, that is, the organisation itself, often saturated with criminal drives" (Mongillo, Vincenzo. (2018). *Criminal responsibility between individual and collective entity*. Turin: G. Giappichelli Publisher, p. 152).

[70] Art. 22: *Nullum crimen sine lege*—No person shall be considered criminally responsible under this Statute unless his or her conduct constitutes a crime within the jurisdiction of the Court at the time it takes place. Art. 23: *Nulla poena sine lege*—Any person convicted by the Court may only be punished in accordance with the provisions of this Statute.

[71] Art. 25: Individual Criminal Responsibility—According to this Statute, the Court shall have jurisdiction to try natural persons.

[72] Art. 24: Non-retroactivity *ratione personae*—No person shall be held criminally responsible under this Statute for conduct prior to the entry into force of the present Statute.

judicial action is especially relevant here, considering accumulation offences, such as the case of atmospheric pollution.[73]

In the case of GHG emissions, it goes back to the concentration of gases over years, since the beginning of the industrial revolution. Thus, limiting criminal prosecution to cases subsequent to the issuance of a hypothetical norm that curbs such conduct (e.g. illegal emissions of GHGs), whether at a national or international level, would be neglecting centuries of gas accumulation, which, in an insignificant/harmless way (like the use of a motor vehicle by an individual) or robust (like a coal plant in operation for decades), contributed to the worsening of CO2 concentration in the atmosphere.

The fact that it is a cumulative damage also implies other obstacles to criminal prosecution. Cumulative offences are collective action offences, meaning they consist of the sum of individual conducts that, practised by numerous agents, cause severe damage to a certain good.[74] This aspect particularly undermines the attribution of responsibilities, as, in addition to the difficulty of individualizing conducts, it challenges a fair application of sanction,[75] considering also the temporal character between the action/omission and the respective consequence (causality).[76]

The current legal reality therefore reveals the impossibility of international criminal law dealing with the phenomenon of anthropogenic climate change, leaving it to national jurisdictions to indirectly attack[77] the problem.

---

[73] "Cumulative offences comprise actions that, considered individually, do not have the power to affect the legal good, acquiring criminal relevance the accumulation of human behaviours. This means that the effective probability of their multiplication constitutes the reason for the inclusion of the figure in the legal-criminal field" (Lima, Vinicius de Melo (2009). The principle of guilt and the cumulative offences. *Journal of the Public Prosecutor's Office of Rio Grande do Sul*, 51–86, p. 54).

[74] Direct accumulation develops in two effects: summative and synergistic. The first is identified by the sum of several individual quotas resulting from simultaneous GHG emissions. The second effect relates to the combination of elements to generate a third effect, usually more harmful, such as the feedback of the global warming chain, such as the melting of the *permafrost* and the polar ice caps, factors that accelerate climate change (Caetano, Matheus Almeida (2016). *Accumulation offences in environmental criminal law*. São Paulo: Pillares, p. 219).

[75] Caetano, Matheus Almeida (2016). *Accumulation offences in environmental criminal law*. São Paulo: Pillares, p. 218.

[76] "Chronic, permanent and cumulative pollutions and degradations, resulting from various agents, lead to considerable environmental damage, however serious obstacles arise in determining the causal link. In the criminal sphere, the difficulties regarding the causal link are no different, the problems related to the space-time coefficients between the facts and the results, the gravity that some of the latter can reach in certain situations, even with irreversible effects and of global reach, as well as several factors 'often lead to insurmountable difficulties in causal determination'" (Caetano, Matheus Almeida (2016). *Accumulation offences in environmental criminal law*. São Paulo: Pillares, p. 221).

[77] A case that seemingly brings ecocide closer to climate change occurred in the district of Porong, Sidoarjo, East Java: "*The incident occurred as a result of drilling for PT. Lapindo Gas, which resulted in hot mudflows and natural gas explosions. Peak period the Lapindo mudflow has been spewing up to 180,000 m of mud per day and emitting hydrogen sulfide gas with a temperature of around 60 °C. The Netherlands Institute for Space Research in Utrecht and the Sidoarjo Mud*

The technical obstacles to the operation of criminal law on the subject, however, do not cover up the seriousness of the risk to global security from climate change. In this sense, with robust scientific backing, it is sought from international institutions the promotion and definition of planetary boundaries[78] as the object of a legal norm.

With well-drawn boundaries, it would be possible, in theory, to establish conducts against climate change that, once perpetrated, would entail the application of a criminal type.[79] A correlation with the crime of ecocide soon emerged, now existing in some countries and projected in others, as well as a proposal at the ICC.

In the current discussion for the construction of ecocide at the international level, the creation of the new crime is often argued as a response to the climate emergency.[80] Indeed, the consequences of global warming, such as extreme temperatures and, mainly, the rise in sea level, are the main flag of the island states Vanuatu and Maldives, when pleading for the inclusion of the crime before the Assembly of Parties at the ICC.[81]

Control Center (PPLS) used a combination of ground-based and satellite observations (TROPOMI) to calculate the amount of gas released into the atmosphere by the Lapindo Mudflow. According to this assessment, the total methane released by the Lapindo Mudflow reached 100,000 tons per year. Long-term consequences of this event include increased vulnerability to climate change, which causes a variety of issues such as seasonal anomalies, disruption of the hydrometeorological cycle, and natural disasters". (Aida, Melly; TAHAR, Abdul Muthalib; DAVEY, Orima (2023). Ecocide in the International Law: Integration Between Environmental Rights and International Crime and Its Implementation in Indonesia. In *3rd Universitas Lampung International Conference on Social Sciences (ULICoSS 2022)* (pp. 572–584). Atlantis Press. https://www.atlantis-press.com/article/125986377.pdf. Accessed on: 10 Jan. 2025).

[78] Planetary boundaries are understood as the establishment of references, to be considered within legal systems, mapped by studies of the processes and systems that regulate the stability and resilience of the Earth system, the interactions of the Earth, oceans, atmosphere and life, which together provide the conditions for the existence of societies. The suppression of these boundaries implies a threat to humanity and a reduction in nature's capacity to contribute to the well-being of populations (Cabanes, Valérie. (2018). Holding States and companies accountable for climate change: from planetary boundaries to the crime of ecocide. In C. Cournil & L. Varison (Org.), *Climate trials between national and international*. Pedone. P. 267–269).

[79] The studies that aim to address climate change As a criminological issue, they are in initial stages, barely raising questions such as inequality, social and ecological justice. It is necessary to situate green criminological discourse considering the harms, impacts and consequences of anthropocentric activity, instead of the exclusive focus on the penal type (legally defined), as is traditional in criminology (White, Rob. (2018). *Climate change criminology*. Bristol: Policy Press).

[80] Cozens and Stoks suggest five connections between climate change and crime: 1. Human behaviour generating climate change; 2. Crime arising from protesting against climate change; 3. Built form mitigations for climate change affect crime; 4. Consequences of climate change affect crime and; 5. Crime affects climate change (Cozens, Paul., & Stoks, Frank. (2024). Climate change and crime—exploring future risks, resilience and crime through environmental design (CPTED). Crime Prevention and Community Safety, 420–439).

[81] Thus argued the ambassador of Vanuatu to the European Union, within the Assembly of the parties of the ICC: "*The threat to our environment, and ultimately our existence as sovereign nations, is becoming ever more severe. Climate change phenomena and related impacts have continuously battered our islands over the last three or four decades, but over the past 4 years Vanuatu has*

However, existing ecocide laws, as well as draft laws, do not contemplate any conduct directly related to the subject of climate change, but indirectly.[82] They still lack a theoretical structure capable of expanding the concept of damage to include violations to the ecosystem and future generations (Pink & White, 2016, pp. 3–19). It is not questioned that the criminalization of certain actions related to anthropogenic climate change is important, on the contrary. It is crucial to identify the main culprits of global warming who, even aware of the damage and methods to mitigate them, do not do so because of the costs and profits involved.[83]

However, despite the political discourse in favour of the crime,[84] it must be admitted that the current design of ecocide prevents criminal prosecution under the theme of climate change. The use of international criminal law has the potential to affect attitudes and behaviours, stigmatizing common and tolerated behaviours. It also has the potential to signal to individuals and companies that even relatively minor decisions are socially and legally relevant (Keenan, 2019, pp. 89–112).

---

experienced disasters and related calamities of unprecedented scale. Sea level rise and other impacts of climate change are increasingly compromising our ability to achieve sustainable development in line with the SAMOA Pathway and the 2030 Agenda. We are not alone with this; societies around the world face similar challenges. Those who contributed the least to the problem are most severely affected. Science indicates that things will get worse, and catastrophic if we do not achieve the rapid and far-reaching transformations necessary to keep temperature rise below 1.5 °C". (Licht, John H. (2019). *General Debate of the 18th Session of the Assembly of States Parties to the Rome Statute of the International Criminal Court*. The Hague, 7 Dec 2019. https://asp.icc-cpi.int/iccdocs/asp_docs/ASP18/GD.VAN.2.12.pdf, accessed on: 28 Jun. 2025).

[82] For example, the statement of Art. 358 of the Russian Penal Code (1996, with Amendment of 2012), reiterated in the legislation of the other ex-Soviet Union States: "The massive destruction of the animal or plant kingdoms, the contamination of the atmosphere or water resources, also the practice of other actions capable of causing an ecological catastrophe, are punishable with imprisonment for a period of 12 to 20 years" (free translation). The generic description of punishable conduct ends up making it impossible to attribute criminal charges to the aggressor, which is why, to date, there has never been punishment for ecocide in the country.

[83] "*One purpose of using international criminal law to address climate change might be to demonstrate that there are identifiable wrongdoers whose actions have contributed to climate change. This approach would rely on the expressive value of the law to mark as wrongful behaviour that has been widespread or socially acceptable, and to attempt to deliberately change norms of behaviour that may be firmly established*" (Keenan, Patrick. J. (2019). International Criminal Law and Climate Change. *Boston University International Law Journal, 37*, 89–112, p. 96).

[84] The reference to human rights is also constant in the discourse for a crime against climate change: "*GHG emissions that are the result of business activities, such as those of the Carbon Majors, have qualitative consequences on the enjoyment of human rights. (...) States have the obligation to adopt and apply legal and institutional frameworks to protect against environmental damage that interfere or may interfere with the enjoyment of human rights and to respond to all human rights violations caused by environmental degradation, including the impairment of human rights in relation to climate change*" (Márquez, Daniel Iglesias (2019). Climate litigation against the carbon majors in the countries of origin: notes from the perspective of business and human rights. *Electronic Journal of International Studies (REEI), 37*, 2–37, p. 3–4).

It must be discussed whether it is the role of ecocide as an international crime to combat climate change directly, by stipulating planetary limits.[85] The expansion of the meaning of the criminal type can have the opposite effect: emptying it as a norm, weakening the potential for practical application as law or treaty.

For this, it would be necessary, mainly, to define a climate crime, with sufficient specificity to satisfy the requirements of due process, and then reveal whether the concepts of ecocide, as they are discussed today, reach those conducts.

In this context, considering ecocide as a mechanism capable of combating directly climate change may, perhaps, be a technically insurmountable barrier, with current technology.[86]

Regardless of the type of judicial prosecution, it is a fact that actions in favour of greater legal protection of the environment are multiplying, boosted by successive climate alerts. With the aim of promoting environmental security, the recently studied cases point— among others—to two key problems: international accountability and damage repair (sanction).

---

[85] "*To estimate the reality and severity of the alleged facts, it is proposed that the Court rely on the concept of planetary boundaries, which would allow scientifically determining the tolerable thresholds of modification of the living and potentially controlling industrial activity. The calculations should be made not where the industrial project is located but in the country where the company's headquarters are located, in order to respect the principle of common but differentiated responsibility in each nation's participation in the destabilisation of the terrestrial ecosystem*" (Cabanes, Valérie. (2018). Holding States and companies accountable for climate change: from planetary boundaries to the crime of ecocide. In C. Cournil & L. Varison (Org.), *Climate trials between national and international*. Pedone, 2018. P. 276).

[86] From the increase in national legislation to international recognition, especially by the Security Council, environmental security is increasingly identified as fundamental to the preservation of peace and human rights, on the international level. The 'ecocide' types, developed to date, do not present tools capable of dealing with the issue of climate change, at least directly.

3.4 Environmental Security and Ecocide: The Environment as a Priority

The process of promoting peace and international security goes through environmental security.[87] In this context, the use of criminal law as a tool to combat environmental crime[88] and against the promotion of massive damage to the environment is revealed in a movement of expansion in national Codes.[89]

The peculiarities of environmental infractions, however, require a different approach from criminal law, as the response sought aims more at the repair/prevention of environmental damage than at the punishment of the accused.[90] The environmental criminal litigation— different from civil[91]—deserves to be analysed separately, considering the international official documents (especially, the Rome Statute), seeking a realistic way[92] to operationalize an international crime in this area.

---

[87] See item 8.1.

[88] Often denounced, but never contested, the penalisation of all branches of law is also observed in environmental matters: "*numerous studies have been devoted to this phenomenon and they have highlighted the richness of environmental criminal law, at least from a quantitative point of view. However, the existence of these environmental offences does not mean that the environmental trial will necessarily take place before the criminal judge*" (Perrier, Jean-Baptiste. (2021). The environmental trial before the criminal judge. In M. Hautereau-Boutonnet & È. Truilhe (Eds.), The environmental trial: from the trial on the environment to the trial for the environment (pp. 57–68). Dalloz, p. 63).

[89] Ecocide is considered a crime in various states, and it is possible to identify current legislative movement towards criminalising the promotion of massive damage to the environment.

[90] Obviously, "*compensation is not absent from other trials, it is one of the objectives sought by criminal justice, when the offence has caused harm to a physical person*" (Perrier, Jean-Baptiste. (2021). The environmental trial before the criminal judge. In M. Hautereau-Boutonnet & È. Truilhe (Eds.), The environmental trial: from the trial on the environment to the trial for the environment (pp. 57–68). Dalloz, p. 63).

[91] Within civil environmental litigation, the resources for the protection of rights "*are far from being anecdotal. However, it is not a question of making them the basis of a plea for such appeals, nor for their transposition in France under this model - which seems in any case unlikely and would find a perfectly suitable alternative in a better use of existing legal avenues. Although it sometimes arouses scepticism, the movement to make environmental principles fundamental can be taken at face value and have tangible jurisdictional consequences. Appeals for the protection of rights therefore deserve to be included, and will undoubtedly deserve to be included more and more, among the trials on the environment having useful effects for the protection of the environment*" (Gay, Laurence., & Stefanini, Marthe Fatin-Rouge. (2021). Appeals for the protection of fundamental rights in comparative law. What justiciability of the right to the environment?. In M. Hautereau-Boutonnet & È. Truilhe (Eds.), The environmental trial: from the trial on the environment to the trial for the environment (pp. 69–94). Dalloz, p. 94).

[92] Certainly, there are authors who do not believe in a real change without a radical alteration of the social fabric itself, advancing in principles of the "*wild law*": "*Deepening our understanding of the requirements of social change is a first order challenge for advocates of Wild Law. In thinking about this work, I am motivated by a slogan promoted by MNS: 'most of what we need to know in order to bring about a nonviolent revolution we have yet to learn'. The disappointing setbacks that*

Over the last 25 years, environmental litigation[93] has developed rapidly, following the technical development of the subject[94] and the importance conferred by States and international organizations. The direction of actions to States and transnational corporations (TNC) as defendants is, however, opposite to the traditional construction of international criminal law, aimed at individuals.[95]

our movements have faced in recent years seem to indicate the continuing validity of such a proposition. Still, it seems clear that a good deal of what we have to learn can be gained from studying the specific successes and shortcomings of sympathetic movements not just in the nineteenth and early twentieth centuries but also in the recent past: and then modifying our practice accordingly" (Burdon, Peter D. (2015). Wild Law: A Proposal for Radical Social Change. New Zealand Journal of Public and International Law, 13, 157–178, p. 177).

[93] Certainly, there are problems in treating damages against the environment as constituting international crimes: "*First, this move is narrowly anthropocentric. It may minimize our ability to appreciate broader attacks on the environment that do not immediately affect human beings but are nonetheless inherently dangerous to the environment. In addition, existing international crimes encompass at best a small portion of environmental harms, even among those that sow devastation on human beings. Finally, 'traditional' international crimes typically require proof of complex elements* (e.g., *embededness in an attack or 'special intent') that have little to do with environmental degradation, which may substantially diminish the likelihood of successful prosecutions. Having to wait for environmental degradation to approach the level of genocide before prosecuting the crime raises the threshold far too high and limits criminal law's effectiveness to deter such crimes*" (Mégret, Frédéric. (2011). The Problem of an International Criminal Law of the Environment. Columbia Journal of Environmental Law, 36(2), 195–257, p. 210).

[94] For example, in the International Court of Justice, "*we must cite the judgment rendered in 1997 in the case of the dam on the Danube between Hungary and Slovakia, the first case submitted to the Court in which the environmental issue was also central. (...) Similarly, a large part of the jurisprudence of the International Tribunal for the Law of the Sea (ITLOS) concerns the environment. The ITLOS also issued two important opinions for the protection of the environment in 2011 and 2015 (1st Feb 2011, Rec ITLOS 10; 2nd Apr 2015, Rec ITLOS 2015.4)*" (Maljean-Dubois, Sandrine. (2021). The opening of the environmental trial in the international order. In M. Hautereau-Boutonnet & È. Truilhe (Eds.), The environmental trial: from the trial on the environment to the trial for the environment (pp. 105–120). Dalloz, p. 106–107). The Gabcikovo-Nagymaros case (Hungary vs. Slovakia), revolved around issues related to violations of international obligations involving the environment, "being one of the first judgments to apply the principle of prevention, which is why it is treated as a benchmark in the field of International Environmental Law" (Thomé, Romeu Faria., & Venancio, Stephanie Rodrigues. (2022). The Gabcikovo-Nagymaros case (Hungary Vs Slovakia): The International Court of Justice and the principle of prevention. *Journal of Law and Sustainability*, *8*(2), p. 20).

[95] Even the identification of the State as a "victim" is of questionable acceptance, when it comes to environmental protection: "*in international law, the principle is that only injured subjects can seek to engage the responsibility of the author of the illicit act. However, the notion of an injured State is strictly understood. Indeed, in general international law does not recognize the popular action, that is the possibility for any State to establish the responsibility of any other State having infringed international legality. (...) this principle however tolerates two exceptions concerning obligations erga omnes due to a group of States or general. Article 48 of the draft articles of the ILC (International Law Commission) on the responsibility of States indeed admits that a State other than an injured State can invoke the responsibility of a third State to defend a collective interest, when "a) The violated obligation is due to a group of States of which it is part, and if the obligation is established for the protection of a collective interest of the group; or b) The violated obligation is due to the international community as a whole*" Maljean-Dubois, Sandrine. (2021). The opening

Thus, considering that all the cases analysed here were perpetrated by States or companies, it is necessary to determine whether international criminal prosecution against natural persons is sufficient to achieve the objectives of an environmental criminal type. Afterwards, it is important to investigate what type of sanction is appropriate, given the peculiarities of criminality against the environment and the massive damages characteristic of the ecocide.

3.5 International Criminal Accountability

There are no available instruments to hold accountable for environmental damage, on an international level, in the criminal field. As demonstrated, even nationally, it is difficult to bring a lawsuit against the State,[96] international organizations,[97] or companies,[98] either due to the absence of specific law or technical restrictions, such as the *forum non conveniens*. The criminal prosecution of natural persons, as seen in the cases of Brumadinho and Mariana, in Brazil, and Bhopal, in India, also faces

of the environmental trial in the international order. In M. Hautereau-Boutonnet & È. Truilhe (Eds.), The environmental trial: from the trial on the environment to the trial for the environment (pp. 105–120). Dallozp. 115).

[96] It is worth stating here the existence, from the end of the nineteenth century, of a doctrinal current in favour of the recognition and possible activation of the criminal responsibility of the State at the international level: "*Minority, it has not succeeded in consecrating this idea, echoes of which have nevertheless resonated several decades later within the International Law Commission*" (Bellivier, F., Eudes, M., & Fouchard, I. (2018). *International Crimes Law*. Paris: Themis Droit, p. 225–226).

[97] The engagement of the responsibility of collective entities directly implicated in the practice of international crimes is widely debated: "*If the principle of the exclusion of the state's criminal responsibility burdens part of the reflection, some elements could nevertheless suggest a possible engagement of a form of responsibility of these actors, or at least some of them. Thus, the cases of groups of people exercising a criminal activity but not having the status of a legal person will be excluded from the next developments: if the Nuremberg trial was an opportunity to examine the role of the SS or the Gestapo in particular, this only had the consequence of qualifying these entities as 'criminal organisations', without implying the imposition of collective sanction, nor inspiring the subsequent admission of the 'ratione personae' competence of other criminal jurisdictions towards them*" (Bellivier, F., Eudes, M., & Fouchard, I. (2018). *International Crimes Law*. Paris: Themis Droit, p. 239).

[98] Unlike international organisations, examples of corporate involvement in the practice of international crimes are relatively numerous and take various forms: "*However, according to the often quoted adage, 'Societas delinquere non potest' (companies do not have the power to commit a crime), which seems to exclude all criminal logic and therefore any possibility of prosecution and judgement in this field. It is true that the examination of the conditions and consequences of an engagement of the responsibility of this legal person reveals the existence of a certain number of difficulties*" (Bellivier, F., Eudes, M., & Fouchard, I. (2018). *International Crimes Law*. Paris: Themis Droit, p. 248).

challenges, not infrequently the occurrence of prescription or acquittal, due to the fragility in the probative construction of the causal link.[99]

Considering the only permanent international criminal court in operation on the planet,[100] criminal responsibility is exclusively individual, according to article 25, only for those over 18 years old, according to article 26, both of the Rome Statute, consecrating the principle of *nullum crimen sine conducta.*[101] Furthermore, the document defines responsibility as subjective (article 30 [1]), requiring proof of the agent's intention to carry out the conduct for the correct imputation of the crime. For this reason, the analysis on the construction and feasibility of ecocide in the international criminal system is restricted to the prosecution of the natural person.

When it comes to *accountability* in environmental policies,[102] three examples of approach can be cited, associated with three distinct mechanisms: the climate accountability of governments, which is ensured by goal governance (nationally determined contributions), and in the dissemination of the climate issue; ecological responsibility of the polluter, ensured by the polluter-pays principle, which encourages the management of damages within the framework of environmental economics,

[99] The construction of causality, that is, the relationship between the author of the facts and the damage caused, is especially intricate when it comes to environmental damage. Gilbert (2014) also raises doubts about the determination of the degree of causality between the supposedly damaging activity and the damage itself for the purpose of criminal liability. In the author's conception, especially in the context of certain episodes of environmental destruction, it can be extremely difficult, if not impossible, to establish causality between the relevant human activity and the damage caused with a sufficient degree of certainty, so as to impose criminal responsibility" (Thome, A. C. R., Nunes, N. A., & Thome, R. L. (2020). Environmental degradation in the Brazilian Amazon and the challenges for the inclusion of the crime of ecocide in the Rome Statute. *Guaju: Brazilian Journal of Sustainable Territorial Development, 6*(2), 178–189, p. 189).

[100] The Malabo Protocol, not yet ratified, "creates a new international criminal jurisdiction of the African Court of Human Rights, including establishing new crimes different from those listed by the Rome Statute of the International Criminal Court, provides not only for cases of individual criminal responsibility, but also for corporate criminal responsibility. Both types of responsibility are innovations of the African regional human rights system. In addition to being the only regional system with international criminal competence alternative to the international jurisdiction of the International Criminal Court" (Leão, H. de G., & Prata, L. (2020). The African Court of Human and Peoples' Rights in 5 reflections. *Cosmopolitan*. Available at: https://www.cosmopolita.org/post/o-tribunal-africano-dos-direitos-humanos-e-dos-povos-em-5-reflex%C3%B5es. Accessed on: 2. Jun. 2025).

[101] Therefore, "the responsibility of legal entities—whether or not they are public law—should be carried out not by International Criminal Law. On this issue, item 4 of the same Article provides that 'the provisions of this Statute on the criminal responsibility of individuals in no way affect the responsibility of the State, according to international law'" (Reiss, Michel Wencland. (2017). *The International Criminal Court in the Context of the Globalisation of Law: Analysis of the Rome Statute based on Anglo-Saxon inspired Criminal Law, on Criminal Law inspired Romano-Germanic and in Brazilian Criminal Law* [Doctoral Thesis, Pontifical Catholic University of Rio de Janeiro], p. 79).

[102] "*Specific to politics (Max Weber), it designates the attitude of the one who must answer for the foreseeable consequences of his actions. It opposes the ethics of conviction, which guides action based on a higher moral duty*" (Estève, Adrien. (2020). *Introduction to environmental political theory*. Armand Colin, p. 187).

and; corporate social responsibility, promoted by ecological seals, which bets on taking ecological issues into account in corporate strategies through environmental management (Estève, 2020, pp. 187–188).

Once a conduct that causes massive damage to the environment fails—or is criminal—the question remains: Is prosecuting only the individual, as is the rule of international criminal law, sufficient to provide the desired environmental protection? Considering that all the damages studied here were perpetrated by States[103] and international corporations, the answer to the question would initially be the inefficiency of the measure, given the exclusion of authorship of the main perpetrators.[104]

In this sense, scholars and enthusiasts of ecocide as an international crime promote debates about the need to expand criminal accountability,[105] to reach legal entities[106] of public and private law. However, the obstacles have not yet been overcome at the international level[107]: lack of a uniform conception of "company";[108] the

[103] For an analysis of the criminal culpability of an individual, more demanding than attributing responsibilities to a State for an internationally wrongful act, see: Pellet, Alain (2007). State Responsibility and Individual Criminal Responsibility in International Law. *Romanian Journal of International Law, 4*, 11–32.

[104] The debate about the link between corruption and other forms of transnational crime is significant, "*enriching individuals, state agents or rebel groups, particularly in the field of environmental damage*" (Bellivier, F., Eudes, M., & Fouchard, I. (2018). *International Crimes Law*. Paris: Themis Droit, p. 251).

[105] The historical experience of recent decades "*has highlighted the growing emergence of a "need for justice" in the international community and the perceived need to provide adequate repressive tools in the face of the most serious offenses to the goods and rights fundamental to the person and the community, thus strengthening the aspiration towards a 'supranational punitive power'*" (Di Landro, Andrea (2018). *Responsibility for authorized activity in the sectors of the environment and territory: Criminal and extrapenal protection tools*. G. Giappichelli Publisher, p. 1).

[106] "The issue of criminal liability of the legal entity is still a very controversial topic that has attracted the attention of criminal doctrine around the world. This mainly due to the increasingly important role played by the legal entity in modern society, which has decisively linked it to the phenomenon of so-called economic crime *in a broad sense* (e.g., economic order, consumer relations, environment etc.) (...). There is also, in this area, a serious and worrying conflict between economic-business freedom and fundamental individual rights" (Bitencourt, Cezar (2002). Criminal Liability of Legal Entity: Foundations and Implications. *Journal of Criminal Law, 13*, 27–38, p. 27).

[107] Although it is not a rule, there are countries that criminally punish legal entities. In Brazil, for example, criminal liability against legal entities is only for environmental crimes (Art. 225, §3°, of the Federal Constitution: "Conducts and activities considered harmful to the environment will subject the offenders, individuals or legal entities, to criminal and administrative sanctions, regardless of the obligation to repair the damages caused").

[108] Companies, defined by internal legislations, do not find a common definition on the international level, known generically, when transnational, as a "group of private companies made up of a parent company and its subsidiaries, and affiliated companies distributed in a very large number of States, characterised by a management unit and a global strategy" (Bellivier, F., Eudes, M., & Fouchard, I. (2018). *International Crimes Law*. Paris: Themis Droit, p. 253).

international obligations that are imposed on them[109]; and reluctance to admit the criminal responsibility of these entities.[110]

The fact is that there is no way to criminally prosecute a company—whether isolated or cumulatively with the individual[111]—at the international level.[112] Aside

[109] Regarding legal entities, note a certain imprecision that involves determining the sources and the scope of the obligations incumbent upon them and, potentially, allowing them to assume their responsibility in case of ignorance of these obligations. A significant progress could then lie in the adoption of a Convention on crimes against humanity, in line with the work of the ILC that explicitly provides for the responsibility of legal persons in this area: "*Pending such developments, positive law relies solely on soft law rules, notably adopted under the auspices of the OECD and the UN, and presented under the names of 'corporate social responsibility' (CSR) or within the framework of the 'Global Compact'*" (Bellivier, F., Eudes, M., & Fouchard, I. (2018). *International Crimes Law*. Paris: Themis Droit, p. 253–254).

[110] Most States do not foresee, internally, criminal sanction to the legal person, refusing to admit that the company, being fictitious, without physical presence and without individual consciousness, can have intent or knowledge required by criminal law: "*Moreover, there is a feeling shared by national legislators that the proof of criminal acts committed by a legal person would be difficult to report and that there would be no appropriate sanctions for it due to the impossibility of imprisonment and the uselessness of the fine penalty with regard to the richest companies*" (Bellivier, F., Eudes, M., & Fouchard, I. (2018). *International Crimes Law*. Paris: Themis Droit, p. 255).

[111] Some legislations also experiment with openly non-cumulative techniques of assigning responsibilities: "*a) Exclusive responsibility - in addition to the criminal figures achievable by our - adopt a principle of speciality in the selection of the crimes-assumption of the responsibility of the collective entity, some legal systems provide, in a general and abstract way, spaces of punishability reserved for the societas. (Ex: Italy); b) Subsidiary responsibility of the entity - in Switzerland, for any hypothesis of crime, the entity responds in an alternative and subsidiary way whenever, due to an organisational gap, the individual author is not identifiable; c) Alternative and mutually exclusive responsibility of individual and entity - in Belgium, the distribution of responsibility between individual and moral person, in all cases where the physical person has been identified and has not acted consciously and voluntarily, is informed by a principle of necessary judicial decumulation: responds, exclusively, the subject who has committed the most serious crime (the most serious fault). In all other cases, the cumulation is only optional; d) Optional punishment of the entity or the physical person - in Germany, the imposition of the Gelbusse (financial penalty) to the entity is left to the discretion of the judge. Some Nordic systems (Finland, Sweden) grant the judge the power not to punish the individual or the entity in situations of 'weakened' guilt or responsibility and in other situations indicated by law. In Spain, instead, the judge is required to "modulate" the pecuniary penalties imposed on the legal person and the physical person, in compliance with the principles of proportionality and ne bis in idem substantial; according to current jurisprudential interpretation, it is not possible to go below the legal minimum limit of the fine*" (Mongillo, Vincenzo. (2018). *Criminal responsibility between individual and collective entity*. Turin: G. Giappichelli Publisher, p. 449).

[112] The question of whether legal persons can commit crimes and incur penalties is not a product of modern times, but has its roots in a very distant past: "*Savigny noted this in 1840, speaking of a question "always much debated"; Delitala reiterated it about a century later, evoking the "age-old and tormented problem"; and Bricola returned to it, at the beginning of the seventies of the last century, at a historical moment in which the "age-old recurring problem" still stood imperiously the dogma societas delinquere et puniri non potest. A perennial dilemma, therefore. But that would not have exhibited such a strong coefficient of enigmaticity if it were not intertwined with a denser question - socio-cultural before even normative - of 'relational' cut. At stake, in fact, are the rela-*

from the political character, that is, the choice not to criminally hold TNC's[113] accountable, international criminal law seems to be built on the individual—human[114]—will to perpetrate a crime.[115] In this aspect, the criminal prosecution of fictitious entities is impaired within the International Criminal Court, as well as in past international courts.[116]

---

tionships between the responsibilities of individual and collective subjects, their respective foundations and possible distributions" (Mongillo, Vincenzo. (2018). *Criminal responsibility between individual and collective entity*. Turin: G. Giappichelli Publisher, p. 1).

[113] In the 10 (ten) years of the ICC, Delmas-Marty reminded that the relationship between mass atrocities and economic activities was already a subject present in Nuremberg, "*where senior businessmen were convicted for their complicity in Nazi crimes for furnishing concentration camps with toxic gas in the knowledge that it would be used for the extermination of humans; for subjecting individuals to forced labour in their factories; for supporting the deportation, assassination or infliction of other forms of mistreatment on victims; for financially supporting the SS perpetrators and for pillaging property in occupied Europe.6 Corporate criminal involvement in international crimes did not end with the Second World War. To the contrary, new developments in the available means of communication in a globalised and more interconnected world create new opportunities, particularly as some transnational corporations wield greater economic power than some states. These corporations have become major players, which have complex relationships with national governments and the local population*" (Delmas-Marty, Mireille (2013). Ambiguities and Lacunae: The International Criminal Court Ten Years On. *Journal of International Criminal Justice, 11*(3), 553–561. https://doi.org/10.1093/jicj/mqt032. Accessed on: 10 Jun. 2025).

[114] It is observed that the reason for the resistance in recognising the criminal responsibility of the legal person, "embraced by the theory of Fiction, lies in the following fact: the moral entity cannot commit crimes because it does not have its own will. Therefore, without being able to act with intent or fault, there is no way to talk about culpability, this presupposition of application of the penalty" (Johannsen, A. P. da S., & Ferreira, A. P. (2012). Brief considerations about the environmental criminal responsibility of the legal person in Brazil and in Spain. *Revista Direito e Política, 7*(3), 1620–1651. https://periodicos.univali.br/index.php/rdp/article/download/5556/2962. Accessed on: 20 Jun. 2025).

[115] International criminal law was born as a reaction to the most serious crimes, capable of undermining the very structure of the international community, trying to break any immunity that opposed its repression. If on the one hand, therefore, international criminal law is based on the recognition of the elementary needs of each human being and each community, "*on the other hand, the normative consolidation of the rules that are an expression of this often clashes with an inability to dialogue, which seems to be based on a sometimes 'misleading linguistic artificiality'. The evolution of international criminal law has led to the emergence of the awareness of the need to start from the individual, in his nature as a free being, as the recipient of rights and duties. The recognition of the individual as a subject of international law goes through a 'personification/humanisation of the normative recipient', and, consequently, a 'linguistic/normative' adaptation of the rules of conduct*" (Di Landro, Andrea (2018). *Responsibility for authorized activity in the sectors of the environment and territory: Criminal and extrapenal protection tools*. G. Giappichelli Publisher, p. 117).

[116] The bases for the recognition of individual responsibility in international law can already be found in the Treaty of Versailles, of 28 June 1919: "*According to art. 227, William II, Emperor of Germany, should have been judged for 'supreme offence against international morality and the sacred authority of treaties'. A real individual responsibility for international crimes was however normatively fixed expressly only from the Nuremberg Charter (art. 613) and Tokyo (art. 114). The principle of individual responsibility found express recognition, with almost identical formulations, at the beginning of the nineties, in the Statutes of the two* ad hoc *Tribunals, respectively for*

The claim, although legitimate, therefore, does not find significant resonance in international doctrinal and legal production,[117] which shows an expansion of understanding about the authorship of international crimes in the short term. The environmental urgency calls for speed in the enhancement of protection systems, through creations/changes—of laws, treaties, conventions—feasible, considering the current development of international criminal law. It is not reasonable to bet on the punishment of legal entities for the practice of massive damage to the environment as the only possibility of effectively safeguarding it.

However, a potentially positive effect of the criminalization of ecocide is its incorporation into the ESG risk assessment criteria (*Environmental, social, and governance*) of companies by credit rating agencies (Oliver, 2024, pp. 87–120). Even if the crime does not directly attack the causes of climate change, the formatting of socio-environmental performance standards can be influenced by a conduct considered harmful to the environment.

The repression of individual criminality, at the international level,[118] can constitute a tool for the mitigation of massive environmental damage, when supported by a production of evidence and construction of a sufficiently strong causal link. In the context of symbolic criminal law,[119] making a leader of a transnational a defendant before an international court is very serious for the company's image, as seen in Brazil. It is not the type of promotion desired by the company, even if it is not the direct target of criminal prosecution.[120]

---

crimes committed in the former Yugoslavia (ICTY), arts. 7 and 23, and for Rwanda (ICTR), arts. 6 and 22. The International Criminal Tribunal for the former Yugoslavia was established with Resolution of the United Nations Security Council no. 827 dated 25 May 1993, 'based on a highly innovative and controversial interpretation of the powers conferred on such a body under Chap. 7 *of the United Nations Charter', a chapter that deals with actions to be developed in the face of threats or violations of peace or acts of aggression. Similarly, with Resolution no. 955 of 8 November 1994, the International Criminal Tribunal for Rwanda was established*" (Di Landro, Andrea (2018). *Responsibility for authorized activity in the sectors of the environment and territory: Criminal and extrapenal protection tools.* G. Giappichelli Publisher, p. 5).

[117] The study on corporate criminality in the ICC "*does appear to be better suited as a mode of liability in such armed conflict where the Court currently operates due to its flexibility. However, there are too few decisions and judgments delivered by the Court to truly establish how well the 'control of the crime' theory and the 'control over an organisation' theory can be applied in the context of armed conflict today*" (Lord, Sofia (2013). *Joint criminal enterprise and the international criminal court: a comparison between joint criminal enterprise and the modes of liability in joint commission in crime under the Rome Statute; can the International Criminal Court apply joint criminal enterprise as a mode of liability?* Thesis in International Criminal Law. Stockholm University).

[118] International criminal repression, despite being individual, reaches various means of agent participation (planner, instigator, leader, participant), in addition to punishing, as in the ICTY, participants of a common criminal enterprise, when willing to contribute to a common criminal desire (Chaumette, Anne-Laure Vaurs. (2009). *The subjects of international criminal law: Towards a new definition of international legal personality?*. Pedone, p. 442–443).

[119] See item 3.6.

[120] However, "*it is difficult to assume that the investigation (extremely delicate and complex) of the possible contribution to ecocide by corporate executives is a priority for any prosecutor while*

Even considering the capacity to produce environmental damage enhanced by large corporate activities, in the end it is individuals who operationalize and promote them,[121] generating legal responsibilities.[122] Thus, the absence of criminal repression of legal entities—at the international level—is not fatal to the intention of environmental protection through an international crime, when the means of building the process are robust.

Obviously, companies are not being exempted from socio-environmental responsibilities. The limited judicial risk of their operation is disproportional to the profits and sometimes caused damages.[123] The international community should, in

---

corporate actors are not expressly included in the Rome Statute. Without an international criminal jurisdiction to pursue human rights violations committed by companies, the current context requires expanding the ICL to legal entities to make it more effective (as pointed out by the Special Tribunal for Lebanon and the Malabo Protocol regarding the African Court). It would be necessary to transfer to the ICL the internal control measures and the international standard of due diligence of human rights introduced by the Guiding Principles on business and human rights" (Scarpello, Andrea, et al. (2021). Ecocide and corporate responsibility: the necessary link to achieve environmental justice. *Electronic Journal of Contemporary International Law (REDIC), 4.* http://sedici.unlp.edu.ar/bitstream/handle/10915/133831/Versi%C3%83%C2%B3n_en_PDF.pdf?sequence=1. Accessed on: 20 Jun. 2025).

[121] Any effort to understand the causes of environmental damage must consider both individuals and larger groups: "*The same is true of efforts to address environmental harm. This includes efforts to change state and corporate behaviour; if such efforts are to be successful, they require knowledge of the myriad ways in which states and corporations impact individuals. And this includes efforts that are directed at individuals. Changing individual behaviour will require changes in the culture, social structure, and infrastructure of societies. The above discussion points to the types of changes that are necessary. For example, any successful change will require such things as reduction in the status attached to ordinary harms, redefinition of gender roles in ways that place less emphasis on consumption, increased costs of engaging in ordinary harms, undermining the specific beliefs that foster the harms, and making alternatives to ordinary harms more available and less costly*" (Agnew, R. (2012). The ordinary acts that contribute to ecocide. In *Routledge International Handbook of Green Criminology* (pp. 70). https://doi.org/10.4324/9780203093658.ch3. Accessed on: 8 Jun. 2025).

[122] In 1987, discussing the inclusion of ecocide in the draft of *The Code*, the ILC pointed out that "*serious damage to the environment should be included in the draft code. There again, the decisive consideration was whether there had been criminal intent to destroy the environment. Without criminal intent there was no criminal responsibility. For example, there might be an accident in a nuclear power plant which caused widespread and serious damage to the environment in neighbouring States. The question of the liability of the author State towards the injured States would certainly arise under international law, but not that of individual criminal responsibility, unless there had been criminal intent on the part of those concerned*" (ILC (1987), *Yearbook of The International Law Commission*, V. 1, p. 40. Available at: http://legal.un.org/ilc/publications/yearbooks/english/ilc_1987_v1.pdf, accessed on: 20 Mar. 2025).

[123] Although there is considerable academic debate over whether criminal sanctions are effective or even necessary when applied to legal entities, "*it is submitted that the accountability of corporations should be recognised under the ICC Statute. In particular, powerful international non-state actors currently face limited risk of accountability under the national laws of some host states—and limited or no liability under international law—would have to act more diligently in the host countries where they operate. This is particularly the case of multinational corporations, but this should also apply to international financial institutions which fund projects that damage the envi-*

consensus, develop a set of mandatory regulations for transnationals,[124] foreseeing sanctions—even civil ones— for deviations. In the international criminal sphere, for now, focus should be on individual prosecution, already consolidated—with reinforced aspects of cooperation between the Court and the States,[125] if the creation of ecocide as a crime is desired, within a "reasonable time frame", otherwise it may become impractical.[126]

It is worth remembering that the jurisdiction of the International Criminal Court is complementary,[127] that is, the priority of processing is still with the States, which should have laws that reach the desired environmental protection.[128] Nothing

---

ronment" (Pereira, Ricardo (2020). After the ICC Office of the Prosecutor's 2016 Policy Paper on Case Selection and Prioritisation: Towards an International Crime of Ecocide? *Criminal Law Forum, 31*(2), 179–224, p. 221).

[124] For example, "*a binding set of law would alleviate pressure on individual developing countries and mandate that all states follow a uniform set of standards, rather than one set for industrialised countries and one for developing nations. TNCs should not have the option to choose to operate in one country* versus *another based on its weak environmental standards*" (Schmidt, T. M. (2005). Transnational Corporate Responsibility for International Environmental and Human Rights Violations: Will the United Nations' "Norms" Provide the Required Means. *California Western International Law Journal, 36*, 217–246, p. 246).

[125] Cooperation with States is a fundamental element for the implementation of international criminal justice, because, just like the ad hoc courts, "*the International Criminal Court is "a giant without arms and legs" that needs state cooperation for the conduct of investigations, for the collection of evidence, to obtain the material availability of investigated and accused persons, especially considering that the international order in question does not contemplate the celebration of trials* in absentia, *and finally, for the execution of the sentence possibly imposed with the conviction*". Regarding the Italian legal system, "*after having hosted the diplomatic conference held in Rome whose works led on 17 July 1998 to the adoption of the Statute establishing the Court, after showing its own activism by being part of the group of so-called 'like-minded' countries that during the same had as their only goal the overcoming of obstacles for the birth of the Court, after becoming the first State signatory of the Statute and only the fourth to have ratified it with the law of 12 July 1999, n. 232, it has 'stained' itself with a regrettable inertia lasting 13 years and interrupted in an absolutely partial way with the approval of the law of 20 December 2012, n. 237, entitled 'Rules for the adaptation to the provisions of the statute establishing the International Criminal Court'*" (Fanchiotti, Vittorio, Miraglia, M., & Pierini, J. P. (2014). *The International Criminal Court: substantive and procedural profiles*. Turin: G. Giappichelli Editore p. 177).

[126] The development of the notion of ecocide reveals that the legal debate in national legislatures still does not reach the discussion about the punishment of legal entities, beyond the States where the criminal prosecution of companies is already a reality.

[127] See item 8.2.

[128] The *International Law Commission*, according to the "'*Draft principles on protection of the environment in relation to armed conflicts, adopted by the Commission on first reading,' Principle 10 on 'Corporate Due Diligence' states that States should take appropriate legislative and other measures 'aimed at ensuring that corporations and other business enterprises operating in or from their territories exercise due diligence with respect to the protection of the environment, including in relation to human health, when acting in an area of armed conflict or in a post- armed conflict situation.' Moreover, the principle of corporate accountability is embedded in Principle 11 which directs States to 'take appropriate legislative and other measures aimed at ensuring that corporations and other business enterprises operating in or from their territories can be held liable for harm caused by them to the environment, including in relation to human health, in an area of*

prevents the crime of ecocide, once added to the ICC, from being established nationally[129]—in the member countries of the Court—with provision for punishment of the legal entity, according to local norms.[130] Taking advantage of the legal structure of the Court, without profound changes in its institutes, is fundamental to the reduction of noise in the discussion for the insertion of a new crime.[131]

A second debate that brings to environmental crimes is the type of appropriate sanction. Again, past ecocide cases—even treated by the judiciary in different ways—and the sanctions provided in the ICC should guide the discussion.

3.6 Sanctions for Ecocide

If the processing of authors of environmental damage is tortuous, the application of appropriate sanction is even more inconsistent, as analysed in cases of ecocide in practice. The discrepancy between the perpetrated damages and the amount of indemnities/reparations in the civil sphere,[132] when existing, is the main characteristic of these judicial processes. More rare, national criminal actions also suffer from a similar problem, at most, condemning individuals to negligible sentences.[133]

---

armed conflict or in a post-armed conflict situation"' (Pereira, Ricardo (2020). After the ICC Office of the Prosecutor's 2016 Policy Paper on Case Selection and Prioritisation: Towards an International Crime of Ecocide? *Criminal Law Forum, 31*(2), 179–224, p. 220–221).

[129] The Supreme Federal Court (STF) of Brazil accepted the possibility of criminal liability of companies independent of the liability of the individual, for environmental crimes, moving away from the theory of double imputation (Friede, Roy Reis (2017). The new paradigm of criminal liability of the legal entity for environmental crime. *Legal Journal of the Higher School of Advocacy of OAB-PR, 2*(1), 15).

[130] Ultimately, it is suggested that Article 21[3] of the Rome Statute provides a suitable and solid legal basis for interpreting and applying the relevant international criminal law in light of intersectionality (Maučec, Gregor. (2021). The International Criminal Court and the Issue of Intersectionality—A Conceptual and Legal Framework for Analysis. *International Criminal Law Review, 21*(1), 1–34, 2021).

[131] "*There seems to be an urgent need for more and more complex regulation and official intervention; yet this is, in our present system of international law and relations, extremely difficult to bring about in a timely and efficient manner. The fact of the matter surely is that these difficulties reflect the increasingly evident inadequacy of the traditional view of international relations as composed of pluralistic separate sovereignties, existing in a world where pressures of many kinds, not least of scientific and technological skills, almost daily make those separate so-called sovereignties, in practical terms, less independent and more and more interdependent. What is urgently needed is a more general realisation that, in the conditions of the contemporary global situation, the need to create a true international society must be faced. It needs in fact a new vision of international relations and law*" (Sands, Philippe (2003). *Principles of international environmental law* (2nd ed.). Cambridge: Cambridge University Press.p. XV).

[132] For example, the compensations defined for the veterans of the Vietnam War did not reach $4000.00 (four thousand dollars) per person (see item 2.1).

[133] In 2010, the president of the American company *Union Carbide Corporation*, Warren Anderson, and some executives of this were criminally convicted in India to sentences of 2 (two) years of

There has long been a discussion about the appropriate penalty for the practice of international crimes.[134] The sanction for environmental infractions has peculiar factors in this scenario, with the impossibility of repairing the damage, due to natural or financial issues of the defendants, with humanity absorbing the loss entirely.

The prison sentence[135]—physical restriction of freedom—is still the main sanction for crimes worldwide.[136] The imprisonment of the convicted[137] is also the tone

prison and fines, for the disaster in Bhopal. Absent from the process, the convicted president died, in 2014, without starting the sentence.

[134] The problem of punishing war crimes has long been on the international agenda: "*Apart from the obligatory mention of the steps taken to bring William II to trial on the basis of the Versailles Treaties, as well as the attempts to establish a permanent organ of criminal justice, operating internationally, as early as January 1942 a commission was established for the punishment of crimes committed during the Second World War. In October of the same year, a United Nations commission for the punishment of war crimes was established. Above all, the 'Moscow declaration' of 30 October 1943, the result of agreements between the US, British and Russian foreign ministers, with the consultation of China, definitively strengthened the project of a jurisdiction over crimes committed during the war, also marking its transition from the sphere of the United Nations to that of the allied governments, at least for the crimes whose genesis or whose effects had not been exhausted in a certain geographical area, therefore destined for condemnation 'by joint decision of the government of the Allies'*" (Masucci, M. (2017). *Structures of international criminal law: interpretation, application, offences*. Turin: G. Giappichelli Editore, p. 3).

[135] Prison, before being considered 'punishment', seen as an institution to detain men against their will, originated in the most remote antiquity: "*It probably goes back as far as the time of the general practice of cannibalism, when future victims were held in stockades to be fattened or to await their turn in contributing the chief course in the menu of their captors Throughout recorded history one frequently meets with references to prisons used for the confinement of political and religious offenders*" (Barnes, Harry Elmer (1921). Historical origin of the prison system in America. *Journal of Criminal Law and Criminology, 12*(1), 35–60. https://scholarlycommons.law.northwestern.edu/cgi/viewcontent.cgi?article=1772&context=jclc. Accessed on: 22 Jun. 2025).

[136] Prison, today, a means of punishment for the majority of crimes, is an innovation of relatively recent origin: "*It is quite impossible to fix the exact date of the general beginning of imprisonment as a punishment for crime, and it may, indeed, be seriously doubted if any such date exists, except in a metaphysical sense. All that can be stated with accuracy is that at the beginning of the eighteenth-century imprisonment was unusual, except as applied to political and religious offenders and debtors, while before the middle of the nineteenth century it was the conventional method of punishing crime in both Europe and America. The eighteenth century was the century of transition from corporal punishment to imprisonment, and, though the process of change was most rapid after 1775, there can be no doubt that the general movement was in progress during the entire period.*" (Barnes, Harry Elmer (1921). Historical origin of the prison system in America. *Journal of Criminal Law and Criminology, 12*(1), 35–60. https://scholarlycommons.law.northwestern.edu/cgi/viewcontent.cgi?article=1772&context=jclc. Accessed on: 22 Jun. 2025).

[137] This change in the understanding of imprisonment, in the Renaissance period, is related to the transformation in the conception of 'time', "which removes the convict from public presence and autonomy in the administration of their time. However, it should be noted that, in the face of huge public clocks controlling the dynamics of life, followed by pocket watches and finally wristwatches, like handcuffs of a life that does not wait for will, but demands action with productive purpose at all times, few are the masters of their time and many are its servants. So that prison will be an instrument of coercion, conditioning and education for the timed life of capitalist society" (Chiaverini, Tatiana (2009). *Origin of the prison sentence*. Master's Dissertation in Philosophy of

of international criminal law, embodied in Article 77, of the Rome Statute.[138] The death penalty, maximum of the ad hoc Courts post-War, was banned from the International Criminal Court.

In addition to the prison sentence,[139] with a maximum limit of 30 years (Article 77 [1][a]), it can also be perpetual (Article 77 [1][b]), the Court can determine the application of a fine and loss of assets originating from the committed crime (Article 77 [2][a] and [b]). The low variation of types of sanctions raises the question of whether the ICC can offer a meaningful response to the repression of massive damage to the environment, given the peculiarities of the crime.[140]

The practice of ecocide, as exemplified by the cases brought in this book, causes severe environmental destruction, where transnational companies and States, using technologies and high economic power, cannot minimize the consequences of the damages satisfactorily. An individual, therefore, has significantly reduced their ability to repair them,[141] making any applied sanction disproportional—to the detriment of society.

It happens that the criminalisation of certain conduct does not have the objective[142] exclusively to repair the damage or imprison (punish) the perpetrator of the

---

Law. Pontifical Catholic University of São Paulo. http://www.dominiopublico.gov.br/download/teste/arqs/cp119708.pdf Accessed on: 22 Jun. 2025).

[138] Article 77, of the Rome Statute: "1. Without prejudice to the provisions of article 110, the Court may impose on the person convicted of one of the crimes provided for in article 5 of this Statute one of the following sentences: a) Imprisonment for a certain number of years, up to a maximum limit of 30 years; or b) Life imprisonment, if the high degree of illegality of the fact and the personal conditions of the convicted justify it, 2. In addition to the prison sentence, the Court may apply: a) A fine, according to the criteria provided for in the Procedural Regulation; b) The loss of products, goods and assets resulting, directly or indirectly, from the crime, without prejudice to the rights of third parties who have acted in good faith".

[139] Although outside the scope of this work, it is worth commenting that imprisonment (especially in prisons), in itself, does not carry, in practice, greater meaning for the convicts in most countries, where overcrowding, mistreatment and social abandonment prevail, little relating to repentance or reflection on the crime committed. For a portrait of the prison experience in Ceará, see: EZEOKEKE, Cornelius Okwudili (2013) *Paradoxes in prison*. Fortaleza: Premius Editora.

[140] "*A more fundamental question lurks beneath any evaluation of the ICC as a mechanism to promote environmental security. Essentially, the ICC represents a punitive, retributive justice paradigm in which certain serious crimes against the international community are to be redressed through the prosecution and imprisonment of selected individuals. The foundational question for international environmental lawyers is whether a punitive methodology will actually promote environmental security*" (Drumbl, Mark A. (2000). International Human Rights, International Humanitarian Law, and Environmental Security: Can the International Criminal Court Bridge the Gaps? *ILSA Journal of International & Comparative Law, 6*, 305–341, p. 331).

[141] For example, the cost of environmental damages caused in the War between Ukraine and Russia are estimated at more than 56 billion dollars (Hryhorczuk, Daniel, et al. (2024). The environmental health impacts of Russia's war on Ukraine. *Journal of Occupational Medicine and Toxicology, 19*(1), 1. https://doi.org/10.1186/s12995-023-00398-y. Accessed on: 10 Jan. 2025).

[142] The legal historian "*Lawrence Friedman identifies three goals of the criminal law: deterrence, punishment, and the setting of 'moral boundaries' to show a society 'where the line lies between good and bad'. The third goal is too often overlooked. Its application to renegade companies and*

infraction.[143] Especially in the international sphere, the symbolic character[144] of an incrimination is a setting of limits[145] to acts definitely reprehensible by the international community, consisting of an argument of deterrence against new criminal practices.[146]

Ecocide at the ICC would represent a symbol[147] not found in all the cases reported in this Chapter: the clear establishment that massive environmental destruction is prohibited, as it is a conduct against the very existence in peace and security of

---

their well- compensated executives has become extraordinarily important to the quality of life in the developed and developing worlds. But white collar criminal prosecutions are not only important because of the immediate effects they can achieve in correcting behaviour that harms public health, worker and consumer safety, and the environment" (Steinzor, Rena (2016). How Criminal Law Can Help Save the Environment. *Environmental Law, 46*, 209–239, p. 234).

[143] 'Psychology of Punishment' suggests that "people punish for a retributivist psychological motivation, but justify their decision in terms of the possibility of producing behavioural change. However, as is peaceful in the psychological literature, punishment as a form of behavioural pedagogy only works under very specific conditions, which are absent from the existing criminal punitive system. In turn, empirical studies on the effects of the extension of the deprivation of liberty on criminality, we try to show that its low preventive efficacy is due to the fact that the risk calculation made by the transgressors has little relation to the abstract text of the criminal law; and that prison can be criminogenic even in short durations, due to the breaking of social ties and the violence experienced by the incarcerated subjects" (Horta, Ricardo Lins (2020). The disheartening function of punishments: revisiting the Theories of Punishment in the light of Experimental Psychology. *Law Review, State and Society*, 1–32. https://doi.org/10.17808/des.0.1346. Accessed on: 22 Jun. 2025).

[144] International crimes reflect the most important values of the international community. Thus, a certain degree of symbolism is identified as inherent to the architecture of international criminal justice (Aksenova, Mariana (2017). Symbolism as a constraint on international criminal law. *Leiden Journal of International Law, 30*(2), 475–499).

[145] The symbolic power of an international crime also contains an important pre-deterrence effect, which shapes the decision-making of actors even before a crime is adopted or prosecuted: "*Pre-deterrence implies creating conditions whereby individuals do not even contemplate taking part in political violence because of certain assumptions about lines not to be crossed, or the moral minima, instilled in their minds. The symbolic role of international criminal law is thus antecedent to its deterrent power. Both goals seek to establish a normative standard that shapes individual decision-making. The difference is in the timing—symbolism starts working before general deterrence and targets even those who do not contemplate offending*" (Aksenova, Mariana (2017). Symbolism as a constraint on international criminal law. *Leiden Journal of International Law, 30*(2), 475–499).

[146] Following this logic, "*a message about the lack of tolerance towards certain conducts is sent to the international society every time a new core crime is recognized. The crime of ecocide is not excluded from this logic and the name of this crime is part of this rhetorical symbolism*" (Pezzot, Romina, & Graf, J.-P. (2022). Ecocide—Legal Revolution or Symbolism? *Völkerrechtsblog*. https://voelkerrechtsblog.org/ecocide-legal-revolution-or-symbolism/. Accessed on: 22 Jun. 2025).

[147] If adopted, ecocide "*would become the symbol of a legal revolution that is taking place: a new shared international core limitation established to protect the environment worldwide. This new shared international core limitation would be a powerful message for humanity since it would also represent a new contract or a new relationship between humanity and the environment*" (Pezzot, Romina, & Graf, J.-P. (2022). Ecocide—Legal Revolution or Symbolism? *Völkerrechtsblog*. https://voelkerrechtsblog.org/ecocide-legal-revolution-or-symbolism/. Accessed on: 22 Jun. 2025).

humanity.[148] In this aspect, the criminalization of this conduct, per se, gains special prominence, elevating its international reprehensibility to the level of crimes against humanity and genocide.

Certainly, symbolic sanction alone will not suffice for practical purposes of effective environmental protection.[149] However, the demand (or even belief) exclusively in the crime of ecocide to "save" the environment is unwarranted. No conduct typified as crime, in isolation, has the ability to prevent or remedy the damages resulting from it.[150] The role of criminal law, as ultima ratio, is to establish the most harmful conducts to the community, imposing the corresponding sanction. This task does not overlap with the obligations of other areas of law, including civil, tax, environmental, all with roles to play, jointly, in the preservation of human ways of life.[151]

In terms of criminal prosecution and sanctioning of individual authors linked to companies or governments for massive environmental crime, for example, the symbolism of the criminal conviction can have a greater meaning to customers/citizens than a settlement or judgement in the civil sphere.[152] If maintaining a corporate

---

148 Public international law, traditionally based on the fragmentation of the territorial environment (existence of multiple sovereign states with their own territories), collides with the inherent and interdependent unity of the natural environment, devoid of rigid borders.

149 The effectiveness of the sanction can be understood, first and foremost, by the effectiveness that the norm derives from the application of the penalty following the violation: "*secondly, the expectation that the norm will be observed in the future by the one to whom it has been applied; finally and more precisely, the effectiveness of the half-penalty in its executive impact. It is particularly with respect to this last point that it seems possible to identify a fundamental weakness in the proposals for the criminalisation of ecocide examined. They indeed appear to be based on a punitive-repressive approach, without considering the feasibility of prescriptive-reparative sanction paradigms. This approach does not seem to adequately value the needs for repair and restoration of the status quo ante, particularly felt in the field of environmental protection, and the role that victims - those who have established qualified relationships with the offended environment - could play in contributing to the definition of the contents and methods of the reparative conduct*" (Molteni, Viola (2021). The long road of the criminalisation of ecocide: legal issues and dynamics of normative and social effectiveness. *Contemporary Criminal Law, 4*, 205–233, p. 217).

150 Intentional homicide is, undoubtedly, the main - and most common - crime typified in the countries of the planet. But, it is also certain, it does not prevent the occurrence of murders: for example, 4039 (four thousand and thirty-nine) violent lethal and intentional crimes (CVLI) were recorded in Fortaleza, in the year 2020, with an average of 336 deaths (among homicides, bodily injuries and robberies followed by death) per month, or 11 (eleven) deaths per day, only in the capital of Ceará (SUPESPCE. Violent lethal and intentional crimes—CVLI. Monthly statistics, Dec. 2020. Available at: https://www.sspds.ce.gov.br/wp-content/uploads/sites/24/2021/01/01-CVLI-Estatisticas-Mensais.pdf. Accessed on: 20 Jun. 2025).

151 In this sense, maintaining an anthropocentric view of law, which considers man as part of the environment, and not the environment as his property (see item 7.5).

152 "Especially in the international arena, where, at times, the damage caused is irreparable, the symbolism of the penalty can bring positive preventive effects, perhaps greater than the repressive character. For example, the case known as 'dieselgate', in 2015, triggered a succession of investigations, initiated by the American Environmental Agency (US EPA), in the face of diesel engines manipulated by Volkswagen to present nitrogen gas emission levels lower than reality. The resulting criminal processes have already led engineers, managers and directors of the transnational to prison, in addition to the application of high fines. There is no doubt that, in this case, the penal

image of respect for the environment was unimportant, there would be no need to practice *greenwashing* (green makeup),[153] frequently denounced by various NGOs.[154]

Furthermore, criminal punishment can be considered to be the first stage of transitional justice, where damage repair (rehabilitation, memorialization, apology, and guarantees of non-repetition), information about the reality of events (truth commissions, reports, and educational programmes), and institutional reform mechanisms (amendment of laws and related norms) are the next stages to criminal prosecution (Rodeiro, 2024, pp. 47–79).

Indeed, the sanctions provided for in the Rome Statute do not seem sufficient to repress a crime like ecocide.[155] But, considering the existing laws and bill proposals on the subject, no legal system appears completely capable of dealing with massive environmental damage. Under these conditions, international criminalization, complementary to national ones, can focus on the emblematic aspect of criminal repression,[156] setting a universal limit to environmental destruction. The mere

character of the actions amplified the reflection throughout the automotive industry, having reverberations in Germany against other companies, such as Audi, BMW and *Porsche*. Here, the imprisonment of the involved does not repair the environmental damage caused in any way, but certainly tarnishes the, perhaps, main asset of these companies: the image" (Brochado Neto, Djalma Alvarez, & Mont'Alverne, T. C. F. (2020). Massive damage to the environment: crime in war, but not in peacetime? Intergovernmental organisations and the next step in global environmental governance. *Science and Peace, XI*(2), 37–55. https://scienzaepace.unipi.it/index.php/it/call-for-papers/item/download/430_e5761931728ba84456238f2abebf5ac7.html. Accessed on: 22 Jun. 2025).

[153] The disclosure, by public or private companies, to the public of positive environmental practices, while, however, performing actions adverse to the socio-environmental interests they disclose, is called "*green make-up washing, the so-called greenwashing". This term is applied when environmental and social concepts used to form a public responsible image of a company do not match with their actual management, sometimes negative and that causes problems and degradation. in the environment, social problems or health and safety at different levels*" (Medeiros, Tatiana Dilma Fernandes de Oliveira, & Pitassi, C. (2018). Eco-Innovation in the Corporations Operating in the International Market. *Journal of Management and Sustainability, 8*(1), 75–92, p. 77).

[154] United Nations Environment Programme (UNEP). (2021). Global Climate Litigation Report: 2020 Status Review. https://wedocs.unep.org/bitstream/handle/20.500.11822/34818/GCLR.pdf?sequence=1&isAllowed=yUNITED NATIONS ENVIRONMENT PROGRAMME. Global Climate Litigation Report: 2020 Status Review. 2021, p. 19, available at: https://wedocs.unep.org/bitstream/handle/20.500.11822/34818/GCLR.pdf?sequence=1&isAllowed=y, accessed on: 10 Jun. 2025.

[155] At this point, it is worth remembering the existence of a crime—indirect—against the environment in the Rome Statute, when it is carried out in times of war (Article 8[2][b][iv]): "*The inclusion of Article 8(2)(b)(iv) in the Rome Statute represents a significant advance for international law. For the first time, the world community has recognized both that environmental damage caused by unnecessary military attacks should be prohibited even when that damage does not directly harm human interests and that the only effective sanction for such attacks is individual criminal responsibility*" (Heller, Kevin Jon, & Lawrence, J. C. (2007). The Limits of Article 8(2)(b)(iv) of the Rome Statute, The First Ecocentric Environmental War Crime. *Georgetown International Environmental Law Review, 20*, 1–40).

[156] The discussion about 'justice' and punishment is beyond the scope of this work. It can be briefly mentioned that the fair sanction is the one that reconciles the law's forecast with the evidence built

existence of the new crime would serve, at least, to officially name—the most serious conducts against the environment as ecocide,[157] avoiding excessively disparate treatments between similar cases.

Going beyond this symbolic function, the definition of an international sanction for ecocide would have the power to harmonize, by virtue of the Rome Statute, the penalties in the signatory States, combating ecological *dumping*.[158] With this objective, it would be necessary to amend Article 77 of the Statute, to provide, among the applicable penalties,[159] for damage repair (where possible), prohibition of contracting with public service (public administration) for work in the environmental field and reversal of the fine in favour of the victims of the event.[160]

The main point is: the lack of an international definition of ecocide compromises the identification of cases of massive destruction of the environment around the

---

in the process, that is, it takes place within the judiciary, in criminal prosecution: "*the use of the integrative analysis of the concept of 'justice' as well as consideration of its axiological immanent essence, provide, in our opinion, sufficient grounds for defining this legal category as a special type of state activity carried out by courts and judges by consideration and resolution in a special procedural form of legal conflicts, assigned to their jurisdiction, and by making binding decisions, ensured by measures of state coercion, in order to restore and protect violated legal interests and rights*" (Pankova, Olga, & Migachev, Y. (2020). Justice in the Contemporary World. *BRICS Law Journal, 7*(1), 119–147, p. 146). For more about the perception of justice for perpetrators of international crimes, see: Bijleveld, Catrien, et al. (2022). Sanctioning Perpetrators of International Crimes: A Vignette Study. *International Criminal Law Review, 1*(aop), 1–22.

157 In the end, the question is not really whether punitive sanction, proactive protection or environmental justice should constitute the dominant approach to promoting environmental security: "*instead, a polycentric approach blending all three paradigms might maximize policy results. Such a multifaceted approach could promote environmental security by criminally punishing the most invidious offender, dissuading the negligent offender through incentive-based schemes, cleaning up blighted communities, according individuals a medium to air grievances, and encouraging the global community to equally shoulder the environmental externalities of industrialization*" (Drumbl, Mark A. (2000). International Human Rights, International Humanitarian Law, and Environmental Security: Can the International Criminal Court Bridge the Gaps? *ILSA Journal of International & Comparative Law, 6*, 305–341, p. 340).

158 "Ecological dumping is an illicit form of promoting the external competitiveness of environment-intensive products, in whose production a country specialises, at the expense of the accelerated degradation of national natural resources, and in violation of the PPP. Ecological dumping occurs when a country specialises in the production of environment-intensive goods, not because it has a true comparative advantage in the production of these goods, but only due to state interventions or 'absences' that allow it to maintain 'abnormally' low prices for these products (lower than the prices practiced internally)" (Aragão, Alexandra. (2014). *The polluter pays principle: cornerstone of community environmental policy* (Vol. 1). Institute The Right for a Green Planet, p. 203).

159 The doctrine names as 'accessory penalties', the sanctions, on the international level, beyond imprisonment: "*the judges can first confiscate his assets (...) the International Criminal Court can pronounce pecuniary fines*" (Frouville, Olivier de (2012). *International criminal law: sources, incriminations, responsibility*. Paris: Pedone, p. 473–474).

160 In Neyret's proposal for the "Ecocide" and "Ecocrimes" Conventions, the author suggests punishments for legal entities (transnational companies), such as the dissolution of the moral person, temporary or definitive closure of activities and prohibition of partnerships with the State, in addition to compensation to the victims, after publicising the conviction (Neyret, Laurent (2015). *From ecocrimes to ecocide: criminal law to the rescue of the environment*. Brussels: Bruylant, p. 417).

world, provoking a plurality of legal responses and, consequently, penalties. After the definition of genocide in 1933, and ratification in its own Convention in 1948, various genocidal situations were soon exposed, including the Holocaust.[161] The same should occur with ecocide.[162]

As will be seen in the next chapter, the development of ecocide, after its recognition in the Vietnam War, remained related to the war context in *The Code*, equated to crimes against humanity and genocide, to only in the 1990s, jump to conducts in peacetime. However, even in the most modern bill projects, ecocide seems distant from the direct repression of actions/omissions that cause climate change.

References

Agnew, R. (2012). The ordinary acts that contribute to ecocide. In *Routledge international handbook of green criminology* (p. 70). Routledge. https://doi.org/10.4324/9780203093658.ch3

Aida, M., Tahar, A. M., & Davey, O. (2023). Ecocide in the international law: Integration between environmental rights and international crime and its implementation in Indonesia. In *3rd Universitas Lampung international conference on social sciences (ULICoSS 2022)* (pp. 572–584). Atlantis Press. https://www.atlantis-press.com/article/125986377.pdf

Aksenova, M. (2017). Symbolism as a constraint on international criminal law. *Leiden Journal of International Law, 30*(2), 475–499.

Aragão, A. (2014). *The polluter pays principle: Cornerstone of community environmental policy* (Vol. 1). Institute The Right for a Green Planet.

Barnes, H. E. (1921). Historical origin of the prison system in America. *Journal of Criminal Law and Criminology, 12*(1), 35–60. https://scholarlycommons.law.northwestern.edu/cgi/viewcontent.cgi?article=1772&context=jclc

Bellivier, F., Eudes, M., & Fouchard, I. (2018). *International crimes law*. Themis Droit.

Bijleveld, C., et al. (2022). Sanctioning perpetrators of international crimes: A Vignette study. *International Criminal Law Review, 1*, 1–22.

Bitencourt, C. (2002). Criminal liability of legal entity: Foundations and implications. *Journal of Criminal Law, 13*, 27–38.

Burdon, P. D. (2015). Wild law: A proposal for radical social change. *New Zealand Journal of Public and International Law, 13*, 157–178.

Cabanes, V. (2018). Holding states and companies accountable for climate change: From planetary boundaries to the crime of ecocide. In C. Cournil & L. Varison (Org.), *Climate trials between national and international*. Pedone.

Caetano, M. A. (2016). *Accumulation offences in environmental criminal law*. Pillares.

[161] In the twentieth Century, "*government violence and repression claimed the lives of tens of millions of people by either directly killing them or by placing them in situations where they were likely to starve, fall ill, and die. In its most extreme form—genocide—this repression seeks to 'destroy, in whole or in part, a national, ethnical, racial or religious group, as such.' Since the end of World War II, social scientists have documented over forty cases of genocide and at least one hundred non-genocidal campaigns of mass killing*" (Wayne, Carly, & Zhukov, Y. M. (2022). Never again: The holocaust and political legacies of genocide. *World Politics, 74*(3), 367–404. https://doi.org/10.1017/S0043887122000053. Accessed on: 25 Jun. 2025).

[162] It is not intended here, obviously, to compare the severities of ecocide and genocide. The equivalence as international crimes is made in the sense of defining them as reprehensible behaviours by all, as they are contrary to the very existence of humans in peace and security.

Canali, L. (2018). Climate litigation against companies: Assessment and prospects. In C. Cournil & L. Varison (Eds.), *Climate trials between the national and the international* (pp. 68–83). A. Pedone Editions.
Chaumette, A.-L. V. (2009). *The subjects of international criminal law: Towards a new definition of international legal personality?* Pedone.
Chiaverini, T. (2009). Origin of the prison sentence. Master's Dissertation in Philosophy of Law. Pontifical Catholic University of São Paulo. http://www.dominiopublico.gov.br/download/teste/arqs/cp119708.pdf.
Climate Case Chart. (2019). Milieudefensie et al. v. Royal Dutch Shell plc..
Conectas Human Rights. (2019). *Climate litigation in practice: Strategies for climate litigation in Brazil.*
Cozens, P., & Stoks, F. (2024). Climate change and crime—exploring future risks, resilience and crime through environmental design (CPTED). *Crime Prevention and Community Safety*, 420–439.
Delmas-Marty, M. (2013). Ambiguities and lacunae: The international criminal court ten years on. *Journal of International Criminal Justice, 11*(3), 553–561. https://doi.org/10.1093/jicj/mqt032
Di Landro, A. (2018). *Responsibility for authorized activity in the sectors of the environment and territory: Criminal and extrapenal protection tools.* G. Giappichelli Publisher.
Drumbl, M. A. (2000). International human rights, international humanitarian law, and environmental security: Can the international criminal court bridge the gaps? *ILSA Journal of International & Comparative Law, 6*, 305–341.
Duthoit, L. (2020). Milieudefensie et al v. Shell (2019). In C. Cournil (Ed.), *The great climate affairs, confluence of rights*. International, Comparative and European Rights.
Estève, A. (2020). *Introduction to environmental political theory*. Armand Colin.
Fanchiotti, V., Miraglia, M., & Pierini, J. P. (2014). *The international criminal court: Substantive and procedural profiles*. G. Giappichelli Editore.
Friede, R. R. (2017). The new paradigm of criminal liability of the legal entity for environmental crime. *Legal Journal of the Higher School of Advocacy of OAB-PR, 2*(1), 15.
Frouville, O. d. (2012). *International criminal law: Sources, incriminations, responsibility*. Pedone.
Gay, L., & Stefanini, M. F.-R. (2021). Appeals for the protection of fundamental rights in comparative law. What justiciability of the right to the environment? In M. Hautereau-Boutonnet & È. Truilhe (Eds.), *The environmental trial: From the trial on the environment to the trial for the environment* (pp. 69–94). Dalloz.
Griffin, P. (2017). *The carbon majors database: CDP carbon majors report 2017*. Carbon Disclosure Project (CDP) UK. http://www.truevaluemetrics.org/DBpdfs/Carbon/CDP/CDP-Carbon-Majors-Report-2017.pdf
Hautereau-Boutonnet, Mathilde. (2018). Les procès climatiques par la "doctrine du procès climatique". In Christel Cournil & Leandro Varison (Orgs.), Les procès climatiques: Entre le national et l'international (pp. 31–46). : Pedone.
Heede, R. (2014). Carbon majors. Accounting for carbon and methane emissions. *Methods & Results Report*. Climate Mitigation Services. https://climateaccountability.org/pdf/MRR%209.1%20Apr14R.pdf. Accessed June 25, 2025.
Heller, K. J., & Lawrence, J. C. (2007). The limits of article 8(2)(b)(iv) of the Rome statute, the first ecocentric environmental war crime. *Georgetown International Environmental Law Review, 20*, 1–40.
Horta, R. L. (2020). The disheartening function of punishments: Revisiting the theories of punishment in the light of experimental psychology. *Law Review, State and Society*, 1–32. https://doi.org/10.17808/des.0.1346
Hryhorczuk, D., et al. (2024). The environmental health impacts of Russia's war on Ukraine. *Journal of Occupational Medicine and Toxicology, 19*(1), 1. https://doi.org/10.1186/s12995-023-00398-y
Intergovernmental Panel on Climate Change (IPCC). (2018). *Global warming of 1.5°C. Special report of the intergovernmental panel on climate change*. https://www.ipcc.ch/pdf/special-reports/sr15/sr15_spm_final.pdf.

Intergovernmental Panel on Climate Change (IPCC). (2021). *Climate Change 2021: The physical science basis. Contribution of working group I to the sixth assessment report of the Intergovernmental Panel on Climate Change*. Cambridge University Press.

Intergovernmental Panel on Climate Change (IPCC). (2023). Climate change 2023: Synthesis report. *Summary for Policymakers*. https://www.ipcc.ch/report/ar6/syr/downloads/report/IPCC_AR6_SYR_SPM.pdf.

Johannsen, A. P. d. S., & Ferreira, A. P. (2012). Brief considerations about the environmental criminal responsibility of the legal person in Brazil and in Spain. *Revista Direito e Política, 7*(3), 1620–1651. https://periodicos.univali.br/index.php/rdp/article/download/5556/2962

Keenan, P. J. (2019). International criminal law and climate change. *Boston University International Law Journal, 37*, 89–112.

Lameira, V. (2017). Climate Change: Litigation strategies and the role of the judiciary in combating the causes and effects of global warming in the Brazilian context. *Journal of the Public Prosecutor's Office of Rio de Janeiro, 64*, 197.

Leão, H. de G., & Prata, L. (2020). The African court of human and peoples' rights in 5 reflections. Cosmopolitan. https://www.cosmopolita.org/post/o-tribunal-africano-dos-direitos-humanos-e-dos-povos-em-5-reflex%C3%B5es.

Licht, J. H. (2019). *General Debate of the 18th Session of the Assembly of States Parties to the Rome Statute of the International Criminal Court*. The Hague, 7 Dec 2019. https://asp.icc-cpi.int/iccdocs/asp_docs/ASP18/GD.VAN.2.12.pdf.

Lima, V. d. M. (2009). The principle of guilt and the cumulative offences. *Journal of the Public Prosecutor's Office of Rio Grande do Sul*, 51–86.

Lin, J. (2015). The first successful climate negligence case: A comment on Urgenda foundation v. the state of The Netherlands (Ministry of Infrastructure and the Environment). *Climate Law, 5*(1), 65–81.

Liston, G. (2020). Enhancing the efficacy of climate change litigation: How to resolve the 'fair share question' in the context of international human rights law. *Cambridge International Law Journal, 9*(2), 241–263.

Lord, S. (2013). Joint criminal enterprise and the international criminal court: A comparison between joint criminal enterprise and the modes of liability in joint commission in crime under the Rome statute; can the International Criminal Court apply joint criminal enterprise as a mode of liability? Thesis in International Criminal Law. Stockholm University.

Maljean-Dubois, S. (2021). The opening of the environmental trial in the international order. In M. Hautereau-Boutonnet & È. Truilhe (Eds.), *The environmental trial: From the trial on the environment to the trial for the environment* (pp. 105–120). Dalloz.

Márquez, D. I. (2019). Climate litigation against the carbon majors in the countries of origin: Notes from the perspective of business and human rights. *Electronic Journal of International Studies (REEI), 37*, 2–37.

Masucci, M. (2017). *Structures of international criminal law: Interpretation, application, offences*. G. Giappichelli Editore.

Maučec, G. (2021). The international criminal court and the issue of intersectionality—a conceptual and legal framework for analysis. *International Criminal Law Review, 21*(1), 1–34.

Mégret, F. (2011). The problem of an international criminal law of the environment. *Columbia Journal of Environmental Law, 36*(2), 195–257.

Medeiros, T. D., de Oliveira, F., & Pitassi, C. (2018). Eco-innovation in the corporations operating in the international market. *Journal of Management and Sustainability, 8*(1), 75–92.

Michelot, A. (2019). Climate justice: Facing the responsibility of climate change? *International Journal of Bioethics and Science Ethics, 30*(2), 17–39.

Misonne, D. (2020). Netherlands v. Urgenda (2019). In C. Cournil (Ed.), *The major climate cases, confluence of rights* (p. 209). International, Comparative and European Rights.

Molteni, V. (2021). The long road of the criminalisation of ecocide: Legal issues and dynamics of normative and social effectiveness. *Contemporary Criminal Law, 4*, 205–233.

Mongillo, V. (2018). *Criminal responsibility between individual and collective entity*. G. Giappichelli Publisher.

Neto, B., Alvarez, D., & Mont'Alverne, T. C. F. (2020). Massive damage to the environment: Crime in war, but not in peacetime? Intergovernmental organisations and the next step in global environmental governance. *Science and Peace, XI*(2), 37–55. https://scienzaepace.unipi.it/index.php/it/call-forpapers/item/download/430_e5761931728ba84456238f2abebf5ac7.html

Neyret, L. (2015). *From ecocrimes to ecocide: Criminal law to the rescue of the environment*. Bruylant.

Oliver Yébenes, M. (2024). Climate change, ESG criteria and recent regulation: Challenges and opportunities. *Eurasian Economic Review, 14*(1), 87–120.

Pankova, O., & Migachev, Y. (2020). Justice in the contemporary world. *BRICS Law Journal, 7*(1), 119–147.

Peel, J., & Osofsky, H. M. (2020). Climate change litigation. *Annual Review of Law and Social Science, 16*, 21–38.

Pellet, A. (2007). State responsibility and individual criminal responsibility in international law. *Romanian Journal of International Law, 4*, 11–32.

Pereira, R. (2020). After the ICC Office of the Prosecutor's 2016 policy paper on case selection and prioritisation: Towards an international crime of ecocide? *Criminal Law Forum, 31*(2), 179–224.

Perrier, J.-B. (2021). The environmental trial before the criminal judge. In M. Hautereau-Boutonnet & È. Truilhe (Eds.), *The environmental trial: From the trial on the environment to the trial for the environment* (pp. 57–68). Dalloz.

Pezzot, R., & Graf, J.-P. (2022). Ecocide—legal revolution or symbolism? *Völkerrechtsblog*. https://voelkerrechtsblog.org/ecocide-legal-revolution-or-symbolism/

Pink, G., & White, R. (2016). Collaboration in combating environmental crime. Making it matter. In G. Pink (Ed.), *Environmental crime and collaborative state intervention*. Palgrave Macmillan.

Reiss, M. W. (2017). *The International Criminal Court in the Context of the Globalisation of Law: Analysis of the Rome Statute based on Anglo-Saxon inspired Criminal Law, on Criminal Law inspired Romano-Germanic and in Brazilian Criminal Law* [Doctoral Thesis, Pontifical Catholic University of Rio de Janeiro].

Ripple, W. J., et al. (2024). The 2024 state of the climate report: Perilous times on planet earth. *Bioscience, 74*(12), 812–824.

Rodeiro, M. (2024). *Responding to ecocide through transitional justice* (pp. 47–79). Diálogos.

Sands, P. (2003). *Principles of international environmental law* (2nd ed.). Cambridge University Press.

Schmidt, T. M. (2005). Transnational corporate responsibility for international environmental and human rights violations: Will the United Nations' "Norms" provide the required means. *California Western International Law Journal, 36*, 217–246.

Scarpello, A., et al. (2021). Ecocide and corporate responsibility: The necessary link to achieve environmental justice. *Electronic Journal of Contemporary International Law (REDIC), 4*. http://sedici.unlp.edu.ar/bitstream/handle/10915/133831/Versi%C3%83%C2%B3n_en_PDF.pdf?sequence=1

Steinzor, R. (2016). How criminal law can help save the environment. *Environmental Law, 46*, 209–239.

Thome, A. C. R., Nunes, N. A., & Thome, R. L. (2020). Environmental degradation in the Brazilian Amazon and the challenges for the inclusion of the crime of ecocide in the Rome statute. *Guaju: Brazilian Journal of Sustainable Territorial Development, 6*(2), 178–189.

Thomé, R. F., & Venancio, S. R. (2022). The Gabcikovo-Nagymaros case (Hungary vs Slovakia): The international court of justice and the principle of prevention. *Journal of Law and Sustainability, 8*(2).

United Nations Environment Programme (UNEP). (2021). *Global climate litigation report: 2020 status review*. https://wedocs.unep.org/bitstream/handle/20.500.11822/34818/GCLR.pdf?sequence=1&isAllowed=y.

United Nations Environment Programme (UNEP). (2023). *Global climate litigation report: 2023 status review*. https://wedocs.unep.org/bitstream/handle/20.500.11822/43008/global_climate_litigation_report_2023.pdf?sequence=1&isAllowed=y.

Van Dijk, N., Linehan, J., & Lawrence, P. (2018). Introduction to the special issue: Imagining a different future, overcoming barriers to climate justice. *University of Tasmania Law Review, 37*(2), 1–24.

Wayne, C., & Zhukov, Y. M. (2022). Never again: The holocaust and political legacies of genocide. *World Politics, 74*(3), 367–404. https://doi.org/10.1017/S0043887122000053

White, R. (2018). *Climate change criminology*. Policy Press.

Chapter 4
Development of the Notion of Ecocide

The human and environmental consequences of the use of Agent Orange during the Vietnam War triggered diverse reactions. The global nature of environmental degradation received much attention among lawyers, politicians, and civil society, with some consensus on the need for actions at the international level; however, there was no convergence on what measures were necessary (Malhotra, 2017, p. 49).

In the legal field, after the events in Indochina, the academic discussion about ecocide sought to understand it, from the perspective of whether to require intent to commit it to the context of prohibition, in times of war or also in times of peace. As environmental disasters occurred not directly linked to armed conflicts, the need for an international legal approach became more explicit.[1]

At the level of the United Nations Organisation, environmental protection was seen connected to international peace and security, in the following decades.[2] The

[1] There is also an increase in awareness about the situation of disaster victims, bringing attention to the importance of adequate national and international legal norms and structures for prevention, mitigation and responses to these events: "*International Disaster Response Law has developed significantly in recent years, as shown by the increasing number of relevant treaties which have been signed and ratified worldwide. The codification of norms addressing various aspects related to disaster prevention, management, and post-disaster recovery occurred over a strikingly short period of time, very often as a reaction to new kinds of disasters. This resulted in* ad hoc *developments of IDRL, which sometimes caused significant overlapping and contradictions. The need for better synchronization and co-ordination of codification activities has been highlighted several times by scholars, and this inspired the International Law Commission to focus its attention on these issues*" (Guttry et al., 2012).

[2] The international protection of the environment "*is a viable objective, even upon the most positivistic conception of international relations, because of the mutual dependence of states (for the collective survival of their peoples) on responsible environmental management and development activities. In other words, we are linked in mutual self-interest by the 'indivisibility of global biospheric processes'. As a result, environmental depletion is a non- military threat to the life and well-being of societies. On an extreme view, environmental degradation could itself be seen as a form of warfare*" (Reilly, 1995, p. 783).

D. A. Brochado Neto, *Ecocide*, https://doi.org/10.1007/978-3-032-07757-8_4

involvement of the Security Council was, however, restrained, limiting itself to pointing out the link between the deterioration of the environment and natural resources—as an element of armed disputes, resulting in political instability—and planetary security.[3]

It fell to the *International Law Commission* (ILC), of the UN, the forays[4] into a possible international codification of criminal environmental protection, mainly in the 1980s and 1990s. After the study, the final text excluded the existence of an environmental crime committed by an individual,[5] maintaining criminal liability for severe destruction of the environment in a war context.[6]

The idea of "ecocide", obscured at the international level, was reached, in the 1990s, by some States. First, Vietnam (1990),[7] followed by Russia (1996) and, in the following years, the newly created nations after the dissolution of the Soviet Union included in their criminal codes the crime (Cabanes, 2018, p. 276), with vague typification and difficult subsumption of practical case (taxativity).

Even with this initial Asian impulse, the exclusion of the crime at the international level cooled the discussion in other regions, especially after the creation of the International Criminal Court, accepting the final draft of the ILC, in 1998. The theme would be renewed with the return of the environmental agenda in the climate sphere, evidenced by the successive reports of the IPCC, pointing to a need for global action against the greenhouse effect.[8]

Tied—in discourse—to the climate crisis, ecocide returned to legislative houses as bill proposals in recent years, bringing definitions and varied scopes. The

[3] "*The case against the Security Council's involvement is premised on the idea that 'defining environmental issues in terms of security risks is in itself a risky operation. 'The concern is that 'we may end up contributing more to the militarization of environmental politics than to the de-militarization of security politics'. 'This is not because the urgency of international environmental problems does not warrant attention at the highest level, but rather because their characterisation as a 'security concern' could import all the defects of the present statist machinery of international law as a justification for further centralisation of power 'and even a rationale for armed attack*" (Reilly, 1995, p. 784).

[4] The ILC has already dealt, in its projects, with responsibilities in general and transboundary environmental damages, such as, for example, in the *Draft Articles on State Responsibility*, in 2001, when it made several references to the duty to prevent such damages (Jodoin & Saito, 2012, p. 143).

[5] The provision of the environmental crime perpetrated by an individual (art. 26) "*was removed from the Code altogether. The final version adopted by the ILC only mentioned the intentional creation of 'widespread, long-term and severe damage to the natural environment' within a war context under Article 8.23 Thus, Article 8 is the only provision in international law to hold a perpetrator responsible for environmental damage. However, this article limits the crime to wartime situations and to intentional damage, and its threshold is considered to be too high*" (Malhotra, 2017, p. 53).

[6] Later, embodied in the Rome Statute, Article 8, 8(2)(b)(iv).

[7] In three Penal Codes, 1990 (art. 278), 1999 (art. 342) and 2015 (art. 422), Vietnam chose to criminalise ecocide, treating it as a crime against humanity (Link: https://ihl-databases.icrc.org/customary-ihl/por/docs/v2_cou_vn_rule45, accessed on: 20 Jun. 2025).

[8] Link: https://www.ipcc.ch/reports/

diversity, however, comes unaccompanied by better legal technique, as it brings various obstacles to the application of the crime,[9] as was perceived in countries where the infraction already exists. This fact can be explained, in part, by the absence of theoretical-doctrinal in-depth analysis on the theme "international criminal law",[10] more specifically "ecocide".

It is undeniable, however, the recent development of studies on the crime, including analyses on its best definition, at the international level.[11] Even so, the technical obstacles, such as the need for the agent's intention for the characterisation of ecocide, the construction of the causal link and the liability for damages, carry difficulties of practical application, in addition to legal incompatibilities between the various legal systems, which, per se, prove problematic in international criminal law.

In this context, the role of the *International Law Commission* is particularly relevant.[12] The conception of a Code of international crimes requires the construction of a system that contemplates the different national legal cultures, both of substantive and procedural law, without, however, forgetting the international character and peculiarities of the document. It is revealing, therefore, that in its elaboration, the

---

[9] Among the ecocide projects for the ICC, for example, it is suggested that climate change be an aggravating circumstance of the definition, a fact that would greatly hinder ratification and insertion of the crime at the national levels, considering the subsidiary character of the Court (Chiarini, 2022).

[10] Restricted to wars, international criminal law has theoretical depth especially regarding crimes against humanity and genocide, today enshrined in the Rome Statute. Hence the attempt to link ecocide with the two crimes (items 3.1.1 and 3.1.2): "*The majority of genocide literature does not seriously or thoroughly analyze the connection between genocide and the destruction of nonhuman nature, otherwise known as ecocide. In this respect, most genocide and human rights scholarship remains anthropocentric, such that only the destruction of and the dignity of human life is considered to be of consequence. The term 'ecocide' was coined in 1970 by a group of scientists to describe the devastation being wrought to the land in Vietnam as a result of chemical weapons like Agent Orange. Lawyer and activist Polly Higgins later defined ecocide as 'extensive damage to, destruction of or loss of ecosystem(s) of a given territory, whether by human agency or by other causes, to such an extent that peaceful enjoyment by the inhabitants of that territory has been severely diminished'. Because "ecocide" is still a relatively under-theorized subject, the term covers a wide array of acts and harms*" (Eichler, 2020, p. 107).

[11] For example, the amendment project to the Rome Statute, presented by the foundation *Stop Ecocide Earth*, in June 2021, and basis of the official proposal to the Assembly of Parties, in 2024, whose elaboration involved various specialists in international criminal law, among judges, lawyers and students (Link: https://ecocidelaw.com/definition/#definition/). The definition of ecocide reached by the group is already used by politicians to propose the crime in national legislations, such as Scotland (Link: https://www.dailyrecord.co.uk/news/scottish-news/scotland-could-first-county-make-24762289).

[12] McCaffrery warns of the little attention to the ILC's initial work on the project of the Code of international crimes: "*The Draft Code of Offenses Against the Peace and Security of Mankind has received far too little attention, both publicly and in scholarly circles, and I encourage anyone at all interested in the subject to write about it. It is a subject on which the Commission*" (Bassiouni et al., 1986).

inclusion of ecocide (treated here as the act of causing severe damage to the environment),[13] an episode detailed below, was considered.

4.1 From the Project of *The Code* to the Rome Statute

The *International Law Commission* (ILC)[14] was established at the UN General Assembly in 1948,[15] as a permanent institution for the codification and progressive development of international law (Morton, 2000, p. 1), in compliance with the provisions of art. 13 (1) (a) of the United Nations Charter.[16] Since 1981, the Commission is composed of 34 members,[17] elected for 5 years, in a process similar to the election of the judges of the International Court of Justice, with independent action from their countries (governments) of origin. Indeed, the aim is to achieve a scientific reformulation of the law by independent experts, avoiding political appointments.[18]

Since then, the ILC has drafted, for example, the Vienna Convention on Diplomatic Relations (1961) and the Vienna Convention on the Law of Treaties

[13] As the construction of an international crime, it is difficult to fit serious offenses against the environment as conduct against humanity: "*The idea that an international crime arises if the actus reus 'shocks the conscience of mankind' is ambiguous. Attacks on the environment do not categorically 'shock the conscience of mankind': some may, others may not, and whether they do will depend on the audience. To some extent, certain behaviours appear shocking only after offences have been defined and socially designated as grave. Moreover, the shocking character of certain offences has never been conceived of as an autonomous source of international criminalisation, but rather serves as a way of rhetorically reinforcing the perceived gravity of those offences. More importantly, the current human rights-oriented bases for international criminal law are decidedly anthropocentric*" (Mégret, 2011, p. 208).

[14] Link: https://legal.un.org/ilc/

[15] Resolution 174 (II) of the UN General Assembly.

[16] Charter of the United Nations, article 13. 1.: The General Assembly shall initiate studies and make recommendations, aimed at: (a) promoting international cooperation in the political field and encouraging the progressive development of international law and its codification.

[17] Statute of the ILC, article 2 (Link: https://legal.un.org/ilc/texts/instruments/english/statute/statute.pdf).

[18] The politicisation of the election of the Commission's members occurred gradually, especially in the 70s, when, for example, the UN General Assembly failed to select the correct quota for the Asian continent, leaving it underrepresented. The problems in the election, coupled with the "brain drain" from the ILC to international courts, characterised a certain decline in the quality of the work. The fourth decade (1980–1989) of the Commission was characterised by a robust agenda and conclusion of two conventions (Morton, 2000, pp. 11–17). Regarding the discussion about the legitimacy of the Commission, see: Bravo (2015, p. 163).

(1969). Regarding international crimes,[19] the Commission was twice tasked with drafting a Code of Crimes Against Peace and Security of Humanity.[20]

The first draft took place shortly after the creation of the Institute, was submitted to the General Assembly in 1950, and adopted by the Commission in 1954 (Morton, 2000, p. 38). The text proposes the creation of an International Criminal Court, also listing ten offences against peace and security of humanity.[21] At the time—during the Cold War—the qualification of various acts of war as a crime was problematic, leading to the interruption of the document's elaboration by the General Assembly, while waiting for the definition of the crime of aggression (Morton, 2000, p. 41). It should be noted that there is no mention of the environment in this first project drafted by the Commission.

The second draft was requested through resolution 36/106,[22] of the UN General Assembly, on 10 December 1981. In the discussion on *The Code*, various countries made suggestions of crimes, such as the use of atomic weapons (or other weapons of mass destruction), mercenarism, *apartheid*, racial discrimination, slavery, colonialism, terrorism, drug trafficking, and destruction of the environment (Morton, 2000, p. 42).

The Commission, as a way to organise the work from the 1954 project, focused on the new draft on offences against peace and security of humanity as crimes for international law,[23] through an exhaustive list, excluding references to the internal

---

[19] "*International criminal law has developed on an* ad hoc *basis and includes over three hundred treaties that have evolved over the past 175 years (1996). These treaties define international crimes and place a duty upon participating states to criminalise the conduct prescribed by the treaties and to prosecute accused offenders and punish those convicted or extradite the accused to another state willing to prosecute. (…). The crimes considered by the International Law Commission in the drafting of its Code of Crimes, however, must pass a higher standard, namely, they must constitute a threat to the 'peace and security to mankind'*" (Morton, 2000, p. 21).

[20] Bassiouni criticises the way the UN conducted the development of the Code: "*One problem with developing an enforceable Code of Offences Against the Peace and Security of Mankind is that no U.N. body has ever been vested with complete responsibility for producing a draft. Instead, three bodies have shared that responsibility. First, the International Law Commission (ILC) began working on the Draft Code itself. Second, another "Special Committee" of the General Assembly was given the responsibility for drafting a statute for an international criminal court. Third, there was the Special Committee on Defining Aggression, which in 1974 finally produced a document. To have different bodies dealing with the same subject is thus clearly unproductive. It would have made more sense for the same body to deal with all questions relating to the same subject since enforcement must be tailored to the crimes intended to be enforced*" (Bassiouni et al., 1986).

[21] Link: https://legal.un.org/ilc/texts/instruments/english/commentaries/7_3_1954.pdf

[22] Link: https://documents-dds-ny.un.org/doc/RESOLUTION/GEN/NR0/407/32/IMG/NR040732.pdf

[23] The nature of current criminal acts and their definitions in applicable international instruments and customary international law indicate that there are no common or specific doctrinal foundations that constitute the necessary legal basis to include certain conduct as an international crime. However, the following requirements can be listed as bases: "*(1) existing international conventions which consider the act in question an international crime; (2) recognition under customary international law that such conduct constitutes an international crime; (3) recognition under general principles of international law that such conduct is or should be deemed violative of interna-*

law of the countries (Morton, 2000, p. 42). Thus, included in the initial debates, in addition to the behaviours listed in the first draft, was severe environmental destruction,[24] a direct reflection of the events that occurred in the Vietnam War, in the previous decade.

During the first years of the work, even under criticism,[25] environmental protection through international criminal law always permeated, sometimes tangentially, the discussions of the ILC.[26] In 1991, the most significant movement in favour of an environmental crime was made, with the proposal of Article 26 to the project:

> **Article 26**
> Wilful and severe damage to the environment—An individual who wilfully causes or orders another individual to cause widespread, long-term and severe damage to the natural environment shall, on conviction thereof, be sentenced [to]... (ILC, 1991, p. 234)

The idea was to restrict the scope of the crime to the most severe situations to the environment, therefore using the severity of the damage and its duration as criteria. There was also an agreement among the members of the Commission to only include intentional behaviours in the article, excluding accidental damages caused by negligence. It was, therefore, fundamental to establish the agent's intention to perpetrate the environmental damage.[27]

---

tional law and about which there is a pending draft convention before the United Nations; and (4) prohibition of such conduct by an international convention though not specifically stating that it constitutes an international crime and which is also recognized in the writings of scholars as such" (Bassiouni, 1983, p. 27).

[24] In the Report of the 36th Session, the conducts of colonialism, *apartheid*, severe damage to the environment, economic aggression, use of nuclear weapons and mercenarism were considered possible to be included in the Code project. Regarding the environment, "*Article 19 of part 1 of the draft articles on State responsibility recognizes that, under certain conditions, causing serious damage to the environment may be considered as an international crime*" (ILC, 1984, p. 16).

[25] For Bassiouni, in 1986, "*The ILC's debates as to what the code should include (ratione materiae) are baffling. Consider for example the application of loose criteria which lead to the inclusion of "mercenarism" and environmental violations" as international crimes (however one may wish to define them since they are not recognized as international crimes) while overlooking certain recognized ones such as "war crimes," "slavery," and others. Furthermore, none of the weaknesses of the Nuremberg and Tokyo Trials has been cured by the work of that Special Rapporteur. The crimes are vaguely defined, ambiguous in their meaning, and the elements of each offence are far from being discernible*" (Bassiouni et al., 1986).

[26] In 1987, the crime of ecocide was nominally remembered, as a viable conduct to be included in *The Code*: "*Crimes against the peace and security of mankind might therefore be characterised as acts which seriously jeopardised the most vital interests of mankind, violated the fundamental principles of jus cogens and threatened individual nations, ethnic groups, civilisation and the right to life. Perhaps the Special Rapporteur could also consider the relationship between the provisions of the draft code and those of article 19 of part 1 of the draft articles on State responsibility. He would also not object if the list of international crimes included 'ecocide', as a reflection of the need to safeguard and preserve the environment, as well as the first use of nuclear weapons, colonialism, apartheid, economic aggression and mercenarism*" (ILC, 1987, p. 56).

[27] If the damage occurred for a purpose other than environmental destruction, the situation should not be covered by the Code: "*The scope of the article was further limited by the requirement that the causing of the damage must be wilful. There had been general agreement in the Drafting*

In the discussions, the practical difficulties of determining the widespread, serious, and long-lasting nature of the damage were also raised, albeit superficially.[28] That is, by requiring a long-term damage to frame the behaviour as a crime, any probability of applying the provision could be excluded. Even so, Article 26 was adopted and incorporated into the project, only removing the term "another individual" from the proposed text (ILC, 1991, p. 236).

As a way to make the Code drafted in 1991 more acceptable to the international community,[29] a significant reduction in the number of crimes (a maximum of six offences) was suggested in 1995, suppressing,[30] among others, the provision on serious environmental crimes.[31] The removal from the agenda of ecocide did not occur in a traditional way, through agreements between the parties, highlighting the political character (and little recorded, in documents) of the unilateral decision of the Commission's leadership.[32] As a reaction from the ILC members themselves to the

---

Committee that the causing of accidental damage, even as a result of negligence, should not come within the terms of the article. On the other hand, the concept of intent proposed by the Special Rapporteur had been deemed to be too broad and difficult to interpret. In the view of the Drafting Committee, the causing of damage that was a likely consequence of an act committed for a different purpose should not fall within the ambit of the Code, and only such harm as was the direct consequence of a deliberate act should be covered. That notion was conveyed by the word "wilful"" (ILC, 1991, p. 235).

[28]"*Mr. BEESLEY said that he was not opposed to adoption of the article although he had certain reservations in that regard. They arose from the fear that, probably inevitably, a lengthy investigation would be necessary before it was possible to determine accurately whether or not the harm caused to the natural environment was widespread, long-term and severe, and that might divest the article of its substance. The Drafting Committee's proposed text was, however, the best possible one in the circumstances*" (ILC, 1991, p. 235).

[29]The 1991 draft was not received with enthusiasm by the States, especially as it extended far beyond the accusations made in Nuremberg: "*some of these 'new' crimes were as obscure as intervention (Article 17) or 'any other form of alien domination' (Article 18)*" (Tomuschat, 1996, p. 242).

[30]Despite only representatives of three States having opposed ecocide in the *draft*, the suppression of several of the proposed crimes was unilateral, by decision of the president of the Commission Ahmed Mahiou (Schwegler, 2017, p. 75).

[31]"The draft articles on colonial domination and other forms of alien domination and wilful and severe damage to the environment were equally unpopular with Governments that expressed an opinion on them. Although article 19 of the draft articles on State responsibility characterizes as international crimes both colonial domination and other forms of alien domination and serious damage to the human environment, for the time being these draft articles do not seem to have convinced Governments. It will be necessary to wait until developments in international law confirm or reverse the tendency to consider these acts as crimes" (ILC, 1995, p. 35).

[32]The criticisms, among the members, of the text of Article 26 focused mainly on the need to prove the author's intent in causing environmental damage, since, as reminded by several countries, these often occur without the direct intention of the agent. However, instead of removing the volitional character, the crime was completely excluded, without due debate: "*Reactions within the ILC to the announcement of the withdrawal of Article 26 were recorded only in part. Based on the observations recorded at the time, what we do know is that the decision taken was not based on agreement between the parties. Subsequent off-the-record discussions between ILC members failed to further the progress of the debate about the law of ecocide: in 1995 it was decided at least twice to*

suggestion (then realised), a working group was established to examine the possibility of contemplating in the project the subject of wilful and serious damage to the environment (Tomuschat, 1996, p. 242).

The report on the subject was presented to the ILC in March 1996, prepared by the jurist Christian Tomuschat (ILC, 1996b, p. 22). In the document, the rapporteur states that, even with some reservations, the vast majority of the Commission's members were in favour of including offences against the environment in *The Code*, suggesting a division between environmental crimes as a war crime and as crimes against humanity (ILC, 1996b, p. 25).

Brought to the plenary, an agreement was reached on the referral of serious offences against the environment under the mantle of war crimes for further refinement by the drafting committee, while a motion—to have them also reviewed as crimes against humanity—was narrowly defeated.[33] The adopted text, in the end, included environmental damage as a crime (Article 20, war crimes, item *g*) only in the case of armed conflict, when used as a method or means of war—not justified by military necessity—with the intention of causing widespread, long-term, and severe damage to the natural environment, severely harming the health or survival of the local population (Tomuschat, 1996).

In December 1997, the UN General Assembly issued a resolution guiding the establishment of an international criminal court (UN, 1998a), requesting a draft, prepared by a Preparatory Committee, for presentation at the Rome Conference, to be held in June 1998. The Rome Statute of the International Criminal Court would be adopted in mid-July of the same year,[34] taking advantage of the last *draft* sculpted by the *International Law Commission*, defining the crimes within the jurisdiction of this new Court.

The individual and intentional conduct of causing massive damage to the environment in times of peace was, therefore, purged from the jurisdiction of the ICC, even before analysis by the Preparatory Committee to the Rome Conference.

Undeniable, however, is the visible increase, since the 1990s, in the field of study "international criminal law" (Tallgren, 2002, p. 562), both quantitatively and qualitatively. The performance of the ILC, a Commission embedded in the body of the United Nations with the aim of progressively developing international law and its codification, is relevant in this sense. In announcing the possible crimes liable to criminal prosecution in the international arena, the body understands that certain

---

hold informal meetings 'to facilitate the consultations and ensure a truly frank exchange of views" (Gauger et al., 2013, p. 10).

[33] The revision of the wording for environmental crimes, even in a context of war, revealed a fear of criminalising the use of atomic weapons, a recurring theme throughout the Cold War: "*One cannot escape the impression that nuclear arms played a decisive role in the minds of many of those who opted for the final text which now has been emasculated to such an extent that its conditions of applicability will almost never be met even after humankind would have gone through disasters of the most atrocious kind as a consequence of conscious action by persons who were completely aware of the fatal consequences their decisions would entail*" (Tomuschat, 1996, p. 243).

[34] Rome Statute of the International Criminal Court, link: https://www.icc-cpi.int/sites/default/files/RS-Eng.pdf

behaviours "are simply wrong and should be punished",[35] requiring, at the very least, discussion at the international level. Combining this assertion with the gradual recognition, by the Security Council, that serious transnational environmental offences affect the peace and security of humanity, violating "customary rules" and "universal values" (Pereira, 2020, pp. 191–192), the fate of certain behaviours—the most serious—as international crimes is envisaged.

For now, serious offences against the environment are considered an international crime only in the strict context of war. From an environmental point of view, however, there is no reason why it should not be equally reprehensible to cause such damage in times of peace. In this respect, the development of crimes against humanity is a conceptual precedent: these latter were gradually and completely dissociated from war crimes, where armed conflict is the essential element (Mégret, 2011, p. 246).

Another moment when severe environmental damage was related to unlawful acts on the international level, even if not immediately evident (Misutra, 2018, p. 204), occurred during the study of improving the crime of genocide.

4.2 Equating to Genocide

The crime of genocide[36] is well outlined in international criminal law since 1948, embodied in the Convention for the Prevention and Punishment of the Crime of Genocide[37] (Resolution 260 of the UN General Assembly), defined as the practice of certain acts (listed in Article II), during war or in times of peace, with the intention of destroying, in whole or in part, a national, ethnic, racial, or religious group.[38] It is one of the legacies of the Nuremberg trial[39]—and, consequently, of the

[35] "*But how positivistic, rational, utilitarian and 'real' can international criminal justice be? This is not a question easy to pose. The unambiguously devastating quantity and quality of the suffering of the victims of serious international crimes calls for intuitive-moralistic answers, in the manner of '[c]ertain things are simply wrong and ought to be punished. And this we do believe.' To feel compelled nevertheless to subject also international criminal law to the question 'why?' bears the risk of being misunderstood, the risk of being defined in terms of for or against the violence and injustice the crimes represent*" (Tallgren, 2002, p. 564).

[36] The term "genocide" was coined by the Polish lawyer Raphael Lemkin, in 1933, linking the concepts of "barbarism" and "vandalism", as a form of physical and cultural destruction of human social groups (Crook & Short, 2014, p. 305).

[37] Link: https://www.un.org/en/genocideprevention/documents/atrocity-crimes/Doc.1_Convention%20on%20the%20Prevention%20and%20Punishment%20of%20the%20Crime%20of%20Genocide.pdf, accessed on: 20 Apr. 2025.

[38] The Genocide Convention was ratified by 152 States, being recognized as an international crime in 1946, by the UN General Assembly (A/RES/96-I).

[39] The crime of genocide was not included in the Statute of the Nuremberg Military Tribunal, which is why there are no trials for this crime in the post-Second World War, in observance of the principle of legality (even though it is an exceptional court). The 1948 Convention would soon correct this gap (Bellivier et al., 2018, p. 146).

foundations of international criminal law—in the post-War (Tomuschat, 2006, p. 843). Until the end of the 1970s, however, there was no direct correlation between this crime and the perpetration of environmental damage.

Environmental destruction in Vietnam drew international attention to the need for legal protection of the environment. The increase in academic debate around the concept of ecocide (a term that originates inspired by the word "genocide") and civil society awareness of the serious consequences of environmental damage pressured states to address the issue.

During the 1970s, the idea of expanding the 1948 Genocide Convention led to an extensive UN investigation, before the ILC to delve into the topic, on how it could be improved, including the possibility of criminalising ecocide alongside genocide (Gauger et al., 2013, p. 6). To this end, a report was prepared—by the Subcommission on Prevention of Discrimination and Protection of Minorities—for the UN Human Rights Commission, in 1978.[40]

In the report, ecocide is discussed as an international crime similar to genocide, noting that, although not legally defined, its essential meaning is well understood: it denotes various measures of devastation and destruction, aimed at damaging and destroying the ecology of geographical areas, to the detriment of human life, animal life, and plant life (Ruhashyankiko, 1978, p. 128).

However, it was considered that the term "ecocide", at the time, had no precise legal meaning, leading states, during discussions, to allocate the crime in a different context from genocide. For the rapporteur, the "exaggerated extension of the notion of genocide to cases that maintain a very distant connection with this idea is likely to harm the effectiveness of the Convention itself" (Ruhashyankiko, 1978, p. 134).

Following the Ruhashyankiko report, the concept of ecocide resurfaced in 1985, when the Subcommission reconsidered the expansion of the Convention on Genocide, this time reported by Benjamin Whitaker (Crook & Short, 2014, p. 308). Again, some members proposed expanding the definition of genocide, to include cultural genocide, called "ethnocide", and ecocide, understood as adverse changes to the environment, sometimes irreversible, through for example, nuclear explosions, chemical weapons, severe pollution and acid rain, or destruction of the rainforest, which threaten the existence of entire populations, deliberately or with criminal negligence.[41]

---

[40] The Subcommission was asked to consider adding ecocide and reintroducing the cultural method to the Convention: "Special Rapporteur Mr. Nicodème Ruhashyankiko prepared the study, with the final draft published in 1978. At this time, many sub-commission members were supportive of the idea that additional instruments be adopted.80 Within the sub-commission, Mr. Abdelwahab Bouhdiba voiced support for criminalising ecocide: 'any interference with the natural surroundings or environment in which ethnic groups lived was, in effect, a kind of ethnic genocide because such interference could prevent the people involved from following their own traditional way of life'" (Crook & Short, 2014, p. 308).

[41] The report noted that indigenous groups are often the silent victims of ecocide, as emphasised by the study on Indigenous Populations (E/CN.4/Sub.2/1983), requiring urgent attention to cases of physical destruction of these communities (genocide) and destruction of cultures (ethnocide), rein-

It was argued, by some members of the Subcommission, that cultural ethnocide and ecocide are crimes against humanity, rather than genocide, thus deserving better attention, with the possibility of formulating a separate protocol, in the absence of consensus (Whitaker, 1985, p. 17), which in fact did not happen.

The final report took place at the 38th Session, in November 1985 (UN, 1985). It was recommended that the Special Rapporteur Whitaker deepen the investigation into the expansion of the Convention on Genocide, with the aim of including cultural and ecocidal means of promoting genocide, to report at the 40th Session, which did not happen. It is not clear in the UN records why the review of the Convention did not proceed (Crook & Short, 2014, p. 308).

Undoubtedly, the connection between genocide and ecocide is more visible when considering indigenous communities,[42] past and present. The massive destruction of the environment as a way to decimate original populations,[43] aiming to occupy their lands (and natural/energy resources), is the most subtle way to extinguish a population group, without resorting to traditional acts of violence.[44] The exploitation of tar sands in Alberta, Canada, is a current example, where the legal consequences do not reach the criminal sphere, due to the absence of legal precision.

Despite this, most of the literature on genocide does not seriously or fully analyse the connection between the crime and the destruction of non-human nature, as is the case with ecocide. This fact remains evident given the almost exclusively anthropocentric approach to genocide and human rights, in such a way that massive environmental damage is considered only a collateral effect of an injury to human dignity (Eichler, 2020, p. 107).

The inclusion of ecocide as a genocidal method, therefore, remained, like *The Code*, frustrated. It is important to highlight, however, the approach of the UN Subcommission to the crime, which sought to codify it in a pre-existing Convention. The members, when not influenced directly by the opinion of the States, they were often favourable to the addition, broadening the concept of genocide.

---

forced by the increasing attention given by United Nations bodies to the issue (Whitaker, 1985, p. 17).

[42] The community defines itself "as a collectivity that has the legal capacity to self-identify, for example, as tribal or indigenous, but that lives, moreover, vulnerably due to over-dependence, historically, on a certain terrestrial territory and its components from which it derives its Right to life" (Monebhurrun et al., 2016, p. 462).

[43] Environmental devastation of this kind functions as a slow genocide, eroding the health of the people, their sovereignty as a nation and the land, all of which are an integral part of their group identity: "*Because this form of genocide might occur over such a long period of time, it may not always be immediately recognizable as genocide, especially when compared to other genocides like the Holocaust, the Rwandan genocide, or the Bosnian genocide*" (Eichler, 2020, p. 109).

[44] After the industrial revolution, the Euro-North-American logic became increasingly focused on the elimination of indigenous peoples to gain access to their territory for the purpose of resource extraction: "*When indigenous peoples who have a physical, cultural and spiritual connection to their land are forcibly dispossessed and estranged from their lands, they invariably experience 'social death', and thus, genocide*" (Crook & Short, 2014, p. 310).

It is necessary to recognise, however, that inserting ecocide into the 1948 Convention as a means of committing genocide would require much more than an adaptation of it to the treaty; it would be necessary to review the very definition of genocide, rewriting it away from the colonialist view, which separates nature from man,[45] to achieve the protection of the environment directly, not just as a consequence of human protection.

The link between genocide and ecocide, nevertheless, recently served as an argument before the International Criminal Court. Environmental destruction was used as a basis for the complaint filed by the Articulation of Indigenous Peoples of Brazil (APIB) against the president of Brazil, Jair Bolsonaro, to the ICC Prosecutor's Office, in August 2021.[46] The piece was based on the "International Dossier of complaints from the indigenous peoples of Brazil" (APIB, 2021), which points out various conducts that would characterise the genocide perpetrated by the accused, among them, the impact of invasions, deforestation, illegal mining, and mining in Indigenous Lands, in addition to the spread of the Covid-19 pandemic on isolated peoples or those of recent contact.[47] As can be seen, the environmental issue would be peripheral, only as an element to configure (prove) the genocide, a crime within the jurisdiction of the Court, and technically cannot be called ecocide, due to the lack of provision in the Rome Statute.

To elevate ecocide as a means to commit genocide[48] is, in fact, to simplify a serious crime against the environment. It would, in practice, condition the criminal prosecution of a conduct that causes massive environmental destruction to the strict purpose restrictions of genocide (specific intent to decimate a national, ethnic, racial, or religious group). For this reason, the maximum environmental crime found greater legal foundation when equated to crimes against humanity.

---

[45] For Eichler, "this addition would not only help capture some cultural components lost in the transition from Lemkin's definition to the UN's but also mitigate some of the anthropocentric and Western biases of the UN definition and provide Indigenous peoples and other groups with more leverage for contesting climate change and other devastating acts against nonhuman nature" (Eichler, 2020, p. 118).

[46] Link: https://apiboficial.org/2020/12/15/tribunal-penal-internacional-comeca-a-analisar-denuncia-contra-bolsonaro-por-crimes-contra-a-humanidade-e-incitac%CC%A7a%CC%83o-ao-genocidio-de-povos-indigenas-no-brasil/, accessed on: 22 Apr. 2025.

[47] The Munduruku peoples, the indigenous people who live in the TI Yanomami, the Guarani-Mbya, Kaingang, the Guarani-Kaiowá, the Tikuna, Kokama, the Guajajara and the Terena were listed (Link: https://apiboficial.org/2021/08/09/inedito-apib-denuncia-bolsonaro-em-haia-por-genocidio-indigena/, accessed on: 18 Apr. 2025).

[48] Genocide is often considered the "crime of crimes", as it connects to sensitive and controversial indictments (Bellivier et al., 2018, p. 144).

4.3 Equating to Crimes Against Humanity

The so-called "crimes against humanity" have been legally known since the end of the Second World War,[49] but, despite being contemporary to the crime of genocide, they never had their own Convention like the latter. Similarly, they were initially conditioned to the existence of an armed conflict,[50] but, given the broad content of protection to all humanity,[51] they were gradually detached from war.

This category of crimes was first typified in article 6 (c), of the Charter of the Nuremberg Military Tribunal,[52] in analogous norms elaborated for the Tribunal for the Far East,[53] and in the *Allied Control Council Law* N° 10,[54] bringing practically identical definitions, encompassing the following acts: murder, extermination, reduction to a condition analogous to that of a slave, deportation and other inhuman acts committed against civilian populations, before or during the war, as well as persecution for political, racial, or religious reasons, whether such acts are crimes or not under the domestic law of the countries where they have been committed (Japiassú, 2009, p. 37).

---

[49] The "laws of humanity" were originally introduced into international law in the St. Petersburg Declaration, in 1868, with the purpose of renouncing the use of certain explosive projectiles, in times of war: "*They next appeared in the preamble to the Hague Convention of 1899, in which States Parties agreed to serve the 'interests of humanity' even during armed conflicts and, consequently, to protect populations and belligerents under the 'law of humanity'*" (Nollez-Goldbach, 2017, p. 92).

[50] Crimes against humanity were only considered when within an armed conflict also in the Statute of the International Criminal Tribunal for the former Yugoslavia (ICTY), but disconnected from the war for the International Criminal Tribunal for Rwanda (ICTR) and for the International Criminal Court (ICC) (Nollez-Goldbach, 2018, p. 66).

[51] The reference to 'humanity' remains largely implicit and vague in international norms and jurisprudence; it is not properly defined, nor is its nature or content fully developed: "*the legal concept of humanity firstly refers, in the law of war, to an abstract moral value directed and limiting war atrocities. The conception of humanity as a victim thus characterizes crimes against humanity, while a biological understanding of it is currently developing as a result of bioethics. Humanity also points to existence of a worldwide community of interests underlying a concept of humanity centred on solidarity. This results, finally, in a fundamental transformation of the international systems that is now grounded on the protection of humanity. It did not lead though to a paradigm shift from the traditional centrality of State sovereignty*" (Nollez-Goldbach, 2017, p. 91).

[52] Article 6, (c): "*Crimes against humanity: namely, murder, extermination, enslavement, deportation, and other inhumane acts committed against any civilian population, before or during the war, or persecutions on political, racial or religious grounds in execution of or in connection with any crime within the jurisdiction of the Tribunal, whether or not in violation of the domestic law of the country where perpetrated*" (UN, 1945).

[53] Article 5 (c), Charter of the International Military Tribunal for the Far East, 1946. Available at: https://www.un.org/en/genocideprevention/documents/atrocity-crimes/Doc.3_1946%20Tokyo%20Charter.pdf, accessed on: 20 Apr. 2025.

[54] Article II 1 (a), Control Council Law No. 10, Available at: https://www.legal-tools.org/doc/ffda62/pdf/, accessed on: 20 Apr. 2025.

There has never been disagreement about the inclusion of crimes against humanity,[55] despite the absence of a specific international document (and, consequently, its definitions), in the project of the *The Code*. On the contrary, there is a normative and jurisprudential trend (of international courts) of legal extension of the concept. The first important development was to detach them from war crimes,[56] significantly increasing the possibilities of application in law.

In 1984, during the drafting of the document in *International Law Commission*, in one of the discussions about the behaviours compatible with the crime under study, considered the inclusion of massive environmental damage in crimes against humanity, considering the technological development at the time.[57] The protection of the environment was not then only a matter that concerned man in his singularity, but all of humanity.[58]

In the fourth report of the *draft*, in March 1986, the Commission recalled the growing importance of environmental problems, which would justify the inclusion of a specific provision in the draft Code.[59] In the draft of Article 12 (Acts that constitute crimes against humanity), it was proposed that "any serious violation of an international obligation of essential importance for the safeguarding and preservation of the human environment" would reach the crime (ILC, 1986, p. 85).

The ILC, in 1989 (41st Session), pointed out that the inclusion of serious damage to the human environment among crimes against humanity was favourably received

[55] "It can also be highlighted that the disapproval of crimes against humanity has been frequent within the international community. The Universal Declaration of Human Rights, from 1948, prohibits, in its articles 4 and 5, slavery, the slave trade, torture, and cruel, inhuman or degrading treatment or punishment" (Japiassú, 2009, p. 37).

[56] In Nuremberg, they existed autonomously to war crimes and crimes against humanity (as well as crimes against peace), but crimes against humanity, recognised as customary international law, were linked to the period—and circumstance—of war (ICJ, 2018, p. 3).

[57] "The question arises whether it should not in some cases be made a crime against humanity. Some members thought not. However, the Commission considered that, although just any damage to the environment could not constitute a crime against humanity, the development of technology and the considerable harm it sometimes did—for example, to the atmosphere and to water—might lead to certain kinds of damage to the human environment being regarded as crimes against humanity. It was pointed out that there were conventions prohibiting certain tests which could harm the environment. Although those conventions were primarily concerned with military tests, the essential reason for the prohibition seemed to have been the damage done to the environment. This applied in particular to the treaties prohibiting nuclear weapons in the atmosphere, in outer space, on the seabed and the ocean floor and in the subsoil thereof" (ILC, 1984, p. 16).

[58] The concern about environmental issues went beyond the humanity of the present, it also included, within the limits of common sense, future generations: "The incommensurable character of this interrelation would give this matrix value such importance that it would found the necessity of a supranational crime—ecocide—likely to guarantee a penal protection similar to that guaranteed by the crime against humanity or genocide" (Neyret, 2015, p. 93).

[59] The Commission, to substantiate the *draft*, cites Article 19, paragraph 3 (d) of the Draft on the International Responsibility of States: "'*a serious breach of an international obligation of essential importance for the safeguarding and preservation of the human environment, such as those prohibiting massive pollution of the atmosphere or of the seas' is an international crime*" (ILC, 1986, p. 61).

by the Commission.[60] A discussion was raised about the need to demonstrate intent in the commission of the crime, in order to distance it from accidental behaviours. Some members, however, argued that the severe consequences to the human population required that massive damage to the environment be considered crime, regardless of whether there was intent to commit it (ILC, 1989, p. 64). At this point, ecocide had two viable paths in the *The Code*: act considered as a crime against humanity or an autonomous offence, like that of Article 26 (1991 draft).

As seen, ecocide was removed from the project of "Code of crimes against peace and security of humanity", in the text adopted in 1996a, before the start of the Rome Conference, in 1998. The requirement of an armed conflict to characterise crimes against humanity was abandoned, but it was established the need for criminal behaviours to occur intentionally, within a widespread or systematic attack against a civilian population, in pursuit as a policy of a State or an Organisation (Bellivier et al., 2018, pp. 139–141).

Since then, despite the proposals presented, the possibility of prosecuting episodes of massive environmental degradation in the category of crimes against humanity has not been widely discussed (Misutra, 2018, p. 210).

Of the points raised, by part of the doctrine,[61] as favourable to the inclusion of ecocide in crimes against humanity,[62] one can cite the greater ease, in theory, of proving the *mens rea* in the latter, as it would only be necessary to know that the severe environmental damage was part of a widespread and systematic attack against the civilian population, and not the specific intent necessary for the perpetration of genocide.[63]

Article 7 of the Rome Statute[64] lists eleven behaviours, all reflecting the understanding of the notion of crimes against humanity, built from customary international law (Misutra, 2018, p. 208). There is no mention in the provision to destruction of the environment. Today codified, this category of crimes is focused on the protection of civilian populations. Unlike crimes against humanity and genocide, ecocide has not established itself in a final form (Greene, 2019, p. 32), which makes it

[60] Starting from a previously presented draft (seventh report), the Commission suggests the following wording to the *draft* of Article 14: "Crimes against humanity include: (…) 6. Any serious and intentional damage to a vital human good, such as the human environment" (Chiarini, 2022, p. 12).

[61] Some authors argue for the possibility of evolving the interpretation of human rights violations, in light of the "social context and changes in society", to achieve environmental protection (Durney, 2018, p. 415).

[62] For example, in recent doctrine, lawyer Polly Higgins argued that ecocide would be the fifth crime against peace, forgotten during the drafting of *The Code*, raising the possibility of fitting it among crimes against humanity (Gauger et al., 2013).

[63] Also, "crimes against humanity are susceptible to include activities of a lesser degree of gravity than those required under the crime of genocide. Thus, the category of crimes against humanity appears more suitable to prosecute acts of environmental destruction, such as the performance of extractive activities or the disposal of hazardous wastes, carried out for the purpose of economic development" (Misutra, 2018, p. 210).

[64] Link: https://www.icc-cpi.int/sites/default/files/RS-Eng.pdf. Accessed on: 18 Apr. 2025.

difficult to understand who is the victim of the latter, whether the environment or the human being.[65]

Just like in genocide, the massive destruction of the environment could function as a means to perpetrate crimes against humanity.[66] This approach would highlight the anthropocentric character of crime against nature, for adaptation to existing crime groups.[67] Again, ecocide is of utmost importance to the survival of humanity itself to submit to the conditions of the international crime of Article 7 of the Rome Statute.

The experience of considering ecocide as a crime against humanity already exists in some countries, but, with superficially and generically definitions, there is no record of criminal convictions for the most serious crime against the environment. In any case, the evolution of its definition is notable, from the studies of ecocide in the codes and in the bill projects, as demonstrated in the next chapter.

References

APIB. (2021). *International dossier of complaints from Brazil's indigenous peoples 2021*. Articulation of Indigenous Peoples of Brazil (APIB).

Bassiouni, M. C. (1983). The penal characteristics of conventional international criminal law. *Case Western Reserve Journal of International Law, 15*, 27.

Bassiouni, M. C., et al. (1986). Draft code of offenses against the peace and security of mankind. *Proceedings of the Annual Meeting (American Society of International Law), 80*, 120–135. Retrieved April 3, 2025, from http://www.jstor.org/stable/25658302

Bellivier, F., Eudes, M., & Fouchard, I. (2018). *Law of international crimes*. Themis Law.

Bravo, L. F. (2015). *Il diritto internazionale come professione* (1st ed.). Università degli Studi di Trento.

Cabanes, V. (2018). Holding states and companies accountable for climate change: From planetary boundaries to the crime of ecocide. In C. Cournil & L. Varison (Eds.), *Climate trials: Between national and international* (pp. 265–278). Pedone.

[65] The most advanced concept of humanity today is victim-centred: "*This is guaranteed by the international criminal order that has been growing increasingly over the past two decades and it is enforced by the decisions of both the ICT's and the ICC. Nonetheless, nowhere is this understanding of humanity defined; it is only implied. Yet it constitutes the basis of an international crime*" (Nollez-Goldbach, 2017, p. 98).

[66] In the context of crimes against humanity, "environmental destruction could arguably fall within four categories of act. First, the prohibition of 'extermination, or intentional infliction of conditions of life …calculated to bring about the destruction of part of the population.' Second, the deportation or forcible transfer of a population. Third, persecution through the intentional and severe deprivation of fundamental rights contrary to international law. And fourth, it could be considered an example of 'other inhumane acts', provided the destruction occurred 'as part of a widespread or systematic attack directed against any civilian population, with knowledge of the attack' (Killean, 2020, p. 330).

[67] For Tsilonis, "ecocide could be criminalised through already existing core crimes within the ICC framework, such as genocide and crimes against humanity. This would necessarily imply adopting an anthropocentric approach, as both crimes have human beings at their centre. It is nevertheless a possibility to protect the environment, even if only as a tool for humans." (Tsilonis, 2024, p. 275).

Chiarini, G. (2022, April 1). Ecocide: From the Vietnam war to international criminal jurisdiction? Procedural issues in-between environmental science, climate change, and law. *Cork Online Law Review*.

Crook, M., & Short, D. (2014). Marx, Lemkin and the genocide-ecocide nexus. *International Journal of Human Rights, 18*(3), 298–319.

Durney, J. (2018). Crafting a standard: Environmental crimes as crimes against humanity under the international criminal court. *Hastings Environmental Law Journal, 24*(2), 413.

Eichler, L. J. (2020). Ecocide is genocide: Decolonizing the definition of genocide. *Genocide Studies and Prevention, 14*(2), 104–121.

Gauger, A., et al. (2013). *The ecocide project: Ecocide is the missing 5th crime against peace*. University of London, Human Rights Consortium.

Greene, A. (2019). The campaign to make ecocide an international crime: Quixotic quest or moral imperative? *Fordham Environmental Law Review, 30*(3), 1.

Guttry, A. D., Gestri, M., & Venturini, G. (2012). *International disaster response law*. TMC Asser Press.

ILC. (1984). *Report of the International Law Commission on the work of its thirty-sixth session, V. 2, A/39/10*. Retrieved April 4, 2025, from https://legal.un.org/ilc/documentation/english/reports/a_39_10.pdf

ILC. (1986). *Yearbook of the international law commission, 36th session. V. 2, Part One*. Retrieved April 20, 2025, from https://legal.un.org/ilc/publications/yearbooks/english/ilc_1986_v2_p1.pdf

ILC. (1987). *Yearbook of the International Law Commission, 1987, V. 1*. Retrieved February 23, 2025, from http://legal.un.org/ilc/publications/yearbooks/english/ilc_1987_v1.pdf

ILC. (1989). *Yearbook of the international law commission, 41st session. V. 2, Part Two*. https://legal.un.org/ilc/publications/yearbooks/english/ilc_1989_v2_p2.pdf

ILC. (1991). *Draft code of crimes against the peace and security of mankind. Titles and texts of articles adopted by the Drafting Committee: Parts One and Two; articles 1–26 - reproduced in A/CN.4/SR.2236, V. 1*. Retrieved April 3, 2025, from https://legal.un.org/ilc/documentation/english/a_cn4_l459.pdf

ILC. (1995). *Thirteenth report on the draft code of crimes against the peace and security of mankind*, by Mr. Doudou Thiam, Special Rapporteur, A/CN.4/466.

ILC. (1996a). *Draft code of crimes against the peace and security of mankind*. https://legal.un.org/ilc/texts/instruments/english/draft_articles/7_4_1996.pdf

ILC. (1996b). *Document on crimes against the environment*, prepared by Mr. Christian Tomuschat, member of the Commission. ILC(XLVIII)/DC/CRD.3.

Japiassú, C. E. A. (2009). *International criminal law*. Del Rey.

Jodoin, S., & Saito, Y. (2012). Crimes against future generations: Harnessing the potential of individual criminal accountability for global sustainability. *McGill Journal of Sustainable Development Law, 7*, 115.

Killean, R. (2020). From ecocide to eco-sensitivity: 'Greening' reparations at the international criminal court. *The International Journal of Human Rights, 25*(2), 323–347.

Malhotra, S. (2017). The international crime that could have been but never was: An English school perspective on the ecocide law. *Amsterdam Law Forum, 9*(3), 49–70.

Mégret, F. (2011). The problem of an international criminal law of the environment. *Columbia Journal of Environmental Law, 36*(2), 195–257.

Misutra, A. (2018). Is there space for environmental crimes under international criminal law? The impact of the Office of the Prosecutor Policy Paper on case selection and prioritization on the current legal framework. *Columbia Journal of Environmental Law, 43*(1), 181–226.

Monebhurrun, N., et al. (2016). The legal definition of "community". *International Law Review, 13*(3), 444–471. Retrieved June 10, 2025, from https://www.cienciasaude.uniceub.br/rdi/article/view/4472

Morton, J. S. (2000). *The international law commission of the United Nations*. University of South Carolina Press.

Neyret, L. (Ed.). (2015). *From ecocrimes to ecocide: Criminal law to the rescue of the environment*. Bruylant.
Nollez-Goldbach, R. (2017). Crimes against humanity: The concept of humanity in international law. In P. Kastner (Ed.), *International criminal law in context* (pp. 91–98). Routledge.
Nollez-Goldbach, R. (2018). *La Cour Pénale Internationale*. Presses Universitaires de France.
Pereira, R. (2020). After the ICC Office of the prosecutor's 2016 policy paper on case selection and prioritisation: Towards an international crime of ecocide? *Criminal Law Forum, 31*(2), 179–224.
Reilly, B. (1995). "Clear and present danger": A role for the United Nations Security council in protecting the Global Environment. *Melbourne University Law Review, 20*(30), 763–804.
Ruhashyankiko, N. (1978). *Study of the question of the prevention and punishment of the crime of genocide*. United Nations Economic and Social Council. Retrieved April 20, 2025, from https://digitallibrary.un.org/record/663583
Schwegler, V. (2017). The disposable nature: The case of ecocide and corporate accountability. *Amsterdam Law Forum, 9*(3), 71.
Tallgren, I. (2002). The sensibility and sense of international criminal law. *European Journal of International Law, 13*(3), 561–595.
Tomuschat, C. (1996). Crimes against the environment. *Environmental Policy and Law, 26*(6), 242–243. Retrieved April 3, 2025.
Tomuschat, C. (2006). The legacy of Nuremberg. *Journal of International Criminal Justice, 4*(4), 843.
Tsilonis, V. (2024). *The jurisdiction of the international criminal court* (2nd ed.). Springer.
UN. (1945). *Charter of the international military tribunal*. Retrieved April 20, 2025, from https://www.un.org/en/genocideprevention/documents/atrocity-crimes/Doc.2_Charter%20of%20IMT%201945.pdf
UN. (1946). *Charter of the international military tribunal for the far east*. https://www.un.org/en/genocideprevention/documents/atrocity-crimes/Doc.3_1946%20Tokyo%20Charter.pdf
UN. (1948). *Convention on the prevention and punishment of the crime of genocide*. https://www.un.org/en/genocideprevention/documents/atrocity-crimes/Doc.1_Convention%20on%20the%20Prevention%20and%20Punishment%20of%20the%20Crime%20of%20Genocide.pdf
UN. (1969). *Vienna Convention on the Law of Treaties*. http://www.planalto.gov.br/ccivil_03/_ato2007-2010/2009/decreto/d7030.htm
UN. (1981). *Statute of the International Law Commission*. https://legal.un.org/ilc/texts/instruments/english/statute/statute.pdf
UN. (1985). *Report of the subcommission on the promotion and protection of human rights*. Subcommission on Prevention of Discrimination and Protection of Minorities. Economic and Social Council. Geneva, 38th sess. 4 Nov. 1985. Retrieved April 20, 2025, from https://digitallibrary.un.org/record/116304?ln=en
UN. (1998a, January 28). *Resolution 52/160, A/RES/52/160*. Retrieved April 3, 2025, from https://documents-dds-ny.un.org/doc/UNDOC/GEN/N98/762/49/PDF/N9876249.pdf
UN. (1998b). *Rome Statute of the International Criminal Court*. https://www.icc-cpi.int/sites/default/files/RS-Eng.pdf
UN. (2018). *The international court of justice: Custodian of the archives of the international military Tribunal at Nuremberg*. ICJ.
UN. (2021). *International Dossier of complaints from Brazil's indigenous peoples 2021*. https://apiboficial.org/2021/08/09/inedito-apib-denuncia-bolsonaro-em-haia-por-genocidio-indigena/
Whitaker, B. C. G. (1985). *Special rapporteur on prevention and punishment of the crime of genocide*. Economic and Social Council. Retrieved April 20, 2025, from https://digitallibrary.un.org/record/108352?ln=en

Chapter 5
Ecocide in National Legislation

Following the international surge in ecocide studies, which occurred during the Vietnam War and subsequently by the *International Law Commission*, some countries developed their own criminal provisions in national legislation concurrent with the draft of *The Code*.

This normative evolution, however, was localised, restricted to the Asian continent, and, like international environmental and criminal law itself, lacked coordination and theoretical depth.[1] After Vietnam, in 1990, the states that succeeded it, also include ecocide as a crime in their legislation, are all countries remaining from the dissolution of the Soviet Union, in addition to Russia itself (Cabanes, 2018, p. 276), which is evident when analysing the similarity of the texts.

It is also noticeable, with the recent return of international criminal law's attention to the environment, an increase in legal technique in the criminal definitions created in recent years, such as in Colombia,[2] in addition to the bills presented in national assemblies and before the International Criminal Court. The approaches, however, are sometimes different,[3] which reinforces the need for a top-down

[1] The fact that many environmental infractions are created after public protests for distinct incidents indicates the level of difficulty in establishing a coherent system of criminal offences intended to protect the environment: "*The few notable evolutions that have emerged remain somewhat haphazard and uncoordinated. Their subject matter, the intensity of the prohibitions involved, and the modes of enforcement vary considerably. This uncoordinated approach is in stark contrast to the many areas of international criminal law that have become highly structured over the years, most notably through the operation of international criminal tribunals. Moreover, there is no commonly agreed upon criminological theory of the uses of criminal law to better protect the environment*" (Mégret, 2011, p. 201).

[2] Article 333 of the Colombian Penal Code, amended by Law 1121, of August 2021.

[3] Fragmentation in the field of environmental law can be more interesting, from the point of view of global environmental governance: "*a disaggregated perspective could create opportunities to see global environmental governance as a regulatory intervention that does not occur at any one specific level, but rather as one that involves many tasks, activities, objectives, elements and actors.*

D. A. Brochado Neto, *Ecocide*, https://doi.org/10.1007/978-3-032-07757-8_5

perspective, at least regarding the conceptualisation of ecocide (which would be done by force of a treaty, like the Rome Statute). The standardisation of the most serious environmental crime, whose consequences are often transnational, would have the power to provide a better legal response, and consequently, environmental protection.[4]

What is clear is a perspective of improving the current legislative framework (in quality and quantity), in order to justify environmental protection based on cooperation between peoples, whose side effect is to reveal the lack of normative provision concerning "organised environmental delinquency".[5] Various countries today, recognising this gap, discuss the inclusion of ecocide in their national legislation, if not officially, through Bills of Law, but through specialised doctrine,[6] with influence among policy promoters.

In the following topics, a list of the definitions of "ecocide" currently existing in the world will be made, as well as the main bills in national progress; afterwards, the proposed amendment to the Rome Statute, presented before the Assembly of the Parties of the International Criminal Court in 2024, will be analysed, with the aim of pointing out confluences or inconsistencies in the general notion of the crime.

This list of national and international initiatives is scattered and partially included in information *hubs* about ecocide, especially the *Ecocide Law,*[7] which is usually cited as a source by the vast majority of doctrine, in articles and books, and by the legislators themselves, when justifying their proposals. In this book, an attempt was made to expand it as much as possible, to locate all possible initiatives, to date, on the subject, in the form of law or bills.

It is necessary to make a note: it is not intended here to use tools of comparative law in order to attest quality or effectiveness among the laws of the States, since, for this, it would be necessary to delve into the legal systems individually, in addition

---

Another benefit is that a global focus allows considerable methodological freedom" (Kotzé, 2014, p. 552).

[4] It is certain that, in general, a *bottom-up* approach carries numerous advantages, especially when it comes to the environment, with peculiarities inherent to each State, in addition to being able to achieve greater local legal protection, given the unnecessary need for international multilateral consensus for the elaboration of a certain norm. Thus, "*domestic environmental constitutionalism could 'level the playing field' as it were and be driven primarily by nation-states which would arguably regard a bottom-up approach less threatening to their sovereignty than a once-off top-down approach*" (Kotzé, 2012, p. 229).

[5] "Both the dimension of the international plan and that of domestic law are today recognisably unsatisfactory for the pursuit and dissipation of illicit ecological trade" (Suxberger & Dos Reis, 2020, p. 148).

[6] For example, in Argentina, the "*Penal Code does not contain a special figure referring to ecological damage as a crime, but it sanctions cases of poisoning of waters or food or medicinal substances, but does not contemplate cases of damage to the atmosphere, to the soils,* etc." (Fernández et al., 2021).

[7] Link: https://ecocidelaw.com/ and https://www.stopecocide.earth/. Accessed on: 13 Dec. 2024.

to being attentive to the comparability of sources; words and concepts of comparison, of circulation and imitation; the language or culture barrier; the translation.[8]

What matters here is, in an international context, to identify which legal elements and difficulties are revealed to the actors who try to codify ecocide,[9] considering its inspiration of internationalist origin and of global interest, starting with Vietnam.

Ecocide as a crime defined by law is still an exception in criminal codes around the world. Although the existence of environmental crimes (prohibition of hunting and fishing, for example) is common, there is a constant gap in legislation when it comes to massive destruction of the environment. The dimension of the latest environmental damages and the insufficiency of the legal response, however, have exposed this deficiency.

The context of the creation of the term "ecocide" (defoliant gas attacks during the Indochina War in the 1960s and 1970s), therefore, served as a stimulus for the first state to codify it as a crime.

5.1 Vietnam (1990)

Concurrent with the advancement of studies on ecocide at the ILC, whether as an autonomous crime or as a crime against humanity, in 1989 (Chiarini, 2022, p. 12), Vietnam, a country that suffered the attacks of Agent Orange against its forests during the Indochina War, drafted its own law against massive environmental damage.

The Penal Code of 1990 (art. 278) provided that committing ecocide, "destroying the environment, in times of peace or war, would constitute a crime against humanity".[10] The simplicity of the law, without explanatory norm, was repeated in the Penal Code of 1999 (art. 342), which was further amended in 2009:

> **Article 342: Crimes against humanity**
>
> -Crimes against mankind. Those who, in peace time or war time, commit acts of annihilating en-mass population in an area, destroying the source of their livelihood, undermining the cultural and spiritual life of a country, upsetting the foundation of a society with a view to undermining such society, as well as other acts of genocide or acts of ecocide or destroying the natural environment, shall be sentenced to between ten years and twenty years of imprisonment, life imprisonment or capital punishment.[11]

---

[8] It would therefore be necessary to pay attention to "the prudence with which the author must choose and make his sources speak, must think about the terminology used, must know and understand the environment in which the rights that are compared were elaborated, and possibly related, must, finally, meditate on the meaning and interest of "your comparison" (Soleil, 2021).

[9] At various times, national legislators base their proposals on debates, laws and suggestions of foreign text, revealing their international nature and a search for a global definition of the crime under analysis.

[10] Link: https://ihl-databases.icrc.org/customary-ihl/por/docs/v2_cou_vn_rule45, accessed on: 20 Apr. 2022.

[11] Vietnam Penal Code, 1999. Link: https://wipolex.wipo.int/en/text/184118, accessed on 20 Jun. 2025.

The maintenance of ecocide as a crime against humanity also occurred in the current Vietnamese Penal Code, of 2015, in Chap. XXVI (disturbance of peace, crimes against humanity, and war crimes). This time, the term "ecocide" was omitted, with environmental destruction remaining as a way to commit the former:

Article 422: Crimes against humanity

1. Any person who, whether in peacetime or wartime, commits genocide against population of an area, destroys sources of living, cultural or spiritual life of a nation or sovereign territory, upsets the foundation of a society in order to sabotage it, or commits other acts of genocide, or destroys of the environment shall face a penalty of 10–20 years' imprisonment, life imprisonment, or death.
2. This offence is committed under pressure or order given by superior officers, the offender shall face a penalty of 10–20 years' imprisonment.[12]

It is important to note that, in the 1999 and 2015 Codes, ecocide and genocide were considered behaviours included in crimes against humanity. Despite Vietnam not being a State Party to the Rome Statute—and therefore not directly subject to the International Criminal Court[13]—the inspiration for this understanding came from the discussions of the International Law Commission.

Before the confirmation of what would be the crimes of The Code, the idea of having at least four groups was concrete: crimes against humanity, genocide (in Vietnamese law, included in the first), war crimes, and crime of aggression (Morton, 2000, p. 41). The 2015 Code, a direct reflection of the previous codes, brings, in addition to the above, the crime of mercenarism[14] (recruiting, training, employing, or working as a mercenary).

Thus, the lack of depth of what would be "ecocide" seen during the ILC debates reflected in the Vietnamese texts, vague and unusable as legislative reference, at least on the international level. This weakness is also verified in the texts produced by the countries resulting from the dissolution of the Soviet Union in the 1990s.

5.2 Countries Dismembered from the Extinct Soviet Union (1996—2003)

After Vietnam, other countries in Asia and Eastern Europe also included ecocide in their national penal codes, to refer to the most serious environmental crimes that cause or may cause massive destruction to the natural environment (Estupiñan-Silva, 2016, p. 39).

---

[12] Vietnam Penal Code, 2015. Link: https://wipolex.wipo.int/en/text/446020, accessed on: 20 Jun. 2025.

[13] Here is a caveat of universal jurisdiction, possibility conferred in the Statute itself, when activated by the UN Security Council.

[14] Articles 424 and 425 of the Vietnam Penal Code of 2015 (Link: https://wipolex.wipo.int/en/text/446020, accessed on: 20 Jun. 2025).

Russia, a state that signed but did not ratify the Rome Statute,[15] was the first among them. Prior to this, the country (in its various configurations) has always been involved in the development of international criminal law, implementing legislation on crimes that, in the future, would be termed "serious violations of international humanitarian law".[16]

However, legislative and academic activities in this field diminished with the advancement of the Cold War and the socioeconomic stagnation of Russian society.[17] Thus, from the late 1980s, the development of international criminal law, compared to the European experience, was contained.

The last proactive movement in this regard was the inclusion of Chap. 34 in the Russian Criminal Code, of 1996.[18] Among others, the crimes of genocide (art. 357), use of prohibited methods of war (art. 356), and public appeals to trigger an aggressive war (art. 354) were defined. Ecocide, dissociated from war, was typified in art. 358:

> **Article 358. Ecocide**
> Massive destruction of the animal or plant kingdoms, contamination of the atmosphere or water resources, and also commission of other actions capable of causing an ecological catastrophe, shall be punishable by deprivation of liberty for a term of 12 to 20 years.[19]

Like Vietnam, Russia also sought inspiration in the discussions originating from the *International Law Commission*, even naming the Chap. 34[20] with the same

---

[15] Russia signed on September 13, 2000, but on November 30, 2016, it expressed its intention not to become part of the Rome Statute of the International Criminal Court (Link: https://treaties.un.org/Pages/ViewDetails.aspx?src=TREATY&mtdsg_no=XVIII-10&chapter=18&clang=_en#9, Accessed on: 21 Jun. 2025).

[16] Following Russian initiatives, conferences were held in 1868, 1874, and 1899. In the 1940s, the Union of Soviet Socialist Republics (USSR) actively participated in the Nuremberg and Tokyo trials, as well as conducting national trials against Nazis. In Russian academic circles, the Nuremberg trial is considered the greatest achievement of Soviet diplomacy and its theory of international criminal law (Esakov, 2017, p. 372).

[17] Furthermore, the aversion to the legacy of the International Criminal Court for the former Yugoslavia, based on a close political alliance with Serbia, undermined confidence in the then embryonic International Criminal Court (Esakov, 2017, p. 376).

[18] The provisions relating to universal jurisdiction (section 12(3)) and prescription (sections 78(5), 83(4)) are the only vestiges of international criminal law in the general part of the Russian Penal Code.

[19] Russian Penal Code, 1996, Link: https://legislationline.org/taxonomy/term/15719, accessed on: 20 Jun. 2025.

[20] The existence of this Chapter in Russian legislation, even considered problematic for practical application, stands out among the BRICS countries, when only Brazil and South Africa, in addition to Russia itself, establish the constitutional right to a favourable environment for all, guaranteed directly by the State. "*However, in India there is no rule directly regulating the right of everyone to a favourable environment, which is an omission that needs to be rectified. China's Constitution also lacks any provision guaranteeing the right of citizens to a favourable environment, but it does establish the obligation of the state to protect the environment. Furthermore, the provisions of Russian environmental legislation that regulate civil (property) liability for environmental offences may be of interest to the other BRICS countries in terms of procedures for compensation for lawful*

denomination of *The Code*: "Crimes against peace and security of mankind". Again, the provision mirrors the moment at the time of the studies on ecocide, with vagueness and imprecision incompatible with international criminal law.[21]

The collapse of the USSR, in 1991, redesigned the map of the region, emerging several post-Soviet nations,[22] whose Russian influence was (and still is) determinant. Of the 15 new internationally recognised states, 9 [23] included, at different periods, ecocide as a crime in their national criminal codes.

The Criminal Code of Kyrgyzstan[24] of 1997 (amended in 2006), repeated, in art. 374, the crime stipulated in Russian art. 358. It copied, including Chap. 34, naming it "Crimes against peace and security of mankind", similar to Tajikistan[25] (1998), which typified ecocide in art. 400, of Belarus[26] (1999), in art. 131 of the Belarusian

harm, as well as the three-tiered system of the structure of environmental harm (economic, environmental and social) that was formulated by scientific doctrine (and adopted by the legislator) and its practical importance for calculating the amount of compensation. Structures of individual parts of the Russian Penal Code (Article 358'Ecocide') or administrative sanctions (administrative suspension of environmentally hazardous activities) can be very useful in practice" (Anisimov & Kayushnikova, 2019, p. 99).

[21] For example, the lack of specificity of what constitutes "massive destruction" or "ecological catastrophe", for the international field, would make practical application unfeasible, as it allows for a wide—or restricted, depending on the judge—discretion sufficient to fit all—or no—cases of environmental damage.

[22] For the Russian Federation, there are currently still six unrecognised states in the post-Soviet space: the Pridnestrovian Moldavian Republic (Transnistria, 1990), the Republic of South Ossetia (1990), the Republic of Nagorno-Karabakh (Artsakh, 1991), the Republic of Abkhazia (1994), the People's Republic of Lugansk (2014) and the People's Republic of Donetsk (2014), "*all of them have been formed as a result of armed conflicts between a state vigorously pursuing the policy of national unification and a minority residing compactly*" (Tolstykh et al., 2019, p. 81). With regard to the last two territories, Donetsk and Lugansk, inserted in Ukraine, their independence was recognised by Russia, in February 2022, during the invasion of that country (Link: https://www.jurist.org/news/2022/02/putin-signs-decrees-recognizing-independence-of-eastern-ukraine-regions/, accessed on: 4 Jun 2025).

[23] Kyrgyzstan, Kazakhstan, Tajikistan, Uzbekistan, Belarus, Georgia, Ukraine, Moldova, and Armenia.

[24] "*Article 374. Ecocide. Massive destruction of the animal or plant kingdoms, contamination of the atmosphere or water resources, and also commission of other actions capable of causing an ecological catastrophe, shall be punishable by deprivation of liberty for a term of 12 to 20 years*" (Kyrgyzstan Penal Code, 1996, link: https://wipolex.wipo.int/en/text/248664, accessed on: 20 Jun. 2025).

[25] "*Article 400. Ecocide. Mass destruction of flora and fauna, poisoning the atmosphere or water resources, as well as commitment of other actions which may cause ecological disasters is punishable by imprisonment for a period of 15 to 20 years*" (Tajikistan Penal Code, 1998, Link: https://www.legislationline.org/download/action/download/id/1707/file/207b8150765af2c85ad6f5bb8a44.htm/preview, accessed on: 20 Apr. 2022). It should be remembered that Tajikistan has been a signatory to the Rome Statute since 5 May 2000 (UN, Link: https://treaties.un.org/Pages/ViewDetails.aspx?src=TREATY&mtdsg_no=XVIII-10&chapter=18&clang=_en, accessed on: 20 Jun. 2025).

[26] Crimes against peace and humanity are set out in Chap. 17 of the Belarusian Penal Code of 1999, amended in 2012. Within it, is Art. 131, ecocide: Deliberate mass destruction of flora or fauna, or

Criminal Code, of Ukraine[27] (2001), in art. 441, of Moldova[28] (from 2002, amended in 2016), in art. 136, and of Armenia[29] (2003), in art. 396 of the Criminal Code.

Kazakhstan also did so, including in its Criminal Code (first, in that of 1997, transposing to article 169 of the current Code,[30] of 2014, with amendment of 2016), not making a distinction for offences in peacetime or wartime. The Code also adopted, in its Chap. 4, the name of the *The Code*, including a series of crimes against peace and the security of humanity. Among them are the majority of "traditional" crimes for international law— genocide, war crimes, and crimes of aggression— among others. It should be noted that, as in Russia and Kyrgyzstan, crimes against humanity are not included in the Penal Code so far, but some of its defining characteristics are shared by the so-called "extremist crimes".[31]

The Penal Code of Uzbekistan (1994, with amendment of 2002) has a chapter on crimes against peace and humanity (Chap. 8), but separated them from massive damages against the environment, allocating them in Chap. 14, of "crimes related to

---

poisoning of the atmospheric air or of water resources, or the practice of other intentional acts, capable of causing an ecological catastrophe (ecocide), will be punished with a prison sentence of ten to fifteen years. "*Article 131. Ecocide. Deliberate mass destruction of the plant or animal world, or poisoning of the atmospheric air or water resources, or the commission of other intentional actions, capable of causing an ecological disaster (ecocide), are punishable by deprivation of liberty for a term of ten to fifteen years*" (Belarus Penal Code, 1999).

[27] Ukraine calls its Chap. XX of the Penal Code (2001) "Crimes against peace, humanity's security and international legal order". Regarding ecocide: "*Article 441—Ecocide. Mass destruction of flora and fauna, poisoning of air or water resources, and also any other actions that may cause an environmental disaster, shall be punishable by imprisonment for a term of eight to fifteen years*"

[28] The Moldovan Penal Code, unlike the others, includes, in art. 135, offences against humanity. As for ecocide: "Article 136—Ecocide. The intentional mass destruction of the flora or fauna, the intoxication of the atmosphere or water resources, as well as the commission of other actions that may cause or that have caused an ecological disaster, shall be punished by imprisonment from 10 to 15 years. Moldova ratified the Rome Statute on 12 October 2010, being since then a State Party of the ICC.

[29] The Armenian Penal Code, in art. 390, lists several criminal behaviours that would constitute "serious violation of international humanitarian law during armed conflicts". Ecocide is classified in the "*Article 394—Ecocide. Mass destruction of flora or fauna, poisoning the environment, the soils or water resources, as well as implementation of other actions causing an ecological catastrophe, is punished with imprisonment for the term of 10 to 15 years.*

[30] "*Article 169. Ecocide. Mass destruction of vegetable or animal world, poisoning of the atmosphere, land andwater resources, as well as commission of other actions, caused or could cause ecological disaster or environmental emergency, – shall be punished by imprisonment for the term of ten to fifteen years*" (Kazakhstan Penal Code, 2014).

[31] At first glance, the Kazakhstan Penal Code seems to include various conducts of crimes against humanity, despite not directly criminalising the latter. "*However, under Kazakhstan's penal law, these do not fall (except Article 174) within the ambit of crimes against the peace and security of mankind (of which crimes against humanity are a part), and hence are not subject to the provisions of international and domestic penal law regarding the non-applicability of statutes of limitations. Such common crimes are also exempted from ICL [international criminal law] rules on universal jurisdiction. If crimes against humanity were integrated into Kazakhstan's penal legislation in the future, these aspects of the General Part of ICL should be taken into account*" (Sayapin, 2020, p. 5).

the protection and conservation of the environment". Article 196 brings the closest provision to ecocide, despite not naming it:

Article 196. Pollution of the Natural Environment

Pollution or damage of land, water, or atmospheric air, resulted in mass disease incidence of people, death of animals, birds, or fish, or other grave consequences—shall be punished with fine from one hundred to two hundred minimum monthly wages or deprivation of certain right up to five years, or correctional labor up to three years.

The same acts resulted in death of a person—shall be punished with arrest from three to six months, or imprisonment up to three years and deprivation of certain right.

Uzbekistan has done important work in implementing crimes against peace and the security of humanity[32] in its internal criminal law.[33] The fact of typifying conducts close to ecocide, even without naming it as such, is relevant, as it added in its definition, in art. 196, palatable elements for a practical process, by indicating possible results for environmental damage. However, by pointing out "pollution" as the only means of causing such damage, it restricts the scope of the rule, by force of the principle of legality.

Finally, the Penal Code of Georgia (1999, with amendment of 2021), features in Section 14 (offences against humanity), Chapter XLVII (crimes against humanity, peace and security, and against international humanitarian law). More closely reflecting international concerns, the chapter contains crimes against humanity (art. 408), crime of aggression (arts. 404 and 405), genocide (art. 407), and crimes against international humanitarian law (arts. 411, 412, and 413). It also adds crimes on weapons of mass destruction (art. 406) and ecocide (art. 409), maintaining the structure of the criminal provision similar to the neighbours of the continent, but subdivided the penalty according to the period in which the crime is committed:

Article 409: Ecocide

1. Ecocide i.e. contamination of the atmosphere, soil, water resources, mass destruction of fauna or flora, or any other act that could have led to an ecological disaster, shall be punished by imprisonment for a term of twelve to twenty years.
2. The same act committed during armed conflicts, shall be punished by imprisonment for a term of fourteen to twenty years or by life imprisonment.

Georgia, unlike most Asian countries, is a signatory to the Rome Statute[34] since 5 September 2003, having, including, investigation authorised by the Prosecutor of the ICC in progress, for alleged crimes committed in armed conflict, occurred between 1 July and 10 October 2008, in the region of South Ossetia and surroundings.[35]

---

[32] Despite the progress, Uzbekistan is not known for respecting human rights norms, when, for example, it allows forced and child labour (Narine, 2015, p. 103).

[33] The country continues studies to project its Penal Code to the reality of international law, approaching crimes today considered international (Sayapin, 2019, p. 23).

[34] Kyrgyzstan (8/12/1998), Armenia (1/10/1999), Uzbekistan (29/12/2000), and Ukraine (20/01/2000) signed the Rome Statute, but did not ratify the document internally.

[35] The commission of crimes against humanity (murder, forced population transfer, and persecution) and war crimes (attacks on civilian population, intentional murder, intentional attacks on

The Georgian criminal law incorporated the crimes instituted in the International Criminal Court, but did so, with regard to war crimes, insufficiently,[36] without description of the various crimes that the Statute mentions. This implies in the difficulty of this Court being effective, since it depends on national authorities to function effectively, in addition to compromising its performance, in respect to the principle of complementarity (Birkett, 2019, p. 355).

The differences between the criminal definitions "ecocide" are, in general, not very significant, with poor description of the crime, its circumstances and elements, varying the sanctions of the penalty of fine (with restrictions of right, in Uzbekistan) to life imprisonment (Georgia, in case of war) and the death penalty (Vietnam).

The good intention of the legislators to positivise the act of causing massive damage to the environment, however, ran into the precariousness of studies on ecocide, hitherto developed. It must also be considered the lack of political will for this, as seen in the debates of the ILC, maintaining a vague and ambiguous text, but difficult to subsume a concrete case to the criminal norm.[37]

The criminal norms on ecocide—and, in general, on international crimes in Asia were strongly influenced by the context discussed in the *International Law Commission*, in the 1980s and 1990s. The return of attention to the environment through criminal law, at the end of the 2000s, promoted a revisitation to the theme, this time with different theoretical foundations, giving rise to more modern laws, like that of Ecuador.

---

peace forces, property destruction, and looting) are being investigated (ICC, Georgia, Link: https://www.icc-cpi.int/georgia, accessed on: 20 Jun. 2025).

[36] There is only one provision, in art. 413, d), stipulating punishment for the commission of war crimes provided for in international agreements signed by the country, and not punished by arts. 411 and 412.

[37] Even so, the cases effectively judged and sanctioned "within the framework of this definition of crime are however marginal. State hesitations in this regard, in our opinion, are an indicator of the need for transnational harmonisation, of the circulation of international legal norms and relations in the fight against environmental crime, and of the international pressures to which States are subjected" (Estupiñan-Silva, 2016, p. 40).

5.3 Ecuador (2014)

The legal system of environmental protection in Ecuador is a pioneer on the planet,[38] breaking the anthropocentric paradigm. Based on the philosophy of *Buen Vivir*,[39] the original Ecuadorian legislator produced, in 2008, a plurinational Constitution[40] that, for the first time in a Charter, created the "rights of nature", in its Chap. 7.[41] That is, nature becomes not a mere object, but a subject of rights. Nature, or *Pacha Mama* (Mother Earth),[42] can, therefore, be the author of lawsuits, claim rights and, above all, must be recognised as "inalienable life".[43]

---

[38] Bolivia followed the same path the following year, in 2009.

[39] The philosophy of *Buen Vivir*—or "Good Living"—is an alternative path that seeks harmony with nature, reciprocity and solidarity among individuals and communities, opposed to the concept of perpetual accumulation: "it surpasses the traditional concept of development and its multiple synonyms, introducing a much more diversified and, certainly, complex vision (...) Let's make it clear that, as the Ecuadorian Constitution states, the human being, being the centre of attention, is the fundamental factor of the economy. And, in this sense, rescuing the need to strengthen and dignify work, any form of labour precarisation is abolished. However, this reasoning is incomplete. And here arises a key element: the centre of attention should not only be the human being, but the human being living in community and in harmony with nature" (Acosta, 2019).

[40] "Plurinationality refers to a new conception of social organisation that seeks to rescue the plurality of ethnic and cultural visions in order to rethink the State, says Acosta. In this way, collective rights stand out as an important characteristic for the formation of this State" (Jacques, 2021, p. 114).

[41] "Art. 71.—Nature or Pacha Mama, where life is reproduced and realised, has the right to have its existence and the maintenance and regeneration of its life cycles, structure, functions and evolutionary processes fully respected.

Any person, community, people or nationality may demand the public authority to comply with the rights of nature. To apply and interpret these rights, the principles established in the Constitution will be observed, as appropriate.

The State will encourage natural and legal persons, and collectives, to protect nature, and will promote respect for all the elements that form an ecosystem.

Art. 72.—Nature has the right to restoration. This Restoration will be independent of the obligation that the State and natural or legal persons have to compensate individuals and collectives that depend on the affected natural systems.

In cases of severe or permanent environmental impact, including those caused by the exploitation of non-renewable natural resources, the State will establish the most effective mechanisms to achieve restoration, and will adopt appropriate measures to eliminate or mitigate harmful environmental consequences" (Constitution of the Republic of Ecuador, 2008).

[42] "Bolivia and Ecuador emerge as the spearhead: they have societies with a stronger position against this threat to Humanity caused by disconnection from Nature, which is justified by the influence of their significant indigenous population, which began to have a voice with the processes of democratisation in Latin America, at the end of the last century. Consistent with this position, Ecuador and Bolivia took bold and avant-garde measures. Internally, the two countries mark the non-anthropocentric turn in the field of Law, constitutionalising, respectively, the proposals of Good Living and Living Well, synthesised as Harmony with Nature, by Fernando Huanacuni and David Choquehuanca, in Bolivia" (Moraes, 2018, p. 22).

[43] "Pachamama is an Andean term that reconnects the human being to the subalternised Amerindian motherland through the Eurocentric colonisation that subjugated the conquered peoples. (...) It is

The constitutional provisions (art. 71, 72, and 73) were put to test before the Ecuadorian judiciary, in December 2010, when the Vilcabamba River sued, along with two landowners in the region, the Provincial Government of Loja, in the south of the country, for irregular disposal of excavation waste for a road.[44] In a second-degree decision, in March 2011, the Provincial Court condemned the defendant to, among other measures, apologise to society for starting the construction works without prior environmental licensing, through an official publication.[45]

Ecuador, which has already suffered massive environmental disasters,[46] does not mention in its legal system the term "ecocide", but distributes, in three articles of the Penal Code, conducts that cause serious damage to water (art. 251),[47] soil (art.

---

important to emphasise that Pachamama is life, strength and totality, the one that emanates survival and fertility, therefore, Zaffaroni explains that the incorporation of Pachamama into constitutional law would be nothing less than the incorporation of a universal archetype existing in every human being as a result of the survival experiences of the species throughout evolution" (Dutra, 2021, p. 854).

[44] "The case of the Vilacamba River was one of the first actions to invoke nature as a subject of law, Pachamama in the courts in Ecuador. The river follows the road in the city of Vilacamba and Quinara, located in the Province of Loja. It was nature the entity of the action, not as an object, but as a subject of law, which is worth recognising to surpass the Western idea of legal personality" (Brito, 2021, p. 186).

[45] Provincial Court of Justice of Loja, *Protection Action* number 11121-2011-0010, 30 March 2011, Available at: https://elaw.org/system/files/ec.wheeler.loja_.pdf, accessed on: 1 Jul. 2025.

[46] Before the 2008 Constitution conferred the ownership of rights to nature, Ecuador faced a series of lawsuits, in the country and in the United States, against the oil company *Chevron Corporation*, for 8 years (1993 to 2001). For 30 years, the multinational drilled about 340 oil wells, built 18 central production stations and extracted about 1.5 billion barrels of crude oil, transported by 1500 km of pipelines. "*Among others, Chevron regularly 'sprayed roads with crude oil for maintenance and dust control, and deliberately dumped tons of toxic drilling and maintenance wastes [...I into the environment without treatment or monitoring,' "acts which constitute a breach of its contractual obligations. Several consequences arise from Chevron's practices and can be summarised as follows: innumerable rivers and streams were contaminated, which rendered fishing impracticable and polluted the sources of drinking water. Chevron's activities also negatively impacted the vegetation and polluted the soils. (...) The health consequences continued as toxic substances spread on land and in the water. Eventually, pollution led to loss of flora and fauna, and soils became sterile*" (Crasson, 2017, p. 31). The case was even discussed as to whether it constituted crimes against humanity, promptly dismissed by the Prosecutor of the International Criminal Court (Lambert, 2017).

[47] "*Article 251—Crimes against water. The person who, in contravention of current regulations, contaminates, dries up or alters the bodies of water, springs, sources, ecological flows, natural surfaced or underground waters of the hydrographic basins and in general the hydrobiological resources or discharges into the sea causing serious damage, will be punished with a deprivation of freedom of three to five years. The maximum penalty will be imposed if the infringement is perpetrated in a space of the National System of Protected Areas or if the infringement is perpetrated with a profit motive or with methods, instruments or means that result in extensive and permanent damage*" (Comprehensive Organic Criminal Code of Ecuador, 2016).

252),[48] and air (art. 253).[49] All crimes are within Chap. 4 (offences against the environment and nature or *pacha mama*).

In common, despite the low penalties compared to the dimension of the damage (3 to 5 years in prison), the crimes indicate that the dosimetry will be maximum, when instruments or means that result in extensive and permanent damage are used to commit the conduct. There is provision even for criminal punishment of legal entities (art. 258),[50] sanctioned by a fine proportional to the penalty of deprivation of liberty.

The crimes also take care to list various conducts, such as contaminating, draining, or altering bodies of water, affecting or damaging the fertile layer of forest lands, causing erosion or desertification. The criminal provisions condition their accomplishment to the non-compliance with existing norms, that is, it is possible that an administrative authorisation to carry out a massive destruction of the environment (through a work pollutant of national magnitude, with involvement in oil extraction, for example) prevents the penal incidence of the conducts.

There is also a provision in the Ecuadorian Penal Code, in the provisions on the application of the law over time (Title V), pointing out that legal actions—and the serving of the sentence—for environmental damages are imprescriptible (art. 16, [4]).[51]

[48] "*Article 252—Crimes against soil. The person who, in contravention of current regulations, in relation to the plans of territorial and environmental planning, changes the use of forest soil or the soil intended for the maintenance and conservation of native ecosystems and their ecological functions, affects or damages its fertile layer, causes erosion or desertification, causing serious damage, will be punished with a deprivation of freedom of three to five years. The maximum penalty will be imposed if the infringement is perpetrated in a space of the National System of Protected Areas or if the infringement is perpetrated with a profit motive or with methods, instruments or means that result in extensive and permanent damage*" (Comprehensive Organic Criminal Code of Ecuador, 2016).

[49] "*Article 253—Air pollution. The person who, in contravention of current regulations or for not adopting the measures required in the standards, contaminates the air, the atmosphere or other components of the airspace at levels such that serious damage to natural resources, biodiversity and human health results, will be punished with a deprivation of freedom of one to three years*" (Comprehensive Organic Criminal Code of Ecuador, 2016).

[50] "*Article 258—Penalty for legal persons. In the crimes provided for in this Chapter, if criminal responsibility is determined for the legal person, it will be punished with the following penalties: 1. Fine of one hundred to three hundred basic unified salaries of the general worker, temporary closure, confiscation and the remediation of environmental damage, if the crime has a penalty of deprivation of freedom of one to three years. 2. Fine of two hundred to five hundred basic unified salaries of the general worker, temporary closure, confiscation and the remediation of environmental damage, if the crime has a penalty of deprivation of freedom of three to five years.3. Fine of five hundred to a thousand basic unified salaries of the general worker, definitive closure, confiscation and the remediation of environmental damage, if the crime has a penalty of deprivation of freedom greater than five years*" (Comprehensive Organic Criminal Code of Ecuador, 2016).

[51] "*Article 16 (…) The infractions of aggression to a State, genocide, crimes against humanity, war crimes, forced disappearance of persons, embezzlement, bribery, extortion, illicit enrichment and legal actions for environmental damage are imprescriptible both in action and in penalty*" (Comprehensive Organic Criminal Code of Ecuador, 2016).

As can be seen, despite the non-existence of ecocide, there are provisions that, in a manner similar to modern projects, try to punish the most destructive behaviours against the environment. Ecuador also opened an alternative path to the relationship with nature, inserting into the legal universe tools that consider it as part holder of rights[52]—and that can directly enjoy them—in an ecocentric view of the Constitution itself.

The influence of traditional Ecuadorian indigenous communities gave a different, more holistic approach,[53] to ecocide, compared to the studies carried out by the *International Law Commission*, and consequently, to the laws created by Asian countries. Ecuador did not nominally criminalise ecocide, but typified several of its conducts, distributed in the three articles of Section Two, Chap. 4, of the Penal Code.

However, it should be highlighted that it is crucial to give a name and a format to the conduct of promoting extreme environmental damage: ecocide. Identifying it, whether from an anthropocentric (more common) or biocentric (especially characteristic of Andean countries) perspective, will promote awareness around similar environmental disasters globally, contributing to the construction of new ways of cultural and social recognition of the condition of those who suffer the consequences of the damages (Varona, 2020, p. 668).

At this point, Colombia went further, in July 2021.

5.4 Colombia (2021)

The Political Constitution of Colombia,[54] from 1991, does not expressly create the rights of nature, like the Ecuadorian or Bolivian, but it is peaceful in doctrine and jurisprudence[55] that the Colombian Magna Carta contains ideological charge (in

[52] The impacts of mining and oil exploration brought massive protests, some of them violent, from indigenous communities throughout the country: "Nature rights were inextricably entwined with their daily lives, a symbiosis captured in the word "Pachamama," not simply a belief but a way of relating to everything else around them" (Houck, 2017, p. 40).

[53] The rights of nature inspired civil society to create the International Tribunal for the Rights of Nature, in 2014, with the aim of discussing, problematising and making recommendations about the environment (Maloney, 2016, p. 130). For more information, see: https://www.rightsofnature-tribunal.org/, accessed on: 10 Jun. 2025.

[54] Political Constitution of the Republic of Colombia, Available at: http://www.secretariasenado.gov.co/constitucion-politica. Accessed on: 2 Jul. 2025.

[55] A common argumentative profile in Colombian jurisprudence is the critical approach to the concept of sustainable development, with the consequent adherence to new ecocentric doctrines on the rights of nature, when, for example, the Supreme Court recognised, judging the deforestation in the Colombian Amazon, that the system is moving from an anthropocentric model of environmental law to an "anthropic ecocentric", motivating the principle of solidarity, declined both towards Nature and, above all, towards future generations (Bagni, 2018, p. 44).

Chap. 3) —which radiates throughout the Document—with the essence of commitments to environmental protection.[56]

The jurisprudential broadening[57] of the constitutional approach to the treatment of the environment is compatible with the principle of progressivity of economic, social, and cultural rights in Colombia. Thus, environmental protection must increase[58]—and not decrease—in the drafting of laws and their judicial interpretation, prohibited the setback (Arango, 2006, p. 154).

In the penal field, Law 2.111,[59] from July 2021, replaced Title XI (Of the crimes against natural resources and the environment), from arts. 328 to 339 (Special part of the crimes in general) of the Penal Code of Colombia[60] (2000). The innovation[61] came in Chap. II (of the damages to natural resources), which included in the Colombian legal system the crime of ecocide[62] (art. 333):

---

[56] The language of the Colombian Constitution was influenced by the international debate on the relationship between development, sustainability and environmental protection: "*In articles 79 and 80 const. it affirms the right to enjoy a healthy environment and the duty of the State to protect the diversity and integrity of the environment and to conserve areas of special ecological importance. In addition, the State commits to plan the management and use of natural resources, to ensure their sustainable development, their conservation, restoration or replacement. The Constitution, therefore, not only refers to the concept of a healthy environment, but defends on multiple occasions the need to guarantee the "ecological" dimension of other rights such as property or economic development*" (Bagni, 2018, p. 39).

[57] In Colombia, "*numerous courts have recognised the rights of at least eight rivers and/or river basins,30 including the Atrato River Basin, which the Constitutional Court held to be an 'entity subject to rights to protection, conservation, maintenance and restoration by the State and ethnic communities'*" (Wilson, 2020, p. 66).

[58] An example of expanding environmental protection through the interpretation of constitutional norms is the case Future Generations v. Minister of the Environment and others (Supreme Court of Justice, April 5, 2018, M.P: L. Villabona, File: 11001-22-03-000-2018-00319-01), "*a group of 25 youth plaintiffs sued the Colombian government and several other entities, arguing that the government's failure to prevent deforestation violates plaintiffs' fundamental rights. The Supreme Court of Colombia recognised that the fundamental constitutional rights of life, health, minimum subsistence, freedom, and human dignity were substantially linked to the environment and the ecosystem. The court ordered the government to formulate and implement action plans to address deforestation in the Amazon region*" (United Nations Environment Programme, 2020, p. 40).

[59] Congress of Colombia, Law 2.111, of 29th July 2021.

[60] Penal Code of Colombia, Law 599 of 2000, Link: https://leyes.co/codigo_penal.htm, accessed on: 10 Jun. 2025.

[61] The Law, in addition to changes in the procedural code, also included in the Colombian Penal Code the new crimes of wildlife trafficking (article 328A), illicit handling of exotic species (article 329), deforestation (article 330) and promotion and financing of deforestation (article 330 A).

[62] "Article 333. Damage to natural resources and ecocide. Whoever, in breach of existing regulations, destroys, renders useless, makes disappear or causes a serious environmental impact or in any other way damages the natural resources referred to in this title or those associated with these, will incur imprisonment of sixty (60) to one hundred and thirty-five (135) months and a fine of one hundred sixty-seven (167) to eighteen thousand seven hundred and fifty (18,750) minimum monthly legal wages.

Paragraph 1. For the purposes of this article, ecocide is understood as the massive damage and serious and systemic widespread destruction of ecosystems.

Article 333. Damage to natural resources and ecocide

Whoever, in violation of current regulations, destroys, renders useless, makes disappear or causes serious environmental impact or in any other way damages the natural resources referred to in this title or associated with them, incurs a prison sentence of sixty (60) to one hundred and thirty five (135) months and a fine of one hundred and sixty seven (167) to eighteen thousand seven hundred and fifty (18,750) legal monthly minimum wages.

§ 1° For the purposes of this article, ecocide is understood as the massive damage and widespread, serious and systemic destruction of ecosystems.

§ 2° A serious environmental impact is understood as the alteration of environmental conditions generated as a result of the affectation of environmental components, eliminating the integrity of the system and putting its sustainability at risk.

Among the natural resources referred to in Title XI, liable to protection from the crime of ecocide (*caput* of art. 333), are the specimens, products or parts of fauna, forest resources, floristic, hydrobiological, coral, biological, or genetic resources of Colombian biodiversity (art. 328). In this case, Colombian law offers a list of legal goods significantly larger and more detailed than in the Ecuadorian case, in three articles.

The explanatory norms (§§ 1° and 2°) are important to confer greater precision to the meaning of "ecocide" and "serious environmental impact", imposing technical limits on the applicability of the criminal definition. For Colombian law, the crime occurs when the agent, violating some regulation, causes damage to natural resources or alters the conditions of a certain environment, eliminating it or putting its sustainability at risk.

It is undeniable that the Colombian norm, despite the increase in environmental protection, is of an anthropocentric character, treating nature as a "resource", to promote socio-economic development, while doing little to safeguard planetary integrity (Du Toit & Kotzé, 2022, p. 3).

The penalty dosimetry for ecocide also evidences the little relevance of the new crime compared to crimes with direct property consequences. The sanction for the massive destruction of the environment is from 5 to 11 years and 3 months in prison; the crime of creating websites to capture personal data (art. 269G), with some aggravating circumstance (art. 269H), for example, confers a penalty on the agent between 6 and 14 years in prison.

Colombian criminal law already suffered from questions about its effectiveness, regarding environmental crimes, in the Penal Code of 1980 (Law 100), repealed by the current Code (2000), because the environment was, at the time, classified under "Crimes against economic and social order", where the protected legal good was contemplated from an eminently economic aspect (Cabrera Izquierdo et al., 2020, p. 410).

Paragraph 2. By serious environmental impact is understood, the alteration of environmental conditions that is generated as a consequence of the affectation of the environmental components, eliminating the integrity of the system and putting its sustainability at risk" (Penal Code of Colombia, 2000).

With the advent of the new Code, the environment emerges as an autonomous legal good, but the marks of symbolic law remain,[63] especially due to the lack of technical-juridical investments, such as the creation of a specialised justice (with technically qualified people in the area), better distribution of administrative competences and environmental education (educational, research, and administrative sectors).[64]

In addition, the country faces criticism for increasing the protection of environmental law, but failing to protect its environmentalists (Alonso, 2021), evidenced by the late ratification of the Escazú Agreement,[65] a regional tool for access to information, justice, and public participation in environmental matters.

The difficulties of applying national legislation related to the environment are not exclusive to Colombia. From this, it is commendable the proactivity of the legislature in including ecocide as a crime in the Penal Code, detailing it beyond the generic texts drafted by Asian countries. The pioneering of Latin America, both in the adoption of a new definition and in the recognition of the rights of nature, offers new tools to discuss the directions of international criminal law, in the environmental field.

In the French case, civil society was crucial to the inclusion of ecocide in domestic legislation.

5.5 France (2019–2021)

Among European countries, France maintains prominence in the discourse on the criminal protection of the environment. The 21st Conference of the Parties (COP-21) of the United Nations Framework Convention on Climate Change was held between November and December 2015, where paths were discussed to limit the average temperature increase of the planet below 2° Celsius. As a result of the Summit Meeting, the Paris Agreement was signed (UN, Paris Agreement, 2015), establishing strategies and objectives (assumption of targets) among the countries that ratify

---

[63] The Colombian Judiciary has difficulties in prosecuting environmental crimes, especially those of greater magnitude: "*In the information provided by the Attorney General's Office it is evident that there are many environmental criminal offenses that materially happen, but unfortunately the jurisdictional action is not sufficient to control and sanction the offenders, thus coinciding with the doctrinal position that environmental criminal law is a symbolic law*" (Cabrera Izquierdo et al., 2020, p. 401).

[64] "*That this new law provides instruments to protect and defend nature is something irrefutable in my opinion, however and being consistent with what was expressed in another column I consider that 'the protection of the environment cannot be left solely to the penal system but in addition to this it is necessary to prevent, intervene or suspend, timely, bad practices of companies and individuals, carry out social actions that solve needs of 'nutrition and employment and carry out pedagogical activities that shape and transform behaviours'*" (Pérez, 2021).

[65] Colombia was, until now, the last country to ratify the treaty, in September 2024. Link: https://www.cepal.org/pt-br/acordodeescazu, accessed on: 13 Dec. 2024.

it. After the meeting, France sought to take a leading political role in international environmental issues of relevance,[66] including among them a penal reflection on massive environmental damage.

In 2019, the National Assembly reviewed a Bill (no. 2353/2019[67]) for the recognition of the crime of ecocide. The intention was to include, after Chap. III of Book IV of the French Penal Code, a new Chapter (III Bis–Ecocide), punishing natural and legal persons:

> **Chapter III Bis—Ecocide**
> Section 1—Extensive, irreversible and irreparable damage to an ecosystem
> Art. 413-15.—An ecocide is any concerted and deliberate action tending to directly cause extensive, irreversible and irreparable damage to an ecosystem, committed in knowledge of the consequences that would result and which could not be ignored.
> Ecocide is punishable by twenty years of criminal imprisonment and a fine of €10,000,000 or, in the case of a company, 20% of the total global annual turnover of the previous financial year.
> Art. 413-16.—The public and direct provocation, by all means, to commit an ecocide is punishable by seven years of criminal imprisonment and a fine of €5,000,000 if this provocation has been followed by effect.
> If the provocation has not been followed by effect, the facts are punished with two years of imprisonment and a fine of 100,000 euros.
> Art. 413-17.—Participation in a group formed or agreed to participation, characterised by one or more material acts, of one of the crimes defined in articles 413-15 is punishable by a prison sentence of twenty years and a fine of € 10,000,000, or, in the case of a company, 20% of the total annual global turnover from the previous year.

The initiative also provided for the imprescriptibility of the crime and the universal jurisdiction of the French court (arts. 6 and 7 of the Penal Code). Attentive to international discussions on the subject, the French parliamentarian supporters of the initiative deliberately maintained a restrictive definition of the offence,[68] sticking to deliberate destructive acts, with massive consequences to the environment.

---

[66] Indeed, the European Union as a whole has engaged in the environmental theme, especially on climate change, converging with the French conception: "*the European Union has every interest in defending climate justice. Indeed, this can allow to link the sectoral competences of the EU, support the promotion of its model of solidarity and be an element of reinforcement of its influence in the world by the promotion of multilateral cooperation as a political message in climate negotiations and beyond. The EU, as an organisation displaying global aspirations, has taken important steps to become a major actor in climate justice, particularly in the areas of development assistance and adaptation to climate change*" (Jouzel & Michelot, 2020, p. 82).

[67] *National Assembly, Proposal for Law recognising the crime of ecocide n° 2353/2019*. Available at: https://www.assemblee-nationale.fr/dyn/opendata/PIONANR5L15B2353.html. Accessed on: 22 Jun. 2025.

[68] In the words of the rapporteur, Christophe Bouillon, "*I do not wish to criminalise an accident, an involuntary act even unreasonable, a negligence even guilty; we already have legal instruments for this. The objective is to strike hard for the most odious acts, the most deliberate, the most destructive, those whose consequences are massive and irreparable on the scale of human life. It is because the scope of the offence is deliberately very narrow that I propose to punish it with such heavy penalties and by such exceptional means.*" (National Assembly, 2019).

The Project,[69] however, was rejected by the National Assembly, on12 December 2019,[70] despite the significant debate held in the House. Among the main reasons for the filing, doubt was pointed out about the need for the new crime, given the rules already existing in the country.[71] Another aspect mentioned was the indefiniteness about various concepts necessary to characterise ecocide, such as "ecosystem", "widespread damage", and "irreversible", there being no validation, until then, international.

This project was proposed by direct stimulus from civil society. In the same year, in 2019, the *Convention Citoyenne pour le Climat*[72] began, with the aim of developing and submitting to the Parliament's consideration measures to reduce, at least, 40% of GHG emissions by 2030, within a logic of social justice.[73] In the end, a report with 149 proposals (Citizens' Convention for Climate, 2021) was generated, among them the protection of ecosystems through legislation on ecocide, considering the planetary limits. The proposal included a wording for the crime, punishable

[69] It is important to mention the previous project for recognition of the crime of ecocide, presented in March 2019, to the French Senate, which proposed to include arts. 230-1 to 230-3 in the Penal Code: "*An ecocide constitutes the fact, in execution of a concerted action tending to the total or partial destruction or degradation of an ecosystem, in times of peace as in times of war, to seriously and durably harm the environment and the living conditions of a population.*

Ecocide is punished by twenty years of criminal imprisonment and a fine of 7,500,000 €." (Senate. Bill recognising the crime of ecocide no. 384, 19 Mar. 2019. Available at: http://www.senat.fr/leg/ppl18-384.html. Accessed on: 23 May. 2025). The project was rejected shortly after, on 2nd of May 2019, with criticisms that would resemble proposal no. 2353/2019 (Link: http://www.senat.fr/dossier-legislatif/ppl18-384.html. Accessed on: 23 Jun. 2025).

[70] National Assembly. Text no. 369, 12 Dec. 2019. Available at: https://www.assemblee-nationale.fr/dyn/15/textes/l15t0369_texte-adopte-seance. Accessed on: 23 May. 2025.

[71] Parliamentarian Didier Paris criticised: "*First of all, do we really need a new text? The question arises because we already have a complete set of rules: ten years of imprisonment for what falls under offences, not crimes—you are right to make the difference—, which is not nothing, especially in order to fight against pollution in the high seas that you have pointed out. Whether these incriminations are in the penal code or in the environmental code, what difference does it make to the magistrates? They know how to refer to a text wherever it is.*" (National Assembly, 2019).

[72] A *Citizens' Convention for Climate* was composed of French citizens, gathered 150 people, drawn in a way representative of French society, operating between October 2019 and June 2020 (Link: https://www.conventioncitoyennepourleclimat.fr/)

[73] The French pioneering, by admitting the direct intervention of civil society for the discussion, among others, of ecocide, translating it into an institutional initiative, was highlighted in the European doctrine, considered an advance in the approach to the theme (Fronza, 2021).

for intentional conduct (art. 522.1, in the Penal Code)[74] and negligent (committed with recklessness, art. 522.2, of the Penal Code).[75]

In response to the Convention's Report,[76] Bill No. 3875 was proposed in the National Assembly,[77] in February 2021, with the aim of valuing the French demand for a participatory democracy and justice in the ecological transition. Among the various measures, it was understood to strengthen the criminal repression of attacks on the environment, and, when irreversible, it was termed ecocide.[78]

The Bill was passed (Law No. 2021–1104, then called "Climate and Resilience Law")[79] with amendments, on 22 August 2021. Ecocide was included in the Environmental Code, articles L231–1, L231.2, and L231–3:

Article L231-1

The conduct, in manifestly deliberate violation of a particular duty of caution or safety provided for by law or regulation, of emitting into the air, discharging, dumping or allowing to flow into surface or underground waters or into the sea within the limits of territorial waters, directly or indirectly, one or more substances whose action or reactions lead to serious and lasting harmful effects on health, flora, fauna, with the exception of the damages mentioned in articles L. 218-73 and L. 432-2, or serious alteration of the normal water supply system is punishable by five years imprisonment and a fine of one million euros, this amount being increased up to five times the benefit derived from the practice of the offence.

Paragraph 1 of this article applies only:

---

[74] "Art. 522–1.—Constitutes a crime of ecocide, any action that has caused serious ecological damage consisting of a manifest and non-negligible exceeding of at least one of the planetary limits [defined in article L XXX of the environmental code] and whose author knew or should have known that there was a high probability of this exceeding.

The crime of ecocide is punished by twenty years of criminal imprisonment and a fine of [10,000,000 €] the amount of which can be increased, in a proportionate manner to the benefits derived from the breach, to 20% of the last known turnover at the date of the commission of the facts" (Citizens' Convention for Climate, 2021).

[75] "*Art. 522–2—Constitutes a crime of imprudence of ecocide, any violation of a duty of care or safety provided by law, regulation or an international convention having directly or indirectly caused serious ecological damage consisting of a manifest exceeding of the planetary limits [in the sense of article L.XXX of the environmental code], if it is established that the author of the facts has not performed the normal diligences taking into account, where appropriate, the nature of his missions or his functions, his competences as well as the power and the means at his disposal.*

The crime of ecocide is punished by five years of imprisonment and a fine of 1,000,000 € the amount of which can be increased, in a proportionate manner to the benefits derived from the breach to 10% of the last known turnover at the date of the commission of the facts" (Citizens' Convention for Climate, 2021).

[76] Even before its conclusion, the Citizens' Convention lost strength, with the repeal of provisions that indicated the submission of the final recommendations, without a referendum filter, to parliament, or determined the direct regulatory application, which would cause significant turbulence in the French legal system (Torney, 2021, p. 387).

[77] *National Assembly, Proposal for combating climate change and strengthening resilience to its effects no. 3875/2021*. Available at: https://www.assemblee-nationale.fr/dyn/15/textes/l15b3875_projet-loi. Accessed on: 23 Jul. 2025.

[78] Explanatory memorandum of Bill 3875/2021.

[79] Link: https://www.vie-publique.fr/loi/278460-loi-22-aout-2021-climat-et-resilience-convention-citoyenne-climat. Accessed on: 22 Jul. 2025.

1° In relation to emissions to the atmosphere, only if the emission limit values set by decision of the competent administrative authority are exceeded;

2° In relation to dumping operations and the use of authorised substances, only in case of non-compliance with the requirements established by the competent administrative authority.

Harmful effects on health or damage to flora or fauna that may last at least seven years are considered lasting.

The limitation period for public action for the offence mentioned in the first paragraph runs from the discovery of the damage.

Article L231-2

The conduct of abandoning, depositing or causing to deposit waste, in conditions contrary to Chapter I of Title IV of Book V, and the fact of managing waste, in the sense of article L. 541-1-1, without satisfying the requirements on the characteristics, quantities, technical conditions of waste management and treatment processes implemented, defined in articles L. 541-2, L. 541-2-1, L. 541-7-2, L. 541-21-1 and L. 541-22, when causing substantial degradation of fauna and flora or the quality of air, soil or water are punished with three years imprisonment and a fine of €150,000.

The limitation period for public action for the offence mentioned in the first paragraph of this article runs from the discovery of the damage.

Article L231-3

The offence provided for in article L. 231-1 constitutes ecocide when the acts are committed with intent.

Also constitute ecocide the offences provided for in article L. 231-2, committed intentionally, when causing serious and lasting damage to health, flora, fauna or air quality.

The prison sentence provided for in articles L. 231-1 and L. 231-2 is increased to ten years imprisonment. The fine provided for in the same articles L. 231-1 and L. 231-2 is increased to 4.5 million euros, this amount may be increased up to ten times the advantage derived from the practice of the offence.

Harmful effects on health or damage to flora, fauna or the quality of soil or surface or underground waters that may last at least seven years are considered lasting.

The limitation period for public action for the offence mentioned in the first paragraph of this article runs from the discovery of the damage.[80]

As seen, ecocide is recognised as an aggravating factor (offence)[81] of the crimes provided for in articles L231-1 and L231-2 of the Environmental Code, when committed with intent, causing serious and lasting damage (at least 7 years). The absence of a specific crime of ecocide—with its downgrading to an offence—is contested by civil society and doctrine, given the disregard by the National Assembly of the decision in the Citizens' Convention for the Climate, which expressed the desire for the criminalisation of the conduct.

Indeed, ecocide in the French system, treated as an offence, is a lesser criminal offence than a crime, and still defined by successive references to other offences,

---

[80] French Environmental Code Available at: https://www.legifrance.gouv.fr/codes/id/LEGITEXT000006074220/

[81] In the French penal system, there are differences, in the strict sense, between crime, offence and contravention (art. 111-1, of the French Penal Code). Crimes, the most serious infractions, carry heavier penalties (imprisonment, life imprisonment, etc.), while in offences the penalties, considered correctional (art. 131-3, of the Penal Code), reach a maximum of 10 years in prison. Finally, contraventions (art. 131-12, of the same code) are the lightest infractions, with sanctions such as fines, deprivation or restriction of rights (Guinchard & Debard, 2018).

which hampers the clarity of the institute (Baudouin, 2021). Among other criticisms of the Law, it is pointed out the missed opportunity to, in the absence of recognition in international law, define it internally, correctly allocating it as a crime, according to the severity of the massive environmental damages.[82]

Another significant obstacle lies in the criterion of intentionality (proof of will—the active desire, in the theory of crime—to commit ecocide) and the illegality of the conduct, restricting the application of the crime to a previous violation of a norm, excluding its application when the conduct, even causing massive environmental damage, has administrative authorisation.

The Climate Law has multiple dimensions, with reinforcement in the repressive environmental aspect (Dufourq, 2021), toughening penalties and creating crimes and offences. However, the retreat of the French government[83] in the construction of ecocide—timidly increasing the punishment for massive damage to the environment—exposed the difficulty in defining and instituting the crime, whether for technical or political reasons.[84]

Even so, the 2019 and 2021 Bills of Law highlight the increase in debates about the need to establish more severe measures in dealing with environmental crime, when causing massive damage, whether by natural or legal persons. At this moment, the concern with climate change is the catalyst for the discussion about ecocide, even though the crime, per se, does not combat it directly.[85] On the external plane, France maintains support for the inclusion of the offence in the list of international crimes.

Concurrently, other countries in the world have taken on the task of seriously discussing the inclusion of the crime in domestic legislation through bills of law (PL), with different approaches, but all more detailed, tuned—to some extent—with the doctrine and the appeals of civil society. This is the topic of the next chapter.

---

[82] The recognition of ecocide in domestic law "*would allow for punishment commensurate with the gravity of the most serious harms that could be inflicted, knowingly, on the environment on French territory and/or by French leaders and companies (and to deter the commission of such harms). Then, international law is created thanks to precedents in domestic law*" (Baudouin, 2021, pp. 3–4).

[83] For the Government, the recognition of ecocide as a crime could only be done on a global scale, to then gain contours nationally (Lenormand, 2022).

[84] The treatment reserved for ecocide in the climate law allows us to doubt the French intentions: "*By refusing to recognise the crime of ecocide in its criminal law, France has missed the opportunity to be a driving force of a movement that will eventually impose itself as inevitable. Worse, by reducing ecocide to an obscure and unsuitable offence, it creates a precedent that could lower the future discussions within the European Union and internationally*" (Baudouin, 2021, p. 16).

[85] The climate issue imposes new modes of cooperation, new concepts and/or new legal principles and a broad reflection on the conditions of a global climate governance (Michelot, 2018).

5.6 Chile (2023)

Chile has undergone a significant legal movement, resulting from the Plebiscite[86] of 2020, when the population decided (almost 80% of the votes) (Venaglia, 2020) to elect a Constituent Assembly to draft the new Constitution, replacing the Charter of the dictatorship of Augusto Pinochet. This process was in charge of the *Convención Constitucional*, but the project was rejected after a popular vote, on 4 September 2022 (BBC News World, 2022).

The current Constitution,[87] of 1980, in terms of environmental protection, is limited to establishing the right to live in an environment free from contamination (art. 19, n° 8°). The rejected text gave significantly greater attention to this topic, creating a specific Chapter for the environment. In it, the rights of nature are recognised (§ 297); it imposes the duty of the State to take actions in the face of the climate crisis (§ 296); and recognises the right to informed participation in environmental matters (§ 308).[88]

With the contestation of the current Charter and discussion about the new main legal text of the country,[89] several legislative proposals remained pending, among them the Bill on environmental crimes and environmental damage (Bulletin n° 12.398–12, message 339–366),[90] without movement since November 2022. The

[86] Since 18 October 2019, Chile has been oppressed by large social protests: "*What first meant a discomfort for the increase in the metro fare and the violence of the state apparatus, transmuted into a general discomfort directed at an entire system and political class that was inherited from the civil-military dictatorship and maintained in the subsequent 30 years of democracy*" (Dulci & Sadivia, 2021).

[87] Political Constitution of the Republic of Chile, of 24 October 1980. Available at: https://www.camara.cl/camara/doc/leyes_normas/constitucion_politica.pdf. Accessed on: 2 Jun. 2025.

[88] The draft of the Charter also includes statutes on water (§ 309 and following), minerals (§ 324 and following), as well as establishing the minimum environmental principles to be observed: the principles of progressive justice, preventive, environmental, intergenerational solidarity, responsibility and fair climate action (§ 307).

[89] A new Charter was submitted to another plebiscite, with doubts about approval: "Public support for the new document fell dramatically in recent weeks, with voters intending to reject the new constitution surpassing those who plan to approve it for the first time in early April. But the Cadem research institute recorded on Sunday (15) its first increase in "yes" voters since the end of March, with a jump of 3 points to 38% since the beginning of May, while "no" voters fell 2 points to 46%" (Villegas & Ramos, 2022). In fact, in December 2023, the Chilean population rejected for the second time the new Constitution, largely written by conservative parliamentarians, maintaining the old Charter in force (Bartlett, 2023).

[90] Chilean environmental management has been strengthened in recent years with the development of various instruments and the creation of a new institutional framework on the matter, composed by the Ministry of the Environment, Superintendency of the Environment, Environmental Assessment Service and Environmental Courts. However, the supervisory competences, dispersed in various sectoral bodies, belong exclusively to the Superintendency of the Environment, in charge of sanctioning infractions, punishing them administratively. There is, therefore, no special legislation on environmental criminal offences, despite the existence of some specific definitions scattered in various regulatory bodies (Bill, initiated in message from H. E. the President of the Republic, on environmental crimes and environmental damage. Bulletin N° 12.398-12, Message

measure aimed to fill a gap in the Chilean legislative system, given the lack of a specific document to deal with the subject.[91]

The aforementioned PL did not explicitly provide for ecocide, but included a provision against massive environmental damage (arts. 2 to 4):

Articles 2-4

Art. 2—Whoever, intentionally, causes loss, reduction, deterioration or significant damage to the environment or to one or more of its components will be punished with a sentence of lesser imprisonment in its minimum to medium degree and a fine of 501 to 700 monthly fiscal units.

If the conducts provided for in this article are committed with recklessness, the penalty will be lesser imprisonment in its minimum degree and a fine of 100 to 500 monthly fiscal units.

Art. 3—If the conducts provided for in the previous article seriously affect the object of protection of a national reserve, a national park, a natural monument, a forest reserve, a marine park, a marine reserve, a protected coastal marine zone for multiple uses or a nature sanctuary, they will be punished with a sentence of lesser imprisonment in its medium to maximum degree and a fine of 801 to 1000 monthly fiscal units.

If the conduct is perpetrated with recklessness, the penalty will be lesser imprisonment in its medium degree and a fine of 701 to 800 monthly fiscal units.

Art. 4—For the purposes of articles 2 and 3, the loss, reduction, damage or deterioration is significant when any of the following circumstances apply:

1° when it affects the basic properties of one or more components of the environment, considering its location, state, vulnerability, scarcity, representativeness or capacity for permanence or regeneration, with harmful effects that are prolonged or prolongable over time in a relevant spatial area;

2° it is irreversible or difficult to reverse, in terms of its existence or the ecosystem services it provides;

3° when it seriously affects the life or subsistence of species classified as extinct, extinct in the wild or critically threatened; or

4° when it causes serious damage to the health of the population.

As can be seen, the Project included an explanatory norm, to define the penal scope of the term "significant damage". For the Chilean penal system, however, penalties such as those stipulated are considered lenient,[92] consisting, in the most serious hypothesis, of lesser imprisonment, in medium to maximum degrees.[93]

N° 339-366. Available at: https://www.camara.cl/legislacion/ProyectosDeLey/tramitacion.aspx?prmID=12927&prmBOLETIN=12398-12. Accessed on: 2 Jun, 2025).

[91] The Chilean Penal Code, from 1874, did not bring, until 2023, any provision on the environment, that is, almost 150 years of absence of the theme in the penal sphere.

[92] The penalty for the crime provided for in art. 2, for example, is similar to the penalty for the crime of simple theft in Chile.

[93] The penalties for crimes in Chile (art. 59 of the Penal Code) are applied according to 5 (five) scales, having a wide diversity. For example, among the penalties of imprisonment or seclusion, they can vary between minor seclusion in minimum degree (approximately 2 months to 1 year and a half) to major seclusion in maximum degree (approximately 3 to 5 years), up to perpetual imprisonment. The table implies, at times, problems when legal reductions or increases are made (Calderón, 2016).

Stimulated by the expanded environmental approach conferred in the draft of the new Charter, a Bill was proposed in the Chilean Chamber of Deputies[94] (Bulletin no. 14537–12, Legislature 369, of 18 August 2021) to include ecocide in the Penal Code. Considering the dimension of environmental damage—which goes beyond local jurisdictions— commonly seen,[95] the Initiative is based on the impacts of environmental destruction on humanity, citing global climate changes, forest fires, focusing on the consequences for Chile, a country that concentrates 80% of the glaciers in South America.[96]

The Project also draws a panorama of ecocide on the international level, highlighting the proposals and support for the inclusion of the crime in the Rome Statute, mentioning the resolutions on the subject of the European Parliament and the recommendations of Belgium and Spain. The crime would also be imprescriptible.[97]

The Initiative proposes to include ecocide in art. 161-D, of the Chilean Penal Code, detailing it in the following articles:

> **Article 161-D.**
>
> The author, accomplice or cover-up of the crime of ecocide, that is, any omission or unlawful or arbitrary act committed knowingly that there is a substantial probability that it will cause serious damage that is extensive or long-lasting to the environment, will be punished with the penalty of minor imprisonment in its maximum degree to major imprisonment in its medium degree and a fine of 900 to 9,000 monthly tax units.
>
> Likewise, all persons who appear before the environmental authority as holders of the projects or activities that cause the damage will be considered authors of the crime of ecocide. In the case of legal persons, their legal representatives will be responsible.
>
> **Article 161-E.**
>
> For the purposes of the provisions in the previous article, it will be understood that there is an arbitrary act or omission when it implies a lack of reasonableness in acting or omitting; lack of proportion between the motives and the end to be achieved; absence of adjustment between the means used and the objective to be obtained, or even the non-existence of the facts that support an act, when they clash against logic and straight reason.

---

[94] Bill that Modifies the Penal Code to create and sanction the crime of Ecocide. Bulletin N° 14,537–12, Legislature N° 369. Available at: https://www.camara.cl/legislacion/ProyectosDeLey/tramitacion.aspx?prmID=15019&prmBOLETIN=14537-12. Accessed on: 13 Dec. 2024.

[95] Ecocide is a behaviour of exposure to suicidal risk, usually mediated, in the long term, that produces homicidal anticipation of the death of others or oneself: "*the fact that ecocide is also a suicide accompanied by a homicide would allow, apparently, to approach it from the perspective of national penal codes, which usually typify the crime of homicide. However, the uniqueness of ecocide is that its breadth and concept surpass the environmental damage, suicide and common homicide and even combined*" (…) "*The power of the State or a ruler in the territory that it occupies or governs is not unlimited. In other words, they have a duty of care, but not the power to use or destroy the territory in the name of sovereignty or property*" (Neira et al., 2019).

[96] Ecocide Bill, statement of reasons (Bulletin n° 14537-12, Legislature n° 369). Available at: https://www.camara.cl/verDoc.aspx?prmID=14762&prmTIPO=INICIATIVA. Accessed on: 3 Jun. 2025.

[97] The Project includes art. 94-ter in the Penal Code: "*Article 94 ter.- The criminal action will not prescribe regarding the crime described and sanctioned in article 161-D*" (Ecocide Bill, statement of reasons (Bulletin n° 14537-12, Legislature n° 369). Available at: https://www.camara.cl/verDoc.aspx?prmID=14762&prmTIPO=INICIATIVA. Accessed on: 3 Jun. 2025).

Serious damage will be understood as any affectation that generates the loss, decrease, detriment or significant impairment inflicted on the environment or one or more of its components, in any of the following circumstances:

1°—Affect species categorised as extinct, extinct in the wild, critically endangered or endangered or vulnerable;

2°—Endanger the health of one or more people;

3°—Affect the functions and ecosystem services.

Extensive damage will be understood as damage that goes beyond a limited geographical area, reaches a significant set of species according to the characteristics of the affected area, crosses the borders states or affects the entirety of an ecosystem or a species or a large number of human beings.

Damage will be understood as lasting if it is irreversible, irreparable or cannot be repaired through its natural regeneration within a reasonable period.

The environment will be understood as the global system made up of natural and artificial elements of a physical, chemical or biological, sociocultural nature and their interactions, in permanent modification by human or natural action and that governs and conditions the existence and development of life in its multiple manifestations.

Article 161-F.

When the crime contemplated in article 161-D is caused by negligence or imprudence, the immediately lower degree of the designated corporal punishment will be imposed and a fine that does not exceed half of the maximum.

The design of ecocide for Chile in the Bill is characterised by the detailing of the terms used, through explanatory notes, in order to reduce the discretion of the rule's applicator, especially regarding the temporal duration and extent of environmental damage. Even so, the proposed definition presents certain complexity for its subsumption to a practical case, for example, by linking the occurrence of damage (art. 161-E) to "a large number" of human victims affected (without defining what this number would be) or conditioning its recognition to changes in the functions and services of the ecosystem (considering that any conduct against the environment causes, in varying degrees, changes in this).

Unlike the Project of environmental crimes, the penalties for ecocide are higher, revealing the importance of the good to be protected. The fact of punishing the legal entity (Law No. 20.393) and negligent conducts also demonstrates the legislator's attention to the most common situations of committing the crime.

As it stands, the Chilean initiative, veiled inspiration in the 2021 Amendment Proposal to the Rome Statute, is one of the most relevant on the subject, seeking to make the offence viable, from an operational point of view, and a landmark in the criminal system of Latin America.

While the aforementioned Project has stalled since its proposal,[98] Law 21.595, of 7th August of 2023, finally included crimes against the environment in the Chilean Penal Code:

---

[98] Despite parliamentary effort, the initiative has been stalled in the Chamber since its proposal (Link: https://www.camara.cl/legislacion/ProyectosDeLey/tramitacion.aspx?prmID=15019&prmBOLETIN=14537-12. Accessed on: 13 Dec. 2024).

Article 305

The person who, without having subjected their activity to an environmental impact assessment, knowingly being obliged to do so:

1. Discharges polluting substances into maritime or continental waters.
2. Extracts continental waters, whether surface or underground, or maritime waters.
3. Discharges or deposits polluting substances in the soil or subsoil, continental or maritime.
4. Discharges lands or other solids into wetlands.
5. Extracts components of the soil or subsoil.
6. Releases polluting substances into the air. The penalty will be imprisonment or minor confinement in its medium to maximum degrees if the offender commits the act being obliged to subject their activity to an environmental impact study.

Article 308. The person who, by discharging, depositing or releasing polluting substances, or extracting waters or components of the soil or subsoil, seriously affects the maritime or continental waters, surface or underground, the soil or the subsoil, whether continental or maritime, or the air, or animal or plant health, the existence of water resources or the supply of drinking water, or who seriously affects wetlands by discharging into them lands or other solids, will be punished:

1. With the penalty of imprisonment or major confinement in its minimum degree, if the serious affectation is perpetrated with the circumstances provided for in articles 305, 306 or 307.
2. With the penalty of imprisonment or minor confinement in its maximum degree to major imprisonment in its minimum degree in cases not included in the preceding number, and provided that they are not authorised to do so.

Article 309.—The person who, through reckless imprudence or mere imprudence or negligence with violation of the regulations, incurs in the facts indicated in the previous article, will be punished:

1. With the penalty of imprisonment or minor confinement in its maximum degree, if the serious affectation is perpetrated with the circumstances provided for in articles 305, 306 or 307.
2. With the penalty of imprisonment or minor confinement in any of its degrees in cases not included in the preceding number.[99]

Articles 310 and following provide for a crime similar to ecocide, considered as massive damage to the environment:

Article 310

Whoever seriously affects one or more environmental components of a virgin region reserve, a national park, a natural monument, a national reserve or an internationally important wetland, will be punished with imprisonment or a greater prison sentence in its minimum degree.

The same penalty will be imposed on whoever, violating an environmental qualification resolution or without having submitted their activity to an environmental impact assessment and being obliged to do so, seriously affects a glacier.

The penalty will be imprisonment or lesser imprisonment in its maximum degree if any of the acts indicated in the previous sections is perpetrated by reckless negligence or by mere negligence or violation of the regulation.

---

[99] Penal Code of Chile, of 12 November 1874. Amended by Law 21.595, of 17 August 2023. Available at: https://bcn.cl/2f6m7. Accessed on: 13 Dec. 2024.

Article 310 bis.

For the purposes of the three previous articles, serious deterioration of one or more environmental components will be understood as the adverse alteration produced in any of them, provided that any of the following circumstances occur:

1. Have relevant spatial extension, according to the ecological or geographical characteristics of the affected area.
2. Have effects prolonged over time.
3. Be irreparable or difficult to repair.
4. Reach a significant set of species, according to the characteristics of the affected area.
5. Impact species categorised as extinct, extinct in the wild, critically threatened or endangered or vulnerable.
6. Put the health of one or more people at serious risk of severe damage.
7. Significantly affect the services or ecosystem functions of the environmental element or component.

In the case of the events provided for in no. 1 of article 308 and in the first and second paragraphs of article 310, if the serious damage causes irreversible damage to an ecosystem, the maximum of the indicated penalties will be applied.[100]

The Code also provides for a fine penalty (art. 311) and accessory sanctions (art. 311 bis), such as a perpetual ban on entering the affected area.

Despite the detail, with explanatory notes, the content of the standard still lacks taxativity. For example, when stating that it is considered serious environmental deterioration when the effects are prolonged over time (art. 310 bis, 2), it is not clear what period to consider, leaving the discretion of the judge to decide. Also, characterising the crime when the damage is irreparable or difficult to repair (art. 310 bis, 3) is to condition it to the evaluative and technical capacities of the moment, being problematic to define what is "difficult" in the strict context of criminal law.

Now, the Chilean Penal Code covers all the elements that make up the international definition of ecocide promoted by the foundation *Stop Ecocide International*, including its arbitrary character. Chile was, therefore, the first country to approve a Bill based on the international *draft*.[101] However, the law misses the opportunity to name the crime. It is crucial to define the most serious actions against the environment as ecocide. By naming them, the actions pass through the cultural imaginary as a serious crime against the planet, bringing fundamental symbolic repercussion to a crime whose full repair of the damage is almost always impossible. Public and business attention is different for the commission of a simple environmental crime and for an ecocide, with much more negative emphasis on the latter.

Belgium was the most recent country to include ecocide as a crime in domestic legislation.

---

[100] Penal Code of Chile, of 12 November 1874. Amended by Law 21.595, of 17 August 2023. Available at: https://bcn.cl/2f6m7. Accessed on: 13 Dec. 2024.

[101] The new crimes will allow to reach "*the serious impacts on the environment that were not previously sanctioned and that were also not considered in our Penal Code. This also means that the representatives of the various economic activities that generate environmental damage will have to take greater care and take measures to avoid any illicit or arbitrary act that seriously impacts the environmental surroundings, or they risk having to serve sentences of up to ten years in prison*" (Vallejos et al., 2023).

5.7 Belgium (2023)

On 8 July 2000, Belgian parliamentarian Samuel Cogolati filed a resolution proposal (Cogolati, 2020) in the Chamber of Representatives of Belgium, with the aim of promoting the inclusion of the crime of ecocide in the Rome Statute, in support of Vanuatu's proposal,[102] and in domestic criminal law. The proposal was fully aware of the political movement about the crime at the moment, highlighting its international character.

The inclusion of ecocide as a national crime came along with a revolution of Belgian criminal law itself,[103] with the approval by the House of Representatives of the Bill (Cogolati, 2024) which introduces book II of the Penal Code, renewing the penal law, almost 150 years old.[104]

Ecocide is now set out in art. 94 of the new Code (Cogolati, 2024):

Art. 94. The crime of ecocide

§ 1o. The crime of ecocide, as defined below, whether committed in peacetime or in wartime, is punishable in accordance with the provisions of this Title.

The crime of ecocide consists of deliberately committing, by action or omission, an illegal act that causes serious, widespread and long-term damage to the environment, knowing that this act is causing such damage, provided that this act constitutes a violation of federal legislation or an international instrument that is binding on the federal authority or if the act cannot be located in Belgium.

For the purposes of paragraph 2, the following definitions apply:

a) "serious damage": damage that results in highly harmful negative changes, disturbances or losses to any component of the environment, including substantial repercussions on life or health human, biodiversity or natural, cultural or economic resources for society;

b) "extensive damage": damage that extends beyond a limited geographical area, crossing regional or state borders or that are suffered by an entire ecosystem or species or by a significant number of human beings;

c) "long-term damage": irreversible damage or that cannot be repaired by natural regeneration within a reasonable period of time;

d) "environment": the Earth, its ecosystems, biosphere, cryosphere, lithosphere, hydrosphere, atmosphere and outer space.

§ 2. This crime is punishable with a level 6 sentence.

---

[102] At the time, Vanuatu only expressed support for the crime of ecocide in the ICC. Only in 2024 was there an official proposal before the Assembly of State Parties.

[103] "The idea of reforming Belgium's century-old and heavily convoluted criminal code first arose under the previous government of Charles Michel. In 2015, then Minister of Justice Koen Geens entrusted the redrafting to two respected criminal law experts, Damien Vandermeersch and Joëlle Rozie. The main goals were to restructure the law for better readability, simplify its logic, and modernise its substance. Like its predecessor, the new Code was structured into two books, the first of which dealt with general provisions relating to the material and mental elements of crime, rules on participation, and criminal attempts, among others. Book II, by contrast, reconfigured the substance of Belgian criminal law, abolishing some offences, adjusting penalties, and introducing some new crimes—although there was no mention of ecocide yet" (Bertram, 2024).

[104] Even new, the Code does not escape criticism, prioritising, for example, property crimes over bodily harm (Chini, 2024).

Art. 94 also defines several key concepts, establishing the penalty as level 6, close to the maximum (level 8) in the country, that is, punishable with a prison sentence between 15 and 20 years for individuals and a fine between 1.2 million euros and 1.6 million euros for legal entities.

After France, Belgium officially considers ecocide as a crime defined by law. The penalty is established as level 6, close to the maximum (level 8) in the country. The article also seeks to define some concepts, such as serious, extensive, and long-term damage. However, as can be seen, the parameters do not seem precise enough to identify when a case is ecocide and when it is not. For example, it is difficult to prove procedurally a "serious" damage, when it causes "highly harmful" changes, if the discretion of the terms "highly" and "harmful" is evident. Technical expertise alone will not suffice; it will be necessary to define, through jurisprudence, the necessary parameters in practice. In addition, the law requires the accumulation of damages (serious, extensive, and long-lasting), unlike the Bill for the ICC, which considers them alternatively. It is, therefore, the Belgian law more restrictive.

There are other problems, when, for example, the elements *actus reus* and *mens rea*[105] are observed. In addition, the 2022 legislative proposal removed the "arbitrary" element, requiring, therefore, that the conducts be strictly illegal, considering them only in front of the Belgian federal law and international instruments of which the country is a signatory (Bertram, 2024), as criticised by Sophie Rohonyi, in February 2024, in the House of Representatives.[106]

Despite the criticisms, the evolution of the crime of ecocide as law, especially those developed recently, is notable. Regardless of the format, all recipients of the norm will have to pay attention to the new crime, promoting public policies, changes in business routines and in popular culture.

Concurrently, other countries in the world have taken on the task of seriously discussing the inclusion of the crime in domestic legislation through bills (PL), with different approaches, but all more detailed, tuned—to some extent—with the doctrine and the appeals of civil society. This is the topic of the next chapter.

---

[105] Studied in Chap. 6, item 6.4.

[106] "The member however regrets that the crime of ecocide only concerns acts or omissions falling within federal competences. Thus, large-scale pollution of a river will be excluded from the scope of the crime of ecocide, even if this pollution meets all the other conditions of application provided, which is inconsistent with the objective of this incrimination. Ms. Hugon had urged the federated entities to also legislate in terms of ecocide (see DOC 3518/006, p. 38). The speaker fears however that this may lead to fundamentally different devices, given that the political sensitivities of certain federated entities are opposed to the incrimination of ecocide. It would therefore be necessary to consider refederalising material criminal law. What do the authors of Article 94 think of this risk of fundamental divergence of regulations?" (Chamber of Representatives of Belgium, 2024).

References

Acosta, A. (2019). *The good living: An opportunity to imagine other worlds*. Editora Elefante.

Alonso, J. (2021, December 26). *Colombia pursues environmental crimes but does not protect its ecologists*. DW News. Retrieved June 20, 2025, from https://p.dw.com/p/42DV5

Anisimov, A., & Kayushnikova, J. (2019). Trends and prospects for legislative regulation of legal responsibility for environmental offences in BRICS countries: Comparative law. *BRICS Law Journal, 6*(1), 82–101.

Arango, R. (2006). The prohibition of regression in Colombia. In C. Courtis (Ed.), *Not one step back* (pp. 153–172). Ed. Del Puerto.

Bagni, S. (2018). The rights of nature in Colombian and Indian jurisprudence. *Juridical Review Right, 7*(9), 33–53.

Bartlett, J. (2023, December 18). *Chile votes to reject new conservative constitution which threatened rights of women*. The Guardian. Retrieved December 13, 2024, from https://www.theguardian.com/world/2023/dec/18/chile-votes-reject-conservative-constitution-referendum-womens-rights

Baudouin, C. (2021, September 23). *Ecocide: The missed opportunity*. Our Affair to All. Retrieved June 2, 2025, from https://notreaffaireatous.org/wp-content/uploads/2021/09/Ecocide-_-loccasion-manquee.pdf

BBC News World. (2022, September 4). *Chile rejects proposal for new constitution*. Retrieved July 5, 2025, from https://www.bbc.com/portuguese/internacional-62791155

Bertram, D. A. (2024). Ecocide à la Bruxelloise. *Verfassungsblatt, 3*, 517–520. Retrieved December 13, 2024, from https://hdl.handle.net/1814/77259

Birkett, D. J. (2019). Twenty years of the Rome statute of the international criminal court: Appraising the state of national implementing legislation in Asia. *Chinese Journal of International Law, 18*(2), 353–392.

Brito, A. G. (2021). Pachamama and the web of life: Between the risk society, deep ecology, and the indigenous worldview. *Academic Space Journal, 230*(2), 186.

Cabanes, V. (2018). Making states and companies accountable in the face of climate change: From planetary limits to the crime of ecocide. In C. Cournil & L. Varison (Eds.), *Climate trials: Between the national and the international* (pp. 265–278). Pedone.

Cabrera Izquierdo, L., Lastra Mier, R. E., & Vergara, A. R. (2020). Environmental crimes in Colombia: Analysis from the perspective of national policies for the protection of natural resources. *Readings on Environmental Law, 20*, 388–417.

Calderón, G. O. (2016). Some problems of application of rules of legal determination of the penalty in the Chilean Penal Code. *Law Review, 11*(22), 766–793. Retrieved June 2, 2025, from https://papers.ssrn.com/sol3/Delivery.cfm/SSRN_ID3081212_code1369244.pdf?abstractid=3081212&mirid=1

Chamber of Representatives of Belgium. (2024, February 13). Bill. *DOC 55 3518/010. Introducing Book II of the Penal Code. Report of the second reading*. Retrieved December 13, 2024, from https://www.dekamer.be/FLWB/PDF/55/3518/55K3518010.pdf

Chiarini, G. (2022, April 1). Ecocide: From the Vietnam war to international criminal jurisdiction? Procedural issues in-between environmental science, climate change, and law. *Cork Online Law Review*.

Chini, M. (2024, February 27). *After 150 years, Belgium has a new penal code*. The Brussels Times. Retrieved December 13, 2024, from https://www.brusselstimes.com/937483/after-150-years-belgium-has-a-new-penal-code

Citizens' Convention for Climate. (2021). *The proposals of the citizens' convention for climate. Report*. Retrieved July 25, 2025, from https://www.lecese.fr/sites/default/files/pdf/Convention/ccc-rapport-final.pdf

Cogolati, S. (2020, July). *Resolution Proposal n° 1429/001*. Chamber of Representatives of Belgium. Retrieved December 13, 2024, from https://www.lachambre.be/FLWB/PDF/55/1429/55K1429001.pdf

Cogolati, S. (2024, February 13). *Bill. DOC 55 3518/011. Introducing Book II of the penal code*. Chamber of Representatives of Belgium. Retrieved December 13, 2024, from www.dekamer.be/FLWB/PDF/55/3518/55K3518013.pdf

Comprehensive Organic Criminal Code of Ecuador. (2016). Retrieved June 10, 2025, from https://vlex.ec/vid/codigo-organico-integral-penal-631464447

Constitution of the Republic of Ecuador. (2008). Retrieved July 2, 2025, from https://www.ambiente.gob.ec/wp-content/uploads/downloads/2018/09/Constitucion-de-la-Republica-del-Ecuador.pdf

Crasson, A. (2017). The case of Chevron in Ecuador: The need for an international crime against the environment? *Amsterdam Law Forum, 9*(3).

Du Toit, L., & Kotzé, L. J. (2022). Reimagining international environmental law for the Anthropocene: An earth system law perspective. *Earth System Governance, 11*, 100132.

Dufourq, P. (2021, September 9). *Law "climate and resilience": Aspect of criminal law*. Dalloz News. Retrieved May 24, 2022, from https://www.dalloz-actualite.fr/flash/loi-climat-et-resilience-aspect-de-droit-penal#.Yp-hZKjMLDc

Dulci, T. M. S., & Sadivia, V. A. (2021). The social outbreak in Chile: Towards a new constitutionalism? *Katálysis Magazine, 24*, 43–52. Retrieved June 2, 2025, from https://www.scielo.br/j/rk/a/xfp9XCkzSSDrWgtp7M5JyTF/?lang=es&format=html

Dutra, G. K. M. (2021). The meaning of Pachamama for life on earth. *Development and Environment, 58*(2), 850–856.

Esakov, G. (2017). International criminal law in Russia: Missed crimes waiting for a revival. *Journal of International Criminal Justice, 15*(2), 371–392.

Estupiñan-Silva, R. (2016). Transnational challenges and responses to environmental crimes. *International Law Journal, 13*(3), 29–48.

Fernández, R. I. T., Villada, J. L., & Cattán, M. A. C. (2021). Inclusion of environmental crimes in the Argentine penal code. *Omnia. Law and Society, 4*(4), 55–77. Retrieved June 10, 2025, from http://revistas.ucasal.edu.ar/index.php/RO/article/view/311/330

Fronza, E. (2021). Sanction without sanctioning? Problems and perspectives of the new international crime of ecocide. *La Legislazione Penale*, 1–15. Retrieved July 2, 2025, from http://www.lalegislazionepenale.eu/wp-content/uploads/2021/03/Fronza_LP.pdf

Guinchard, S., & Debard, T. (2018). *Lexicon of legal terms* (25th ed.). Dalloz.

Houck, O. A. (2017). Noah's second voyage: The rights of nature as law. *Tulane Environmental Law Journal, 31*(1), 1–50.

Jacques, F. V. S. (2021). The "Buen Vivir" and the construction of a new society. *New NAEA Notebooks, 23*(3), 114.

Jouzel, J., & Michelot, A. (2020). What climate justice for France? *Revue de l'OFCE, 165*(1), 71–96.

Kotzé, L. J. (2012). Arguing global environmental constitutionalism. *Transnational Environmental Law, 1*(1), 199–233.

Kotzé, L. J. (2014). Fragmentation revisited in the context of global environmental law and governance. *The South African Law Journal, 131*, 548–582.

Lambert, C. (2017). Environmental destruction in Ecuador: Crimes against humanity under the Rome statute? *Leiden Journal of International Law, 30*, 707–729.

Lenormand, A. (2022, January 11). *Climate and resilience law: What to remember about measures on judicial protection of the environment and climate assessment*. Bank of Territories. Retrieved June 3, 2022, from https://www.banquedesterritoires.fr/loi-climat-et-resilience-ce-quil-faut-retenir-des-mesures-sur-la-protection-judiciaire-de

Maloney, M. (2016). Building an alternative jurisprudence for the earth: The international rights of nature tribunal. *Vermont Law Review, 41*(1), 129–142.

Mégret, F. (2011). The problem of an international criminal law of the environment. *Columbia Journal of Environmental Law, 36*(2), 195–257.

Michelot, A. (2018). International protection of the climate and state sovereignty. *VertigO, 18*(1). Retrieved July 3, 2025, from https://doi.org/10.4000/vertigo.19685

Moraes, G. D. O. (2018). *Harmony with nature and rights of Pachamama*. UFC Editions.

Morton, J. S. (2000). *The international law Commission of the United Nations*. University of South Carolina Press.

Narine, M. (2015). Disclosing disclosure's defects: Addressing corporate irresponsibility for human rights impacts. *Columbia Human Rights Law Review, 47*(1), 84–159.

National Assembly. (2019, November 27). *Report made on behalf of the Commission of Constitutional Laws, Legislation and General Administration of the Republic on the Bill recognising the crime of ecocide no. 2353*. Retrieved May 23, 2025, from https://www.assemblee-nationale.fr/dyn/15/rapports/cion_lois/l15b2447_rapport-fond

Neira, H., Russo, L. I., & Subiabre, B. A. (2019). Ecocide. *Philosophy Journal, 76*, 127–148. Retrieved June 3, 2025, from http://www.scielo.cl/scielo.php?script=sci_arttext&pid=S0718-43602019000200127&lng=es&nrm=iso

Penal Code of Colombia. (2000). Retrieved June 10, 2025, from https://leyes.co/codigo_penal/333.htm

Pérez, G. Y. V. (2021, August 8). *What was missing from the environmental crimes law 2111 of July 29, 2021*. Voz Jurídica. Retrieved June 20, 2025, from https://www.vozjuridica.com/columnista-abogada-gloria-yaneth-velez-perez/lo-que-le-falto-a-la-ley-de-delitos-ambientales-2111-de-julio-29-de-2021-columna-de-la-abogada-gloria-yaneth-velez-perez-juridicaasesora

Sayapin, S. (2019). Crimes against the peace and security of mankind in the revised edition of the criminal code of the Republic of Uzbekistan. *Review of Central and East European Law, 45*(1), 1–23.

Sayapin, S. (2020). The implementation of crimes against the peace and security of mankind in the penal legislation of the Republic of Kazakhstan. *Asian Journal of International Law, 10*(1), 1–11.

Soleil, S. (2021). Comparative history of law and its methodological challenges. *Journal of the Law School of UFRGS, 47*, 03–20. Retrieved June 10, 2025, from https://www.seer.ufrgs.br/index.php/revfacdir/article/view/121033/65990

Suxberger, A. H. G., & Dos Reis, R. F. M. (2020). Organised crime in environmental crimes: International normative frameworks and possible responses. *Journal of Environmental Law and Society, 10*(1), 148.

Tolstykh, V., Grigoryan, M., & Kovalenko, T. (2019). Legal systems of the post-soviet non-recognised states: Structural problems. *Russian Law Journal, 7*(2), 81–100.

Torney, D. (2021). Deliberative mini-publics and the European green Deal in turbulent times: The Irish and French climate assemblies. *Politics and Governance, 9*(3), 380–390.

UN, Paris Agreement. (2015). Retrieved June 22, 2025, from https://unfccc.int/sites/default/files/english_paris_agreement.pdf

United Nations Environment Programme. (2020). *Global climate litigation report: 2020 status review*. Sabin Center for Climate Change Law.

Vallejos, R., Espinosa, D., & Poblete, F. (2023, October 18). *Chile is the first country to turn ecocide into law*. Chile Without Ecocide. Retrieved December 13, 2024, from https://chilesinecocidio.org/2023/10/18/chile-es-el-primer-pais-en-convertir-el-ecocidio-en-ley/

Varona, G. (2020). Restorative pathways after mass environmental victimisation: Walking in the landscapes of past ecocides. *Onati Socio-Legal Series, 10*(3), 664–685.

Venaglia, G. (2020, October 25). *Plebiscite: Chile decides to replace Constitution made in Pinochet's dictatorship*. CNN Brazil. Retrieved June 2, 2025, from https://www.cnnbrasil.com.br/internacional/apuracao-no-chile-larga-com-amplo-apoio-a-nova-constituicao/

Villegas, A., & Ramos, N. (2022, April 17). *First draft of the new Constitution of Chile is delivered*. CNN Brazil. Retrieved June 2, 2025, from https://www.cnnbrasil.com.br/internacional/primeiro-rascunho-da-nova-constituicao-do-chile-e-entregue/

Wilson, G. (2020). Envisioning nature's right to a stable climate system. *Sea Grant Law & Policy Journal, 10*(1), 60.

Chapter 6
The Bills on Ecocide

The projection given to ecocide in the international panorama—as the greatest crime against the environment—in recent years has sparked a wave of debates for its inclusion in national legislations, as done in Colombia and, partially, in France.

Various propositions were formalised as Bill Projects,[1] mainly in Europe and in the American continent, gaining significant popular support in many cases, such as the *Convention Citoyenne pour le Climat*. What these proposals have in common is the concern with the growth of occurrences that promote massive environmental damage, climate changes,[2] and the fragility of legal documents to address them, especially the criminal ones.

It is necessary, however, to study them in order to verify if—in the current scientific/political moment[3]—there is a unity of understanding about what is, effectively, ecocide, a circumstance that, in the 1980s, served as a basis for excluding it from *The Code*.

What becomes clear is the international vocation of ecocide, even in discussions about the crime in terms of domestic law. The justifications for the PLs are

[1] In addition to legal propositions, there are numerous researchers, in different States, who echo the idea of criminalising ecocide as a way to increase national environmental protection, especially in countries where the collective right to a healthy environment is recognised, such as in India (Chadha & Singh, 2024).

[2] The fight against climate change through criminal law is a controversial issue, as, as seen, the existing laws and projects do not address the main causes of global warming, namely, greenhouse gas emissions. Furthermore, studies on the criminal liability of individuals or companies for climate change are still in their infancy.

[3] It is not intended here, it is repeated, to discuss—in depth—the political viability of ecocide, but it is not denied that it, politics, is unavoidable as the only way to make the crime viable, both nationally and internationally (with the drafting and approval of laws and treaties). The coherence of the institute necessarily passes through political agreement for this. The proliferation of proposals before the legislatures and the ICC indicate, at least, greater attention from this spectrum to massive environmental damage and criminal law.

D. A. Brochado Neto, *Ecocide*, https://doi.org/10.1007/978-3-032-07757-8_6

commonly based on international debates (from the *International Law Commission* to the most recent propositions in the ICC), with direct citations to the approaches of other countries, mentioning the projects presented and foreign doctrine.

In some situations, the ecocide bill project is leveraged by local situations, when the magnitude of a specific environmental damage exposes a gap in the legislation to reach it. This is the case of Brazil, when, after the disasters of Mariana and Brumadinho, the PL 2.787/2019 was presented in May 2019.

Before delving into the topics, it is important to highlight that the study of bill projects can, at first, seem of little use, since, as a project, it is susceptible to significant changes during its progress with, including, the probability of not becoming law, like most of the PLs presented to legislative houses. These, only as propositions, do not have any compelling force, do not create or extinguish obligations; they are, therefore, in theory, irrelevant to the legal system.

However, this understanding is incorrect. First, the analysis of bill projects by the doctrine (researchers of law and other areas) is crucial for the proper functioning of the legal system, after all a PL may not become law, but almost every law was once a PL.[4] The lack of attention to projects and, therefore, of technical discussion, sometimes, leads to approvals of conflicting norms, without social support or, as is reasonably common, unconstitutional (despite prior internal control), either by form or content.[5] Public consultations[6] conducted in Brazil are a way to attract popular participation to projects, in addition to hearings. However, this means is underused in the absolute majority of PLs, except some case of great media repercussion or as a political propaganda tool for a certain voter base.[7]

Second, a study of the PLs provides, in addition to a possible improvement of the project itself, a panorama of the entrails of the State in the formation of its norms, serving as a parameter to verify the influences of the doctrine and also national and foreign debates on the subject. It is in this aspect that this work stands, to detail how ecocide is treated at this moment by the countries that are willing to classify it. It seeks to illuminate also what can be expected from the evolution of (international) criminal law, in the environmental field, since the PLs represent the future of legal systems.

---

[4] This is dealt with here in a broad, more common way, given that there are laws originated from unilateral acts, such as decrees, etc.

[5] In 2017, in Brazil, 8 out of 10 laws questioned in Direct Actions of Unconstitutionality were judged provided by the Federal Supreme Court (Matsuura, 2018).

[6] For more information, see: https://www12.senado.leg.br/ecidadania/comofunciona consultapublica

[7] As an example, the public consultation on the PL 27/2018 (Chamber) Brazilian obtained just under 25 thousand votes, to add, in the Environmental Crimes Law (Law 9.605/98) provision on the legal nature of non-human animals (e-Citizenship. Available at: https://www12.senado.leg.br/ecidadania/visualizacaomateria?id=133167, accessed on: 14 Dec. 2024), while the Suggestion 9/2018, for the printed vote in 100% of the ballot boxes had more than 3 million votes (e-Citizenship. Available at: https://www12.senado.leg.br/ecidadania/visualizacaomateria?id=132598, accessed on: 14 Dec. 2024).

In this aspect, the multilateral international influence is significant on the propositions of ecocide, confirming the global character of the crime, as revealed by the most recent proposal to the International Criminal Court.

In this chapter, it is sought to bring as many Bill Projects in progress in the world as possible. Even aware of the thankless task of identifying—in different legal systems, with various legislative processes—the matter in progress in countries with varied languages, it is attempted here to collect the discussion around ecocide as faithfully as possible in legislative houses in recent years.

The Brazilian Congress, finally, began its work on the subject in 2019.

6.1 Brazil (2019–2024)

Following the successive environmental disasters of Mariana and Brumadinho,[8] in November 2015 and January 2019, respectively, with nearly 300 (three hundred) deaths and, to date, uncertainty about the progress of criminal proceedings against the accused (acquitted in the first instance, in the case of Mariana), Brazilian politicians were urged to amend the penal law. At that time, it became clear that there was no legal (penal) provision to reach the extent of the damage resulting from the two events.

The environmental crimes pointed out by the accusing body were ephemeral, in their penalties, given the complexity—probative in the construction of the causal link—which undoubtedly pointed to the prescription of those. The termination of criminal actions for homicide (in the form of eventual intent), in both cases,[9] exposed the difficulty of attributing crimes with more severe sanctions to agents in cases of massive environmental damage. The legislator, then, proposed to close this gap.[10]

Several federal deputies jointly presented, in May 2019, Bill 2.787/2019 (Chamber of Deputies, 2019a), to include in the Environmental Crimes Law (Law 9.605/1998) two new crimes: causing a dam break (art. 60-A) and ecocide (art. 54-A). In the justification of the project, the authors restricted themselves to commenting on the disasters of Mariana and Brumadinho, to substantiate the first crime

[8] Both disasters occurred due to collapses of tailings dams, after successive errors and negligence by those responsible for their conservation, as well as suspicions of corruption and absence of the State, causing deaths of numerous living beings (including hundreds of humans), destruction of natural habitats and extinction of native species.

[9] HC 1033377-47.2018.4.01.0000, TRF-1, 4th Chamber, Federal Judge Olindo Menezes, judged on April 23, 2019, for Mariana, and RHC 151.405—MG (2021/0228782-1), Rel. Min. Olindo Menezes (Federal Judge Convoked From TRF-1), judged on Oct. 19, 2021, for Brumadinho.

[10] The PL, authored by Federal Deputy Zé Silva and others, is the result of the External Commission specifically designed to follow the investigations related to the rupture in Brumadinho-MG and the inspection of other dams (CexBruma, Link: https://www.camara.leg.br/internet/comissoes/comissoes-especiais/historico/56/cexbruma.pdf, accessed on: 8 Jan. 2025).

and changes related to increasing the value of fines.[11] Still in the Chamber of Deputies, an amendment was proposed to the ecocide to condition it to the recognition of the state of public calamity (Janones, 2019).

After approval in the Chamber, the PL reached the Senate in June 2019, where it was amended in the Environment Committee, under the rapporteurship of Senator Alessandro Vieira.[12] The crime of ecocide remained, until now, thus defined:

> **Ecocide**
>
> Art. 54-A. Causing a large-scale environmental disaster or that produces a state of public calamity, with significant destruction of flora or animal mortality, as a result of atmospheric, water or soil contamination or pollution.
>
> Penalty—imprisonment, from 4 (four) to 12 (twelve) years, and a fine.
>
> § 1° If the crime is negligent:
>
> Penalty—detention, from 1 (one) to 3 (three) years, and a fine.
>
> § 2° If the crime results in the death of a person, the penalty is applied regardless of the penalty provided for the crime of homicide. (Vieira, 2019)

Senator Carlos Heinze argued that, in the form of the originally proposed wording, the law could create an objective criminal responsibility, in disagreement with constitutional principles. He therefore presented an amendment[13] to change the wording of the *caput* of art. 54-A, in September 2019, including the need for a technical report to attest to the extent of the damage:

> **Article 54-A**
>
> Causing an ecological disaster due to non-compliance with legislation, the terms of the environmental license and its conditions and that generates a state of public calamity due to significant atmospheric, water or soil contamination, according to a technical report from the competent environmental authority attesting to the extent of the damage (…)

The Opinion of the Environment Committee was approved (Federal Senate, 2019), on 10 October 2019, awaiting analysis of the Amendment by Senator Fabiano Contarato. If there is an amendment in the Senate, the PL must return to the Chamber of Deputies for a new vote, before the presidential sanction and the consequent formal change of the environmental law.

---

[11] "The painful tragedies of Mariana, at the end of 2015, and of Brumadinho, at the beginning of this year of 2019, clearly exposed that the penal legislation on this subject is still weak. Today, the responsibility for occurrences like this must be framed based on broad crimes, which generate legal questions and delay judicial processes. With the specific definition, greater effectiveness in criminal prosecution will be achieved, a necessary advancement in the face of recent events" (Chamber of Deputies, 2019b).

[12] The proceedings in the Senate Environment Committee took place between August and October 2019 (Link: https://www25.senado.leg.br/web/atividade/materias/-/materia/137437, accessed on: 8 Jan. 2025).

[13] "Despite the fact that the state of public calamity is caused by an abnormal situation, caused by disasters, causing damage and losses that imply a substantial compromise of the response capacity of the public power of the affected entity and that the same is established through a ministerial ordinance, it is necessary that the typification is based on a technical report from the competent environmental authority that attests to the extent of the damage" (Heinze, 2019).

In July 2019, a study of the project was presented—by this author—to the office of Senator Alessandro Vieira, containing some observations for discussion, with the intention of improving it, in line with Brazilian jurisprudence and legislation. Two points dealt with the punishment of the legal entity, advocating for a specific sanction for this, preventing the mere conversion to the generic fine penalty of art. 21, clause I,[14] of Law 9.605/1998, in order to avoid the rapid prescription of the crime.[15]

Another point addressed was the possibility, according to the project of the crime of negligent ecocide (art. 54-A, § 1°), of incidence of the benefits of arts. 27 and 28 of Law 9.605/1998, which provide for the possibility of subsidiary application of Law 9.099/95 (Special Civil and Criminal Courts) regarding measures of a depenalising nature, that is, the criminal transaction and the conditional suspension of the process, for crimes committed in environmental law.[16] The disproportionality of the massive damage to the environment and the sanction would be evident, a factor that would weaken the deterrent character of the new crime, despite the seriousness of the crime.

Finally, it was noted the need to qualify the wording of the crime, to define the terms "disaster" and "significant destruction" in *caput*, which, as they stand, can give rise to various interpretations, including, prevent the application of the crime (What is the limit between regular damage and a disaster? What is the difference between destruction and significant destruction?). Despite there being no international consensus on the definition of ecocide, it would be important to enhance the project with explanatory norms of such designations, exposing that the referred acts affect the planet's security when they cause, together or cumulatively, certain results.[17]

---

[14] Art. 21. The penalties applicable separately, cumulatively or alternatively to legal entities, in accordance with the provisions of Art. 3, are: I—fine; II—restrictive of rights; III—provision of services to the community (Law 9.605/1998, Available at: http://www.planalto.gov.br/ccivil_03/leis/l9605.htm. Accessed on: 8 Jan. 2025).

[15] It was also claimed the removal—in a textual way—of the necessary double imputation (possibility of prosecuting only the company, regardless of accusation against an individual). For some years in national jurisprudence and doctrine, there was doubt about the possibility of criminal imputation of the legal entity without the identification of a physical person author. The theory of necessary double imputation, initially guided by the STJ (e.g.: EDcl in REsp 865.864/PR), soon found solution in the Federal Supreme Court, in the Extraordinary Appeal 548181/PR, reported by Minister Rosa Weber. After, the STJ changed its understanding (Ex.: RMS 39.173/BA) to follow the decision in the STF. However, despite the subject being settled in the Superior Courts, among first and second degree magistrates there are decisions that embrace different currents, supported by the judge's motivated free conviction, given the absence of express legal provision. There is, even, such a provision in the PL of the new Penal Code (PL 236/2012), under consideration in the Federal Senate.

[16] According to the sanction stipulated in the PL, the culpable ecocide would have a penalty of detention, from 1 (one) to 3 (three) years, and a fine. Thus, it would be within the scope of incidence of the benefits granted to infractions of lesser offensive potential.

[17] For example, "(a) extensive, durable and severe degradation of air or atmosphere, soils, waters, aquatic environments, fauna or flora, or their ecological functions; (b) death, permanent disability or severe incurable diseases to a population, or the permanent dispossession of the latter from their

The Federal Senate responded to the report (at the request of Senator Alessandro Vieira),[18] through Technical Note No. 4.502/2019, prepared by the Legislative Consultancy of the Senate, in August of 2019. Commenting on the observations made, the body did not consider prudent to indicate a specific penalty for the legal entity, pointing out that "it is up to the Judiciary, in its task of assessing the seriousness of the crime, to estimate the gradation of the punishment." It argued that a change in this sense would distort the very Environmental Crimes Law.[19]

The suggestion to detail the definitions of the terms "disaster" and "significant destruction" was accepted, leaving it up to the Consultancy to draft an amendment to the proposition, aiming to distinguish the crime of pollution[20] from the crime of ecocide. The increase in penalty for the crime of negligent ecocide was also accepted, in order to escape it from the reach of art. 89 of Law 9.099, of 1995.[21]

Finally, the legislative consultants stated they do not consider a specific law such as that of ecocide, "the best place to resolve the judicial controversy regarding the prescription of penalties, as each law should deal with a single theme", a role suitable for another law,[22] proper to amend the Brazilian Penal Code.[23]

There was no previous discussion about the format of an "ecocide law" for Brazil, this being the first time there is a technical debate[24] on the subject (when

---

lands, territories or resources; (c) The extinction or risk of extinction of species of native fauna or flora of a certain region" (Martin-Chenut et al., 2015).

[18] STC No. 2019-09829.

[19] It is up to the Judiciary to estimate the severity of the crime to, within the legal parameter, set the penalty. However, that Power cannot sanction beyond—or below—the legal provision. The suggestion was in the sense of avoiding disproportionate penalties (to a massive damage) and, mainly, the prescription, which, in the case of the fine penalty, is 2 years (art. 114, I, of the Brazilian Penal Code), a negligible time for the progress of a complex process like that of ecocide.

[20] Law 9.605/1998, art. 54: To cause pollution of any nature at levels that result or may result in damage to human health, or that cause the death of animals or significant destruction of flora: Penalty—imprisonment, from one to four years, and a fine. § 1 If the crime is culpable: Penalty—detention, from six months to one year, and fine.

[21] Provision that created the conditional suspension of the process, for crimes whose minimum penalty is equal to or less than one year.

[22] Although the attempt by the Senate's legal consultancy to compartmentalise the subjects by PL's is commendable, it is known of the Brazilian legislator's ability to create "anomalous laws" (in Brazil, they are called "jabuticaba laws"), when it inserts a legal provision without direct linkage to the theme of a certain Bill, either due to poor drafting technique or intentionally, to avoid deep discussion on the subject, for example, PL 9.206/17 (Gomes, 2022). It should be noted, this would not be the case of the proposition presented, as it directly affects the theme, "environmental crime", dealing specifically with the prescription for this case.

[23] Brazilian Penal Code, Decree-Law 2.848, of 7 December 1940. Available at: http://www.planalto.gov.br/ccivil_03/decreto-lei/del2848compilado.htm. Accessed on: 2 May 2025.

[24] Among the few comments on the PL, it is common to raise the requirement for actions beyond the criminal sphere, such as promoting awareness and prevention, especially against corporate crimes: "At this point, it is essential to revisit the hypothesis established by Sutherland, when he exposes that the negligence of the State and society regarding corporate crimes is especially due to the fact that many people adopt similar behaviours in their daily practices. Thus, everything indicates that the interruption of environmental devastation in the country will not be possible through

already approved in the Chamber of Deputies), pointing out the generally transnational character of the crime,[25] hence the importance of an international approach, in addition to the revision according to national law.

It should be noted that, once the PL is approved, the disasters of Mariana and Brumadinho would not fit—at least for Brazilian law—as ecocide, but would pierce the new definition of article 60-A, that is, to cause a dam break,[26] in respect to the principle of speciality of criminal law. The peculiarity of the crime draws attention, directly related to what happened in the mining waste lakes. It would be left to ecocide to punish other massive damages to the environment, caused by practices in disagreement with the legislation.

The Brazilian PL also deviates from other projects (and existing crimes) in terms of international influence, reflecting in the proposed wording. The legislator was concerned with criminalising the destruction massively exploiting the commotion over Brumadinho and Mariana, but little sought international references on ecocide (to take advantage of the scientific knowledge accumulated since the 1970s). The vague and generic terms, such as those in the proposed article, have already been the subject of questioning in the ILC, and have proven fatal to the application of the crime in national legislations, barely distinguishing it from the crime of pollution, already existing in the Environmental Crimes Law.

The fact is that one cannot escape the influence of large corporations, when drafting laws, either directly or indirectly. The possible repercussion of a new rule on the activities of a transnational is already reason for caution from the legislator, especially when the new rule imputes conducts—within the practice of a company that deals with natural resources[27]—as criminal, possibly affecting both natural and legal persons.

The favourable political conjuncture to the project, after pressure from civil society (including social organisations, researchers, and environmentalists) for greater environmental protection in the face of successive disasters, runs into the conservative approach of the legislator when proposing the new law, which is reluctant to improve the existing rule.[28]

---

the expansion of criminal law, but with the diffusion of a new mentality and new values" (Boldt, 2019).

[25] Although there is no international criminal provision to deal with massive transnational environmental damage, "it is irrefutable the impossibility of locally restricting the effects caused by offences to the environment. The environmental problem is an evident fact of the emergence of a transnational logic" (Piffer & Miglioranzi De Rosso, 2019, p. 121).

[26] PL 2.787/2019, "art. 60-A Causing the rupture of a dam by disregarding legislation, technical standard, license and its conditions or determination of the environmental authority and the dam safety supervisory entity: Penalty—imprisonment, from 2 (two) to 5 (five) years, and fine. Single paragraph. If the crime is negligent: Penalty—detention, from 1 (one) to 3 (three) years, and fine".

[27] Information about sustainability in companies is increasingly relevant to investors, it is essential to know the methodologies of different ESG rating and index providers, which should pay attention, among other points, to legislation, including criminal (Yébenes, 2024).

[28] The power of transnationals in the cases of Mariana and Brumadinho exposes the asymmetry between the parties and the interests involved, constructing in the media a narrative where the

In June 2023, members of the Chamber of Deputies (among them, Federal Deputy Célia Xakriabá, only the third indigenous parliamentarian in the history of Brazil), presented Bill 2.933/2023 (Brazil. Chamber of Deputies, 2023), to include the crime of ecocide in Brazil. The proposal was built in civil society—among the responsible, the Ecoe Brasil group—based on the definition of the crime made by the Panel of Independent Experts, still in 2021:

> **CHAPTER V : CRIMES AGAINST THE ENVIRONMENT**
>
> Section VI-A—Ecocide
>
> Art. 69-B. To commit illegal or reckless acts with the awareness that they generate a substantial probability of serious and widespread or long-term damage to the environment:
>
> Penalty—imprisonment from 5 to 15 years and a fine.
>
> § 1° For the purposes of the provision in the caput, the following are considered:
>
> I—illegal act: that which is in disagreement with the current law, license or authorisation issued by environmental agencies.
>
> II—reckless act: that with knowledge of the risk of creating clearly excessive damage in relation to the social and economic benefits foreseen in an activity;
>
> III—serious damage: damage that implies very serious adverse changes, disturbance or damage to any element of the environment, including serious impacts on human life, biodiversity or natural, cultural or economic resources;
>
> IV—widespread damage: damage that extends beyond a limited geographical area, crosses national borders or is suffered by an entire ecosystem or species or by a large number of beings;
>
> V—long-term damage: irreversible damage or that cannot be repaired through natural recovery within a reasonable period of time.
>
> § 2° The crime of ecocide is directed at high-ranking officials responsible for decisions that lead to the promotion, planning, financing, agency, contracting, management and execution of activities that fall under the hypothesis provided for in the caput of this article.
>
> § 3° The crime of ecocide does not apply to indigenous and traditional populations who continue to live in their traditional way and in their territories.

The new Project, built under the proposal of Amendment to the Rome Statute (therefore, similar to the law approved in Belgium),[29] conditions the recognition of ecocide to the practice of acts in non-compliance with the law (*lato* sensu) or (alternatively) reckless, meaning risk of disproportion between damages and social and economic benefits.

---

companies have positive evaluations; while the Public Power is the guilty party (impersonal, can bear the burden of negative evaluations), either due to the delay in creating the law, or due to lack of inspections/corruption: "In this judgement, a positive evaluation refers to economic and financial achievements from the company (…) Judgements with negative polarity were associated with law regulatory bodies, (…) judging the attitudes of the Legislative Power that, by not approving laws, collectively instils fear in the population due to the uncertainties that a new accident may happen (…). Reading the two texts, one can perceive a power asymmetry in the discourses of social actors according to the roles they occupy in society, with little regard for the suffering of the victims and minimal action to restore the way of life of people and the environment. The mining company Vale and the public power jointly hold economic and legal power and act with disregard for the problems of the victims, residents and environment affected by the dam breaks more than once" (Andrade & Araes, 2021).

[29] See item 5.7.

In this format, ecocide would be a crime of danger, with the material damage being mere exhaustion of the crime. It is undeniable that in a serious conduct, such as terrorism, it is interesting to repress acts prior to the damage, called "preparatory acts". There is also in the law the possibility of criminally punishing reckless management[30] of a financial institution, which, imprudently,[31] assumes excessive risks, disregarding market safety standards.

However, the transfer of the understanding of "reckless" from crimes against the financial system to environmental law, in the criminal sphere, brings complications. At first, it can be stated that all activities Human activities, to varying degrees, impact the environment, the so-called ecological footprint. Humanity itself depends on various activities that cause significant environmental impact.[32] The measurement of the risks of the economic/social benefit being greater or lesser than the environmental damage is extremely challenging. Connect this to an evidentiary context in the criminal field and it is almost impossible to construct a borderline behaviour that the law needs to define.

The environmental damages themselves are challenging to measure. Take the case of Mariana, for example, where, to this day, the extent of the environmental destruction is unknown, more than 5 years after the disaster.

The Bill also draws attention for its second and third paragraphs. The *Draft* makes it clear that the crime is intended for high-ranking officials—making the crime proper—with decision-making power over, among other activities, the management and execution of the illegal or reckless conducts provided for in the *caput*. It seems problematic a legal provision that limits the defendants, for two aspects: first, it excludes potentially criminal people, but who do not belong to the

---

[30] Thus provides the Law of crimes against the national financial system: "Art. 4° Fraudulently manage a financial institution: Penalty—Imprisonment, from 3 (three) to 12 (twelve) years, and fine. Sole paragraph. If the management is reckless: Penalty—Imprisonment, from 2 (two) to 8 (eight) years, and fine". (Brazil. Law of crimes against the national financial system. Law 7.492/86, of June 16, 1986. Available at: https://www.planalto.gov.br/ccivil_03/leis/l7492.htm. Accessed on: Dec 14, 2024).

[31] Even with the terminology of negligent crime, the crime of reckless management is considered intentional, in the form of eventual intent (STJ, HC 101.570/RJ, Rel. Minister Maria Thereza Moura, sixth Panel, judged on 21/09/2010, DJE 11/10/2010).

[32] "When commentators casually propose criminalizing all high-impact activities (i.e. those with 'severe' impacts), they appear to assume that such activities are rare and peripheral and thus easily outlawed. It is likely that most people underestimate the extent to which their lives as they currently know them rely on high-impact activities. This includes transportation, food production, energy production, construction and so on. Of course, all of these activities need to be radically rethought. But even with the best strategies, operations that sustain hundreds of millions of people can have startlingly high impacts.

For those who are surprised by this, I have elsewhere outlined some constraints of science, demographics, and logistics: your survival entails some footprint; we have a huge human population which strains carrying capacity; and sometimes collective activity, serving hundreds of millions of people, is efficient. In other words, if we must tolerate a certain footprint for an individual to meet a particular need (eg food), then an activity providing that need for hundreds of millions of people might have a very large footprint." (Robinson, 2024).

decision-making top. Second, it appears to criminalise business activity, since it is the larger corporations—which, as a rule, are capable of causing massive environmental damage—that are commonly pointed out as villains of the environment, but many operate with respect for the laws and for the benefit of humanity, such as energy production, mineral extraction, and transport (Robinson, 2024).

Finally, Bill 2.933/23 seeks, in §2, to remove the incidence of the rule from indigenous and traditional populations who "continue living in their traditional way and in their territories". The idea, as explained in the justification of the Bill, is to avoid instrumentalisation against "certain more vulnerable and unprotected social groups" (Brazil. Chamber of Deputies, 2023, p. 15) Indeed, there are no reports of regular activities of the original Brazilian peoples that result in massive damage to the environment. It is certain that this clause will not prevent prosecution if these activities significantly exceed the traditional way of life, exposing their own existence to risk.

One year after the protocol of this Bill, a third Bill (Bill 2.875/2024) (Brazil. Chamber of Deputies, 2024) was presented by Federal Deputy Pedro Aihara, also in the Chamber of Deputies, in July 2024, to criminalise ecocide. The Project includes articles 54-A, 54-B, and 54-C to the Environmental Crimes Code:

> **Article 54-A**
>
> To commit ecocide, thus considered any unlawful or arbitrary act perpetrated with the awareness that there is a high probability that it will cause serious, extensive or long-lasting damage to the environment.
>
> Penalty—imprisonment from 5 (five) to 10 (ten) years, and a fine.
>
> §1 For the purposes of this article, it is considered:
>
> I—arbitrary: the act of reckless imprudence that generates manifestly excessive damage in relation to the social or economic advantage that is foreseen;
>
> II—serious: the damage that causes very adverse changes, disturbances or notable damage to any element of the environment, including the effects on human life or natural, cultural or economic resources;
>
> III—extensive: the damage that goes beyond a limited geographical area, overflows state borders or affects the entirety of an ecosystem or a species or a large number of human beings;
>
> IV—long-lasting: the irreversible damage or that cannot be repaired by natural regeneration within a reasonable period.
>
> § 2 The penalty will be increased by one-third to half if:
>
> I—it results in serious injury or death of someone;
>
> II—it causes irreparable damage to species threatened with extinction;
>
> III—it is committed in conservation units, in their buffer zones or in permanent protection areas;
>
> IV—it affects sources of drinking water supply.
>
> § 3 If the crime is committed by a legal entity, the sanctions provided for in articles 21 and 22 of this Law will be applied, without prejudice to other sanctions.
>
> **Art. 54-B**
>
> The conviction for ecocide will include the obligation to repair the damages caused, by restoring the degraded environment, whenever possible.
>
> Single paragraph. When the restoration of the degraded environment is not possible, the convicted person must compensate for the damages caused through alternative measures, which will be defined by the competent environmental agencies.

> Art. 54-C. The Union, the states, the Federal District and the municipalities, in their respective spheres of competence, will promote actions to prevent and minimise the effects of ecocide, with the aim of ensuring the protection of the environment and the preservation of life in all its forms, including:
>
> I—promotion of educational actions at all levels of education, in order to raise awareness among the population about the importance of protecting the environment and the risks of ecocide;
>
> II—support for research and development of technologies for the recovery of degraded areas and the remediation of environmental damage, including the reintroduction of species and the restoration of ecosystems.

This wording has similarities with Bill 2.933/23, such as the need for the practice of an unlawful or arbitrary act, with knowledge of the probability of massive environmental damage. In other words, it is still a crime of danger carried out in the form of eventual intent. The crime also brings explanatory notes (such as serious, extensive, and lasting) and the obligation of repair or compensation for the damage (art. 54-B).

As a crucial difference, the Bill brings an aggravating factor (art. 54-A, §2°), when some damage actually happens. This detail is important, because, unlike the previous Project, the consequence of the unlawful action that materially brings a harmful result deserves greater sanction (even though they seem to increase the penalty slightly, given the gravity of the crime). This project is attached to Bill 2.933/23 in Parliament.

There is time to change, as these are projects still in progress. The Brazil should serve as a guide on global environmental issues. With a unique repertoire of available natural resources (biomes, forests, culture), the country is the most interested in protecting such heritage, taking the lead in the international discussion on environmental protection, including the study on ecocide.

Finally, it should be noted that there are movements, at least at the municipal level, of recognition of the rights of nature in Brazil. At least two rivers have been declared as "living beings, holders of inherent rights": the Laje Komi-Memen River,[33] in Rondônia, and the Mosquito River,[34] in Porteirinha and Serranópolis, state of Minas Gerais. This advance contrasts with the anthropocentric approach of the Brazilian legal system, but undoubtedly confers significant rights on the entities mentioned.

Other South American countries, however, are ahead on the subject, for now, in the attempt to provide legal safeguard to the environment. In addition to Ecuador,

---

[33] Brazil. Municipal City Hall of Guajará-Mirim/RO. Law No. 2.579/2023 Of 28 June 2023. Provides for the recognition of the rights of the Laje River—Komi Memen—in the municipality of Guajará-Mirim and its classification as a specially protected entity. and gives other provisions. 28 June 2023. Available at: https://sapl.guajaramirim.ro.leg.br/media/sapl/public/normajuridica/2023/2743/lei_2579.pdf. Accessed on: 14 Dec. 2024.

[34] Brazil. Municipal City Hall of Porteirinha/MG. Law No. 2.251, of 15 April 2024. Provides for the recognition of the rights of the Mosquito River, a tributary of the Gorutuba River, in the Municipality of Porteirinha and its classification as a specially protected entity and gives other provisions. 15 April 2024. Available at: https://sapl.guajaramirim.ro.leg.br/media/sapl/public/normajuridica/2023/2743/lei_2579.pdf. Accessed on: 14 Dec. 2024.

Bolivia is the second country to recognise the "rights of nature", an ecocentric approach to the protection of legal goods.

6.2 Bolivia (2020)

Bolivia does not expressly have in its Constitution (Political Constitution of the State of Bolivia, 2009) the "rights of nature", as in Ecuador, despite that opening the possibility of ecocentric approaches to infraconstitutional legislation. The preamble of the Charter announces the need for respect to *Madre Tierra*, and art. 8 (I) defines the principles, values, and purposes of the State, among them the *suma qamaña* (*vivir bien*).[35] There is also a provision, in art. 255 (II) (7), determining that the negotiation, signature, and ratification of international treaties will be governed by the principle of harmony with nature and defence of biodiversity.[36]

The Bolivian Constitution, thus, intensified environmental concern, defining new foundations and conceptions related to the earth and to Pachamama.[37] However, this new constitutional perspective fits the healthy environment as a right of people to quality of life, which confirms a still anthropocentric view of the document (Calaça et al., 2018).

The rights of nature were textually recognised, on the other hand, in infraconstitutional legislation.[38] The *Ley de Derechos de la Madre Tierra,*[39] of December 2010, does so (collective subject of public interest, art. 5°), establishing the rights of Mother Earth (art. 7°), the obligations of the State and duties of society (art. 8°) and how these rights will be exercised (art. 6°). This last article declares that all Bolivian

[35] "*Article 8. I. The State assumes and promotes as ethical-moral principles of the plural society: ama qhilla, ama llulla, ama suwa (do not be lazy, do not be a liar or a thief), suma qamaña (live well), ñandereko (harmonious life), teko kavi (good life), ivi maraei (land without evil) and qhapaj ñan (noble path or life)*" (Political Constitution of the State of Bolivia, 2009).

[36] "*Article 255. (…). II. The negotiation, subscription and ratification of international treaties will be governed by the principles of: (…). 7. Harmony with nature, defence of biodiversity, and prohibition of forms of private appropriation for the exclusive use and exploitation of plants, animals, microorganisms and any living matter*" (Political Constitution of the State of Bolivia, 2009).

[37] The provisions relevant to environmental protection are in articles 33 and 34, 342 to 347, 348 to 358 and 373 of the Bolivian Constitution.

[38] Bolivian environmental law, "already with some seeds sown by the (new) Bolivian Constitution of 2009, by the 'People's Agreement' of 2010 and by the Universal Declaration of the Rights of Mother Earth of 2010, sought a new paradigm and to find it followed patterns identical to that of the aforementioned World People's Conference on Climate Change and the Rights of Mother Earth". In this context, Law 71 of 2010, "constituted the 'starting shot' of the new paradigm of Bolivian environmental law". In a second moment, "the Law of Mother Earth and of Integral Development for Well-being17 was approved by the Plurinational Legislative Assembly on September 5, 2012 and promulgated by President Evo Morales on October 15, 2012" (Almeida, 2017, p. 1068).

[39] Law No. 71, December 21, 2010, *Law of Rights of Mother Earth*. Available at: https://www.lexivox.org/norms/BO-L-N71.html. Accessed on: May 2, 2025.

men and women are part of the community of beings that make up Mother Earth, that is, it removes the preponderance of the human being over nature. There is also a provision that creates the Defender of Mother Earth (art. 10), whose mission is to ensure the fulfilment of the rights provided for Pachamama.

In this scenario, the Bill[40] 137/2020 was presented to the Chamber of Deputies, of the Plurinational Legislative Assembly of Bolivia, which creates mechanisms for the protection of Mother Earth, and, among them, defines the crime of ecocide, amending the Penal Code[41] Bolivian (Decree Law No. 10.426/1972). In the justification of the project, the legislators affirm that the massive damage and destruction of ecosystems of Mother Earth are endangering her life, it being necessary to recognise limits to human activities, which should develop without threatening the continuity of vital cycles, structure, and functioning of nature.[42]

The Project intends to include art. 365 in the Penal Code:

Article 365 (ecocide):

Whoever causes serious and significant damage to Mother Earth, endangering the continuity of her vital cycles, structure and functioning, will be punished with imprisonment from (15) fifteen to (30) thirty years, without prejudice to civil and/or environmental liability that may arise from the damages caused.

The penalty will be aggravated up to the maximum provided in this article when:

1. The damages caused to Mother Earth are irreversible.
2. The crime has been committed in a place declared Natural Heritage, in protected areas, places that perform custodial functions, rescue or in RAMSAR areas [wetlands].
3. The practice of the illicit results in the death of one or more people, affect the livelihoods of indigenous peasant peoples and/or cause serious damage to human health and/or food security.[43]

For the Bolivian legislator, ecocide is a massive and significant damage to biodiversity, ecosystems, and the rights of *Madre Tierra*, "which threatens the existence and functioning of life systems", endangering the continuity of the vital cycles of nature, affecting the capacity for regeneration (being, commonly, irreversible).[44] Thus, given its gravity, the crime would have as maximum penalty the limit allowed in the country (thirty years).

It should be noted that this Bill takes place in the context of the Framework Law of Mother Earth, whose objective is to protect the rights of the Earth, establishing

---

[40] Bill Against Ecocide and Protection of Mother Earth, PL 137-20. Available at: https://diputados.gob.bo/wp-content/uploads/2022/05/PL-101-2021-2022.pdf. Accessed on: May 2, 2025.

[41] Bolivian Penal Code, of August 23, 1972. Available at: https://www.oas.org/juridico/spanish/gapeca_sp_docs_bol1.pdf. Accessed on: May 2, 2025.

[42] PL 137/2020 is based on the provisions of Law 71/2010, providing tools for the protection of Mother Earth (Bill Against Ecocide and Protection of Mother Earth, PL 137-20. Available at: https://diputados.gob.bo/wp-content/uploads/2022/05/PL-101-2021-2022.pdf. Accessed on: May 2, 2025, p. 3).

[43] Bill Against Ecocide and Protection of Mother Earth, PL 137-20. Available at: https://www.vicepresidencia.gob.bo/IMG/pdf/proyecto_ley_contra_el_ecocidio.pdf. Accessed on: May 2, 2025.

[44] Bill Against Ecocide and Protection of Mother Earth, PL 137-20. Available at: https://www.vicepresidencia.gob.bo/IMG/pdf/proyecto_ley_contra_el_ecocidio.pdf. Accessed on: 2 May 2025.

the imprescriptibility of any crime related to it. Another Bolivian norm that criminalises conduct on this theme is the Environmental Law[45] (Law 1.333/1992), which typifies, in Chapter V, Title IX, some environmental crimes (art. 103 to 115), referring some conducts to crimes of the Penal Code.

The Bolivian Project is considered an advance in the country,[46] as it fills a legal gap against conducts that cause great environmental damage. However, issues such as corporate responsibility (mining cooperatives held protests against the Ecocide Bill in August 2021 in La Paz) and the structural lack of supervisory bodies are obstacles to the approval of the PL (Ledezma, 2022). As a consequence, the two texts do not have regular progress in Parliament.

The fact that countries like Ecuador and Bolivia have textually assumed the rights of nature has stimulated international initiatives for environmental protection by itself, such as the institution, for example, of the International Tribunal for the Rights of Nature and Mother Earth,[47] created by civil society.[48]

One of the unifying foundations of social mobilisation for the idealisation of this Tribunal were anthropogenic climate changes and the consequent environmental disasters, extinction of species, deterioration of ecological communities, among other effects (Maloney, 2016, p. 131). This argument also underpins the Mexican projects on ecocide.

6.3 Mexico (2020–2021)

Mexico (United Mexican States) is a federal republic and, as such, has a decentralised legal system, so that each state—as in Brazil, for example—has its own Constitution.[49] The competence in criminal legislative matters, however, is broader

---

[45] Bolivia's Environmental Law, of 27 April 1992. Available at: https://sea.gob.bo/digesto/CompendioII/N/129_L_1333_01.pdf. Accessed on: 2 May 2025.

[46] Note the existence of PL 275/2020 – 2021, which proposes the crime of ecocide with simplistic wording, including art. 138 bis to the Bolivian Penal Code (Bill "Ecocide", PL 275-20. Available at: https://diputados.gob.bo/leyes/pl-n-275-2020-2021/. Accessed on: 14 Dec. 2024).

[47] Link: https://www.rightsofnaturetribunal.org/. Accessed on: 22 May 2025.

[48] In January 2014, members of civil society, Global Alliance for the Rights of Nature, held the world's first International Tribunal for the Rights of Nature and Mother Earth in Quito, Ecuador. "Since that time, the International Tribunal has met in Lima, Peru and Paris, France in parallel with the Conference of Parties for UN climate change negotiations, and Regional Chambers of the International Tribunal have been held in the United States and Australia". The main sources of the Tribunal are "the Universal Declaration of the Rights of Mother Earth (UDRME). Additionally, for cases from Ecuador and Bolivia, the Tribunal can refer to the Ecuadorian Constitution and Bolivia's Framework Act for the Rights of Mother Earth and Holistic Development to Live Well 2012, respectively, as these existing domestic legal instruments explicitly recognize the rights of nature" (Maloney, 2016, p. 130).

[49] "The spatial scope of validity of the norms is determined by the territory where they are applicable. The Mexican Republic is composed of free and sovereign States in terms of their internal regime, but united in a Federation. In addition, it includes the Federal District, which is the seat of

for the federative units, which can create crimes,[50] as in the neighbouring United States of America.

Thus, in addition to a broad federal law that deals with environmental protection[51] (*General Law of Ecological Balance and Environmental Protection*), there are some states where ecocide is already typified. In October 2019, the inclusion of the crime in the Penal Code of the State of Jalisco was approved:

> **Article 289 Bis**
>
> The crime of ecocide is committed by those who:
>
> I. Cause the destruction or total loss of an ecosystem that covers an area of at least ten hectares;
>
> II. Cause irreparable damage to an ecosystem that covers an area of at least ten hectares; or
>
> III. Cause damage to an ecosystem whose damage and impacts last for at least four months.
>
> The person responsible for the crime of ecocide will be sentenced to three to ten years in prison and a fine of five hundred to fifty thousand times the daily value of the Measurement and Update Unit.
>
> The previous penalties will increase by a third when the ecocide occurs in protected natural areas, as declared by the competent authority. (Penal Code for the State of Jalisco, 1982)

It is interesting to note that the law describes minimum limits for the destroyed area (10 hectares) and minimum recovery time for impacts (4 months). Although these choices of dimension and duration are discretionary (and, to a certain extent, short), without scientific basis, they point to a security regarding the application of the norm, avoiding judicial discretion in this aspect.

In 2023, it was the capital Mexico City that internalised the crime in its Penal Code:

---

the Powers of the Union and capital of the United Mexican States. For their part, the States have as the basis of their territorial division, political and administrative organization, the free Municipality" (Supreme Court of Justice of the Nation, 2006).

[50] Article 73, clause XXI, of the Mexican Constitution establishes the Union's minimum competence to legislate on criminal law: "Article 73. The Congress has the power: (…). XXI. To issue: (a) The general laws that establish at least, the types of crimes and their penalties in matters of kidnapping, forced disappearance of persons, other forms of illegal deprivation of liberty, human trafficking, torture and other cruel, inhuman or degrading treatment or punishment, as well as electoral" (Political Constitution of the United Mexican States, 5 Feb. 1917).

[51] It is worth mentioning that Mexican laws on environmental matters are different from each other not only because of their federal or local nature, but also because of the hierarchy of the legal systems to which they correspond: "Within the federal framework, there are the Political Constitution, Federal Laws, Treaties and International Agreements, Mexican Official Standards and, in some cases, judicial precedents, for example. On the other hand, there are differences between casual environmental legislation, sectoral environmental legislation, and properly environmental legislation. Thus, the process of forming Mexican Environmental Law has caused the dispersion of the norms in multiple regulations, making their knowledge difficult. As Raúl Brañes points out, perhaps the most complicated thing is its structural heterogeneity, which is expressed in countless omissions, reiterations and contradictions" (García, 2012, p. 3).

Article 346 bis

The crime of ecocide is committed by those who intentionally cause serious damage to the environment, by emitting pollutants, carrying out risky activities or affecting the natural resources of Mexico City.

A sentence of five to twelve years in prison and a fine of 5,000 to 10,000 Current Measurement and Update Units will be applied to those who:

I. Cause the destruction, total loss or irreparable damage to an ecosystem that covers an area of at least ten hectares;

II. Cause damage to an ecosystem whose effects and impacts last for at least four months;

III. Cause damage to an ecosystem where an endemic or threatened species lives or exists; or

IV. Cause water and soil pollution by chemical spills.

The previous penalties will increase by a third when the ecocide is committed in Areas of Environmental Value and Protected Natural Areas under the jurisdiction of Mexico City.

In addition to the sanctions provided for in this article, those who commit this crime will be obliged to compensate and fully repair the damage, based on the provisions of article 16 of the Political Constitution of Mexico City (Penal Code for the Federal District, 2002). (…)

Again, as in the law in Jalisco, the legislator chose to define a minimum area and recovery time for the configuration of ecocide. It also provides for the duty of reparation and compensation as a result of the criminal sanction.

The Penal Code for the State of Chiapas[52] (located in the south of Mexico, on the border with Guatemala) provides, in art. 457:

Article 457

Ecocide is a deliberate conduct, which consists in causing serious damage to the environment due to the emission of pollutants, the performance of risky activities or the affectation of natural resources under the jurisdiction of the State of Chiapas. A prison sentence of five to twelve years and a fine of two thousand to twenty thousand days of the current minimum wage will be imposed on those who: (…)

The aforementioned article, included in the state Penal Code in 2020, presents twelve subsections, with descriptions of behaviours that constitute the crime, all of them causing serious damage to the environment. In addition to Chiapas, there is a Bill, from November 2021, for the crime of ecocide also in Michoacán, in order to prevent the "destruction of the ecosystems" of the state (Press Release 228/2021, 2021).

At the national level, some initiatives to reform the Federal Penal Code to include ecocide have emerged since 2018. The first of these, already discarded (by agreement with the Board), was presented by deputy María Victoria Mercado Sánchez, from the Parliamentary Group of the Citizen Movement. The proposal was to add articles 421 and 421 Bis to the Code, defining the crime as:

---

[52] The Crime is in the Twenty-First Title (Environmental Crimes), Chapter II is provided, which deals exclusively with Ecocide (Penal Code for the State of Chiapas, 14 Mar. 2007. Available at: https://www.congresochiapas.gob.mx/new/Info-Parlamentaria/LEY_0012.pdf?v=Mjc=. Accessed on: 22 May 2025).

Article 421. Commits the crime of Ecocide:

I. Whoever causes serious damage, destruction or loss of the ecosystems of a certain territory, whether by human mediation or other causes, in such a way that the peaceful enjoyment of this territory by its inhabitants is severely diminished.

Article 421 bis. A sentence of one to nine years in prison and the equivalent of three hundred to three thousand days of fine will be applied.

The sanction referred to in the article will be increased by half in the case of public servants.[53]

Other initiatives are still in progress in the Mexican legislative houses. Presented by Senator Samuel Alejandro García Sepúlveda, in March 2020, the proposal includes art. 416 Bis in the Federal Penal Code:

Article 416. Bis

Commits the crime of ecocide who, by himself or by an interposed person derived from the activities he exercises, causes serious, massive and extensive damage, of surface and temporality, to natural resources, flora, fauna, water quality, soil, subsoil or environment, whose result is the affectation of a certain ecosystem.

For such crime, twelve to twenty years of imprisonment and the equivalent of five hundred to three thousand days of fine will be imposed.

An additional penalty of up to two years in prison and a fine of up to a thousand days will be applied when the behaviours described in this article are practiced by public servants to obtain profit or economic benefit.[54]

The Senator justified his proposal by citing global climate changes and their impacts on the Mexican environment, especially the loss of biodiversity. He listed various international instruments of which Mexico is a part, to demonstrate the legal gap on behaviours that cause massive damage, enumerating some countries that already have the crime typified in law.[55]

The appeal to environmental disasters that have occurred in the country also underpins the Initiative proposed by Deputy Karem Zobeida Vargas Pelayo, in April 2021, which amends art. 421 of the Federal Penal Code:

Article 421

Ecocide is considered the irreparable damage and destruction of an ecosystem due to causes directly related to human activity or derived from it.

I. The penalty for committing the crime of ecocide will be two and up to ten years in prison.[56]

---

[53] Available at: http://sil.gobernacion.gob.mx/Archivos/Documentos/2018/01/asun_3659459_20180124_1516809481.pdf. Accessed on: 22 May 2025.

[54] Available at: http://sil.gobernacion.gob.mx/Archivos/Documentos/2020/03/asun_4025989_20200324_1584567385.pdf. Accessed on: 22 May 2025.

[55] Secondary Law Initiative, of 24 Mar. 2020, Available at: http://sil.gobernacion.gob.mx/Archivos/Documentos/2020/03/asun_4025989_20200324_1584567385.pdf. Accessed on: 22 May 2025.

[56] Article 414-Bis. The crime of ecocide is committed by those who destroy, authorise or order, totally or partially, the destruction of flora or fauna, the pollution of the atmosphere or water resources and any other action that may cause ecological damage.

For such a crime, penalties of ten to fifteen years of imprisonment and from eight hundred to five thousand days fine. (Secondary Law Initiative, of 23 September 2021, Available at: http://sil.

The definition, simpler, is similar to the Initiative proposed by Senator Raúl Paz Alonzo, in September 2021. In this, however, the statement of reasons is more robust, tracing the evolution, since the Stockholm Conference, in 1972, of environmental protection at the international level, with the aim of highlighting the need for legislative increment. The project also lists the countries where the crime already exists, even remembering the Mexican support for the inclusion of ecocide in the International Criminal Court, of which it is a part. The wording of the new art. 414 Bis was thus proposed:

> **Article 414-Bis**
>
> The crime of ecocide is committed by whoever destroys, authorises or orders, in whole or in part, the destruction of flora or fauna, the contamination of the atmosphere or water resources and any other action that may cause ecological damage.
>
> For such crime, ten to fifteen years of imprisonment and eight hundred to five thousand days of fine will be imposed.

The last initiative, more aligned with the international definition proposed for the Rome Statute, was presented by Deputy Karina Marlen Barrón Perales, a member of the *Parliamentary Group of the Institutional Revolutionary Party*, in July 2023. The text adds article 417 bis to the Federal Penal Code:

> **Article 417 bis**
>
> A penalty of 10 to 15 years in prison and a fine of 1,000 to 1,500 days will be applied to anyone who commits any illegal or arbitrary act knowing that there is a high probability of causing serious, extensive or lasting damage to the environment.[57]

In general, the proposals have higher penalties than the sanctions stipulated for other environmental crimes in the Mexican Federal Penal Code, which demonstrates the relevance of the subject for the country (López & López, 2020, p. 259). However, the initiatives define ecocide in a generic way, without detailing the conducts and limits for the legal application of the norm. Aside from technical issues, the topic faces challenges for insertion at the federal level, such as the lack of awareness and public understanding of the importance of environmental protection, in harmony with economic growth, in addition to political and administrative corruption.[58]

---

gobernacion.gob.mx/Archivos/Documentos/2021/09/asun_4219660_20210923_1632404003.pdf. Accessed on: 22 May 2025).

[57] Initiative with Project of Decree by which an article 417 Bis is added to the Federal Penal Code, of 30 July 2023, Available at: http://sil.gobernacion.gob.mx/Archivos/Documentos/2023/07/asun_4585203_20230718_1689699416.pdf. Accessed on: 14 Dec. 2024.

[58] "Another significant factor is the presence of political and administrative corruption, as well as the control exercised by organised crime, phenomena that prevail in much of the national territory. These elements contribute to the complexity and hinder the implementation of stricter environmental laws and the penalisation of ecocide. Corruption facilitates the illegal exploitation of natural resources and the evasion of environmental sanctions, while organised crime can directly interfere in environmental governance through threats and violence. (…). The question of whether the regulation of ecocide should be at the national or international level also adds an additional layer of complexity to the challenge. Criminal law experts suggest that the national criminal frame-

Mexico, a country that suffers numerous problems related to the environment,[59] has global importance in ecological protection, evidenced in the plurality of environmental laws and proposals for the crime of ecocide, in addition to supporting the inclusion of this in the Rome Statute. In this aspect, it is natural that the expositions of reasons for the Initiatives to change the law are based on the international movement of parliamentarians[60] and civil organisations to transform ecocide into a crime, inserting into the national debate the external context: laws of other countries, global anthropogenic climate changes and the proposals for the ICC, now officially submitted for consideration at the Assembly of States Parties.

Several countries—like some already presented here—used the definition format of ecocide proposed by the Independent Expert Panel, in 2021, as a model for internal Bills, with minor changes.

6.4 Independent Expert Panel for the Legal Definition of Ecocide (2021)

On the international level, ecocide as a crime within the jurisdiction of the ICC has gained strength in recent years. Among the initiatives for the creation of the crime, the proposal developed by the Independent Expert Panel for the Legal Definition of Ecocide, led by the *Stop Ecocide Foundation*, deserves prominence.

In November 2020 (coinciding with the 75th anniversary of the opening of the Nuremberg trials of high-ranking Nazi officials, in 1945), various experts in international criminal law and jurists formerly linked to other International Courts, joined together to develop the definition of ecocide,[61] in order to submit it[62] to the Assembly of the Parties of the International Criminal Court. The result was announced in June 2021, in the format of a proposal to amend the Rome Statute, with comments from the authors (Sands & Sow, 2021).

---

work is insufficient to address the crime of ecocide and advocate for placing it alongside genocide in international criminal law" (Gómez-Rodríguez et al., 2024).

[59] Among the most recent environmental problems, mention should be made of the expansion (megaprojects) of wind farms, based on environmentalism of market and climate change mitigation programmes, resulting in a slow "industrial genocide" in the Isthmus of Tehuantepec region (Dunlap, 2018, p. 566).

[60] For example, Senator Raúl Paz pointed out, in a speech in the Mexican Senate, to the environmental emergency that the country is going through and the lack of compliance with international agreements on the subject, highlighting that currently there are only economic penalties for those who commit ecocide, despite the effects being irreversible (Senadores de México, 2021).

[61] In addition to the experts directly involved in the project, such as Phillipe Sands, Dior Fall Show, Kate Mackintosh (UCLA School of Law), Valérie Cabanes and Jojo Mehta, the Panel conducted a public *online* consultation, with hundreds of suggestions analysed, between November 2020 and February 2021 (Stop Ecocide International, 2020).

[62] This submission is through a State Party.

Ecocide would be the fifth crime within the jurisdiction of the ICC, included in art. 8 ter:

> **Article 8 ter**
>
> Ecocide
>
> 1. For the purpose of this Statute, "ecocide" means unlawful or wanton acts committed with knowledge that there is a substantial likelihood of severe and either widespread or long-term damage to the environment being caused by those acts.
>
> 2. For the purpose of paragraph 1:
>
> a. "Wanton" means with reckless disregard for damage which would be clearly excessive in relation to the social and economic benefits anticipated;
>
> b. "Severe" means damage which involves very serious adverse changes, disruption or harm to any element of the environment, including grave impacts on human life or natural, cultural or economic resources;
>
> c. "Widespread" means damage which extends beyond a limited geographic area, crosses state boundaries, or is suffered by an entire ecosystem or species or a large number of human beings;
>
> d. "Long-term" means damage which is irreversible or which cannot be redressed through natural recovery within a reasonable period of time;
>
> e. "Environment" means the earth, its biosphere, cryosphere, lithosphere, hydrosphere and atmosphere, as well as outer space.

The Proposal was developed taking advantage of the terms used in the Rome Statute—such as *wanton* (negligence)—and in different international documents—as *widespread* (widespread), *severe* (severe), and *long-term* (long-term),[63] in order to find support in the structure of the drafting. Thus, there was a concern in the text and in the form to make the initiative viable in relation to existing codes and to international criminal law.

Two conditions were thought of to identify the criminal act: a substantial probability that the conduct (commission or omission) will cause severe and widespread or long-term damage to the environment and requirement of evidence that the acts are illegal or arbitrary.[64] This latter requirement opposes the essence of ecocide, ecocentric by nature, foreseeing, on the contrary, that if environmental destruction is—in some way— legal, there will be no crime, that is, it conditions it to an anthropocentric bias (this view guides the Rome Statute itself).

---

[63] The three terms cited are mentioned in two articles of the First Additional Protocol to the Geneva Conventions, 1977 (API, link: https://ihl-databases.icrc.org/ihl/INTRO/470#:~:text=It%20extends%20the%20protection%20of,detailed%20provisions%20on%20medical%20transportation), in the Environmental Modification Convention (ENMOD, link: https://www.un.org/disarmament/enmod/) and in the Rome Statute, in the description of the crime against the environment in times of war (art. 8[2][b][iv]).

[64] There are activities that are legal, socially beneficial and operated responsibly to minimise impacts that, however, cause serious damage, maintaining balance within a concept of sustainable development: "*With these two thresholds, the prosecution would need to prove a substantial likelihood of causing severe and either widespread or long-term damage through acts or omissions that are either unlawful or wanton*" (Sands & Sow, 2021).

It is important to highlight that ecocide as proposed is a crime of danger[65] (threat) and not of material result. The guilt for the infraction is linked to the creation of a dangerous situation, and not necessarily to a specific result: it is the practice of acts with knowledge of the substantial probability of causing severe and widespread or long-term damage that is criminalised.[66] The result should influence, in this case, at the time of the dosimetry of the penalty.

The document had in its first year repercussion among various States, receiving support for the proposition from the European Union[67] and from various countries, such as Scotland,[68] France, Mexico, New Guinea (West Papua),[69] Belgium,[70] Finland,[71] Denmark, Cyprus,[72] Bangladesh,[73] Samoa, and Iceland. Chile adapted the

[65] The crime of danger requires significantly greater than the principle of proportionality, given that the prediction of damage is hypothetical (Beade, 2022).

[66] This would not be the first crime with this characteristic in the Rome Statute. For example, regarding genocide (art. 6), "*the crime consists in carrying out actions intended to reach that goal. Endangerment is also key to Articles 35(3) and 55(1) API, which prohibit the use of 'methods or means of warfare which are intended, or may be expected to cause, widespread, long-term and severe damage to the natural environment*'" (Sands & Sow, 2021).

[67] In the 2021 Annual Report, the European Parliament stated, about the right to a safe and healthy environment: "*is aware of the close link that exists between human rights, a healthy environment, biodiversity and the fight against climate change and welcomes the call by the United Nations for global recognition of the right to a safe, clean, healthy and sustainable environment; insists on the essential role played by human rights defenders related to the environment and by local and indigenous populations in preserving such an environment, despite the threats of violence that those responsible for harmful environmental practices and those who profit from them often put on them; encourages the Union and the Member States to promote the recognition of ecocide as an international crime under the Rome Statute of the ICC and asks the Commission to study the relevance of the qualification of ecocide for Union law and its diplomacy; invites the Union and the Member States to take bold initiatives to combat the impunity of environmental crime at the global level*" (European Parliament, 2022).

[68] Link: https://www.parliament.scot/chamber-and-committees/votes-and-motions/votes-and-motions-search/S6M-00483. Accessed on: 4 Jun. 2025.

[69] Link: https://www.ulmwp.org/press-release-west-papuan-leaders-pledge-to-make-ecocide-a-serious-crime-in-worlds-third-largest-rainforest. Accessed on: 4 Jun. 2025.

[70] As early as July 2020, the House of Representatives of Belgium presented a resolution proposal for the inclusion of ecocide in the Rome Statute and in domestic law. Legally speaking, "international instruments relating to the environment have begun to include provisions requiring the State to criminalise certain behaviours offensive to the environment, such as the Basel Convention of 22 March 1989 on the transboundary movements of hazardous wastes and their disposal, which has set up a control system to prevent damage" (Chamber of Representatives of Belgium, 2020).

[71] Statement by the Finnish Minister of Foreign Affairs Pekka Haavisto, in December 2021, at the Assembly of States Parties of the International Criminal Court (Link: https://www.youtube.com/watch?v=RDyepTLExaA. Accessed on: 4 Jun. 2025).

[72] Link: https://www.stopecocide.earth/new-breaking-news-summary/cyprus-ecocide-raised-in-house-of-representatives-complete-with-t-shirt. Accessed on: 4 Jun. 2025.

[73] Statement by the Prime Minister of Samoa Fiamé Naomi Mata'afa, in December 2021, at a side event to the Assembly of States Parties of the International Criminal Court (Link: https://www.youtube.com/watch?v=Q7EQegJVCvE. Accessed on: 4 Jun. 2025).

definition and included it in the Penal Code,[74] in 2023. Others, like Scotland, the United Kingdom, and Peru, have Bills based on the proposal.

The new Project for the ICC was widely celebrated among environmentalists,[75] with international dissemination.[76] As a starting point for a global discussion on the inclusion of ecocide in the structure of international criminal law, the initiative was successful.[77] The Panel of experts tried to demonstrate that, with the legal techniques available today, it is possible to develop the structure of a crime against the most destructive conducts to the environment, without resorting to unrealistic transformations of international law— traditionally slow to drastic changes—despite being necessary, given the environmental crisis of the planet.

In this aspect, by forging an amendment to the Rome Statute using its own building blocks, the Panel extended the existing environmental crime (during a war, as a military objective) to situations of peace. Considering that there have never been cases in the International Criminal Court about the first mode, it would hardly be the case for the second, if approved, since no conduct was described in the Project. The result is, in this case, a symbolic definition.[78]

The criticisms of the new definition are, after all, predominantly from criminal lawyers and internationalists.[79] Besides the perennial discussion about the need for

[74] Law 21.595, of 7 August 2023.

[75] For example, *Global Alliance for the Rights of Nature* (GARN, Link: https://www.garn.org/ecocide/) and *Climate Tracker* (Link: https://climateactiontracker.org/)

[76] For illustration, *The Guardian* (Link: https://www.theguardian.com/environment/2021/jun/22/legal-experts-worldwide-draw-up-historic-definition-of-ecocide. Accessed on: 4 Jun. 2025) and Peace Palace Library (Link: https://peacepalacelibrary.nl/blog/2021/legal-definition-ecocide. Accessed on: 4 Jun. 2025).

[77] There are many questions about the real chances of the proposal being approved by the Rome Statute: "And in that the definition of ecocide has already been extremely successful: no other topic in international law was covered as broadly in the news and blogosphere this year. Governments, the EU, the UN Secretary General, the Pope, and so many others are talking about it. Ecocide cannot be removed from our minds and the international community's agenda—it is here to stay and all the technical drafting questions will be discussed along the way" (Pezzot & Graff, 2022).

[78] Not listing any criminal acts "is a strong (and indeed desirable!) statement that all forms of environmental harm, regardless of the nature of the act, should entail individual criminal responsibility (provided that the additional threshold requirements of the act being 'unlawful or wanton' and the perpetrator having had 'knowledge that there is a substantial likelihood of severe and either widespread or long-term damage to the environment being caused by those acts' are fulfilled). This symbolic statement, however, comes at the expense of legal certainty, a basic pillar of criminal law required for its justifiability and enforceability" (Kersting, 2021).

[79] Of the main criticisms, as will be demonstrated in the following Chapters, is the anthropocentric commitment of the Project, which seeks to be politically palatable to States of different political and economic spectrums: "This is because, by compromising its design, the Panel's vision of ecocide is now unlikely to appeal to either (i) states that want to see change (the 'progressive' states) or (ii) states that wish to preserve the status quo (the 'regressive' states). It should be acknowledged before proceeding that the idea of progressive and regressive states sitting in a neat dichotomy is an oversimplification: the attitudes in different countries to environmental protection is a complex, varied and constantly evolving phenomenon". (Winter, 2024, p. 197).

an autonomous crime for environmental protection, the proposed crime has technical deficiencies.

Next, we briefly study how some countries have adapted the new definition to national legislations, in the form of Bills.

6.4.1 Italy (2023)

Italy is yet another European country to discuss ecocide in the national Parliament.[80] Previously, in 2022, the country had already taken a significant step towards environmental protection, amending two articles of the Constitution, now more aligned with European Directives.[81]

Article 9 announced that "the Republic promotes the development of culture and scientific and technical research" and "protects the landscape and the historical and artistic heritage of the Nation". It came to include[82] that it also "protects the environment, biodiversity and ecosystems, also in the interest of future generations", relegating to State laws the regulation of the ways and forms of animal protection. This was the first amendment in the first part of the Charter (fundamental principles) since its inception in 1948.

Another amended article was 41, which deals with the economic freedom of private initiative. The text came to limit this freedom not only when contrasting with social utility but also environmental.[83]

In response to the new constitutional commands, the parliamentarian Filiberto Zaratti— with three other parliamentarians—presented in the Senate, on 24 July2023, Bill 1325, to introduce the crime of ecocide[84] in the country:

---

[80] In Catalonia (Spain), there has been, since 2023, a Project for the inclusion of ecocide in the Spanish Penal Code (Link: https://www.stopecocide.earth/2024/hearings-on-proposed-ecocide-bill-begin-in-catalan-parliament. Available on: 18 Dec. 2024).

[81] For example, the Treaty of Nice. Link: https://www.europarl.europa.eu/about-parliament/pt/in-the-past/the-parliament-and-the-treaties/treaty-of-nice. Accessed on: 18 Dec. 2024.

[82] "Art. 9. The Republic promotes the development of culture and scientific and technical research. It protects the landscape and the historical and artistic heritage of the Nation. It protects the environment, biodiversity and ecosystems, also in the interest of future generations. The law of the State regulates the ways and forms of protection of animals." (Constitution of the Italian Republic, 1948).

[83] "Art. 41. Private economic initiative is free. It cannot take place in contrast with social utility or in a way that causes damage to health, the environment, safety, freedom, human dignity. The law determines the programs and appropriate controls so that public and private economic activity can be directed and coordinated for social and environmental purposes." (Constitution of the Italian Republic, 1948).

[84] Italy. Bill Proposal 1325. Introduction of the crime of ecocide. Senate of the Republic. 24 July 2023. Available at: https://www.camera.it/leg19/126?leg=19&idDocumento=1325. Accessed on: 18 Dec. 2024.

Article 1

(Purpose and object)

1. In implementation of Articles 9 and 41 of the Constitution and in compliance with international agreements, this law, also for the purpose of protecting the interest of future generations, lays down fundamental principles on the prevention and repression of crimes against the environment and makes provisions for the introduction of the crime of ecocide.

Article 2

(Definitions)

1. For the purposes of this law, the crime of ecocide shall be any unlawful or arbitrary act committed with knowledge that there is a substantial probability that the same act will cause serious and widespread or long-term damage to the environment or an ecosystem.

2. For the purposes of this law, the following are defined as:

(a) "arbitrary act" means an act that fails to take into account harm that would clearly be disproportionate to the anticipated social and economic benefits;

(b) "serious damage" means damage that results in very serious alterations, disruptions, or consequences to any element of the environment, including serious impacts on human life or natural, cultural, or economic resources;

(c) "widespread damage" means damage that extends beyond a limited geographic area, crosses state boundaries, or is suffered by an entire ecosystem or species or a large number of human beings;

(d) "long-term damage" means damage that is irreversible or cannot be repaired through natural recovery within a reasonable period of time;

(e) "environment" means the Earth, its biosphere, cryosphere, lithosphere, hydrosphere and atmosphere, and outer space;

(f) "ecosystem" means a significant geographic area in which plants, animals and organisms, as well as weather and landscape interact;

(g) "public concerned" means persons affected or likely to be affected by the offenses under this Law; persons with sufficient interest or evidence of injury to a right, as well as organizations promoting environmental protection, shall be deemed to be affected.

3. The acts referred to in paragraph 1 must be committed intentionally and with awareness of the widespread and systematic nature of the actions in the scope of which they are carried out. The acts referred to in paragraph 1 shall also be considered intentional when the perpetrator knew or should have known of the high probability that the same acts could adversely affect the safety of the ecosystem.

Article 3

(Instigation, aiding, abetting and attempting)

1. Unless the act constitutes a more serious crime, instigation, aiding and abetting and attempt to commit the crime of ecocide shall be punished by imprisonment of three to six years. The punishment referred to in this article shall also apply when the act is committed abroad by an Italian citizen.

Article 4

(Sanction)

1. Unless the act constitutes a more serious crime, anyone who violates the provisions of this law shall be punished by imprisonment for a term of twelve to twenty years. The punishment referred to in this Article shall also apply when the act is committed abroad by an Italian citizen.

Article 5

(Obligations of the convicted person)

1. With the judgment of conviction for the crimes provided for in this law, the benefit of the suspension of the sentence may be subject to full compensation for the damage and the execution of the safety, reclamation and restoration of the places.

Article 6

(Prescription)

1. The statute of limitations referred to in Article 157 of the Criminal Code shall not apply to the crime of ecocide.

Article 7

(Protection of persons who report ecocide crimes or cooperate in the investigation)

1. The Minister of Justice, by his own decree, within six months from the date of entry into force of this law, shall establish the necessary measures to ensure the protection of persons who report ecocide crimes, provide evidence or cooperate in the investigation.

The Project, clearly inspired by the definition developed by the Panel of Experts, has some important peculiarities. Art. 2, item 3, defines that the crime must be recognised when the acts are committed with intention and knowledge of their widespread and systematic consequences. That is, it requires direct intent. Also, however, it recognises eventual intent (or even conscious guilt, for Brazilian law) when it points out that the perpetrator commits the crime if he knew or should have known of the high probability that his acts could adversely affect the security of the ecosystem.

By applying a penalty of twelve to twenty years in prison, Art. 4 also provides for a possibility of extraterritoriality of the law, when it determines its application when the crime is committed by Italians abroad. There is also provision for repair/restoration of damages (Art. 5) and the imprescriptibility of the crime, moving away from the rules of Art. 157 of the Italian Penal Code.[85]

Art. 7 brings an interesting provision, which sets a deadline for the Minister of Justice to create devices that guarantee the protection of people who report ecocide crimes or who in some way cooperate with the investigation.

Despite the normative advance, Italy does not escape criticism regarding its environmental treatment, especially regarding the climate commitments assumed by the Italian government.[86]

Even so, the Italian Bill demonstrates an interesting local adaptation of the international definition, revealing the increase in the level of discussion about the crime.

---

[85] Italy. Penal Code of the Italian Republic. Text of the Royal Decree n. 1398, 19 October 1930. Available at: https://www.altalex.com/documents/codici-altalex/2014/10/30/codice-penale. Accessed on: 18 Dec. 2024.

[86] "The Italian climate cause, Universal Judgement, is built on the basis of the danger posed by an omission by the Italian State that does not respect the limits marked by the Intergovernmental Panel on Climate Change (IPCC). The legal strategy consists in asking the public administration not to compensate for previous damages, but to avoid causing others. The request is not to do: not to carry out those actions (the exceeding of the level of Co_2 gas emissions) that with certainty—based on the forecasts and limits established State by State by the IPCC—would cause certain damage (Chiaramonte, 2023, pp. 186–187).

6.4.2 Scotland (2023)

In November 2023, the Scottish Parliament supported a public consultation (Lennon, 2023) to gauge the receptivity of a Bill to include ecocide, in the mould of the definition developed by the Independent Expert Panel. The consultation was open from 8th November 2023 to 9th February 2024. A total of 3379 responses to the questionnaire (which had 11 questions) were received, from representatives of public and private companies, professionals in the field, as well as the general public (86% of the total) (Lennon, 2024).

The main question was: "Which of the following best expresses your view of the proposed Bill (Fully supportive/Partially supportive/etc.)?". The response was clear: 95% of those consulted fully supported the Bill. Thus, the Bill was presented for analysis to the Scottish Parliament, on 12th November 2024. The text, at the moment (Lennon, 2023, p. 7), is the same as defined in 2021 by the Panel of Experts:

> The proposed definition of ecocide is: 'unlawful or wanton acts committed with knowledge that there is a substantial likelihood of severe and either widespread or long-term damage to the Scottish environment being caused by those acts'.

The document proposes prison sentences between 10 and 20 years, in addition to financial sanctions (10% of global turnover, for three years) for companies. The project justifies the increase in light of the traditional sanctions for environmental crimes in Scotland, which do not exceed 5 years, at most. Now, the *Draft* must proceed through Parliament (Scottish Parliament, 2024).

The Netherlands, in the same year, followed a similar step.

6.4.3 Netherlands (2023)

A public consultation was held[87] in the Netherlands, between the months of July and August 2023, to know the opinion of people (89%) and interested parties (NGOs, companies, etc.) about the Bill that criminalises ecocide in the country. As in Scotland, the majority were in favour of the intensification of the penal law against massive environmental damage.[88]

The proposal (Tweede Kamer der Staten-Generaal, 2023–2024), initiated by Deputy Van Raan,[89] was presented to Parliament on 30th November 2023, to amend the Penal Code (of mainland and Caribbean Netherlands) to include the crime of ecocide:

---

[87] Link: https://www.internetconsultatie.nl/ecocidewet/document/12259. Accessed on: 20 Dec. 2024.

[88] Link: https://www.internetconsultatie.nl/ecocidewet/reacties/datum/23. Accessed on: 20 Dec. 2024.

[89] On 17 April 2024, Parliamentarian Christine Teunissen took up the defence of the project.

Article 153

1. As guilty of ecocide shall be punishable by imprisonment for not more than fifteen years or a fine of the sixth category whoever intentionally by act or omission causes serious and widespread or serious and prolonged damage to the environment, or creates a danger of such damage, this being in any case all danger meeting the damage criterion for ecocide.

2. For the purposes of subsection 1:

a. by environment is meant: the whole of conditions and influences within the physical living environment which are important for the protection of people, animals, plants and goods, of water, soil and air and of scenic, natural scientific and cultural-historical values and of the control of the climate, as well as of the relations between them.

b. damage to the environment classified as:

1°. widespread, if the damage occurs in a more than limited geographical area, crosses national borders, or concerns an important part of an ecosystem, a large number of people or a large number of a certain animal or plant species;

2°. long-term, if the damage is irreversible or cannot be restored by natural recovery within a reasonable time; and

3°. serious, if the damage results in a very serious adverse change or changes, disruption or disturbance of one or more components of the environment.

The crime is consummated with the damage effectively caused or with the creation of a danger of causing it. The article also details what is meant by environment, repeating the definition of the terms "widespread", "long-term", and "serious" from the international project. The proposal, finally, provides for a fine and up to 15 years in prison as punishment.

Currently, the Bill is being prepared for debate in the Parliament.

The United Kingdom began discussing ecocide in Parliament in 2021. The real progress, however, occurred at the end of 2023.

6.4.4 *The United Kingdom (2023)*

The first suggestions of the crime of ecocide in the United Kingdom were initially incorporated as amendments (287 and 293D) to the Environment Bill[90] of 2021. Baroness Bennett of Manor Castle proposed to the Parliament to add, after art. 133 of the new law being voted on, the crime as set out by the *Ecocide Law Foundation*. In the end, the Law was sanctioned, in November 2021, without the Baroness's amendments: the first, withdrawn from the agenda;[91] the second, was not even put to the vote.[92]

In November 2023, the "Ecocide Bill" (House Of Lords, 2023) was presented by Baroness Rosie Boycott, with the aim to fill the existing gap in criminal legislation

---

[90] UK Environment Act 2021 (Link: https://www.legislation.gov.uk/ukpga/2021/30/contents/enacted. Accessed on: 5 Jun. 2025).

[91] Amendment (287) clause 133 to the Environment Act (available at: https://bills.parliament.uk/bills/2593/stages/15298/amendments/87844. Accessed on: 5 Jun. 2025).

[92] Amendment (293D) clause 133 to the Environment Act (available at: https://bills.parliament.uk/bills/2593/stages/15298/amendments/88127. Accessed on: 5 Jun. 2025).

regarding accountability for serious environmental damage. The Bill provides for punishment for any entity, natural or legal registered in the United Kingdom, that commits the crime:

1 Offence of ecocide

It is an offence of "ecocide" for a person, company, organisation, partnership or any other legal entity registered in the United Kingdom, to be in breach of section of this Act.

2 Ecocide for the purposes of this Act, "ecocide"—

(a) as it applies to an individual, means unlawful or wanton acts or omissions committed by persons of superior responsibility who had knowledge, or should have had knowledge, that there was a substantial likelihood of severe and either widespread or long-term damage to the environment being caused by those acts;

(b) as it applies to a company, organisation, partnership or other legal entity, means strict liability for unlawful or wanton acts or omissions with a substantial likelihood of severe and either widespread or long-term damage to the environment being caused by those acts.

3 Sentencing

(1) The Secretary of State must by regulations establish defences and penalties for offences under sections 1 and 2 within 12 months of the day on which this Act is passed.

(2) Before establishing the defences and penalties under subsection (1), the Secretary of State must carry out a public consultation and take advice from the Sentencing Council as to the most appropriate defences and penalties.

The Bill details the responsibility of the superior in command:

4 Superior responsibility

1. Any director, senior manager, partner, leader and or any other person in a position of superior responsibility is responsible for offences committed by members of staff under their authority, and is responsible as a result of their authority over such staff where they fail to take all reasonable measures within their power to prevent or to stop all steps that lead to the commission of the crime of ecocide.
2. A superior is responsible for offences committed by staff under their effective authority as a result of their failure to exercise authority properly over such staff where they failed to take all reasonable measures within their power to prevent or stop the commission of a crime or to submit the matter to the competent authorities for investigation.
3. A person responsible for aiding, abetting, counselling or procuring the commission of an offence is regarded as responsible for an offence under this section.

Among other details, the Proposal, like the wording developed by the Panel of Experts, refines the concepts in the *caput* of the crime:

10 Interpretation

In section 2—

"acts" includes an act or a failure to act;

"environment" means the earth, its biosphere, cryosphere, lithosphere, hydrosphere and atmosphere as well as outer space;

"long-term" means damage which is irreversible or which cannot be redressed through natural recovery within a reasonable period of time;

"severe" means damage which involves very serious adverse changes, disruption or harm to any element of the environment, including serious impacts on human life or natural, cultural or economic resources;

"wanton" means with reckless disregard for damage;

"widespread" means damage which extends beyond a limited geographic area, to impact upon an ecosystem or species or a significant number of human beings.

The Project is in its first reading, in the House of Lords,[93] awaiting movement since May 2024.

The international definition was incorporated into three Bills in Peru, in 2024.

6.4.5 *Peru (2024)*

Peru, a country that shares a significant part of the Amazon Rainforest with Brazil, suffers from a succession of ecological disasters (forest fires; water contamination by mining waste; oil spills at sea, as caused by Repsol, in January 2022), highlighting the need for a more robust environmental criminal law.

Taking advantage of the definition developed by the Panel of Experts, three Bills on ecocide were presented to Parliament, by Congressmen Américo Gonza Castillo (PL 7866/2023),[94] Isaac Mita Alanoca (PL 7941/2023),[95] both in May 2024, and Ruth Luque Ibarra, in June of the same year (PL 8274/2023).[96] All seek to incorporate the crime into the Peruvian Penal Code. The texts are similar, with the first Project being the most complete:

> **Article 305-A.- Ecocide**
>
> Whoever provokes, carries out or omits acts that cause or may cause serious, extensive and long-lasting damage to the environment or its components, environmental quality or environmental health or the integrity of ecological processes, will be punished with a prison sentence of not less than seven (7) years and not more than twenty (20) years and with three hundred and sixty-five to seven hundred and thirty days-fine.
>
> The same penalty will apply to shareholders, partners, associates, managers, directors, administrators or legal representatives of a legal person.
>
> For the purposes of this article, the following will be understood:
>
> a) By serious damage, it will be understood as that damage that causes very adverse changes, disturbances or notorious damages in the atmosphere, the soil, the subsoil, terrestrial, maritime or underground waters, including serious impacts on human life, natural, cultural or economic resources;
>
> b) By extensive, it will be understood as that damage that goes beyond a limited geographical area or exceeds state borders or affects the entirety of an ecosystem or a species or a large number of human beings;
>
> c) By long-lasting, it will be understood as that damage that is irreversible or that cannot be mitigated through natural recovery processes during a reasonable period of time.[97]

---

[93] Link: https://bills.parliament.uk/bills/3531. Accessed on: 5 Jan. 2025.

[94] Link: https://www.stopecocide.earth/s/PL-7866-2023-CR-LPDerecho1.pdf. Accessed on: 5 Jan. 2025.

[95] Link: https://drive.google.com/file/d/1EMkmF-MgdzoEuM16aR4BUtHTUQz2YCVB/view. Accessed on: 5 Jan. 2025.

[96] Link: https://ruthluque.com/pl-8274-2024-cr-ley-que-incorpora-el-delito-de-ecocidio-en-el-codigo-penal/. Accessed on: 5 Jan. 2025.

[97] PL 7866/2023, Link: https://www.stopecocide.earth/s/PL-7866-2023-CR-LPDerecho1.pdf. Accessed on: 5 Jan. 2025.

In this case, the crime of ecocide, like the Dutch Bill, is consummated with the damage or the generation of danger of damage. It also points to the possibility of punishing leaders of legal entities,[98] concluding the text with norms explanatory of the terms "serious", "long-lasting", and "extensive".

The proposals should be discussed in Parliament in a unified manner, to strengthen the claim.

In the same year, it was Azerbaijan's turn to have its own Bill on ecocide.

6.4.6 *Azerbaijan (2024)*

The Constitution of the Republic of Azerbaijan, of 1995, amended in 2002, enshrines the right of citizens to a healthy and clean environment.[99] However, like most States, the country faces significant environmental challenges[100] since its independence from the Soviet Union, in 1991, a few months before its dissolution. In addition to disorderly industrial advancement, the country suffers from the consequences of wars against Armenia and severe environmental damage in the occupied territories, with rampant and irregular exploitation of natural resources.[101]

Between 11 and 22 November 2024, the 29th Conference of Parties on Climate Change (COP 29) took place in Baku, the capital of Azerbaijan. Amid discussions about climate financing,[102] the country's president, Ilham Aliyev, announced that he had proposed a change in national legislation, internally creating the crime of eco-

[98] There are questions in Peru as to whether a legal entity can be criminally prosecuted, especially with the advent of Law 30.424, which defined administrative infractions for companies whose directors commit crimes (Díaz, 2020).

[99] "The Constitution also outlines the division of environmental responsibilities between central and local bodies. The 1992 Law on Environmental Protection and Utilization of Natural Resources introduced, among other things, the polluter-pays principle, opened the door for the use of economic instruments, envisaged the bridging of the gap between existing and international environmental standards, and enhanced the role of public awareness." (Asian Development Bank, 2005. p. 29).

[100] "The extensive use of both subterranean and surface resources, the construction of large industrial complexes, the construction of reservoirs, canals, and drainage networks, advances in energy and communication infrastructure, road construction in mountainous regions, urban expansion, and agricultural expansion due to deforestation in lowland and foothill regions have all contributed to increased anthropogenic pressures on the environment. This has resulted in significant environmental degradation and an increasing load on the environment's separate components: air, water, and soil." (Mammadov, 2023, p. 7).

[101] "Environmental degradation in the occupied territories has reached such a fast and unobstructed pace that even Armenia-based environmental organisations raised a red flag. Valuable species of trees, including nut-trees, oaks, Eldar's pine-tree, persimmon and others that are under special protection are subjected to felling and cutting for timber, which is exported out of the occupied territories for furniture, barrel and rifle production. Many species of trees for a long time are on the verge of disappearance." (Ministry of Foreign Affairs of the Republic of Azerbaijan, 2016, p. 15).

[102] Link: https://www.un.org/en/climatechange/cop29. Accessed on: 18 Dec. 2024.

cide. The proposal, presented on 8 October 2024 to Parliament, includes Article 104–1 in the Penal Code of Azerbaijan:

> **Article 104-1. Ecocide**
> Mass destruction of flora and fauna, poisoning of the atmosphere, of the land or of water resources, or intentional practice of other actions that harm the environment, when these actions cause an ecological disaster or create a real threat of an ecological disaster -
> will be punished with imprisonment for a period of ten to fifteen years.

The project differs significantly from the definition brought by the Panel of Experts, but agrees on an important aspect, not previously seen in other *drafts*: it provides for the crime even without the occurrence of damage, just the creation of a threat of massive damage. That is, ecocide could be consummated without a material result.

Voted and approved in the third Reading, the Bill continues its course in the legislative House.[103]

6.4.7 International Criminal Court (Pacific Islands, 2024)

After the declaration of Vanuatu and Maldives, in 2020, in support of the crime of ecocide in the ICC, and the drafting of a definition by the Independent Expert Panel, in 2021, some Party country remained to formally present a proposal to amend the Rome Statute.

At the twenty-third session of the Assembly of the Parties to the ICC, in September 2024, Vanuatu, accompanied by Fiji and Samoa,[104] officially proposed the Amendment to the Rome Statute for the inclusion of ecocide, using the definition prepared by the Panel of Experts (ICC. Assembly of States Parties, 2024). Thus was the proposed wording for the crime:

> **Article 8ter Ecocide**
> 1. For the purpose of this Statute, "ecocide" means unlawful or wanton acts committed with knowledge that there is a substantial likelihood of severe and either widespread or long-term damage to the environment being caused by those acts.
> 2. For the purpose of paragraph 1:
> (a) "Wanton" means with reckless disregard for damage which would be clearly excessive in relation to the social and economic benefits anticipated;
> (b) "Severe" means damage which involves very serious adverse changes, disruption or harm to any element of the environment, including grave impacts on human life or natural, cultural or economic resources;

---

103 "It was observed that taking such a step on the eve of the international event COP29 in our country has a symbolic meaning and is a clear example of how Azerbaijan promotes the protection of the environment as a value belonging to humanity as a whole" (Link: https://www.meclis.gov.az/news.php?id=5713&lang=az. Accessed on: 18 Dec. 2024).

104 Most recently, the Democratic Republic of Congo formally endorsed the creation of the crime of ecocide (Link: https://www.stopecocide.earth/2024/drc-joins-pacific-island-nations-in-call-for-an-international-crime-of-ecocide. Accessed on: 15 Dec. 2024).

(c) "Widespread" means damage which extends beyond a limited geographic area, crosses state boundaries, or is suffered by an entire ecosystem or species or a large number of human beings;

(d) "Long-term" means damage which is irreversible or which cannot be redressed through natural recovery within a reasonable period of time;

(e) "Environment" means the earth, its biosphere, cryosphere, lithosphere, hydrosphere and atmosphere, as well as outer space."

It was also proposed,[105] consequently, amendment to the book *Elements of Crimes*:[106]

Article 8ter Ecocide

Introduction

The term 'acts' includes single acts or omissions, as well as cumulative acts or omissions.

Elements

1. The perpetrator committed acts that were substantially likely to cause severe and either widespread or long-term damage to the environment.
2. The perpetrator knew of the substantial likelihood of severe and either widespread or long-term damage to the environment being caused by those acts.
3. The acts were

(a) unlawful, meaning contrary to applicable national or international law, or

(b) wanton, meaning that the foreseeable damage would be clearly excessive in relation to the foreseeable social and economic benefits.

4. The perpetrator

(a) was aware of the factual circumstances that established the unlawfulness of the acts; or

(b) recklessly disregarded damage which would be clearly excessive in relation to the social and economic benefits anticipated.

The proposal, in its explanatory comments, reminds us that the term "acts" encompasses actions or omissions, isolated or cumulative, maintaining the standard of the Rome Statute. Regarding the elements, Vanuatu explains that the terms "severe", "widespread", "long-term", and "environment" are also borrowed from international law, specifically adapted from the definitions of humanitarian and environmental law, in the 1970s and 1990s.[107]

The damage must be massive ("severe") in all cases, being, alternatively or cumulatively, long-term or extensive. The mental element addressed there remains

---

[105] The proposal suggests that it will likely be necessary to also review the book Rules of Procedure and Evidence, to adapt it to environmental crime (Link: www.icc-cpi.int/sites/default/files/Publications/Rules-of-Procedure-and-Evidence.pdf. Accessed on: 17 Dec. 2024).

[106] Link: https://www.icc-cpi.int/sites/default/files/Publications/Elements-of-Crimes.pdf. Accessed on: 17 Dec. 2024.

[107] "The terms "severe", "widespread", "long-term", and "environment" are defined in paragraph 2 of Article 8 ter. The definitions are adapted from international humanitarian law and environmental law, as explained in the Panel's commentary. The terms "severe", "widespread" and "long-term" appear in the 1977 First Additional Protocol to the Geneva Conventions ('API') (Arts 35(3) and 55(1)), in Article 8(2)(b)(iv) of the Rome Statute, in the 1976 Convention on the Prohibition of Military or any other Hostile Use of Environmental Modification Techniques ("ENMOD"), and in the 1991 International Law Commission draft of an international crime of wilful and severe damage to the environment." (ICC. Assembly of States Parties, 2024, p. 10).

somewhat problematic, no more than for other crimes in the Statute, as the proposal itself reminds us.[108]

The project also notes that the crime is not intended for all human activities that cause environmental damage: the legality[109] of the conduct is then of interest, relegating the regulation of lawful and socially beneficial activities to other areas of law, respecting the position of criminal law as ultima ratio. There is also an appeal to environmental law for the definition of what is arbitrary ("wanton"), with this area of law pointing out, with its own tools, the existence of an imbalance between damages and social benefits.[110]

As can be seen, the definition of the Panel of Experts was fully maintained in the official proposal. The novelty focuses on the alteration of the elements of the crime, detailing a little more the conduct and the perpetrator.

Therefore, the same criticisms that the definition elaborated by the Panel of Experts receives are applicable to the Amendment Project currently at the ICC.

There is no doubt that ecocide meets the requirements of different theories of criminalisation, such as the principle of harm and the theory of human rights, fitting into the narrow focus of the Rome Statute. But, legitimacy as a crime is only part of the equation (Bertram, 2024, p. 2).

At the same time, the construction of an international crime comes from the legal gap existing in most countries—that is, local—of greater protection when massive damage to the environment occurs, which usually affects more than one nation. This interaction also occurs at the level of justification, as presented, when the proposals

108 "Article 30 provides the default mental element for Rome Statute crimes where no mental element is otherwise stated. With respect to consequences, the default standard has been interpreted to require an awareness of a near certainty that the consequences will occur. Given that environmental harms often cannot be anticipated with "near certainty", the Panel concluded that the default mens rea standard was too narrow and would not capture highly culpable conduct. (…). The proposed Art 8 ter specifies a mental element, displacing the default rule of Article 30. The standard is "knowledge that there is a substantial likelihood" of the prohibited environmental damage. The standard is akin to national law standards such as recklessness or dolus eventualis." (ICC. Assembly of States Parties, 2024, p. 11).

109 The requirement that the act be illegal, considering national and international laws, is more relevant for the former, as there are few prohibitive international norms in the criminal field: "For this reason, it is unsurprising that both the Belgian ecocide provision and the EU Directive require unlawfulness as a precondition for criminal liability. However, they define unlawfulness in relation to the wealth of administrative regulations in domestic or EU law, which is significantly broader than international law in this respect. Moreover, the EU Directive further contains an open clause that requalifies nominally law-abiding conduct as unlawful if a legal license was obtained by fraud, extortion, coercion or was otherwise in breach of "substantive legal requirements". The latter solution would also be thinkable at the international level, allowing ecocide to evolve dynamically with international environmental legal doctrines that clarify what counts as unlawful." (Bertram, 2024, p. 3).

110 "The term "wanton" employs a balancing test akin to the balancing test in Article 8(2)(b)(iv), the war crime of disproportionate attacks. However, the test is modified for a broader peacetime context. As noted by the Panel, the test refers to environmental principles, which balance long-term social, economic, and environmental harms and benefits, through the concept of sustainable development." (ICC. Assembly of States Parties, 2024, p. 12).

are based on arguments produced in the national and international spheres, highlighting the global character of ecocide.

What should be observed is the unmistakable demonstration of the current importance of the theme,[111] in view of the debates in various parliaments and specialised groups, with different approaches, evidently due to the visible massive damage to the environment and its most serious consequences, climate change. Such engagement is crucial for the concept of ecocide to take shape and gain strength (Voigt, 2021), towards codification as an instrument in favour of nature.[112]

References

Almeida, L. F. M. (2017). From the law of mother earth and integral development for the well-being Bolivian or from the ecocentrism of cocktail molotov. *Lisbon: Luso-Brazilian Legal Journal, 3*(5), 1057–1090.

Andrade, M. L. C. V. O., & Araes, C. R. (2021). After Mariana and Brumadinho: A discursive analysis of news about neglect. *GEL Journal, 18*(3), 264–284.

Asian Development Bank. (2005). *Country environmental analysis: Azerbaijan*. ADS. Retrieved December 18, 2024, from https://www.adb.org/sites/default/files/institutional-document/32178/aze-cea.pdf.

Beade, G. A. (2022). The crimes of danger and constitutional proportionality: A restructuring of criminal responsibility under the basic guidelines of the principle of proportionality. *Ius et Praxis, 28*(3), 191–201.

Bertram, D. A. (2024). *Towards an international crime of ecocide. TOAEP Policy Brief, 2024/157*. Retrieved December 13, 2024, from https://hdl.handle.net/1814/77482

Boldt, R. (2019). Ecocide, crime against humanity? *Bulletin of the Brazilian Institute of Criminal Sciences, 27*(326), 19–20. Retrieved May 10, 2025, from https://www.ibccrim.org.br/noticias/exibir/7183/

Brazil. Chamber of Deputies. (2023). *Bill No. 2.933, of June 5, 2023. Typifies the crime of ecocide, inserting it in Law No. 9.605, of February 12, 1998, which "provides for criminal and administrative sanctions derived from conducts and activities harmful to the environment, and gives other provisions"*. Retrieved December 14, 2024, from https://www.camara.leg.br/proposicoesWeb/fichadetramitacao?idProposicao=2367513

Brazil. Chamber of Deputies. (2024). *Bill No. 2.875, of 12 July 2024. Amends Law No. 9.605, of 12 February 1998, to typify ecocide as a crime*. Brasília, Chamber of Deputies. Retrieved December 14, 2024, from https://www.camara.leg.br/proposicoesWeb/prop_mostrarintegra?codteor=2454663&filename=PL%202875/2024

Calaça, I. Z. P., et al. (2018). Nature as a subject of rights: Bioethical analysis of the constitutions of Ecuador and Bolivia. *Latin American Journal of Bioethics, 18*(1), 155–171.

Chadha, S. K., & Singh, V. (2024). Ecocide: Should destruction of environment be punishable? *Journal of Higher Education Theory and Practice, 24*(2), 36–46. Retrieved January 10, 2025, from https://johetap.com/index.php/JHETP/article/download/3/3

[111] "The remarkable legal inscription of the rights of Mother Earth or Pachamama, in Ecuador and Bolivia, and the global campaigns for Earth law and ecocide law are inspiring and important" (Ray, 2016, p. 133).

[112] The challenges will undoubtedly be greater than those overcome in the adoption of the crime of aggression. This last process, however, serves as a learning experience for ecocide (Chin, 2023).

Chamber of Deputies. (2019a). *Bill No. 2.787, of 5 May 2019. Amends Law No. 9.605, of 12 February 1998, to typify the crime of ecocide and the criminal conduct of the person responsible for a dam break disaster; and provides other measures*. Brasília, Chamber of Deputies. Retrieved January 8, 2025, from https://www.camara.leg.br/proposicoesWeb/fichadetramitacao?idProposicao=2201529

Chamber of Deputies. (2019b). *Bill No. 2.787, of 5 May 2019. Amends Law No. 9.605, of 12 February 1998, to typify the crime of ecocide and the criminal conduct of the person responsible for a dam break disaster; and provides other measures*. Brasília, Chamber of Deputies. Retrieved January 8, 2025, from https://www.camara.leg.br/proposicoesWeb/prop_mostrarintegra?codteor=1744716&filename=PL+2787/2019

Chamber of Representatives of Belgium. (2020). *Resolution proposal: Aiming to include the crime of ecocide in the Rome Statute of the Criminal international and Belgian criminal law. DOC 55 1429/001*. Chamber 2°, 8 Jul. 2020. Retrieved June 4, 2025, from https://www.lachambre.be/FLWB/PDF/55/1429/55K1429001.pdf

Chiaramonte, X. (2023). Killing the house? On the problematic implications of ecocide. *Jura Gentium, 1*, 173–197.

Chin, S. (2023). Lessons learned from the adoption of the crime of aggression: Ecocide to chart its own path. In *'An international crime of ecocide: New perspectives' symposium*. UCLA. The Promise Institute for Human Rights. Retrieved December 16, 2024, from https://ecocidelaw.com/wp-content/uploads/2023/08/5-Chin-Lessons-learned-from-the-adoption-of-the-crime-of-aggression.pdf

Constitution of the Italian Republic, 1948. Retrieved December 18, 2024, from https://www.governo.it/it/costituzione-italiana/2836

Díaz, J. E. C. (2020). ¿Criminal or administrative responsibility of the legal entity?: Some scopes from the Law No. 30424. *Ius Inkarri, 9*(9), 403–427. Retrieved January 5, 2025, from https://revistas.urp.edu.pe/index.php/Inkarri/article/view/3693/6617

Dunlap, A. (2018). The 'solution' is now the 'problem': Wind energy, colonisation and the 'genocide-ecocide nexus' in the Isthmus of Tehuantepec, Oaxaca. *International Journal of Human Rights, 22*(4), 550–573.

European Parliament. (2022). *Human rights and democracy in the world—Annual report 2021*.

Federal Senate. (2019). *Opinion no. 29, of 2019. From the Environmental Committee, on bill no. 2787, of 2019, which amends law no. 9.605, of 12 February 1998, to typify the crime of ecocide and the delinquent conduct of the person responsible for a dam break disaster; and provides other measures*. Retrieved January 8, 2025, from https://legis.senado.leg.br/sdleg-getter/documento?dm=8023535&ts=1630423535915&disposition=inline

García, L. E. G. (2012). The environment in the Mexican legal system. *Amicus Curiae, 2*(3), 3.

Gomes, T. A. R. (2022). Law 13.606/2018: The (un)constitutional attempt to improve the enforceability of the tax credit. *Journal of the Federal Regional Court of the 1st Region, 34*(1). Retrieved May 12, 2025, from https://rtrf1.emnuvens.com.br/trf1/article/view/368

Gómez-Rodríguez, J.-M., Pérez, W. A. A., & Guevara, E. L. S. (2024). Ecocide in Mexico: Current situation and challenges. *KAIRÓS, Journal of Economic, Legal and Administrative Sciences, 7*(13), 126–144. Retrieved December 14, 2024, from https://kairos.unach.edu.ec/index.php/kairos/article/download/367/302

Heinze, L. C. (2019, September 18). *Amendment No. 1—CMA. Bill No. 2.787/2019*. Federal Senate. Retrieved January 8, 2025, from https://legis.senado.leg.br/sdleg-getter/documento?dm=8012552&ts=1630423535661&disposition=inline

House of Lords. (2023, November 30). *Ecocide Bill. Baroness Boycott. Introduce the crime of ecocide; and for connected purposes*. Retrieved January 5, 2025, from https://bills.parliament.uk/publications/53197/documents/4084

ICC. Assembly of States Parties. (2024, December 1). *Report of the Working Group on Amendments. ICC-ASP/23/26. Proposal submitted by Vanuatu to amend the Rome Statute. Annex II, Article 8ter Ecocide*. Retrieved December 7, 2024, from https://asp.icc-cpi.int/sites/default/files/asp_docs/ICC-ASP-23-26-ENG.pdf

Janones, A. (2019). *Opinion delivered in Plenary*. Bill No. 2.787/2019. Chamber of Deputies. Retrieved January 8, 2025, from https://www.camara.leg.br/proposicoesWeb/prop_mostrarintegra?codteor=1769205&filename=Parecer-CMADS-25-06-2019

Kersting, N. (2021). *On symbolism and beyond: Defining ecocide*. Völkerrechtsblog. Retrieved June, 2025, from https://voelkerrechtsblog.org/on-symbolism-and-beyond/

Ledezma, V. (2022, March 24). *Bill against ecocide will incorporate corporate responsibility*. ANA Bolivia. Retrieved May 10, 2025, from https://anabolivia.org/proyecto-de-ley-contra-el-ecocidio-incorporara-responsabilidad-empresarial/

Lennon, M. (2023, November 8). *Proposed Ecocide (Prevention) (Scotland) Bill*. Central Scotland Region. Retrieved December 17, 2024, from https://www.parliament.scot/-/media/files/legislation/proposed-members-bills/ecocide-consultation.pdf

Lennon, M.. (2024, November 12). *Proposed Ecocide (Prevention) (Scotland) Bill. Summary of consultation responses*. Retrieved December 17, 2024, from https://www.parliament.scot/-/media/files/legislation/proposed-members-bills/monica-lennon-ecocide-consultation-summary-2-(2).pdf

López, Z. R., & López, T. R. A. (2020). Ecocide in Mexico: Conceptualisation through an analysis of the national and international jurisdiction. *Scientific Journal, 5*(16), 246–267.

Maloney, M. (2016). Building an alternative jurisprudence for the earth: The international rights of nature tribunal. *Vermont Law Review, 41*(1), 129–142. Retrieved May 22, 2025, from http://www.readingfromtheleft.com/PDF/CochabambaDocuments.pdf

Mammadov, G. (2023). General situation of aggravation of environmental problems in Azerbaijan. *Journal of Endemism: Biodiversity & Environment, 1*(2), 7. Retrieved December 17, 2024, from https://ebe.wcu.edu.az/uploads/files/1.Mammadov_V1_No2.pdf

Martin-Chenut, K., Neyret, L., & Perruso, C. (2015). Towards the internationalisation of criminal environmental protection: From ecocrimes to ecocide. *International Law Review, 12*(2).

Matsuura, L. (2018). Eight out of ten laws were judged unconstitutional by the STF in 2017. In *Yearbook of Justice Brazil 2018*. Legal Consultant.

Ministry of Foreign Affairs of the Republic of Azerbaijan. (2016). *Illegal economic and other activities in the occupied territories of Azerbaijan*. Report by the Ministry of Foreign Affairs of the Republic of Azerbaijan. Retrieved December 18, 2024, from https://mfa.gov.az/files/shares/MFA%20Report%20on%20the%20occupied%20territories_March%202016.pdf

Penal Code for the Federal District. (2002, July 16). Retrieved December 14, 2024, from https://paot.org.mx/centro/codigos/df/pdf/2024/COD_PENAL_DF_11_01_2024.pdf

Penal Code for the State of Jalisco. (1982, September 2). Retrieved December 14, 2024, from https://mexico.justia.com/estatales/jalisco/codigos/codigo-penal-para-el-estado-libre-y-soberano-de-jalisco/

Pezzot, R., & Graff, J.-P. (2022). *Ecocide: Legal revolution or symbolism?* Völkerrechtsblog. Retrieved June 5, 2025, from https://voelkerrechtsblog.org/ecocide-legal-revolution-or-symbolism/

Piffer, C., & Miglioranzi De Rosso, A. L. (2019). Ecocide as an instrument of transnational environmental protection. *Point of View Legal, Caçador (SC), 8*(2), 114–125.

Political Constitution of the State of Bolivia. (2009, February 7). Retrieved May 2, 2025, from https://www.oas.org/dil/esp/constitucion_bolivia.pdf

Press Release 228/2021. (2021, November 18). *Reyes Galindo proposes initiative to sanction ecocide in Michoacán*. State Congress of Michoacán. Retrieved May 22, 2025, from http://congresomich.gob.mx/reyes-galindo-propone-iniciativa-para-sancionar-el-ecocidio-en-michoacan%EF%BB%BF/

Ray, G. (2016). Writing the ecocide-genocide knot: Indigenous knowledge and critical theory in the endgame. *South as a State of Mind, 8*, 1–41. Retrieved July 30, 2025, from http://www.documenta14.de/en/south/895_writing_the_ecocide_genocide_knot_indigenous_knowledge_and_critical_theory_in_the_endgame

Robinson, D. (2024). *Ecocide: A call to discuss some hard conundrums*. EJIL: Talk! Retrieved December 14, 2024, from https://www.ejiltalk.org/ecocide-a-call-to-discuss-some-hard-conundrums/

Sands, P., & Sow, D. F. (2021). *Independent expert panel for the legal definition of ecocide: Commentary and core text*. Stop Ecocide Foundation. Retrieved May 20, 2025, from https://static1.squarespace.com/static/5ca2608ab914493c64ef1f6d/t/60d7479cf8e7e5461534dd07/1624721314430/SE+Foundation+Commentary+and+core+text+revised+%281%29.pdf

Scottish Parliament. (2024, November 12). *Proposed Ecocide (Prevention) (Scotland) Bill*. Monica Lennon, Central Scotland, Scottish Labour. Retrieved December 14, 2024, from https://www.parliament.scot/bills-and-laws/proposals-for-bills/proposed-ecocide-prevention-scotland-bill

Senadores de México. (2021). *Sen. Raúl Paz (PAN) calls for prison sentences for ecocide* [Video]. YouTube. Retrieved June 1, 2025, from https://www.youtube.com/watch?v=UIlGAx6u_w8

Stop Ecocide International. (2020). *Top international lawyers to draft definition of "Ecocide"*. Retrieved May 20, 2025, from https://www.stopecocide.earth/prelaunch-expert-drafting-panel

Supreme Court of Justice of the Nation. (2006). *The Mexican legal system* (4th ed.). Supreme Court of Justice of the Nation. Retrieved May 22, 2025, from https://www.scjn.gob.mx/sites/default/files/material_didactico/2016-11/Sistema-Juridico-Mexicano.pdf

Tweede Kamer der Staten-Generaal. (2023–2024). *Legislative proposal by member Van Raan amending the Criminal Code and the BES Criminal Code in connection with the criminalisation of ecocide (Ecocide Criminalisation Act) (Bill 36 475)*. Retrieved January 7, 2025, from https://www.tweedekamer.nl/downloads/document?id=2023D47626

Vieira, A. (2019, September 18). *Opinion of the Environment Committee. Bill No. 2.787/2019*. Federal Senate. Retrieved January 8, 2025, from https://legis.senado.leg.br/sdleg-getter/documento?dm=8013400&ts=1630423535730&disposition=inline

Voigt, C. (2021). *"Ecocide" as an international crime: Personal reflections on options and choices*. EJIL: Talk! Retrieved June 4, 2025, from https://www.ejiltalk.org/ecocide-as-an-international-crime-personal-reflections-on-options-and-choices/

Winter, E. (2024). Stop ecocide international's blueprint for ecocide is compromised by anthropocentrism: A new architect must be found. *Israel Law Review, 57*(1), 175–209. https://doi.org/10.1017/S0021223722000218. Retrieved January 10, 2025.

Yébenes, M. O. (2024). Climate change, ESG criteria and recent regulation: Challenges and opportunities. *Eurasian Economic Review, 14*(1), 87–120. Retrieved December 14, 2024, from https://link.springer.com/content/pdf/10.1007/s40822-023-00251-x.pdf

Chapter 7
The Path of Ecocide as an International Crime

Ecocide as a norm has been a reality since the 1990s, with the first codifications in Vietnam and the former Soviet republics, undergoing an increase in number and legal quality in the last decade. The practical difficulties in defining it, however, have been the subject of debates since the discussions in the *International Law Commission*, in the 1980s. It is certain that, in the face of the worsening of environmental issues and the mismatch with national and international legislation, the topic has gained strength in parliaments in the form of bill proposals and, subsequently, existing laws.

The obstacles to the creation of the most serious environmental crime[1] were attacked differently by States, with greater or lesser levels of detail regarding the offense, significant variations in penalties and approaches (ecocentric or anthropocentric). What remains constant is the desire to prosecute conducts that cause massive damage to the environment.

It is also noted that national legislators seek as source/foundation for the law proposals an international focus, in consonance with the generally transboundary characteristic of those damages. This fact imposes a systematic investigation of the

[1] The very idea of the crime "ecocide" is criticised by some authors, as a construction linked to historical-colonial contexts, to the detriment of the Global South: "It is thus important to situate the proposed new crime of ecocide within the histories and continuation of colonial practices, as these practices are intimately tied to different environmental injustices. This is even more important given that critical legal scholars have shown how the ICL project has not only been silent on colonial power dynamics but has actually reproduced colonial and racial legacies by reinforcing problematic assumptions about the Global South as a place of disorder, backwardness, and lawlessness needing external interventions, including in the form of international criminal trials ending the local 'culture of impunity'. While it may be too early to say, the dangers of employing the same 'civilising' discourse in relation to the entangled socio-ecological crises are not to be taken lightly." (Cusato, Eliana, & Jones, E. (2024). The 'imbroglio' of ecocide: A political economic analysis. *Leiden Journal of International Law, 37*(1), 42–61. doi:10.1017/S0922156523000468. Accessed on: 10 Jan. 2025, p. 50).

D. A. Brochado Neto, *Ecocide*, https://doi.org/10.1007/978-3-032-07757-8_7

existing definitions and in legal proceedings, in order to verify how the identified problems were attempted to be overcome.

Before this study, however, it is worth asking: Will the International Criminal Court be the most qualified Court for the task of combating massive damage to the environment?

The Permanent Court of International Justice (1922–1946), predecessor of the International Court of Justice (ICJ)[2], inaugurated an era today characterised by the multiplication of international courts,[3] segmented and thematic (Lima & De Andrade, 2015, pp. 373–398). The fragmentation of law is not reflected only in the proliferation of Courts but also in the creation of specialized normative systems (Lima & De Andrade, 2015, pp. 373–398), sometimes resulting in the formation of "self-contained regimes",[4] with their own norms. For the environmental field, this compartmentalisation is more useful, given the difficulty in uniformly regulating issues of environmental protection.[5]

In this context, simultaneously with the increasing attention given to the environment, the idea of a specific international Court for the matter developed. The first movement in this direction took place in 1986, in Rome, during the International Forum on "Justice and Environment". The need for the creation of a supranational

---

[2] Link: https://www.icj-cij.org/en.

[3] The fragmentation of international law is seen by some as a product of the proliferation of international courts, corresponding, in theory, to the development of divergent and conflicting jurisprudential orientations. To maintain the unity of law, it should be kept within the competence of the International Court of Justice, to assume customary international law and to interpret treaties exclusively. For others, the multiplication of international courts determines a progress of international law: the specialisation of jurisdiction would limit the overlap of competences, creating a legal fabric connected by common principles (Cassese, Sabino (2009). *I Tribunali di Babele: i giudici alla ricerca di un nuovo ordine globale*. Roma: Donzelli editore, p. 8).

[4] These regimes are mainly characterised by specialisation in relation to the norms of general international law, as well as their own accountability systems, such as, for example, the World Trade Organisation. On self-contained regimes, see: Simma, Bruno, & Pulkowski, D. (2006). Of planets and the universe: Self-contained regimes in international law. *European Journal of International Law, 17*(3), 483–529, p. 488. Available at: https://academic.oup.com/ejil/article-pdf/17/3/483/8734931/chl015.pdf. Accessed on: 10 Jun. 2025.

[5] Despite international disputes over environmental issues being taken to existing international courts, "there is a severe limitation to the environmental defence itself. The ICJ, although it has already advanced towards a jurisprudential construction that protects the environment, is an example of these limitations. (...). It should be noted that the ICJ itself established, in 1993, in the face of environmental demands that were already emerging at the time, a permanent special chamber for issues related to the Environment—the Special Environment Chamber. In the early 90s, of seven cases under analysis by the Court, two involved environmental issues. The existence of this chamber, however, does not bind the litigating parties to resort to it, it is just an alternative" (Lima, Lucas Carlos, & De Andrade, M. C. (2015). An international court for the environment and its insertion in the debate about the fragmentation of international law. *Revista da Faculdade de Direito da UFMG, 67*, 373–398, p. 378. Available at: https://web.direito.ufmg.br/revista/index.php/revista/article/view/1745. Accessed on: 12 Jun. 2025).

environmental protection agency and a global environmental Court was expressed,[6] with the aim to protect the environment and impose sanctions on those who cause environmental damage.[7]

Three years after the Forum, the Foundation of the International Court of the Environment was established,[8] led by Italian Amedeo Postiglione,[9] with the aim of developing, among others, an International Environmental Tribunal. Regarding international criminal law, the social organisation supports the creation of an International Environmental Tribunal ad hoc or the inclusion of environmental crimes in the International Criminal Court.

As for the construction of a specific tribunal on the environment, there are criticisms in the doctrine[10] against this initiative. Among the main arguments, the fragmentation of international law with the multiplication of Courts, the scope of international law matters beyond the environmental theme that touch on the demands and the existence of tribunals that, in theory, already have the capacity to deal with these issues are pointed out (Lima & De Andrade, 2015, pp. 373–398).

Among the existing Courts with an environmental theme, the International Tribunal for the Law of the Sea (ITLOS) is mentioned as a means of resolving disputes on this matter.[11] Even so, the target of disputes—whether in specific spaces on environmental law or traditional ones, such as the ICJ[12]—are predominantly nations, unrelated to criminal issues and punishments for natural persons.

---

[6] For some authors, a new Ecocide Convention could be negotiated: "As part of this Convention, an International Environmental Court could be convened to hear cases involving transnational environmental crime. Under this proposal, the Convention could include ecocentric provisions relating to, for example, restitution and recovery for the affected territory, or injunctions to prevent further ecological damage. In addition, the Convention would not be bound by the prior restrictions of the Rome Statute, and could require a less stringent mens rea" (Greene, Anastacia, 2019). The campaign to make ecocide an international crime: Quixotic quest or moral imperative? *Fordham Environmental Law Review, 30*(3), 1–44, p. 44).

[7] Pirro, D. (2006). Project for an International Court of the Environment–Origins and Development. In T. Greiber (Coord.), *Judges and the Rule of Law: creating links—environment, human rights and poverty* (pp. 13–20). IUCN Publications Service Unit.

[8] *International Court of the Environment Foundation* (ICEF).

[9] For Postiglione, the environment is a substantive human right, decisive to the fate of the planet, related to information, participation and access, whose protection is the only means of ensuring respect for human rights (Postiglione, Amedeo (2010). Human rights and the environment. *The International Journal of Human Rights, 14*(4), 524–541, p. 534).

[10] For example, see: Pedersen, Ole W. (2012). An international environmental court and international legalism. *Journal of Environmental Law, 24*(3), 547–558. Available at: https://academic.oup.com/jel/article-abstract/24/3/547/391058?login=false. Accessed on: 10 Jun. 2025.

[11] The disputes relating to the Court Convention concern the delimitation of maritime zones, navigation, conservation and management of living sea resources, protection and preservation of the marine environment and marine scientific research (International Tribunal for the Law of the Sea—ITLOS. Available at: https://www.itlos.org/en/. Accessed on: 10 Jun. 2025).

[12] For example, the International Court of Justice, in complex issues involving environmental themes, makes use of experts from the area, who provide "the *input* scientific to the collegiate body and, thus, contribute, ultimately, to the legitimacy of the sentence" (Lima, Lucas Carlos, & De Andrade, M. C. (2015). An international court for the environment and its insertion in the debate

The fact that the International Criminal Court is the only—criminal—permanent court in operation, dedicated to the prosecution of the most serious crimes, judging individuals, in addition to having initially considered—when drafting the *The Code*—the inclusion of environmental issues, makes it the most viable place to receive a crime against the environment.[13]

Considering the focus of this book, the analysis will stick to the possibility of including ecocide in the ICC, taking into account national approaches (laws and bill proposals) and international (proposal to amend the Rome Statute) to the main obstacles to the creation of the crime.

It is known that, in the context of international legislation, there is a delicate balance between the imprecision of the definition and the specificity.[14] Among national initiatives, few have presented detailed deepening of the crime, with explanatory norms of certain terms (like "serious environmental impact"[15] or "significant damage"[16]), which makes explicit two aspects: influence of the debates that took place on the international level (when they encountered similar difficulties) and inconsistency in defining the offence. These two characteristics converge insofar as the very conduct— massive destruction of the environment—understood as a crime was born from an international event, the attacks with Agent Orange, in the Vietnam War.

Since then, it is also at the international level that the main contours of the crime[17] (of which undoubtedly national legislators take advantage), culminating in the most

---

about the fragmentation of international law. *Revista da Faculdade de Direito da UFMG, 67*, 373–398, p. 387. Available at: https://web.direito.ufmg.br/revista/index.php/revista/article/view/1745. Accessed on: 12 Jun. 2025).

[13] Ecocide is also indicated as a possible crime within the study for a Mercosul Criminal Court: "there are elements that we they conclude that criminal organisations are heavily involved in the practice of environmental crimes, a result of corporate institutional arrangements that seek to deconstruct/disregard the legal instruments of environmental protection, requiring specialisation of their definition, operational means of prevention and confrontation, given that such behaviours have been causing serious environmental damage, for the current and future generations" (Marinho, Ronaldo. (2019). *Mercosul Criminal Court: confronting transnational criminal organisations*. Lumen juris, p. 137).

[14] On the one hand, if a provision is too vague, the States will not be willing to agree, due to the risk of its interpretation being unpredictable. On the other hand, it is difficult to obtain consensus from a significant number of States on a very specific wording, since a more open formulation can encompass more nuances and thus accommodate slightly different views among the potential signatories: "*In international criminal law however, the principle of legality adds another dimension to the debate, which the panel failed to address appropriately. Defining the criminal acts cannot be left to prosecutors or judges, whose sphere of responsibility is and must be limited to interpretation of the law*" (Kersting, Natascha. (2021, July). On Symbolism and Beyond: Defining Ecocide. *Völkerrechtsblog*. Available at: https://voelkerrechtsblog.org/on-symbolism-and-beyond/. Accessed: Jun. 2025).

[15] Art. 333, §§ 1° and 2°, of the Colombian Penal Code.

[16] Art. 4, of the Bill on environmental crimes of Chile.

[17] For Pellet, the concern is the legal pointillism that excessively limits the discretion of judges, especially in the field of international criminal law, when "the criminal imagination of men is, unfortunately, limitless and it is impossible to foresee in advance the forms that the crimes of

recent proposal to amend the Rome Statute. It is the reactivation of the debate (started in *The Code*) about the inclusion, in times of peace, of an environmental crime in the international criminal structure, as interest of the global community itself, to the detriment of the merely local cut.

7.1 The Problems of Ecocide in the International Criminal Court

Despite the criticisms of old and recent attempts to define ecocide, the modern maturity of understanding the crime is notorious, as seen by the profusion of parliaments, governments, and researchers who discuss it. The question that arises is: How ready is the crime to be seriously considered for inclusion in the list of crimes within the jurisdiction of the International Criminal Court?[18]

The analysis about the suitability of amendment projects to the Statute of Rome goes through the study of the mechanisms of modification of the Treaty itself,[19]

tomorrow will take. It would certainly have been wiser to stick to very general and 'open' definitions and to leave it to the jurisprudence and the wisdom of the Judges to specify the 'constituent elements'" (Pellet, Alain. (2003). For the International Criminal Court, anyway!—Some remarks on its jurisdiction and referral. *International Criminal Law Review*, *1*(1–2), 91–110, p. 99).

[18] One could question the opposite: would the ICC be ready to receive a crime with a purely environmental bias, considering that the Court is not specialised in social justice, let alone environmental?: "ICC judges have been eager to emphasise that the Court's mandate is limited to retributive justice in the form of assessing the charges brought against the individual at trial and excludes 'political or even humanitarian goals', such as 'to restore social justice and to heal the wounds' of the afflicted communities. Yet, the insights from critical environmental law scholarship suggest that normative choices are inevitable when environmental justice is concerned. As discussed, even if the ICC adopts the linear and reductionist mentality of IEL and assumes away the complexities of environmental assessments and their socio-ecological implications, this would still be a normative choice". (Minkova, Liana Georgieva. (2024). Ecocide, sustainable development and critical environmental law insights. *Journal of International Criminal Justice*, *22*(1), 81–97, p. 96).

[19] The practical issue of inserting/amending a new provision in the Rome Statute is provided for in the Treaty itself, allowing for deep changes (article 121) and of an institutional nature (art. 122). In the former, a proposal from at least 1 (one) State Party is required, which will be submitted to the Secretary-General of the United Nations, who is responsible for communicating to the other signatories (article 121 [1]). After 3 (three) months of this notification, the State Parties will decide, by majority, whether the proposal should be examined (article 121 [2]). The quorum to accept a change is 2/3 of the State Parties (article 121 [3]), valid for all who ratify it, when it comes to arts. 5, 6, 7 and 8 (the crimes under the Court's jurisdiction), 1 (one) year after acceptance (article 121 [5]). It should be remembered that the Statute has already undergone reform, originally provided for in article 123, in order to reassess the list of crimes in article 5. The first Review Conference of the Rome Statute of the International Criminal Court took place in Kampala, capital of Uganda, between May and June 2010 (Link: https://asp.icc-cpi.int/reviewconference/rome-statute-amendment-proposals. Accessed on: 10 Jun. 2025), where, among other things, the elements of the crime and the crime of aggression were discussed, the latter activated in 2017 (Assembly of States Parties to the International Criminal Court, 16th Session, New York, 14 Dec. 2017. Available at: https://asp.icc-cpi.int/sites/asp/files/asp_docs/ASP16/ICC-ASP-16-22-ENG.pdf. Accessed on: 10 Jun.

considering the thematic compatibility[20] and structural of the new crime. The most recent change to the Statute—inclusion of the crime of aggression—had an advantage, as there was already a "space reservation",[21] waiting for a better definition, which came a posteriori. Including ecocide will be much more complex. For this book, what matters is the current level of understanding of ecocide and the problems that have prevented—and prevent—its recognition as an international crime to this day.

The proposal of the *Stop Ecocide Foundation*, formalised with the Assembly of Parties in 2024, reflects this new moment of understanding about ecocide. Not forgetting the origins of the crime, the Panel of experts incorporated into the document current concerns,[22] seeking to draft a wording compatible with existing international documents on the reported themes, especially the Rome Statute.

However, in addition to embracing the structural problems of the Statute, the project encounters its own challenges, similar to those revealed in the existing and proposed national crimes. When it comes to environmental crimes, in the sense of serious and extensive damage[23] to the environment, there are problems in adjusting behaviours to a single universal definition.[24] The notion of massive environmental

2025). In addition, Trinidad Tobago, in 2009, proposed the inclusion of the crime of international drug trafficking (Trinidad Tobago, Proposal for Amendment to the Rome Statute, C.N.737.2009. TREATIES-9, 29 Oct. 2009. Available at: https://treaties.un.org/doc/Publication/CN/2009/CN.737.2009-Eng.pdf. Accessed on: 10 Jun. 2025).

[20] There is no material prohibition in the Rome Statute to the amendment of any theme, once the procedures set out in articles 121 to 123 of the document are followed.

[21] Chin, Shirleen. (2023). Lessons Learned from the Adoption of the Crime of Aggression: Ecocide to Charter its own Path. *'An International Crime of Ecocide: New Perspectives' Symposium*. UCLA. The Promise Institute for Human Rights. Available at: https://ecocidelaw.com/wp-content/uploads/2023/08/5-Chin-Lessons-learned-from-the-adoption-of-the-crime-of-aggression.pdf. Accessed on: 16 Dec. 2024.

[22] In defining the term "*widespread*" (generalised), the Panel justified that the requirement, for recognition of the crime of ecocide, of setting a certain geographical area is inadequate, when it comes to damage to certain climate systems, for example, which do not have predefined spaces (Sands, Phillipe, & Sow, D. F. (2021). *Independent expert panel for the legal definition of ecocide: Commentary and core text*. Stop Ecocide Foundation, p. 10. Available at: https://static1.squarespace.com/static/5ca2608ab914493c64ef1f6d/t/60d7479cf8e7e5461534dd07/1624721314430/SE+Foundation+Commentary+and+core+text+revised+%281%29.pdf. Accessed on: 20 May. 2025).

[23] The very notion of harm "is an evolving concept that reflects the diverse and contested aspects of our individual and collective lived experience. While harm, like crime, is a socially constructed process, it retains a substantially broader theoretical and imaginative scope, which enables zemiologists to challenge presupposed understandings, attitudes, perceptions, and experiences that might otherwise be neglected". (Burns, Reece (2023). From meaning to ecocide: The value of phenomenology for green criminology. *Critical Criminology, 31*(4), 1137–1154, p. 1138).

[24] Indeed, "there is no single definition or meaning of what environmental crimes are either in national legal systems or in international law. Furthermore, much has been discussed about the question of which acts or omissions that cause environmental harm should be criminalised and how to ascertain which social harms should form part of this definition" (Lora, Libia Arenal (2021). The legal regulation of crimes against the environment in international law: Challenges for

damage for legal purposes has transactional and intergenerational implications,[25] as does the damage itself. All of this results in cost, which is commonly transferred to future generations.[26] The technical and political difficulties, therefore, merge.[27]

The definition proposed by the *Stop Ecocide Foundation*—like all national definitions —bears little resemblance to the concept of genocide, the inspiration for the term ecocide.[28] Moving away from this and crimes against humanity, with the intention of avoiding the technical restrictions of both crimes, the Panel of experts sought to take advantage of the symbolic capital of the term "genocide",[29] but placing it closer to an ecocentric view, despite not being so in practice. According to the wording of the norm, the crime allows a cost-benefit analysis in the case of lawful environmental damage[30] (limiting the *actus reus* to "unlawful" acts to be defined by

---

the definition of ecocide as an international crime. *Anuario Iberoamericano de Derecho Internacional Penal, 9*, 1–20, p. 18).

[25] Public interest has been selectively used worldwide to establish future generations as victims of environmental crimes: "A vital concept, especially in regards to human interest, is the notion of intergenerational equity. What are the implications of such concepts in regards to the notion of Earth Rights and addressing the needs of the nonhuman environmental victim? Here the problem once again rests upon both what are considered the essential attributes of this sort of victim, and over what time period" (White, Rob (2016). Four problems for specialist courts in dealing with nonhuman environmental victims. In T. Spapens, R. White, & W. Huisman (Eds.), *Environmental crime in transnational context: Global issues in green enforcement and criminology* (pp. 139–153). Routledge, p. 148).

[26] Environmental crime is usually perceived with low value by magistrates and judges, as objectively reflected in the outcomes of sentences, "although this is due to a variety of definitional, investigatory, evidentiary and social reasons, and there is some indication that this is changing" (White, Rob (2016). Four problems for specialist courts in dealing with nonhuman environmental victims. In T. Spapens, R. White, & W. Huisman (Eds.), *Environmental crime in transnational context: Global issues in green enforcement and criminology* (pp. 139–153). Routledge, p. 139).

[27] Arifin points out four groups of challenges to the construction of ecocide: definition and scope; legal and jurisdictional obstacles; corporate responsibility and; political resistance (Arifin, R., et al. (2024). Ecocide as the serious crime: A discourse on global environmental protection. In *IOP Conference Series: Earth and Environmental Science*. IOP Publishing. Available at: https://iopscience.iop.org/article/10.1088/1755-1315/1355/1/012004/meta. Accessed on: 10 Jan 2025).

[28] "The essence of genocide is the desire to rid the world of specific groups, as reflected in the protected group and specific intent requirements. There is nothing 'group-like' about the definition of Ecocide (…). And it would be neither desirable nor practically possible to limit the crime to the destruction of specific groups of animals or plants. But the proposed crime is not a form of genocide; it is much closer in nature and structure to a crime against humanity" (Heller, Kevin Jon (2021). Skeptical thoughts on the proposed crime of "ecocide" (that isn't). *Opinio Juris*. Available at: http://opiniojuris.org/2021/06/23/skeptical-thoughts-on-the-proposed-crime-of-ecocide-that-isnt/. Accessed on: 12 Jun; 2025).

[29] Heller, Kevin Jon (2021). Skeptical thoughts on the proposed crime of "ecocide" (that isn't). *Opinio Juris*. Available at: http://opiniojuris.org/2021/06/23/skeptical-thoughts-on-the-proposed-crime-of-ecocide-that-isnt/. Accessed on: 12 Jun; 2025.

[30] "In sum, you either take an ecocentric view (as implicit in the term "ecocide") and then prohibit and criminalise any (lawful or not) serious and intentional environmental damage, or you opt for a more anthropocentric view (allowing, inter alia, for a cost-benefit analysis) but then do not, in fact, advocate a crime of ecocide" (Ambos, Kai (2021). Protecting the environment through interna-

national legislation), that is, as assumed by the Panel itself,[31] it is not a crime to cause "serious and widespread or long-term damage to the environment", as long as humans benefit sufficiently from the destruction.[32]

The need to demonstrate the agent's intention—in the Amendment Proposal—goes beyond the knowledge that their actions will cause damage to the environment, but also that the same damage will be clearly excessive in relation to the anticipated social and economic benefits.[33] In addition to the evidentiary difficulty, "negligence" (*wanton*), understood as "reckless disregard", is confused with eventual intent,[34] when the author assumes the risks (is indifferent to the possibility of damage occurring), which may bring incompatibility with the text of the Rome Statute.[35]

tional criminal law? *EJIL: Talk!*. Available at: https://www.ejiltalk.org/protecting-the-environment-through-international-criminal-law/. Accessed on: 9 May. 2025).

[31] "b. 'Unlawful or wanton acts' - This second threshold is necessary because not all acts likely to cause severe and widespread or longterm damage to the environment are illegitimate, or even undesirable. International criminal law, like environmental law, must permit legitimate development" (Sands, Phillipe, & Sow, D. F. (2021). *Independent expert panel for the legal definition of ecocide: Commentary and core text.* Stop Ecocide Foundation, p. 10. Available at: https://static1.squarespace.com/static/5ca2608ab914493c64ef1f6d/t/60d7479cf8e7e5461534dd07/1624721314430/SE+Foundation+Commentary+and+core+text+revised+%281%29.pdf. Accessed on: 20 May. 2025).

[32] Heller, Kevin Jon (2021). Skeptical thoughts on the proposed crime of "ecocide" (that isn't). *Opinio Juris*. Available at: http://opiniojuris.org/2021/06/23/skeptical-thoughts-on-the-proposed-crime-of-ecocide-that-isnt/. Accessed on: 12 Jun; 2025.

[33] Article 8 ter, 1 and 2 (a), of the Amendment Proposal (Sands, Phillipe, & Sow, D. F. (2021). *Independent expert panel for the legal definition of ecocide: Commentary and core text.* Stop Ecocide Foundation, p. 10. Available at: https://static1.squarespace.com/static/5ca2608ab914493c64ef1f6d/t/60d7479cf8e7e5461534dd07/1624721314430/SE+Foundation+Commentary+and+core+text+revised+%281%29.pdf. Accessed on: 20 May. 2025).

[34] The Panel, mindful of Art. 30 of the Statute, decided to expand the understanding of *mens rea*, to punish, as well as those who commit the crime with the will to do so, the agent who acts with eventual intent, that is, with awareness of a substantial probability of the occurrence of serious and widespread or long-term damage: "This mens rea is sufficiently onerous to ensure that only those persons with significant culpability for grave damage to the environment will be held responsible" (Sands, Phillipe, & Sow, D. F. (2021). *Independent expert panel for the legal definition of ecocide: Commentary and core text.* Stop Ecocide Foundation, p. 10. Available at: https://static1.squarespace.com/static/5ca2608ab914493c64ef1f6d/t/60d7479cf8e7e5461534dd07/1624721314430/SE+Foundation+Commentary+and+core+text+revised+%281%29.pdf. Accessed on: 20 May. 2025).

[35] In addition to the facts that the concepts of "recklessness" and "eventual intent" cannot be equated and there are numerous different definitions for each of them, "*the actual wording of the proposed crime—'knowledge that there is a substantial likelihood'—seems to entail a higher (cognitive) threshold than recklessness or 'dolus eventualis' for the very use of the term 'knowledge'. In other words, if the drafters had clearly wanted to propose a lower subjective threshold they should have formulated the subjective elements of the crime more straightforwardly*" (Ambos, Kai (2021). Protecting the environment through international criminal law? *EJIL: Talk!*. Available at: https://www.ejiltalk.org/protecting-the-environment-through-international-criminal-law/. Accessed on: 9 May. 2025).

The difficulty of punishing perpetrators of environmental damage is exacerbated, in the ICC, by the Court's operational structure. According to its Statute, the inclusion of a new crime would imply, out of respect for the principle of legality (articles 24 and 121 [5]), a temporal and territorial limiter, by allowing prosecution only for conduct committed after 1 year of the amendment's ratification by the countries, in addition to restricting its application to nationals of States Parties that accept the legal change.

The principle of legality will lead to the same consequences in countries where ecocide is typified, especially regarding the non-retroactivity[36] of the norm (*in pejus*). However, the restrictions existing in the ICC regarding territorial (*ratione loci*) and personal (*ratione personae*) competences are overly exclusive, when it comes to massive environmental crimes.

Furthermore, the complementarity of the Court, in relation to national criminal jurisdictions (article 1 of the Rome Statute), requires that international crimes within the ICC's jurisdiction also be crimes in the States Parties,[37] and, mainly, there is procedural forwarding in these.[38] This requirement results in a delayed effective exercise by the international court, a delay that is fatal to the investigation of environmental damage, when prompt repair is sought.

Meanwhile, the Office of the Prosecutor (OTP) of the Court conducted two public consultations to develop a Policy Paper with the aim of promoting accountability for environmental crimes under the Rome Statute. The prosecutor, Karim AA Khan KC, announced the first consultation[39] in February 2024, pointing out that the document will be based, in addition to the Statute, on applicable environmental treaties,

[36] The non-retroactivity of the norm, in international criminal law, is a recent topic, exclusive to the ICC (Article 24 of the Rome Statute), since it is a permanent Court, unlike the others, ad hoc, whose justification for punishing for uncodified crimes rested on the criminalisation of conduct defined by international customs. Otherwise, "How to justify the punishment of conduct carried out even before the creation of the court that judged them, as is the case with the Nuremberg Tribunal? Doesn't this hypothesis precisely constitute what is called a 'court of exception'?" (De Carli, C. V. (2014). Grammar of international criminal law: The languages of crime and punishment. *Cadernos do Programa de Pós-Graduação em Direito/UFRGS, 9*(1), 370–394. Available at: https://www.seer.ufrgs.br/ppgdir/article/download/42767/35171. Accessed on: 12 Jun. 2025).

[37] The preamble states: "Recalling that it is the duty of each State to exercise its respective criminal jurisdiction over those responsible for international crimes" (Decree 4.388/2002, Rome Statute. Available at: http://www.planalto.gov.br/ccivil_03/decreto/2002/d4388.htm. Accessed on: 14 Jun. 2025).

[38] Thus, "being subsidiary to national jurisdiction, the Court cannot intervene in cases that have been investigated and judged internally by the States" (Fabel, Luciana Machado Teixeira., Costa, Beatriz Souza., & Massad, Fernando Antonio. (2022, March). Ecocide in the International Criminal Court: analysis of the feasibility of the court's jurisdiction in cases of mining waste dam breaks. *Legal Journal (FURB), 25*(58), e9905, p. 10. Available at: https://bu.furb.br/ojs/index.php/juridica/article/view/9905. Accessed on: 25 Jun. 2025).

[39] ICC. Office of the Prosecutor. (2024, February 16). *The Office of the Prosecutor launches public consultation on a new policy initiative to advance accountability for environmental crimes under the Rome Statute*. Available at: https://www.icc-cpi.int/news/office-prosecutor-launches-public-consultation-new-policy-initiative-advance-accountability-0. Accessed on: 15 Jan. 2025.

rules of customary international law, and jurisprudence from other international and national courts.

The second public consultation[40] was launched in December 2024. The development of the new document aims to guide the Office to ensure a systematic approach to dealing with environmental crimes from the beginning of the preliminary examination process to the investigations and proceedings, according to the draft[41] previously presented.[42]

The structural criticisms of the ICC, however, cannot compromise the discussion about a crime against massive environmental damage.[43] It is incongruous, in the current state of compression of the importance of a healthy environment for all living beings (including humanity), the existence of a criminal court for the most serious international crimes, absent a formal crime—and, therefore, any process[44]—for the massive destruction of that same environment.

Initially, it is necessary to verify whether the argument of neocolonialism in the ICC's performance, over the last 20 years, can undermine the pretensions of the existence of a truly international crime, such as ecocide. Once this stage is overcome, it is necessary to analyse the functioning of the Court, in conjunction with the peculiarities of environmental crime.

---

[40] ICC. Office of the Prosecutor. (2024, December 18). *ICC Office of the Prosecutor launches second public consultation on a policy initiative to advance accountability for environmental crimes under the Rome Statute*. Available at: https://www.icc-cpi.int/news/icc-office-prosecutor-launches-second-public-consultation-policy-initiative-advance. Accessed on: 15 Jan. 2025.

[41] Link: https://www.icc-cpi.int/sites/default/files/2024-12/2024-12-18-OTP-Policy-Environmental-Crime.pdf. Accessed on: 15 Jan. 2025.

[42] To broaden the reach of the consultation, the Office, coordinated by Professor Kevin Jon Heller, called upon the Promise Institute Europe, linked to the Law School of the University of California (UCLA), to collect as many opinions and technical comments as possible. This Author, representing Unichristus (Brazil), and Gustavo Beade, for the Universidad Austral de Chile, were the co-Hosts for Latin America and the Caribbean.

[43] In terms of *ratione materiae* scope, the introduction of this crime in the Rome Statute is intended to develop existing law, extending the protection of the environment by international criminal law beyond times of armed conflict to times of peace (Negri, Stefania (2022). On meteors and comets: Is the crime of ecocide back to stay? Environmental crimes at the interface of philosophy, the law of state responsibility and international criminal law. *International Criminal Law Review, 1*(aop), 1–30, p. 28).

[44] "It is distressing to contemplate why persons are investigated, prosecuted and punished for various crimes such as theft, to give just one example, whereas they are frequently not investigated, prosecuted and punished for mass atrocities (core crimes) which, besides endangering international peace and security, cause immense suffering and hardship to many human beings and to humankind in general" (Soler, Christopher., et al. (2019). *The global prosecution of core crimes under international law*. TMC Asser Press).

7.2 The Argument of Neocolonialism

Emerging with the advancement of the understanding of international criminal law, allied to the need to promote a permanent Court, respectful of the general principles of criminal law (especially legality and non-retroactivity), with a list of crimes that reached the most serious conduct against peace and security, the International Criminal Court realised the UN's aspiration[45] for a judgement—almost[46]—supranational, in the criminal field. The judicial repression of international crimes accompanied the evolution in the very relations between States, from an international law of coexistence to one of cooperation (Pasquali, 2019, pp. 2–51).

The Rome Statute has a significant number of countries that have ratified it, spread across all continents of the planet. There is no privilege among the States Parties, with regard to judges, procedures, exceptions.[47] Despite this universal vocation,[48] the very legal construction of the Court, located in The Hague, privileges Anglo-Saxon law, even if not expressly so.

However, the Court's performance in the 20 years following its establishment was marked, especially with regard to the cases investigated and prosecuted, by

---

[45] The Rome Statute materialises 'the utopia of an international criminal judge', "*it represents, at the same time, a point of arrival and departure, both of legal and non-legal culture, both of reflection and dogmatic comparison, concretising the effort of the international legislator to modify 'the image [...] of a very fluid and uncertain subject, constantly searching for its own dogmatic identity and 'prisoner' of a continuous tension between the obligation of fidelity to some cornerstones of criminal law of Enlightenment-liberal derivation (legality of crimes and punishments, criminal law of the 'fact', personal criminal responsibility* etc.*) and the need to take into account its own peculiarities (mostly customary or contractual nature of international law, particular heinousness of crimes, commission mostly on a large scale of the same* etc.*)'. In this sense, we can speak of a commitment aimed at achieving a qualitative leap in the face of an international criminal law perceived by many as 'physiologically derogatory with respect to the fundamental guarantees underlying the general principles of liberal-style criminal law*'" (Di Landro, Andrea. (2018). *Responsibility for authorised activities in the areas of environment and territory: Penal and extra-penal protection tools*. G Giappichelli Publisher, p. 1).

[46] The principle of complementarity in the ICC implies that its action will only take place when it is not possible—for various reasons—to achieve a fair trial in the state of origin of the crime (Article 1, of the Rome Statute). Thus, in theory, the jurisdiction of the Court does not overlap with the national one.

[47] The intervention of the Security Council, provided for in the Statute, is the most direct possible form of interference by a State in the activities of the ICC.

[48] International criminal law becomes a place of dialectic between legal cultures; "the juxtaposition of adjectives that refer by their nature to distinct logics, even in some aspects physiologically incompatible, 'criminal' and 'international', raises at first significant perplexities, and, however, it is precisely this hybrid and innovative nature that makes the subject stimulating, offering insights for a renewed reflection on national solutions. International criminal law becomes a place of communication between different legal cultures, both in the phase of codification of the norm itself, and in the implementation and interpretative phase at the level of normative geometries; not by chance international criminal law has been defined as the Silicon Valley of comparison" (Di Landro, Andrea. (2018). *Responsibility for authorised activities in the areas of environment and territory: Penal and extrapenal protection tools*. G Giappichelli Publisher, p. 4).

regional selectivity, centred in Africa.[49] Some States, which previously accepted the limitations of their sovereignty in favour of the Court, began to consider releasing this international bond (Pasquali, 2019, pp. 2–51), under the argument that the Court would serve as a neocolonialist instrument.[50] In addition to the deficient relationship of cooperation between the States and the Court, the cases of Kenya and Uganda are the most relevant regarding the threats of withdrawal from the Rome Statute, through the device inscribed in Article 127[1].[51]

Accusations of racism and neocolonialism[52] against the Court were accompanied by political attacks from States targeted by the investigations, seeking to undermine the credibility and legitimacy of the Tribunal,[53] especially after 2010. In reaction to

[49] To a certain extent, African contexts are comparable to those of many Asian countries: "in the early phase of the Cold War, Asian and African States sharing similar histories of colonialism, liberation wars, and other horrific human rights abuses, envisioned a new multilateral forum outside the UN. They sought to discuss and reflect on their own interests in international affairs as newly independent nations. Most prominently, at the 1955 Asian-African Conference (known as the Bandung Conference), States from both regions declared their vision of sovereignty and the principle of non-interference. The Bandung Conference became the inspiration for Third World solidarity in the struggle against colonialism" (Kim, Heejin. (2017). Missed opportunities in the judicialisation of international criminal law? Asian states in the emergence and spread of the Rome statute system to punish atrocity crimes. *Netherlands Quarterly of Human Rights*, *35*(4), 246–271, p. 267).

[50] "The distrust of African authorities regarding the impartiality and legitimacy of the court exposes the tension relationship between the African Union and the ICC on how to address the issue of impunity on the African continent, openly questioning the 'jurisdictional cosmopolitanism' of the court which presupposes, as is known, the institution of a regime of global citizenship" (Saraiva, Maria Francisca. (2017). The role of African states in the politicisation of the International Criminal Court. *National Defence Institute*, (Jun), 1–8, p. 2).

[51] Rome Statute, Article 127: "1. Any State Party may, by written notification addressed to the Secretary-General of the United Nations, withdraw from this Statute. The withdrawal will take effect 1 year after the date of receipt of the notification, unless it indicates a later date".

[52] Certainly, the criticisms of the ICC due to the selection of values especially western also exist in China, a country not signatory to the Court: "although the substantial Chinese movements in The attacks began with the issuance of arrest warrants against the incumbent president of Sudan, Omar AL-Bashir, in 2009, and then against Muammar Gaddafi, in 2011: "But they clearly intensified with the opening of cases against the incumbent Kenyan president and vice-president, Uhuru Kenyatta and William Ruto, in 2011. A political opposition to the ICC then organised within the African Union (AU) at the initiative of Kenya. The AU thus adopted several resolutions first asking its members not to cooperate with the Court for the execution of arrest warrants against the Sudanese and Libyan presidents, then to the Security Council to suspend proceedings against the Kenyan president and vice-president, as Article 16 of the Statute authorises it" (Nollez-Goldbach, Raphaëlle. (2018). *The International Criminal Court*. Presses Universitaires de France, p. 108–109).

[53] The attacks began with the issuance of arrest warrants against the sitting president of Sudan, Omar AL-Bashir, in 2009, and then against Muammar Gaddafi in 2011: "But they clearly intensified with the opening of cases against the sitting Kenyan president and vice-president, Uhuru Kenyatta and William Ruto, in 2011. A political opposition to the ICC then organized within the African Union (AU) at the initiative of Kenya. The AU thus adopted several resolutions first asking

the opening of an inquiry[54] against the (future) president of Kenya, Uhuru Kenyatta, and his deputy, William Ruto (as well as four other people), the Parliament of this country approved the first motion in favour of leaving the ICC.[55] Due to lack of evidence, the charges against Kenyatta were definitively archived in March 2015.[56]

The case of Uganda, unlike the previous one, began by triggering Article 14 of the Statute, that is, by a complaint from the State Party itself, in 2004.[57] Against Joseph Kony, leader of the Lord's Resistance Army (LRA), President Yoweri Museveni (who had taken power in 1986) brought the case to the ICC Prosecutor's Office, committing to cooperate (in the search and arrest)[58] with the Court, under the terms of Article 89, of the Rome Statute.[59] In a second moment, however, Museveni himself began to accuse the Court of unjustly persecuting African leaders,

its members not to cooperate with the Court for the execution of arrest warrants against the Sudanese and Libyan presidents, then to the Security Council to suspend proceedings against the Kenyan president and vice-president, as Article 16 of the Statute authorizes" (NOLLEZ-GOLDBACH, Raphaëlle. The International Criminal Court. Paris: Presses Universitaires de France, 2018, p. 108–109).

[54] The investigation was opened, *proprio motu*, in March 2010, to analyse the occurrence of crimes against humanity, committed in the context of post-election violence in Kenya, in 2007/2008 (Link: https://www.icc-cpi.int/situations/kenya. Accessed on: 25 Aug. 2025).

[55] In 2013, Kenyatta became President of the Republic and Ruto vice-president: "a few months after this election the Parliament approved a second withdrawal motion. The reasons for this choice, clearly expressed during the parliamentary debate, were centred on the need to protect Kenya's sovereignty and its citizens. It was indeed highlighted that the great powers are not part of the Rome Statute and that the justification put forward by the United States was precisely the protection of its own citizens and soldiers from the risk of proceedings being opened against them for political reasons" (Pasquali, Leonardo. (2019). The limits set by African countries to the institutionalisation of cooperation between States in the judicial repression of international crimes. *Federalismi.it. Journal of Italian Public Law, Comparative, European*, 9, 2–51, p. 6).

[56] ICC. Trial Chamber V. (2015, March 13). *Decision on the withdrawal of charges against Mr Kenyatta*. (ICC-01/09-02111). Available at: https://www.icc-cpi.int/sites/default/files/CourtRecords/CR2015_02842.PDF. Accessed on: 2 Jul. 2025.

[57] ICC, Link: https://www.icc-cpi.int/uganda. Accessed on: 2 Sep. 2025.

[58] Despite an outstanding arrest warrant since 2005, the founder of the LRA group, Joseph Kony, remains at large.

[59] Among the main reasons for Uganda's accession to the ICC, "as for many other African States, there was the declared hope that this would lead to the punishment of those responsible for crimes" (Pasquali, Leonardo. (2019). The limits set by African countries to the institutionalisation of cooperation between States in the judicial repression of international crimes. *Federalismi.it. Journal of Italian Public Law, Comparative, European*, 9, 2–51, p. 8).

expressing support for States intending to withdraw from the Tribunal,[60] like South Africa and Burundi.[61]

The dissatisfaction of signatory countries with the alleged selectivity[62] of the ICC (even in the case of States not investigated, like Namibia),[63] supported by the African Union, culminated in the adoption, in January 2017, of a "Strategy for collective withdrawal" from the Rome Statute, based on Article 127 of the Treaty, which provides for exit as a right, through a unilateral and sovereign act of each State.[64]

---

[60] The attitude of the president of Uganda was considered emblematic of the utilitarian approach of African rulers: "according to various authors, these leaders support the work of the International Criminal Court when the accusations are directed at their enemies (such as rebels or political opponents). Conversely, they fail in their obligations to cooperate and adopt a critical attitude towards the Court itself when the investigations concern a senior African State official, thus demonstrating their desire to protect each other from the risk of having to answer to the ICC for possible crimes" (Pasquali, Leonardo. (2019). The limits set by African countries to the institutionalisation of cooperation between States in the judicial repression of international crimes. *Federalismi.it. Journal of Italian Public Law, Comparative, European*, *9*, 2–51, p. 9).

[61] Of the African countries, only Burundi has effected its withdrawal from the ICC, notifying the UN General Assembly on 28 October 2016 (BURUNDI, C.N.805.2016.TREATIES-XVIII.10 (Depositary Notification), Oct. 2016. Available at: https://treaties.un.org/doc/Publication/CN/2016/CN.805.2016-Eng.pdf. Accessed on: 22 Aug. 2022), confirmed the following year (27 October 2017). The second country to withdraw from the Statute was the Philippines, on 17 March 2018, confirmed in March 2019 (UNITED NATIONS. (2021, October 5). *United Nations Treaty Collection. Rome Statute of the International Criminal Court*. Available at: https://treaties.un.org/Pages/ViewDetails.aspx?src=TREATY&mtdsg_no=XVIII-10&chapter=18&clang=_en#12. Accessed on: 2 Jul. 2025).

[62] Although many varieties of selectivity are not intrinsically reprehensible, "group-based selectivity is contested on the basis that it presents a serious normative challenge and entwines ICL in the continuing repression of Third World peoples. Crucially, this marginalisation occurs not in spite of the resistance of the post-colonial state, but is enabled through that state's structures. Here, ICL becomes an extension of partisan domestic political agendas, often compounding long-standing social patterns that foment ethnic factionalism and socio-economic dispossession, and, in the worst-case scenario, precipitating further atrocity" (Kiyani, Asad. (2016). Group-Based Differentiation and Local Repression: The Custom and Curse of Selectivity. *Journal of International Criminal Justice*, *14*(4), 939–957, p. 955. Available at: https://academic.oup.com/jicj/article/14/4/939/2236031?login=false#41846519. Accessed on: 10 Jun. 2025).

[63] In 2015, "the Minister of Information Tjekero Tweya declared that the Cabinet of Ministers had approved a motion considering a possible withdrawal of the State from the ICC, without indicating a date. The Court was indeed accused of focusing exclusively on African countries, or those in development, and of targeting their rulers. Specifically, Namibian President Geingob had expressed his displeasure with the procedure opened against the President of Kenya, qualifying it as interference in the internal affairs of said State that the ICC should have avoided" (Pasquali, Leonardo. (2019). The limits set by African countries to the institutionalisation of cooperation between States in the judicial repression of international crimes. *Federalismi.it. Journal of Italian Public Law, Comparative, European*, *9*, 2–51, p. 9).

[64] Nollez-Goldbach, Raphaëlle. (2018). *The International Criminal Court*. Presses Universitaires de France, p. 109.

The AU also proposed amendments to the Statute, especially regarding the right of the UN General Assembly to suspend proceedings at the ICC,[65] in case of inaction by the Security Council,[66] and on the immunity of sitting heads of State. Furthermore, it encouraged the proposal of the Malabo Protocol,[67] in 2014, which inaugurates an international criminal jurisdiction of the African Court of Human Rights, expanding the list of international crimes and accepting the main demands of the States targeted by the Hague Court.

However, the policy of opposition to the ICC is not unanimous in Africa. Several States on the continent—such as Senegal, Botswana, Nigeria,[68] etc.—demonstrate support for the Court, understanding the need for international cooperation and reduction of inequalities.[69] Certainly, the concentration of investigations originating from the African continent is notorious in the first 20 years of the Tribunal's operation. But, today, a gradual geographical expansion of the cases is noticeable,

---

[65] The possibility of suspending proceedings at the ICC by The Security Council is already, per se, a target of criticism: "Infinitely more debatable - frankly scandalous to tell the truth—is the other possibility of intervention in the functioning of the Court, open to the Security Council. And one cannot rely on the apparent symmetry it achieves between the triggering of investigations and their suspension - if only because, even when a situation is referred to the Court under Article 13(b), it may not proceed with prosecutions, whereas, in the second case, it has no choice and must comply with the Council's injunction. This is provided for in Article 16 of the Statute, modestly entitled "Suspension of investigation or prosecution" (Pellet, Alain. (2003). For the International Criminal Court, anyway!—Some remarks on its jurisdiction and referral. *International Criminal Law Review, 1*(1–2), 91–110, p. 108).

[66] Situation based on Resolution 377 (V) of the UN General Assembly.

[67] African Union. (2014, June 27). *Malabo Protocol. Protocol on amendments to the Protocol on the Statute of the African Court of Justice and Human Rights*. Available at: https://au.int/sites/default/files/treaties/36398-treaty-0045_-_protocol_on_amendments_to_the_protocol_on_the_statute_of_the_african_court_of_justice_and_human_rights_p.pdf. Accessed on: 20 Jul. 2025.

[68] Even Nigeria, which has a national under investigation at the ICC, expresses support for the Court, unlike Burundi and the Philippines which withdrew in reaction to opened investigations (Nollez-Goldbach, Raphaëlle. (2018). *The International Criminal Court*. Presses Universitaires de France, p. 110).

[69] In contemplating the relationship of the ICC with structural forms of racism, "DeFalco and Mégret observe that the court has been relatively antagonistic towards criticisms of this nature. As the authors note, the question here is not merely one of whether the ICC is a deliberately racist institution, but rather how the 'systemic, pervasive, often obscure perpetuation of racially-based inequalities through the totality of society and its institutions' has impacted the prosecution of international criminal justice" (Phillips, Sara K. (2021). Unpacking "ecocide": A note of caution for international criminalisation. *Stockholm Environment Institute - SEI*. Available at: https://www.sei.org/perspectives/unpacking-ecocide-international-law/. Accessed on: 20 Aug. 2025).

reaching Georgia,[70] Bangladesh/Myanmar,[71] Philippines,[72] Afghanistan,[73] Palestine,[74] Venezuela,[75] and Ukraine.[76] There are also several preliminary analyses underway,[77] which evidences the global search for international criminal justice.[78]

The threats of withdrawal from the Treaty occurred because the ICC has touched sensitive aspects in criminal prosecution, such as investigating current leaders of State Parties.[79] The clear disposition of the Rome Statute for the "irrelevance of

[70] Alleged crimes against humanity and war crimes committed in the context of an international armed conflict between 1 July and 10 October 2008 (Link: https://www.icc-cpi.int/situations/georgia. Accessed on: 2 Sep. 2025).

[71] The Court focuses on "any alleged crimes within the Court's jurisdiction—including but not limited to crimes against humanity, such as deportation and persecution, allegedly committed against the Rohingya population - committed at least in part on the territory of Bangladesh, a State Party to the Rome Statute, or on the territory of any other State Party, insofar as such crimes are sufficiently linked to the situation as described in the Pre-Trial Chamber III's 14 November 2019 decision. The situation as described in this decision encompasses the 2016 and 2017 waves of violence which allegedly took place in Rakhine State, on the territory of Myanmar".

[72] It investigates the occurrence of crimes within the jurisdiction of the Court, including, crime against humanity of murder, committed between 1 November 2011 and 16 March 2019 in the context of the so-called "war on drugs" campaign (Link: https://www.icc-cpi.int/philippines. Accessed on: 2 Jul. 2025).

[73] The ICC investigates crimes against humanity and war crimes committed in Afghanistan since 1 May 2003 (Link: https://www.icc-cpi.int/afghanistan. Accessed on: 2 Jul 2025).

[74] Crimes committed "in the occupied Palestinian territory (Gaza and the West Bank), including East Jerusalem, since 13 June 2014" are being investigated. In January 2015, Palestine acceded to the Rome Statute, depositing its instrument of accession with the UN Secretary-General (Link: https://www.icc-cpi.int/palestine. Accessed on: 2 Jul. 2025).

[75] Crimes against humanity allegedly committed in the territory of Venezuela, from 12 February 2014 onwards, are being investigated (Link: https://www.icc-cpi.int/venezuela. Accessed on: 2 Jul. 2025).

[76] Crimes committed in the context of the situation in Ukraine since 21 November 2013, with the annexation of Crimea by Russia, followed by the 2022 invasion, are being investigated. The investigation began in March 2022 (Link: https://www.icc-cpi.int/ukraine. Accessed on: 2 Jul. 2025).

[77] The Office of the Prosecutor has already received more than 13 (thirteen) thousand communications of alleged situations, few of them reaching the status of investigation (https://www.icc-cpi.int/about/otp, Accessed on: 2 Jul. 2025).

[78] Between 1 November 2017 and 31 October 2018, the ICC prosecutor's office received 673 (six hundred and seventy-three) communications from worldwide, 443 (four hundred and forty-three) of which were outside the Court's jurisdiction (ICC. Office of the Prosecutor. (2018, December 5). *Report on the activities carried out in 2018 in terms of preliminary examination*, p. 9).

[79] The issue of the impact of certain countries' desire to "withdraw from an international organisation of which they are part the competences attributed to it to reappropriate them on the institutionalisation of cooperation between States in the judicial repression of international crimes has indeed arisen in Africa, at the moment when the International Criminal Court has opened investigations and exercised criminal action against Heads of State and other senior State officials of African countries in office. It has, in short, "dared" to affect the hard core of State sovereignty, claiming to subject to trial the physical persons who embody pro tempore the State itself, such as its head of State in office" (Pasquali, Leonardo. (2019). The limits set by African countries to the institutionalisation of cooperation between States in the judicial repression of international crimes. *Federalismi.it. Journal of Italian Public Law, Comparative, European*, *9*, 2–51, p. 41).

official quality" of the individual (Article 27) investigated is one of the most significant advances of the Court, inspired by post-War Tribunals, as a way to minimise the possibility of impunity. That is, the reaction of some countries is not, necessarily, against the International Criminal Court, but against any international institution that supersedes—in some way—the sovereignty (and, especially, the sovereign) of the State.

In this aspect, international organisations themselves would be at risk, at the moment they contradicted national interests. Even the African Union, which encourages non-compliance with the Rome Statute regarding cooperation,[80] would be doomed to the threat of abandonment, if it did not yield to the absolute protection (immunity) of current leaders of States, which evidences a crisis of confidence in international organisations as a whole.

The African regional Criminal Court itself, designed in 2014 by the Malabo Protocol, cannot be implemented: out of 55 (fifty-five) countries, 15 (fifteen) signed, but none ratified or deposited, until May 2019.[81] That is, the scope achieved by the ICC will hardly be dissolved into regional criminal courts,[82] while the greater power of investigation and judgement remains in national jurisdictions.

The maturing of the ICC—through trials for situations spread across the planet—can reduce the noise with some African and Asian States. The Court is a reality,[83] which reacts to preserve its legitimacy.[84] The increase in transparency of decisions

[80] The duty to cooperate with the Court is described in Article 86 of the Rome Statute: "States Parties shall, in accordance with the provisions of this Statute, fully cooperate with the Court in the investigation and prosecution of crimes within its jurisdiction".

[81] List of countries that have signed, ratified the Malabo Protocol. 20 May. 2019. Available at: https://au.int/sites/default/files/treaties/36398-sl-PROTOCOL%20ON%20AMENDMENTS%20TO%20THE%20PROTOCOL%20ON%20THE%20STATUTE%20OF%20THE%20AFRICAN%20COURT%20OF%20JUSTICE%20AND%20HUMAN%20RIGHTS.pdf. Accessed on: 20 Jul. 2025.

[82] Indeed, the regional solution has some advantages: "there is indeed a regional solidarity, the result of political factors and of mutual benefits more strongly felt, which produces as a positive effect, the mitigation of the risk of a negative reaction arising from an intervention considered from the outside, from afar and therefore experienced as the result of a policy of domination by the most powerful States, such as for example the permanent members of the United Nations Security Council or, even, in the case of Africa, as the fruit of a neo-colonial policy. In the specific case, it would also be an application of the principle 'African solutions to African problems', so dear to the standard-bearers of pan-Africanism and held in high consideration by the African Union itself" (Pasquali, Leonardo. (2019). The limits set by African countries to the institutionalisation of cooperation between States in the judicial repression of international crimes. *Federalismi.it. Journal of Italian Public Law, Comparative, European*, *9*, 2–51, p. 47).

[83] If the criticisms and attacks on the ICC reveal its real limits and deficiencies, "it remains nonetheless that the very existence of such a permanent international jurisdiction represents a real success, long unimaginable. What would be of a world where no Court would exist to judge crimes of genocide, crimes against humanity and war crimes? The end of the ICC and the return to jurisdictional nothingness would bring no progress" (Nollez-Goldbach, Raphaëlle. (2018). *The International Criminal Court*. Presses Universitaires de France, p. 114).

[84] Although the feared mass withdrawal has not occurred, "the ICC stands at a turning point regarding its global relevance. Meanwhile, no international criminal court has ever operated within non-

and consistency of definitions of gravity also contribute to minimising perceptions of selectivity (Kiyani, 2016, pp. 939–957), factors that only occur with the practical accumulation of experience of the Court, built under various legal systems.

Just as the nature of the discussion about regional or universal criminal jurisdiction (as the ICC intends to be) is ideological and political, the environmental assessment of "risk" and "damage" for criminal purposes is also.[85] In this prism, it is important to analyse more technical and practical aspects, aimed at the realisation of ecocide in the International Criminal Court, considering it, at the moment, the only Court capable of offering the reach compatible with an international crime against massive damage to the environment.

It is necessary, then, to discuss in greater depth the will of the agent—which is required for the completion of the conduct—and the object protected by the norm, whether the latter protects the environment per se or the human being and its economic activities. Also, considering the specificity of environmental damage, one must study the *actus reus,* as required in the Rome Statute, as a limit to the processing of the crime of ecocide.

For this, a brief analysis will be made on the criminal justice systems in *civil law* and in *common law*, especially within the ICC, as a way to understand their influences on international criminal law.

7.3 Common Law and Civil Law in the ICTY

Initially, it should be highlighted that studying from a legal *civil law* culture makes the researcher accustomed to this system perceive the law first and directly from the text of the law; the original scholar of the *common law* tradition starts with the case,

---

turbulent times. The establishment of the ICC faced strong resistance from powerful political players and was only possible thanks to intensive diplomatic efforts. Many contentious questions discussed at the Rome Conference pose immense challenges to date. However, the progress of the ICC—being the first permanent international criminal court—is continuous. Its consolidation depends on the confidence of the States Parties" (Altunjan, Tanja., & Neugebauer, Konrad. (2019). *Workshop Report: "The International Criminal Court in Turbulent Times"*. Asser Press. Available at: https://zis-online.com/dat/artikel/2019_6_1303.pdf. Accessed on: 20 Jul. 2025).

[85] "The conflicts pertaining to diminished environmental resources, to the impacts of global warming, to differential access and use of nature, and to friction stemming from the cross- border transference of harm are all overlaid by questions of class and state power, and the histories and contemporary manifestations of imperialism and colonialism. Indeed, underpinning many of the ecological pressures and social conflicts occurring "elsewhere" (i.e., in the non-Western world) are processes and decisions made in the metropole—the United States and the European Union. Transnational corporations, in conjunction with hegemonic nation-states and local political elites, are directly implicated in these trends and patterns" (White, Rob., & Kramer, Ronald C. (2015). Critical criminology and the struggle against climate change ecocide. *Critical Criminology*, *23*(4), 383–399. Available at: https://link.springer.com/article/10.1007/s10612-015-9292-5. Accessed on: 20 Jul. 2025).

then, recognises the *case* (judicial opinion) and defines the applicable norm.[86] In international criminal law there is a mix,[87] as demonstrated below, with an attempt at codification (Rome Statute), dissected by jurisprudence (trial of cases, still scarce). Hence the choice, at this moment, for the analysis primarily established in the Treaty.

The Systems[88] *civil law* (from German law, *strafrechtswissenschaft*) and *common law* constitute the predominant source for the construction of dogmatics in the—ongoing—theory of crime in international criminal matters (De Carli, 2014). The influence of States, and their political wills, to consolidate this development was crucial, leaving the technical issues of compatibility between the various legal systems[89] in the background.[90] The lack of theoretical depth on the intersection

---

[86] Given the relevance of jurisprudence in *common law*, it is of utmost importance that lawyers, judges and students "*understand how to read, analyze, and synthesize judicial opinions—what we call case law or simply cases. The prominence of case law—precedent—and the rule of stare decisis are among the defining elements of the U.S. legal system*" (Jaeger-Fine, Toni. (2015). *Mastering The U.S. Legal System: A Beginner's Guide*. Jaeger-Fine Publishing New York, p. 5). It should be noted that, even in the United States, there is a process of codifying norms, imposing new methods of studying law. Even so, the study of cases (decisions with binding force) is determinant in legal practice: "There are few skills more important for a U.S. lawyer or student to possess than the ability to read, understand, analyze, and synthesize cases. A "case" is the word we use to refer to the written decision of a court" (Jaeger-Fine, Toni. (2015). *Mastering The U.S. Legal System: A Beginner's Guide*. Jaeger-Fine Publishing New York, p. 54).

[87] In addition to interpretation, a significant problem—and sometimes forgotten—is the translation of documents and terms: "one of the main curiosities that the theme of multilingualism in international normative acts arouses is whether it is possible to hypothesize a unified interpretative solution, or whether, on the contrary, the hermeneutic criteria that are imposed differ depending on the type of act. Are there, in essence, rules of interpretation applicable to all the international normative acts taken into consideration, or does the different nature of the systems examined justify the application of different hermeneutic rules?" (Pasquali, Leonardo. (2016). Multilingualism in international normative acts and the need for differentiated interpretative solutions (Vol. 12). G Giappichelli Editore, p. 173).

[88] By the ethno-historical theory, it is identified, for each group of legal systems, the dominance of a certain legal idea or legal order: "in the Romanist, the French Code civil; in the Germanic, the German 1897 Civil code; in the Anglo-American, the Common Law, and in the Far Eastern, the Confucian theory of law" (Luts, L. L. (2010). Typologies of Modern Legal Systems of the World. *Journal of Comparative Law*, *5*(1), 28–40, p. 29). For more information on the Soviet system, see: Razi, G. M. (1960). Around the World's Legal Systems. *Howard Law Journal*, *6*(1), 1–29.

[89] In contemporary legal doctrine, the classification of the world's legal systems is based on various criteria: "types of sources of law and model of legislative procedure; elements of general and legal culture; legal traditions; commonality of principles of legal regulation of social relations, unity of terminology, legal categories and concepts; together with complex or aggregate criteria, among which there are: (a) historical genesis, system of sources of law and structure of legal system; (b) distinctive features of law creation orientated towards a particular element of the legal system and legal ideology; (c) methodology of law, infrastructure of law, and structure of procedural law; (d) legal ideology and legal technique; (e) legal style; (f) historical experience and development of law, method of legal thought, legal institutes, types of sources of law, and structural and axiological pre-determined link between them" (Luts, L. L. (2010). Typologies of Modern Legal Systems of the World. *Journal of Comparative Law*, *5*(1), 28–40, p. 31).

[90] It is observed, from a historical perspective, "that state leaders were the masters of the game within the political system of international relations, and they still are largely today, even if the

between the systems, especially in criminal law, causes great difficulties in understanding sensitive institutes, such as the theories of crime, which, per se, encounter various problems in the norm and in the doctrines of the various models of criminal liability.

The internal systems (and the internal norms) were/are determinants for the increase of international criminal law.[91] Thus, it prevailed in the Courts ad hoc,[92] from Nuremberg and Tokyo, the somewhat American approach[93]—winners of World War II—of *common law*, defining the crime in two elements[94]: *mens rea* (subjective aspect of conduct) and *actus reus* (objective aspect), also adopting a bipartite structure in the process (*offense/defenses*). The *civil law*, however, adopts a tripartite theory[95] of crime, designating it as typical, unlawful and culpable.[96]

---

emergence of competing actors comes to disturb a position long unchallenged" (Gounelle, Max. (2006). *The political system of international relations*. Dalloz, p. 45).

[91] It is widely recognized "that domestic rules are crucial for the criminal sanctioning of international crimes, in terms of the classification and criminalization of punishable behaviours and the very existence of universal criminal jurisdiction, as well as the possibility of extradition to a state whose criminal jurisdiction lacks a territorial basi" (Rodríguez Iglesias, Gil Carlos. (2019). The relationship between legal systems. *Spanish Yearbook of International Law*, *1*, 1–8, p. 2. Available at: https://scholar.archive.org/work/ypckl45o2vcmlcrwdru4d7iwuq/access/wayback/http://www.sybil.es/documents/ARCHIVE/Vol23/1_RodriguezIglesias.pdf. Accessed on: 15 Jun. 2025).

[92] It is certain that each criminal court did not seek, when instituting its Statutes, to codify international criminal law itself, but only to organise its criminal jurisdictions for regular functioning, without broader ambitions: "*chaque Statut constitue donc um effort de codification du droit international général en vigueur à l'époque des faits. Mais en même temps, chaque Statut procède à une codification contextualisée, adaptée aux circonstances et aux nécessités de l'institution envisagée*" (Frouville, Olivier de (2012). *Droit international pénal: sources, incriminations, responsabilité*. Paris: Pedone, p. 59).

[93] Even in the United States, there is a replacement of the system of crimes in *common law* by a codification: "The common law continues to play an important role in modern American criminal law, and to the extent that it has been displaced by statutes, our justice system has not improved. Criminal statutes regularly delegate questions about the scope of criminal law to prosecutors, and judges have failed to serve as a check on that power" (Hessick, Carissa Byrne. (2019). The myth of common law crimes. *Virginia Law Review*, *105*(5), 965–1024). The changes also occur in the *civil law* system: "legal systems of the Romano-Germanic type are materially changing, to which the following trend testifies: the growth of the importance of international treaties; the increased significance of judicial precedents; the unification of legal regulation by international legal standards; the coming together of the Romano-Germanic and Anglo- American types of legal systems; the increased significance of general-civilized principles of law" (Luts, L. L. (2010). Typologies of Modern Legal Systems of the World. *Journal of Comparative Law*, *5*(1), 28–40, p. 39).

[94] Indeed, not only *common law* countries use the bipartite system of crime theory.

[95] Obviously, it is not intended here to discuss the position of part of the doctrine that questions culpability as part of the analytical concept of crime, understanding it only as a prerequisite for punishment, as defended by Damásio de Jesus (Reiss, Michel Wencland. (2017). *The International Criminal Court in the Context of Globalisation of Law: Analysis of the Rome Statute based on Anglo-Saxon inspired Criminal Law, Roman-Germanic inspired Criminal Law and Brazilian Criminal Law* [Doctoral Thesis, Pontifical Catholic University of Rio de Janeiro], p. 97. Available at: https://www.maxwell.vrac.puc-rio.br/36273/36273.PDF. Accessed on: 10 Jun. 2025).

[96] De Carli, C. V. (2014). Grammar of international criminal law: The languages of crime and punishment. *Cadernos do Programa de Pós-Graduação em Direito/UFRGS*, *9*(1), 370–394, p. 382.

It should be noted that the three elements of the crime (analytical concept),[97] in *civil law*, must be analysed in order: typicality, unlawfulness, and, finally, culpability.[98] This order is irrelevant, however, in *common law*[99] (regarding *mens rea* and *actus reus*). For the International Criminal Court, an attempt was made to advance in the dogmatics[100] about a theory of international crime, mixing characteristics of various systems.[101] There is, therefore, a debate in doctrine about which of them, for this Court,[102] is more relevant, in order to study—and apply—correctly the insti-

---

Available at: https://www.seer.ufrgs.br/ppgdir/article/download/42767/35171. Accessed on: 12 Jun. 2025. For a study on the differences between the two systems, in relation to international law, see: Matus, Jean Pierre. (2008). *The transformation of crime theory in international criminal law*. Atelier, and Gallant, Kenneth S. (2009). *The principle of legality in international and comparative criminal law*. Cambridge University Press.

[97] For continental Criminal Law, the crime, according to its analytical definition, consists of a typical, illicit and culpable human conduct (Zaffaroni, Eugenio Raúl., Batista, Nilo., Alagia, Alejandro., & Slokar, Alejandro. (2010). *Brazilian criminal law. Theory of crime: historical and methodological introduction, action and typicality* (2nd ed., Vol. II, t. I). Lumen Juris, p. 20).

[98] "The elimination of chance and the overcoming of result-oriented criminal law are, historically, the greatest achievements of the principle of culpability. Only after it has been determined that the causation of the result is not a product of chance, but resulted, in an objectively attributable way, from the author's behaviour, will the other question be formulated — also to be answered with the help of the principle of culpability — as to whether the inner constitution of the agent allows a subjective attribution, if he is 'guilty', in the current sense of the word. The principle of culpability is, therefore, the backbone of both objective and subjective attribution" (Roxin, Claus. (2006). *Studies of criminal law*. Renovar, p. 135).

[99] "The fact is that the struggle between these two approaches to criminal responsibility has dominated theoretical debates in the field of international law for the last 50 years. The problems were, first, which system to adopt, and, second, how to deal with particular issues within the adopted system. In the tripartite system, more rigorous and demanding, the discussion about where to place the subjective elements of the crime (intent and fault); whether in the definition of the crime (typicality), or in culpability. A similar debate occurred within Common Law regarding the crime of murder, as to the characterization of prima facie (intentional) murder and accidental (negligent) murder" (De Carli, C. V. (2014). Grammar of international criminal law: The languages of crime and punishment. *Cadernos do Programa de Pós-Graduação em Direito/UFRGS, 9*(1), 370–394, p. 391. Available at: https://www.seer.ufrgs.br/ppgdir/article/download/42767/35171. Accessed on: 12 Jun. 2025).

[100] For information on the development of the draft for a "general part of international criminal law" of the Rome Statute, see: Clark, Roger S. (2008). Drafting a general part to a penal code: Some thoughts inspired by the negotiations on the Rome Statute of the International Criminal Court and by the Court's first substantive law discussion in the Lubanga Dyilo confirmation proceedings. *Criminal Law Forum, 19*(3–4), 519–552.

[101] In any case, the decision was made to value the agent's will, to the detriment of an exclusive focus on the result: "the final theory of action, with its return to ontic structures and to social reality, successfully managed to bring criminal dogmatics closer to reality, and to return to the theory of action and type the plasticity of true descriptions of events" (Roxin, Claus. (2002). *Criminal policy and legal-criminal system*. Renovar, p. 27).

[102] The Rome Statute uses a language distinct from the *common law* and *civil law* systems, seeking to distance itself from a direct identification with any system: "the trick is to make it work as a sui generis piece of codification, just as the procedural provisions of the Statute are neither those of the common law nor those of the civil law as their respective practitioners and devotees understand

tutes.[103] It is appropriate here, in this work, to highlight the aspects of the theories of crime incorporated in the international system, with the aim of verifying the technical feasibility of an international environmental crime.

It is undeniable, however, that we are still in a considerably rudimentary phase in the process of constructing a General Part of international criminal law,[104] despite the progress promoted by the Rome Statute, which establishes itself as the main codification[105] in the area (mainly due to, respect for the principle of legality).[106] The penal system in the ICC is, in a certain way, mixed, the causal relationship between the type of procedure (adversarial or inquisitive, with predominance of the latter) and the theory of crime effectively adopted[107] is not clearly perceived.

The influence of Roman-Germanic law is determinant for, for example, imposing some important circumstances in the Treaty, such as non-retroactivity and, in the

---

them. They are something new; the general part of the Rome Statute is something new" (Clark, Roger S. (2008). Drafting a general part to a penal code: Some thoughts inspired by the negotiations on the Rome Statute of the International Criminal Court and by the Court's first substantive law discussion in the Lubanga Dyilo confirmation proceedings. *Criminal Law Forum, 19*(3–4), 519-552p. 552).

[103] "These are small samples of the difficulties arising from the need to construct a hybrid dogmatics, which tries to combine legal institutes not yet suitable for such unification. Note that the Statute still maintains the antinomy of error of law and error of fact, while the doctrine of *criminal law* in Europe, for a long time, deals with error of type and error of prohibition" (Azevedo, Tupinambá Pinto de. (2014). Theories of the crime–Roman-Germanic model and Common Law. *Law & Justice*, *40*(2), 205–215, p. 208. Available at: https://revistaseletronicas.pucrs.br/index.php/fadir/article/download/17348/11150. Accessed on: 12 Jun. 2025).

[104] Reiss, Michel Wencland. (2017). *The International Criminal Court in the Context of Globalisation of Law: Analysis of the Rome Statute based on Anglo-Saxon inspired Criminal Law, Roman-Germanic inspired Criminal Law and Brazilian Criminal Law* [Doctoral Thesis, Pontifical Catholic University of Rio de Janeiro], p. 77. Available at: https://www.maxwell.vrac.puc-rio.br/36273/36273.PDF. Accessed on: 10 Jun. 2025.

[105] Certainly, the International Criminal Court, with a more general and permanent vocation than the other criminal courts ad hoc, benefited from the *expertise* of these in its formation, benefiting from the jurisprudence, for example, of the International Criminal Tribunal for the former Yugoslavia (particularly on the definition of crimes). The ICC also differentiated itself by seeking the most precise possible definition of crimes, in order to reduce to the maximum the judge's power of appreciation, favouring legal certainty and respect for the principle *nullun crimen* (Frouville, Olivier de (2012). *Droit international pénal: sources, incriminations, responsabilité*. Paris: Pedone, p. 60).

[106] Article 22, of the Rome Statute (Clementino, Marco Bruno Miranda. (2010). Culpability in International Criminal Law. *CEJ Magazine*, *14*(51), p. 61).

[107] Although the great debate that arose "from the Rome Statute, in which the typification of international crimes is done in the moulds of criminal legality in the style of *Strafrechtswissenschaft* (*nullum crimen, nulla poena sine lege scripta, praevia, stricta, certa*), it has long been asserted a growing approximation between the theory of Roman-Germanic crime and *common law* "(Azevedo, Tupinambá Pinto de. (2014). Theories of the crime–Roman-Germanic model and Common Law. *Law & Justice*, *40*(2), 205–215, p. 207. Available at: https://revistaseletronicas.pucrs.br/index.php/fadir/article/download/17348/11150. Accessed on: 12 Jun. 2025).

procedural scope, absence of the jury.[108] On the other hand, in the construction of the theory of crime, there is a predominance of the concepts of the *common law* system, coming from the ad hoc Courts. This does not imply, however, in the exclusion of other legal systems. The Treaty expressly determines which law is applicable to the Court (article 21), listing, in order of importance, first the Statute itself (with the books on the Constitutive Elements of Crime (ICC, 2011) and the Procedural Regulation (ICC, 2013) in the background), then the treaties and, after, the applicable principles and norms of international law and the general principles of law, taken from the internal law of the different existing legal systems.[109]

The choice made by the States Parties to the Court for the definition of crimes is clearly Anglo-Saxon,[110] despite the Statute not using terms linked to certain legal traditions: the mental elements (*mens rea*; intent *latu* sensu) were replaced by "Psychological Elements" (article 30), while the defensive theses (*defenses*; exclusions of illegality and culpability in the *civil law*) were uniformly called "Causes of Exclusion of Criminal Responsibility" (article 31). The elements of the crimes were set out in a separate book (*Elements of Crimes*), where it is textually exposed that the intention of the agent and the knowledge (article 30 [1])[111] can be inferred from relevant facts and circumstances in the process.[112]

Despite this preference, there are constant movements of the doctrine and of the Court itself in minimizing the differences between the criminal legal systems seeking—the still distant—common link in the theory of crime. Regardless of this, the

---

[108] The presence of the jury court in a certain legal system does not necessarily indicate it to be *common law*, after all there are States *civil law* that adopt the people's court as a model of judgement. Brazil, for example, defines the jury as competent to judge intentional crimes against life, in a system similar to the American jury (Brochado Neto, Djalma Alvarez. (2016). *Representativeness in the Brazilian Jury Court: criticisms of the selection of jurors and proposals in light of the American model* [Master's Dissertation, Federal University of Ceará]. Available at: https://repositorio.ufc.br/bitstream/riufc/23804/1/2016_dis_dabrochadoneto.pdf. Accessed on: 12 Jun. 2025).

[109] Article 21 (1) (c), of the Rome Statute.

[110] "The influence of Common Law is more clearly revealed when studying the exclusions in the aforementioned Statute. It is observed that Anglo-Saxon inspired criminal law simply speaks of *defences*, while continental criminal law divides them into exclusions of illegality or culpability. And the Statute generically deals with exclusions in Article 31, whose marginal heading is 'Causes of Exclusion of Criminal Responsibility'" (Reiss, Michel Wencland. (2017). *The International Criminal Court in the Context of Globalisation of Law: Analysis of the Rome Statute based on Anglo-Saxon inspired Criminal Law, Roman-Germanic inspired Criminal Law and Brazilian Criminal Law* [Doctoral Thesis, Pontifical Catholic University of Rio de Janeiro], p. 118. Available at: https://www.maxwell.vrac.puc-rio.br/36273/36273.PDF. Accessed on: 10 Jun. 2025).

[111] "Article 30. (...) 1. Unless otherwise provided, no person shall be criminally liable and punished for a crime within the jurisdiction of the Court, unless they act with the will to commit it and knowledge of its material elements" (Decree 4.388/2002, Rome Statute. Available at: http://www.planalto.gov.br/ccivil_03/decreto/2002/d4388.htm. Accessed on: 14 Jun. 2025).

[112] The definitions of crimes and all their elements are in the book *Elements of Crimes*, but, despite serving as guidance to judges, they are not binding (De Carli, C. V. (2014). Grammar of international criminal law: The languages of crime and punishment. *Cadernos do Programa de Pós-Graduação em Direito/UFRGS, 9*(1), 370–394, p. 394. Available at: https://www.seer.ufrgs.br/ppgdir/article/download/42767/35171. Accessed on: 12 Jun. 2025).

construction—incipient—of international criminal law necessarily involves constant observation of human rights, understanding it without prioritizing a certain system.

It is important to highlight that the judges of the International Criminal Court come from a variety of national systems, that is, different from the one adopted in the Court (in theory, a hybrid form). This mix of expertises enriches international criminal practice,[113] as their views of law are put to the test in the interpretation of norms and in the cases under judgement.

To apply the definition of a crime to a concrete case, one must verify, successively, the presence of all the constitutive elements (material, the *actus reus*; and psychological, the *mens rea*) contained in the *caput* and in the underlying crime (the paragraphs, conducts described in the article itself).[114] It would then remain to determine the form of responsibility applicable to the author to assess his degree of fault.[115]

For an understanding of the psychological element in the Court,[116] it is necessary to understand how the *mens rea* (*guilty mind*), with a focus on compatibility of what

---

[113] The coexistence "of magistrates from different national legal systems, within all contemporary international courts, seems to me to be healthy, and does not present, in my view, insurmountable difficulties, particularly given the willingness to study each of those systems (*civil law*, *common law*, Islamic law, among others) in the great works of comparative law. More significant, and difficult, seems to me another type of coexistence, that of peers with different conceptions of the very *international judicial function*. Such conceptions, in my view, are independent of the national legal system of origin" (Trindade, Antônio Augusto Cançado. (2010). Contemporary International Courts and the pursuit of the ideal of international justice. *Rev. Fac. Law UFMG*, *57*, 37–68, p. 63).

[114] The assessment of the presence of constitutive elements is fundamental to the correct subsumption of the case to the norm. For example, a homicide, for the Rome Statute, listed in various items of several articles, can constitute a crime against humanity (article 7 [1] [a]), genocide (article 6 [1] [a]) or a war crime (article 8 [2] [a] [i]).

[115] Frouville, Olivier de (2012). *Droit international pénal: sources, incriminations, responsabilité*. Paris: Pedone, p. 73.

[116] The analysis of art. 30 raises a methodological question: whether one should start from a research that aims to find "conceptual traces" of different legal systems, with the aim of interpreting a provision that emerges as an attempt at dialogue between different legal cultures, or, vice versa, from the result, regardless of the national experience, in a context analysis that takes as its exclusive criterion of evaluation the internationalist data in which the norm intends to operate: "*The question as posed is, in reality, fraught with misunderstandings, since, in posing itself in terms of an absolute alternative, it does not take into account the conceptual autonomy of a norm that emancipates itself from national solutions and takes on peculiarities and needs of the internationalist context and, at the same time, the incisiveness of national reflection under two aspects: as an interpretative support for ambiguous "lexical choices" and as a comparison parameter for the coexistence between systems in the perspective of complementarity that outlines its essence* (...) *The solution that seems preferable moves, therefore, from an analysis of the international standard functional to the field in which it is intended to operate and in which the national data becomes a point of reflection for the purpose of reducing to coherence the provision, without however that the same is reflected as an "ordalic hermeneutic" criterion on the "conceptual autonomy" of the provision*" (Wenin, R. (2012). *The mens rea in the Rome Statute*. G. Giappichelli Publisher, p. 13/24).

is required in the Rome Statute with behaviours that cause massive environmental damage.

7.4 The Mental Element and Environmental Crimes

The construction of a crime aims to limit the exercise of punitive power[117] against an individual. The bases for the recognition of individual responsibility in international law date back to the Treaty of Versailles, of June 1919, passing through the Courts ad hoc, finding itself, within the International Criminal Court, inscribed in article 25.[118]

The attribution of international criminal responsibility also depends, on the volitional character[119] of the agent for the commission of the crime, called psychological elements, set out in article 30 of the Treaty.[120] That is, it is not enough for the conduct to be unlawful, the intention of the accused to commit it and his knowledge of the material elements of the crime must be demonstrated[121]:

---

[117] For most legal systems, the imposition of criminal liability goes through two basic requirements: the practice of some act provided for by law as a crime by the person to be held responsible; and "the mens rea or guilty mind with which the act is done. It is not enough that a man has done some act which on account of its mischievous results the law prohibits; before the law can justly punish the act, an inquiry must be made into the mental attitude of the doer" (Sayre, Francis Bowes. (1932). Mens rea. *Harvard Law Review*, *45*(6), 974–1026, p. 974. Available at: https://www.jstor.org/stable/pdf/1332142.pdf?refreqid=excelsior%3Af22543cbd9836c96a090e8c6f2008e16&ab_segments=&origin=. Accessed on: 12 Jun. 2025).

[118] What characterises the Rome Statute in relation to previous regulatory experiences is the express reference to the mental elements for the assessment of individual responsibility: "It is just the case to remark, how different is the affirmation of individual responsibility, from that of the necessity of a psychological requirement for the attribution of the international crime. It can well be said that the first complete affirmation of the principle of guilt is contained precisely in the provision of art. 30 of the Statute" (Wenin, R. (2012). *The mens rea in the Rome Statute*. G. Giappichelli Publisher, p. 10).

[119] This requirement is relatively recent, considering that, in the trial of Adolf Eichmann, after the 2nd World War, the element *mens rea* is almost overlooked, to the detriment of the *actus reus*. For more detail on the topic, from the perspective of the philosophies of Immanuel Kant and Hannah Arendt, see: Druart, Pierre. (2024). Mens Rea in International Criminal Law: A Look at Eichmann's Responsibility in the Light of Kant and Arendt. In *Heritage in War and Peace: Legal and Political Perspectives for Future Protection*. Springer International Publishing. p. 227–238).

[120] The provision of Article 30 has a prominent importance in the Treaty: "It signifies the clear refusal of a purely objective conception of illicit, based on the mere production of a result, and of an understanding of guilt as a mere psychological connection of the agent to the fact" (Faria, Maria Paula Ribeiro de (2006). The psychological elements of crimes provided for in the Rome Treaty. *Law and Justice, Special Issue*, 133–146, p. 133).

[121] Thus, it is inappropriate "the possibility of talking about any form of objective responsibility or without guilt in this seat, which might not be completely inappropriate considering the gravity of the results produced, but which would violate fundamental principles of freedom and personal responsibility and human dignity as those that can be associated with the formulation of a judg-

Article 30: Psychological Elements

1. Unless otherwise provided, no person may be criminally responsible and punished for a crime within the jurisdiction of the Court, unless he acts with the will to commit it and knowledge of its material elements.
2. For the purposes of this article, it is understood that acts intentionally who:
   (a) Regarding a conduct, proposes to adopt it;
   (b) Regarding an effect of the crime, proposes to cause it or is aware that it will take place in a normal order of events.
3. Under this article, "knowledge" is understood as awareness that a circumstance exists or that an effect will occur place, in a normal order of events. The expressions "to have knowledge" and "with knowledge" should be understood in compliance.

For the ICC, the various forms of criminal realisation (provided for in article 25 [3]),[122] assume the intentionality of the agent. This subjective attribution, assessed as prescribed in article 30 of the Rome Statute,[123] only occurs when the agent, deliberately, proposes to adopt the criminal conduct (article 30 [2] [a]), proposes to cause the effect of a crime or knows that this will occur, in a normal order of events (article 30 [2] [b]).

As can be seen, there are no references in the Statute that indicate the institutes related to the subjective element, whether based on the *civil law*[124] or on the *common law*,[125] there being confusion in doctrine about the generic concept of *mens rea*

ment of guilt on the agent" (Faria, Maria Paula Ribeiro de (2006). The psychological elements of crimes provided for in the Rome Treaty. *Law and Justice, Special Issue*, 133–146, p. 134).

[122] Commission, attempt, complicity and instigation, as principal, incitement, among others (Article 25 [3], Rome Statute.

[123] Article 30 of the ICC represents the result of a political commitment "which carries the scars of the compromising seat from which it owes its genesis; however, it emerges the choice in favour of a hermeneutic criterion that binds the community reaction to the gravity of the crime, manifested not only by the intensity of the endangerment of the protected legal good, but also by the 'subjective disvalue of the conduct'" (Wenin, R. (2012). *The mens rea in the Rome Statute*. G. Giappichelli Publisher).

[124] Intent and fault. For more, see: Zaffaroni, Eugenio Raúl., Batista, Nilo., Alagia, Alejandro., & Slokar, Alejandro. (2010). *Brazilian criminal law. Theory of crime: historical and methodological introduction, action and typicality* (2nd ed., Vol. II, t. I). Lumen Juris.

[125] The *mens rea* is divided into four categories of mental attitudes, in successive degrees of intention (implying the gravity of the crime): *purpose* or *intent*, explicit and conscious desire to commit the criminal act (similar to direct intent, in *civil law*); *knowledge*, knowledge that their actions will cause certain damage (certainty); *recklessness*, imprudence, but with a different sense from Roman-Germanic law, closer to eventual intent, when the agent commits a certain action, despite knowing the associated risks; *negligence*, the mildest form, when the agent acts without reasonable care. There is also the so-called *strict liability offences*, consisting of situations in which the agent's will is indifferent, in the mould of objective criminal responsibility. The conceptualisations and fits to concrete cases are confusing to the researcher accustomed to *civil law*, causing, even in practice in countries that adopt this division of mental elements, certain jurisprudential inconsistencies

(the need for the presence of the subjective element of the crime) with an institute of intent, one of the modalities of the subjective element.[126]

The words "vontade" and "intenção", as translated into Brazilian law,[127] were originally recorded in English[128] as *intent* and *knowledge*, respectively. At first glance, the two terms are similar to the first two mental elements of *mens rea*, restricting intent to direct intent[129] (closer to *intent*). According to the explanatory notes of Article 30, it is seen that other mental states are accepted in the ICC, when admitting intent,[130] regarding the consequences of a crime, when wishing to cause them, or being aware that it will cause the result, which is close to eventual intent[131] (in *common law*, close to the understanding of *recklessness*).

---

regarding the mental state of defendants, always judicial innovation (Sayre, Francis Bowes. (1932). Mens rea. *Harvard Law Review*, *45*(6), 974–1026, p. 974. Available at: https://www.jstor.org/stable/pdf/1332142.pdf?refreqid=excelsior%3Af22543cbd9836c96a090e8c6f2008e16&ab_segments=&origin=. Accessed on: 12 Jun. 2025).

[126] Reiss, Michel Wencland. (2017). *The International Criminal Court in the Context of Globalisation of Law: Analysis of the Rome Statute based on Anglo-Saxon inspired Criminal Law, Roman-Germanic inspired Criminal Law and Brazilian Criminal Law* [Doctoral Thesis, Pontifical Catholic University of Rio de Janeiro], p. 159. Available at: https://www.maxwell.vrac.puc-rio.br/36273/36273.PDF. Accessed on: 10 Jun. 2025.

[127] As described in Article 30, of Decree 4.388/2002, which promulgated the Rome Statute in Brazil.

[128] Link: https://www.icc-cpi.int/sites/default/files/RS-Eng.pdf. Accessed on: 14 Jun. 2025.

[129] According to the Roman-Germanic system, it is possible to recognise in the Rome Statute the requirement of a specific intent, as well as the generic intent referred to in Article 30: "Thus, in art. 8°, 2, a), iv) crime of destruction and appropriation of goods, it speaks of an arbitrary destruction and appropriation, in art. 8°, 2), b) xi), war crime of killing or injuring by treachery, of a treacherous conduct, and in numerous war crimes, an intention of the agent is autonomised that is not well known what degree of specificity it holds, but which nevertheless allows them to distinguish from most of the incriminations that do not refer to any specific intent or intention, being satisfied with the operation of the general rules of art. 30°" (Faria, Maria Paula Ribeiro de (2006). The psychological elements of crimes provided for in the Rome Treaty. *Law and Justice, Special Issue*, 133–146, p. 137).

[130] "It is necessary to mention all those cases where less than intention is required. This happens, for example, in art. 28° of the Rome Treaty when it is established that the military leaders are responsible not only if they know, but if they should know, that a subordinate was committing or was going to commit a significant crime. Here touches the problem of 'wilful ignorance' which is, to a large extent, a problem of error (or a fictitious problem of error). In fact, what happens is that, sometimes, the agent can be in error or remain in error as a way to escape criminal responsibility that he would otherwise have, but by remaining in "ignorance" he often has at the same time the awareness of facts that he knows exist, or of results that he knows will materialise" (Faria, Maria Paula Ribeiro de (2006). The psychological elements of crimes provided for in the Rome Treaty. *Law and Justice, Special Issue*, 133–146, p. 137).

[131] This also rules out conscious guilt: "In the case of guilt, the agent, despite the disregard of the duty of caution, believes in the non-occurrence of the result. According to Welzel, despite the carelessness, the agent *could be absolutely sure that he will not harm legal goods*—but the result ends up happening" (Reiss, Michel Wencland. (2017). *The International Criminal Court in the Context of Globalisation of Law: Analysis of the Rome Statute based on Anglo-Saxon inspired Criminal Law, Roman-Germanic inspired Criminal Law and Brazilian Criminal Law* [Doctoral Thesis, Pontifical Catholic University of Rio de Janeiro], p. 162. Available at: https://www.maxwell.vrac.puc-rio.br/36273/36273.PDF. Accessed on: 10 Jun. 2025).

"Knowledge", a requirement that must work cumulatively with "will", is related to the circumstances and consequences of the action. Indeed, there is no intention without knowledge, but there can be the opposite (which is generally irrelevant in criminal law). Knowledge of the circumstances (material elements) emerges as an additional typical element.[132] This rule, at first, is different from what is understood by *knowledge* as a mental state,[133] which is the awareness of possible risks arising from a certain criminal practice, that is, a lower degree of evidentiary requirement than in the Rome Statute.

It is worth remembering that the Treaty admits, in Article 28 (b), the subjective responsibility of the hierarchical superior and subordinates,[134] adopting the doctrine of command responsibility,[135] which results in a dilution of *mens rea*.[136] Even so, it seems clear that the ICC does not reach negligent conduct (or *negligence*, for *common law*), requiring, at least, a level above (*recklessness*), at the level close to eventual intent.[137]

Bringing the psychological elements to ecocide, it is a challenge to establish the necessary *mens rea* to link conduct to massive environmental damage. Following what is currently possible in the Court, excluding the possibility of strict liability offences and negligent modalities, the practice of the crime (destruction of the

---

[132] "The agent must be aware that the effect will occur in the normal course of events, that is, he must anticipate that his conduct will produce the prohibited result. When one talks about the regular course of events or facts, this does not mean that there has to be certainty that the result will occur in any way, but that it will occur unless exceptional circumstances intervene" (Faria, Maria Paula Ribeiro de (2006). The psychological elements of crimes provided for in the Rome Treaty. *Law and Justice, Special Issue*, 133–146, p. 136–140).

[133] For more on the degrees of *knowledge* in *mens rea*, see: Edwards, J. Ll J. (1954). Criminal Degrees of Knowledge. *The Modern Law Review*, *17*(4), 294–314.

[134] Extrapolating from the cases of military leaders, common in war events (Article 28 [a], of the Rome Statute).

[135] The "reconstructed knowledge", or presumed, of the illicit conducts practiced by the subordinates "is found in the expression 'had information that would allow him to conclude', of n° 2 of Article 86° of the PAI, in the expression 'had reasons to know' of n° 3 of the Article 7 of the ICTY Statute and No. 3 of Article 6 of the ICTR Statute and, finally in the expression 'should have had knowledge', of § i) of paragraph a) of Article 28 of the Statute of the International Criminal Court" (Leandro, Francisco José. (2006). The criminal responsibility of military leaders in the Rome Statute (Article 28). *Law and Justice*, (Special), 81–132, p. 110. Available at: https://journals.ucp.pt/index.php/direitoejustica/article/view/11246/10886. Accessed on: 20 Jun. 2025).

[136] Some authors see the provision in Article 28 as the introduction of the theory of wilful blindness (doctrine linked to *knowledge*, in *common law*) in the Statute, expanding to other legal systems (Soares, Jucelino Oliveira. (2019). The theory of wilful blindness and its applicability to financial crimes. *Academic Journal School of the Public Prosecutor's Office of Ceará*, *11*(2), 109–128, p. 113. Available at: http://www.mpce.mp.br/wp-content/uploads/2019/12/ARTIGO-6.pdf. Accessed on: 20 Jun. 2025).

[137] Reiss, Michel Wencland. (2017). *The International Criminal Court in the Context of Globalisation of Law: Analysis of the Rome Statute based on Anglo-Saxon inspired Criminal Law, Roman-Germanic inspired Criminal Law and Brazilian Criminal Law* [Doctoral Thesis, Pontifical Catholic University of Rio de Janeiro], p. 165. Available at: https://www.maxwell.vrac.puc-rio.br/36273/36273.PDF. Accessed on: 10 Jun. 2025.

environment) would remain intentional, or, at least, knowing and assuming the risks of producing the result.

It happens that most of the cases reported as ecocide are located in a grey area, between conduct practiced negligently (primarily in the negligence modality) and with risk assumption (close to eventual intent). Allocating the crime in the Rome Statute, considering its limits to criminal liability, would undermine the chances of prosecuting the offence in the Court, given the difficulty in fulfilling the psychological requirement.[138]

It is important to remember that the Statute itself already criminalises environmental damage caused in the context of war (Article 8 [2][b][v]). The *mens rea*, in this case, is linked to intentions within an armed conflict, with environmental destruction (extensive, long-lasting and serious damage, which are clearly excessive in relation to the overall concrete and direct military advantage anticipated) being just one of the underlying elements of the crime.[139]

Considering that there have never been proceedings in the International Criminal Court on the first crime, this would hardly be the case for the proposal of the *Stop Ecocide Foundation*, if approved, since no conduct was described in the bill.[140] The result in this case is a symbolic definition.

The proposition of the Panel of experts brings changes regarding the psychological elements. The standard *mens rea*, in relation to the effects of a crime (article 30

[138] Behaviours, for example, that cause harm by accumulation would be excluded from the ICC, due to the lack of intention to cause it, individually. The synergistic effect of accumulation (combination of elements to generate a third effect, generally more harmful), cannot be considered, for the purpose of international criminal responsibility (on accumulation offences, see: Caetano, Matheus Almeida. (2016). *The accumulation offences in environmental criminal law*. Pillares, p. 219).

[139] "Ecocide is often deemed a 'peacetime equivalent' to 8(2)(b)(iv). That it is not strictly the case. Indeed, this argument is grounded in the fact that 8(2)(b)(iv), as a war crime, employs a proportionality assessment related to armed conflict. This assessment requires that harm to the natural environment must be 'clearly excessive in relation to the concrete and direct overall military advantage anticipated', thereby placing environmental integrity as secondary to military advancement. The terminology of 'military advantage' indicates quite a low threshold of proof, arguably lower than 'military necessity', thus showcasing that military advantage might have an exculpatory effect for war crimes causing environmental harm." (Bienfait, Isabelle (2024). Unpacking the mens rea of ecocide: Can the ICC adopt a lower fault standard for crimes against the environment? In *Criminal Law Forum*. Dordrecht: Springer Netherlands, p. 376).

[140] Not listing any criminal acts "is a strong (and indeed desirable!) statement that all forms of environmental harm, regardless of the nature of the act, should entail individual criminal responsibility (provided that the additional threshold requirements of the act being 'unlawful or wanton' and the perpetrator having had 'knowledge that there is a substantial likelihood of severe and either widespread or long-term damage to the environment being caused by those acts' are fulfilled). This symbolic statement, however, comes at the expense of legal certainty, a basic pillar of criminal law required for its justifiability and enforceability" (Kersting, Natascha. (2021, July). On Symbolism and Beyond: Defining Ecocide. *Völkerrechtsblog*. Available at: https://voelkerrechtsblog.org/on-symbolism-and-beyond/. Accessed: Jun. 2025).

[2][b]), requires an almost certain awareness that the consequences will occur.[141] Thus, the Panel considered having a narrow margin to fit ecocide, suggesting a mental state of *recklessness* or *dolus eventualis,*[142] considering it sufficiently burdensome to ensure that only people with significant guilt for severe environmental damage will be held accountable.[143]

It should be noted that the Statute, as seen, promotes nuances of criminal liability, considering the peculiarities of each crime. Nothing prevents, for example, the creation of a new crime (surely serious to humanity and the planet)[144]—accompa-

[141] This conception of *mens rea* is in line with the case judged in the US Supreme Court in *Rehaif v. United States* of 2019, which recognised the requirement of culpable knowledge to the federal statute on gun possession by criminals, 18 U.S.C. § 922(g), which was previously treated as strict liability. It was therefore established that proof is required that the defendant was aware of their prohibited status (Mizel, M. L., Serota, M., Cantor, J., & Russell-Fritch, J. (2023). Does Mens Rea Matter?. Wisconsin Law Review, 287–343. Available at: https://heinonline.org/hol-cgi-bin/get_pdf.cgi?handle=hein.journals/wlr2023&section=9. Accessed on: 13 Jan. 2025).

[142] Sands, Phillipe, & Sow, D. F. (2021). *Independent expert panel for the legal definition of ecocide: Commentary and core text.* Stop Ecocide Foundation, p. 10. Available at: https://static1.squarespace.com/static/5ca2608ab914493c64ef1f6d/t/60d7479cf8e7e5461534dd07/1624721314430/SE+Foundation+Commentary+and+core+text+revised+%281%29.pdf. Accessed on: 20 May. 2025.

[143] In fact, this proposed change in understanding of Article 30 aims to broaden the scope of the rule, within the ICC, opening possibilities for damages caused negligently, for the *civil law*: According to almost all national criminal law systems, ICC judges have interpreted Art. 30 (3) to require that the perpetrator is aware that their actions are "almost certain" to bring about the prohibited consequences - a much higher standard of subjective awareness than "substantial likelihood", close to recklessness. Thus, "knowledge" in the definition of ecocide really means *recklessness* or *dolus eventuais*, which raises the question of why the Panel decided to use the term "knowledge". The Panel knows that the drafters of the Rome Statute were overwhelmingly opposed to the inclusion of recklessness in the Rome Statute, considering the crimes too serious to justify such a *mens rea* so restricted (recklessness is only found in the context of child soldiers and superior responsibility). "*But let's be honest: states are not going to be fooled. They will realise that knowledge actually means recklessness in the definition of ecocide. So I don't understand why the IEP didn't simply acknowledge that they think recklessness is more appropriate than knowledge and make the case for ecocide being the third exception to Art. 30's default mens rea*" (HELLER Heller, Kevin Jon (2021). Skeptical thoughts on the proposed crime of "ecocide" (that isn't). *Opinio Juris*. Available at: http://opiniojuris.org/2021/06/23/skeptical-thoughts-on-the-proposed-crime-of-ecocide-that-isnt/. Accessed on: 12 Jun; 2025).

[144] The ICC, it is worth remembering, recognised in 2016, through the Office of the Prosecutor, the gravity of environmental damage as an element to be considered in a prioritisation of case investigation under the jurisdiction of the Court. Therefore, "it seems crucial that, if the jurisdiction of the ICC were extended to include ecocide, it should take into account the scale and gravity of the impact on the environment, for example, the number of victims or the degree of damage caused to the environment" (Pereira, Ricardo (2020). After the ICC Office of the Prosecutor's 2016 policy paper on case selection and prioritisation: Towards an international crime of ecocide? *Criminal Law Forum, 31*(2), 179–224, p. 196). The Policy Paper, however, "reveals that its ambitions with respect to investigating environmental harm were quite modest, and that some commentators may have been raising unrealistic expectations about the Court. Specifically, the Policy Paper noted that environmental damage would be taken into consideration when assessing the gravity of other criminal conducts. However, the Policy Paper did not mention the prosecution of environmental crimes as such." (Minkova, Liana Georgieva (2023). The fifth international crime: Reflections on the defi-

nied by the description of conducts, even general ones—with peculiar rules about mental elements, respecting the parameters of article 30. In fact, it takes advantage of both the nuance between *mens rea* and intent/negligence as the liability of the hierarchical superior, alien to situations of war.[145]

The investigation of the will, to the detriment of the results, may seem an obstacle to processing in cases of massive environmental damage. However, the imposition of criminal sanction only according to the consequences of conduct (which would imply objective liability)[146] finds no support either in the International Criminal Court or in national legislations.[147] The existing definitions of ecocide—and most of the law proposals—require some level of intention or negligence of the agent, which is sufficient for the reprehensibility of the crime.

It is also unquestionable that the level of knowledge required for criminal liability, so discussed in the theories of the crime, undergoes a revolution in the current information age, so that technology assists both decision-makers[148] and justice

---

nition of "ecocide". *Journal of Genocide Research, 25*(1), 62–83. https://doi.org/10.1080/14623528.2021.1964688. Accessed on: 10 Jan. 2025).

[145] "The ICC held that the concept of control could be interpreted in three ways. Having control over the crime included direct perpetration where individuals physically carry out the objective elements of the offense. It also included indirect perpetration, where the individual had control over the mind of those carrying out the physical elements of the offense, even if they did not participate in the actual commission of the crime. Finally, this mode of liability encompasses co-perpetration where the individual has, along with others, control over the offense by virtue of an "essential" task assigned to them" (Kafedžić, Selma (2016). Determining modes of liability in international criminal law: Why the common purpose doctrine is the strongest legal response to mass atrocity crimes. *New Zealand Yearbook of International Law, 14*, 134–179, p. 161–162).

[146] The majority of the members of the Commission for the creation of the Rome Statute "did not want any of the crimes to involve strict liability; they were generally uncomfortable with negligence-based liability; they were generally uncomfortable with liability based on recklessness or its civil law (near) counterpart dolus eventualis. What they could agree upon was a default rule in Article 30 of the Statute17 that 'unless otherwise provided' the 'material elements' had to be committed 'with intent and knowledge'" (Clark, Roger S. (2008). Drafting a general part to a penal code: Some thoughts inspired by the negotiations on the Rome Statute of the International Criminal Court and by the Court's first substantive law discussion in the Lubanga Dyilo confirmation proceedings. *Criminal Law Forum, 19*(3–4), 519–552. p. 526).

[147] Objective liability can, for example, have relevance in the civil sphere, when, within public international law, in the assessment of damages caused by States, in cases of climate litigation, in respect to the principle of environmental responsibility. However, there are those who advocate for criminal repercussions, in these cases, for countries "akin to the legal intention of dolus eventualis (awareness of the likely outcome of an action) Higgins argues that an additional situation in terms of the linkage of the elements of crime and evidence presents itself in the context of climate related ecocide crime. Signing the Paris Agreement within the framework of the United Nations Framework Convention on Climate Change (UNFCCC) accords prior knowledge of duty to limit carbon emissions to state parties (Eradicating Ecocide 2018). Failing to do so, especially on the part of the top carbon emitters, is a potential criminal act" (Ahmed, Nabil. (2017). Proof of ecocide: towards a forensic practice for the proposed international crime against the environment. *Archaeological and Environmental Forensic Science, 1*(2), 139–147, p. 142).

[148] "Thanks to advances in computing technology and environmental science, the decision tools available to environmental policymakers have become quite sophisticated. A variety of modelling

itself. Thus, both computerised predictions about environmental damage and decision-making processes—in short, elements of proof—are exposed to the construction of psychological elements, necessary for criminal imputation.

The next step is to check whether the second element of the crime, the *actus reus*, is a limit to the criminal prosecution of environmental crimes in the International Criminal Court, considering the anthropocentric approach of law.

7.5 Ecocentric and Anthropocentric Approaches in the ICC

When talking about *actus reus*, the second element of the *offense* (which, in *common law*, must be proven in the trial by the prosecution, in addition to the *mens rea),*[149] external data, objective facts are considered, without investigating the subjective aspect of the agent (mental elements). The analysis of the *actus reus* bears resemblance to the judgement of objective formal typicity (Brazil), despite there not being a definition of crime as strict as in *civil law.*[150] The *actus reus* is,

---

software exists for a whole suite of environmental problems from water quality to power plant operations. These models can make projections with varying degrees of confidence. When the model is 95 percent confident in a range of outcomes in terms of statistical lives lost, or deaths prevented, based on the policy choice, it would seem that the prediction has not only statistical, but also criminal, significance. As described earlier, an actor is said to have knowledge of a result if it is 'practically certain' to occur and is said to act recklessly when there is a "substantial risk" of the result. Thus, when armed with the type of modelling now readily available, government entities possess the ability to act at least recklessly, if not knowingly, with regard to indeterminate human lives" (Moffa, Anthony (2018). Environmens rea. *Penn State Environmental Law Review, 1*, 299–346, p. 334).

[149] It is common in customary law to divide (for Brazil, only in the civil sphere) between themes of accusation and defence, opposing them as if they were symmetrical parts, that is, each side produces the evidence of their interest (accusation, evidence that condemns; defence, theses that exempt or reduce the penalty): "It is important to bear in mind that the basis used in England and Wales for not making categorical differences between justifications and excuses is that from the defendant's point of view both produce the same effect —they deny responsibility or prevent punishment—. In this way, it states that «it seems relatively logical to construct the theory of crime in a «procedural» key distinguishing the «offence» (what the prosecution must prove, actus reus and mens rea) from the "defences" (what the defence must prove, that is, any element that denies the existence of an offence, or introduces limitations to the imposition of a penalty in the specific case, such as prescription)" (Pardos, Mariano Melendo. (2009). ¿Strafrechtswissenschaft o Common Law? A propósito de Matus Acuña, Jean Pierre: La transformación de la teoría del delito en el derecho penal internacional. *Revista de Derecho Penal y Criminología, 3*(1), 413–433, p. 420. Available at: https://revistas.uned.es/index.php/RDPC/article/download/24735/19596. Accessed on: 20 Jun. 2025).

[150] The examination of the *actus reus* generates the classification of crimes into four distinct species: action crimes; result crimes; circumstance crimes and omission crimes. Already in the typicality In a formal objective sense, generally, the first element of the crime to be considered is the verb (nucleus), to then determine the legal good and the passive subject (holder of the protected good), as well as the result (if it occurs), to finally "verify the presence of causal link, that is, whether that human conduct under analysis contributed or not to the achievement of the result"

therefore, the commission of the act itself and the connection (causal link) of this with the result (without the depth of the theory of the crime in the Roman-Germanic system).[151]

The Rome Statute does not provide, in its text, for the definition of the *actus reus* or the material elements of the crime, leaving an idea of what it would be in article 30 (1),[152] indicating now in Article 9, that the material elements (constituting the crimes) would be elaborated a posteriori, by a majority of two-third of the members, which indeed occurred[153] in 2010, with the adoption of the book Elements of Crimes.[154]

The *actus reus*, as well as the *mens rea*, is a limiter of punitive power. By requiring the completion of a certain conduct, victim and causal link (allied to the will to commit it), the norm seeks to hold accountable only the agent who caused (or wished to cause) certain damage, in the fair measure of his culpability, to be assessed in the sentence.[155]

As stated, the conducts contained in the Rome Statute—as well as in most penal codes worldwide[156]—are aimed at protecting legal goods related to human rights. In this aspect, the construction of a crime (definition) related to environmental issues reveals a problem. The *actus reus* (the practice of the act in the real world, objec-

---

(Reiss, Michel Wencland. (2017). *The International Criminal Court in the Context of Globalisation of Law: Analysis of the Rome Statute based on Anglo-Saxon inspired Criminal Law, Roman-Germanic inspired Criminal Law and Brazilian Criminal Law* [Doctoral Thesis, Pontifical Catholic University of Rio de Janeiro], p. 104/81. Available at: https://www.maxwell.vrac.puc-rio.br/36273/36273.PDF. Accessed on: 10 Jun. 2025).

[151] For this reason, we are faced with only a similarity with the judgement of typicality, and not identical analyses.

[152] The meaning of this provision is that it assigns different levels of mental element to each of the material elements of the crime in question. It is therefore possible that a single definition of crime may require a different psychological state for each objective element of the offence: "this approach is similar to the one adopted by the Model Penal Code, in 1962, by the American Law Institute. The Model Penal Code's approach is based on the view that, unless some element of mental culpability is proved with respect to each material element of the offence, no valid criminal conviction may be obtained" (Badar, Mohamed Elewa (2008). The mental element in the Rome Statute of the International Criminal Court: A commentary from a comparative criminal law perspective. *Criminal Law Forum, 19*, 473–518, p. 476).

[153] The Elements of Crimes were adopted during the Review Conference of the Rome Statute, in Kampala, which took place between 31 May and 11 June 2010 (Link: https://asp.icc-cpi.int/reviewconference/rome-statute-amendment-proposals. Accessed on: 10 Jun. 2025).

[154] ICC. (2011). *Elements of Crimes*. The Hague: International Criminal Court. Available at: https://www.icc-cpi.int/sites/default/files/ElementsOfCrimesEng.pdf. Accessed on: 20 Jun. 2025.

[155] On the international level, there is—in theory—no hierarchy among crimes (there is no specific sanction for each crime): "it cannot be said that a certain class of international crimes includes more serious facts than conduct prohibited based on different criminal norms. *In abstracto*, all international crimes constitute serious violations of International Law, and no hierarchy in relation to their severity can be, *a priori*, established among them (for example, between war crimes and serious violations of the Geneva Conventions, or between war crimes and crimes against humanity)" (Cretella Neto, José. (2014). *Course of international criminal law* (2nd ed.). Saraiva, p. 117).

[156] With the exception of countries that recognise the rights of nature, such as Bolivia and Ecuador.

tively considered) should, possibly,[157] shift its focus[158] from direct harm to humans to harm to the environment[159] itself. This implies a revision of an anthropocentric approach to an ecocentric one of law.

The perception of man—and his activities—as the sole centre worthy of legal protection is the keynote for international law and for most States. Restricting the analysis to criminal law (in particular, in the definition of *actus reus*), this bias points to the definition of legal goods and recognition of victims channelled in the human being, raising the question whether the object of environmental security is the environment itself or its capacity to sustain the desired and existing levels of human civilisation.

The recognition of the *status* of "victim" is crucial for understanding how environmental damages affect humans and non-humans (meaning to locate living beings and environments within their unique niche and ecological context),[160] as well as essential to understanding the scope of the norm itself. In this context, the proposals for ecocide (national and international) are ambiguous, because, despite conferring

[157] At first glance, human rights and environmentalism may not seem opposed to each other: "As many scholars have argued, the framing of environmental protection as a fundamental condition for ensuring human rights has enabled environmental concerns to move to the top of the global agenda. However, this framing has also prevented the evolution of the norm of environmentalism into conceptions of responsibility similar to those that are in place for human rights (like R2P) or a 'responsibility of care' as proposed by Higgins. The inherent anthropocentrism of the international environmental regime and the duties and responsibilities attached to it, limit the potential of the emergence of this norm" (Malhotra, Saloni (2017). The international crime that could have been but never was: An English school perspective on the ecocide law. *Amsterdam Law Forum, 9*(3), 49–70, p. 62).

[158] For some authors, it is up to the *International Law Commission* the task of clarifying the *actus reus* in ecocide: "The role of ICL will be to clarify the elements of the ecocide crime, including the actus reus which is the red line that it is not supposed to be crossed. After all, the essence of criminal law is to delimit the acts prohibited while trying to affect the freedom of human beings as little as possible. This is exactly what ICL is called to do with the crime of ecocide: to criminalize only those serious acts that destroy the environment, without affecting those economic activities performed in a sustainable manner" (Pezzot, Romina., & Graf, Jan-Phillip. (2022, February 3). Ecocide—Legal Revolution or Symbolism?. *Völkerrechtsblog*. Available at: https://voelkerrechtsblog.org/ecocide-legal-revolution-or-symbolism/. Accessed on: 22 Jun. 2025).

[159] "Human damage can be and often is secondary (it arises out of the primary damage - for instance the polluted waters can give rise to illness). Thus the actus reus (the physical element - the doing of the act) of the crime is the establishment of damage to the territory, not specifically the doing damage directly to the people" (Higgins, Polly (2012). *Earth is our business: Changing the rules of the game*. London: Shepheard-Walwyn Publishers, p. 5).

[160] In this case, the issues revolve around the identification of the principles of justice that should guide the evaluation of non-human victimisation and the problems associated with the elaboration of a "legal ontology" of natural objects. Another problem "focuses on issues of evidence and expertise from the point of view of identifying who speaks for and on behalf of whom. It deals with the question of 'whose voices' are or should be heard in court; how this is, ought or might occur; and specifically, how and to whom does non-human nature communicate its needs" (White, Rob (2016). Four problems for specialist courts in dealing with nonhuman environmental victims. In T. Spapens, R. White, & W. Huisman (Eds.), *Environmental crime in transnational context: Global issues in green enforcement and criminology* (pp. 139–153). Routledge. p. 114/145).

intrinsic value to nature (it is important to preserve it not only for the well-being of humans but also of other species), they are, like current environmental laws, mainly anthropocentric, limiting the scope of the State's responsibility to protect the environment only to the extent necessary to safeguard human beings.[161]

The anthropocentric adoption of law, therefore, creates a hierarchy in relation to the environment. This position of superiority of directly human interests is seen in the laws and bills of ecocide, when they condition the recognition of a criminal conduct (that causes massive environmental damage) to the absence of administrative authorisations for a certain activity. That is, the dimension of the damage or the environmental harm caused by human action does not matter, as long as it is in observance of the legislation and with the proper legal licenses.[162]

The utilitarian perspective of the environment, commonly considered as derived from economic imperatives, is an inherent limitation to international law, relevant to understanding the—so far—failure of ecocide as an international crime.[163]

The proposal of the *Stop Ecocide Foundation* was attentive to this issue, when it defines ecocide as the practice of "unlawful" (*unlawful*) or "negligent" (*wanton*) acts, conditioning its recognition to the execution of a conduct against the law (broad sense) and with "intentional recklessness,[164]" with the damage caused clearly excessive in relation to the anticipated social and economic benefits.[165] Therefore, it

[161] It is possible to affirm that the most important national and international environmental laws have an anthropocentric framework, recognising the fundamental connection between environmental protection and respect for human rights. For example, "the Rio Declaration (1992) is a manifest of anthropocentric environmentalism. (…). Moreover, on 12 December 2015, the Parties to the UN Framework Convention on Climate Change adopted the Paris Agreement, one of the most important climate agreements since the UNCED. The climate negotiators included a strong reference to Human Rights in the agreement" (Malhotra, Saloni (2017). The international crime that could have been but never was: An English school perspective on the ecocide law. *Amsterdam Law Forum, 9*(3), 49–70, p. 63).

[162] For example, the Brazilian PL, the laws in Ecuador, in Colombia and in France.

[163] The value in combining environmental protection and human rights is recognised at the international level: "the way this anthropocentric framing of environmental stewardship constrains the emergence of this institution needs to be highlighted however, to explain the failure of the ecocide law and other ambitious ecocentric environmental projects" (Malhotra, Saloni (2017). The international crime that could have been but never was: An English school perspective on the ecocide law. *Amsterdam Law Forum, 9*(3), 49–70, p. 64).

[164] *Reckless disregard*, here in a sense close to eventual intent (Masucci, M (Org.). (2017). *Structures of international criminal law: interpretation, application, offences*. G. Giappichelli Editore, p. 58).

[165] For the Panel of experts, this limitation to the recognition of ecocide introduces a test of proportionality in the definition, reflecting the principles of environmental law: "much national and international environmental law involves a balancing of environmental harms against social and economic benefits, which is expressed in the principle of sustainable development, and the Panel was mindful that socially beneficial acts, such as housing developments and transport links, can cause severe and either widespread or long-term damage to the environment" (Sands, Phillipe, & Sow, D. F. (2021). *Independent expert panel for the legal definition of ecocide: Commentary and core text*. Stop Ecocide Foundation, p. 10. Available at: https://static1.squarespace.com/

cannot be said that the project changes the anthropocentric bias[166] of the Rome Statute to an ecocentric one,[167] as the focus remains on the human being and their well-being.

The anthropocentric approach also leads to the conclusion that a long-term and widespread destructive conduct to the environment may not be recognised as ecocide, in case there is legal provision for such. In other words, the name given to the harmful result to nature (regardless of the dimension) will depend on the endorsement achieved through administrative bureaucratic procedures.[168] By removing human responsibility[169] for significant changes in the planet—including the climate—the alleged crime may even lose its symbolic power.

static/5ca2608ab914493c64ef1f6d/t/60d7479cf8e7e5461534dd07/1624721314430/SE+Foundation+Commentary+and+core+text+revised+%281%29.pdf. Accessed on: 20 May. 2025).

[166] As ecocide, in the initiative of the *Stop Ecocide Foundation*, was highlighted from crimes against humanity and genocide (completely anthropocentric), the co-author of the project, Philippe Sands, believes it to be the new crime of an ecocentric nature: It‘s been intellectually challenging: there had been no new international crimes since 1945. It‘s really interesting; I‘ve been calling it the ‘Fifth Crime’, but it‘s different from the four previous ones, because it‘s not anthropocentric. And I‘m really clear: I don‘t know what will emerge finding the definition, but it‘s very important for me, personally, that it not be focused on the protection of the human" (Sands, Philippe., et al. (2021, April 24). Defining Ecocide: An interview with Philippe Sands. *Völkerrechtsblog*. Available at: https://voelkerrechtsblog.org/defining-ecocide/. Accessed on: 22 Jun. 2025).

[167] There are authors who consider that the proposal adopts an ecocentric understanding, therefore, this perspective should be extended to the regime of participation and reparation of the victims of the ICC, allowing a more holistic repair to the damage caused (Killean, R., & Newton, E. (2024). From ecocide to ecocentrism: Conceptualising environmental victimhood at the International Criminal Court. *International Review of Victimology*, p. 2–27).

[168] The question is whether the definition of ecocide should distinguish between lawful and unlawful acts, under penalty of restricting the incidence of the crime to unlikely situations: "I don't believe that ecocide should treat lawful and unlawful acts differently, nor do I believe that lawful acts should be subjected to an anthropocentric cost-benefit analysis. But even if you accept both aspects of the IEP's definition, you should be concerned that the wantonness requirement will simply not work in practice. Given the problems of proof that inhere in the cost-benefit analysis and the subjective nature of "reckless disregard," that requirement is likely to acquit at least some ecocide defendants who deserve conviction" (Heller, Kevin Jon (2021). Skeptical thoughts on the proposed crime of "ecocide" (that isn't). *Opinio Juris*. Available at: http://opiniojuris.org/2021/06/23/skeptical-thoughts-on-the-proposed-crime-of-ecocide-that-isnt/. Accessed on: 12 Jun; 2025).

[169] The influence of human activities is so great that, in fact, it has altered the geological era of the planet: "One of the many features that distinguish the Anthropocene is that, in the words of the manager of climate monitoring at the Australian Bureau of Meteorology in January 2013, 'Everything that takes place in the climate system now is taking place on a planet which is a degree hotter than use to be'. The geological era that this new age is said to have replaced is the Holocene, a period that began 12,000 years ago following the last Ice Age. (…) These begin climatic conditions have proved to be very consequential as they freed humans to 'finally make their mark' and shifted their geological status from bit players to 'geological agents'. Today, humans can no longer be conceived of as social actors operating exclusively within a social sphere of human-to-human engagements" (Shearing, Clifford (2020). Criminology and the Anthropocene. In R. White (Ed.), *Environmental crime* (Vol. II, pp. 2–16). Cheltenham: Elgar, p. 2–3).

This fact leads to a larger question, outside the scope of this investigation, involving consumer relations and the determining influence of the capitalist system[170] in the construction of goods that the law must observe and protect.[171] In the critique of anthropocentrism, environmental ethics particularly opposes the commodification of nature.[172] Even among ecocentrists, the restrictive criterion of "life" limits moral obligations towards the environment, by disregarding the oceans, soils, and the atmosphere, for example.[173]

All these elements demand a new legal approach to the link between man and the environment, considering the urgency[174] environmental (scientifically recognised), which cannot wait for the slow structural changes necessary for a significant review of social relations.

---

170 For Napoletano and Clark, there are three important questions that advocates of ecocentric conservation can raise, about this apparent antagonism between environment and capitalism: "1) The way capital extends the same instrumental valuation to humans and non-human nature means that the struggle over conservation is by definition one over social justice, with the converse also being true, that every struggle over social justice affects conservation to some degree. 2) The extent to which this combined struggle is often obscured by alienation from nature, and the corresponding illusion that problems displaced in the social metabolism are resolved, belie normative appeals that neglect the way humanity's relationship with nature is always socially mediated through labor. As a result, a society plagued by hierarchical class antagonisms will necessarily exhibit an antagonistic metabolic relationship with nature and vice-versa, making the struggle against capitalist alienation an important common cause. 3) Conservation efforts at any scale will reverberate through the rate, volume, technical composition, and spatial configuration of the social metabolism, often in unanticipated ways, and will therefore never be politically neutral or free of influence by the underlying imperial capital system and its class rule so long as it operates" (Napoletano, Brian M., & Clark, Brett. (2020). An ecological-marxist response to the half-earth project. *Conservation & Society*, *18*(1), 37–49, p. 47).

171 The climate negotiations led by the UN and the IPCC have resigned themselves to solutions within the logic of imperial ecocide: "the embrace of carbon trading, carbon offsets, geo-engineering and using forests as carbon sinks while commercialising them, are all part of the agenda to deal with the climate crisis. However, these are not real systemic solutions" (Satgar, Vishwas (2018). The Anthropocene and imperial ecocide: Prospects for just transitions. *The Climate Crisis*, 47–68, p. 60).

172 A bias of liberal doctrine would grant supreme value to human interests and participate in the sacralisation of economic rationality in society, that is, "a system of thought that considers our environment as a means to serve ends decided by Man. Living beings (plants, animals), can then be assigned a use value set by the market (a price)" (Estève, Adrien (2020). *Introduction to environmental political theory*. Mallakoff: Armand Colin, p. 55–56).

173 The ecological crisis that we are going through deteriorates a large number of non-organic entities, which should also be taken into account in an ethical reflection, "his ecosophy, however, has important ethical implications, as it imposes a strong limit on human action, capable of destabilising an already precarious ecological balance" (Estève, Adrien (2020). *Introduction to environmental political theory*. Mallakoff: Armand Colin, p. 65). However, his ecosophy has important ethical implications, as it imposes a strong limit on human action, capable of destabilising an already precarious ecological balance.

174 Technically, the law was not prepared to create and incorporate into its international punitive system the crimes of genocide and against humanity, but the emergency conditions of the 2nd World War, especially, demanded a rapid advance of international criminal law.

Criminological theories cannot exist only to explain the victimisation of the human being,[175] especially when this is conceived, in the international legal system, as part of the earth systems.[176] The path for international criminal law might be to take advantage of the theoretical (human rights, crime theory, etc.) and physical structures (courts, treaties, etc.) to be effective.

Even countries with anthropocentric biases[177] of law recognise the healthy environment as a fundamental right, inherent to the very existence of society. A reinterpretation of human rights that promotes environmental protection is necessary, inserting it as a legal good preserved in balance with other goods.[178]

From a subjective point of view, the personal dimension of the environment does not entirely oppose the collective point of view; the public dimension should integrate the role of individuals and civil society. Therefore, there is no contrast between the individualistic and the community view, when the environment is accepted as a priority value for all culture, associating socio-economic development with the living ecosystem of the planet.[179]

---

[175] This theory needs to expand to encompass the entire environment, within the framework of environmental criminology (Eman, K Katja, Meško, G., & Fields, C. (2009). Crimes against the environment: Green criminology and research challenges in Slovenia. *Varstvoslovje, 4*, 574–592, p. 575).

[176] "As we humans have slowly but surely come to recognise this change in our status, we have begun to question foundational assumptions about ourselves as a 'social-only domain', separate from 'the natural world "over-there" that surrounds us' as was formed during the Holocene" (Shearing, Clifford (2020). Criminology and the Anthropocene. In R. White (Ed.), *Environmental crime* (Vol. II, pp. 2–16). Cheltenham: Elgar, p. 3).

[177] Some authors call this current "weak anthropocentrism", as a way to search for a more suitable anthropocentric ethic to the traditional morality of our societies in harmony with the environment: "Weak anthropocentrism shows that we have the necessary ethical resources to criticise the instrumentalisation of nature for human ends, and that several of our personal preferences push us to promote a sustainable and harmonious management of our environment" (Estève, Adrien (2020). *Introduction to environmental political theory*. Mallakoff: Armand Colin, p. 67–68).

[178] In addition to the need for more ecocentric and feasible laws and rights of nature, "certain human rights themselves require a re-interpretation and reformation to 'allow for a new ethical relationship between humanity and nature'. This applies to human rights that can be invoked to justify environmental damage like property and development rights. States that emphasise a libertarian and individualist ideology may discard ecological limitations to civil and political rights, like the property right, on the grounds that the unrestricted enjoyment of such rights are 'essential to personal freedom'. As already established in the discussion on the institution of the market, the role of the state is to protect property, not limit its use beyond what is needed and justified in the interest of society as a whole" (Malhotra, Saloni (2017). The international crime that could have been but never was: An English school perspective on the ecocide law. *Amsterdam Law Forum, 9*(3), 49–70, p. 63).

[179] If individual rights are fundamental rights, constituting the individual's minimum necessary and indispensable content, it cannot be denied that today the environment is essential for every human being: some individual rights such as physical well-being and health are based on the protection of the environment: "this is where the qualitative leap comes in. The right to the environment is not only a right not to suffer restrictions of one's individual rights, but a right-duty to positively intervene to protect assets that are essential for the community, in the spirit of social solidarity"

In other words, the focus would remain on the human being, but the range of social protection would have been expanded, preventing, for example, the prevalence of property rights and development over large-scale environmental damage. Instead of a hierarchy between the values "human life" and "the environment", there would be harmonisation. Criminal law, as ultima ratio, would operate in this scenario.[180]

This interpretation of environmental protection through international criminal law, within a "weak" anthropocentric context, is the line adopted by the European Union, in supporting the "ecocide initiative" within a Resolution dedicated to human rights and democracy in the world.[181] By recognising "the human right to a safe, clean and sustainable environment", the UN endorses this possibility,[182] paving the way for actions with ecocentric characteristics at the national and international levels.

With this perspective, one ceases to criticise an ecocide project that is based on an anthropocentric view, provided that, in conflict with established human rights, the environment is also recognised as such. The practical—and realistic—consequence of this approach is the impossibility of an act (*actus reus*) that causes massive damage to the environment (harmful to the individual, the community and,

(Postiglione, Amedeo (2010). Human rights and the environment. *The International Journal of Human Rights, 14*(4), 524–541, p. 529.).

180 For example, when the offence is of absolute prohibition, such as the destruction of an environmental reserve, and the *mens rea*, in the sense of foreseeing the consequences of the damages, is excluded, the mere intentional practice of the prohibited act is sufficient to hold the accused accountable: "all that must be shown is that the actus reus, which in itself constitutes the offence, resulted from a voluntary act on the part of the prisoner, and in such cases it is obvious that the maxim has no application" (Edwards, J. Ll J. (1954). Criminal Degrees of Knowledge. *The Modern Law Review, 17*(4), 294–314, p. 296).

181 From an anthropocentric point of view, "the criminalisation of ecocide would indeed serve a function of protection of human rights, in line with the approach that has historically shaped the Rome Statute. The approach of the European Parliament, for example, which, as seen, promotes the recognition of ecocide within a Resolution dedicated to human rights and democracy in the world, would seem to be anthropocentric. In the prism of ecocentrism, this perspective would instead be reversed: ecocide would not be exclusively a threat to man, but, more broadly, to the specific violated ecosystem and to all those—human beings and not—who inhabit it" (Molteni, Viola. (2021). The long road to the criminalisation of ecocide: legal issues and dynamics of normative and social effectiveness. *Contemporary Criminal Law, 4*, 205–233, p. 208).

182 "If ever there was an opportunity for international legal norms to explicitly embrace ecocentrism, then this is it; however, there is a very real chance that this opportunity will be lost, unless the ongoing efforts to adopt ecocide pursue a radically different direction. Moreover, while the recent recognition by the UN Human Rights Council of the "human right to a safe, clean and sustainable environment" is significant and could have important benefits for people and nature (Savaresi, 2021), it also remains human-centred, with no attempt by states to recognize, for example, rights of nature in IEL or, at least, the explicit need to safeguard ecological foundations as a prerequisite for the enjoyment of all other human rights" (Du Toit, Louise, & Kotzé, L. J. (2022). Reimagining international environmental law for the Anthropocene: An earth system law perspective. *Earth System Governance, 11*, 1–12, p. 3).

possibly, all of humanity) being excused by the existence of licences or administrative authorisations for it.

To attract the jurisdiction of the International Criminal Court, for example, the damage would need to be severe (like the chemical pollution of Bhopal), clearly disproportionate to the collective benefit and not necessarily affecting the human being,[183] an indirect victim of the attack on the environment.[184] Thus, ecocide should be considered a unique international crime *sui generis*, having as its *ratio legis* the prohibition of causing serious, extensive and lasting damage to the environment, regardless of the legality of the conduct,[185] when disproportionate to the gain as a society (and not just of the stakeholders).

The idea is not to criminalise large-scale industrial activities, which promote improvements and social development to all human activities, such as mining, aviation, or oil extraction. But, when carried out without due control, alongside existing damage mitigation technologies, with a clear imbalance between the monetary

---

[183] One of the concerns of the expert panel of the Stop Ecocide Foundation was about lawful conducts that cause environmental damage, since these, in most States, are not considered criminal: "But the panel was cautious of a definition that would "leapfrog" any and every act that causes severe and either widespread or long-term environmental damage to the level of an 'international crime of ecocide'. In respect of the ICC's jurisdiction over the most serious crime of concern to the international community as a whole, and for reasons of clarity, predictability, legitimacy, but also to address this challenge with a certain degree of realism, the choice was made that for lawful acts, the wantonness of the act would be the "criminalising" element. In this situation, an additional, "unjustifiability" threshold was included: the disproportionality or excessiveness of the environmental damage in relation to anticipated social and economic benefits, and the reckless disregard for such" (Voigt, Christina. (2022). "Ecocide" as an international crime: Personal reflections on options and choices. *EJIL Talk!*, 3 Jul. 2021. Available at: https://www.ejiltalk.org/ecocide-as-an-international-crime-personal-reflections-on-options-and-choices/. Accessed on: 4 Jun. 2025).

[184] There is severe doubt whether ecocide can/should directly combat climate change. It is complicated to align the *actus reus* and *mens rea* in the face of greenhouse gas emissions as an environmental crime (De-Paor, Risteard (2020). Towards criminality climate: Creating a fifth category of crime under the Rome Statute to penalise the aggravation of climate change. Spanish Yearbook of International Law, 36, 289–325, p. 292). In a sense, international criminal law is still in its infancy, "especially with respect to prosecutions before an international criminal court, such that jumping on this particular bandwagon may, to mix metaphors, rock the boat both in relation to international responses to climate change and in relation to international criminalisation in general. To paraphrase some of the reasoning in the literature pertaining to Responsibility to Protect, international criminalisation of climate change induced displacement may be a step too far" (Gilbert, Geoff (2014). International criminal law is not a panacea - Why proposed climate change "crimes" are just another passenger on an overcrowded bandwagon. *International Criminal Law Review, 14*(3), 551–587, p. 587).

[185] Behaviours that cause massive damage to the environment should be prohibited, "produced not only by illicit, dangerous or potentially harmful behaviours, on which there is already a wide but heterogeneous regulatory norm in international law, but also by the development of perfectly lawful activities, which are typical of our productive and consumption model, but which in their development fulfil an accumulative function of dangers in terms of destruction and predation of the natural environment and human life" (Lora, Libia Arenal (2021). The legal regulation of crimes against the environment in international law: Challenges for the definition of ecocide as an international crime. *Anuario Iberoamericano de Derecho Internacional Penal, 9*, 1–20, p. 18).

gains of shareholders, to the detriment of communities and the environment, these conducts, even if legal and authorised, should be recognised as ecocide, when they cause massive environmental destruction.

The clash between human rights and environmentalism, understanding the anthropocentric framing of environmental law[186] as contrary to ecocentric objectives, can be softened with a review of anthropocentrism, moving humans "as masters of nature and recipients of rights against a defenceless environment" (Kotzé, 2014, pp. 252–275) to a position of equality with the environment. This change in understanding—without, necessarily, recognising the rights of nature at the international level—redefines the objective aspect of the conduct[187] (*actus reus*), as it expands the possibilities of identifying the action/omission, the victims and, consequently, the causal link.

Obviously, the utility of international crime depends on the reverberation at the national level, considering, among other things, the complementarity of the ICC in relation to the jurisdictions of the States. That being said, it is necessary to study the competences to judge environmental issues, especially in the criminal field, when the massive damages cross borders or are of concern to the international community. At some point, internal and external competences clash, forcing a review of the sovereign power/duty of States to prosecute an individual criminally.

To understand this relationship, one must question the role of the sovereignty of States in the structure of international criminal justice. The next chapter seeks to expand the discussion on the topic.

---

[186] For Darryl Robinson, the most complex aspect of constructing ecocide is aligning international criminal law with environmental law, especially regarding the 'illegality' of the conduct, considering that all human activity has an environmental impact: "For example, cultivating food has an ecological footprint; thus a major enterprise coordinating activities to provide food for hundreds of millions of people can thereby knowingly contribute to WLS harm through its operations, even if it uses the current best available practices, because of the sheer number of people being fed. An easy reply, to avoid facing the conundrum, is to say that food producers should use more environmentally-sound practices. And they should. But even if they use the best available practices, there is still some impact. Multiplied over a large enough scale, the impact will reach the WLS threshold. The conundrum remains. The solution is not simply to ban large operations, because that may also ban efficiencies of scale: the resulting duplication of tools, activities, energy, and waste may create an even worse net environmental impact. This is why environmental law looks not only at impacts, but also at benefits, adequacy of measures to mitigate harms, and other considerations like eradicating poverty". (Robinson, Darryl (2022). Ecocide: Puzzles and possibilities. *Journal of International Criminal Justice, 20*(2), 313–347. doi.org/10.1093/jicj/mqac021. Accessed on: 12 Jan. 2025, p. 333).

[187] A similar *actus reus* already exists in the Rome Statute, in article 8(2)(b)(iv): "the actus reus must be widespread, severe and cause long-term environmental damage" (Patel, Payal. (2016). Expanding Past Genocide, Crimes Against Humanity, and War Crimes: Can an ICC Policy Paper Expand the Court's Mandate to Prosecuting Environmental Crimes? *Loyola University Chicago International Law Review, 14*(2), 175–193, p. 178).

References

African Union. (2014, June 27). Malabo Protocol. Protocol on amendments to the Protocol on the Statute of the African Court of Justice and Human Rights. Available at: https://au.int/sites/default/files/treaties/36398-treaty-0045_-_protocol_on_amendments_to_the_protocol_on_the_statute_of_the_african_court_of_justice_and_human_rights_p.pdf. Accessed on July 20, 2025.

Altunjan, T., & Neugebauer, K. (2019). *Workshop report: "The International Criminal Court in Turbulent Times"*. Asser Press.

Ambos, K. (2021). Protecting the environment through international criminal law? *EJIL: Talk!*. Retrieved from https://www.ejiltalk.org/protecting-the-environment-through-international-criminal-law/

Arifin, R., et al. (2024). Ecocide as the serious crime: A discourse on global environmental protection. In *IOP conference series: Earth and environmental science*. IOP Publishing. https://doi.org/10.1088/1755-1315/1355/1/012004

Azevedo, T. P. d. (2014). Theories of the crime–Roman-Germanic model and common law. *Law & Justice, 40*(2), 205–215. Available at: https://revistaseletronicas.pucrs.br/index.php/fadir/article/download/17348/11150. Accessed on June 12, 2025

Badar, M. E. (2008). The mental element in the Rome statute of the international criminal court: A commentary from a comparative criminal law perspective. *Criminal Law Forum, 19*, 473–518.

Bienfait, I. (2024). Unpacking the mens rea of ecocide: Can the ICC adopt a lower fault standard for crimes against the environment? In *Criminal law forum*. Springer.

Brochado, N., & Djalma, A. (2016). *Representativeness in the Brazilian jury court: Criticisms of the selection of jurors and proposals in light of the American model* [Master's dissertation, Federal University of Ceará].

Burns, R. (2023). From meaning to ecocide: The value of phenomenology for green criminology. *Critical Criminology, 31*(4), 1137–1154.

Caetano, M. A. (2016). *The accumulation offences in environmental criminal law*. Pillares.

Cassese, S. (2009). *I Tribunali di Babele: i giudici alla ricerca di un nuovo ordine globale*. Donzelli editore.

Chin, S. (2023). Lessons learned from the adoption of the crime of aggression: Ecocide to charter its own path. 'An International Crime of Ecocide: New Perspectives' symposium. UCLA. The Promise Institute for Human Rights.

Clark, R. S. (2008). Drafting a general part to a penal code: Some thoughts inspired by the negotiations on the Rome statute of the international criminal court and by the court's first substantive law discussion in the Lubanga Dyilo confirmation proceedings. *Criminal Law Forum, 19*(3–4), 519–552.

Clementino, M. B. M. (2010). Culpability in international criminal law. *CEJ Magazine, 14*(51).

Cretella Neto, J. (2014). *Course of international criminal law* (2nd ed.). Saraiva.

Cusato, E., & Jones, E. (2024). The 'imbroglio' of ecocide: A political economic analysis. *Leiden Journal of International Law, 37*(1), 42–61. https://doi.org/10.1017/S0922156523000468

De Carli, C. V. (2014). Grammar of international criminal law: The languages of crime and punishment. *Cadernos do Programa de Pós-Graduação em Direito/UFRGS, 9*(1), 370–394.

De-Paor, R. (2020). Towards criminality climate: Creating a fifth category of crime under the Rome statute to penalise the aggravation of climate change. *Spanish Yearbook of International Law, 36*, 289–325.

Druart, P. (2024). Mens Rea in international criminal law: A look at Eichmann's responsibility in the light of Kant and Arendt. In *Heritage in war and peace: Legal and political perspectives for future protection*. Springer.

Du Toit, L., & Kotzé, L. J. (2022). Reimagining international environmental law for the Anthropocene: An earth system law perspective. *Earth System Governance, 11*, 1–12.

Edwards, J. L. J. (1954). Criminal degrees of knowledge. *The Modern Law Review, 17*(4), 294–314.

Eman, K. K., Meško, G., & Fields, C. (2009). Crimes against the environment: Green criminology and research challenges in Slovenia. *Varstvoslovje, 4*, 574–592.

Estève, A. (2020). *Introduction to environmental political theory*. Armand Colin.

Fabel, L. M. T., Costa, B. S., & Massad, F. A. (2022, March). Ecocide in the International Criminal Court: analysis of the feasibility of the court's jurisdiction in cases of mining waste dam breaks. *Legal Journal (FURB), 25*(58):e9905, p. 10. Available at: https://bu.furb.br/ojs/index.php/juridica/article/view/9905. Accessed on June 25, 2025.

Faria, M. P. R. d. (2006). The psychological elements of crimes provided for in the Rome Treaty. *Law and Justice, Special Issue*, 133–146.

Frouville, O. d. (2012). *Droit international pénal: Sources, incriminations, responsabilité*. Pedone.

Gallant, K. S. (2009). *The principle of legality in international and comparative criminal law*. Cambridge University Press.

Gilbert, G. (2014). International criminal law is not a panacea—why proposed climate change "crimes" are just another passenger on an overcrowded bandwagon. *International Criminal Law Review, 14*(3), 551–587.

Gounelle, M. (2006). *The political system of international relations*. Dalloz.

Greene, A. (2019). The campaign to make ecocide an international crime: Quixotic quest or moral imperative? *Fordham Environmental Law Review, 30*(3), 1–44.

Heller, K. J. (2021). Skeptical thoughts on the proposed crime of "ecocide" (that isn't). Opinio Juris. Retrieved from http://opiniojuris.org/2021/06/23/skeptical-thoughts-on-the-proposed-crime-of-ecocide-that-isnt/.

Hessick, C. B. (2019). The myth of common law crimes. *Virginia Law Review, 105*(5), 965–1024.

Higgins, P. (2012). *Earth is our business: Changing the rules of the game*. Shepheard-Walwyn Publishers.

ICC. (2011). *Elements of crimes*. The Hague: ICC. Available at: https://www.icc-cpi.int/sites/default/files/ElementsOfCrimesEng.pdf. Accessed on June 14, 2025.

ICC. (2013). *Rules of procedure and evidence*. The Hague: ICC. Available at: https://www.icc-cpi.int/sites/default/files/RulesProcedureEvidenceEng.pdf. Accessed on June 14, 2025.

ICC. Office of the Prosecutor. (2018, December 5). *Report on the activities carried out in 2018 in terms of preliminary examination.*

ICC. Office of the Prosecutor. (2024a, February 16). The Office of the Prosecutor launches public consultation on a new policy initiative to advance accountability for environmental crimes under the Rome Statute. Available at: https://www.icc-cpi.int/news/office-prosecutor-launches-public-consultation-new-policy-initiative-advance-accountability-0. Accessed on January 15, 2025.

ICC. Office of the Prosecutor. (2024b, December 18). ICC Office of the Prosecutor launches second public consultation on a policy initiative to advance accountability for environmental crimes under the Rome Statute. Available at: https://www.icc-cpi.int/news/icc-office-prosecutor-launches-second-public-consultation-policy-initiative-advance. Accessed on January 15, 2025.

ICC. Trial Chamber V. (2015, March 13). *Decision on the withdrawal of charges against Mr Kenyatta*. (ICC-01/09-02111). Available at: https://www.icc-cpi.int/sites/default/files/CourtRecords/CR2015_02842.PDF. Accessed on July 2, 2025.

Jaeger-Fine, T. (2015). *Mastering the U.S. legal system: A beginner's guide*. Jaeger-Fine Publishing.

Kafedžić, S. (2016). Determining modes of liability in international criminal law: Why the common purpose doctrine is the strongest legal response to mass atrocity crimes. *New Zealand Yearbook of International Law, 14*, 134–179.

Kersting, N. (2021, July). On symbolism and beyond: Defining ecocide. *Völkerrechtsblog*. Available at: https://voelkerrechtsblog.org/on-symbolism-and-beyond/. Accessed June, 2025.

Kiyani, A. (2016). Group-based differentiation and local repression: The custom and curse of selectivity. *Journal of International Criminal Justice, 14*(4), 939–957. p. 955. Available at: https://academic.oup.com/jicj/article/14/4/939/2236031?login=false#41846519. Accessed on June 10, 2025

Kotzé, L. J. (2014). Human rights and the environment in the Anthropocene. *The Anthropocene Review, 1*(3), 252–275.
Leandro, F. J. (2006). The criminal responsibility of military leaders in the Rome Statute (Article 28). *Law and Justice*, 81–132.
Lima, L. C., & De Andrade, M. C. (2015). An international court for the environment and its insertion in the debate about the fragmentation of international law. *Revista da Faculdade de Direito da UFMG, 67*, 373–398.
Lora, L. A. (2021). The legal regulation of crimes against the environment in international law: Challenges for the definition of ecocide as an international crime. *Anuario Iberoamericano de Derecho Internacional Penal, 9*, 1–20.
Luts, L. L. (2010). Typologies of modern legal Systems of the World. *Journal of Comparative Law, 5*(1), 28–40.
Malhotra, S. (2017). The international crime that could have been but never was: An English school perspective on the ecocide law. *Amsterdam Law Forum, 9*(3), 49–70.
Marinho, R. (2019). Mercosul criminal court: Confronting transnational criminal organisations. Lumen juris.
Masucci, M. (Org.). (2017). Structures of international criminal law: Interpretation, application, offences. G. Giappichelli Editore.
Matus, J. P. (2008). *The transformation of crime theory in international criminal law*. Atelier.
Minkova, L. G. (2024). Ecocide, sustainable development and critical environmental law insights. *Journal of International Criminal Justice, 22*(1), 81–97.
Minkova, L. G. (2023). The fifth international crime: Reflections on the definition of "ecocide". *Journal of Genocide Research, 25*(1), 62–83. https://doi.org/10.1080/14623528.2021.1964688
Moffa, A. (2018). Environmens rea. *Penn State Environmental Law Review, 1*, 299–346.
Molteni, V. (2021). The long road to the criminalisation of ecocide: Legal issues and dynamics of normative and social effectiveness. *Contemporary Criminal Law, 4*, 205–233.
Napoletano, B. M., & Clark, B. (2020). An ecological-marxist response to the half-earth project. *Conservation and Society, 18*(1), 37–49.
Negri, S. (2022). On meteors and comets: Is the crime of ecocide back to stay? Environmental crimes at the interface of philosophy, the law of state responsibility and international criminal law. *International Criminal Law Review, 1*, 1–30.
Nollez-Goldbach, R. (2018). *The international criminal court*. Presses Universitaires de France.
Pardos, M. M. (2009). ¿Strafrechtswissenschaft o Common Law? A propósito de Matus Acuña, Jean Pierre: La transformación de la teoría del delito en el derecho penal internacional. *Revista de Derecho Penal y Criminología, 3*(1), 413–433.
Pasquali, L. (2016). *Multilingualism in international normative acts and the need for differentiated interpretative solutions* (Vol. 12). G Giappichelli Editore.
Pasquali, L. (2019). The limits set by African countries to the institutionalisation of cooperation between states in the judicial repression of international crimes. *Federalismi.it Journal of Italian Public Law, Comparative, European, 9*, 2–51.
Patel, P. (2016). Expanding past genocide, crimes against humanity, and war crimes: Can an ICC policy paper expand the court's mandate to prosecuting environmental crimes? *Loyola University Chicago International Law Review, 14*(2), 175–193.
Pedersen, O. W. (2012). An international environmental court and international legalism. *Journal of Environmental Law, 24*(3), 547–558.
Pellet, A. (2003). For the international criminal court, anyway!—Some remarks on its jurisdiction and referral. *International Criminal Law Review, 1*(1–2), 91–110.
Pereira, R. (2020). After the ICC Office of the Prosecutor's 2016 policy paper on case selection and prioritisation: Towards an international crime of ecocide? *Criminal Law Forum, 31*(2), 179–224.
Pezzot, R., & Graf, J.-P. (2022, February 3). *Ecocide—legal revolution or symbolism?* Völkerrechtsblog.

Phillips, S. K. (2021). Unpacking "ecocide": A note of caution for international criminalisation. Stockholm Environment Institute—SEI. Retrieved from https://www.sei.org/perspectives/unpacking-ecocide-international-law/.

Pirro, D. (2006). Project for an International Court of the Environment–Origins and Development. In T. Greiber (Coord.), Judges and the rule of law: Creating links—environment, human rights and poverty (pp. 13–20). IUCN Publications Service Unit.

Postiglione, A. (2010). Human rights and the environment. *The International Journal of Human Rights, 14*(4), 524–541.

Razi, G. M. (1960). Around the world's legal systems. *Howard Law Journal, 6*(1), 1–29.

Reiss, M. W. (2017). *The International Criminal Court in the Context of Globalisation of Law: Analysis of the Rome Statute based on Anglo-Saxon inspired Criminal Law, Roman-Germanic inspired Criminal Law and Brazilian Criminal Law* [Doctoral Thesis, Pontifical Catholic University of Rio de Janeiro], p. 97. Available at: https://www.maxwell.vrac.puc-rio.br/36273/36273.PDF. Accessed on June 10, 2025.

Robinson, D. (2022). Ecocide: Puzzles and possibilities. *Journal of International Criminal Justice, 20*(2), 313–347. https://doi.org/10.1093/jicj/mqac021

Rodríguez, I., & Gil, C. (2019). The relationship between legal systems. *Spanish Yearbook of International Law, 1*(1–8), 2. Available at: https://scholar.archive.org/work/ypckl45o2vc-mlcrwdru4d7iwuq/access/wayback/http://www.sybil.es/documents/ARCHIVE/Vol23/1_RodriguezIglesias.pdf. Accessed on June 15, 2025

Roxin, C. (2002). Criminal policy and legal-criminal system. Renovar.

Roxin, C. (2006). Studies of criminal law. Renovar.

Saraiva, M. F. (2017). *The role of African states in the politicisation of the international criminal court* (pp. 1–8). National Defence Institute.

Sands, P., & Sow, D. F. (2021). *Independent expert panel for the legal definition of ecocide: Commentary and core text*. Stop Ecocide Foundation.

Sands, P., et al. (2021, April 24). Defining ecocide: An interview with Philippe Sands. *Völkerrechtsblog*.

Satgar, V. (2018). The Anthropocene and imperial ecocide: Prospects for just transitions. *The Climate Crisis*, 47–68.

Sayre, F. B. (1932). Mens rea. *Harvard Law Review, 45*(6), 974–1026. p. 974. Available at: https://www.jstor.org/stable/pdf/1332142.pdf?refreqid=excelsior%3Af22543cbd9836c96a090e8c6f2008e16&ab_segments=&origin=. Accessed on June 12, 2025

Shearing, C. (2020). Criminology and the anthropocene. In R. White (Ed.), *Environmental crime* (Vol. II, pp. 2–16). Elgar.

Simma, B., & Pulkowski, D. (2006). Of planets and the universe: Self-contained regimes in international law. *European Journal of International Law, 17*(3), 483–529.

Soares, J. O. (2019). The theory of wilful blindness and its applicability to financial crimes. *Academic Journal School of the Public Prosecutor's Office of Ceará, 11*(2), 109–128.

Soler, C., et al. (2019). *The global prosecution of core crimes under international law*. TMC Asser Press.

Trindade, A. A. C. (2010). Contemporary international courts and the pursuit of the ideal of international justice. *Revista da Faculdade de Direito da Law UFMG, 57*, 37–68.

United Nations. (2021, October 5). United Nations Treaty Collection. Rome Statute of the International Criminal Court.

Voigt, C. (2022). "Ecocide" as an international crime: Personal reflections on options and choices. EJIL Talk!.

Wenin, R. (2012). *The mens Rea in the Rome statute*. G. Giappichelli Publisher.

White, R. (2016). Four problems for specialist courts in dealing with nonhuman environmental victims. In T. Spapens, R. White, & W. Huisman (Eds.), *Environmental crime in transnational context: Global issues in green enforcement and criminology* (pp. 139–153). Routledge.

Zaffaroni, E. R., Batista, N., Alagia, A., & Slokar, A. (2010). Brazilian criminal law. Theory of crime: Historical and methodological introduction, action and typicality (2nd ed., Vol. II, t. I). Lumen Juris.

Chapter 8
Competence and Sovereignty

Discussing sovereignty is to observe the foundations, along with equality,[1] of modern states and international law.[2] This foundation, however, does not have a fixed definition, undergoing evolutions of meanings since the origin of the term, in the sixteenth century.[3] Indeed, sovereignty has never been an instrument of unlimited

[1] Equality, in this sense, compared to other States, in equivalence, without hierarchy.

[2] The term "sovereignty" is among the 10 most important words for international law: "Its destiny is less cursed than in internal debates where it often rubs shoulders with the shadowy figure of the "sovereignist" in poorly enlightened polemics. The reason is simple: the very structure of international law as well as its historical necessity rest on the couple formed by sovereignty and equality characterising the State in its relations with its peers" (Alland, Denis (2021). *The 100 words of international law*. Paris: Que. sais-je?, p. 108).

[3] Jean Bodin was the first author to systematically analyse sovereignty, in 1576, considering it as a criterion for the existence of the Republic itself, as absolute power. Sovereignty was first addressed, however, in the book *Methodus ad Facilem Historiàrum* Cognitionem, of 1566, by the same author. Sovereign power, for Bodin, must differentiate itself from other powers existing in society precisely by the exclusive possession of certain rights (Barros, Alberto Ribeiro de (1996). The concept of sovereignty in the *Methodus* of Jean Bodin. *Speech*, 27(1), 139–155, p. 143. Available at: https://www.revistas.usp.br/discurso/article/download/140419/135461. Accessed on: 25 Jun. 2025). For other authors, sovereignty, however, is not considered an element of the State, as it is understood as "an attribute of the legal order that the State establishes, presented in the figure of the government, which represents the human dimension and projects itself over the territory. In the external sphere, sovereignty presents itself as a necessary adjective-characteristic for the recognition of the personality of the State in international society (Borges, Thiago Carvalho (2011). *Course on public international law and community law*. São Paulo: Atlas, p. 35).

D. A. Brochado Neto, *Ecocide*, https://doi.org/10.1007/978-3-032-07757-8_8

power,[4] especially when considering the relations between states. That is, at the international level, sovereignty is relative.[5]

Even so, few fields of law have remained almost unchanged by the influence of the international plan as criminal law—and the consequent *jus puniendi* of the state. This domain is traditionally considered reserved for sovereign states, not existing in the UN Charter,[6] despite setting values and the protection of human dignity, provision on the criminal area.[7]

States had the right to prosecute and judge any crimes committed in their territories, committed by their nationals within or outside their limits. Third states, however, had no voice in internal matters in criminal matters (Tomuschat, 2006, pp. 830–838).

The exclusively national criminal jurisdiction had its greatest questioning as a result of the incidents in the two World Wars (especially in the Second), in the first half of the twentieth century, when the emergence of international criminal law. Until Nuremberg, the sovereignty of the state was the fundamental pillar of the international legal order. The International (military) criminal courts[8] imposed the

---

[4] On the international plane, "classically, three rights of States revealed the existence of sovereignty: the *justractuum* or right to make treaties, the *juslegationi* or to receive and send diplomatic representatives and the *jusbelli* or to wage war. Now, with the prohibition of war by the United Nations Charter (art. 2, no. 4) this last right is interpreted as mere right of legitimate defence, individual or collective (art. 51 of the same Charter)" (Miranda, Jorge (2006). *Course on public international law*. Principia, p. 195). For a general overview of the evolution of sovereignty, see: Mazzuoli, Valério de Oliveira (2019). *Course on public international law*. Rio de Janeiro: Forense.

[5] "Sovereignty, on the international plane, is, by nature, relative, since there is the sovereignty of another State—change in the concept can reflect in the constitutions, which will cease to have the pretension of providing a totalising regulatory scheme in a sovereign state power, to accept the ordering frameworks of the international community" (Canotilho, José Joaquim Gomes (2003). *Constitutional law and theory of the constitution*. Coimbra: Almedina, p. 329).

[6] Sovereignty "is currently found within the framework of the texts of positive Public International Law, among which the provision in art. 2, § 1, of the United Nations Charter of 1945, according to which the UN is based 'on the principle of sovereign equality of all its members'. Notice that the UN Charter refers to sovereignty with equality (sovereign equality...), which already leads to the understanding that modern sovereignty has limits, found in the very international norms managing the activities of the States" (Mazzuoli, Valério de Oliveira (2019). *Course on public international law*. Rio de Janeiro: Forense, p. 660–661).

[7] The UN Charter leaves to each State, in article 2 (7), the relevant and essentially national issues, without intervention from the Organisation in these matters (except exceptions), as long as they do not affect the sovereignty of other States, which casts doubt on the activity in relation to crimes that cross territorial barriers (Fouchard, Isabelle (2014). *International crimes: Between internationalisation of criminal law and criminalisation of international law*. Brussels: Bruylant).

[8] Nuremberg (International Military Tribunal) ended the protective umbrella that the sovereignty of the State offered to perpetrators. Holding political leaders directly accountable under international law for organised and ordered criminal actions is a necessity in a world where the basic axioms of the international system have changed: "*state sovereignty has lost its absolute character and is counterbalanced by the requirements of human rights protection. The emergence of international criminal justice embodies the concept of international community in the most palpable manner*" (Tomuschat, Christian (2006). The legacy of Nuremberg. *Journal of International Criminal Justice*, 4(4), 830–838, p. 830).

recognition of groups of supranational crimes, thus considered by the umbilical relationship with human rights, as they identify basic goods to the very existence of an international community in peace and security.

This competence in criminal matters is, since Nuremberg, directed at processing the individual, seeking to sanction the natural person, not the States (legal entities of public law) or companies (entities of private law). International competence was also reserved for the most serious crimes,[9] today embodied in the Rome Statute.

In addition, a relationship developed (especially with the advent of the International Criminal Court)[10] of complementarity[11] and co-participation,[12] between national and international jurisdictions, where criminal prosecution begins—in theory and in general —in the country where the infraction occurred. Therefore, despite the competence for certain crimes being shared, the sovereignty of the state remains,[13] exercised in the signing of the Treaty (in this case, the Rome Statute) and in the initial criminal prosecution[14] (as a requirement of ICC jurisdiction), both possible only because they are sovereign states.

---

[9] The list of crimes with the possibility of being internationalised was discussed, under the command of the UN, by the *International Law Commission*, when drafting the Code of crimes against peace and the security of humanity.

[10] For more details on the correlation between national sovereignties and international jurisdiction, see: Cassese, Antonio (2004). Is there an insurmountable conflict between state sovereignty and international criminal justice? In A. Cassese & M. Delmas-Marty (Eds.), *International crimes and international jurisdictions* (pp. 67–82). Barueri: Manole.

[11] "Contrary to what many still suppose in so many countries, national and international jurisdictions, at the beginning of the twenty-first century, are not competitors or conflicting, but rather complementary, in constant interaction in the protection of human rights and in the fight against the impunity of the violators of such rights" (Trindade, Antônio Augusto Cançado (2010). Contemporary international courts and the pursuit of the realization of the ideal of international justice. *Rev. Fac. Direito UFMG*, 57, 37–68, p. 61).

[12] "Indeed, the expansion of international jurisdiction counts on the contribution, the co-participation, of national jurisdictions. International law assigns international functions also to national courts. The expansion of international jurisdiction occurs *pari passu* with the expansion of both personality and international responsibilities, – all pointing to the current construction of a new *jus gentium* of our times" (Trindade, Antônio Augusto Cançado (2010). Contemporary international courts and the pursuit of the realization of the ideal of international justice. *Rev. Fac. Direito UFMG*, 57, 37–68, p. 62).

[13] By forms of implementation of international criminal law, it is understood "the different normative and institutional regimes through which the criminal prosecution of international crimes is exercised, and which imply, on the one hand, the preservation, albeit mitigated, of the criminal jurisdiction of States, and on the other hand, the creation, as a general rule, of mechanisms of complementation or competition between state jurisdictions and international ones or between state jurisdictions" (Oliveira, Marcus Vinícius Xavier de. (2020). *Studies on (criminal) international jurisdiction: forms of implementation, expansion, fragmentation and actio popularis*. Edufro—Publisher of Federal University of Rondônia, p. 38).

[14] There are two regimes for implementing International Criminal Law: "the direct enforcement system, whose exercise of criminal prosecution is carried out by international criminal courts, and which is characterized by the regime applicable to international judicial institutions that have the power to execute their mandates (*have the power of enforcing their orders*) and judgments without going through the States or any other legal authority", executed by the ad hoc Courts, and of indi-

Thus, it is not necessarily the creation of a Court with competence to judge international crimes that results in a supposed reduction of sovereignty of a state. The fragility of the concept of sovereignty comes today from the pressure of historical needs,[15] notably by the international system of protection of human rights, in contrast to its original concept.[16] That is, sovereigns do not have total autonomy on the internal plan to manage their laws and protect their population, there are basic rights to be respected by states.[17]

The jurisdiction of the International Criminal Court is limited to the most serious crimes (*ratione materiae*, Article 5 [1] of the Statute), prosecuting individuals who commit them on the territory of a State Party, or its national (*ratione loci*, Article 12), for an act occurring anywhere. As for substantive law, the offences inscribed in the Statute are (or should be) crimes also in the jurisdictions of the signatory States (in accordance with the complementary nature of the Court).[18]

The location of the offence is, therefore, determinant for the establishment of international jurisdiction, which, in theory, competes with the national one. The complementarity of the Court, therefore, seeks to break with this apparent conflict

---

rect enforcement, "characterized by the exercise of criminal prosecution of proper and/or improper international crimes by States in a regime of international cooperation in criminal matters", based "on the internalization of international obligations in criminal matters and on the creation of international obligations that establish principles, procedures and forms of international cooperation in criminal law" (Oliveira, Marcus Vinícius Xavier de. (2020). *Studies on (criminal) international jurisdiction: forms of implementation, expansion, fragmentation and actio popularis*. Edufro—Publisher of Federal University of Rondônia, p. 44–45).

[15] "The international globalization of problems ('human rights', 'resource protection', 'environment') is there to demonstrate that, if the 'legal constitution of the state centre', territorially delimited, continues to be a political and cultural identity card and a necessary normative mediation of basic structures of justice of a Nation-State, increasingly it must be articulated with other rights, more or less binding and preceptive (hard law), or more or less flexible (soft law), progressively forged by new "political units" ('world city', 'community Europe', 'European house', 'African unity')" (Canotilho, José Joaquim Gomes (2003). *Constitutional law and theory of the constitution*. Coimbra: Almedina, p. 18).

[16] Mazzuoli, Valério de Oliveira (2019). *Course on public international law*. Rio de Janeiro: Forense, p. 741.

[17] "Article 12 of the OAS Charter categorically states that "the fundamental rights of States cannot be restricted in any way". However, notwithstanding the imperativeness of this conventional rule, it is more than known that the rights of States are not absolute. Sometimes, both customs and international treaties impose certain *restrictions* on the basic prerogatives of States, considering the common good of the international society. Such restrictions on the rights of States sometimes affect their *internal sovereignty*, sometimes their *external sovereignty*" (Mazzuoli, Valério de Oliveira (2019). *Course on public international law*. Rio de Janeiro: Forense, p. 747).

[18] "The International Criminal Court emerges as a complementary apparatus to national criminal jurisdiction. The Rome Statute reiterates the idea that the State has the primary responsibility, the legal duty to lend its jurisdiction. However, if this does not occur, the subsidiary responsibility is of the international community. (...) In this way, we understand that the Statute seeks to balance the guarantee of the right to justice, the end of impunity, the sovereignty of the State in light of the Principle of Complementarity" (Piovesan, Flávia (2000). Principle of complementarity and sovereignty. *Journal of Judicial Studies*, 4(11). Available at: http://www.dhnet.org.br/direitos/sip/tpi/textos/tpi_piovesan.html. Accessed on: 25 Jun. 2025).

of jurisdiction,[19] there is also a provision for *ne bis in idem* (Article 20 of the Statute). Thus, the restrictions on the jurisdiction of the State are imposed by international law, which respects the national (including its judicial decisions, except as provided in Article 20 [3]),[20] in the criminal field.[21]

Despite being recent, the existence of the only permanent criminal court[22]—and its doctrinal consequences for sovereignty—is, in a way, peaceful, as to the theoretical foundations of punishment for crimes on the international level. The agreement with the negotiation of a *The Code* and the very creation of the Court (ratified, so far, by 125 countries) confirm the argument.

The most latent difficulties arise when confronting this seemingly harmonious judicial system with transboundary environmental damage. First, one must distinguish between conducts that are national crimes (within the reach of international criminal law) and international crimes (of international criminal law). In this context, although there are, within international environmental law, traditional conflict resolution institutes, regulation of resource exploitation and established principles (such as self-determination and non-intervention), there is no environmental crime in the international sphere (typified in treaty or as *jus cogens*). Therefore, there is only environmental criminal prosecution at the national level.

In this sense, the problems identified when trying to nationally prosecute for massive and transboundary environmental damage are amplified on the international scene. Issues such as liability for damage and appropriate sanctions are

---

[19] Although the complementarity of the Court is relatively clear in the text, in practice it is not simple to establish the distinction between inertia, delay in investigation or zeal, or even the quick trial in the State Party, which points to a discretionary position of the Prosecutor's Office, indicating the start of an investigation (Tsilonis, Victor. (2024). *The Jurisdiction of the International Criminal Court* (2nd ed.). Springer International Publishing, p. 242).

[20] Article 20 [3]: "3. The Court may not try a person who has already been tried by another court, for acts also punished by articles 6, 7 or 8, unless the proceedings in that other court: a) Were intended to shield the accused from his criminal responsibility for crimes within the jurisdiction of the Court; or b) Were not conducted independently or impartially, in accordance with the guarantees of a fair trial recognised by international law, or were conducted in a manner that, in the specific case, is incompatible with the intention to bring the person to justice" (Decree 4.388/2002, Rome Statute. Available at: http://www.planalto.gov.br/ccivil_03/decreto/2002/d4388.htm. Accessed on: 14 Jun. 2025).

[21] Thus, it is understood that the creation of an International Court does not mean taking away the sovereignty of States, which constitutes "a manifest misunderstanding, if not bad faith, which is valid for many cases, with enormous legal-political effects in the context of International Law. A misunderstanding because sovereignty is only the concept used by various disciplines that deal with the legal-political problem of the independence of States *vis-à-vis*, but which never refers to that of International Law. Bad faith because, in the context of International Law, sovereignty can mean many things, but never a power above International Law and the interests of other States" (Oliveira, Marcus Vinícius Xavier de. (2020). *Studies on (criminal) international jurisdiction: forms of implementation, expansion, fragmentation and actio popularis*. Edufro—Publisher of Federal University of Rondônia, p. 74–75).

[22] The existence of a permanent International Criminal Court solves various problems argued in all other international courts, now respecting principles such as anteriority and legality.

influenced by the flexible approach to the concept of sovereignty, in cases where the international aspect of the crime is prominent.

Multilateralism,[23] a characteristic of international environmental law,[24] offers some projections—beyond the responsibility of States—that can be exploited by the criminal sphere. The trends of international environmental legislation point to a path of cooperation between States, given the interest in exercising their sovereignties to exploit natural resources, without, however, causing environmental damage. This obligation ultimately imposes limitations on the freedom of action of the sovereigns (who voluntarily adhered to international treaties on the subject). The interdependence between States, therefore, guarantees rights and limits a presumed absolute sovereignty. Certainly, the benefits of this rearrangement outweigh the individual interests of the States.

Cooperation is also fundamental in the investigation and repression of transnational environmental crimes.[25] The current instruments for this, however, are insufficient to effectively combat them, lacking viable solutions for the criminal prosecution of massive environmental damage. In addition, many crimes occur in territories seen as "ungoverned spaces", where the sovereign is unable to enforce the laws or where state institutions do not fully function.[26]

---

[23] The multilateralism of environmental issues "often leads to various states complaining about the loss of their sovereignty due to environmental agreements, as well as feeling disadvantaged due to the increasing existence of international organisations dedicated to the subject. (...) multilateralism is a characteristic of DIMA and, certainly, should not be confused with loss of sovereignty, but is, indeed, a new form of its expression. Also noteworthy is the fact that the peculiarities of the environmental issue lead to the entry of new actors on the international scene, such as civil associations of various natures, indigenous and traditional peoples and even individuals" (Antunes, Paulo de Bessa (2020). International environmental law: Peculiarities. *Paths of Law: Environmental Law and Sustainable Development*, 17(37), 263–294, p. 276).

[24] The peculiarity of the concept of sovereignty in DIMA finds its origins in the case *Trail Smelter Arbitration*, in the 1940s, when the "principle was established that no state has the right to use or allow the use of its territory in a way that causes damage to other countries or to properties and/or people of third states. Thus, the concept of international responsibility of states was established" (Antunes, Paulo de Bessa (2020). International environmental law: Peculiarities. *Paths of Law: Environmental Law and Sustainable Development*, 17(37), 263–294, p. 277).

[25] The central instruments of traditional police cooperation are rogatory letters, or requests for mutual legal assistance: "the central instrument in traditional law enforcement cooperation is rogatory letters, or requests for mutual legal assistance. How such requests are exchanged is laid down in an extensive patchwork of treaties and conventions drawn up for example in the context of the United Nations, the Commonwealth, the Council of Europe, and bilaterally between states. In addition, the police can exchange information through the Interpol channel" (Spapens, Toine, White, R., & Huisman, W. (Eds.). (2016). *Environmental crime in transnational context: Global issues in green enforcement and criminology*. Routledge, p. 2).

[26] There is also no globally competent police force to enforce international environmental treaties, such as the Convention on International Trade in Endangered Species of Wild Fauna and Flora (CITES) and the International Convention for the Prevention of Pollution from Ships (MARPOL)" (Spapens, Toine, White, R., & Huisman, W. (Eds.). (2016). *Environmental crime in transnational context: Global issues in green enforcement and criminology*. Routledge, p. 2).

As can be seen, the greater interaction between States on the subject has not meant an improvement in the protection of the environment against massive damage,[27] given that there is not, in most countries, even internally, criminal legislation dedicated to the subject. This hesitation of States to provide adequate tools for cases results, as can be seen in international practice, in the entry of new actors into the international legal scenario,[28] which, in a way, has generated perplexities and misunderstandings, which are expressed in ultra-nationalist reactions against a supposed loss of national sovereignty.[29]

Thus, sovereignty is used as an argument for states to deny the trial of international crimes committed on their territory or by their nationals, supported by the principle, among others, of non-intervention.[30] This "return" to some aspects of the rigid concept of sovereignty imposes new difficulties on the international community, to ratify and implement treaties, as well as to enforce international norms (including the UN Charter, violated by successive invasions of sovereign states by members of the Security Council, in disagreement with international rules).[31]

Regardless of the Court, the trial of international crimes often requires the application of national and international law (the internationalised Courts, by definition,

---

[27] In many countries, environmental crimes have low investigation priority and, therefore, the responsible bodies lack resources and personnel: "Environmental crimes often do not produce immediate victims or visible pollution and thus require proactive and intelligence-led-policing, whereas in many countries such concepts have yet to be developed or to be implemented successfully. (…). Specific harms to the environment may not be defined as criminal offences at all. In other cases, the maximum penalty may be so low that proper investigation and transnational law enforcement cooperation may become impossible" (Spapens, Toine, White, R., & Huisman, W. (Eds.). (2016). *Environmental crime in transnational context: Global issues in green enforcement and criminology*. Routledge, p. 2).

[28] "The relativisation of the role of states presents itself dramatically, as a large part of environmental issues are of a regional or global nature, which determines that states must 'give up' part of their sovereignty so that, in collaboration with the other parties of international agreements, they can tackle cross-border pollution or protect global biological diversity" (Antunes, Paulo de Bessa (2020). International environmental law: Peculiarities. *Paths of Law: Environmental Law and Sustainable Development*, 17(37), 263–294, p. 279).

[29] "In recent years, the concept of governance has been challenged by nationalist movements that contest the "loss of sovereignty" and the increasing bureaucratisation of the international order, as a consequence of multilateralism. However, it seems evident that it is in multilateralism that developing countries find the best way to express their common aspirations before the international community, as it is the only way to balance power in the face of superpowers" (Antunes, Paulo de Bessa (2020). International environmental law: Peculiarities. *Paths of Law: Environmental Law and Sustainable Development*, 17(37), 263–294, p. 281).

[30] This flawed line of reasoning repeats itself in different forms, for example, "in the American position on the ICC and the position of non-party states. But, as several contributors to these volumes point out, states cannot appeal to sovereignty-based arguments to claim a veto over prosecutions that are authorized or required by customary international law or treaties binding upon them" (Ferdinandusse, Ward (2004). The interaction of national and international approaches in the repression of international crimes. *The European Journal of International Law*, 15, 1041–1053, p. 1050).

[31] In the most recent examples of military intervention, mention the United States and Russia.

apply both bodies of law). But, undoubtedly, national criminal law also plays an important role in the construction of the jurisprudence of international Tribunals, even if the application of this law itself is not part of their mandate.[32]

Concurrent criminal jurisdiction, national and international, is therefore not a hindrance, but a facilitator for the application of the law—considering the complementarity of the ICC. The confrontation of macro-criminality, given the dimension of the massive damages caused by environmental crimes, if carried out individually by States, will be fruitless, lacking the execution of international cooperation programmes in criminal matters (Oliveira, 2020, p. 99), which expand the possibilities of a more robust criminal prosecution in practice.

It is certain that sovereignty—even internal—does not serve as a shield to practices by States contrary to their own people, who, in fact, confer legitimacy on them. Even with the current nationalist bias, questioning international law, its organs and treaties, sovereignty can only be exercised within a responsibility to protect (R2P),[33] an intrinsic duty of the State.

In the apparent clash between sovereignty and international security, the environment emerges as an element capable of redefining the priorities of States.

8.1 Sovereignty, International Security, and Environment

The interconnectivity between the environment—and its various biomes—as a whole and human actions requires a joint approach to problem-solving. Thinking systemically and complexly about environmental security is a necessity not only driven by facts but also by the progression of conceptual versions of new securities, characteristic of this century (Gaillard, 2016, pp. 41–60).

---

[32] The ad hoc Tribunals have resorted to comparative national law for reasons of interpretation and legitimation: "National courts also necessarily resort to a combination of national and international law. Most legal systems incorporate (parts of) international law by reference, not least in the field of ICL. But even where they do not, international law is often used by national courts to interpret, and sometimes correct or supplement, corresponding national legislation. The extent to which international law can remedy lacunae and harmonize inconsistencies in national law is of great practical importance, since no national law is flawless in its regulation of international crimes. While the current wave of ICC implementing legislation has considerably improved many national laws, deficiencies and incongruities in national implementation will remain a structural feature of ICL, if only because the process of progressive criminalization under customary international law resists complete and timely implementation" (Ferdinandusse, Ward (2004). The interaction of national and international approaches in the repression of international crimes. *The European Journal of International Law*, 15, 1041–1053, p. 1052).

[33] In this regard, the impact on external sovereignty in the humanitarian context may be questioned due to the emergence of the concept of "Responsibility to Protect" (R2P), which limits the exercise of internal sovereignty (Henderson, Christian (2014). The Arab Spring and the notion of external state sovereignty in international law. *Liverpool Law Review*, 35(2), 175–192, p. 187). Under this argument, the Security Council has already determined humanitarian (Resolution 1542, 2004, in Haiti) and military intervention (Resolution 1973, 2011, in Libya).

Attention to the environment as a factor of international security has been positively affirmed within the UN Security Council,[34] especially in the post–Cold War period,[35] when threats to humanity escaped the issues of a war conflict.[36] Sources of non-military international instability—of economic, social, humanitarian, and ecological domain— gained significant projection.

The broadened definition of threats to peace and international security imposed the recognition of the Security Council's competence in environmental matters, when environmental degradation or climate change present risks to the international order.[37] However, despite this new concern, the limits of action of the UN's own security body remain undefined.

For example, the use of military means in rescue missions (direct aid, evacuation of victims, transport of cargo or medical personnel, or in acts of public power (such as the temporary administration of an airport), presumes respect for the sovereignty of the assisted State, with the application of the principle of subsidiarity (intervention when the State cannot act) being extremely rare (Guillot, 2016, pp. 111–122).

---

[34] The process of "environmentalising" security within the UN is all the more interesting as it also allows environmental security to be placed on the agenda: "Indeed, just as technicisation is a relevant manoeuvre to secure the environment while avoiding over-politicisation and the issues of sovereignty that often obstruct cooperation, the "environmentalisation" of security supports efforts to secure the environment" (Maertens, Lucile (2016). When blue turns green: The securitisation of the environment at the UN. In N. Clinchamps et al. (Eds.), *Security and environment* (pp. 79–90). Brussels: Bruylant, p. 79).

[35] The post-Cold War era, particularly shortly after the collapse of the Soviet Union, "*revived hope that the United Nations would finally emerge as the institutionalised consciousness of global security. There is vast literature on the momentous shift within the United Nations in response to Iraq's occupation of Kuwait in 1990–91, and the potential that Soviet endorsement of collective security offered. But two important avenues for research and policy engagement remained underdeveloped*" (Mamlyuk, Boris N. (2014). Uniting for "Peace" in the Second Cold War: A Response to Larry Johnson. *American Journal of International Law, 108*, 129–134, p. 132. Available at: https://www.cambridge.org/core/journals/american-journal-of-international-law/article/uniting-for-peace-in-the-second-cold-war-a-response-to-larry-johnson/CADCCA16FE57685EBAC8BF599898BD61. Accessed on: 26 Jul. 2025).

[36] "The process of détente or depolarisation of International Relations in the form of the triumphalist discourse of liberal democracy and the process of globalisation and integrative regionalisation modified the decision-making behaviour of the UNSC. After its moment of sterilisation during the Cold War period, the UNSC will experience a drastic reduction in the use of the veto by the P-5" (Castro, Thales (2012). *UN Security Council: Unipolarity, consensus and trends*. Curitiba: Juruá, p. 128.).

[37] The syllogism is simple: "*climate change has consequences for peace and international security; the Security Council has primary competence in matters of peace and international security; therefore, it must be able to examine, within the framework of its mandate, issues related to climate change. If the syllogism is simple, its implementation faces many obstacles that our presentation highlights and supports. The most fundamental is undoubtedly that affirming the consequences of climate change in terms of security does not make it a threat to peace and international security recognised by the Security Council*" (Cazala, Julien. (2016). United Nations Security Council and environmental security. In Nicolas Clinchamps et al. (Eds.), *Security and environment*. Bruylant, p. 90).

In the environmental context, international investment in prevention, monitoring, response planning, assistance to disaster victims, support for infrastructure works, promoted by international organisations demonstrate commitment to environmental security, in cooperation on a scale uncommon in other areas.[38] The field of activity of the Security Council, however, is restricted. In the case of an armed conflict, induced or aggravated by climate issues, for example, the Council could take necessary measures to cease the disturbance of peace. In this case, the environmental issue is peripheral, conditioned to the war conflict (Weyers, 2016, pp. 278–283).

It is certain that, in a panorama of globalised problems, the responses also need to be collective. Environmental security and national security[39] were only recently accepted as inseparable,[40] recognising that the possibility of a solution to serious environmental crises lies at the international level, with cooperation between States (Foegle, 2016, p. 384).

This international articulation is, in practice, led by the UN. In the report "An Agenda for Development", the Secretary-General stated that the environment—like peace, the economy, society, and democracy—permeates all aspects of development, not constituting separate concepts, nor can they be addressed without mutual reference.[41] As can be seen, being a cross-cutting and multidisciplinary issue, the relationship between environment and security is addressed in a fragmented way, within the mandates of each body.[42]

---

[38] "This investment in favour of the environment undoubtedly attests to a paradigm shift in terms of security apprehension" (Guillot, Philippe Ch.-A. (2016). International activities in favour of environmental security. In N. Clinchamps et al. (Eds.), *Security and environment* (pp. 111–122). Brussels: Bruylant, p. 122).

[39] Three generations are recognised in terms of environmental security: the first corresponds to a narrow vision of security, restricted to military threats; the second, assigns to States, individually, responsibilities for the strategies of actors in security and defence, treating the environment as an indirect cause, through environmental degradation, of risks and threats to countries; the third bets on cooperation between States for the solution of major environmental problems, constituting a duty of all (Foegle, Jean-Philippe. (2016). Environmental security and national security: the dangerous liaisons?. In Nicolas Clinchamps et al. (Eds.), *Security and environment*. Bruylant, p. 283–384).

[40] In 1990, the Secretary of Defense of the United States, Dick Cheney, stated that the protection of the environment and defense policy do not exclude each other, as it is impossible to choose one at the expense of the other, in a world of security threats and real environmental concerns (Foegle, Jean-Philippe. (2016). Environmental security and national security: the dangerous liaisons?. In Nicolas Clinchamps et al. (Eds.), *Security and environment*. Bruylant, p. 381).

[41] UN Doc. A/48/935, of 6 May 1994. Available at: https://digitallibrary.un.org/record/188719/files/A_48_935-EN.pdf?ln=en. Accessed on: 10 Jul. 2025.

[42] Cautiously, "but significantly, the General Assembly has already begun to build its position on the possible implications of climate change for peace and international security, through Resolution 63/281, of 3 June 2009" (Amorim, João Alberto Alves (2015). *The UN and the environment*. São Paulo: Atlas Publisher, p. 123).

It is up to the States, in mutual agreement,[43] to increase environmental protection collectively, through international bodies and courts[44] with competence for this, which gives legitimacy[45] to the international norm. Certainly, recent nationalist movements to "reclaim sovereignty" prove to be obstacles to the formation of global governance on the subject. In this prism, security, which derives from the concepts of risk and vulnerability, functions as an act of discourse to operationalise the state monopoly of responses to a specific challenge.[46]

---

[43] The responsibility to protect (R2P), considering the healthy environment as a fundamental right, reaches the environmental area. However, it does not imply, subjection to military interventions, already controversial and difficult to carry out, within the Security Council, in a non-war context: "But what might explain such a difference in approach to two actions both of which constitute a use of force and therefore an unlawful intervention? It is arguable that while R2P may have impacted little upon the formal contours of the law to date, it has palpably increased expectations amongst many within the international community that action by the UNSC should be taken in such circumstances. However, as Syria highlights, this expectation is still met with a divided UNSC similar to that which was witnessed for much of the Council's life. As such, while there is a general reluctance to take away the prerogative of the Council in authorizing the use of measures of a direct forcible nature, it seems as if lesser indirect forcible measures have become more acceptable in the face of what may be characterized as an R2P situation" (Henderson, Christian (2014). The Arab Spring and the notion of external state sovereignty in international law. *Liverpool Law Review*, 35(2), 175–192, p. 190).

[44] One might ask, "if States enjoy sovereignty, why do they decide to submit to the rules of International Law? And, once obliged and inserted in an international system that does not have a supranational agent responsible for controlling and applying sanctions, why do they obey this law? The answer lies in the concept of legitimacy. Two elements are important to determine the legitimacy of a norm: authority and control. For a rule to have authority it must be understood by States as law, *as opinio juris*. It must also control the behaviour of States. Thus the practice of States must reflect what the norm or the institution determines" (Platiau, Barros, Granja, A. F., & Vieira, P. B. S. (2006). The legality of preventive intervention and the United Nations Charter. *Brazilian Journal of International Politics*, 49, 179–193, p. 180. Available at: https://www.scielo.br/j/rbpi/a/6hTCYsc9cBFwLFptxbPKCXK/?lang=pt. Accessed on: 22. Jun. 2025).

[45] Legitimacy can be defined as "a property of a rule or rulemaking institutions which itself exerts a pull toward compliance on those addressed normatively because those addressed believe that rule or institution has come into being and operates in accordance with generally accepted principles of right process" (Franck, Thomas M., et al. (1990). *The power of legitimacy among nations*. Oxford University Press, p. 24).

[46] Commonly referred to as "security issues" is the process that "shifts the solution of the problem from the standard institutional routes to the field of extraordinary and fanciful measures, which makes the analysis and real solution of risk and vulnerability difficult" (Amorim, João Alberto Alves (2015). *The UN and the environment*. São Paulo: Atlas Publisher, p. 123).

It is necessary to go beyond the unilateral actions of the States,[47] in dealing with problems of global reach.[48] The recognition, especially in the last two decades, of the environment as a risk factor to international security, as well as alignment with human rights, places the environmental issue on a level that allows it to be discussed as a sensitive good deserving of protection from international criminal law. If, at the time of *The Code*, the environment was a supporting actor, a collateral damage that deserved reprimand in the context of war, today it can be seriously considered for inclusion among the core crimes of the International Criminal Court.[49]

The limits of the ICC's jurisdiction, however, need to be better analysed when considering prosecuting natural persons for massive damage to the environment.

[47] "The weakening of international organisations, the unilateral use of force in disregard of the provisions of the United Nations Charter, the War in Iraq, terrorist actions" are factors that led the High-Level Panel on Threats, Challenges and Changes, convened by Kofi Annan, to present the report *A More Secure World—Our Shared Responsibility*, in 2004, which, among others, listed threats to peace and international security, with which countries should be concerned (Soares, João Clemente Baena (2005). *The United Nations in the face of threats, challenges, changes*. Brazilian Centre for International Relations, p. 3).

[48] In this sense, one should use the tools of integration of international law into environmental law, reconciling the characteristic principles of each legal system, in order to enable the application of the norm within the International Criminal Court. Among the possibilities suggested by the doctrine for this integration, the theory of systemic integration is pointed out "Using framework integration to draw external sources into international law can import significant advantages for the adjudication of environmental harm. Environmental law instruments and principles can inform and instantiate factors, including the lawfulness of conduct harming the environment, as well as the 'severe' element and mens rea 'criteria' of crimes encompassing harm to nature, along with the proposed crime of ecocide. In this way, these external sources can provide legal reference points on which the ICC judiciary can rely in reaching their conclusions. (...) Challenges arise from using framework integration, include exposing the Court to allegations of acting ultra vires and binding States to treaty provisions they may not have signed up to. Yet careful management of these risks can be achieved. Key to this are the four complementary principles, namely, adjudicative coherence, effet utile, substantive proximity, and de-fragmentation of international law." (Gillett, M. (2024). Ecocide, environmental harm and framework integration at the International Criminal Court. The International Journal of Human Rights, 1–37. https://doi.org/10.1080/13642987.2024.2433660, p. 23).

[49] "Despite these dangers, however, the expressivist position is based upon a compelling moral and political recognition: that the very process of bringing ecocide into international consideration, of declaring that the ongoing and mounting devastation of environments locally and globally is inherently unacceptable, is crucially important in a contemporary political moment marked by political leaders publicly rationalizing large-scale environmental sacrifice and even extermination. It is also important at a moment when many of these same political forces are seeking to dismantle international institutions and law". (Branch, Adam., & Minkova, Liana. (2023). Ecocide, the Anthropocene, and the International Criminal Court. *Ethics & International Affairs, 37*(1), 51–79, p. 74).

8.2 The Jurisdiction of the ICC and its Problems for Ecocide

The competence of the International Criminal Court is based primarily on the principle of territoriality and not universality.[50] Thus, only crimes that are committed in the territory of the States that have ratified the treaty—or accepted, the Court's competence—can be judged there.[51]

Before, however, considering making use of the international court, the national judge is, in principle, the ordinary judge of international crimes. International criminal jurisdiction only intervenes—or should be activated—when States cannot or do not want to act against the presumed perpetrator of the offence.[52] This aspect, in general, facilitates criminal prosecution, as it is more feasible to process on site, with the everyday tools of investigation, than to rely on the apparatus of a Court, distant from the country of origin of the damage and lacking cooperation, if the State has the technical capacity for it.[53] The fact that the conduct investigated nationally is considered an international crime pressures local justice, by keeping it under external scrutiny.

---

[50] With the exception of the case of referral to the ICC Prosecutor by the UN Security Council—which can affect any State, even if it is not part of the Rome Statute –, all cases must have occurred within a State Party: "in the other cases in which the Court can activate its jurisdiction—referral by one of the member states or initiation of an investigation by the Prosecutor—it will be necessary that the conduct has been held in a State, or by a citizen of a State, part of the Rome Statute or that has anyway accepted the jurisdiction of the Court" (Molteni, Viola. (2021). The long road of the criminalisation of ecocide: legal issues and dynamics of normative and social effectiveness. *Contemporary Criminal Law*, *4*, 205–233, p. 215).

[51] The acceptance of the jurisdiction of the ICC is automatic, not admitting reservations (art. 12.1), "that is, by ratifying the ICC Statute, the State accepts, regardless of express consent in this regard, the jurisdiction of the court at the same time that it cannot make reservations to certain matters, should submit to the jurisdiction of the body in relation to all crimes of its competence" (Vieira, Susana Camargo., & Andrade, Ana Maria de. (2015). The International Criminal Court: an analysis of its evolution and its competence to judge the crime by terrorism. *Brazilian Journal of International Law*, *2*(1), 115–136, p. 124).

[52] The "secondary" place of international criminal jurisdiction is essentially manifested in the existence of several detailed rules, which limit its fields of intervention (Bellivier, Florence, Eudes, M., & Fouchard, I. (2018). *Droit des crimes internationaux*. Paris: Themis Law, p. 369).

[53] Obviously, the apparent technical ease of local justice does not guarantee that criminal prosecution will occur or that it will be fair (respecting the rules): "there is great variation between judicial systems of various States and, in addition, if an ethical conflict occurred, for example, it becomes almost impossible to demand that the court that will, after all, judge the criminals, be completely free from desires for revenge, formed as it is by human beings, who may belong to ethnicities different from those of the accused (...), in other cases, the Justice of a certain country simply does not want to judge certain citizens of its nationality, like former Heads of State, for internal political issues of the nation" (Cretella Neto, José (2014). *Course of international criminal law*. Saraiva, p. 193). There is also the risk of corruption, involving politicians and justice itself, factors with less influence in a permanent international court.

Thus, international jurisdiction[54]—dealing with the ICC—does not aim to suppress the national one, but to offer a complement, when it is unfeasible to prosecute in the country of origin, with the symbolism[55] of recognising an individual's conduct as unacceptable, incompatible with the very existence of humanity in peace and security.

One of the striking features of the ICC's constitutive instrument is the independence of the Court,[56] although this is questionable given the possibility of intervention by the Security Council in the progress of investigations and proceedings. Undoubtedly, the interaction of the Court with the UN's highest security body both expands (article 13 [b], of the Rome Statute) and compresses (article 16) its jurisdiction.

Even so, the ICC's jurisdictional reach is undeniable today. Despite being reduced, in the material sense (there are, rightly, few crimes), the Court can act all over the planet, if one considers the authorisation of the Security Council. Even without this—remote[57]— possibility, more than half of the world's countries have

[54] Three generations of international criminal courts can be identified: the first, consisting of the Post-War Military Courts, breaking the idea of sovereignty as a prohibition of external interference and immunity from jurisdiction; the ad hoc Tribunals (for ex-Yugoslavia and Rwanda), created by resolutions of the Security Council, are pointed out as second generation; the third corresponds to the ICC, created by treaty as a permanent court. A new generation is also pointed out, composed of hybrid international courts (mixing international and national judges), such as the Special Court for Sierra Leone, Cambodia, East Timor, Kosovo, Bosnia-Herzegovina and Lebanon (Cretella Neto, José (2014). *Course of international criminal law*. Saraiva, p. 146, 157, 184 and 208).

[55] "As the evolution of IEL is yet to reach a more general stage in the imposition of criminal liability, the possible deterrent or even pre-deterrent effect of an international criminal regime on gross environmental wrongs might produce the necessary stimuli to encourage those involved to abide by rules preserving the environment. As noted by Kersting, employing ICL as 'a vehicle to combat environmental destruction already carries significant symbolic weight'—whether or not the agreed definition of 'ecocide' is ecocentric or anthropocentric. The combined Rechtsgut-harm (eng 'risk of harming') approach, broadened to include the 'risk to harm' and 'harm to oneself', can be regarded as reflective of the prevention principle". (Palarczyk, Danuta. (2023). Ecocide before the international criminal court: Simplicity is better than an elaborate embellishment. In *Criminal Law Forum* (pp. 147–207). Springer Netherlands, p. 157).

[56] The independence of the Court in the face of unequivocal political pressures is crucial to its proper functioning: "in this sense, some precautions were taken to preserve its autonomy, such as its conception as an independent body from the UN (although there is a relationship of cooperation between the institutions) and the autonomy granted to the prosecution to activate, on its own initiative, independent of provocation, the jurisdiction of the court (article 15.1)" (Vieira, Susana Camargo., and Andrade, Ana Maria de. (2015). The International Criminal Court: an analysis of its evolution and its competence to judge the crime by terrorism. *Brazilian Journal of International Law*, *2*(1), 115–136, p. 125).

[57] It is not palatable to believe that there would be consensus among the permanent members of the Security Council to authorise the prosecution of international crimes occurring in countries of the Council itself—or their allies—and non-signatories of the Rome Statute, in a deadlock similar to that which occurred during the Cold War. Moreover, "it seems no surprise that the USA is less inclined than Europe to trust in courts or prosecutors—who can be considered as agents who show deficiencies in being accountable to States or their superiors—who decide on the universal juris-

already ratified the Rome Statute, which signifies an advance in international criminal law.[58]

The problem for ecocide, as the ultimate environmental crime, lies, in addition to the technical difficulties of defining the offence, in the lack of consensus in national jurisdictions on the penal treatment of the environment. Macro-criminality has only recently been considered in various legislations, with uncertainties about how to approach it in law, with a great discrepancy between sanctions, conducts, and requirements of laws (or bills).

This insecurity regarding ecocide, taken to an international court already insecure about its jurisdictional reach,[59] makes, a priori, it difficult to envisage the expansion of the list of crimes within its competence. However, as already demonstrated in the latest official initiatives (for example, in the European Union) and civil society (such as the proposed amendment to the Rome Statute and the Citizens' Convention for Climate, in France), there is technical and political predisposition for this, considering the development and maturity of the Court,[60] with more than two decades of existence.

As a tool for international protection (criminal recrimination), an offence of ecocide in the International Criminal Court would be as close as possible—in a realistic view—to a universal jurisdiction,[61] since it is already admitted in the text ratified by

diction of certain States" (Cretella Neto, José (2014). *Course of international criminal law.* Saraiva, 2014, p. 249).

[58] Certainly, as already mentioned, the number of signatory countries (123) is relevant, but it does not, in practice, guarantee the applicability of the Court's jurisdiction, as some of the world's largest powers—members of the Security Council—are not on the list, such as Russia, the United States and China.

[59] The relationship of the Court with the Security Council is one of the most controversial aspects of the Rome Statute, since the Court's action is not subordinate to the Council (as the five permanent members intended), but some decisions are conditioned on what is determined by the UN body. These aspects "may favour a selective, asymmetrical and potentially discriminatory justice but are far from exhausting the possibilities of politicisation of the court's action. The problem has other dimensions, perhaps less known, such as the issue of politicisation promoted by the States parties to the Statute. Indeed, the African countries parties to the Statute and the African Union, which was born with the task of accelerating the process of integration of the African continent, have actively promoted a discourse of discrediting the court, accusing it of neocolonialism and selectivity in the cases brought to trial" (Saraiva, Maria Francisca. (2017). The role of African states in the politicisation of the International Criminal Court. *National Defence Institute*, (Jun.), 1–8, p. 1).

[60] "Innovation and the progressive development of Law are inevitable, if we are willing to rise to the challenges of our time" (Trindade, Antônio Augusto Cançado (2010). Contemporary international courts and the pursuit of the realization of the ideal of international justice. *Rev. Fac. Direito UFMG*, 57, 37–68, p. 65).

[61] The "concept of universal jurisdiction" conceives the Rome Statute as a legislative act of the international community: "Indeed, a fundamental factor for the selection of the crimes to be within the jurisdiction of the ICC was that they constitute 'the most serious crimes of international concern'. Even though the four categories of crimes within the Statute did not have agreed precise definitions, a wide majority of States adopted their definition and made them universally applicable. (…) Most agree that the offenses subject to the universality principle are very limited in num-

more than a hundred countries of the Rome Statute. The endorsement would imply admission, by these States, of the crime within their own national jurisdictions, bringing a harmony not seen today.

Considering the groups of crimes within the ICC's competence, it is necessary to analyse whether the environment finds support in the set of imperative norms of public international law, deserving of criminal protection due to the importance that the matter reaches on the international scene.

8.2.1 *Jus Cogens and Ecocide*

The competence *ratione materiae*[62] of the International Criminal Court was not chosen randomly. The four groups of international crimes listed in article 5 of the Rome Statute (crimes against humanity, genocide, war crime, and aggression), are in theory, offences considered the most serious against the international community, even dispensing with codified norm to be considered imperative.

Such crimes—especially the first three—found reverberation in the Military Criminal Courts post—World War II and in the subsequent ones, as violations of human rights, serving as the basis for the construction of *The Code* and, subsequently, the Rome Statute. There is consensus among scholars that all these offences are considered *jus cogens,*[63] rules that hold the highest hierarchical position among all other norms and principles, and, as such, are considered peremptory and non-

---

ber. The crimes within jurisdiction of the ICC are generally deemed subject to universal jurisdiction. However, as mentioned above, the specific definitions of these crimes are not, in some cases, rest entirely on customary international law. Nevertheless, this does not deprive these crimes of their status as crimes under international law but posits them as crimes under treaty law" (Galand, Alexandre Skander (2018). *UN Security Council referrals to the International Criminal Court: Legal nature, effects and limits*. Leiden: Brill, p. 88–89).

[62] It is verified, from article 5 and following of the Rome Statute, that the material jurisdiction of the ICC is broader than that of the two International Criminal Courts (Rwanda and ex-Yugoslavia). Regarding first to genocide (art. 6), crimes against humanity (art. 7) and war crimes (art. 8), there is no fundamental difference between the three Statutes, except that the ICC's is more detailed and usefully complemented by the Elements of Crimes, provided for in article 9 of the Statute and adopted by the Assembly of States Parties in 2002 (Bellivier, Florence, Eudes, M., & Fouchard, I. (2018). *Droit des crimes internationaux*. Paris: Themis Law, p. 372).

[63] The idea of *jus cogens* is prescribed in article 53 of the First Vienna Convention on the Law of Treaties: "Article 53—Treaty in Conflict with a Mandatory Norm of International Law. General (*jus cogens*)—A treaty is null and void if, at the time of its conclusion, it conflicts with a mandatory norm of general international law. For the purposes of this Convention, a mandatory norm of general international law is a norm accepted and recognised by the international community of States as a whole, as a norm from which no derogation is permitted and which can only be modified by a subsequent norm of general international law of the same nature" (Vienna Convention on the Law of Treaties). The opening for the Security Council to indicate the ICC Prosecutor to prosecute any country, even not a signatory to the Rome Statute, for committing any of the crimes there typified, demonstrates the understanding that these are norms *jus cogens*, applying to all members of the international community, a universally imperative and non-derogable right.

derogable (Bassiouni, 1996, pp. 63–74); they are, thus, beyond the will or agreement of the subjects of international law, playing a prominent role, in the confrontation between all other principles and rules.[64]

However, there is no agreement on what constitutes a peremptory norm and how a particular norm rises to this level.[65] In short, the disagreements among criminal lawyers are significant regarding the path for a particular international crime to achieve the status of *jus cogens*.

Seeking to understand how a particular crime can be understood as *jus cogens* for international criminal law is relevant for two aspects: first, it gains support to be included in the select list of offences (in the Rome Statute) considered inadmissible against all of humanity; second, it imposes consequences[66] related to jurisdiction and to States (character *erga omnes*).

Positive international criminal law does not offer—nor the practice of States[67]—explicit norms that define the characterisation of a certain crime as *jus cogens*. While some authors consider it as a reflection of customary law,[68] most researchers

---

[64] And, "with its own legal force, with the inherent effects on the subsistence of contrary norms and acts" (Miranda, Jorge (2006). *Course on public international law*. Principia, p. 123).

[65] The basic reasons for disagreement are "the significant differences in philosophical premises and methodologies of the views of scholarly protagonists. These differences apply to sources, content (the positive or norm-creating elements), evidentiary elements (such as whether universality is appropriate or less will suffice), and value-oriented goals (for example, preservation of world order and safeguarding of fundamental human rights). Furthermore, there is no scholarly consensus on the methods by which to ascertain the existence of a peremptory norm, nor to assess its significance or determine its content. Scholars also disagree as to the means to identify the elements of a peremptory norm, to determine its priority over other competing or conflicting norms or principles, to assess the significance and outcomes of prior application, and to gauge its future applicability in light of the value-oriented goals sought to be achieved" (Bassiouni, M. Cherif (1996). International crimes: "Jus cogens" and "obligatio erga omnes". *Law and Contemporary Problems*, 59(4), 63–74, p. 67. Available at: https://www.jstor.org/stable/pdf/1192190.pdf?refreqid=excelsior%3A6ece53b8b95b107fe4d426ad66d5c297&ab_segments=&origin=&acceptTC=1. Accessed on: 10 Jul. 2025).

[66] For Bassiouni, "the implications of jus cogens are those of a duty and not of optional rights; otherwise jus cogens would not constitute a peremptory norm of international law. Consequently, these obligations are non-derogable in times of war as well as peace" (Bassiouni, M. Cherif (1996). International crimes: "Jus cogens" and "obligatio erga omnes". *Law and Contemporary Problems*, 59(4), 63–74, p. 65. Available at: https://www.jstor.org/stable/pdf/1192190.pdf?refreqid=excelsior%3A6ece53b8b95b107fe4d426ad66d5c297&ab_segments=&origin=&acceptTC=1. Accessed on: 10 Jul. 2025).

[67] The practice of States shows that, most of the time, "impunity has been allowed for jus cogens crimes, the theory of universality has been far from being universally recognized and applied, and the duty to prosecute or extradite is more inchoate than established, other than when it arises out of specific treaty obligations" (Bassiouni, M. Cherif (1996). International crimes: "Jus cogens" and "obligatio erga omnes". *Law and Contemporary Problems*, 59(4), 63–74, p. 66. Available at: https://www.jstor.org/stable/pdf/1192190.pdf?refreqid=excelsior%3A6ece53b8b95b107fe4d426ad66d5c297&ab_segments=&origin=&acceptTC=1. Accessed on: 10 Jul. 2025).

[68] For D'Amato, for example, the sources of *jus cogens* are the same as customary law: "many legal disputes arise precisely because neither side has previously consented to the same rule. As Lauterpacht argued, to say that prior consent must be shown in order to reach a legal conclusion in

understand custom[69] as one of the possible characteristics to recognise a norm *jus cogens.*[70]

In this sense, the traditional legal bases (before the existence of the ICC) for identifying a certain norm as *jus cogens* are (1) international pronouncements, called *opinio juris* (Dahlman, 2012), reflecting the recognition that certain crimes are thus considered by general customary law; (2) language in the preambles or other provisions of applicable treaties, indicating a superior status of these offences in international law; (3) significant number of States that have ratified treaties related to these crimes; and (4) the international investigations ad hoc and criminal proceedings (Bassiouni, 1996).

Certainly, these requirements cannot be seen in a static and cumulative way.[71] Certain crimes affect the interests of the global community as a whole, as they threaten peace and security or shock the conscience of humanity. If both elements are present in a certain crime, it can be concluded that it is part of *jus cogens.*[72]

---

any given international dispute is tantamount to rejecting the possibility of the existence of the vast majority of the rules of international law" (D'Amato, Anthony A. (1969). The concept of special custom in international law. *American Journal of International Law*, *63*(2), 211–223, p. 211).

[69] The customary legal norm, according to the Statute of The Hague Court, "results from 'a practice accepted as being law'. this expression informs of the material element of custom, namely the practice—the repetition, over time, of a certain way of proceeding in a given factual framework -, and its subjective element, namely the conviction that this is done not without reason, but because it is necessary, just, and consequently legal" (Rezek, Francisco (2016). *Public international law: Elementary course*. Saraiva, p. 156).

[70] Nevertheless, many norms considered as *jus cogens* are customary norms: "some commentators have persuasively argued that jus cogens norms can also arise from general principles of law. This is supported by the language of Article 53 of the Vienna Convention on the Law of Treaties, which refers to peremptory norms of 'general international law,' a term which, we have seen, in turn includes general principles of law. Moreover, I have elsewhere suggested that general principles of moral law that reflect essential ethical principles should be classified as jus cogens norms. The criteria used to identify jus cogens general principles of law should be similar, but not identical, to those for customary norms" (Lepard, Brian. (2010). Defining Jus Cogens Customary Norms. In B. Lepard, *Customary International Law: A New Theory with Practical* (pp. 243–260). Cambridge University Press).

[71] "Instead, each one of these crimes must be examined separately to determine whether it has risen to a level above that stemming from specific treaty obligations, so that it can therefore be deemed part of general international law applicable to all states irrespective of specific treaty obligations. To pursue the approach suggested, it is also necessary to have a doctrinal basis for determining what constitutes an international crime and when in the historical legal evolution of a given crime it can be said to achieve the status of jus cogens" (Bassiouni, M. Cherif (1996). International crimes: "Jus cogens" and "obligatio erga omnes". *Law and Contemporary Problems*, 59(4), 63–74, p. 65. Available at: https://www.jstor.org/stable/pdf/1192190.pdf?refreqid=excelsior%3A6ece53b8b95b107fe4d426ad66d5c297&ab_segments=&origin=&acceptTC=1. Accessed on: 10 Jul. 2025).

[72] The argument is less convincing, although still strong enough, if only one of these two elements is present. Implicit in the first, and sometimes in the second element, is the fact that "the conduct in question is the product of state- action or state-favouring policy. Thus, essentially, a jus cogens crime is characterised explicitly or implicitly by state policy or conduct, irrespective of whether it is manifested by commission or omission. The derivation of jus cogens crimes from state policy or

Threats to peace and security are essentially political judgements. Thus, what was considered, at the beginning of the century, as a risk to civilisation, today has its range diversified beyond warlike conduct and derived from these.[73] It is in this context that the idea of the obligation of environmental protection[74] as *jus cogens.*[75] Among the main arguments advanced is the close relationship between the protection of the environment and the protection of human rights.[76]

---

action fundamentally distinguishes such crimes from other international crimes. Additionally, crimes which are not the product of state action or state-favouring policy often lack the two essential factors which establish the jus cogens status of a particular crime, namely a threat to the peace and security of mankind and conduct or consequences which are shocking to the conscience of humanity" (Bassiouni, M. Cherif (1996). International crimes: "Jus cogens" and "obligatio erga omnes". *Law and Contemporary Problems*, 59(4), 63–74, p. 70. Available at: https://www.jstor.org/stable/pdf/1192190.pdf?refreqid=excelsior%3A6ece53b8b95b107fe4d426ad66d5c297&ab_segments=&origin=&acceptTC=1. Accessed on: 10 Jul. 2025).

[73] Only recently principles with the characteristic of *jus cogens* are "proclaimed in solemn texts, international and national, are taken as decision criteria for the purpose of conflict resolution and they seek to confer full awareness. And this development of the *jus cogens* has as a backdrop some factors or trends not always coinciding: the new awareness of the primacy of people's rights, after the cataclysms caused by totalitarian regimes and the Second World War; the new demands for peace and collective security and the crisis of sovereignty; the idea of self-determination of peoples and the emergence of new states committed to remaking the international order; and the impulse given by the internationalist science" (Miranda, Jorge (2006). *Course on public international law*. Principia, p. 124).

[74] "Currently, environmental protection is present in the agenda of any discussion about public governance, due to the environment the environment not being able to recover from the damage it is suffering at the same rate as the natural resources that are being demanded from it to ensure the global standard of consumption. A healthy environment presents itself as a permanent discussion because it is an essential condition for the maintenance of life on Earth. Environmental issues will always be in discussion and should make up the agenda of any discussions, whether they are academic, political, ethical, etc., under penalty of making life unviable" (Galvão, Silvano Macedo. (2020). *Jus cogens environmental: non-derogability of the Human Right to a Healthy Environment*. Dialética Publisher).

[75] There is a growing movement to declare that transboundary environmental damage be defined as a violation of norms *jus cogens*, defined as imperative norms that are so binding for States that their violation is contrary to the fundamental norms of International Law (Dunn, Brian. (2002). The mexicali tire pile: smoke on the horizon. *Georgetown International Environmental Law Review, 14*, 409–427, p. 415).

[76] In addition, the following arguments can be mentioned: "(i) the particular object of protection of certain environmental norms, such as the ozone layer or the climate, which constitute values or goods common to all States; (ii) the acceptance of the prohibition relating to intentional environmental damage during an armed conflict, which is included in articles 35(3) and 55 of the first Additional Protocol to the Geneva Conventions; (iii) the imperative nature of certain environmental norms seems confirmed by the inclusion of environmental protection as a norm whose violation would be likely to give rise to an international crime (in the previous version of the CDI Articles) or by the reaction of the international community in relation to the destruction of the environment during the Gulf War; (iv) the ICJ acknowledged the importance of environmental protection in the Gabcikovo-Nagymaros case by giving it the status of an essential interest and mentioning it in relation to article 64 of the Vienna Convention, which refers to the emergence of new norms of jus cogens" (Viñuales, Jorge E. (2008). The protection of the environment and its normative hierarchy in international law. *International Law: Rev. Colomb. Int. Law*, 13, 11–44, p. 23–24).

The *International Law Commission*, in 2014, decided to focus on *jus cogens*, in a long-term work programme,[77] with the aim of developing a *Draft* of a Convention for consideration by the General Assembly of the UN. The first Report (ILC, 2016b) was released in March 2016, presenting an overview of the institute, concluding that, despite knowing its characteristics, there is no formula for identifying the norms of *jus cogens* in contemporary international law (ILC, 2016b).

In the latest report, from January 2022, it became clear that, despite achieving a draft of the Convention on the subject (ILC, 2022b), there is still no consensus on specific characteristics of *jus cogens* and its consequences in international relations. Several States expressed the opinion that the *Draft* of Conclusions is based more on doctrine and academic knowledge than on practice.[78] The Rapporteur Dire Tladi pointed out that there are, in fact, two variations of the argument of the "lack of practice of States": the first is that there simply is not enough practice; the second asserts that the Commission chose not to rely on existing practice,[79] focusing only on doctrine and theory. Both were rejected by the majority of countries, who recognise[80] the difficulty of compiling judicial decisions where a conflict between *jus cogens* and a common norm (national or international) was analysed.

---

[77] ILC analytical work guide, link: https://legal.un.org/ilc/guide/1_14.shtml. Accessed on: 15 Jul. 2025.

[78] For example, the United States "*stated that, as a general matter* "[t]here is little State practice related to peremptory norms of general international law", noting that the commentary "cites no examples" and that it is "not aware of any examples of" any new rules of international law conflicting with existing jus cogens norms, and that the incidences of existing treaties violating later-emerging jus cogens are exceedingly rare. Its concrete recommendation to address this matter was for the Commission to clearly identify in the commentary where it is engaged in the process of progressive development. The Netherlands, also, while endorsing "the general approach of the" Commission on the topic, lamented the fact that the draft conclusions "rely more on judicial decisions and scholarly writings than on State practice". Similarly, Israel stated that it was concerned by the approach of the Special Rapporteur, which, notwithstanding the views of "various States" and "several members", had "relied greatly on theory and doctrine rather than on a thorough survey of State practice…". (…) Similarly, Malaysia, while applauding the quality of the reports of the Special Rapporteur, expressed the view that the conclusions proposed in those reports were based on doctrine and theory. Like the United States, Turkey also expressed its reservation about the topic as a whole on the grounds that there was insufficient State practice and case law" (ILC. (2022a, January). *Fifth report on peremptory norms of general international law (jus cogens) by Dire Tladi, Special Rapporteur*. (A/CN.4/747), p. 8., §14. Available at: https://documents-dds-ny.un.org/doc/UNDOC/GEN/N21/284/83/PDF/N2128483.pdf. Accessed on: 18 Jul. 2025). Nevertheless, countries such as Germany, Great Britain and the Nordic countries expressed support for the format of the *Draft* (§§15–18).

[79] For countries like the United States and the Netherlands, the preliminary conclusions and their comments are based more on judicial decisions and academic writings, considering "practice" an act of violation, which, for the Rapporteur, demonstrates a very narrow view of what "practice" is (ILC. (2022a, January). *Fifth report on peremptory norms of general international law (jus cogens) by Dire Tladi, Special Rapporteur*. (A/CN.4/747), p. 9, §18–19. Available at https://documents-dds-ny.un.org/doc/UNDOC/GEN/N21/284/83/PDF/N2128483.pdf. Accessed on: 18 Jul. 2025).

[80] "Indeed, many States explicitly stated that they supported the approach of the Commission. Spain, for example, stated that it "commends the Commission and the Special Rapporteur for their efforts to base the draft conclusions and the commentaries thereto on practice, jurisprudence and

The Commission also did not escape questions about the displacement of human rights—at least in certain aspects—outside the concept achieved of *jus cogens*. Economic, social, and cultural rights are absent from the discussion of peremptory norms in the ILC, despite considering human rights indivisible.[81]

Despite the criticisms, the preliminary draft,[82] approved in May 2022, describes in 23 Conclusions, among others, the definition of a mandatory norm of general international law (*jus cogens*); how to identify it, in two criteria[83]; the sources (customary international law, more common, treaties and the general principles of law); consequences of the conflict between treaties and norms *jus cogens*; obligations of States; and a non-exhaustive list of norms *jus cogens* (without prejudice to the existence or subsequent emergence of others similar).

---

doctrine on the topic". South Africa, for example, stated that the "Commission has managed to deliver a well-balanced text of draft conclusions, supported by practice and judicial decisions of international courts and tribunals. Cyprus also expressed its support for the work of the Commission.38 Japan, for its part, having stressed the importance of achieving a balance between 'theory and reality', expressed its support for the Commission's decision to be guided by the Vienna Convention, describing this decision as 'sensible'" (ILC. (2022a, January). *Fifth report on peremptory norms of general international law (jus cogens) by Dire Tladi, Special Rapporteur*. (A/CN.4/747), p. 9, §20. Available at: https://documents-dds-ny.un.org/doc/UNDOC/GEN/N21/284/83/PDF/N2128483.pdf. Accessed on: 18 Jul. 2025).

[81] The study of human rights proclaims the indivisibility of fundamental rights: "During the debates in the International Law Commission in 2019 the issue did not even arise. To be entirely accurate, there was an isolated reference by a member of the Commission, who challenged the methodology of the Special Rapporteur, arguing that if the prohibition of apartheid were included in a list of jus cogens norms then the right to safe drinking water might just as well be added. The sense of observation as not to lament the exclusion of economic, social and cultural rights but rather to warn that without a more rigorous methodology insignificant or trivial matters might be deemed jus cogens. The exclusion of economic, social and cultural rights is nothing more than a remnant of conservative and even archaic visions of fundamental rights. In contemporary society, there is a consensus that certain entitlements, many of them codified in Articles 22 to 26 of the Universal Declarations of Human Rights, in the International Covenant on Economic, Social and Cultural Rights, and in a range of specialised and regional instruments, are as fundamental to modern life as the prohibitions of torture and slavery. The COVID-19 pandemic manifested a global understanding of the significance of public health and of the right to a minimal level of medical care" (Schabas, William A. (2021). *The Customary International Law of Human Rights*. Oxford University Press, p. 67).

[82] ILC. (2022, May 11). *Peremptory norms of general international law (jus cogens). Texts of the draft conclusions and Annex adopted by the Drafting Committee on second reading*. (A/CN.4/L.967). Available at: https://documents-dds-ny.un.org/doc/UNDOC/LTD/G22/339/00/PDF/G2233900.pdf. Accessed on: 18 Jul. 2025).

[83] Conclusion 4: "To identify a peremptory norm of general international law (jus cogens), it is necessary to establish that the norm in question meets the following criteria: (a) it is a norm of general international law; and (b) it is accepted and recognised by the international community of States as a whole as a norm from which no derogation is permitted and which can be modified only by a subsequent norm of general international law having the same character" (ILC. (2022, May 11). *Peremptory norms of general international law (jus cogens). Texts of the draft conclusions and Annex adopted by the Drafting Committee on second reading*. (A/CN.4/L.967). Available at: https://documents-dds-ny.un.org/doc/UNDOC/LTD/G22/339/00/PDF/G2233900.pdf. Accessed on: 18 Jul. 2025).

There is no provision directly related to the environment among the norms exemplified as *jus cogens.*[84] However, the openness conferred by the document to new norms with such status was celebrated by States interested in the subject. Micronesia,[85] a country directly threatened by the rise in sea levels, due to climate change, recognised an opportunity to visualise the protection of the environment in the provisions of the *Draft*, endorsing the non-exhaustive nature of the list[86] of norms *jus cogens*, of Conclusion 23.

There seems to be insufficient evidence of the necessary acceptance and recognition by States of the non-derogable nature of environmental obligations as norms *jus cogens.*[87] In this vein, however, it may be unnecessary to seek validation of the

[84] Included in Conclusion 23, in the non-exhaustive list, as norms with jus cogens status are: "(a) The prohibition of aggression; (b) The prohibition of genocide; (c) The prohibition of crimes against humanity; (d) The basic rules of international humanitarian law; (e) The prohibition of racial discrimination and apartheid; (f) The prohibition of slavery; (g) The prohibition of torture; (h) The right of self-determination" (ILC. (2022, May 11). *Peremptory norms of general international law (jus cogens). Texts of the draft conclusions and Annex adopted by the Drafting Committee on second reading*. (A/CN.4/L.967). Available at: https://documents-dds-ny.un.org/doc/UNDOC/LTD/G22/339/00/PDF/G2233900.pdf. Accessed on: 18 Jul. 2025).

[85] "Micronesia fully endorsed the Commission's reference in its commentary to draft conclusion 23 to obligations "of essential importance for the safeguarding and preservation of the human environment, such as those prohibiting massive pollution of the atmosphere or of the seas" as peremptory norms of general international law (jus cogens). The protection of natural environments of importance to the international community as a whole—such as the ocean and the atmosphere—satisfied the stipulation in draft conclusion 3 that peremptory norms of general international law reflected and protected fundamental values of the international community. Those values included ensuring safe and healthy natural environments for present and future generations. While such environments might be subject to various legal regimes where there was a clear demarcation between the right of sovereignty and other State rights, it was indisputable that the harmful impact of any activity on any part of a natural environment would spread to other parts of the environment. The wide range of multilateral environmental agreements and processes pertaining to natural environments attested to the paramount importance that the international community placed on the conservation, protection and sustainable use of such natural environments and their resources" (UN General Assembly. (2019, November). *Mr. Mulalap (Federated States of Micronesia), 74th Session, A/C.6/74/SR.24, §99*. Available at: https://documents-dds-ny.un.org/doc/UNDOC/GEN/N19/338/66/PDF/N1933866.pdf. Accessed on: 20 Jul. 2025).

[86] The Commission did not wish to provide a complete list of existing *jus cogens* norms. Instead, "as is clear from the carefully written commentary, the Commission has simply provided in draft conclusion 23 and the annex a list of some of the norms that have been 'referred to' in prior work of the Commission, without assessing whether those norms, as of 2019, are 'jus cogens' or are properly formulated as such" (Murphy, Sean D. (2020). Peremptory Norms of General International Law (jus cogens) and other Topics: The seventy-first session of the international law commission. *American Journal of International Law*, *114*(1), 68–86, p. 71).

[87] However, "the report of a United Nations special rapporteur indicated that there is certain support for the acknowledgment of the erga omnes character of obligations regarding global atmospheric degradation. Moreover, the special rapporteur's publications identified norms related to the protection of the environment as possible norms of jus cogens that have not previously been recognised by the ILC. Thus, greater ambition among States to recognise their obligations toward the environment in light of the climate crisis would be necessary for environmental norms to reach the status of jus cogens. Additionally, legal activism at the local and international levels could be a useful tool

protection of the environment—in its entirety—as a mandatory norm, when international criminal law offers a more suitable path to the specificity of ecocide.

Certainly, the prohibition of killing someone is not, per se, identified as a norm *jus cogens*, being so when the murder characterises a crime against humanity or a genocide, for example. Similarly, not every environmental damage deserves such quality. It is its massive scale that gives imperativeness to the prohibition of the conduct.

Due to its scope, ecocide comprises an exception among the countless environmental damages identified daily, being, in this magnitude, inadmissible, regardless of its legality (conformity with a certain norm). Thus, it could, in this restricted field, compose the list of the most serious international crimes, under the same foundations that justified the recognition of the others (apart from the situation of war).

Thinking of the "prohibition of ecocide" as a hierarchically superior norm (alongside others with the status of *jus cogens*)[88] is not, in this aspect, an inapplicable theory. International law, like all law, is embedded in the world of life, and cannot be isolated from social dynamics.[89] The development of studies about the environment is significantly more relevant and accurate today than at the end of the 1940s, as is the knowledge of human impacts and the consequences for future generations. This science cannot be disregarded, in the name of a stagnant preservation of the scope of international criminal law.

Despite the ILC's timidity in dealing with the environment and *jus cogens*, the Commission simultaneously takes on other topics of international law, directly related to the environmental issue, revealing the current and urgent nature of the topic. The Commission has been studying, since 2008, the "Protection of persons in

---

to unify the international community's consent that environmental protection is a crucial and universal value" (Cervantes, Miguel Ángel Marmolejo., Roeben, Volker., & Solís, Lisa Reilly. (2022). Global Climate Change Action as a Jus Cogens Norm: Some Legal Reflections on the Emerging Evidence. *Environmental Policy and Law*, *44*, 1–15, p.14–15).

[88] In 2001, the ILC adopted "a new draft of articles on international responsibility in which the terms crimes and offences had been eliminated and in which it speaks of 'serious violations of obligations emanating from imperative norms of international law', in other words, serious violations of norms of *jus cogens*. Note that, if the new expression translates what was previously understood as international crime, it does not consist of any violation of a norm of *jus cogens*, but only of serious violations" (Nasser, Salem Hikmat (2005). Jus cogens: Still this unknown. *GV Law Review*, 1(2), 161–178, p. 173).

[89] The existence of international law "is only explained, and justified, by the social function it must fulfil: to regulate behaviours within a given society. (...) The existence of a general international law, enforceable to all States, regardless of acceptance or participation in the norm-forming process, and can even, in some cases, impose itself on States that have always objected to these norms, is an idea that has gained currency and is passively accepted by many. (...) Even when the idea of the normative hierarchy of international law does not reach such extremes, it seems to have prevailed the idea that States, the main producers of legal norms, both internal and international, do not have the freedom to legislate contrary to superior norms or a more or less precise notion of international legal order" (Nasser, Salem Hikmat (2005). Jus cogens: Still this unknown. *GV Law Review*, 1(2), 161–178, p. 161–162).

the event of disasters";[90] since 2011, the "Protection of the environment in relation to armed conflicts"[91] and; since 2018, the "Rise in sea level in relation to international law". In all these cases, the approach is at the level of duty and accountability of States.

The Commission also delved into the "Protection of the atmosphere",[92] with studies initiated in 2013. The draft was approved by the UN General Assembly, through Resolution 76/112 (UN General Assembly, 2021), in December 2021. It was defined that States have the obligation to protect the atmosphere, exercising due diligence in taking appropriate measures, in accordance with the applicable rules of

---

[90] ILC's analytical work guide on Protection of people in case of disasters, link: https://legal.un.org/ilc/guide/6_3.shtml. Accessed on: 15 Jul. 2025. In the 2016 adopted Draft, the Commission defines 'disaster' as "a calamitous event or series of events resulting in widespread loss of life, great human suffering and distress, mass displacement, or large-scale material or environmental damage, thereby seriously disrupting the functioning of society" (ILC. (2016a). *Draft articles on the protection of persons in the event of disasters* Available at: https://legal.un.org/ilc/texts/instruments/english/draft_articles/6_3_2016.pdf. Accessed on: 20 Jul 2025). It should be understood that it is not the environmental or property loss per se that would be covered by the draft article, but rather the impact of such loss on people (Bartolini, Giulio. (2017). A universal treaty for disasters? Remarks on the International Law Commission's Draft Articles on the Protection of Persons in the Event of Disasters. *International Review of the Red Cross*, *99*(906), 1103–1137).

[91] ILC's analytical work guide on Sea-level rise in relation to international law, link: https://legal.un.org/ilc/guide/8_9.shtml. Accessed on: 15 Jul. 2022. On the scope and methodology of the Commission, the Presidents of the Study Group stated: "The relationship between these scientifically proven facts and the topic included in the Commission's programme of work was set forth in the 2018 syllabus in defining the scope of the topic: the Commission will only deal with 'the legal implications of sea-level rise', and not with 'protection of environment, climate change per se, causation, responsibility and liability'. Notwithstanding these limitations, and as emphasized in the syllabus in outlining the method of work of the Commission on this topic, the Study Group's efforts 'could contribute to the endeavours of the international community to respond to [the] issues' provoked by sea-level rise, and the topic 'reflects new developments in international law and pressing concerns of the international community as a whole'" (ILC. (2022c, April 19). *Sea-level rise in relation to international law. Second issues paper by Patrícia Galvão Teles and Juan José Ruda Santolaria, Co-Chairs of the Study Group on sea-level rise in relation to international law*. (A/CN.4/752, §51), p. 16. Available at: https://documents-dds-ny.un.org/doc/UNDOC/GEN/N22/276/29/PDF/N2227629.pdf. Accessed on: 15 Jul. 2025).

[92] ILC's analytical guide to the work on Protection of the Atmosphere. In the Statement on the Draft, the Chairperson of the Group, Patrícia Galvão Teles, commented on the scope of the *Draft*, exclusive to atmospheric pollution and degradation: "The present draft guidelines do not deal with and are without prejudice to questions concerning the polluter-pays principle, the precautionary principle and the common but differentiated responsibilities principle" (Teles, Patrícia Galvão. (2021a, 2021b, May). *Protection of the atmosphere. Statement of the Chairperson of the Drafting Committee*. ILC. Available at: https://legal.un.org/ilc/documentation/english/statements/2021_dc_chair_statement_poa.pdf. Accessed on: 15 Jul. 2022). Questioning how international law can promote protection to people in the context of climate change, Teles states that, in any case, the study in this area should seek to present the existing international legal protections for people affected by sea-level rise in a holistic and coherent way, identifying areas for further development, in order to facilitate the work of States, international organisations and other relevant stakeholders (Teles, Patrícia Galvão. (2021a, 2021b). Remarks by Patrícia Galvão Teles. In *Proceedings of the ASIL Annual Meeting* (pp. 158–161). Cambridge University Press).

international law, to prevent, reduce, or control atmospheric pollution and degradation (UN General Assembly, 2021).

The proliferation of national laws and treaties dealing with environmental protection[93] as a norm of characteristics *erga omnes,*[94] that is, with a duty (Gaja, 2011, pp. 151–160) to be observed by all.[95] In other words, the protection of the environment does not function as an absolute norm, since its respect can be limited within the bounds of proportionality and necessity. But, when it comes to massive damages, the understanding should be for total prohibition, similar to the crimes set out in the Rome Statute.[96]

Thus, even with the uncertainty about the understanding of environmental protection as *jus cogens*, there is minimal reluctance regarding the qualification of the said principle as an obligation *erga omnes* (Viñuales, 2008, pp. 11–44), where a global and generic obligation of protection would fit. The full prohibition would be restricted to ecocide.

The increasing judicialisation of the environment, the proliferation of new crimes—and bills—in national legislations and the plurality of studies, resolutions,

---

[93] Despite there being no formal recognition at the customary level of a general category of environmental crimes, "some treaties do impose an obligation on States to criminalise within their domestic legal orders acts that may result in severe damage to the environment" (Negri, Stefania (2022). On meteors and comets: Is the crime of ecocide back to stay? *International Criminal Law Review*, 1(aop), 1–30, p. 3).

[94] There is a clear link between *erga omnes* obligations and *jus cogens* norms, as both seek to preserve the aforementioned "fundamental values" of international society: "It should be noted, however, that the field of international environmental protection is rich in presenting distinct legal qualifications for similar phenomena. Thus, while certain environmental rules can be considered of an *erga omnes* nature and, therefore, of general imposition for all, others are merely guidelines or action programmes that fit only into the concept of *soft law* (...) This relationship becomes even closer when it comes to the protection of human rights, since the obligation that States have to protect people under their jurisdiction (an obligation that may not fit into the concept of *jus cogens* in all cases) has, at the very least, an *erga omnes* character. Also included in this category are several rules of international humanitarian law (*jus in bello*) and on international environmental protection" (Mazzuoli, Valério de Oliveira (2019). *Course on public international law*. Rio de Janeiro: Forense, p. 203).

[95] The obligations *erga omnes* are "obligations imposed on all, as they aim to ensure the fundamental values of international society; they are obligations of respect for the rights of others (..) and also of individuals (...). They differ from the norms of *jus cogens* because they do not have the hierarchical superiority that these hold in the field of International Law, as well as not being unconditional or immune to any type of derogation, as are the norms of *jus cogens*" (Mazzuoli, Valério de Oliveira (2019). *Course on public international law*. Rio de Janeiro: Forense, p. 204).

[96] Indeed, several human rights treaties expressly provide for the possibility of suspending certain human rights in case of public emergency: "In summary, the arguments that have been advanced to support the imperative nature of certain norms relating to environmental protection do not seem conclusive. This does not imply that at least some of these norms do not enjoy a certain hierarchy in international law in relation to other possible qualifications" (Viñuales, Jorge E. (2008). The protection of the environment and its normative hierarchy in international law. *International Law: Rev. Colomb. Int. Law*, 13, 11–44, p. 27).

and treaties on the environment at the international level[97] reinforce the idea that this legal good is fundamental to the survival of humanity, paving the way for the understanding of the prohibition of ecocide as *jus cogens*.[98]

As a current example of validation of this argument, the General Assembly of the UN, on July 28, 2022, approved a resolution[99] to recognise access to a clean and healthy environment as a universal human right, pointing out that environmental damage has negative, direct and indirect, implications for the effective enjoyment of all human rights (United Nations, 2022).

It is certain that the principle of non-retroactivity, set out in the Rome Statute (Article 24), facilitates[100]—at least politically—the inclusion of ecocide in the list of international offences, given the overcoming of the fear of persecutions for past occurrences, which, in theory, should happen, if the crime is recognised as a norm *jus cogens*, in its original conception.[101]

---

[97] It can be discussed whether there is a formation of a custom, in dealing with the environmental issue: "custom is composed of two elements: state practice, its objective component, and *opinio juris* (...) Practice consists of acts and omissions that are attributable to a state, in the exercise of its activities in the executive, legislative or judicial sphere (...) The *opinio juris* is the subjective component of custom and is present when states do or refrain from doing a certain conduct because they recognize that they had the legal obligation to act in that way" (Brant, Leonardo Nemer Caldeira., & Biazatti, Bruno de Oliveira. (2017). The formation of international custom today. *THEMIS: Revista da Esmec*, *15*, 125–169, p. 136/154).

[98] For Bassiouni (in 1996, before the existence of the International Criminal Court), three additional considerations should be taken into account to determine whether a particular international crime has reached the status of *jus cogens*: "The first has to do with the historical legal evolution of the crime. Clearly, the more legal instruments that exist to evidence the condemnation and prohibition of a particular crime, the better founded the proposition that the crime has risen to the level of jus cogens.32 The second consideration is the number of states that have incorporated the given proscription in their national laws.33 The third consideration is the number of international and national prosecutions for the given crime and how they have been characterized" (Bassiouni, M. Cherif (1996). International crimes: "Jus cogens" and "obligatio erga omnes". *Law and Contemporary Problems*, 59(4), 63–74, p. 70. Available at: https://www.jstor.org/stable/pdf/1192190.pdf?refreqid=excelsior%3A6ece53b8b95b107fe4d426ad66d5c297&ab_segments=&origin=&acceptTC=1. Accessed on: 10 Jul. 2025).

[99] UN General Assembly. (2022b, July). *The human right to a clean, healthy and sustainable environment* (Resolution A/76/L.75). Available at: https://digitallibrary.un.org/record/3982508/files/A_76_L.75-EN.pdf?ln=en. Accessed on: 20 Jan. 2025.

[100] The theory of *jus cogens* limits the "autonomy of the will of sovereign entities (*jus dispositivum*) in the international sphere, thus doing so with a view to ensuring public order (*ordre public*) on the world stage" (Mazzuoli, Valério de Oliveira (2019). *Course on public international law*. Rio de Janeiro: Forense, p. 208–209). Thus, ecocide, by obeying the principles of the Rome Statute, would preserve the freedom of the State to ratify it—or not—as a valid norm for its country, distancing the argument against international crimes of the Tribunals ad hoc.

[101] For some authors, the international environmental norm closest to being recognized as *jus cogens* is the principle *no-harm*: "The only potential for the development of an environmental jus cogens norm would be if States were to eventually recognize the peremptory nature of the no-harm principle, which, considering the slow development of customary environmental law norms, is unlikely to occur anytime soon. Until that happens, it is more likely that the normative force of peremptory norms could be extended into the environmental domain through human rights con-

It is worth noting that there is no such requirement in the Statute to include a new crime in the existing list. The digression made here aims to provide arguments for this, since the offences recognised there are considered as norms *jus cogens*, which underpin their validity among all States Parties and beyond (in the case of activation by the Security Council).

Ecocide, as environmental protection, reaches the goods protected in the Rome Statute, namely, human rights.[102] The umbilical relationship of these with the environment[103] cannot be disregarded,[104] even in a context of norms and treaties with anthropocentric biases.[105] The good to be protected—the environment—from

structions, and specifically by addressing environmental protection through those environmentally incidental human rights norms that are currently recognized as having jus cogens status. While it would be far more preferable if explicitly clear environmental jus cogens norms were to be created, we believe using incidental human rights norms for environmental protection holds considerable potential in the short term. States, global judicial institutions such as the ICJ, and global civil society, if they do take their socio-ecological obligations seriously in the Anthropocene, must embark as soon as possible on utilizing this possibility" (Kotzé, Louis. J., & Muzangaza, W. (2018). Constitutional international environmental law for the Anthropocene? *Review of European, Comparative & International Environmental Law*, 27(3), 278–292, p. 291).

[102] It is possible to infer that "supervisory bodies, both global and regional, have considered the relationship between environmental damage and internationally protected human rights. However, in virtually all instances, the petitions were not based on the specific right to a sound environment, but on rights to life, property, health, information, cultural rights, etc. Nevertheless, underlying all the demands were various types of environmental aggression, such as pollution, water contamination, deforestation, loss of biodiversity, among others" (Fonseca, Fúlvio Eduardo. (2010). Notes and reflections on international jurisprudence in environmental matters: The participation of individuals and non-governmental organisations. *Environment and Society*, *13*(2), 243–259, p.253–254).

[103] The most serious infractions against the environment are situated at the highest level of hierarchy of criminal charges: "from the point of view of values, its rapprochement with the crime against humanity could be explained by the attachment of the natural environment to the notion of common heritage of humanity already present in international law" (Neyret, Laurent. (2018). The transformation of the crime against humanity. In M. Delmas-Marty, et al., *The crime against humanity* (pp. 80–116). University Presses of France, p. 97–98).

[104] In the words of Sylvia Steiner, former judge of the ICC: "fundamental rights are born when they can, and must be born. But, once born, there is no return. There is no way to go back. They can be added to other rights, but they are here to stay (...). This is, in my opinion, the situation of International Criminal Justice. The result of a slow evolution, which had as a significant milestone the creation of the post-Second World War Tribunals (...) it established the concept of the inadmissibility of the exception derived from the doctrine of Acts of State or due obedience, the non-existence of immunities for Heads of State, and the international competence to prosecute and judge those who have committed the most serious crimes that threaten peace and the survival of humanity. Regarding these principles, I include them among the principles of protection of fundamental rights and, therefore, they cannot be reversed" (Steiner, Sylvia (2012). *10 years of the International Criminal Court: Sylvia Steiner responds*. Inter-American Court of Human Rights, p. 35. Available at: https://www.corteidh.or.cr/tablas/r33220.pdf. Accessed on: 20 Jul. 2022).

[105] About the *Policy Paper*, developed in 2016 by the Prosecutor of the ICC, it is noted that "reflects the divide between the anthropocentric and ecocentric perspectives of environmental protection. This duality can be inferred from the distinction between crimes committed 'by means of the destruction of the environment' and crimes 'that result in the destruction of the environment'. This

massive damage is vital for States and for society.[106] In this sense, environmental protection, through ecocide, as destruction of this very good, can have the force of norm *jus cogens*.

Once the possibility of recognising attention to the environment (or, at least, some specific aspect of this attention) as *jus cogens* has been determined, it is necessary to analyse how to enhance the protection of the good, in the international criminal field, through a universal jurisdiction, without the limiting obstacles of the Security Council, when blocked by its permanent members.

8.2.2 *Universal Jurisdiction and Resolution 377 (V) of the UNGA*

The dimension of the damage caused by an ecocide—as proposed here—is of global relevance. In this context, criminal judicial prosecution needs, in the same way, to reach as many States (i.e., territories) as possible, in order to configure a true system of worldwide protection through the criminalisation of the conduct.

The jurisdiction of the International Criminal Court is initially, as seen, restricted to States Parties. However, there is a possibility of expansion, set out in Article 13 [b] of the Rome Statute, making the Court competent to judge a crime provided for it occurred anywhere on the planet. For this, the UN Security Council must denounce the situation to the Prosecutor of the ICC, so that the investigation against an individual for the commission of the offence in a non-signatory country (or that has not accepted the jurisdiction of the Court, according to Article 12 [3])[107] can begin.

This provision has already been activated, in conjunction with Article 16 of the Statute (which provides for the suspension of an investigation). In March 2005, the

---

means that the Prosecutor considers both environmental crimes where the victim is the environment itself—which will in any case raise serious factual and evidentiary challenges, especially in terms of causation and attribution—and environmental crimes that are a means to perpetrate a humanitarian atrocity amounting to genocide or a crime against humanity" (Negri, Stefania (2022). On meteors and comets: Is the crime of ecocide back to stay? *International Criminal Law Review*, 1(aop), 1–30, p. 23).

[106] "*By positing the legitimacy of jus cogens in the common good though, have we not returned to an anachronistic philosophy that undermines value pluralism? It is true; in some sense jus cogens itself admits an interaction between law and morality; fact and norm. But this does not mean that jus cogens is posited in some metaphysical superior will or state of nature that violates the fact that reasonable persons may reasonably differ. On the contrary, jus cogens is grounded in the social facts of international community. It admits of a society which, despite apparent differences, does not shy away from the prospective task of reconciling competing values, and cooperating to achieve communal ends*" (RETTER, Mark. *Jus cogens*: towards an international common good?. Transnational Legal Theory, v. 2, n. 4, p. 1–53, 2011, p. 53).

[107] NOLLEZ-GOLDBACH, Raphaëlle. The International Criminal Court. Paris: Presses Universitaires de France, 2018, p. 51.

Security Council issued Resolution 1593,[108] referring the situation in Darfur, western region of Sudan (a country not a signatory to the Rome Statute),[109] to the Prosecutor of the International Criminal Court, to investigate crimes against humanity, war crimes, and subsequently, genocide, promoted by its autocratic president Omar Hassan al-Bashir.

In February 2011, another case led the Security Council to extend the jurisdiction of the ICC, this time in the Libyan Arab Jamahiriya (a country also not a member of the Court), for the use of violence against civilians. Resolution 1970[110] referred the complaint to the ICC Prosecutor, on the grounds of non-compliance with the "duty to protect" (R2P) of the State, imposing a series of restrictions against the leader of Libya at the time, Muammar Gaddafi.[111]

It can therefore be stated that there is indeed legal provision—and used in practice— for universal jurisdiction,[112] in the international criminal sphere.[113] Universal

---

[108] The Security Council determined that the investigation should observe crimes committed from 1 July 2002, that is, the date of the entry into force of the International Criminal Court. (UN Security Council, Resolution 1593, Mar. 2005, S/RES/1593 (2005). Available at: https://digitallibrary.un.org/record/544817/files/S_RES_1593%282005%29-EN.pdf?ln=en. Accessed on: 25 Jul. 2022).

[109] It was not necessary to leave room for customary international law in relation to the definition of crimes. This did not prevent the Court from referring to customary law: "*in Omar Al-Bashir, the Pre-Trial Chamber I stated that the immunity of head of state should be inapplicable also with respect to non-party states. The decision was not only based upon the ICC Statute, but also on the alleged customary norm*" (CZAPLIŃSKI, Władysław. Customary International Law as a Basis of an Individual Criminal Responsibility. In: KRZAN, Bartłomiej (Ed.). Prosecuting International Crimes: A Multidisciplinary Approach. Leiden: Brill Nijhoff, p. 53–69, 2016, p. 61).

[110] UN Security Council, Resolution 1970, Feb. 2011, S/RES/1970 (2011). Available at: https://documents-dds-ny.un.org/doc/UNDOC/GEN/N11/245/58/PDF/N1124558.pdf?OpenElement. Accessed on: 25 Jul. 2022.

[111] The Court requested assistance from the Security Council, in July 2011, to arrest and present the three defendants, Muammar Gaddafi, his son Saif Al-Islam Gaddafi and the head of Libyan intelligence Abdullah Al-Senussi. The latter two were arrested, while the former was killed in October 2011, in Libya (Pre Trial Chamber I. Request to the members of the UN Security Council who are not States Parties to the Rome Statute for the arrest and surrender of Muammar Mohammed Abu Minyar Gaddafi, Saif Al-Islam Gaddafi and Abdullah al-Senussi. Situation in the Libyan Arab Jamahiriya. ICC-01/11-01/11, 4 Jul. 2011. Available at: https://www.icc-cpi.int/sites/default/files/CourtRecords/CR2011_08698.PDF. Accessed on: 25 Jul. 2022).

[112] "There are many international instruments that establish express clauses of universal jurisdiction for certain crimes, those considered jus cogens, such as crimes against humanity, genocide, war crimes, apartheid, torture (...). The rule, in conclusion, is that States, by themselves or in conjunction with the international community, have the duty to prosecute and judge the authors of serious violations of human rights and humanitarian law" (Steiner, Sylvia (2012). *10 years of the International Criminal Court: Sylvia Steiner responds*. Inter-American Court of Human Rights, p. 32. Available at: https://www.corteidh.or.cr/tablas/r33220.pdf. Accessed on: 20 Jul. 2025).

[113] "It should not go unnoticed that both the principle of universal jurisdiction and that of complementarity, among others, call for a greater approximation, if not interaction, between the international and national legal systems" (Trindade, Antônio Augusto Cançado (2010). Contemporary international courts and the pursuit of the realization of the ideal of international justice. *Rev. Fac. Direito UFMG*, 57, 37–68, p. 57).

jurisdiction,[114] however, is a predominantly national phenomenon (extraterritorial criminal jurisdiction), before being launched as a principle of international law for the most serious crimes. Thus, various States have, in their internal regulations, openings for the local judiciary to act in cases of crimes—the most serious ones—occurring anywhere, without any connection with the judging country.

This form of criminal jurisdiction—extraterritorial[115]—has as its rule of connection the international nature of the crime, combined with the purpose of the international society in achieving criminal accountability (Oliveira, 2020), based on the legal-political concept of *actio popularis.*[116] That is, the State acts on behalf of the international community because it has an interest in preserving world order as a member of this community (Bassiouni, 2002, pp. 945–1001).

The way of implementing universal jurisdiction is, however, different, depending on the State, so that real universality encounters obstacles within the laws and judiciaries themselves.[117] It is common for States to establish jurisdiction to defendants

---

[114] "In truth, the remote origin of the principle of universal jurisdiction is found in the Code of Justinian (483–565), from the sixth century. It was recognised as a general principle applicable to international crimes and also to various national crimes by jurists such as Francisco de Vitória (1483–1546), in the sixteenth century, and Hugo Grotius (1583–1645) in the following century. During the Middle Ages, the cities of northern Italy exercised jurisdiction over bandits (called *assassini*, *banditi* and *vagabondi*), suspected of committing crimes outside the limits of the city-state. (...). The doctrine found wide application in combating acts of international piracy (*international piracy*), the oldest international crime recognised as such" (Cretella Neto, José (2014). *Course of international criminal law*. Saraiva, p. 240–241).

[115] "The *principle of universal jurisdiction* reflects the notion that certain crimes are so abominable and aberrant, that all States have—in theory, at least—an interest in ensuring that the criminals are brought to trial. The principle thus provides, the legal basis for the courts of any country to judge suspects in cases involving these crimes, regardless of the location of the facts or the nationalities of the criminals or their victims" (Cretella Neto, José (2014). *Course of international criminal law*. Saraiva, 2014, p. 246–247).

[116] "The *actio popularis* was based on the idea that both the State and any citizen had legitimacy to judicially claim the protection of public interests, constituting, in this sense, a '*qui tam action*', expression that originates from the sentence '*qui tam pro domino rege quam pro se ipso in hac parte sequitur*', from which emerges the idea of a joint responsibility and concurrent legitimacy between citizens and the state. This 'qui tam' therefore constitutes the main reason why most legal systems of the Roman-Germanic family, at least in their phases of republican and/or democratic regimes, have ensured 'actiones populares' for the citizen to propose judicial measures aimed at the protection of public interests" (Oliveira, Marcus Vinícius Xavier de. (2018). The 'actio popularis' and (n) the International (Criminal) Law. *City Law Journal*, *10*(1), 532–571, p. 536. Available at: https://www.e-publicacoes.uerj.br/index.php/rdc/article/download/30188/23365. Accessed on: 28 Jul. 2025).

[117] Although this type of jurisdiction has been available for domestic criminal investigations for international crimes since the early 1950s, "most countries, even after implementing the Rome Statute have opted for a limited type of jurisdiction whereby the presence of a perpetrator in the country carrying out the criminal investigation is required (...) However, the notion of universal jurisdiction where no link at all is required between the state initiating investigations or prosecutions and the perpetrator of international crimes—called universal jurisdiction in absentia—has gained some currency in Europe in the last 15 years" (Rikhof, Joseph. (2009). Fewer places to

residing in the country,[118] or when there is some important connection between the crime and the State. Even so, in the exercise to judge serious violations of human rights, for example, there are manifestations from Spain, France, Germany, and Italy,[119] as well as Belgium, in 2005, and Senegal, in 2006.[120] After 2008, processes with expanded jurisdiction are also observed in Finland, Norway, Sweden, and Argentina.[121]

The technique also has its negative effects.[122] Unrestrained exercise can cost disturbances in world order, as well as serve as an argument to justify deprivations of individual human rights, when used as a political tool for abusive purposes.[123] It

---

hide? The impact of domestic war crimes prosecutions on international impunity. In *Criminal Law Forum* (pp. 1–51). Springer Netherlands, p. 31).

[118] The concentration of universal jurisdiction trials on residents may partially reflect that, in several States, "universal jurisdiction statutes only authorize the exercise of universal jurisdiction against residents. It may also be a consequence of logistical considerations given that it is generally easier to investigate, prosecute and try people already residing in the prosecuting state. Concentrating on residents—as well as the statutory and legal requirements established to that effect—may also reflect a 'no safe haven' conception of the role of states in the universal jurisdiction regime. According to Langer, under the 'no safe haven' conception, the role of states is not to give refuge to participants in international crimes—in contrast with the alternative 'global enforcer' conception of the role of states in the universal jurisdiction regime under which states may prevent and punish core international crimes committed anywhere in the world" (Langer, Máximo, & Eason, M. (2019). The quiet expansion of universal jurisdiction. *European Journal of International Law*, 30(3), 779–817, p. 813–814. Available at: https://escholarship.org/content/qt4c24b3n9/qt4c24b3n9.pdf. Accessed on: 26 Jul. 2025).

[119] TOLEDO, André de Paiva; BIZAWU, Kiwonghi. International legal conditions for intervention in the Amazon. Paths of Law, v. 16, n. 3, p. 91–122, 2019, p. 106.

[120] ANNONI, Danielle; MENDONÇA, Camila Dabrowski de Araujo. Mixed courts: an analysis of the concept. Nomos, v. 35, n. 1, p. 101–134, 2015, p. 116.

[121] In total, "there have been 34 universal jurisdiction trial verdicts on crimes against humanity, genocide, torture and war crimes in the decade 2008–2017. This means an increase of 88.88 per cent in the number of universal jurisdiction trials over core international crimes if we take as the base the number of trials in the decade 1998–2007 and an increase of 425 per cent if we take as the base the number of trials in the decade 1988–1997" (Langer, Máximo, & Eason, M. (2019). The quiet expansion of universal jurisdiction. *European Journal of International Law*, 30(3), 779–817, p. 794. Available at: https://escholarship.org/content/qt4c24b3n9/qt4c24b3n9.pdf. Accessed on: 26 Jul. 2025).

[122] For Cretella Neto, there are still obstacles of a legal, political, and ethical nature to the application of the principle: "a) there is no guarantee that national courts can judge international crimes with more justice and impartiality, given the existence of cultural, historical or political ties with one of the parties in the dispute; b) it is difficult to ensure that there will be no political persecution, as criminal prosecution may be just a pretext to do so; c) the exercise of universal jurisdiction implies interference in the sovereignty and immunity of States, especially when committed by state agents; and d) the application of the principle to countries that are not parties to certain conventions may have a deleterious impact in cases of transition from autocratic regimes to democracy" (Cretella Neto, José (2014). *Course of international criminal law*. Saraiva, p. 260).

[123] Furthermore, universal jurisdiction is not as well established in conventional and customary international law as "its ardent proponents, (major human rights organizations referred to above), profess it to be. These organizations have listed countries relying on universal jurisdiction when, in fact, the legal provisions they cite do not stand for that proposition, or at least not as unequivo-

would ultimately create frictions between States that compromise global security, precisely what is intended to be guaranteed: international security.[124]

Despite such difficulties, it is certain that impunity in cases of the most serious crimes against humanity is the target of States on the international level. If the national structures, per se, present fluctuations and insecurities in the application of the principle of universal jurisdiction, at the international level, there is a reinforcement on the subject[125] with the existence and practice of the ICC.

Undoubtedly, the jurisdiction of the International Criminal Court is more limited[126] (considering its expansion by Article 13 [b] as an exception) than that of the States that admit to universality. However, the scope of the ICC cannot be disregarded, after all, in addition to the 125 signatory countries, it is possible to reach other potential criminal situations with the help of the Security Council.

A virtual barrier to a true universal jurisdiction in the ICC is the inaction of the Security Council, when the issue, external to the States Parties, involves the interests of any of the members with veto power—which is not hard to imagine. But, this deadlock would not occur for the first time. The United Nations has already experienced this moment during the Cold War.

---

cally as represented" (Bassiouni, M. Cherif. (2002). Universal jurisdiction for international crimes: historical perspectives and contemporary practice. In M. Cherif Bassiouni (Ed.), *Post-Conflict Justice* (pp. 945–1001). Brill Nijhoff, p. 946).

[124] "It is impossible not to notice the tension that exists between International Criminal Law and the international system as it currently presents itself, as States try to avoid the censure of their policies and conduct, as well as those of their nationals, made by *extra* or *supranational* entities, while at the same time they seek to enforce the law in their territories. Maintaining state sovereignty, in the tradition of Westphalia, seems difficult to reconcile with the legal norm established by International Law" (Cretella Neto, José (2014). *Course of international criminal law*. Saraiva, p. 250).

[125] By taking the trial to a supranational level, in theory, it moves away from direct influences of state policies (such as, for example, absolute protection of their nationals from an external trial), since the jurisdiction of the International Tribunal has already been authorised by treaty: "Until the ICC treaty is renegotiated to avoid what Kissinger sees as its "short comings and dangers," he recommends that the U.N. Security Council determine which cases warrant an international tribunal. That option was rejected during the Rome negotiations on the ICC because it would allow the council's five permanent members, including Russia and China as well as the United States, to exempt their nationals and those of their allies by exercising their vetoes. As a nation committed to human rights and the rule of law, the United States should be embracing an international system of justice, even if it means that Americans, like everyone else, might sometimes be scrutinized" (Roth, Kenneth (2001). The case for universal jurisdiction. *Foreign Affairs*, 150–154, p. 154).

[126] The most controversial issue in the negotiation of the Rome Statute was the jurisdiction of the Court: "the 'question of questions of the entire project' was whether the Court would exercise universal jurisdiction or would need the consent of every State concerned with the crime. Like Hans-Peter Kaul pointed out, the conflicting principles were universality versus State sovereignty. Article 12, which provides for the preconditions for the exercise of jurisdiction, was until the last minute before the adoption of the Statute 'a make-or-break provision'. It was also felt essential that the SC be empowered to refer situations to the future permanent international criminal court" (Galand, Alexandre Skander (2019). *UN Security Council referrals to the International Criminal Court: Legal nature, effects and limits*. Leiden: Brill. Available at: https://library.oapen.org/bitstream/handle/20.500.12657/37984/9789004342217_webready_content_text.pdf?sequence=1. Accessed on: 22 Jul. 2025, p. 28).

The inertia of the Council (better said, the lack of unanimity among the permanent members) in the face of security situations and threats to international peace prompted the UN General Assembly, which, on November 3, 1950, adopted Resolution 377 (V) (UN General Assembly, 1950), in response to the strategy of the Union of Soviet Socialist Republics (USSR) to block any determination of the Council on measures to be taken to protect the Republic of Korea, against the aggression launched by the military forces of North Korea (Tomuschat, 2008). The resolution, called[127] "Uniting for Peace" (*Uniting for Peace*), provides as follows:

Resolution 377 (V) "Uniting for Peace"

Reaffirming the importance of the exercise by the Security Council of its primary responsibility for the maintenance of international peace and security, and the duty of the permanent members to seek unanimity and to exercise restraint in the use of the veto,

Reaffirming that the initiative in negotiating the agreements for armed forces provided for in Article 43 of the Charter belongs to the Security Council, and desiring to ensure that, pending the conclusion of such agreements, the United Nations has at its disposal means for maintaining international peace and security;

Conscious that failure of the Security Council to discharge its responsibilities on behalf of all the Member States, particularly those responsibilities referred to in the two preceding paragraphs, does not relieve Member States of their obligations or the United Nations of its responsibility under the Charter to maintain international peace and security;

Recognizing in particular that such failure does not deprive the General Assembly of its rights or relieve it of its responsibilities under the Charter in regard to the maintenance of international peace and security;

Recognizing that discharge by the General Assembly of its responsibilities in these respects calls for possibilities of observation which would ascertain the facts and expose aggressors; for the existence of armed forces which could be used collectively; and for the possibility of timely recommendation by the General Assembly to Members of the United Nations for collective action which, to be effective, should be prompt;

Resolves that if the Security Council, because of lack of unanimity of the permanent members, fails to exercise its primary responsibility for the maintenance of international peace and security in any case where there appears to be a threat to the peace, breach of the peace, or act of aggression, the General Assembly shall consider the matter immediately with a view to making appropriate recommendations to Members for collective measures, including in the case of a breach of the peace or act of aggression the use of armed force when necessary, to maintain

[127] Resolution 377 (V) is also "known as 'Uniting for the Maintenance of Peace' or 'Dean Acheson Resolution', named after the American Secretary of State at the time, its great promoter and idealist" (Brant, Leonardo Nemer Caldeira (2005). The conflict of competence between the General Assembly and the Security Council in the light of Article 12, paragraph 1 of the United Nations Charter. *Brazilian Journal of Political Studies*, 92, 135–148, p. 142).

> or restore international peace and security. If not in session at the time, the General Assembly may meet in emergency special session within 24 h of the request therefor. Such emergency special session shall be called if requested by the Security Council on the vote of any seven members, or by a majority of the Members of the United Nations.[128]

Since the adoption of the Resolution,[129] the General Assembly has made use of the *Uniting for Peace* 12 or 13 times, depending on how the first case is characterised.[130] In total, 8 cases were invoked by the Security Council itself,[131] while another 4 cases originated in the General Assembly (Security Council Report, 2013).

In the last of these, the Council, through Resolution 2623,[132] of January 2022, decided to convene a Special Emergency Session of the General Assembly, to examine the issue of the Russian invasion of Ukraine, resulting in Resolution ES-11/1

[128] UN General Assembly. (1950, November 3). *Resolution 377 (V) "Uniting for Peace"*. Available at: https://www.un.org/en/sc/repertoire/otherdocs/GAres377A(v).pdf. Accessed on: 22 Jul. 2025.

[129] The Resolution also established a Peace Observation Commission to observe and report on the situation in any area where there was international tension, "the continuance of which was likely to endanger the maintenance of peace or security. It also established a Collective Measures Committee to study and report to the Security Council and General Assembly on methods which might be used to maintain and strengthen international peace in accordance with the purposes and principles of U.N. Chart" (Ali, S. Nasir. (1958). Uniting for peace. *The Indian Journal of Political Science*, *19*(2), 115–123, p. 118).

[130] The first case is recorded in General Assembly Resolution 498 (V), still timid, for calling for the cessation of hostilities from China against the Korean peninsula (UN General Assembly. (1951, February). *Resolution 498(V)*. History and Public Policy Program Digital Archive, United Nations documentation center. Available at: http://digitalarchive.wilsoncenter.org/document/116196. Accessed on: 25 Jul. 2025).

[131] The penultimate one, from January 1982, dealt with the crisis in the Middle East, about the territories occupied by Israel (UN General Assembly. (1982, February). *Resolution 500*. United Nations Digital Library. Available at: https://digitallibrary.un.org/record/31560. Accessed on: 25 Jul. 2025).

[132] UN Security Council. (2022, February 2). *Resolution 2623*. (S/RES/2623). Available at: https://documents-dds-ny.un.org/doc/UNDOC/GEN/N22/271/32/PDF/N2227132.pdf?OpenElement. Accessed on: 25 Jul. 2025.

(UN General Assembly, (2022a) of the Assembly,[133] in March of the same year.[134] Thus, regardless of the format of use—and responses—of Resolution 377 (V), it is a fact that, when it comes to international security and threat to peace, there is a tool[135] to escape the veto power in the Security Council.[136]

Finally, the General Assembly, in the face of the indiscriminate attack by Israel on the Gaza Strip, which caused humanitarian and environmental catastrophes,[137]

---

[133] It is unlikely that this Resolution will be the last word of the General Assembly on the war in Ukraine. The outcome of the first meeting of the Emergency Special Session, Resolution ES-11/1, did not go as far "as some of these prior resolutions, but it did return to a legal characterization that it has long avoided: aggression. It deplored "in the strongest terms the aggression by the Russian Federation against Ukraine in violation of Article 2 (4) of the [UN] Charter" and condemned Russia's declaration as to the necessity of this "'special military operation.'" It demanded Russia to "cease its use of force against Ukraine" as well as to "immediately, completely and unconditionally withdraw all of its military forces from the territory of Ukraine within its internationally recognized borders." It also condemned "all violations of international humanitarian law and violations and abuses of human rights," demanding that parties to the conflict "fully comply with their obligations under international humanitarian law to spare the civilian population." It recalled the obligations under Article 2(2) of the UN Charter, that all member states, "in order to ensure to all of them the rights and benefits of membership, shall fulfil in good faith the obligations assumed by them in accordance with the [UN] Charter" (Ramsden, Michael. (2022). Uniting for Peace: The Emergency Special Session on Ukraine. *Harvard International Law Journal*).

[134] Although the ICC Prosecutor has initiated an investigation into the situation in Ukraine, there are limitations to the jurisdictional reach of this Court, particularly on the crime of aggression: "as Russia is not an ICC state party, and the Security Council is unable to make a referral of the situation due to Russia's veto, the crime of aggression cannot be prosecuted at the ICC in this situation. The establishment by the Assembly of an ad hoc tribunal over the crime of aggression represents one legal option to redress this impunity gap" (Ramsden, Michael. (2022). Uniting for Peace: The Emergency Special Session on Ukraine. *Harvard International Law Journal*).

[135] However, it should be noted that, despite its use a few times throughout history (notably in the case of Namibia's independence in 1981), a significant group of States is reluctant to consider actions taken based on this Resolution as legitimate (Weiss, Thomas G. (2005). *Overcoming the Security Council reform impasse: The Implausible* versus *the Plausible*. Friedrich-Ebert-Stiftung, Dialogue on Globalization, 14).

[136] The General Assembly can "take upon itself a situation that threatens peace when, 'due to the lack of unanimity among the permanent members, the Security Council fails to exercise its responsibility...'. In reality, it matters little whether the case remains on the list of issues submitted to the Council, it is necessary and sufficient that the Council is prevented from acting for the General Assembly to consider itself authorised to make recommendations" (Brant, Leonardo Nemer Caldeira (2005). The conflict of competence between the General Assembly and the Security Council in the light of Article 12, paragraph 1 of the United Nations Charter. *Brazilian Journal of Political Studies*, 92, 135–148, p. 145).

[137] The environmental catastrophe is evidenced in the UNEP report, which preliminarily pointed out the reconstruction challenges: "Restoring safe living conditions for a densely-populated, water-scarce and contaminated strip of land will also require exceptionally careful planning. Incorporating environmental dimensions into such planning will be necessary from the very start. Planning to rebuild hospitals, schools and homes should incorporate analysis of potential contaminants, so that high-risk areas can be avoided; and be sensitive to possible land instability arising from destroyed tunnels. Clearance of debris also requires an understanding of the contaminants such debris contains, to ensure the clearance and disposal does not spread and further contaminate soil or water, and thus create new risks to Gaza's inhabitants." (United Nations Environment

approved, still in December of 2024, Resolution[138] A/RES/ES-10/26. In it, despite there being no mention of *Uniting for Peace*, the UNGA demonstrates that the inertia—even partial, in this case[139]—of the Security Council, authorises a more insinuating action regarding international security.

It is possible, given this panorama, to construct another function—derived from its secondary responsibility—for the General Assembly, taking advantage of the legal and practical framework developed in recent decades. Imagine the following situation: a serious crime and an attack on peace or international security occurs in a country not a signatory to the Rome Statute, committed by a national of Russia, China, or the United States. As the case, in theory, is not part of the original jurisdiction of the International Criminal Court, a resolution[140] of the Security Council would be necessary to determine the opening of an investigation by the Court's Prosecutor (through Article 13 [b]), based on the Council's competences, set out in Chap. 7, of the UN Charter.[141]

It happens that the State, a permanent member and natural of the agent, can veto the hypothetical resolution, if the situation is submitted to the Council. We would be facing a deadlock similar to what originated as Resolution 377 (V) of the UN General Assembly. At the heart of the matter, we would return to impunity, now in the face of an international crime.

Provoked, the Assembly would meet exceptionally to approve a new resolution, in the face of the risk to peace and international security, deciding to refer the case to the ICC Prosecutor,[142] since, according to Article 13 (b) of the Rome Statute, it

---

Programme. (2024). *Environmental impact of the conflict in Gaza: Preliminary assessment of environmental impacts*. Available at: https://wedocs.unep.org/bitstream/handle/20.500.11822/45739/environmental_impact_conflict_Gaza.pdf. Accessed on: 20 Jan. 2025).

[138] UN General Assembly. (2024, December). *Demand for ceasefire in Gaza: resolution / adopted by the General Assembly*. (Resolution A/RES/ES-10/26). Available at: https://digitallibrary.un.org/record/4070093?ln=en&v=pdf. Accessed on: 20 Jan. 2025.

[139] After several uses of the Veto Power and approval of less broad resolutions (for example, Resolution 2728, of March 2024, which determined a ceasefire during Ramadan), finally, in June, the Security Council approved Resolution 2735 (2024), in June of 2024, which forwarded a total ceasefire, with the release of hostages and prisoners (Security Council. (2024, June). *Resolution 2735 (2024) [on ceasefire in the Gaza Strip]*. Available at: https://digitallibrary.un.org/record/4051310?ln=en&v=pdf. Accessed on: 20 Jan. 2025).

[140] This Resolution limits the action of the Prosecutor to the terms set forth therein, under penalty of inherent normative conflict (Galand, Alexandre Skander (2018). *UN Security Council referrals to the International Criminal Court: Legal nature, effects and limits*. Leiden: Brill, p. 101).

[141] United Nations. (1945, June). *Charter of the United Nations*. Available at: https://unric.org/pt/wp-content/uploads/sites/9/2009/10/Carta-das-Na%C3%A7%C3%B5es-Unidas.pdf. Accessed on: 22 Jun. 2025.

[142] In addition to referring the case to the Prosecutor, for the investigation to be effective, it is still necessary to count on the cooperation of States: "this is legally unproblematic insofar as State-parties are concerned. However, mandatory cooperation of non-parties has to be founded on some other legal basis, principally a binding UN decision. That the UNGA cannot bind members outside internal organizational matters has been challenged by some scholars, referring to equivocation in the drafting history as to the scope of UNGA powers. Furthermore, UN practice demonstrates that

would be up to the Security Council, "acting under Chap. 7 of the United Nations".[143] The situation exemplifies a less aggressive use of *Uniting for Peace*, which can authorise, in certain cases, even the use of force.

The Assembly, under the mantle of Resolution 377 (V),[144] would act only in the case of failure—inaction—on the part of the Security Council, as set out in the UN Charter (Chap. 7) and endorsed by the International Court of Justice,[145] exercising its share of responsibility for maintaining peace and international security. The Court's activity will also respect its complementary character, in relation to the local State of the investigation, because, even if the country is not part of the Rome Statute, the principles of international criminal law must be respected, among them the *ne bis in idem* and the founder of the Court, of complementarity. After all, Resolution 377 (V),[146] the Statute itself and its opening in Article 13 (b) have the same objective: to prevent impunity for the commission of an international crime.

---

the concept of a 'recommendation' is not static, but evolving; it has been used by the UNSC to 'authorize' enforcement action. On this basis, there is some support for UNGA resolutions assuming binding effect where this reflects the will of the UN membership to confer on the body authoritative competencies, as with the UNGA's regulation of trustee and mandated territories" (Ramsden, Michael., & Hamilton, Tomas. (2017). Uniting against impunity: the UN General Assembly as a catalyst for action at the ICC. *International & Comparative Law Quarterly*, *66*(4), 893–921, p. 916).

[143] Article 13 (b), Rome Statute: "The Security Council, acting under Chap. 7 of the Charter of the United Nations, may refer to the Prosecutor any situation in which one or more of these crimes appears to have been committed".

[144] The use by the General Assembly of this Resolution "outlines the undeniable merit of this body in trying to enforce the specific purpose around which the Organization was "essentially created, that is, the maintenance of international peace and security" (Brant, Leonardo Nemer Caldeira (2005). The conflict of competence between the General Assembly and the Security Council in the light of Article 12, paragraph 1 of the United Nations Charter. *Brazilian Journal of Political Studies*, 92, 135–148, p. 148).

[145] The International Court of Justice recognised that the UN Charter gives the Security Council primary, but not exclusive, competence on the subject of maintaining peace and international security, legitimising the actions of the General Assembly in relation to concrete issues, such as peace mission determinations (Amorim, João Alberto Alves (2015). *The UN and the environment*. São Paulo: Atlas Publisher, p. 57, and Brant, Leonardo Nemer Caldeira (2005). The conflict of competence between the General Assembly and the Security Council in the light of Article 12, paragraph 1 of the United Nations Charter. *Brazilian Journal of Political Studies*, 92, 135–148, p. 145). "Determinations made in recommendations and decisions, unlike declarations, may

have causative effect. This effect occurs when law is applied on the basis of a determination. Imagine that the ICJ were to acknowledge as an internal UN customary norm that, based on a sufficiently constant and uniform practice of recommendations combined with an opinio juris, the GA is not precluded from recommending measures to maintain peace and security when it determines that the SC is paralysed by a lack of unanimity among its permanent members" (Öberg, Marko Divac. (2005). The legal effects of resolutions of the UN Security Council and General Assembly in the jurisprudence of the ICJ. *European Journal of International Law*, *16*(5), 879–906, p. 905).

[146] For some authors, the Resolution itself is without utility: "there is no reason to use Uniting for Peace in order to call emergency special sessions. The Assembly is in session all year around. If States want to use it to highlight a particular emergency or crisis, that is a policy question. There is no longer any concern that the Assembly cannot consider any dispute or situation that is also before

The referral of a situation, whether by the UN General Assembly or the Security Council (whose members, it is important to remember, are also part of the General Assembly), does not remove the independence of the Prosecutor's Office to freely evaluate the case, and may even archive it, if there are no minimum indications of the crime.

Therefore, the principle of universal jurisdiction would have its maximum reach, respecting current norms of international law, textual or customary. This relativised conception of universal jurisdiction—given the condition[147] of referring a situation to the Prosecutor's Office—would avoid some particularly serious problems in terms of effectiveness and efficiency, which demand a considerable price for the internal and international legitimacy of the institution (Oliveira, 2020, p. 56).

It is an exceptional situation,[148] following the exceptionality that is the competence of the Court itself.[149] However, it represents an additional way to combat

---

the Council. The ICJ advisory opinion in the 'Wall' case disposed of that. The Assembly has adopted "voluntary sanctions" provisions with and without reference to Uniting for Peace; hence, it is not needed for that purpose. As regards the Assembly recommending the use of force pursuant to Uniting for Peace, the Assembly can do so only within the limited context of supporting the exercise by States of their inherent right to individual or collective self-defense under Article 51 of the Charter. Otherwise, for the Assembly to recommend the use of coercive force would be of dubious legal validity and States who followed such a recommendation would risk violating Article 2 (4) of the Charter and thus being held internationally responsible for having committed an internationally wrongful act" (Johnson, Larry D. (2014). "Uniting for Peace": Does it still serve any useful purpose? *American Journal of International Law*, 108, 106–115, p. 115. Available at: https://www.cambridge.org/core/journals/american-journal-of-international-law/article/uniting-for-peace-does-it-still-serve-any-useful-purpose/90BD2F453491596D637D6C94DE621953. Accessed on: 26 Jul. 2025).

[147] According to Cassese, there are two theories about the expansion of the principle of universal jurisdiction, called "absolute" and "conditional" (Cassese, Antonio (2004). Is there an insurmountable conflict between state sovereignty and international criminal justice? In A. Cassese & M. Delmas-Marty (Eds.), *International crimes and international jurisdictions* (pp. 67–82). Barueri: Manole, p. 67).

[148] Even if the objective of the "Uniting for Peace" resolution was to resolve the injustices of the veto, it is not a panacea: "Public frustration with the unequal power wielded by UN members is unlikely to completely subside with the emergence of a more powerful General Assembly. However, the UN Charter was never truly intended to reflect the sovereign equality of its membership. The dominant structural feature of the Charter, the veto, is the product of an unlikely international compromise that would never have been reached in the absence of a prevailing role for the Allied powers of the Second World War" (Carswell, Andrew J. (2013). Unblocking the UN Security Council: The Uniting for Peace Resolution. *Journal of Conflict and Security Law*, 18(3), 453–480, p. 479. Available at: https://academic.oup.com/jcsl/article-pdf/18/3/453/2570836/krt016.pdf. Accessed on: 22 Jul. 2025).

[149] Certainly, there are those who argue against the possibility of the ICC prosecuting someone from a non-signatory state of the Rome Statute, even with the provision of art. 13 (b), as it threatens one of the most fundamental principles of international legal order—that a state does not incur rights and obligations arising from a treaty without its consent: "the efficacy of legal rules is a basic requirement of any legal system but because the international legal order is a defective legal order in this sense—lacking as it does a police force that can enforce its rules, it needs states as a consent-based legal order. To attempt to dismiss that consent which lies at the heart of the system is what will, in the words of Ambassador John Bolton, make 'the ICC die on its own'" (Iyi, John-

impunity,[150] for times when the Security Council is blocked, when the majority of members with veto power are not States Party to the ICC.[151]

For a massive environmental crime, this possibility is crucial to achieve the objectives of a crime in the ICC, reaching as many spaces as possible, especially considering the symbolic nature of the penalty.[152] Certainly, the opening given to the UN General Assembly could work in favour of building a less selective structure,[153] as to whom to prosecute.

Mark (2019). Re-thinking the authority of the UN Security Council to refer nationals of non-party states to the ICC. *Netherlands International Law Review*, 66(3), 391–417, p. 414. Available at: https://link.springer.com/article/10.1007/s40802-019-00144-4. Accessed on: 26 Jul. 2025).

[150] Despite the criticisms, even at the time of the Resolution, the relevance and importance of the document was clear: "The affirmative conclusions we arrived at on the ground of the interpretation of both the Charter and the Resolution must not lead us to an erroneous judgment on the importance of the Resolution. It is most important. In the first place its importance is political. In the prevailing circumstances it is a substantial step for preserving peace and strengthening the United Nations. Middle-sized and small Powers obtained a larger part of material and moral responsibility with regard to the maintenance of peace. As to the legal aspects, the Resolution is undoubtedly a step 'in the evolution of the law of the United Nations, in the sense that evolution is inherent in every new regulation, although it might be in accordance with existing provisions. Every new disposition, every resolution of the General Assembly elaborating in more detail the provisions of the Charter and other sources of the law of the United Nations, adds new elements to that law. The same is the effect of the practice, the day-to-day application of the Charter. It gives concrete shape to the principles and provisions of the Charter and of the law of the United Nations in general and interprets their sense and meaning. In that way every law, and thus also the law of the United Nations, is subject to perpetual transformation. Hence, such an important act as the Resolution necessarily produces transformations in the legal system of which it becomes a part" (Andrassy, Juraj (1956). Uniting for peace. *American Journal of International Law*, 50(3), 563–582, p. 582).

[151] The reform of the Security Council has been debated for decades, but does not seem close to happening. Meanwhile, in cases of deadlock on issues of international security and peace, the use of Uniting for Peace "is not the complete solution to these calls, and the need, for Security Council reform, but, in the interim, it can be a practical solution to unblocking the Security Council in some limited circumstances" (Melling, Graham., & Dennett, Anne. (2017). The Security Council veto and Syria: responding to mass atrocities through the "Uniting for Peace" resolution. *Indian Journal of International Law, 57*(3), 285–307, p. 307. Available at: https://link.springer.com/article/10.1007/s40901-018-0084-9. Accessed on: 26 Jul. 2025).

[152] In the context of massive environmental crimes, the possibility of individual attribution for an international crime can serve as a deterrent to certain behaviours, especially when practised in the business environment, when the company's reputation is of fundamental commercial importance.

[153] "Although the universal jurisdiction regime, unlike the ICC regime, has not been an international criminal law enforcement regime exclusively or even mainly for Africa, it has been selective in the sense indicated above. Its proponents have tended to leave these selectivity problems aside or to consider them an improper result of political calculations by political branches. But even if these political considerations were improper or morally wrong, an important implication of this article would be that selectivity is such a structural feature of universal jurisdiction that any justification of actual universal jurisdiction statutes, prosecutions, and trials should explain why it is not invalidated by selectivity" (Langer, Máximo. (2011). The diplomacy of universal jurisdiction: The political branches and the transnational prosecution of international crimes. *American Journal of International Law, 105*(1), 1–49, p. 49. Available at: https://www.cambridge.org/core/journals/american-journal-of-international-law/article/div-classtitlethe-political-branches-and-the-transna-

The use of the veto in the Security Council—as well as peace operations[154]—is questioned far beyond (Trahan, 2020, pp. 73–100) the referrals of cases to the ICC Prosecutor's Office. Even so, it constitutes a serious impediment to the investigation of the most serious crimes, national or international. This part of the work tries to demonstrate that there are tools available to mitigate the problem.

The feasibility of ecocide as an international crime depends on the reach that the norm can achieve. The problems of the International Criminal Court—a relatively recent Court, with 20 years of existence and, certainly, pioneering—can be discussed, for improvement, but its importance for the international criminal system is unquestionable.

It is therefore necessary to point out the reasons why it is understood that ecocide—as a crime under construction in the international criminal system—has sufficient maturity to be included in the Rome Statute, also evolving, in view of environmental urgency and the need for development of planetary security systems.

References

Ali, S. N. (1958). Uniting for peace. *The Indian Journal of Political Science, 19*(2), 115–123.

Alland, D. (2021). *The 100 words of international law*. Que sais-je?.

Amorim, J. A. A. (2015). *The UN and the environment*. Atlas Publisher.

Andrassy, J. (1956). Uniting for peace. *American Journal of International Law, 50*(3), 563–582.

Antunes, P. d. B. (2020). International environmental law: Peculiarities. *Paths of Law: Environmental Law and Sustainable Development, 17*(37), 263–294.

Barros, A. R. d. (1996). The concept of sovereignty in the *Methodus* of Jean Bodin. *Speech, 27*(1), 139–155.

Bartolini, G. (2017). A universal treaty for disasters? Remarks on the international law commission's draft articles on the protection of persons in the event of disasters. *International Review of the Red Cross, 99*(906), 1103–1137.

Bassiouni, M. C. (1996). International crimes: "Jus cogens" and "obligatio erga omnes". *Law and Contemporary Problems, 59*(4), 63–74. Available at: https://www.jstor.org/stable/pdf/1192190.pdf?refreqid=excelsior%3A6ece53b8b95b107fe4d426ad66d5c297&ab_segments=&origin=&acceptTC=1. Accessed on July 10, 2025

Bassiouni, M. C. (2002). Universal jurisdiction for international crimes: Historical perspectives and contemporary practice. In M. Cherif Bassiouni (Ed.), *Post-conflict justice* (pp. 945–1001). Brill Nijhoff.

Bellivier, F., Eudes, M., & Fouchard, I. (2018). *Droit des crimes internationaux*. Themis Law.

Borges, T. C. (2011). *Course on public international law and community law*. Atlas.

tional-prosecution-of-international-crimesdiv/0425F8FD48E3FC4D257051D4EA231015. Accessed on: 26 Jul. 2025).

[154] The format of "peace operations" and the use of force, in recent decades, are criticised for the reproduction of mandates regardless of their applicability to the context of the conflict for which they are authorised: "the future legitimacy of peace operations, and indeed the UNSC, are far from guaranteed. The current lock on Chap. 7 mandates satisfies neither international interests in maintaining security, nor the goals of saving lives and ending civil wars" (Howard, Lise Morjé, & Dayal, A. K. (2018). The use of force in UN peacekeeping. *International Organization*, 72(1), 71–103, p. 100).

Branch, A., & Minkova, L. (2023). Ecocide, the Anthropocene, and the international criminal court. *Ethics & International Affairs, 37*(1), 51–79.

Brant, L. N. C. (2005). The conflict of competence between the General Assembly and the security council in the light of article 12, paragraph 1 of the United Nations charter. *Brazilian Journal of Political Studies, 92*, 135–148.

Brant, L. N. C., & Biazatti, B. d. O. (2017). The formation of international custom today. *THEMIS: Revista da Esmec, 15*, 125–169.

Canotilho, J. J. G. (2003). *Constitutional law and theory of the constitution*. Almedina.

Carswell, A. J. (2013). Unblocking the UN security council: The uniting for peace resolution. *Journal of Conflict and Security Law, 18*(3), 453–480.

Cassese, A. (2004). Is there an insurmountable conflict between state sovereignty and international criminal justice? In A. Cassese & M. Delmas-Marty (Eds.), *International crimes and international jurisdictions* (pp. 67–82). Manole.

Castro, T. (2012). *UN Security Council: Unipolarity, consensus and trends*. Juruá.

Cazala, J. (2016). United Nations Security Council and environmental security. In N. Clinchamps et al. (Eds.), *Security and environment*. Bruylant.

Cervantes, M. Á. M., Roeben, V., & Solís, L. R. (2022). Global climate change action as a Jus Cogens norm: Some legal reflections on the emerging evidence. *Environmental Policy and Law, 44*, 1–15.

Cretella Neto, J. (2014). *Course of international criminal law*. Saraiva.

D'Amato, A. A. (1969). The concept of special custom in international law. *American Journal of International Law, 63*(2), 211–223.

Dahlman, C. (2012). The function of opinio juris in customary international law. *Nordic Journal of International Law, 81*(3), 327–339.

Dunn, B. (2002). The Mexicali tire pile: Smoke on the horizon. *Georgetown International Environmental Law Review, 14*, 409–427.

Ferdinandusse, W. (2004). The interaction of national and international approaches in the repression of international crimes. *The European Journal of International Law, 15*, 1041–1053.

Foegle, J.-P. (2016). Environmental security and national security: The dangerous liaisons? In N. Clinchamps et al. (Eds.), *Security and environment* (p. 384). Bruylant.

Fonseca, F. E. (2010). Notes and reflections on international jurisprudence in environmental matters: The participation of individuals and non-governmental organisations. *Environment and Society, 13*(2), 243–259.

Fouchard, I. (2014). *International crimes: Between internationalisation of criminal law and criminalisation of international law*. Bruylant.

Franck, T. M., et al. (1990). *The power of legitimacy among nations*. Oxford University Press.

Gaillard, É. (2016). Environmental security: A systemic, complex and prospective notion. In N. Clinchamps et al. (Eds.), *Security and environment* (pp. 41–60). Bruylant.

Gaja, G. (2011). Obligations erga omnes, international crimes and jus cogens: A tentative analysis of three related concepts. In J. Weiler, A. Cassese, & M. Spinedi (Eds.), *International crimes of state* (pp. 151–160). De Gruyter.

Galand, A. S. (2018). *UN security council referrals to the international criminal court: Legal nature, effects and limits*. Brill.

Galand, A. S. (2019). *UN Security Council referrals to the international criminal court: Legal nature, effects and limits*. Brill. Available at: https://library.oapen.org/bitstream/handle/20.500.12657/37984/9789004342217_webready_content_text.pdf?sequence=1. Accessed on: 22 Jul. 2025

Galvão, S. M. (2020). *Jus cogens environmental: Non-derogability of the human right to a healthy environment*. Dialética Publisher.

Gillett, M. (2024). Ecocide, environmental harm and framework integration at the international criminal court. *The International Journal of Human Rights*, 1–37.

Guillot, Philippe Ch.-A. (2016). International activities in favour of environmental security. In N. Clinchamps et al. (Eds.), Security and environment (pp. 111–122). : Bruylant.

Henderson, C. (2014). The Arab spring and the notion of external state sovereignty in international law. *Liverpool Law Review, 35*(2), 175–192.

Howard, L. M., & Dayal, A. K. (2018). The use of force in UN peacekeeping. *International Organization, 72*(1), 71–103.

ILC. (2016a). Draft articles on the protection of persons in the event of disasters.

ILC. (2016b). First report on jus cogens by Dire Tladi, Special Rapporteur. (ILC A/CN.4/693). p. 44., §72. Available at: https://documents-dds-ny.un.org/doc/UNDOC/GEN/N16/063/77/PDF/N1606377.pdf. Accessed on July 18, 2025.

ILC. (2022a, January). Fifth report on peremptory norms of general international law (jus cogens) by Dire Tladi, Special Rapporteur. (A/CN.4/747).

ILC. (2022b, May 11). Peremptory norms of general international law (jus cogens). Texts of the draft conclusions and Annex adopted by the Drafting Committee on second reading. (A/CN.4/L.967). Available at: https://documents-dds-ny.un.org/doc/UNDOC/LTD/G22/339/00/PDF/G2233900.pdf. Accessed on July 18, 2025).

ILC. (2022c, April 19). Sea-level rise in relation to international law. Second issues paper by Patrícia Galvão Teles and Juan José Ruda Santolaria, Co-Chairs of the Study Group on sea-level rise in relation to international law. (A/CN.4/752, §51).

Iyi, J.-M. (2019). Re-thinking the authority of the UN Security Council to refer nationals of non-party states to the ICC. *Netherlands International Law Review, 66*(3), 391–417.

Johnson, L. D. (2014). "Uniting for Peace": Does it still serve any useful purpose? *American Journal of International Law, 108*, 106–115.

Kotzé, L. J., & Muzangaza, W. (2018). Constitutional international environmental law for the Anthropocene? *Review of European, Comparative & International Environmental Law, 27*(3), 278–292.

Langer, M. (2011). The diplomacy of universal jurisdiction: The political branches and the transnational prosecution of international crimes. *American Journal of International Law, 105*(1), 1–49.

Langer, M., & Eason, M. (2019). The quiet expansion of universal jurisdiction. *European Journal of International Law, 30*(3), 779–817.

Maertens, L. (2016). When blue turns green: The securitisation of the environment at the UN. In N. Clinchamps et al. (Eds.), *Security and environment* (pp. 79–90). Bruylant.

Mazzuoli, V. d. O. (2019). *Course on public international law*. Forense.

Melling, G., & Dennett, A. (2017). The security council veto and Syria: Responding to mass atrocities through the "Uniting for Peace" resolution. *Indian Journal of International Law, 57*(3), 285–307.

Miranda, J. (2006). *Course on public international law*. Principia.

Molteni, V. (2021). The long road of the criminalisation of ecocide: Legal issues and dynamics of normative and social effectiveness. *Contemporary Criminal Law, 4*, 205–233.

Murphy, S. D. (2020). Peremptory norms of General international law (jus cogens) and other topics: The seventy-first session of the international law commission. *American Journal of International Law, 114*(1), 68–86.

Nasser, S. H. (2005). Jus cogens: Still this unknown. *GV Law Review, 1*(2), 161–178.

Negri, S. (2022). On meteors and comets: Is the crime of ecocide back to stay? *International Criminal Law Review, 1*, 1–30.

Neyret, L. (2018). The transformation of the crime against humanity. In M. Delmas-Marty et al. (Eds.), *The crime against humanity* (pp. 80–116). University Presses of France.

Nollez-Goldbach, R. (2018). *The international criminal court*. Presses Universitaires de France.

Öberg, M. D. (2005). The legal effects of resolutions of the UN Security Council and General Assembly in the jurisprudence of the ICJ. *European Journal of International Law, 16*(5), 879–906.

Oliveira, M. V. X. d. (2020). *Studies on (criminal) international jurisdiction: Forms of implementation, expansion, fragmentation and actio popularis* (p. 99). Edufro—Publisher of Federal University of Rondônia.

Oliveira, M. V. X. d. (2018). The 'actio popularis' and (n) the international (criminal) law. *City Law Journal, 10*(1), 532–571.

Palarczyk, D. (2023). Ecocide before the international criminal court: Simplicity is better than an elaborate embellishment. In *Criminal law forum* (pp. 147–207). Springer.

Piovesan, F. (2000). Principle of complementarity and sovereignty. *Journal of Judicial Studies, 4*(11).

Platiau, B., Granja, A. F., & Vieira, P. B. S. (2006). The legality of preventive intervention and the United Nations Charter. *Brazilian Journal of International Politics, 49*, 179–193.

Ramsden, M., & Hamilton, T. (2017). Uniting against impunity: The UN General Assembly as a catalyst for action at the ICC. *International & Comparative Law Quarterly, 66*(4), 893–921.

Ramsden, M. (2022). Uniting for peace: The emergency special session on Ukraine. *Harvard International Law Journal.*

Rezek, F. (2016). *Public international law: Elementary course*. Saraiva.

Rikhof, J. (2009). Fewer places to hide? The impact of domestic war crimes prosecutions on international impunity. In *Criminal law forum* (pp. 1–51). Springer.

Roth, K. (2001). The case for universal jurisdiction. *Foreign Affairs*, 150–154.

Saraiva, M. F. (2017). The role of African states in the politicisation of the international criminal court. *National Defence Institute*, 1–8.

Security Council Report. (2013, October). Security Council Deadlocks and Uniting for Peace*:* An Abridged History.

Security Council. (2022, February 2). Resolution *2623.* (S/RES/2623).

Security Council. (2024, June). Resolution 2735 (2024) [on ceasefire in the Gaza Strip].

Schabas, W. A. (2021). *The customary international law of human rights*. Oxford University Press.

Soares, J. C. B. (2005). *The United Nations in the face of threats, challenges, changes*. Brazilian Centre for International Relations.

Spapens, T., White, R., & Huisman, W. (Eds.). (2016). *Environmental crime in transnational context: Global issues in green enforcement and criminology*. Routledge.

Steiner, S. (2012). *10 years of the international criminal court: Sylvia Steiner responds*. Inter-American Court of Human Rights.

Teles, P. G. (2021a, May). *Protection of the atmosphere. Statement of the Chairperson of the Drafting Committee*. ILC.

Teles, P. G. (2021b). Remarks by Patrícia Galvão Teles. In *Proceedings of the ASIL annual meeting* (pp. 158–161). Cambridge University Press.

Tomuschat, C. (2006). The legacy of Nuremberg. *Journal of International Criminal Justice, 4*(4), 830–838.

Tomuschat, C. (2008). Uniting for peace. *United Nations Audiovisual Library of International Law*. Available at: https://legal.un.org/avl/ha/ufp/ufp.html. Accessed on July 26, 2025

Trahan, J. (2020). Questioning unlimited veto use in the face of atrocity crimes. *Case Western Reserve Journal of International Law, 52*, 73–100.

Trindade, A. A. C. (2010). Contemporary international courts and the pursuit of the realization of the ideal of international justice. *Revista da Faculdade de Direito UFMG, 57*, 37–68.

Tsilonis, V. (2024). *The jurisdiction of the international criminal court* (2nd ed.). Springer.

United Nations. (1945, June). *Charter of the United Nations.*

United Nations. (2022). UN General Assembly declares access to clean and healthy environment a universal human right. *Climate and Environment*. Available at: https://news.un.org/en/story/2022/07/1123482. Accessed on July 28, 2025

United Nations Environment Programme. (2024). Environmental impact of the conflict in Gaza: Preliminary assessment of environmental impacts.

UN General Assembly. (1950, November 3). *Resolution 377 (V) "Uniting for Peace*". Available at: https://www.un.org/en/sc/repertoire/otherdocs/GAres377A(v).pdf. Accessed on July 22, 2025.

UN General Assembly. (1951, February). *Resolution 498(V).* History and public policy program digital archive, United Nations documentation center.

UN General Assembly. (1982, February). Resolution 500. United Nations Digital Library.

UN General Assembly. (2021, December 9). *Protection of the atmosphere* (Resolution 76/112), Guideline 3. Available at: https://documents-dds-ny.un.org/doc/UNDOC/GEN/N21/389/40/PDF/N2138940.pdf. Accessed on July 15, 2025.

UN General Assembly. (2022a, March 1). Eleventh emergency special session, Aggression against Ukraine. (A/ES-11/L.1). Available at: https://documents-dds-ny.un.org/doc/UNDOC/LTD/N22/272/27/PDF/N2227227.pdf?OpenElement. Accessed on July 25, 2025.

UN General Assembly. (2022b, July). *The human right to a clean, healthy and sustainable environment* (Resolution A/76/L.75).

UN General Assembly. (2024, December). *Demand for ceasefire in Gaza: resolution/adopted by the General Assembly*. (Resolution A/RES/ES-10/26).

Vieira, S. C., & Andrade, A. M. d. (2015). The international criminal court: An analysis of its evolution and its competence to judge the crime by terrorism. *Brazilian Journal of International Law, 2*(1), 115–136.

Viñuales, J. E. (2008). The protection of the environment and its normative hierarchy in international law. *International Law: Revista Colombiana de International Law, 13*, 11–44.

Weiss, T. G. (2005). Overcoming the security council reform impasse: The implausible versus the plausible. Friedrich-Ebert-Stiftung, Dialogue on Globalization. (p. 14).

Weyers, L. (2016). The "securitisation" of climate change seen by an internationalist lawyer. In N. Clinchamps et al. (Eds.), *Security and environment* (pp. 278–283). Bruylant.

Chapter 9
Conclusion

Upon a cursory analysis of the current international penal system, a paradox becomes evident: it is considered an international crime to destroy the environment during wartime—when almost everything is permitted—while the same conduct, if committed in times of peace, is not classified as a crime. Although this is clearly incongruent, it reflects the progressive development of international criminal law and the evolving relationship between humans and the environment.

The evolution of the idea of—as the most serious crime against the environment—was examined in parallel with the development of international criminal law, with the aim of assessing whether the concept, once confined to academic discussions between the 1970s and 1990s, now possesses sufficient technical structure and practical relevance to be included under the jurisdiction of the International Criminal Court, the leading institution within the international penal system.

In this context, this study sought to contribute to the open questions surrounding the initiative to define ecocide as an international crime. It was grounded in the analysis of recent large-scale environmental disasters, existing ecocide legislation and proposals around the world, and an assessment of the ICC as a suitable forum to prosecute such crimes.

Ecocide first emerged as a concept in response to a systematic attack on the environment carried out by the United States through the use of herbicides as a military strategy during the Vietnam War, in the late 1960s. The environmental disaster prompted Arthur Galston to coin the term *ecocide* as part of a campaign against the use of chemical weapons in future conflicts. The success of that scientific campaign was solidified by the ratification of the Geneva Protocol by the United States, prohibiting the use of such weapons.

However, the use of Agent Orange was not the only example of massive environmental destruction in the decades that followed. Other cases, such as oil exploitation in Nigeria's Niger Delta and Canada's Alberta tar sands, the chemical disaster in Bhopal, India, and the collapses of tailings dams in Brumadinho and Mariana, Brazil, also caused severe and lasting damage to the environment—resulting from

D. A. Brochado Neto, *Ecocide*, https://doi.org/10.1007/978-3-032-07757-8_9

conduct that ranged from negligence and risk assumption to, in some cases, direct intent.

What these events have in common is a diffuse legal response, marked by difficulty in determining individual and collective, national and international accountability. One major obstacle is the lack of specific legal frameworks for addressing such extreme cases. In criminal law, this normative void is particularly severe. Prosecutions are often limited to minor environmental offenses, with sanctions that are insignificant when compared to the magnitude of the harm caused.

In seeking more severe punishments, national prosecutors tend to focus on the harm caused to humans—whether through fatalities, as in the Brazilian cases, or health damage. In both scenarios, difficulties in fitting the facts to existing legal provisions and establishing causation mean that criminal prosecution is often unsuccessful, further exposing the absence of a specific offense.

The increase in environmentally harmful conduct since the 1970s[1] reflects a growing international awareness of humanity's capacity to negatively alter the planet. Climate change—especially resulting from greenhouse gas (GHG) emissions—has become a central concern, officially recognized by the United Nations as one of the greatest challenges facing humanity in the twenty-first century. States, whether individually or collectively, have signed documents committing to mitigate climate change, particularly through the ratification of international treaties such as the Paris Agreement.

Climate litigation has emerged as a mechanism to hold actors—States and companies—accountable when they fail to comply with these commitments. The lawsuits typically aim to reduce GHG emissions, lessen vulnerability to climate impacts, provide reparations, and manage risk. Still in its early stages, this form of litigation has yet to demonstrate consistent success regarding environmental outcomes. Nevertheless, it is undoubtedly a valuable tool within the broader field of environmental protection.

The ongoing alerts[2] issued by climate-related documents—particularly those from the IPCC—have supported a growing movement among institutions, scientists, policymakers, and civil society to make more assertive use of legal instruments, including criminal law, in addressing climate change. However, there is currently no law that criminalizes GHG emissions per se; thus, there is no legal basis for prosecuting individuals or entities for contributing specifically to

[1] Despite the various efforts to respond to the issues of transnational environmental crimes, "*it is evident by the incessant rise of environmental crimes that, the issue of the development of international environmental criminal law remains episodic and quite limited in scope. The prohibition under Protocol-I of Geneva Convention is less concerned with protecting the environment than it is with regulating war*" (Pathak, P. (2016). International environmental crime: A growing concern of international environmental governance. *US-China Law Review*, 13(5), 397).

[2] For example, see: Armstrong McKay, D. I., et al. (2022). Exceeding 1.5 °C global warming could trigger multiple climate tipping points. *Science*, 377(6611). https://www.science.org/doi/10.1126/science.abn7950 . Accessed on: 10 Jan. 2025.

anthropogenic climate change. *Ecocide*, as a proposed international crime, has been quickly embraced as a potential legal mechanism for this purpose.

Nonetheless, the structure of the proposed crime does not directly address climate change, except in cases where the conduct in question results in GHG emissions as a secondary effect. In other words, ecocide is not currently a fully adequate legal instrument to prosecute climate-related conduct, and attempting to expand its scope too broadly risks undermining its legal coherence and feasibility as a criminal offense.

The search for appropriate mechanisms to prosecute large-scale environmental harm—treating the environment as a protected legal interest—raises two especially sensitive issues: criminal liability and the imposition of suitable sanctions. With respect to the former, corporate criminal liability is currently non-existent in the international criminal system, which remains strictly focused on individual accountability.

In this regard, limiting proposals to the possibility of punishing corporations—arguably the main agents responsible for large-scale environmental harm—may ultimately hinder the inclusion of ecocide under the jurisdiction of the International Criminal Court (ICC), due to incompatibility with the current legal framework. It is therefore more prudent to identify the advantages already offered by the existing system. The prosecution of individual criminal liability may serve as an effective tool, especially when supported by robust evidence and a sufficiently strong causal link. Command responsibility, in the context of symbolic criminal law, when applied to the leader of a transnational corporation, generates an extraordinary and reputationally damaging outcome—something undesirable for the corporation itself—thus functioning as a deterrent. It may also serve, as an administrative instrument, to reinforce the implementation of ESG (Environmental, Social, and Governance) standards, encouraging corporate governance to give greater attention to environmental matters, particularly in industries most sensitive to such issues.

In the international context, sanctions carry a distinct significance, especially considering the scale of the protected legal interests and the magnitude of the damage typically involved. The conventional functions of punishment in national systems—retribution, reparation, and deterrence—do not hold the same prominence in international criminal law, where the priority lies in discouraging impunity. Therefore, questions surrounding proportionality and the severity of ICC penalties are secondary when compared to the symbolic impact of criminalizing ecocide, which would represent a concrete response to environmental destruction and would establish the conduct as an international crime—empowering national enforcement by States Parties.

For the purposes of this work, ecocide is defined as the act of causing, by any means, massive environmental destruction in a way that renders recovery (resilience) unfeasible in the short term, directly or indirectly affecting human populations—either through the physical degradation of ecosystems or through the extinction of species—within a given natural area, with cross-border repercussions for one or more States, regardless of whether the conduct was administratively authorized, and committed with knowledge, or with a duty to know, of its environmental consequences.

It thus became necessary to reframe the concept of ecocide as an autonomous crime and examine its conceptual and practical development. The events of the Vietnam War brought international attention to the need to recognize the environment as a protected legal interest in *The Code*, the draft *Code of Crimes Against the Peace and Security of Mankind* developed by the International Law Commission (ILC). In 1991, ecocide was included in the draft as the intentional infliction of widespread environmental damage, but it was ultimately excluded from the final version, although it inspired discussions during the drafting of the Rome Statute of 1998.

Indeed, the crime of ecocide was not as well developed as other crimes in the draft—such as crimes against humanity, genocide, and war crimes—which had already been examined by post–World War II tribunals and codified through treaties. In that context, ecocide lacked precise definition and failed to meet the criteria of *jus cogens*, a key threshold for identifying the most serious international crimes. Attempts to classify ecocide as equivalent to genocide or crimes against humanity were unsuccessful, revealing a clear incompatibility with those legal categories—even though some countries already considered ecocide to fall under those headings.

The international setback did not extinguish interest in criminalizing ecocide at the national level. Vietnam was the first country to do so, in 1990, classifying it as a crime against humanity, though without offering detailed provisions—reflecting the vagueness of international discussions at the time.

Subsequently, Russia incorporated ecocide into its Criminal Code in 1996, drawing inspiration from the ILC's original formulation: it defined the crime as the massive destruction of fauna or flora, or other actions causing an ecological catastrophe. Between 1997 and 2003, nine former Soviet republics followed suit,[3] criminalizing similar conduct. These national laws share a focus on large-scale environmental destruction but generally do not provide a detailed description of the elements or scope of the offense.

As the international recognition of the environment as a legal good advanced—and successive environmental disasters accumulated—legal thinking around ecocide began to evolve. Two interpretive trends emerged: one framing environmental protection as essential for human well-being and another advancing protection for the environment per se, thereby breaking with anthropocentric paradigms. Ecuador pioneered the latter approach by recognizing nature (*Pacha Mama*) as a subject of rights. Its legislation criminalizes serious harm to water, land, and air, with aggravating circumstances for permanent or large-scale damage. Although it does not use the term "ecocide," Ecuador punishes conduct closely aligned with that definition.

Colombia, in contrast, explicitly included the crime of ecocide in its Criminal Code in 2021. It criminalizes conduct that causes serious environmental impact,

---

[3] Kyrgyzstan, Kazakhstan, Tajikistan, Uzbekistan, Belarus, Georgia, Ukraine, Moldova, and Armenia.

characterizing it as the alteration of environmental conditions, destruction of system integrity, and endangerment of sustainability. Notably, the offense is drafted with greater specificity, respecting the principle of legal certainty (*nullum crimen sine lege*) and enhancing clarity for users of the law.

In France, the debate over ecocide was galvanized by the 2019 *Convention Citoyenne pour le Climat*, which aimed to incorporate civil perspectives into climate policy through a social justice lens. The group ultimately proposed the creation of ecocide as a crime, in both its intentional and negligent forms. However, the draft law passed by the National Assembly in 2021 downgraded the offense to an aggravating factor for existing environmental crimes—falling short of international technical standards. While ecocide is now formally recognized in France, it is considered a lesser offense and defined primarily through references to other crimes, which limits its clarity and practical applicability. This legislative retreat has been interpreted as a sign of insufficient governmental commitment to the environmental agenda, despite official rhetoric in favour of stronger protections.

Several countries remain in earlier stages of discussion, with ecocide bills still pending in their legislative branches. In Brazil, a bill has been under consideration since 2019, prompted by the Mariana and Brumadinho disasters. These cases revealed the absence of a legal provision capable of addressing the scale of harm involved. The proposed bill, however, remains vague, as it conditions recognition of the crime on a state-of-emergency declaration by the Executive Branch. It also creates a separate crime for dam collapse, which—under the principle of specialty—would exclude the Minas Gerais cases from being prosecuted as ecocide. A technical note from the Federal Senate has acknowledged the political challenges[4] of drafting a criminal offense that could be meaningfully applied to powerful[5] potential offenders.

In Bolivia, the ecocide bill—like Ecuador's legislation—is grounded in the recognition of nature's rights, as established in the country's sub-constitutional framework. Introduced in 2020, the bill defines ecocide as causing massive and significant harm to biodiversity, ecosystems, and the rights of Mother Earth, threatening the existence and functioning of life systems. The legislator's aim is to fill a normative gap, ensuring greater environmental protection in response to challenges posed by climate change.

In Mexico, the state of Chiapas defines ecocide in its local legislation, while Michoacán has a bill under review. At the federal level, other initiatives are also underway. These efforts typically define ecocide as causing serious, large-scale, and extensive damage to natural resources or the environment, resulting in the harmful alteration of ecosystems.

[4] The political context in the years following the Project were detrimental to its progress, certainly due to the Government that assumed the presidency of Brazil, in 2018, little inclined to environmental issues.

[5] Brazil is among the countries in the world that punish legal entities for the practice of environmental crimes.

In 2021, the definition of ecocide proposed by the Independent Expert Panel, under the auspices of the Stop Ecocide Foundation, was presented as a model for legislation worldwide. It served as the basis for new laws enacted in Chile and Belgium. From 2023 onward, countries such as Brazil, Italy, Scotland, the Netherlands, the United Kingdom, Peru, and Azerbaijan have used this definition as a reference in their ongoing legislative proposals.

The proposal aimed to serve as the basis for the inclusion of ecocide as a crime under the jurisdiction of the International Criminal Court. The document was carefully drafted in alignment with the terminology and legal concepts established in the Rome Statute and other major international instruments, incorporating notions such as "wanton" (recklessness), "widespread" (generalized), "severe" (serious), and "long-term." It represents the most refined articulation of the concept of ecocide to date.

The expert panel defined ecocide as a crime of endangerment: liability is based on the creation of a hazardous situation, with the perpetrator knowing of a substantial likelihood of causing serious, widespread, or long-term environmental harm. The proposal received support from various States and the European Union and is currently under official consideration by the Assembly of States Parties to the ICC.

The degree of legal precision reached at the national level, echoing developments in international proposals, should remain a model for future legislative initiatives. It reflects the growing recognition of ecocide as a technically feasible and normatively sound criminal offense.

What emerges clearly is the evolution of the ecocide concept: initially vague and restricted to wartime scenarios in the 1970s, it has matured into a potential legal instrument for addressing massive environmental destruction in peacetime. The level of specificity now attained—coupled with advancements in environmental monitoring, assessment, and investigative technologies—supports the understanding of ecocide as a viable international crime, on par with genocide and crimes against humanity.

Accordingly, this study examined the main obstacles to recognizing ecocide under the jurisdiction of the ICC, including a critical analysis of the Court itself as the most suitable venue for prosecuting such conduct.

The proposal developed by the Ecocide Law Foundation was the first to gain traction among States Parties and inspired legislative initiatives at the national level. However, it has drawn criticism, particularly for including a legality clause that limits criminal liability to conduct that violates existing domestic laws. This means that even severe environmental damage may not qualify as ecocide if it is administratively authorized.

The ICC itself has not been immune to criticism—particularly during its first two decades—chiefly for concentrating prosecutions in African States. This gave rise to accusations, especially from those States, that the Court was a tool of Western neo-colonialism. That narrative, however, has been challenged by recent developments, including the African Union's movement to establish a regional criminal court that would exclude jurisdiction over incumbent heads of State.[6] Despite its early shortcomings, the ICC has gradually sought international legitimacy—arguably its greatest challenge—and these criticisms no longer fully apply.[7]

In pursuit of such legitimacy, the ICC did not adopt a single legal tradition. Instead, it operates within a hybrid system that draws from both civil law and common law. While this approach is essential for a Court with universal aspirations, it raises practical challenges, especially regarding applicable law in specific cases.

The identification of the mental element is crucial to international criminal prosecution. In this aspect, the concept of *mens rea* is more significant than intent, for the purpose of criminal liability. The practice of conduct with intention—proven in process—is a mandatory requirement for conviction. Regarding environmental crimes, this requirement becomes an obstacle, considering the theoretically negligent character, characteristic of environmental disasters. It happens that the Rome Statute, within a syncretism of legal systems, defines the volitional character as an element of crimes, but admits the existence of a minimum level of intention, close to eventual intent (approximately *recklessness*), which allows reaching situations where the agent is aware of the probability of damages occurring, assuming the risk of carrying them out.

The other element of the *offence*, the *actus reus*, required to be prosecuted at the international level, relates to the objective facts, which must also be proven by the prosecution. At this point, the anthropocentric design of the crime, that is, considering the human being as the object of the norm and the only victim, can prove problematic for the international criminalisation of conduct against the environment. If there is no injury to some legal good of direct value to man, there is no crime. The transformation of a legal analysis to an ecocentric bias, however, is not a sine qua non condition to prosecute ecocide. It is that, as the crime involves massive destruction of the environment, a review of the "environment" as a universal right, as recognized by the UN, allows the description of conducts (and damages) without the direct identification of harm to the human being (as in crimes against humanity, for example).

The jurisdiction of the ICC was also studied, considering the question about the redefinition of the sovereignty of States, to the detriment of a supranational Court. The relationship between international courts and national jurisdictions is, since Nuremberg and Tokyo, one of complementarity and co-participation, when criminal prosecution begins at the local level. This respect for national jurisdiction is the keynote of the jurisdiction of the International Criminal Court, not necessarily implying a supposed reduction of a State's sovereignty. The jurisdiction, restricted

---

[6] Malabo Protocol.

[7] "*Since only states wield real power, the risk is that international institutions will be ineffective or lack universal legitimacy when they try to deal with offenses such as war crimes. Even when world courts are established by general agreement (for example, the International Criminal Court set up by UN Rome Statute of 17 July 1998), their judgments will not necessarily be accepted as legitimate and binding, so long as powerful states are in a position to disregard them*" (Hobsbawm, E. (2007). *Globalization, democracy and terrorism*. London: Little, Brown, p. 24).

(*ratione materiae*) to the most serious conducts against international security and peace, emerges as a positive aspect, in a presumed criminalisation of ecocide, given the nature—commonly—transnational of the damages and consequences of the crime. The Court's main objective—to reduce spaces for impunity—would remain especially relevant for this type of crime, preserving the possibility of criminal prosecution by the justice of the crime's own location.

The "environment" issue is increasingly highlighted as an element maintaining international peace and security, the subject of multiple multilateral actions between States to ensure the use and reduction of risks arising from today's environmental problems.

In this context, the recognition of the importance of preserving a healthy environment by the UN, in 2022, paves the way for the identification of ecocide—as conduct that causes massive destruction—as *jus cogens*, the first condition to consider the crime among those present in the Rome Statute. The idea of a group of more serious conducts against humanity and international coexistence is not stagnant, as pointed out by the *International Law Commission*. This set of crimes should reflect the risks of an era, according to the advances of technology and society. The highlighted relevance, on a rise since 1970, of the environment allows us to affirm today that, within the limited scope of ecocide, massively destroying the environment is an unacceptable conduct, contrary to the harmonious existence of the international community.

Taking care of an environmental crime, whose borders cannot be determined by norms, it is important that the Court, the destination of ecocide, has the greatest possible jurisdiction. In this aspect, the ICC has more than half of the world's countries as State Parties, and its jurisdiction can be increased through article 13 [b] of the Rome Statute. This provision opens space for the UN Security Council, by resolution, to authorize prosecution in a State that is not part of the ICC. It is proposed here that, in case of deadlock of the Council—as often seen especially during the Cold War—the UN General Assembly could perform its role, by force of its Resolution 377. (V), performing its secondary function in ensuring peace and security of the international community. In this way, the possibility of a truly universal jurisdiction of the ICC is recognized, a condition not achieved by any international Court.

As investigated in the book, it is concluded that the ecocide as a crime is viable, with technical maturity and breadth of discourse—in various forums and national and international parliaments—sufficient to consider it a relatively well-defined conduct (taking into account the malleability of the definitions of consolidated crimes such as genocide and crimes against humanity). It was also found that the most appropriate place to accommodate the new crime is the International Criminal Court. *The Code*, the base project of the Rome Statute, considered the inclusion of ecocide among the main international crimes, as early as the 1980s. Unlike that time, which did not allow for the creation of an International Court, the existence of the ICC, with the ratification of 124 countries, reveals the strength of this model of international justice, even working on its legitimacy, two decades later.

This fact leads to the analysis of the moment to discuss, again, the inclusion of ecocide in the select list of international crimes. As seen, the advancement of studies on the crime is a reflection of the desire for greater environmental protection, in all public and private spheres. Ecocide fills a legal gap—in various countries and internationally—against destructive conduct to the environment in times of peace, increasingly common, with diffuse legal responses. The establishment of the crime in the ICC symbolizes an affirmation of the umbilical connectivity between human values and the environment, inseparable in a society that aims to be fair and secure. The successive environmental crises—amplified by climate change[8]—announce the moment as suitable to debate ecocide as this symbol, of the inadmissibility of causing massive environmental damage.

Subjectively, between aspirations of environmentalist support for the crime—which advocate for its recognition as the only way to save the planet[9]—and pragmatism— ecocide as a possible and limited tool, within a broader legal framework—this author chose the second approach.

The characteristics of massive environmental damage, as well as the national treatment given to the crime, reveal the intrinsically international nature of ecocide, used by States as inspiration or justification for their internal legislation. By representing the most serious crime against the environment, it automatically gains relevance in official discourses and among civil society, amplified by scientific reports about human impacts on nature. If the mobilisation—and disapproval—collective about a conduct is a requirement for the recognition of an international crime, ecocide has shown, especially in recent years, enough strength to be considered as such.

The book, certainly, does not exhaust the debate of the creation of the crime on the international level, needing to deepen in aspects such as the production of evidence in environmental crimes, the development of criminal liability of the legal

[8] The urgency imposed by the climate crisis well illustrates the importance of using existing tools to face new threats to the international community as a whole (Minha, Donna (2020). The possibility of prosecuting corporations for climate crimes before the International Criminal Court: All roads lead to the Rome Statute? *Michigan Journal of International Law*, 41(3), 491–540. https://repository.law.umich.edu/cgi/viewcontent.cgi?article=2095&context=mjil. Accessed on: 9 May. 2025).

[9] It should be highlighted that researchers from other areas—with arguments beyond criminal law—are the ones who most vocally advocate for ecocide as an international crime, for example: "*We have a right to live on this planet peacefully: to breathe clean air, to drink clean water, to enjoy the climate, the land and the seas our forebears enjoyed. It is not a right exclusively enjoyed by our species. It is a right closely interlinked to the right to life. The over-exploitation of our limited resources has led us to a precipice—the very survival of our species, and much of life on earth, is at stake. We have the means to slow down and possibly reverse the unprecedented harm caused by the activities of individuals, states and corporations. This will require selfless international cooperation to curtail and change every aspect of our energy-hungry existence. These changes will have to be underpinned by law. Primary amongst these laws should be the recognition that those who continue to assault our peaceful enjoyment of the planet will be stopped. There is a compelling case for the introduction of a fifth Crime against Peace—the crime of Ecocide*" (Mehta, Sailesh, & Merz, P Prisca (2015). Ecocide—a new crime against peace? *Environmental Law Review*, 17(1), 3–7. https://doi.org/10.1177/1461452914564730. Accessed on: 9 May 2025).

person, and the improvement of international cooperation (*Fusion centers*, information sharing, etc.). The basis developed here can, finally, offer the ballast for the construction of ecocide as an effective crime, with international respect, standardizing the repression of the practice of massive environmental damage.

References

Armstrong McKay, D. I., et al. (2022). Exceeding 1.5°C global warming could trigger multiple climate tipping points. *Science, 377*(6611) https://www.science.org. https://doi.org/10.1126/science.abn7950

Hobsbawm, E. (2007). *Globalization, democracy and terrorism*. Little, Brown.

Mehta, S., & Merz, P. P. (2015). Ecocide—a new crime against peace? *Environmental Law Review, 17*(1), 3–7. https://doi.org/10.1177/1461452914564730

Minha, D. (2020). The possibility of prosecuting corporations for climate crimes before the International Criminal Court: All roads lead to the Rome Statute? *Michigan Journal of International Law, 41*(3), 491–540. https://repository.law.umich.edu/cgi/viewcontent.cgi?article=2095&context=mjil.

Pathak, P. (2016). International environmental crime: A growing concern of international environmental governance. *US-China Law Review, 13*(5), 397.